EYEWITNESS *TRAVEL GUIDES*

FLORIDA

DORLING KINDERSLEY
LONDON • NEW YORK • SYDNEY • MOSCOW

DK

A DORLING KINDERSLEY BOOK

PROJECT EDITOR Emily Hatchwell
ART EDITORS Janice English, Robert Purnell
EDITORS Freddy Hamilton, Jane Oliver,
Naomi Peck, Andrew Szudek
DESIGNERS Jill Andrews, Frank Cawley, Dawn Davies-Cook,
Eli Estaugh, Simon Oon, Edmund White
MAP CO-ORDINATORS Emily Green, David Pugh
RESEARCHER Fred Brown

MANAGING EDITOR Vivien Crump
MANAGING ART EDITOR Jane Ewart
DEPUTY EDITORIAL DIRECTOR Douglas Amrine
DEPUTY ART DIRECTOR Gillian Allan

PRODUCTION David Proffit
PICTURE RESEARCH Monica Allende
DTP DESIGNERS Lee Redmond, Ingrid Vienings

CONTRIBUTORS
Ruth and Eric Bailey, Richard Cawthorne, David Dick,
Guy Mansell, Fred Mawer, Emma Stanford, Phyllis Steinberg

MAPS
EMS Ltd, East Grinstead (UK)

PHOTOGRAPHERS
Max Alexander, Dave King, Stephen Whitehorne, Linda Whitwam

ILLUSTRATORS
Richard Bonson, Richard Draper,
Chris Orr & Assocs, Pat Thorne, John Woodcock

Film outputting bureau Graphical Innovations (London)
Reproduced by Colourscan (Singapore)
Printed and bound by G. Canale & C. (Italy)

First published in Great Britain in 1997
by Dorling Kindersley Limited
9 Henrietta Street, London WC2E 8PS

Every effort has been made to ensure that the information in this
book is as up-to-date as possible at the time of going to press.
However, details such as telephone numbers, opening hours,
prices, gallery hanging arrangements and travel information are
liable to change. The publishers cannot accept responsibility for
any consequences arising from the use of this book.

We would be delighted to receive any corrections and
suggestions for incorporation in the next edition. Please write to:
Deputy Editorial Director, Eyewitness Travel Guides,
Dorling Kindersley, 9 Henrietta Street, London WC2E 8PS.

This book makes reference to various trademarks, marks and
registered marks owned by the Disney Company and Disney
Enterprises, Inc.

THROUGHOUT THIS BOOK, FLOORS ARE REFERRED TO IN ACCORDANCE WITH
AMERICAN USAGE, IE THE "FIRST FLOOR" IS AT GROUND LEVEL.

Previous pages: Roller coaster at Busch Gardens near Tampa

CONTENTS

HOW TO USE
THIS GUIDE 6

**A Tiffany window in
St Augustine (see p199)**

INTRODUCING
FLORIDA

PUTTING FLORIDA ON
THE MAP *10*

A PORTRAIT OF
FLORIDA *16*

FLORIDA THROUGH
THE YEAR *32*

THE HISTORY OF
FLORIDA *36*

MIAMI
AREA BY AREA

MIAMI AT A GLANCE *54*

**Rollerbladers, a common feature
of Florida's seaside resorts**

Dolphins entertaining the crowds at Sea World *(see pp164–7)*

U-peel shrimp, a classic dish

A woman taking in the view from
a snow-white Florida beach

Tourists enjoying the traditional
Key West sunset *(see p286)*

Villa Vizcaya, Miami

HOW TO USE THIS GUIDE

THIS GUIDE HELPS you to get the most from your visit to Florida. It provides expert recommendations as well as detailed practical information. *Introducing Florida* maps the whole state and sets Florida in its historical and cultural context. *Miami Area by Area* and the six regional chapters describe all the important sights, using maps, pictures and illustrations. Features cover topics from architecture to food and sport. Hotel and restaurant recommendations can be found in *Travellers' Needs*, while the *Survival Guide* includes tips on everything from transport to personal safety.

MIAMI AREA BY AREA
Miami is divided into three sightseeing areas. Each has its own chapter, which opens with a list of the sights described. A fourth chapter, *Further Afield*, covers outlying sights. All sights are numbered and plotted on an *Area Map*. Descriptions of each sight follow the map's numerical order, making sights easy to locate within the chapter.

Sights at a Glance lists the chapter's sights by category: Museums and Galleries, Streets and Neighbourhoods, Historic Buildings, for example.

All pages relating to Miami have red thumb tabs.

1 Area Map
For easy reference, the sights are numbered and located on a map. Sights are also shown on the Miami Street Finder on pages 96–101.

A locator map shows where you are in relation to other areas of the city centre.

2 Street-by-Street Map
This gives a bird's-eye view of the heart of each sightseeing area.

A suggested route for a walk is shown in red.

Stars indicate the sights that no visitor should miss.

3 Detailed information
All the sights in Miami are described individually, with addresses, opening hours and other practical information. The key to the symbols used in the information block is found on the back flap.

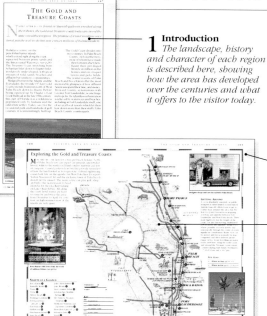

1 Introduction
The landscape, history and character of each region is described here, showing how the area has developed over the centuries and what it offers to the visitor today.

FLORIDA AREA BY AREA

Apart from Miami, Florida has been divided into six regions, each of which has a separate chapter. The most interesting cities, towns and places to visit in each area are numbered on a *Pictorial Map*.

Each region of Florida can be quickly identified by its colour coding, shown on the inside front cover.

2 Pictorial Map
This shows the main road network and gives an illustrated overview of the whole region. All entries are numbered, and there are also useful tips on getting around the region by car and public transport.

3 Detailed information
All the important towns and other places to visit are described individually. They are listed in order, following the numbering given on the Pictorial Map. Within each town or city there is detailed information on important buildings and other sights.

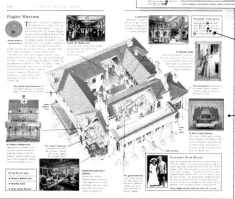

The Visitors' Checklist provides all the practical information you will need to plan your visit to all the top sights.

4 Florida's top sights
These are given two or more full pages. Historic buildings are dissected to reveal their interiors; art galleries have colour-coded floorplans to help you locate the best exhibits; theme parks are shown in a bird's-eye view, with the top attractions picked out.

Introducing
Florida

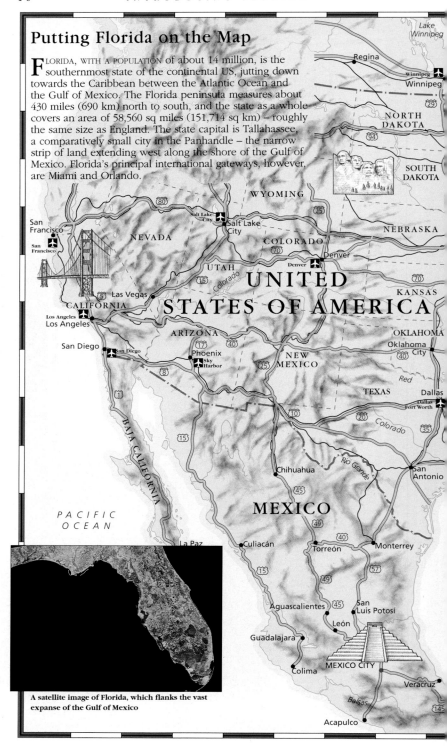

Putting Florida on the Map

F LORIDA, WITH A POPULATION of about 14 million, is the southernmost state of the continental US, jutting down towards the Caribbean between the Atlantic Ocean and the Gulf of Mexico. The Florida peninsula measures about 430 miles (690 km) north to south, and the state as a whole covers an area of 58,560 sq miles (151,714 sq km) – roughly the same size as England. The state capital is Tallahassee, a comparatively small city in the Panhandle – the narrow strip of land extending west along the shore of the Gulf of Mexico. Florida's principal international gateways, however, are Miami and Orlando.

Lake Winnipeg

Regina

Winnipeg
Winnipeg

NORTH DAKOTA

SOUTH DAKOTA

WYOMING

NEBRASKA

San Francisco
San Francisco

NEVADA

Salt Lake City
Salt Lake City

COLORADO

Denver
Denver

KANSAS

UTAH

Colorado

UNITED

Las Vegas

CALIFORNIA

STATES OF AMERICA

Los Angeles
Los Angeles

ARIZONA

OKLAHOMA

Oklahoma City

San Diego
San Diego

Phoenix
Sky Harbor

NEW MEXICO

Red

TEXAS

Dallas
Dallas
Fort Worth

Colorado

BAJA CALIFORNIA

Chihuahua

Rio Grande

San Antonio

PACIFIC OCEAN

MEXICO

La Paz

Culiacán

Torreón

Monterrey

Aguascalientes

San Luis Potosí

León

Guadalajara

MEXICO CITY

Colima

Veracruz

Balsas

A satellite image of Florida, which flanks the vast expanse of the Gulf of Mexico

Acapulco

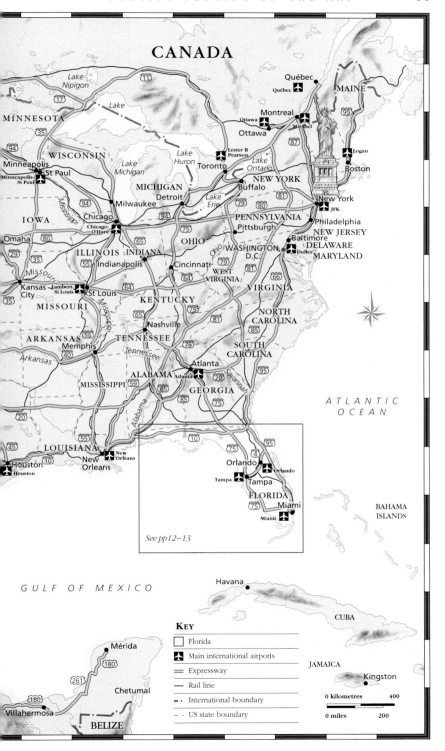

CANADA

Lake
Nipigon

Lake

MINNESOTA

17

Québec
Québec ✈

MAINE

95

35

94

WISCONSIN

Lake
Michigan

Lake
Huron

Ottawa ✈
Ottawa

Montreal
Mirabel

Logan ✈
Boston

Minneapolis
St Paul
Minneapolis-
St Paul ✈

94

Lester B
Pearson ✈
Toronto

Lake
Ontario

87

IOWA

Milwaukee
Chicago
Chicago-
O'Hare ✈

Detroit

MICHIGAN

94

Buffalo

NEW YORK

79

81

New York
JFK ✈

Statue of Liberty

Omaha

80

ILLINOIS INDIANA

65

55

75

Lake
Erie

OHIO

Cincinnati

79

PENNSYLVANIA
Pittsburgh

Philadelphia
NEW JERSEY

79

Indianapolis

64

WEST
VIRGINIA

WASHINGTON,
D.C.
Dulles ✈

Baltimore
DELAWARE
MARYLAND

79

35

Kansas
City

Lambert-
St Louis ✈
St Louis

64

81

MISSOURI

KENTUCKY

75

VIRGINIA

85

55

Nashville

81

NORTH
CAROLINA

ARKANSAS

55

TENNESSEE

Memphis

40

Tennessee

75

SOUTH
CAROLINA

95

Arkansas

MISSISSIPPI

59

ALABAMA

65

Atlanta
Atlanta ✈

85

Atlanta
70

Savannah

GEORGIA

75

ATLANTIC
OCEAN

20

45

LOUISIANA

55

10

New Orleans ✈
New
Orleans

75

4

95

Orlando
Orlando ✈

Houston ✈
Houston

Tampa ✈
Tampa

FLORIDA

75

Miami

BAHAMA
ISLANDS

Miami ✈

See pp12–13

GULF OF MEXICO

Havana

CUBA

Mérida

180

261

Chetumal

KEY

☐ Florida

✈ Main international airports

═ Expressway

— Rail line

-•- International boundary

-- US state boundary

JAMAICA

Kingston

0 kilometres   400

0 miles   200

180

Villahermosa

BELIZE

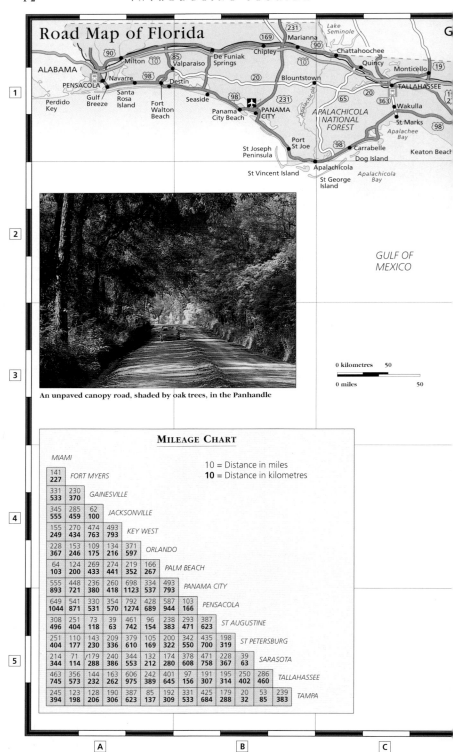

Road Map of Florida

An unpaved canopy road, shaded by oak trees, in the Panhandle

GULF OF MEXICO

0 kilometres 50

0 miles 50

MILEAGE CHART

10 = Distance in miles
10 = Distance in kilometres

MIAMI												
141 **227**	FORT MYERS											
331 **533**	230 **370**	GAINESVILLE										
345 **555**	285 **459**	62 **100**	JACKSONVILLE									
155 **249**	270 **434**	474 **763**	493 **793**	KEY WEST								
228 **367**	153 **246**	109 **175**	134 **216**	371 **597**	ORLANDO							
64 **103**	124 **200**	269 **433**	274 **441**	219 **352**	166 **267**	PALM BEACH						
555 **893**	448 **721**	236 **380**	260 **418**	698 **1123**	334 **537**	493 **793**	PANAMA CITY					
649 **1044**	541 **871**	330 **531**	354 **570**	792 **1274**	428 **689**	587 **944**	103 **166**	PENSACOLA				
308 **496**	251 **404**	73 **118**	39 **63**	461 **742**	96 **154**	238 **383**	293 **471**	387 **623**	ST AUGUSTINE			
251 **404**	110 **177**	143 **230**	209 **336**	379 **610**	105 **169**	200 **322**	342 **550**	435 **700**	198 **319**	ST PETERSBURG		
214 **344**	71 **114**	/179 **288**	240 **386**	344 **553**	132 **212**	174 **280**	378 **608**	471 **758**	228 **367**	39 **63**	SARASOTA	
463 **745**	356 **573**	144 **232**	163 **262**	606 **975**	242 **389**	401 **645**	97 **156**	191 **307**	195 **314**	250 **402**	286 **460**	TALLAHASSEE
245 **394**	123 **198**	128 **206**	190 **306**	387 **623**	85 **137**	192 **309**	331 **533**	425 **684**	179 **288**	20 **32**	53 **85**	239 **383**	TAMPA

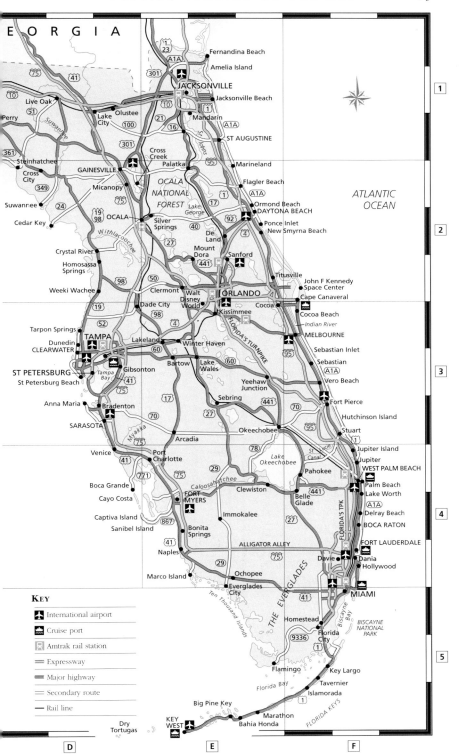

EORGIA

Fernandina Beach
Amelia Island
JACKSONVILLE
Jacksonville Beach
Live Oak
Lake City
Olustee
Mandarin
Perry
ST AUGUSTINE
Steinhatchee
Cross Creek
GAINESVILLE
Palatka
Marineland
Cross City
Micanopy
Flagler Beach
OCALA NATIONAL FOREST
Suwannee
OCALA
Ormond Beach
DAYTONA BEACH
Cedar Key
Silver Springs
Lake George
Ponce Inlet
New Smyrna Beach
Crystal River
De Land
Homosassa Springs
Mount Dora
Weeki Wachee
Sanford
Titusville
Clermont
Walt Disney World
ORLANDO
John F Kennedy Space Center
Cape Canaveral
Dade City
Kissimmee
Cocoa
Cocoa Beach
Indian River
Tarpon Springs
TAMPA
Lakeland
Winter Haven
MELBOURNE
Dunedin
CLEARWATER
Bartow
Lake Wales
Sebastian Inlet
ST PETERSBURG
Gibsonton
Sebastian
St Petersburg Beach
Yeehaw Junction
Vero Beach
Anna Maria
Bradenton
Sebring
Fort Pierce
SARASOTA
Hutchinson Island
Venice
Arcadia
Okeechobee
Stuart
Port Charlotte
Lake Okeechobee
Jupiter Island
Jupiter
WEST PALM BEACH
Boca Grande
Pahokee
Palm Beach
Cayo Costa
FORT MYERS
Clewiston
Lake Worth
Captiva Island
Belle Glade
Delray Beach
Sanibel Island
Immokalee
BOCA RATON
Bonita Springs
FORT LAUDERDALE
Naples
ALLIGATOR ALLEY
Davie
Dania
Hollywood
Marco Island
Ochopee
THE EVERGLADES
MIAMI
Everglades City
Homestead
BISCAYNE NATIONAL PARK
Florida City
Ten Thousand Islands
Biscayne Bay
Flamingo
Key Largo
Florida Bay
Tavernier
Islamorada
Big Pine Key
KEY WEST
Marathon
Bahia Honda
FLORIDA KEYS

ATLANTIC OCEAN

KEY

International airport
Cruise port
Amtrak rail station
Expressway
Major highway
Secondary route
Rail line

Dry Tortugas

Miami

THE METROPOLIS often referred to simply as Miami, or Greater Miami, is more accurately called Dade County. It covers 2,000 sq miles (3,220 sq km) and incorporates many districts and several cities. In this book, Miami has been divided up into three sightseeing areas: Miami Beach, including the resort of South Beach, Downtown and Little Havana, more traditionally urban areas, and the leafy suburbs of Coral Gables and Coconut Grove.

Coral Gables: Miami's most desirable residential district, laid out around a series of canals

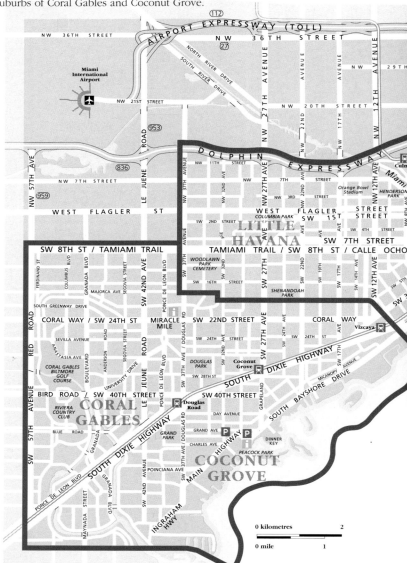

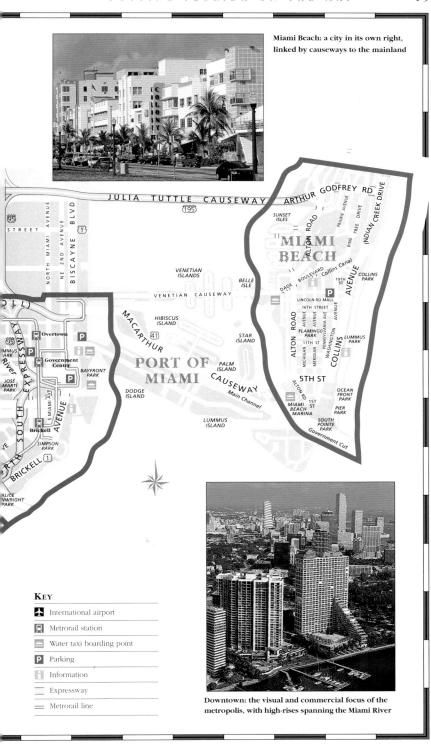

Miami Beach: a city in its own right,
linked by causeways to the mainland

JULIA TUTTLE CAUSEWAY

ARTHUR GODFREY RD

I95

STREET

NORTH MIAMI AVENUE

NE 2ND AVENUE

BISCAYNE BLVD

1

SUNSET ISLES

PRAIRIE AVENUE

PINE TREE DRIVE

INDIAN CREEK DRIVE

MIAMI BEACH

ALTON ROAD

VENETIAN ISLANDS

BELLE ISLE

Collins Canal

COLLINS PARK

DADE BOULEVARD

VENETIAN CAUSEWAY

19TH ST

COLLINS AVENUE

LINCOLN RD MALL

16TH STREET

HIBISCUS ISLAND

ALTON ROAD

FLAMINGO PARK

AVENUE

PENNSYLVANIA AVE

WASHINGTON AVENUE

LUMMUS PARK

Overtown

P

P

MACARTHUR

41

STAR ISLAND

11TH ST

MICHIGAN AVENUE

MERIDIAN AVENUE

COLLINS

Government Center

P

I95

MMUS
ARK

BAYFRONT PARK

PORT OF MIAMI

PALM ISLAND

5TH ST

JOSÉ
MARTI
PARK

River

DODGE ISLAND

CAUSEWAY

Main Channel

ALTON RD

OCEAN FRONT PARK

SOUTH EXPRESSWAY

S MIAMI AVE

MIAMI BEACH MARINA

1ST ST

PIER PARK

LUMMUS ISLAND

SOUTH POINTE PARK

Government Cut

Brickell

BRICKELL

AVENUE

SIMPSON PARK

1

ALICE
NWRIGHT
PARK

Downtown: the visual and commercial focus of the
metropolis, with high-rises spanning the Miami River

A PORTRAIT OF FLORIDA

FOR THE MAJORITY OF FLORIDA'S 40 million plus annual visitors, the typical travel poster images of Florida – sun, sea, sand and Mickey Mouse – are reason enough to jump on the next plane. The Sunshine State deserves its reputation as the perfect family holiday destination, but Florida is much richer in its culture, landscape and character than its stereotypical image suggests.

It is easy to turn a blind eye to what lies beyond the Florida coast, where the beaches are varied and abundant enough to satisfy every visitor – whether you want simply to relax beneath azure skies or make the most of the state's fine sports facilities. However, great rewards await those who put aside their suntan lotion and beach towel to explore.

Beach buggie, Daytona Beach

The lush forests, the rolling hills of the north, the colourful displays of bougainvillea and azaleas in spring shatter the myth that Florida's landscape is totally dull and flat. Wherever you are, it is only a short trip from civilization to wild areas, such as the Everglades, which harbour an extraordinary diversity of plant and animal life, and where alligators and snakes are living reminders of the inhospitable place that Florida was not much more than 100 years ago. By world standards the state was a late developer (most of its "historic districts" date only from the early 1900s), but Florida boasts the nation's oldest town: St Augustine, where a rare wealth of well-preserved buildings provide a glimpse of life in the 18th century.

Both climatically and culturally, Florida is a state divided – a bridge between temperate North America and tropical Latin America and the Caribbean. In the north, roads are lined with stately live oak trees and people speak with a southern drawl,

The unspoilt, watery landscape near Flamingo in Everglades National Park

◁ A typical scene in South Beach, Miami, where rollerblades and minimal clothing are the norm

A local resident enjoying some leisurely fishing off Naples pier, on the shores of the Gulf of Mexico

while, in the south, shade from the subtropical sun is cast by palm trees and the inhabitants of Miami are as likely to speak Spanish as English.

PEOPLE AND SOCIETY

The state "where everyone is from somewhere else", Florida has always been a cultural hotch-potch. The Seminole Indians, who arrived in the 17th century, have been in Florida longer than any other group. They live mostly on reservations, but you see them by the roadside in some southern areas selling their colourful, hand-made crafts. The best candidates for the title of "true Floridian" are the Cracker farmers, whose ancestors settled in the state in the 1800s; their

A stall selling clothes made by Seminole Indians

name comes perhaps from the cracking of their cattle whips or the cracking of corn to make grits. Unless you explore the interior, you probably won't meet a Cracker; along the affluent, heavily populated coast, you'll rub shoulders mainly with people whose roots lie in more northerly states.

North Americans have poured into Florida since World War II; the twentieth most populous state in the US in 1950, Florida is now ranked fourth. The largest single group to move south has

Miami Cubans playing dominos

been the retirees, for whom Florida's climate and lifestyle of leisure (plus its tax concessions) hold great appeal after a life of hard work. But this is not a land of walking sticks and zimmer frames; you'll see many older people playing a round of golf or enjoying a spot of fishing or a browse around one of Florida's state-of-the art shopping malls. While super-rich communities like Palm Beach fit the conservative and staid image that some people still have of Florida, the reality is very different. An increasing number of the new arrivals are young people, for whom Florida is a land of opportunity, a place to have fun, enjoy the good life. It is this younger generation which has helped turn Miami's South Beach, where beautiful bodies pose against a backdrop of Art Deco hotels, into one of the trendiest resorts in the US.

A refreshing ride in one of Florida's popular water parks

There has also been large-scale immigration from Nicaragua, Haiti and other countries in the region, and Miami has a large Cuban community. Here, salsa and merengue beats fill the air while exuberant festivals fill the calendar. The ethnic diversity is also celebrated in the local food: as well as genuine recreations of Caribbean and other ethnic dishes, you can enjoy the exciting and innovative dishes that have emerged with the craze for cross-cultural cuisine.

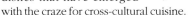

Oranges, Florida's juiciest crop

source of revenue has been agriculture, in particular citrus fruits, vegetables and cattle; the first grow mostly in central Florida, where fruit trees can stretch as far as the eye can see. High-tech industry is significant too, while the proximity of Miami to Latin America and the Caribbean has made it the natural route for US trade with the region. Florida's warm climate has also generated high-profile moneyspinners: spring baseball training draws teams and lots of fans south, while the fashion trade brings models by the dozen and plenty of glamour to Miami.

ECONOMICS AND TOURISM

Economically, Florida is not in bad shape compared with other US states. For most of its history, the state's main

It is tourism, however, that fills the state's coffers. Walt Disney World may appear to dominate the tourist industry, but Florida makes the most of all its assets: its superb beaches, its location within easy striking distance of the Bahamas and the Caribbean (the state's cruise industry is flourishing) and its natural habitats. After decades of unbridled development, Florida has finally learnt the importance of safeguarding its natural heritage. Vast areas of land have already disappeared beneath factories, condos and cabbage fields, but those involved in agriculture and industry are being forced to act more responsibly, and water use is now being strictly monitored. Florida's remaining natural treasures, from its swamps to its last remaining panthers, are now protected for posterity.

Flamingos, seen in some parks and a popular icon

The Landscape of Florida

FLORIDA'S LANDSCAPE is relentlessly low lying, the
highest point in the state being just 345 ft (105 m)
above sea level. The rare, rolling hills of the Panhandle
provide some of the loveliest countryside in the state,
whose flat peninsula is otherwise dominated by grass-
land and swamp, punctuated by forests and thousands
of lakes. Great swathes of the natural landscape have
had to surrender to the onslaught of urban development and agriculture – second only to tourism as the
state's main economic resource. However, you can still
find areas that are surprisingly wild and unpopulated.

Wetlands *consist mainly of
tree-covered swamps, like this
cypress swamp, and more
open, grassy marshes.*

Pensacola ·   · Tallahassee   APALACHICOLA NATIONAL FOREST   Panama City   Gainesville   Ocala   Withlacoochee   Hillsborough   St Petersburg ·   · Tampa   · Sarasota

0 kilometres 50
0 miles 50

Sandy beaches
*account for over
1,000 miles (1,600 km)
of Florida's coastline. In
contrast to the coral sand
on the Atlantic side, the
fine quartz sand in the
Panhandle is so white
that legend has it that
unscrupulous traders
sold it as sugar during
World War II.*

FLORIDA'S SINKHOLES

Many of Florida's 30,000 lakes and ponds started out as a
sinkhole, or "sink". This curious phenomenon, which occurs
mainly in northern Florida, is a result of the natural erosion
of the limestone that forms the bedrock of much of the state.
Most sinkholes form gradually, as the soil sinks slowly into
a depression. Others appear much more dramatically, often
after heavy rain, when an underground cavern collapses
beneath the weight of the
ground above. The largest
recorded sinkhole occurred in
Winter Park in 1981. It swal-
lowed half a dozen cars and a
house, and formed a crater
over 300 ft (90 m) in diameter.
There is no sure way to predict
sinkhole development and
many homeowners take out
sinkhole insurance.

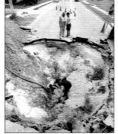

**City workers surveying a sink-
hole in the middle of a road**

Barrier islands,
formed by the piling
up of drifting sand, ring
much of Florida's coast.

KEY

▦	Main urban areas
▦	Main wetland areas
▦	Main forested areas
– –	Intracoastal Waterway
▼	Cattle
🐚	Fish and seafood
◉	Citrus fruit
⚜	Sugar cane
✿	Tobacco
✿	Peanuts

The Intracoastal Waterway is a natural but dredged channel, whose main section along the east coast is a continuation of a route that begins further north, in the state of Maryland; some of the Florida sections were dredged back in the 1880s. It is a popular boating route *(see p342)*.

Forest, mostly pine, covers 50 per cent of the state's land area, but more than half of this is grown for commercial use.

Cattle were shipped from Florida to market in Cuba under the Spanish. Today, Florida is second only to Kentucky in the raising of beef cattle in the southeastern states, its industry based largely on the Brahma, a hardy breed of cattle originally from India. The state's principal cattle ranching country lies along the Kissimmee River, and the town of Kissimmee is known as the "cow capital of Florida" (see p177).

Florida's citrus industry produces over 70 per cent of the citrus fruits consumed in the US. Oranges are grown mainly for their juice, for which the state is famous.

Sugar cane thrives on the rich soil south of Lake Okeechobee (see p124). Once reliant on migrant labourers from the Caribbean, who cut the cane by machete, the industry is now largely mechanized.

The Florida Keys are a chain of fossilized coral islands, many of which are tiny and uninhabited.

Urban growth is the inevitable result of the constant influx of migrants from other US states and abroad, as well as of the general movement of people from rural to urban areas. The southeastern coast of Florida is almost completely built up – as seen at Delray Beach, which straddles the Intracoastal Waterway on the Gold Coast.

Jacksonville

OCALA NATIONAL FOREST

Daytona Beach

Orlando

Kissimmee

Fort Pierce

Lake Okeechobee

Caloosahatchee

Palm Beach

Fort Myers

Miami Canal

Naples

Fort Lauderdale

MIAMI

Tamiami Canal

THE EVERGLADES

FLORIDA KEYS

Key West

St Johns

Wildlife and Natural Habitats

FLORIDA'S GREAT VARIETY of habitats and wildlife is due in part to the meeting of temperate north Florida with the subtropical south. Other factors include the state's humidity, sandy soils, low elevation and proximity to the sea. Some plants and animals can live in several habitats, while others can survive only in one. The bird life in Florida is particularly rich in winter, when migratory birds arrive from the colder northern states.

A tropical hardwood hammock in southern Florida

COASTAL AREAS

Florida's coasts are rich in wildlife despite the often exposed conditions. Apart from wading birds, many animals remain hidden during the day. Some lie buried in the sand, while others, such as turtles, leave the sea only in darkness. Salt marshes and lagoons, protected from the ocean by dunes, are a particularly rich habitat.

Saltwater lagoons are fertile territory for fish and shellfish.

Horseshoe crabs emerge from the ocean in great hordes, usually in spring. They congregate on the beaches to breed.

Ocean

Shrubs on the dunes are "pruned" by the sea's salty spray and bent by the wind.

Limestone bedrock

Clay, sand and shells

The bald eagle, an endangered species found by the sea and in some inland areas, has a wingspan of 7 ft (2 m).

Dunes, shaped by the wind and waves, shift all the time but are stabilized by the roots of sea oats and other plants.

The sea grape, which grows on dunes mainly in southeast Florida, is named after the oval fruit that hangs in grape-like clusters.

PINE FLATWOODS

These woods, where pines tower over an understory of plants and shrubs, cover about half of Florida, and are often interspersed with swamps and other habitats. They thrive when swept by fire periodically, and the plants and animals that live here have adapted to survive the difficult conditions.

Saw palmetto, as well as shrubs such as wax myrtle, do well in the open woodlands.

Slash pine is the most common tree in the flatwoods.

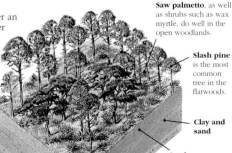

Clay and sand

Sand

White-tailed deer are solitary creatures. Those in Florida are smaller than the white-tailed deer found in more northerly states of the US.

Pygmy rattlesnakes are well camouflaged to blend easily into a background of grass and scrub.

The red-bellied woodpecker nests in dead trees and may use the same nest in successive years.

FRESHWATER SWAMPS

Many swamps have been drained to make way for agriculture or development, but they are still found all over Florida. They are often dominated by cypress trees, which are well suited to the watery conditions, requiring little soil to grow. The dwarf cypress is the most common species, the grander giant or bald cypress tree being rare these days.

White ibis find ample food in freshwater marshes and swamps. They nest in large colonies in high trees or among reeds.

Peat

The bob-cat has a distinctive short tail, facial ruff and spotted coat.

Cypress trees often form a "dome". The trees at the water's edge are shorter than those at the centre.

Sawgrass

Cypress knees are special roots that supply oxygen to the tree, which would otherwise die in the wet soil.

Water and organic matter

Anole lizards are usually green but can change to dark brown, depending on body heat or levels of stress.

Water lilies are the most spectacular freshwater flowering plants. The large leaf is a common resting site for frogs.

HARDWOOD FORESTS

These are among the most verdant habitats in the state. Hardwood-dominated forests are called "hammocks". Unlike the tropical hardwood hammocks of southern Florida, those in the north are dominated by the splendid live oak tree, interspersed with other species such as hickory and magnolia.

Spanish moss, like other epiphytes or air plants, grows on (but does no harm to) its host tree.

Wild turkeys are easily recognized by their coloured plumage and "beard".

Magnolia, one of the oldest known flowering plants, is characterized by its showy ornamental flowers and aromatic bark.

Cabbage or sabal palm

Live oak

Sand and clay

Hammocks occur mainly in patches or narrow bands along rivers.

Opossums are proficient climbers, with hands, feet and tail well adapted to grasping thin branches.

Armadillos are mainly nocturnal. When threatened they roll into a ball, the hard "armour" protecting the soft body from predators such as bobcats.

Hurricanes in Florida

Hurricane Hunters logo

A HURRICANE IS A TROPICAL CYCLONE with wind speeds of at least 74 mph (119 km/h). One in ten of the hurricanes to occur in the North Atlantic hits Florida – which means an average of one every two years. The hurricane season runs from 1 June to 30 November, though the greatest threat is from August to October. The Saffir-Simpson Hurricane Scale, which measures the winds and ocean flooding expected, categorizes hurricanes from one to five; category five is the worst, with winds of over 155 mph (249 km/h). Hurricane names come from a recognized alphabetical list of names, which rotates every six years. Originally, only women's names were used, but since 1979 both men's and women's names have been alternated.

Monument to the 1935 hurricane *(see p280)*

The areas of Florida most likely to be hit by a hurricane are the southeast coast, including the Florida Keys, the west coast of the Everglades and the western Panhandle.

THE LIFE OF A HURRICANE

The development of a hurricane is influenced by several factors – primarily heat and wind. First the sun must warm the ocean's surface enough for water to evaporate. This rises and condenses into thunderclouds, which are sent spinning by the earth's rotation. The hurricane moves forward and can be tracked using satellite images like this one. On hitting land, the storm loses power because it is cut off from its source of energy – the warm ocean.

A boat lifted out of the water onto Miami's Rickenbacker Causeway by the force of the hurricane

An apartment building after its façade was ripped off by Andrew's ferocious winds

A tent camp, set up to house some of the 250,000 left temporarily homeless by Hurricane Andrew

HURRICANE ANDREW

On 24 August 1992 Hurricane Andrew devastated South Florida. It measured "only" four on the Saffir-Simpson Scale (less than the 1935 hurricane that hit the Florida Keys), but it was the nation's costliest ever natural disaster, causing $25 billion worth of damage. Astonishingly, only 15 people died in Florida (and 23 in the country as a whole) from the direct effects of Hurricane Andrew.

The Eye
While encircled by the fastest winds, the "eye" at the heart of the storm is a calm area. Once the eye has passed by, the winds return to their full force.

MONITORING A HURRICANE

Using satellites, computer models and radar, the National Hurricane Center in Miami can detect a hurricane long before it reaches Florida. The most detailed information, however, is provided by pilots known as Hurricane Hunters, who fly in and out of the hurricane gathering data.

The damage from a hurricane is greatly reduced by preparedness: television and radio bulletins keep the public informed, and everyone is encouraged to plot the route of the storm on special hurricane tracking maps.

Trees bent by hurricane force winds

1 Hurricane Alerts
The issuing of a Hurricane Watch is the first indication that a hurricane could hit Florida. This means that a storm may arrive within 36–48 hours. A Hurricane Warning heralds the storm's likely arrival within 24 hours. Airports are likely to close during these alerts.

Traditional hurricane alert flag

2 Evacuation
Emergency management officials may issue evacuation orders via the local news media before a hurricane hits. People living in high-rise buildings, mobile homes and low-lying areas are particularly vulnerable. Signs bearing the hurricane symbol direct people along safe routes. The Red Cross shelters those with nowhere else to go.

Evacuation sign

3 The All Clear
After a hurricane dissipates or moves on, the all clear is given for people to return home. However, safety is still a concern after the storm due to downed power lines, flooding and clean-up related accidents.

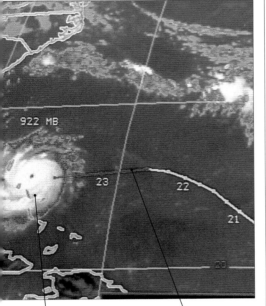

A typical hurricane is 300 miles (480 km) wide and can rise 50,000–60,000 ft (15,250–18,300 m) above the ocean. It moves forward at a speed of 10–45 mph (15–70 km/h).

Many hurricanes, including Andrew, form off Africa and then move west across the Atlantic.

THE STORM SURGE

Most damage and deaths during a hurricane are a result not of wind and rain but of flooding from the storm surge. This wall of water is whipped up by fierce winds near the eye of the storm and then crashes onto the shore; it can span over 50 miles (80 km) and reach a height of 20 ft (6 m) or more.

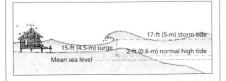

17-ft (5-m) storm tide
15-ft (4.5-m) surge   2-ft (0.6-m) normal high tide
Mean sea level

Shipwrecks and Salvage

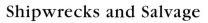

THE WATERS OFF FLORIDA are littered with thousands of shipwrecks which have accumulated over hundreds of years. Many sank during storms at sea, while others were tossed onto the reefs off the Keys. The salvaged wrecks picked out on the map are those that have had a large amount of their cargo recovered. Spain's treasure ships are the greatest prize among salvagers, just as they were once the favoured target of pirates. In museums all over Florida everyday objects and treasure offer an insight into the lives and riches of the Spanish.

Lighthouses
Since the 1800s, lighthouses like the one at Jupiter have helped ships stay on course.

The Atocha
Florida's best-known Spanish wreck, which sank in 1622, was located by Mel Fisher (see p110) in 1985 after a 16-year search. The treasure, worth an estimated $300 million, included coins, gold bars and jewellery.

The Florida Keys
were ideal territory for "wreckers" *(see p289),* who rescued and then sold the cargo from ships that foundered on the nearby reef.

From Mexico

Salvaging Treasure
Salvaging has always required ingenuity. This manuscript from 1623 shows a Spanish technique invented to rescue sunken treasure in the Keys.

MEXICO

From South America

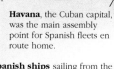

Havana

Havana, the Cuban capital, was the main assembly point for Spanish fleets en route home.

Spanish ships sailing from the New World would pick up the Gulf Stream and tradewinds near Florida to aid their journey back across the Atlantic.

KEY

⚓	Salvaged wreck
⚓	Unsalvaged wreck
↗	Shipping route

TREASURE SEEKERS

It took Mel Fisher more than 100 court hearings to establish his right to keep the treasures of the *Atocha*. Federal law states that wrecks located up to 3 miles (5 km) offshore belong to the state in whose waters they are found, but the law is unclear when it comes to ships lying outside that limit. Amateurs who find coins with metal detectors on land can keep what they find, but in Florida a licence is required to remove anything from an offshore wreck within its jurisdiction.

A treasure hunter on the beach

WHERE TO SEE SPANISH TREASURE IN FLORIDA

Maritime Museum of the Florida Keys see p278

McLarty Treasure Museum see p110

Mel Fisher's Maritime Museum see p288

Mel Fisher's Treasure Museum see p110

Museum of Man in the Sea see p224

St Lucie County Historical Museum see p111

A Spanish treasure fleet that sank here in 1715 *(see p110)* is still being salvaged. Amateurs scour nearby beaches for coins that are sometimes washed up after a storm.

To Spain

Spanish Ships

Caravels and galleons transported treasure back to Spain. These ships could carry a crew of around 200. The chests of gold and silver were usually kept under guard in a room on the lower deck.

Blackbeard

Notorious for his cruelty – and also for his habit of setting fire to hemp cords attached to his hat in order to intimidate his victims – Blackbeard preyed on Spanish ships in the early 18th century. He was killed by the British Navy in 1718.

BAHAMAS

Hispaniola and nearby Tortuga were favourite haunts of French and English pirates, who would launch attacks on Spanish ships from here.

TORTUGA

0 kilometres 200

0 miles 200

CARIBBEAN SEA

HISPANIOLA

Florida's Architecture

BUILDINGS IN FLORIDA are perhaps most interesting as a reflection of the way in which the state was settled. Early pioneers built simple homes, but aspirations grew from the railroad era onwards. Entrepreneurs, eager to lure people southwards, imitated styles with which northerners would be familiar. This trend, plus the speed of settlement, meant that Florida never really developed an indigenous style. But the Sunshine State has some quirky and memorable architecture, often inspired by the need to adapt to the warm climate.

High-rise architecture in downtown Jacksonville

FLORIDA'S VERNACULAR STYLE

The early pioneers of the 1800s built houses whose design was dictated mainly by the climate and the location: the most identifiable common elements are the devices to maximize natural ventilation. Local materials, usually wood, were used. Original "Cracker" homes, so named after the people who built and lived in them *(see p18)*, don't survive in great numbers, but the vernacular style has influenced Florida's architecture ever since.

A chickee, the traditional simple home of Florida's native Indians

The brick chimney replaced the original one, which was made of mud and sticks.

A dog trot, or open walk-through, was often added if, as here, the original house was extended.

The roof, here made of cypress shingle, was usually steeply pitched.

The McMullen Log House, a pine log cabin completed in 1852, is a typical Cracker dwelling. It is now preserved in Pinellas County Heritage Village. (See p238.)

Overhanging eaves shade both the porch and the windows.

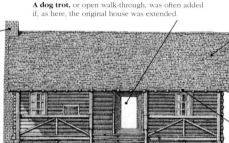

THE GILDED AGE

From the 1880s, the railways and tourism brought new wealth and ideas from outside the state. The love affair with Mediterranean Revivalism began and can be seen in Flagler's brick hotels in St Augustine. Wood was still the favoured material, though, and was used more decoratively – most famously in Key West. Other concentrations of Victorian houses are found in Fernandina Beach *(see p192)* and Mount Dora *(see p206)*.

A tower fulfilled a decorative more than a practical purpose.

Gabled roofs were popular, and could be high enough to fit in an attic.

Ventilation was still a primary concern, hence the generous number of windows.

Verandas that wrapped around the house were quite common.

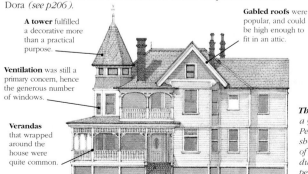

Moorish tower, Tampa Bay Hotel

The McCreary House, a Queen Anne home in Pensacola dated c.1900, shows the refinement of vernacular styles during the Victorian period. (See p217.)

THE FANTASY OF THE BOOM YEARS

The most notable buildings of the period 1920–50 set out to inspire romantic images of faraway places. Each new development had a theme, spawning islands of architectural styles from Moorish to Art Deco – the latter in Miami's South Beach district *(see pp58–63)*. Mediterranean Revivalism dominated, however. Its chief exponents were Addison Mizner in Palm Beach *(see pp114–17)* and George Merrick in Coral Gables *(see pp78–81)*.

The Art Deco Greystone Hotel in Miami's South Beach

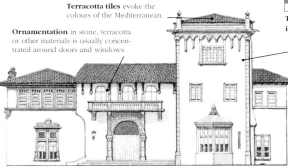

Terracotta tiles evoke the colours of the Mediterranean.

Ornamentation in stone, terracotta or other materials is usually concentrated around doors and windows.

Balconies, turrets and irregular roof levels are all recurrent features.

Palm Beach mansions are primarily Spanish Revival in style. This one on South Ocean Boulevard was built by Julius Jacobs, one of Mizner's chief designers, in 1929.

POSTWAR ARCHITECTURE

Many of Florida's most striking modern buildings are either shopping malls or public buildings, such as theatres or sports stadiums, which are often as impressive for their scale as for their design. More of a curiosity are the new towns of Seaside and Disney's Celebration *(see p150)*, which have arisen out of nostalgia for small-town America and as a reaction to the impersonal nature of the modern city.

Van Wezel Performing Arts Hall in Sarasota *(see p254)*

Large sash windows allow abundant sunlight and sea breezes to enter the house.

Seaside, a piece of award-winning town planning in Florida's Panhandle, has houses with picket fences and other quaint pseudo-Victorian features. (See p222.)

A veranda on the second floor offers a shady place to sit or enjoy the ocean views.

Wood, characteristic of vernacular architecture in Florida, is the favoured material in Seaside.

Neon signs along International Drive, Orlando

THE HIGHWAY

In the 20th century, the flood of visitors and settlers speeding southwards along Florida's highways has spawned buildings unique to the road. Alongside the drive-in banks and restaurants are buildings shaped like ice cream cones or alligators – designed to catch the eye of the motorist driving past at speed. Such outlandishness, aided too by colourful neon signs, breaks up the monotonous strip of motels and fast food outlets.

Spectator Sports in Florida

FLORIDA OFFERS A FINE CHOICE of sports entertainment. The greatest variety and number of events can be seen in Miami *(see p94)* and the southeast, but there are games to watch wherever you are in the state. The spring is the busiest time in most fields of sport. Professional teams are relatively new in Florida and their popularity is often exceeded by that of their college counterparts; collegiate competitions can easily draw crowds of over 80,000 highly partisan fans. Participation sports are described on pages 340–43.

College football crunch match at the Gator Bowl in Jacksonville

AMERICAN FOOTBALL

FLORIDA PRESENTLY boasts three teams in the National Football League (NFL): the Miami Dolphins, the Tampa Bay Buccaneers and, since 1995, the Jacksonville Jaguars. The Miami Dolphins are the most successful, having appeared five times in the Super Bowl. They won it in 1973, completing the first ever unbeaten, no-tie season in NFL history – a feat yet to be repeated. The home game season runs from September to December *(see p94)*.

Florida holds more college bowl games than any other state. The best teams are the Seminoles of Tallahassee, the Hurricanes out of Miami and the Gators from Gainesville; their rivalry is fierce.

Around New Year's Day there is a glut of important and popular college games. The three favourites are the Citrus Bowl in Orlando, the Orange Bowl Classic in Miami and the annual Gator Bowl clash in Jacksonville.

BASEBALL

SINCE WORLD WAR I, Florida's warm climate has made it a favourite spring training site for major league baseball teams. They each return to the same town every year, pumping millions of dollars into the local economy and bringing much prestige. The towns identify strongly with their visitors, whose names are often borrowed by the local Florida State League teams.

Training starts in late February and in March the teams take part in friendly games in the so-called **Grapefruit League**. These games, which take place throughout the week, attract huge crowds, with fans often coming from outside the state. For dates and tickets contact the individual stadiums in advance.

Set up in 1993, the Florida Marlins were the state's first professional baseball team. Second to enrol were the Tampa Bay Devil Rays, who are based at St Petersburg's Tropicana Field stadium *(see p339)*. The baseball season runs from April to August.

GRAPEFRUIT LEAGUE: WHO PLAYS WHERE

Atlanta Braves
Walt Disney World.
((407) 939-2044.

Baltimore Orioles
Fort Lauderdale.
((954) 776-1921.

Boston Red Sox
Fort Myers. ((941) 334-4700.

Chicago White Sox
Sarasota. ((941) 954-7699.

Houston Astros
Kissimmee. ((407) 933-2520.

LA Dodgers
Vero Beach. ((407) 569-6858.

Minnesota Twins
Fort Myers. ((800) 338-9467.

New York Yankees
Tampa. ((813) 879-2244.

Philadelphia Phillies
Clearwater. ((813) 442-8496.

St Louis Cardinals
St Petersburg.
((813) 894-4773.

A complete list is available from the Florida Sports Foundation (see p343).

HORSE RACING AND POLO

FLORIDA BOASTS the USA's second largest thoroughbred industry, centred on Ocala *(see p208)*. The Miami region is home to the most famous races, including the prestigious Florida Derby in March and the Breeder's Cup in November, both staged at

LA Dodgers baseball team, at Vero Beach for spring training

Gulfstream Park in Hallandale. In the spring you can see horses being trained at Hialeah Park *(see p48)* in Miami. Racing also takes place at Tampa Bay Downs during the winter months.

Polo is particularly popular along the Gold Coast, where the top tournament is the Challenge Cup, held in January in West Palm Beach *(see p122)*. With horses galloping over a field as big as nine football pitches, and players hitting balls at up to 110 mph (176 km/h), games can be very exciting. At half time, spectators join in the traditional divot-stamping ritual, in which the scuffed-up turf is trodden flat.

Jai alai, claimed by its fans as the oldest and fastest game in the world

Horse racing at Gulfstream Park, Florida's premier venue

RODEOS

ARCADIA IS THE main centre for professional competition, with two big rodeos a year *(see p261)*, but in February and July crowds also flock to Kissimmee for the Great Silver Spurs Rodeo. Participants from all over the US compete for big purses and top national rankings in bronco riding and other contests. Numerous amateur rodeos can be seen in Davie *(see p133)* and Kissimmee *(see p177)*, all year round.

JAI ALAI

FLORIDA'S GAME of jai alai, a kind of pelota which originated in Europe, is virtually unique in the US *(see p133)*.

Matches take place on a three-walled court, where players use a curved wicker basket to catch and hurl the ball, generating speeds in excess of 150 mph (240 km/h). The back wall is made of granite to absorb the resultant force.

Games are usually played by eight teams of one or two players. After the first point the winners stay on to meet the next team. This goes on until one team has seven points. An evening usually consists of 14 such games.

Jai alai is played all year round in indoor stadiums known as frontons. One of the main attractions is the chance to gamble, and millions are wagered every year.

MOTOR RACING

AUTO AND MOTORCYCLE racing are big in Florida. The season starts in February at the Daytona International Speedway *(see p204)*, one of the world's fastest tracks, with two very popular races. The Rolex 24, like its elder brother at Le Mans, runs all day and all night, and the Daytona 500 is a season highlight for the National Association of Stock Car Auto Racing (NASCAR).

The Daytona 500, first held in 1959

Other big races take place in Hialeah (Miami), Homestead, Pensacola and Sebring (near Orlando). Hot rods come to Gainesville in March for the Gatornationals, the top drag racing event on the Atlantic seaboard. Motorcycles also race at Daytona.

BASKETBALL

PROFESSIONAL basketball is fairly new in Florida, with Orlando Magic and Miami Heat the only Florida teams in the NBA (National Basketball Association). Orlando Magic is famous for its 1992 signing of Shaquille O'Neal, later sold for $120 million. The season is October to April. College games are also very popular.

Orlando in action

GOLF AND TENNIS

GOLF TOURNAMENTS abound in Florida, birthplace of golf ace, Jack Nicklaus. Top of the bill are the Bay Hill Invitational in Orlando and the PGA Tournament Players Championship in Ponte Vedra Beach near Jacksonville; both are held at the end of March.

Tennis is another big favourite. Key Biscayne's Crandon Park is famous for its annual Lipton International Players Championship in March, which pulls huge crowds.

FLORIDA THROUGH THE YEAR

WITH ITS WARM CLIMATE, Florida is a year-round destination, but the difference in the weather between north and south means it has two distinct tourist seasons. In south Florida (including Orlando) the busiest time is from October to April, when Americans come to enjoy the mild winters. Most will have left well before summer arrives, when it can be uncomfortably hot. Orlando's theme parks still attract families with kids on school holidays, but in summer the Panhandle sees the biggest crowds. Be warned that prices in the relevant high season can be double those charged during the rest of the year. Whatever time of year you visit, you are bound to encounter a festival of some kind, although apart from national holidays (see p35) few of these are Florida-wide. For a full list contact the local tourist office.

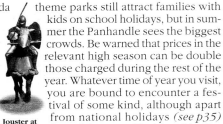

Jouster at Sarasota fair

SPRING

IN LATE FEBRUARY, college students invade Florida for the Spring Break. They pour in by the thousand from all over the US and for the next six weeks Florida's coastal resorts are heaving, putting pressure on accommodation, particularly in Daytona Beach and Panama City Beach.

Baseball training (see p30) is also a big attraction in the spring. In the north, feast your eyes on the blooming azaleas and dogwood trees.

MARCH

Sanibel Shell Fair (first week). Shell collectors and artists come to Sanibel Island (see pp264–5) to learn, show their collections and pick up prizes.
Florida Strawberry Festival (first week), Plant City near Tampa. Feast on strawberry shortcake and country music at this popular shindig.

Little Havana's Calle Ocho, hub of the party at Carnival Miami

Daytona Beach swarming with pleasure seekers on Spring Break

Medieval Fair (first weekend), Sarasota. Magicians, costumed performers and human chess games entertain at this celebration of the Middle Ages.
Motorcycle Races (early Mar), Daytona Beach (see pp204–205). Bikers converge from all over the US, on both vintage and ultramodern bikes.
Carnival Miami (second Sunday). Revel at the nine-day street party in Miami's Latin district (see pp74–5).
St Augustine Arts and Crafts Festival (last weekend). Skilled craft artists offer their wares among the city's historical sites.
Festival of the States (late Mar–early Apr), St Petersburg. The three weeks of fun include parades, coronation balls, jazz bands and nightly fireworks.

APRIL

Antique Boat Festival (first weekend), Mount Dora (see p206). Antique boats race on the lake as visitors attend exhibitions in the pretty town.
Springtime Tallahassee (all month). One of the South's biggest festivals, this extended extravaganza features parades, balloon races, great food and a variety of live music.
Easter (April). Celebrate sunrise services at the Castillo de San Marcos (see pp200–201) and take carriage rides around St Augustine.
Conch Republic Celebration (late Apr–early May), Key West. Party all week with parades, bed races, dancing and other events honouring the town's founding fathers.

MAY

SunFest (first week), West Palm Beach. A week-long mix of cultural and sporting events.

Emblem of the Conch Republic

Isle of Eight Flags Shrimp Festival (first weekend), Fernandina Beach. Sample the local prawns and other seafood delicacies while you peruse the craft stalls.
Destin Mayfest (third weekend). Locals and visitors alike flock to the sound of live jazz on the Destin Harborwalk.

AVERAGE DAILY HOURS OF SUNSHINE

Hours

12
9
6
3
0

Jan Feb Mar Apr May Jun Jul Aug Sep Oct Nov Dec

Sunshine Chart
The chart gives figures for the whole of Florida. The west coast near St Petersburg, which boasts an average of 361 days of sunshine per year, enjoys more sun than elsewhere, but blue skies are a fairly consistent feature everywhere. Even in southern Florida's wetter summer months, the clouds generally disperse quickly.

Young boy in patriotic colours at a Fourth of July celebration

SUMMER

TEMPERATURES and humidity rise as summer progresses, with only Atlantic breezes and almost daily afternoon storms to bring some relief. Florida's hurricane season *(see pp24–5)* is also underway. Travellers on a tight budget can make the most of the off-season hotel prices in the south.

The big summer holiday is Independence Day on 4 July, which is celebrated with street pageants, fireworks extravaganzas, barbecues, picnics and mass cooling off in the sea.

JUNE

Monticello Watermelon Festival *(all month)*, Monticello *(see p229)*. The harvest is celebrated in back-country style with barbecues and hoedowns.
Goombay Festival *(first weekend)*, Coconut Grove, Miami *(see p82)*. A Bahamian party offering a parade, great food and Caribbean music.

Fiesta of Five Flags *(early Jun)*, Pensacola. Two weeks of festivities include parades, marathons and fishing rodeos as well as the re-enactment of Tristan de Luna's beach landing in 1559.
Downtown Venice Street Craft Festival *(mid-Jun)*. Quiet, romantic Venice spruces up its downtown streets for this very popular craft bazaar.

JULY

America Birthday Bash *(4 Jul)*, Miami. The city sounds off with fireworks at midnight, preceded by picnics and fun and games for all the family, in the biggest Independence Day celebration in south Florida.
Silver Spurs Rodeo *(early Jul)*, Kissimmee *(see p177)*. Witness the antics and marvel at the skills at the state's oldest rodeo (also held in February).
Hemingway Days Festival *(mid-Jul)*, Key West. The city offers up a week of author signings, short story contests,

theatrical productions and a very entertaining Hemingway lookalike competition.
Florida International Festival *(late Jul–early Aug)*, Daytona Beach. This world-famous music festival features pop, jazz and classical music.

AUGUST

Boca Festival Days *(all month)*, Boca Raton. This celebration features an art-and-craft fair, barbershop quartet performances and a sand castle building contest.
Annual Wausau Possum Festival *(first Saturday)*, Wausau. This town north of Panama City Beach honours the marsupial with activities such as greased-pole climbing and corn-bread baking, and offers the chance to sample possum-based dishes.
Carrollwood Twilight Arts and Crafts Festival *(first weekend)*, Tampa. The city's fast-paced lifestyle slows a little for this large art show.

Bearded contenders at the Hemingway Days Festival lookalike contest

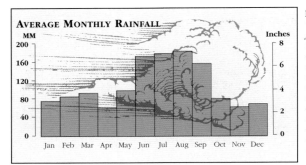

AVERAGE MONTHLY RAINFALL

Jan Feb Mar Apr May Jun Jul Aug Sep Oct Nov Dec

Rainfall Chart
The chart gives figures for the whole state. The north-south climatic divide means that, for example, October is the driest month in the Panhandle but the wettest in the Keys. The rule is that southern Florida is wetter than the north in summer (when short, sharp downpours are the norm), while in winter it's the reverse.

AUTUMN (FALL)

THE TEMPERATURES begin to cool, and although storms are still a threat, the weather is pleasant. The autumn months are usually quiet: the beaches, attractions and highways are all much less crowded.

Thanksgiving, on the fourth Thursday in November, is the highlight of autumn for many, when families come together to eat turkey and pumpkin pie. It is followed by the biggest shopping day of the year and commercially launches the countdown to Christmas.

SEPTEMBER

Las Olas Art Fair *(early Sep)*, Fort Lauderdale. Las Olas Boulevard is the main drag for this street fair offering art displays, tasty food and music.
St Augustine's Founding Anniversary *(Saturday nearest 8th)*. This period-dress re-enactment of the Spanish landing in 1565 is held near the spot where the first settlers stepped off their ships.

Sleek craft on display at the Fort Lauderdale Boat Show

OCTOBER

Destin Fishing Rodeo *(all month)*. The "World's Luckiest Fishing Village" welcomes hordes of competitive anglers for this frenzy of fishing that includes a two-day seafood festival in the first week.
Jacksonville Jazz Festival *(mid-Oct)*. This is an unusual combination of art and craft exhibitions mixed with three days of international jazz stars competing and performing.

Boggy Bayou Mullet Festival *(mid-Oct)*, Valparaiso and Niceville. These twin cities near Fort Walton Beach celebrate the local fish with fine food, arts and entertainment.
Fort Lauderdale Boat Show *(late Oct)*. The largest in-water boat show in the world draws yachting enthusiasts to four separate city locations.
Fantasy Fest *(last week)*, Key West. This wild, week-long Halloween celebration features gay festivities, masked balls, a costume contest and lively street processions.
Johns Pass Seafood Festival *(last weekend)*, Madeira Beach. This popular festival attracts seafood lovers to Johns Pass Village *(see p238)*.
Guavaween *(last Saturday)*, Tampa. This zany Halloween parade pokes fun at the life and history of the city, especially at an early attempt to grow guavas in the area.

NOVEMBER

Apalachicola Seafood Festival *(first weekend)*. The fishing fleet is blessed, net-making lessons are given and oyster-shucking-and-eating contests are held at Florida's oldest and biggest seafood festival.
Orange Bowl Festival *(early Nov–late Feb)*, Miami. This youth festival presents over 20 sporting and cultural events.
Festival of the Masters *(second weekend)*, Walt Disney World. Artists from across the country show their work in Downtown Disney *(see p162)*.
Miami Book Fair International *(mid-Nov)*. Publishers, authors and bookworms congregate in downtown Miami for this cultural highlight.

Costumed revellers out on the streets for Key West's Fantasy Fest

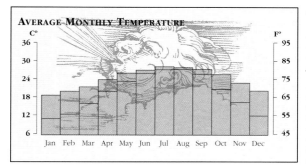

AVERAGE MONTHLY TEMPERATURE

Temperature Chart
This chart gives the average temperature in Miami and Jacksonville, the higher level being the figure for Miami. In the north, even in winter, the evenings are only mildly chilly, and snow is very rare, although it's too cold for swimming. In southern Florida, the hot summer temperatures are exacerbated by the high humidity.

WINTER

WINTER MONTHS are full of excitement in anticipation of Christmas and New Year. The flood of "snowbirds" from the north intensifies. The celebrities arrive too – some to relax, others to perform during the state's busiest entertainment season. The crowds multiply at Walt Disney World and the Magic Kingdom is at its most colourful.

DECEMBER

Winterfest Boat Parade
(early Dec), Fort Lauderdale. Boats decked with lights cruise the Intracoastal Waterway in a magical night-time display.
King Orange Jamboree Parade *(31 Dec)*, Miami. Huge event to herald the New Year, parodied the previous night by the outrageous King Mambo Strut in Coconut Grove.

Santa on the Intracoastal Waterway for a sunny Florida Christmas

JANUARY

Orange Bowl *(New Year's Day)*, Miami. Fans of college football flock to the eponymous stadium *(see p95)* for the big postseason game.
Greek Epiphany Day *(6 Jan)*, Tarpon Springs. Ceremonies, feasts and music at the Greek Orthodox Cathedral *(see p237)*.

Pirates arriving for mock invasion at Tampa's annual Gasparilla Festival

Art Deco Weekend *(mid-Jan)*, Miami Beach. Take tours and dance to 1930s music at this street party in the stunning Art Deco district *(see pp58–65)*.

FEBRUARY

Gasparilla Festival *(second Monday)*, Tampa. A boisterous party, with boat parades and locals in appropriate dress, in memory of the pirates who ravaged the coast *(see p249)*.
Speed Weeks *(first three weeks)*, Daytona Beach. These motor races build up to the famous Daytona 500 on the final Sunday *(see pp204–205)*.
Florida Citrus Festival *(mid-Feb)*, Winter Haven near Orlando. The citrus harvest is honoured at this country fair.
Coconut Grove Arts Festival *(mid-Feb)*, Miami *(see p82)*. This avant-garde art show is one of the country's largest.
Florida State Fair *(mid-Feb)*, Tampa. Carnival rides, corn on the cob, big-name performers and even alligator wrestling can be enjoyed at this big fair.

Miami Film Festival *(mid-Feb)*. The Film Society of America hosts a broad array of films over ten days *(see p337)*.
Swamp Cabbage Festival *(last weekend)*, La Belle, east of Fort Myers. This celebration features rodeos and dancing, and you can sample delicacies made from the edible heart of the honoured state tree.

PUBLIC HOLIDAYS

New Year's Day (1 Jan)
Martin Luther King Day (3rd Mon, Jan)
President's Day (3rd Mon, Feb)
Memorial Day (last Mon, May)
Independence Day (4 Jul)
Labor Day (1st Mon, Sep)
Columbus Day (2nd Mon, Oct)
Election Day (1st Tue, Nov)
Veterans Day (11 Nov)
Thanksgiving (4th Thu, Nov)
Christmas Day (25 Dec)

THE HISTORY OF FLORIDA

AT FIRST GLANCE, Florida appears to be a state with very little history. However, behind the state's modern veneer lies a long and rich past that has been moulded and formed by many different nationalities and cultures.

Until the 16th century, Florida supported a large indigenous population. Many of its tribes had complex political and religious systems which demonstrated a high degree of social organization. However, after Ponce de León first sighted "La Florida" in 1513, Spanish colonization quickly decimated the Indians through warfare and disease.

The next 250 years saw little development; Florida was merely an outpost of Spain's more successful Caribbean colonies and a refuge for slaves and Seminole Indians *(see p271)* fleeing British rule to the north. Only after Britain took control in 1763 did Florida really begin to thrive. For the next 60 years Spain, England and America fought over Florida before it became an American territory in 1821.

Henry Flagler

American attempts to remove the Seminoles from Florida led to conflicts which lasted for over 65 years. Soon after the Seminole Wars came the Civil War – by its end in 1865, the state was in ruins. However, Florida soon recovered. Entrepreneurs like Henry Flagler built a network of railways and luxurious hotels which attracted wealthy tourists from the north.

Tourism flourished during the early 20th century and by 1950 had become Florida's leading industry.

As the state opened up, agriculture expanded and migrants began to flood in. The recession of the 1920s and '30s was only a short hiatus in the state's growth, and between 1940 and 1990 the population increased sixfold.

Today, Florida is home to a sizeable Hispanic community, with a strong Cuban presence as well as many other ethnic groups. Economic inequalities have led to social problems, and the state's relentless urbanization has put a strain on the environment, however Florida is still booming.

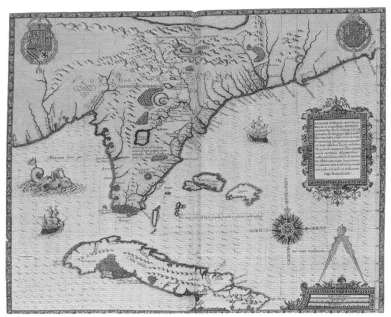

Theodore de Brys' 16th-century map of Florida, one of the earliest in existence

◁ **An early postcard from Florida, a popular holiday destination in the 1920s**

Prehistoric Florida

Stone tool

FLORIDA WAS ONCE part of the volcanic chain that formed the Caribbean islands. This eroded over millions of years and was submerged. When the land finally re-emerged, Florida was connected to North America.

Humans first arrived in Florida after the last Ice Age and formed distinct tribes. Some developed from nomadic hunter-gatherer societies to ones with permanent settlements along Florida's bountiful rivers and rich seaboard. A high degree of religious and political organization was common to many groups by around AD 1000, and was manifested especially in the building of burial and temple mounds.

EARLY TRIBAL CONTACTS

— *Areas in contact*

Human Effigy Vessel
This painted, ceramic burial urn dates from AD 400–600. Such vessels were often very ornate and usually depicted birds and animals. "Kill holes" were often made in the pots to allow the soul of the pottery to accompany that of the dead.

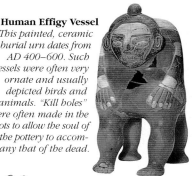

Pots were often incised. This added to the surface area of the vessel and increased its resistance to heat, as well as making it more aesthetically pleasing.

Copper headdress plates were made of hammered copper that came from as far away as the Great Lakes.

FLORIDA'S PREHISTORIC TRIBES
Agriculture and burial mounds, traits shared with groups elsewhere in the southeast US, were associated with the Timucua and other tribes in north Florida. Southern tribes, such as the Calusa and Tequesta, left a legacy of wood carvings and midden mounds, which indicate a diet based on fish and shellfish.

Calusa wood carving

MARCO ISLAND'S SECRET
In 1896, a unique discovery was made on Marco Island *(see p270)*. Many Calusa Indian artifacts of perishable organic material were found perfectly preserved in swampland. However, once out of the protective mangrove sludge the objects quickly crumbled away. Today, sadly just one or two of these extraordinary pieces, which include ceremonial items such as carvings and masks, survive.

Fired Bowl
Made c.AD 800, this ceramic bowl probably had a ceremonial use. Markings help archaeologists to identify the pot's makers.

TIMELINE

c.10,000 Palaeo-Indian stone tools are first made by Florida's earliest inhabitants

Atlatls or throwing sticks, part of the tool-kit after 6000 BC

10,000 BC	9000 BC	8000 BC	7000 BC	6000 BC	5000 BC

The mastodon, an Ice Age animal that once lived in Florida

c.7500 The temperature rises and people start to hunt smaller animals like deer and include more plant foods in their diet

c.5000 The first semi-permanent settlements are built along the St Johns River, creating large midden mounds

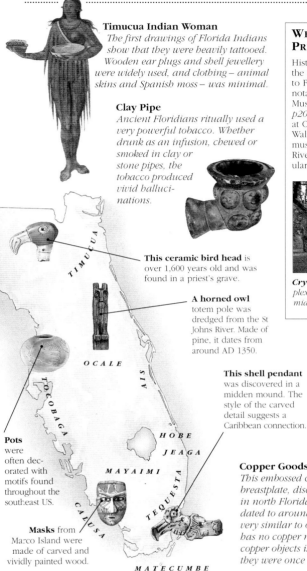

Timucua Indian Woman
The first drawings of Florida Indians show that they were heavily tattooed. Wooden ear plugs and shell jewellery were widely used, and clothing – animal skins and Spanish moss – was minimal.

Clay Pipe
Ancient Floridians ritually used a very powerful tobacco. Whether drunk as an infusion, chewed or smoked in clay or stone pipes, the tobacco produced vivid hallucinations.

This ceramic bird head is over 1,600 years old and was found in a priest's grave.

A horned owl totem pole was dredged from the St Johns River. Made of pine, it dates from around AD 1350.

This shell pendant was discovered in a midden mound. The style of the carved detail suggests a Caribbean connection.

Pots were often decorated with motifs found throughout the south-east US.

Masks from Marco Island were made of carved and vividly painted wood.

Copper Goods
This embossed copper breastplate, discovered in north Florida and dated to around AD 1300, is very similar to one from Georgia. Florida has no copper reserves; the presence of copper objects is thought to indicate that they were once traded as prestige goods.

OCALE

TIMUCUA

AIS

TOCOBAGA

HOBE

JEAGA

MAYAIMI

CALUSA

TEQUESTA

MATECUMBE

WHERE TO SEE PREHISTORIC FLORIDA

Historical museums all over the state contain items relating to Florida's prehistory. Most notable is the Natural History Museum in Gainesville *(see p209)*. Temple mound sites at Crystal River and Fort Walton Beach both have museums attached – Crystal River *(p236)* is in a particularly attractive setting.

Crystal River's Indian complex consists of well-preserved midden and temple mounds.

4000 BC	3000 BC	2000 BC	1000 BC	AD 1	AD 1000

c.1000 Northern Florida sees a shift from a basic hunter-gatherer economy to one of cultivation. The settled communities develop more complex societies and the first burial mounds are built

c.1000 Political systems and religious practices develop and temple mounds are built. Increased contact with tribal groups outside Florida

c.3000 From this time, Florida enjoys a climate that is similar to today's

c.2000 The first crude pottery appears in Florida

A temple structure, built on top of a burial mound

c.800 First evidence of corn (maize) being grown in north Florida

Spanish Florida

AFTER JUAN PONCE DE LEON first sighted Florida in 1513, several Spanish conquistadors attempted unsuccessfully to colonize and find gold in the region. The French were the first to establish a fort in 1564, but it was soon destroyed by the Spanish: the Gulf Stream carried Spanish treasure ships from other New World colonies past Florida's coast, and it was vital that "La Florida" did not fall into enemy hands. The Spanish introduced Christianity,

Spanish crucifix

horses and cattle. European diseases, in addition to the brutality of the conquistadors, decimated local Indian populations. Britain, keen to expand her American colonies, led several raids into Florida in the 1700s, in an attempt to supplant Spanish rule.

SPANISH FLEET SEA ROUTES

— *Sea routes*

Ribault's column, erected in 1562 *(see p193)*, marked the French claim to north Florida.

Juan Ponce de León
While searching for gold, Ponce de León found land that he named Pascua Florida, *after the Feast of Flowers (Easter).*

El Adelantado JUAN PONCE *Descubridor de la Florida.*

Maize, native to Florida, was a staple crop for the Indians.

FORT MOSE

Runaway slaves escaping the harsh conditions in the British Carolinas fled to Florida, where, as in other Spanish colonies, slaves enjoyed certain rights. The Spanish saw the advantage of helping Britain's enemies and in 1738 created Fort Mose, near the garrison town of St Augustine, for the runaways. This fort, with its own militia and businesses, is regarded as North America's first independent black community.

Black militiaman in the Spanish colonies

FLORIDA'S FIRST SETTLEMENT

The Huguenot, René de Laudonnière, founded "La Caroline", Florida's first successful European settlement, in 1564. Another Frenchman, Le Moyne, painted the Indians greeting the colonizers.

TIMELINE

1513 Ponce de León discovers Florida. He tries to establish a Spanish colony eight years later, but is unsuccessful

Hernando de Soto's signature

1622 The Spanish ships *Atocha* and *Santa Margarita* sink during a hurricane

c.1609 *A History of the Conquest of Florida* is published by Garcilasso Inca del Vega

1520	1540	1560	1580	1600	1620

1528 Pánfilo de Narváez lands in Tampa Bay with 600 men, in search of El Dorado, the land of gold

1539 Hernando de Soto arrives at Tampa Bay with 600 men, but he dies by the Mississippi River three years later

1566 The Jesuits arrive in Florida

1565 Pedro Menéndez de Avilés founds San Agustín (St Augustine) after defeating the French

Cross-section of the Atocha

Hernando de Soto
De Soto was the most ruthless of the conquistadors. His search for gold led to the massacre of many Indians; only a third of his own party survived.

(see p253).

WHERE TO SEE SPANISH FLORIDA

In St Petersburg, the De Soto National Memorial marks the spot where de Soto landed (see p253). A reconstruction of Fort Caroline (p193) lies just outside Jacksonville. However, the best place to see the Spanish legacy is in St Augustine (pp196–9) and its imposing Castillo de San Marcos, (pp200–201).

Nuestra Senora de la Leche is a shrine in St Augustine founded by de Avilés in 1565.

Silver and Gold Hair Ornament
Indian artifacts made of precious metals fuelled the Spanish myth of El Dorado. In fact, the metals came from Spanish wrecks.

René de Laudonnière surveys the offerings of the Indians.

Sir Francis Drake
Spain's power in the New World colonies worried the British. Drake, an English buccaneer, burned down St Augustine in 1586.

Codice Osune
This 16th-century manuscript depicts members of Tristan de Luna's expedition to Florida. In 1559, a hurricane destroyed his camp at Pensacola Bay, defeating his attempts at colonization.

Athore, the chief of the Timucua, shows the French colonizers his tribe worshipping at Ribault's column.

1670 The Treaty of Madrid defines the Spanish claim to the New World

The pirate Blackbeard's flag

1718 Blackbeard, who terrorized the east coast of Florida, is killed off North Carolina

1740 The British, based in Georgia, besiege the Castillo de San Marcos

1763 Under the Treaty of Paris, Britain gets Florida and returns recently captured Cuba to Spain

1640	1660	1680	1700	1720	1740	1760

1687 The first eight slaves fleeing the British plantations in the Carolinas arrive in Florida

1693 The Spanish establish Pensacola, which is permanently settled five years later

1702 The British raze St Augustine to the ground

Castillo de San Marcos, St Augustine

1756 Castillo de San Marcos is completed

The Fight for Florida

A PLENTIFUL SUPPLY of hides and furs, and the opportunity to expand the plantation system, attracted the British to Florida. After taking control in 1763, they divided the colony in two. Florida was subsidized by Britain and so stayed loyal during the American Revolution. However, Spain regained West Florida in 1781 and then East Florida was handed back two years later.

Hide boot

American slaves fled to Florida creating antagonism between Spain and the US. This was exacerbated by Indian raids to the north and an Indian alliance with the runaway slaves, giving the US a pretext for invading the colony. General Andrew Jackson led unlawful raids, and even occupied West Florida, thus provoking the First Seminole War.

BRITISH FLORIDA 1764–83

☐ *East Florida*
☐ *West Florida*

The Spanish Caste System
Few Spanish women came to the colonies, so Spanish men often took black or Indian wives. A hierarchical caste system emerged – with those of pure Spanish blood at the top.

Fort George was the main British fortification at Pensacola.

A drummer kept the marching beat, and led soldiers into battle.

Brazier
Used for warmth during northern Florida winters, a brasero *could also smoke out mosquitos in summer.*

THE CAPTURE OF PENSACOLA
In 1781, after a month-long siege, the Spaniard Bernardo de Gálvez defeated the British and captured Pensacola for Spain. His victory undoubtedly helped the bid for independence made by the rebel American colonies.

TIMELINE

1776 American Revolution leaves Britain's reserves heavily depleted and British loyalists begin to abandon Florida

1783 Under the Second Treaty of Paris, Britain recognizes American independence, gains the Bahamas and Gibraltar, and returns Florida to the Spanish, who start to colonize it in earnest

1785–1821 Several Spanish-American border disputes occur

| 1765 | 1770 | 1775 | 1780 | 1785 | 17 |

British soldier in the American Revolution

1781 Under de Gálvez, the Spanish land at Pensacola and capture West Florida

1782 US Congress chooses the bald eagle as the emblem of the new republic

US emblem

General Jackson
An ambitious soldier, Andrew Jackson led unauthorized raids into Florida and eventually conquered it. His successes made him the ideal candidate to become Florida's first American governor in 1821 and later, the seventh US president.

William Bartram's Illustrations
In 1765, William Bartram was appointed the royal botanist in America. He documented Florida's wildlife and her indigenous peoples.

Bernardo de Gálvez, the 27-year-old Spanish governor of Louisiana, was wounded in action in the battle for Pensacola.

WHERE TO SEE THE FIGHT FOR FLORIDA

The Kingsley Plantation *(see p193)* near Jacksonville is the state's oldest surviving plantation house. Pensacola's historic Seville District *(p216)* was laid out by the British during their occupation, and St Augustine *(pp196–9)* contains several buildings dating from this era; they include the British Government House, and the charming Ximenez-Fatio house, from the second period of Spanish rule.

***Kingsley Plantation** occupies a lovely setting at the mouth of the St Johns River.*

Political Cartoon
This cartoon shows the horse America throwing his master. British loyalists in East Florida were dismayed by the loss of the Colonies after 1783, and soon chose to leave Florida.

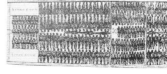

The Slave Trade
Slavery fuelled the plantation system. The journey from Africa to America could take months, and slaves were so tightly packed on board ship that many died en route.

1803 The US buys Louisiana and pushes east, creating Florida's present western boundary. The US claims West Florida

1800 Spain cedes West Florida's Louisiana territories to the French

1808 A law banning the slave trade is enacted by the US Congress, but it is widely ignored

Slave manacles

1817 First Seminole War begins

1795	1800	1805	1810	1815

1795 Spain cedes territory north of the 31st parallel to the US

The Patriots of East Florida's flag

1812 American patriots capture Amelia Island, demanding that the US annexes East Florida from the Spanish. Their attempt fails but instils the feeling that Florida should belong to America

1819 To settle Spain's $5-million debt to the US, all Spanish territories east of the Mississippi (including Florida) are ceded to the US.

Antebellum Florida

Pelican, by
JJ Audubon

AFTER FLORIDA BECAME PART of the US in 1821, American settlement proceeded apace and the plantation system was firmly established in north Florida. The settlers wanted good land, so the Federal government tried to remove all Indians to west of the Mississippi; resulting conflicts developed into the Second and Third Seminole Wars. After Abraham Lincoln, an opponent of slavery, was elected president in 1860, Florida became the third state to secede from the Union. During the ensuing Civil War it saw little action; Florida's chief role was to supply food to the Confederates, especially beef and salt.

INDIAN LANDS 1823–32

☐ *Indian reservation land*

Slave cabins were log huts, built away from the main residence.

Overseer's cabin

Barn and stables

Well

Osceola

The influential Indian leader Osceola refused to move from Florida with his tribe. In 1835 he started the Second Seminole War, during which many plantations were destroyed.

UNCLE TOM'S CABIN

In 1852, Harriet Beecher Stowe, a religious northerner who spent her later years in Florida, published a novel that helped to change the face of America. *Uncle Tom's Cabin* is a tale about a slave who, having rescued a white child, is sold to a sadistic master and is eventually flogged to death. It was hugely successful and furthered the cause of the anti-slavery lobby. During the Civil War, President Lincoln joked that Mrs Stowe was the "little woman who started this big war".

Poster for *Uncle Tom's Cabin*

Cotton

The principal cash crop on plantations was cotton. It required intensive labour and the work was gruelling – especially picking the cotton off the spiny bushes.

TIMELINE

1821 Jackson becomes governor of the territory of Florida

1823 Treaty of Moultrie Creek requires the Seminoles to move from north to central Florida

1832 Under the Treaty of Payne's Creek, 15 Seminole chiefs cede their land in Florida to the US and agree to move west

1835 Second Seminole War begins

Early horse-drawn train

1820	1825	1830	1835	1840

Osceola refusing to sign 1832 treaty

c.1824 The Indian village of Talasi is chosen as the site of the new state capital and is renamed Tallahassee

1832 JJ Audubon, the naturalist, visits Key West

1842 Second Seminole War ends

1829 General Jackson becomes President of the US

1836 The first railways in Florida begin operating

Paddlesteamer
During the Seminole and Civil Wars, steamboats were used to transport troops and supplies to the interior.

Chief Billy Bowlegs
In 1855, a group of surveyors pillaged Indian land. Chief Billy Bowlegs retaliated, so starting the Third Seminole War. He surrendered in 1858, however other Seminoles retreated deep into the Everglades.

Goodwood House was built in a grand style that befitted its wealth and importance within the local community.

Laundry

Privy

Guest House

Spring House

The kitchen was in a separate building because of the risk of fire.

PLANTATION LIFE
Antebellum plantations such as Goodwood (see p229), reconstructed here, were almost self-sufficient. They had their own laws and some housed over 200 slaves, who tended cotton, maize and other crops.

WHERE TO SEE ANTEBELLUM FLORIDA
Gamble Plantation (see p252) sheds light on the lifestyle of a wealthy plantation owner, while at Bulow Plantation (p202) and Indian Key (p280) you can see the ruins of communities destroyed by the Seminoles. The Museum of Science and Discovery (p194) in Jacksonville contains Civil War artifacts, including some from the US army steamboat *Maple Leaf*. Key West's East Martello Tower (p286) and Fort Zachary (p288), and Fort Clinch (p192), in the northeast, are fine examples of 19th-century forts.

The East Martello Tower *was built by Union forces to defend Key West's Atlantic coast.*

Battle of Olustee
In February 1864, Union forces, including two Negro regiments, were defeated by Confederate troops in the northeast. Some 10,000 men fought in the six-hour battle; 2,000 were injured and 300 died.

1845	1850	1855	1860	1865

1845 On 4 July Florida becomes the 27th state to join the United States of America. The Capitol building in Tallahassee is completed

1848 John Gorrie invents an ice-making machine

1855 Third Seminole War begins; three years later 163 Indians surrender (including Billy Bowlegs) and are forcibly removed from Florida

1861 Civil War begins

1865 The northern army is defeated at the Battle of Natural Bridge. The Civil War ends in the same year

Florida's first state seal

1852 Harriet Beecher Stowe publishes the anti-slavery epic, *Uncle Tom's Cabin*

1860s Scottish merchants found Dunedin on Florida's west coast

Confederate Civil War bond

Florida's Golden Age

A FTER THE CIVIL WAR Florida's economy was devastated, but its fine climate and small population meant it was a land ripe for investment. The railroad barons Henry Flagler and Henry Plant forged their lines down the east and west coasts of Florida during the late 1880s and '90s, and tourists followed in increasing numbers, stimulating the economy. A diverse agricultural base also sheltered Florida from the depression of the 1890s which ravaged other cotton-producing states. Fortunes were made and fine mansions were built. Blacks were less fortunate; most lost the right to vote, Ku Klux Klan violence grew, and segregation was the norm.

José Martí,
Cuban hero

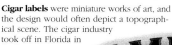

GROWTH OF THE RAILWAYS

— *Railways by 1860*

— *Railways by 1890*

— *Overseas Railroad by 1912*

Steamboat Tourism
Before the advent of the railways, tourists explored Florida's interior by paddlesteamer. Steamboats plied scenic rivers such as the Oklawaha and the St Johns.

Cigar labels were miniature works of art, and the design would often depict a topographical scene. The cigar industry took off in Florida in the late 1800s.

Jacob Summerlin
After the Civil War, Jacob Summerlin, the "King of the Crackers" (see p18), made his fortune by selling beef to Spanish Cuba. His wild cattle were descended, ironically, from animals that had been introduced to Florida by the conquistadors.

GRAND HOTELS
Both Plant and Flagler built opulent palaces for rich tourists who used the railways to escape the northern winters; these "snowbirds" would spend the winter season in style, in towns like Tampa and St Augustine.

TIMELINE

1869 The first black Cabinet member is appointed as Secretary of State for Florida

A Ringling Brothers' circus act

1885 Vincente Ybor transfers his cigar industry to Tampa

1870 More than 100 blacks are killed by the Ku Klux Klan in Jackson County

1892 In the election, only 11 per cent of blacks remain eligible to vote

1870	1875	1880	1885	1890

1884 Ringling brothers set up their travelling circus

1891 The Cuban, José Martí, makes a speech in Tampa to drum up support for his independence movement

1868 Vote granted to all male American citizens aged 21 and over, including blacks

1870s Steamboats start to take tourists, as well as goods, into the interior of Florida

1886 Flagler starts construction of the Florida East Coast Railroad

Rail Travel
Many rich tourists had private railway carriages. Henry Flagler's is today at his former Palm Beach home (see p120).

(see p120)

WHERE TO SEE THE GOLDEN AGE

St Augustine *(see pp196–9)* boasts several of Flagler's buildings, including what is today the Lightner Museum. The Tampa Bay Hotel is now the Henry B Plant Museum *(p244)*, and Fernandina has some fine examples of steamboat architecture *(p192)*. On Pigeon Key *(p282)* you'll find Flagler's Overseas Railroad construction camp.

(see pp196–9), (p244), (p192), (p282)

Spanish-American War
When America joined Cuba's fight against Spain in 1898, Florida boomed. Thousands of troops converged on Tampa, Miami and Key West, and money from the nation's coffers poured in to support the war effort.

Flagler College *in St Augustine was once Henry Flagler's magnificent Ponce de Leon Hotel.*

The Tampa Bay Hotel, built by Henry Plant in 1891, operated as a hotel until 1932. It had 511 rooms, and during the Spanish-American War served as the officers' quarters.

Gilded Rocking Chair
Representative of the decorative excesses of the 19th century, this rocking chair from the Lightner Museum (see p199) is elaborately embellished with scrolls and swans.

(see p199)

The Birth of a Nation
On its release in 1915, this epic film provoked a resurgence of violence by the Ku Klux Klan in Florida.

The Hillsborough River and nearby Tampa Bay helped turn Tampa into one of the three largest Gulf ports by 1900.

1895 Blossoming citrus groves are hit by the "Great Freeze". Julia Tuttle sends some orange blossom to Flagler in Palm Beach to persuade him to continue his railway to Miami

1905 The University of Florida is established at Gainesville

Motoring on the sands at Daytona Beach

1918 Prohibition starts in Florida

1895	1900	1905	1910	1915

Orange blossom

1898 Teddy Roosevelt and his "Rough Riders" arrive in Tampa en route to fight in the Spanish-American War in Cuba

1903 Alexander Winton sets a 68-mph (109-km/h) land speed record on the hard sand at Daytona Beach

1912 Flagler steams into Key West

1915 Dredging doubles the size of Miami Beach

1916 Florida's cotton crop is wiped out by the boll weevil

Boom, Bust and Recovery

Early Pan Am poster

LIKE THE REST OF THE US, Florida saw times of both rapid growth and depression during the first half of the 20th century. Excited by the rampant development during the 1920s land boom, northerners poured in, many as "Tin Can Tourists" in their Model T Fords. Then, in 1926, three years before the Wall Street Crash, a real estate slump ruined many in the state. But economic recovery came earlier than in the rest of the US too, with the the growth of tourism and the introduction of federal schemes; many unemployed fled to Florida from the north looking for work. During and after World War II, the state continued to prosper; in the 1950s it was boosted by the launch of the NASA space programme.

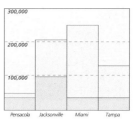

POPULATION FIGURES

☐ *1920*   ☐ *1950*

Land Boom
At the height of the boom, prime land could fetch $26,000 per acre ($11,600 per hectare). A great many northerners were bankrupted after unwittingly investing in swampland.

Hurricane of 1926
On 18 September a hurricane hit South Florida, destroying 5,000 homes. Locals said the winds "blowed a crooked road straight".

THE AMERICAN DREAM IN FLORIDA
Florida's warm winter climate and economic upswing attracted floods of northerners. Many who first came as visitors returned to settle, and foreign immigrants also favoured the state. It was a land of opportunity with rapid urban growth and industries that provided good jobs – even the young could expect a good standard of living.

TIMELINE

1928 The Tamiami Trail between Tampa and Miami is officially opened

1929 The first commercial flight between Miami to Havana is made by Pan American World Airways

1931 Ernest Hemingway buys a house in Key West

1935 Hurricane destroys Flagler's Overseas Railroad

1920	1925	1930	1935	1940

1931 Hialeah Park race track opens after pari-mutuel betting *(see p133)* is legalized

Horse race at Hialeah Park

1939 Gangster Al Capone retires to an estate on Palm Island in Miami

1926 Florida land prices crash, two banks collapse and a hurricane hits the southeast and the Everglades, and devastates Miami

Tin Can Tourists
Each winter, this new breed of tourist loaded up their cars and headed south. They stayed en masse in trailer parks, sharing their tinned food and enjoying the Florida sun.

WHERE TO SEE BOOMTIME FLORIDA

The Wolfsonian Museum *(see p65)* and Miami Beach's Art Deco buildings *(pp56–65)* shouldn't be missed. Mizner's whimsical Palm Beach legacy *(pp114–19)* is also worth visiting. Frank Lloyd Wright's college in Lakeland *(p252)* is very impressive; Henry Ford's winter home in Fort Myers *(p262)* is more modest.

Miami Beach *contains a striking assortment of recently restored Art Deco buildings.*

Zora Neale Hurston
Zora wrote about the lives of rural blacks. Her best known novel, Their Eyes Were Watching God, *was written in 1937.*

Roosevelt's New Deal
The president's New Deal, which allowed farmers to borrow money, helped Florida to recover from the Great Depression. Writers and photographers documented the policy's effects.

World War II
Florida was a training ground for many thousands of troops from 1941–5. War reduced tourism, but the camps helped the economy.

Citrus Industry
Florida became the largest citrus producer in the country, helping it to survive the Depression of the 1930s.

1947 President Truman opens Everglades National Park

Racing car in the Daytona 200

1959 Lee Perry wins the first Daytona 200 race at the Daytona Speedway

1954 The first span of the Sunshine Skyway bridge over Tampa Bay opens

1945	1950	1955	1960

1945 On 5 December, the disappearance of Flight 19 starts the myth of the Bermuda Triangle

1958 The first Earth satellite, *Explorer I,* is launched from Florida after NASA chooses Cape Canaveral as the site of its satellite and rocket programmes

1942 In February, German U-boats torpedo a tanker just off the coast of Florida, in full view of bathers

NASA logo

The Sixties and Beyond

Theme park dolphin

SINCE 1960, FLORIDA has flourished. Tourism has expanded at an unprecedented rate, and countless hotels have been built to cater to all budgets. Theme parks like Walt Disney World and the Kennedy Space Center, home to NASA's space programme, have brought both worldwide fame and crowds of visitors to the Sunshine State. The population has also grown rapidly, through migration from within the US and from abroad; modern Florida is home to many ethnic groups. African-Americans were helped by the Civil Rights movement in the 1960s, but today there is tension between them and the large Hispanic community, which includes the biggest Cuban population outside Cuba. The negative effects of development have led to increased steps to protect natural resources: conservation has become a key issue.

6 million			
4 million			
2 million			
Ages 0–19	Ages 20–44	Ages 45–64	Ages 65+

STATE POPULATION FIGURES

☐ *1960*   ☐ *2000*

Conservation

One way Floridians can support the conservation movement is by buying a special licence plate. Money raised goes to the cause depicted.

Steam forms when water floods the launch-pad at blast off.

The Cuban Exodus
Over 300,000 Cubans have fled to Florida since Castro took over Cuba in 1959. Early arrivals came on "freedom flights", but later refugees had to make the perilous trip by sea on flimsy rafts.

Martin Luther King
The Civil Rights movement reached Florida in the 1960s. Martin Luther King Jr, the movement's most prominent leader, was arrested while on a march in St Augustine in 1964.

SPACE SHUTTLE
To replace the rockets used in Apollo missions, NASA designed a thermally protected space shuttle that wouldn't burn up on re-entry into the earth's atmosphere. The first manned shuttle was launched in 1981 (*see pp186–7*).

TIMELINE

1964 Martin Luther King Jr is arrested and imprisoned in St Augustine

Alan Shephard, NASA astronaut

1969 Apollo II is launched from Cape Canaveral. Buzz Aldrin and Neil Armstrong are the first men to walk on the moon

1973 Dade County is made officially bilingual, and English-Spanish road signs are erected

1977 Snow falls on Miami in January

1965	1970	1975

1962 Cuban missile crisis

1967 Orange juice becomes Florida's state beverage

1971 The Magic Kingdom, Walt Disney's first venture in Florida, opens in Orlando at a cost of $700 million

1976 Florida is the first US state to restore the death penalty

1961 Alan Shephard. becomes the first US man in space

Cinderella Castle, in the Magic Kingdom

The external tank is the only part of the shuttle that is not re-used.

Miami Vice
Miami has a reputation for crime and violence. This was graphically portrayed in the 1980s' TV show, Miami Vice.

Naturalization
Becoming a US citizen is the dream of many immigrants. Mass ceremonies see thousands pledge an oath of allegiance together.

WHERE TO SEE MODERN FLORIDA

Florida has plenty of fine modern architecture, from the skyscrapers in downtown Miami *(see pp68–73)* and Jacksonville *(see p194)* to the Florida Aquarium in Tampa *(see p248)*. To see a more nostalgic approach to modern architecture, visit Seaside in the Panhandle *(see p222)*.

Downtown Miami's *modern skyscrapers create a distinctive and impressive city skyline.*

Blast off catapults the shuttle into orbit. About 7.3 million lbs (3.3 million kg) of thrust is produced.

Florida's Elderly
Just under 20 per cent of Florida's population is over 65 years old. Many retirees are attracted to the state by its low taxes and easy, outdoors lifestyle.

Caribbean Cruises
Tourism is big business in Florida, and cruises in state-of-the-art ships are an increasingly popular holiday choice.

1980 125,000 Cubans arrive in Florida in the Mariel boatlift, which is begun by Fidel Castro and lasts for five months

1981 The maiden voyage of the Space Shuttle is launched

1982 Key West declares itself the "Conch Republic" for just one week

Symbol of the Conch Republic

1986 The space shuttle *Challenger* explodes, killing all seven crew members

1990 General Noriega, the former ruler of Panama, faces drugs charges in Miami

1992 Hurricane Andrew wreaks havoc in south Florida

Cuban refugees

1993 The Task Force on Tourist Safety is created

1994 Another influx of Cubans arrives in Florida

1995 Florida celebrates 150 years as a state

1980	1985	1990	1995

MIAMI AREA
BY AREA

Miami at a Glance

MIAMI HAS BEEN CALLED the Magic City, because what was merely a trading outpost a century ago now sprawls for 2,000 sq miles (5,200 sq km) and boasts a population of two million. Visitors are most likely to remember Miami for its fun-filled South Beach, for its lustrous beaches and for the Latin and Caribbean culture that permeates daily life. Most of Greater Miami is not the violent, drug-crazed city you might imagine, and it is surprisingly popular with families. Even so, be sure to follow safety guidelines on page 348.

Little Havana*, the original heart of the city's Cuban community, is Miami's most welcoming neighbourhood. Life in the streets is fun, with domino games and buzzing cafés.* (See pp74–5.)

The Biltmore Hotel *epitomizes Coral Gables, the exclusive mini-city developed during the 1920s real estate boom. Tales of celebrity guests and Mafia murders add to the mystique of the luxurious hotel.* (See pp78–81.)

CORAL GABLES AND COCONUT GROVE
(see pp 76–85)

The "International Villages" *are clusters of ethnic architecture, from French to Chinese, hidden away along the shady steets of Coral Gables. A tour of them will provide a taste of Miami's prettiest suburb.* (See pp78–9.)

Coconut Grove Village *is a small, friendly area where the focus is on entertainment. Enjoy a relaxing amble or shop in the daytime, before heading for the restaurants and bars, which come to life in the evening.* (See p82.)

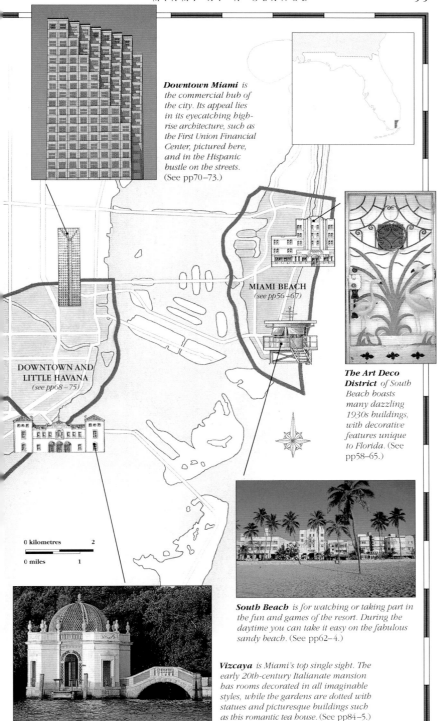

Downtown Miami is the commercial hub of the city. Its appeal lies in its eyecatching high-rise architecture, such as the First Union Financial Center, pictured here, and in the Hispanic bustle on the streets. (See pp70–73.)

MIAMI BEACH
(see pp56–67)

DOWNTOWN AND LITTLE HAVANA
(see pp68–75)

The Art Deco District of South Beach boasts many dazzling 1930s buildings, with decorative features unique to Florida. (See pp58–65.)

0 kilometres 2

0 miles 1

South Beach is for watching or taking part in the fun and games of the resort. During the daytime you can take it easy on the fabulous sandy beach. (See pp62–4.)

Vizcaya is Miami's top single sight. The early 20th-century Italianate mansion has rooms decorated in all imaginable styles, while the gardens are dotted with statues and picturesque buildings such as this romantic tea house. (See pp84–5.)

MIAMI BEACH

NOW OFTEN REFERRED TO as the American Riviera, a century ago Miami Beach was a sandbar accessible only by boat. It was the building of a bridge to the mainland in 1913 that enabled real estate investors like millionaire Carl Fisher to begin developing the island. The resort they created from nothing took off in the 1920s, becoming a spectacular winter playground. The devastating hurricane of 1926 and the 1929 Wall Street Crash signalled the end of the boom, but Miami Beach bounced back in the 1930s with the erection of hundreds of Art Deco buildings, only to decline again after World War II. In another metamorphosis, Miami Beach is on the rise once again. As a result of a spirited

Sea horse on the façade of the Surfcomber Hotel

preservation campaign, South Beach (the southern part of Miami Beach) has been given a new lease of life. It boasts the world's largest concentration of Art Deco buildings, whose funky colours are no less arresting than the local population of body builders, fashion models and drag queens. Anything goes in South Beach, where the mood veers between the chic and the bohemian – hence its nickname SoBe, after New York's hip SoHo district. The Art Deco hotels along Ocean Drive are everyone's favourite haunt but there are other diversions, from trendy shops to higher-brow art museums. The district north of SoBe tempts few people, but what the two areas do share is a superb sandy beach unbroken mile after mile.

SIGHTS AT A GLANCE

Museums and Galleries
Bass Museum of Art **9**
Sanford L Ziff Jewish Museum **3**
The Wolfsonian Foundation **5**

Streets and Neighbourhoods
Central Miami Beach **10**
Collins and Washington Avenues **4**
Española Way **6**
Lincoln Road Mall **7**
Ocean Drive **1**

Beaches
The Beach **2**

Monuments
Holocaust Memorial **8**

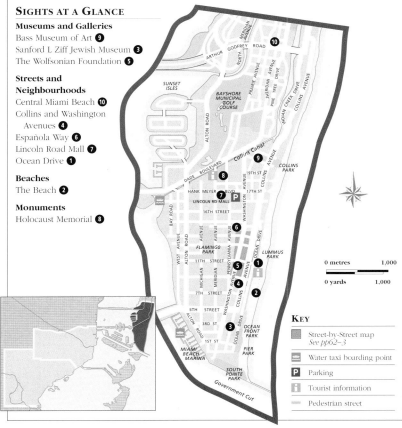

KEY

▨	Street-by-Street map *See pp62–3*
⛴	Water taxi boarding point
P	Parking
ℹ	Tourist information
▥	Pedestrian street

0 metres 1,000
0 yards 1,000

◁ **The Marlin Hotel, a classic South Beach establishment, illuminated in colourful neon**

Ocean Drive: Deco Style

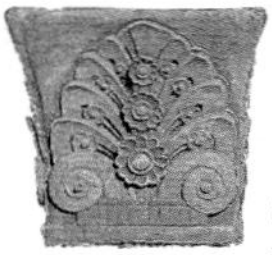

Deco detail, South Beach

THE CREAM of South Beach's Art Deco District, which consists of some 800 preserved buildings, is found on Ocean Drive. Its splendid array of buildings illustrates Miami's unique interpretation of the Art Deco style, which took the world by storm in the 1920s and '30s. Florida's version, often called Tropical Deco, is fun and jaunty. Motifs such as flamingos and sunbursts are common, and South Beach's seaside location inspired features more befitting an ocean liner than a building. Using inexpensive materials, architects managed to create an impression of stylishness for what were, in fact, very modest hotels. The best of the buildings along Ocean Drive are illustrated here and on pages 60–61.

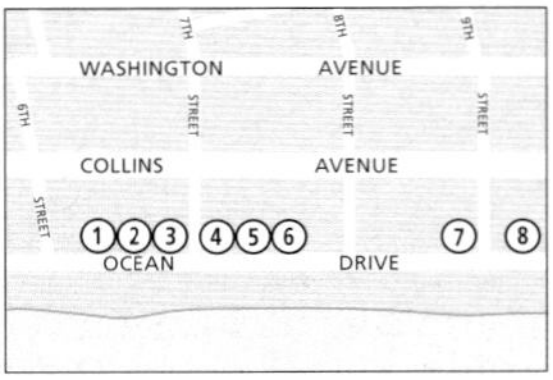

OCEAN DRIVE: 6TH TO 9TH STREETS

White, blue and green were popular colours in the 1930s and '40s; they echo Miami's tropical vegetation and the ocean.

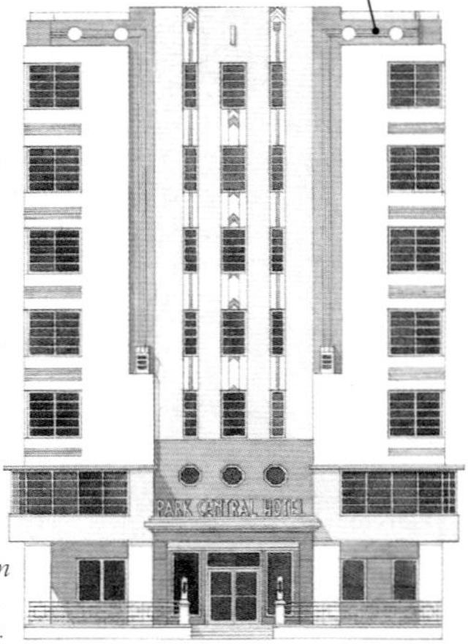

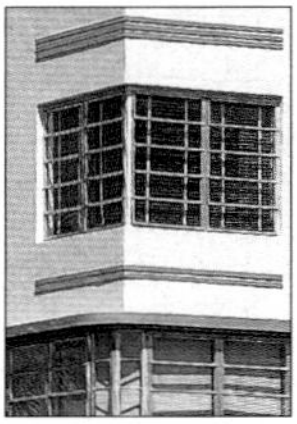

Windows are often continuous around corners.

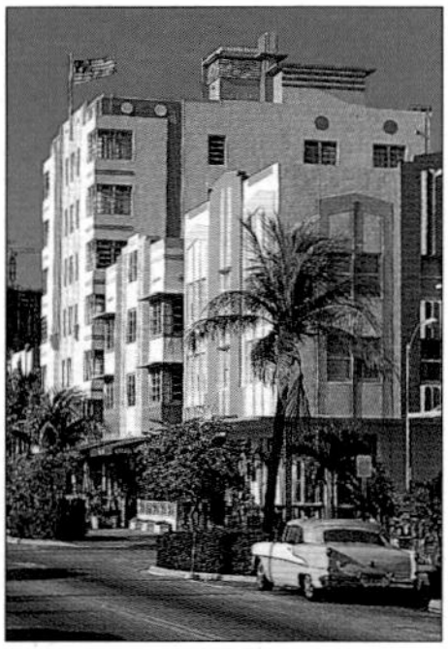

View along Ocean Drive

[1] ***Park Central*** *(1937)*
Henry Hohauser, the most famous architect to work in Miami, designed this hotel. It has fine etched windows.

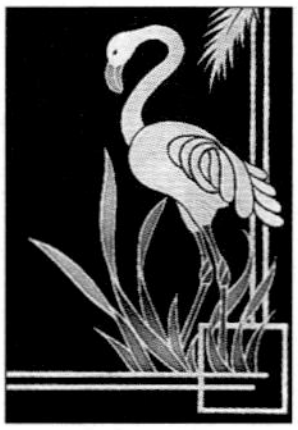

A flamingo is etched into glass doors in the Beacon's lobby.

Angular edges exemplify the influence of Cubism.

Bands of windows give plenty of light and, when open, encourage the circulation of cooling sea breezes.

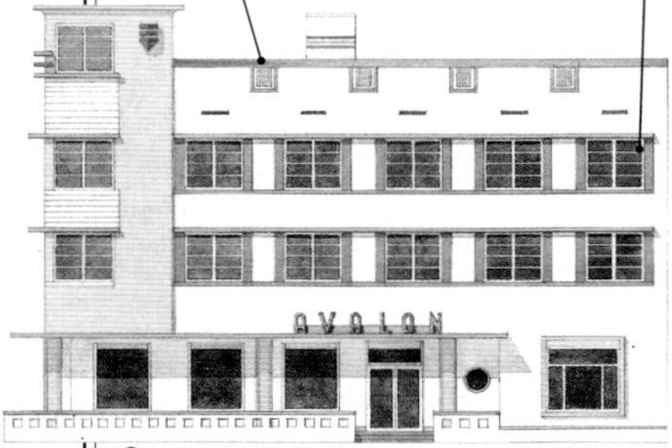

[4] ***Avalon*** *(1941)*
The Avalon is a fine example of Streamline Moderne. The lack of ornamentation and the asymmetrical design are typical, as is the emphasis on horizontal as opposed to vertical lines.

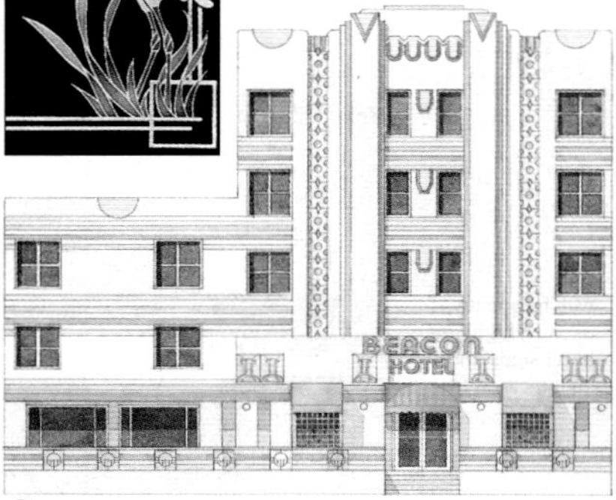

[5] ***Beacon*** *(1936)*
The traditional abstract decoration above the ground floor windows of the Beacon has been brightened by a contemporary colour scheme, an example of Leonard Horowitz's Deco Dazzle (see p65).

ART DECO: FROM PARIS TO MIAMI

The Art Deco style emerged following the 1925 Exposition Internationale des Arts Décoratifs et Industriels Modernes in Paris. Traditional Art Deco combined all kinds of influences, from Art Nouveau's flowery forms and Egyptian imagery to

the geometric patterns of Cubism. In 1930s America, Art Deco buildings reflected the belief that technology was the way forward, absorbing features that embodied the new Machine Age and the fantasies of science fiction. Art Deco evolved into a style called Streamline Moderne, which dominates along Ocean Drive. However, few buildings in South Beach stick to just one style. Indeed it is the creative mix of classic Art Deco details with streamlining and tropical motifs that has made the architecture along Ocean Drive so unique.

Deco-style postcard of the Avalon Hotel

The Berkeley Shore, behind Ocean Drive on Collins Avenue, has classic Streamline Moderne features such as this stepped parapet.

Colour has been used to give the idea of vertical fluting.

Circles, as decoration or as windows, were inspired by the portholes used in ship design.

The lobby of the Majestic has splendid brass elevator doors.

Bas-relief friezes are a recurrent decorative element on Ocean Drive façades.

② **Imperial** (1939)
The design of the Imperial echoes that of the earlier Park Central next door.

③ **Majestic** (1940)
This hotel was the work of Albert Anis, the architect also responsible for the nearby Avalon and Waldorf hotels.

Racing stripes are typical of Streamline Moderne.

"Eyebrows", flat overhangs above the windows, are ideal for providing shade against the unrelenting Miami sun.

This ornamental lighthouse is one of the most evocative examples of Ocean Drive's "architecture for the seashore".

Neon lighting was frequently used to highlight hotel signs and architectural features, so that they could be enjoyed after dark.

Porthole windows

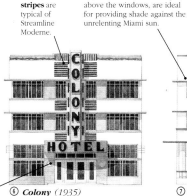

⑥ **Colony** (1935)
One of Henry Hohauser's finest hotels, the Colony has Ocean Drive's most famous neon sign and an interesting mural in the lobby.

⑦ **Waldorf Towers** (1937)
The maritime influence on the design of the Waldorf and some other hotels led to the coining of the phrase "Nautical Moderne".

Ocean Drive: Deco Style

THREE PRINCIPAL ART DECO styles exist in South
Beach: traditional Art Deco, the more futuristic
Streamline Moderne and the Mediterranean Revival,
which is derivative of French, Italian and Spanish
architecture. The unusual injection of Mediterranean
Revival influences along Ocean Drive is noticeable
mainly between 9th and 13th streets.
Here too, however, you will find
some of South Beach's most classic
Art Deco buildings.

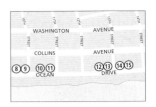

**OCEAN DRIVE:
9TH TO 13TH STREETS**

The central tower recalls
both a ship's funnel and
the totems of American
Indian culture.

The window arches and
columned porch are evocative
of Mediterranean architecture.

Coloured strips,
or "racing stripes",
give a feeling of
speed and
motion.

The railings edging
the roof imitate those
on a ship's deck.

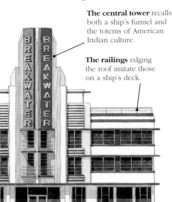

⑧ *Breakwater (1939)*
The Breakwater, by Anton Skislewicz, is a classic
Streamline Moderne hotel with its racing stripes and a
striking central tower. It also has one of Ocean Drive's
better interiors, with etched glass and a terrazzo floor.

⑨ *Edison (1935)*
Hohauser (see p58) experimented
here with Mediterranean Revivalism,
although he was preceded by the
architect of the nearby Adrian.

The sign for the Leslie
hotel is simple, like the
building – in contrast
with the more exube-
rant Carlyle next door.

Flat roofs are the norm along
Ocean Drive, but these are
often broken by a tower or
other vertical projection.

**Corner
windows**

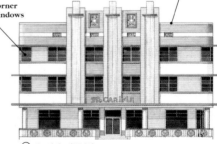

⑫ *Leslie (1937)*
This classic Art Deco hotel's coat of
bright yellow paint is typical of the
colour schemes currently in favour
along Ocean Drive (see p64).

⑬ *Carlyle (1941)*
With its three storeys and three vertical columns,
the Carlyle makes use of the classic Deco divisions,
sometimes known as the "holy three". Most hotels
along Ocean Drive have three floors.

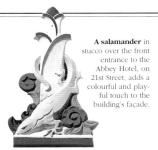

A salamander in stucco over the front entrance to the Abbey Hotel, on 21st Street, adds a colourful and playful touch to the building's façade.

PRESERVING SOUTH BEACH

The campaign to save the Art Deco architecture of South Beach began in 1976, when Barbara Capitman (1920–90) set up the Miami Design Preservation League – at a time when much of the area was destined to disappear under a sea of high-rises. Three years later, one square mile (2.5 sq km) of South Beach became the first 20th-century district in the USA's National Register of Historic Places. Battles still raged against developers throughout the 1980s and '90s, when candlelit vigils helped save some buildings.

Barbara Capitman in 1981

Vertical fluting occurs frequently along Ocean Drive.

"Eyebrow" overhangs shade the windows.

⑩ Clevelander *(1938)*
This hotel's architect, Albert Anis, used classic Deco materials – such as glass blocks in the hotel's bar, now a top South Beach nightspot.

Terracotta tiles

Reinforced concrete was the most common building material used along Ocean Drive, with walls then generally covered in stucco.

A veranda is a prerequisite for most Ocean Drive hotels.

⑪ Adrian *(1934)*
With its subdued colours and chiefly Mediterranean inspiration, the Adrian stands out among neighbouring buildings.

The frieze recalls the abstract designs of the Aztecs.

The terrazzo floor in the bar is a mix of stone chips and mortar – a cheap version of marble that brought style at minimal cost.

The corners of the building are beautifully rounded.

⑭ Cardozo *(1939)*
A late Hohauser work and Barbara Capitman's favourite hotel, this is a Streamline masterpiece, in which the detail of traditional Art Deco is replaced with curved sides, aerodynamic racing stripes and other expressions of the modern age.

⑮ Cavalier *(1936)*
With its sharp edges, this traditional Art Deco hotel provides quite a contrast to the later Cardozo next door.

Street-by-Street: South Beach

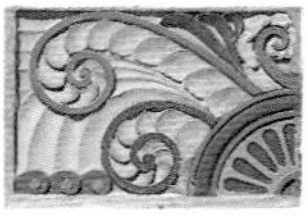

Decoration on the Netherlands Hotel

THE ART DECO DISTRICT of South Beach, which runs from 6th to 23rd streets between Lenox Avenue and Ocean Drive, has attracted more and more visitors since the 1980s. Helped by the interest shown by celebrities such as Gloria Estefan and Michael Caine, the area has been transformed into one of the trendiest places in the States. For many visitors the Deco buildings serve merely as a backcloth for a hedonistic playground, where days are for sleeping, lying on the beach or long workouts at the gym, evenings for dancing into the early hours. But whether your passions are social or architectural, the route shown can be enjoyed both during the day and at night – when a sea of neon enhances the party atmosphere.

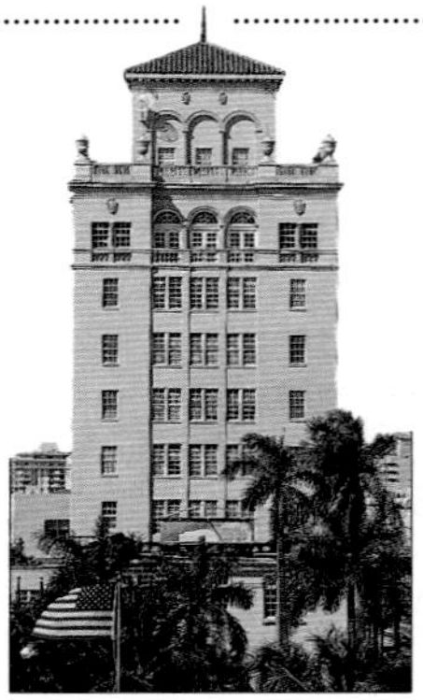

The Old City Hall, a 1920s Mediterranean-style building, ended its service as city hall in 1977, but it remains a distinctive South Beach landmark, towering over the surrounding streets.

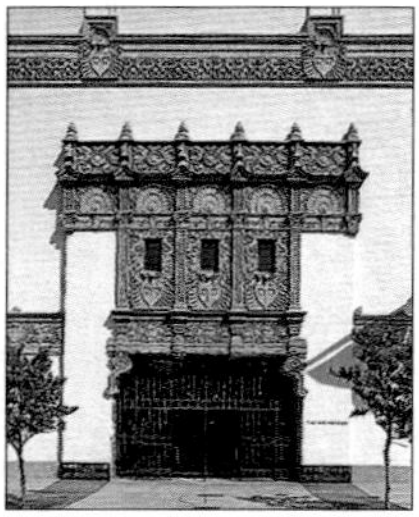

Wolfsonian Foundation
The Wolfsonian, with a striking Spanish Baroque-style relief around its main entrance, houses an excellent collection of fine and decorative arts 5

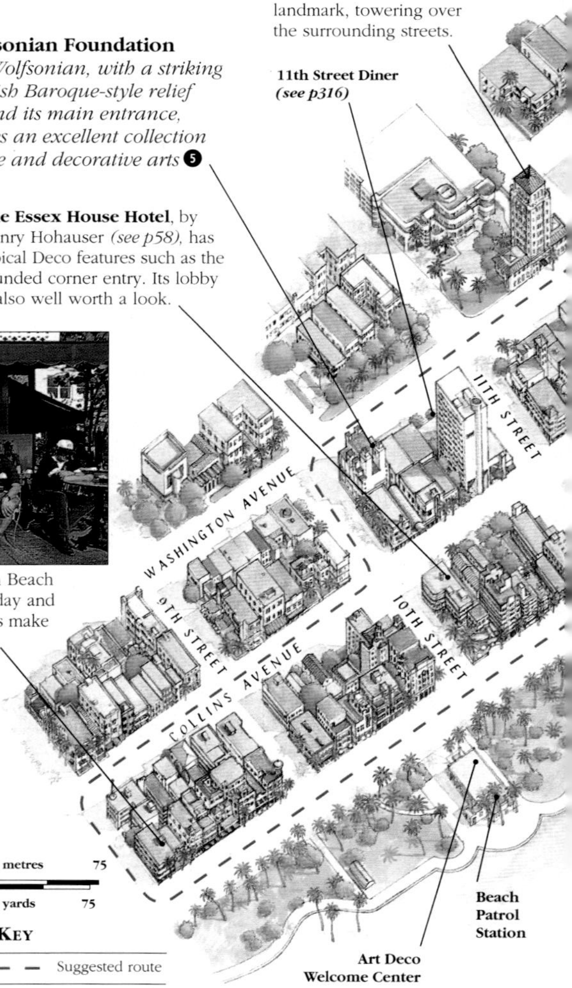

11th Street Diner *(see p316)*

The Essex House Hotel, by Henry Hohauser *(see p58)*, has typical Deco features such as the rounded corner entry. Its lobby is also well worth a look.

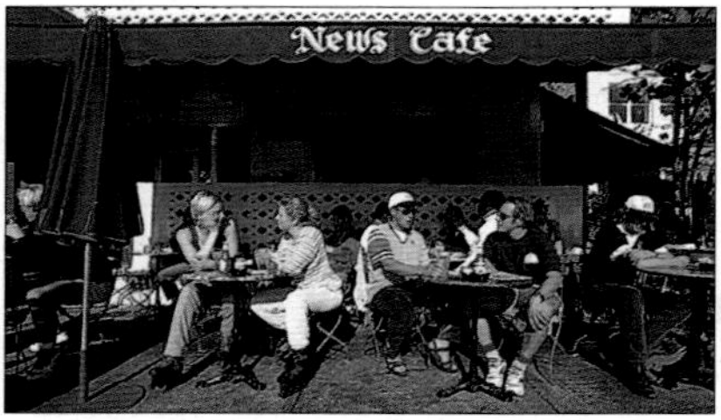

The News Café is a favourite South Beach haunt *(see p330)*, open 24 hours a day and always buzzing. The pavement tables make it a prime spot for people-watching.

Beach Patrol Station

Art Deco Welcome Center

0 metres 75

0 yards 75

KEY

— — Suggested route

ART DECO TOURS

The Miami Design Preservation League lays on excellent 90-minute walking tours from the Art Deco Welcome Center (1001 Ocean Drive) on Thursdays and Saturdays; bicycle tours run every two weeks on Sunday mornings. The league also organizes an Art Deco Week-end (see p35). *For information call the Art Deco Welcome Center on (305) 672-2014.*

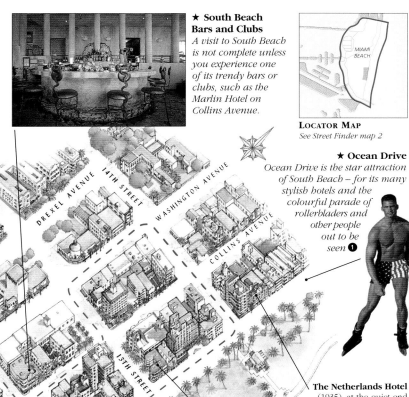

★ **South Beach Bars and Clubs**
A visit to South Beach is not complete unless you experience one of its trendy bars or clubs, such as the Marlin Hotel on Collins Avenue.

LOCATOR MAP
See Street Finder map 2

★ **Ocean Drive**
Ocean Drive is the star attraction of South Beach – for its many stylish hotels and the colourful parade of rollerbladers and other people out to be seen ❶

The Netherlands Hotel
(1935), at the quiet end of Ocean Drive, boasts colourful stucco decoration.

The Cardozo Hotel, among the cream of Ocean Drive's Deco buildings, marked the start of a new era of restoration in South Beach when it reopened in 1982. It is now owned by Gloria Estefan.

Lummus Park

The Amsterdam Palace is a rare private residence on Ocean Drive *(see p64)*.

★ **The Beach**
Sand extends for 10 miles (16 km) up the coast. The beach changes atmosphere depending on where you are, being at its broadest and liveliest in South Beach ❷

STAR SIGHTS

★ **South Beach Bars and Clubs**

★ **Ocean Drive**

★ **The Beach**

South Beach

Ocean drive has the best known Deco buildings in South Beach. But there are wonderful discoveries to be made on Collins and Washington avenues too, as well as further west in quieter residential streets such as Lenox Avenue, where you'll find doors etched with flamingos, and other Deco features.

The Amsterdam Palace, one of Ocean Drive's few non-Deco buildings

South Beach is best explored on foot since parking is difficult. If you don't wish to walk, join the locals on rollerblades or bicycles, both of which can be hired locally.

Ocean Drive ❶

Map 2 F3, F4. 🚌 *C, H, K.* 🛈 *1001 Ocean Drive, (305) 672-2014.*

Spending time at one of the bars or cafés on the seafront is arguably the best way to experience Ocean Drive. It is effectively a catwalk for a constant procession of well-toned flesh and avant-garde outfits; even the street cleaners look cool in their pith helmets and white uniforms, while policemen in skintight shorts cruise past on mountain bikes. A more active exploration,

however, needn't involve much more than a stroll to appreciate the finer points of Art Deco design; feel free to pop into hotel lobbies to admire the interior decor.

One building you cannot enter is the Mediterranean Revival Amsterdam Palace at No. 1114, built in 1930, which the fashion designer Gianni Versace purchased in 1993 for $3.7 million. Nearby, behind the Art Deco Welcome Center, the Beach Patrol Station is a classic Nautical Moderne building *(see p59),* with ship's railings along the top and porthole windows; it still functions as the base for local lifeguards.

There is little to lure you south of 6th Street, but from South Pointe Park, at the tip, you can sometimes get a good view of cruise liners entering Government Cut *(see p73).*

The Beach ❷

Map 2. 🚌 *FM, L, H, S.*

Much of the sand flanking Miami Beach was imported a few decades ago, and it continues to be topped up to counter coastal erosion. The vast stretches of sand are still impressive, however, and in high season people flock to swim and lie in the sun.

Up to 5th Street the beach is popular with surfers. The immense beach beyond is an extension of SoBe's persona, with colourful lifeguard huts and hordes of posing bathers. Alongside runs Lummus Park, where you still find old Jewish folk chatting in Yiddish – evidence of the district's pre-gentrification era. Around 21st Street the clientele on the beach is predominantly gay.

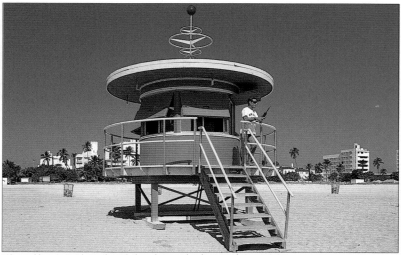

Lifeguard huts in South Beach, with the colours and style to match Ocean Drive

Sanford L Ziff Jewish Museum of Florida ❸

301 Washington Ave. **Map** 2 E4.
📞 (305) 672-5044. 🚌 H, W.
🕐 10am–5pm Tue–Sun. ● Jewish hols. 🎫 ♿ 📷

THIS MUSEUM occupies the first synagogue to have been built in Miami Beach, in 1936. When large numbers of Jews arrived in the 1930s, they often faced fierce anti-Semitism – local hotels carried such signs as "No Jews or Dogs". Today, however, the Jews are a vital, if ageing, part of Miami Beach's community.

The once dilapidated synagogue reopened in 1995 as a museum and research centre of Jewish life in Florida. With its colourful stained-glass windows and other Deco features, the building is almost as memorable as the exhibitions held here.

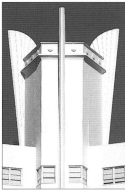

The unmistakable tower of the Delano Hotel on Collins Avenue

Collins and Washington Avenues ❹

Map 2. 🚌 W, C, H, L. ⓘ 1920 Meridian Ave, (305) 672-1270.

THESE STREETS are much scruffier than Ocean Drive: stores sell kinky clothes or tattoos, and there is an altogether more Hispanic flavour. However, some of South Beach's top nightclubs can be

CHANGING COLOURS IN SOUTH BEACH

Art Deco buildings were originally very plain, typically in white with only the trim in bright colours; the paint never extended to the backs of the buildings since money was too tight in the 1930s to allow anything more than a jazzy façade. In the 1980s, designer Leonard Horowitz created the "Deco dazzle" by smothering some 150 buildings in colour. Purists express dismay at this reinvention of the look of South Beach, but advocates argue that the Deco details are better highlighted than ever. Both colour schemes are used these days.

Touching up the colour on the Cardozo Hotel on Ocean Drive

found here (see p95), and there is an abundance of modest Art Deco buildings worth seeing. The Marlin Hotel, at 1200 Collins Avenue, is one of the district's finest Streamline buildings. It has been rejuvenated by Christopher Blackwell, founder of Island Records and the owner of several of Ocean Drive's best known buildings. Behind, at 1300 Washington Avenue, Miami Beach Post Office is one of SoBe's starker Deco creations; a mural inside shows the arrival of Ponce de León (see p40) and his battle with the Native Indians.

North up Collins past Lincoln Road the buildings are interesting rather than beautiful. High-rise 1940s hotels such as the Delano and Ritz Plaza still bear Deco traits, particularly in their towers inspired by the futuristic fantasies of comic strips such as Buck Rogers and Flash Gordon. The strikingly non-Deco interior of the luxury Delano Hotel (see p297) is well worth seeing, with its billowing white drapes and original Gaudí

and Dali furniture. Just off Collins, on 21st Street, is a little-heralded cluster of hotels, notably the Governor, a chrome-trimmed beauty by Henry Hohauser (see p58).

The Wolfsonian Foundation ❺

1001 Washington Ave. **Map** 2 E3.
📞 (305) 531-1001. 🚌 C, H, K, W.
🕐 11am–6pm Tue–Sat, noon–5pm Sun. 🎫 free entry 6–9pm on Thu.
🚫 ♿ 📷

THIS STURDY 1920s building (see p62) used to be the Washington Storage Company, where Miami's richer residents stored their valuables while travelling up north. Now it is a repository for a superb collection of decorative and fine arts from the period 1885–1945, primarily from North America and Europe. Eclectic selections from the Foundation's 70,000 objects include furniture, posters and sculpture. The exhibitions focus on the social, political and aesthetic significance of design in that era.

Electric kettle (1909) in the Wolfsonian

Española Way, a leafy Mediterranean-style shopping street

Española Way ❻

Map 2 E2. 🚌 C, K, H, W.

BETWEEN WASHINGTON and Drexel avenues, Española Way is a tiny, pretty enclave of Mediterranean Revival buildings, where ornate arches, capitals and balconies adorn salmon-coloured, stuccoed frontages. Built from 1922–5, it is said to have been the inspiration for Addison Mizner's Worth Avenue in Palm Beach *(see pp114–15)*.

Española Way was meant to be an artists' colony, but instead became an infamous red-light district. Over the last couple of decades, however, its intended use has been resurrected in its dozen or more boutiques and offbeat art galleries *(see p93)*.

Lincoln Road Mall ❼

Map 2 E2. 🚌 H, S, C.
South Florida Art Center 🕿 *(305) 674-8278.* ◐ *5–10pm Wed–Sat.* ◑ *Thanksgiving, 25 Dec, 1 Jan.* ♿

WHAT IS PRESENTLY the most up-and-coming and cultural corner of South Beach has had a roller coaster of a history. Developer Carl Fisher *(see p57)* envisaged it as the "Fifth Avenue of the South" when it was planned in the 1920s, and its stores did indeed become the height of fashion. Four decades later, Morris Lapidus (designer of the Fontainebleau Hotel) turned the street into one of the country's first pedestrian

malls, but this did not prevent Lincoln Road's decline in the 1970s; the ugly concrete pavilions that Lapidus introduced may not have helped.

The street's revival was initiated by the setting up of the South Florida Art Center (SFAC) here in 1984. Between Lenox and Meridian avenues there are three exhibition areas and some dozen studios which double as work-in-progress and selling space, as well as other independent galleries *(see p93)*. Many people will probably find the art too experimental for their sitting rooms.

The galleries are most reliably open in the evenings. Then the mall comes alive, as theatre-goers frequent the restored Art Deco Lincoln and Colony theatres *(see p94)*, and those searching for a less intense

alternative to Ocean Drive can hang out at voguish restaurants and cafés such as the Van Dyke at 846 – Lincoln Road's answer to the News Café *(see p62)*. At night, too, the Streamline Moderne Sterling Building at No. 927 looks terrific, its glass blocks emanating a wondrous blue glow.

Holocaust Memorial ❽

1933–45 Meridian Ave. **Map** 2 E1.
🕿 *(305) 538-1663.* 🚌 A, FM, G, L.
◐ *9am–9pm daily.* ♿

MIAMI BEACH has one of the largest populations of Holocaust survivors in the world, hence the great appropriateness of Kenneth Treister's gut-wrenching memorial, finished in 1990. The centrepiece is an enormous bronze arm and hand stretching skywards, representing the final grasp of a dying person. It is stamped with a number from Auschwitz and coated with nearly 100 life-size bronze statues of men, women and children in the throes of unbearable grief. Around this central plaza is a tunnel lined with the names of Europe's concentration camps, a graphic pictorial history of the Holocaust and a granite wall inscribed with the names of thousands of victims.

The Holocaust Memorial

Winers and diners outside the Van Dyke Café, Lincoln Road Mall

Coronation of the Virgin (c.1492) by Domenico Ghirlandaio

Bass Museum of Art ⑨

2121 Park Ave. **Map** 2 F1. ☎ *(305) 673-7530.* 🚌 *K, G, L, S.* ⏰ *10am–5pm Tue–Sat (1–9pm on 2nd & 4th Wed of every month), 1–5pm Sun.* ⏺ *public hols.* 🚫 ♿

THIS MAYAN-INFLUENCED Deco building was erected in 1930 as the city's library and art centre. As a museum it came of age in 1964 when philanthropists John and Johanna Bass donated their own art collection, made up mainly of European paintings, sculpture and textiles from the 15th to 17th centuries.

Gallery space is divided between permanent displays and temporary exhibitions. Highlights of the Bass collection include a small number of Renaissance works, paintings from the northern European schools, featuring pictures by Rubens and Dürer, and giant 16th-century Flemish tapestries. Among the modern works are lithographs by Fernand Léger and Toulouse-Lautrec.

Trompe l'oeil view of the Fontainebleau Hotel, Central Miami Beach

SHOOTING FASHION IN MIAMI BEACH

Thanks to its combination of Art Deco buildings, palm trees, beach and climate, South Beach is one of the world's most popular places for fashion shoots. Around 1,500 models live here, but this doesn't include the thousands of hopefuls who flock here uninvited during the season and swan about looking cool in the bars and on the beach. The season runs from October to March, when the weather in Europe and northern America is too poor for outdoor shoots.

Stroll around SoBe in the early morning and you cannot fail to spot the teams of directors, photographers, make-up artists and their assistants – as well as, of course, the models themselves. Ocean Drive is the top spot for shoots, but you can surprise a team at work even in the quieter back streets.

Photographer and crew shooting a model in Miami Beach

Central Miami Beach ⑩

Map 2 F1. 🚌 *G, J, L, S, T, FM, C.* **Lady Lucille Cruise** *(305) 534-7000.*

MIAMI BEACH north of 23rd Street, sometimes called Central Miami Beach, is a largely unprepossessing sight, with endless 1950s and '60s high-rise apartments separating the Atlantic from busy Collins Avenue. A boardwalk running all the way from 23rd to 46th Street overlooks a narrow beach, frequented primarily by families.

The most eye-catching sight in the area is the **Fontainebleau Hotel** (pronounced "Fountain-blue" locally). When driving up Collins Avenue to 44th Street, be sure to avoid driving right through the wall across the road: it is painted with a trompe l'oeil arch and image of the Fontainebleau, which in reality is hidden behind.

Completed in 1954, the curvaceous Fontainebleau is apparently the nearest the architect Morris Lapidus (b.1903) could get to his client's wishes for a modern French château style. The hotel's dated grandeur still impresses, particularly the lobby with Lapidus's signature bow ties on the tiles and the pool complete with waterfall. The hotel was an ideal setting for the James Bond film, *Goldfinger,* in the 1960s.

From outside the Fontainebleau you can take a cruise on the *Lady Lucille* around the millionaires' mansions of Biscayne Bay *(see p71)*. The boat heads first up Indian Creek, which has its own array of smart properties – but these are far less extravagant than those out in the bay.

DOWNTOWN AND LITTLE HAVANA

WHEN THE DEVELOPMENT of Miami took off with the arrival of the Florida East Coast Railroad in 1896, the early city focused on one square mile (2.5 sq km) on the banks of the Miami River, site of the present downtown area. Wealthy industrialists from the northern US set up banks and other institutions, and built winter estates along Brickell Avenue. This is now the hub of Miami's financial district that was spawned by a banking boom in the 1980s. Downtown's futuristic sky-scrapers, bathed nightly in neon, demonstrate the city's status as a major financial and trade centre.

Even after World War II, Miami was still little more than a resort. It was largely the arrival of Cuban exiles

Brass state seal, Dade County Courthouse

from 1959 onwards *(see p50)* that turned Miami into a metropolis. The effect of this Cuban influx is visible most clearly on the streets both Downtown and just across the river in Little Havana. The chatter, faces, shop signs and food make both districts feel more like an Hispanic city with an American flavour than the other way around.

Downtown and Little Havana are enjoyable as much for their atmosphere as for their sights. Downtown has the Metro-Dade Cultural Center, with one of Florida's best historical museums, but tourists are catered for primarily at the shopping-cum-entertainment mall of Bayside Marketplace, which is also a starting point for relaxing boat trips around Biscayne Bay.

SIGHTS AT A GLANCE

Museums and Galleries
Metro-Dade Cultural Center ❷

Historic Buildings
US Federal Courthouse ❶

Modern Architecture
Brickell Avenue ❺

Neighbourhoods
Little Havana ❻

Shops and Restaurants
Bayside Marketplace ❸

Boat Trips
Biscayne Bay Boat Trips ❹

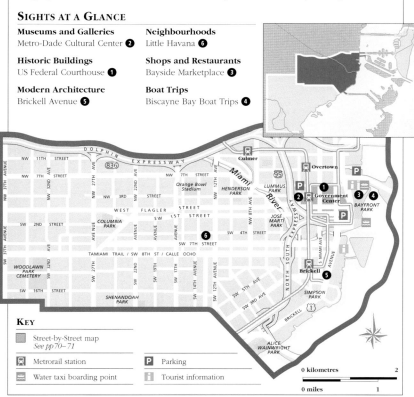

KEY

▨	Street-by-Street map *See pp70–71*
🚇	Metrorail station
⛴	Water taxi boarding point
🅿	Parking
ℹ	Tourist information

0 kilometres 2
0 miles 1

◁ **The striking NationsBank building towering over the Miami River, Downtown**

Street-by-Street: Downtown

OWNTOWN'S SKYLINE IS SUBLIME. It undoubtedly looks best from a distance, particularly at night, but the architecture can also be enjoyed close-up. The raised track of the Metromover gives a good view; or you can explore at ground level, which allows you to investigate the handsome interiors of some of Downtown's public buildings.

The commercial district that lurks beneath the flash high-rises is surprisingly down-market, full of cut-price jewellery and electronics stores, but the Latin street life is vibrant: cafés specialize in Cuban coffee and street vendors sell freshly peeled oranges, Caribbean-style. Flagler Street, Downtown's main thoroughfare, is the best place to get the Hispanic buzz. Visit during weekday office hours; the streets can be unsafe at night.

The Downtown Skyline is a monument to the banking boom of the 1980s. There is an excellent view of it from the MacArthur Causeway.

US Federal Courthouse
This detail from the mural inside the courtroom depicts Miami's transformation from a wilderness to a modern city ❶

Dade County Courthouse has an impressive lobby, with ceiling mosaics that feature this copy of the earliest version of Florida's state seal, complete with mountains.

| 0 metres | | 150 |
| 0 yards | | 150 |

KEY

– – – 　Suggested route

STAR SIGHTS

★ Metro-Dade Cultural Center

★ NationsBank Tower

★ Metro-Dade Cultural Center
This large complex, with a Mediterranean-style central courtyard and fountains, contains the only museum in downtown Miami ❷

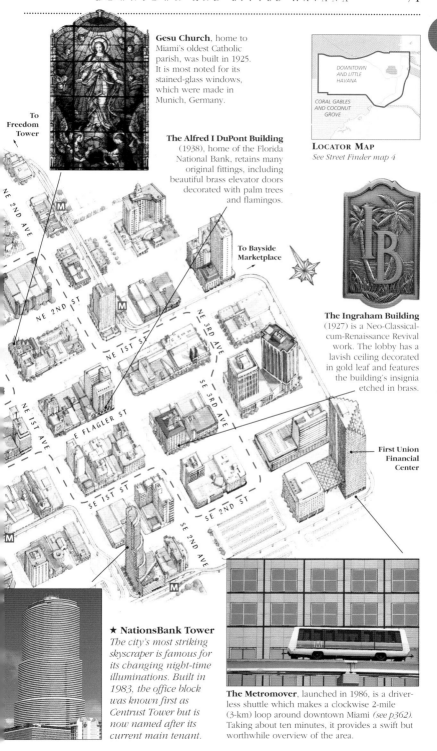

Gesu Church, home to Miami's oldest Catholic parish, was built in 1925. It is most noted for its stained-glass windows, which were made in Munich, Germany.

To Freedom Tower

The Alfred I DuPont Building (1938), home of the Florida National Bank, retains many original fittings, including beautiful brass elevator doors decorated with palm trees and flamingos.

LOCATOR MAP
See Street Finder map 4

DOWNTOWN AND LITTLE HAVANA

CORAL GABLES AND COCONUT GROVE

To Bayside Marketplace

The Ingraham Building (1927) is a Neo-Classical-cum-Renaissance Revival work. The lobby has a lavish ceiling decorated in gold leaf and features the building's insignia etched in brass.

First Union Financial Center

★ **NationsBank Tower**
The city's most striking skyscraper is famous for its changing night-time illuminations. Built in 1983, the office block was known first as Centrust Tower but is now named after its current main tenant.

The Metromover, launched in 1986, is a driverless shuttle which makes a clockwise 2-mile (3-km) loop around downtown Miami *(see p362)*. Taking about ten minutes, it provides a swift but worthwhile overview of the area.

Downtown

DOWNTOWN'S grand early 20th-century buildings, scattered among more modern high-rises, are very evocative of the confidence of those boom years. The Mediterranean Revival and Neo-Classical styles were both popular. A fine example of the latter is Freedom Tower (1925) on Biscayne Boulevard, modelled very loosely on the Giralda in Seville. At first home to the now-defunct *Miami News*, its role and name changed in the '60s when it became the reception centre for Cubans fleeing Castro's Revolution *(see p50)*. It now stands empty.

Downtown also has a few Deco buildings, such as the Burdines store on Flagler Street *(see p92)*.

Freedom Tower (1925)

US Federal Courthouse ❶

301 N Miami Ave. **Map** 4 E1.
🄲 *(305) 536-4548.* Ⓜ *Arena/State Plaza.* 🄾 *8am–5pm Mon–Fri.* ⚫ *public hols.* 🄳

THIS IMPOSING Neo-Classical building, finished in 1931, has hosted a number of high-profile trials, including that of

Manuel Noriega, the former Panamanian president, in 1990. It has a pleasant, thoroughly Mediterranean courtyard, but the main attraction (for the casual visitor at least) is the mural entitled *Law Guides Florida's Progress (see p70)* on the second floor; this was designed by Denman Fink, famous for his work in Coral Gables *(see p80)*. Public access to the courthouse is often restricted, especially during important cases.

Metro-Dade Cultural Center ❷

101 West Flagler St. **Map** 4 E1.
🄲 *(305) 375-3000.* Ⓜ *Government Center.* 🚌 *21, 77.* 🄾 *10am–5pm Mon–Fri (till 9pm on Thu), noon–5pm Sat & Sun.* 🄳

DESIGNED BY the celebrated American architect Philip Johnson in 1982, the Metro-Dade Cultural Center is an art gallery, museum and library rolled into one.

Visitors from out of town will probably find the Historical Museum of Southern Florida, which concentrates on pre-1945 Miami, of most interest. There are informative displays on the Spanish colonization and Seminole culture among other topics, but it is the old photographs that really bring Miami's history to life: these capture everything from the hardships endured by the early pioneers to the fun and games of the Roaring Twenties.

The Miami Art Museum of Dade County, across the plaza from the historical museum,

Bathers in 1920s Miami, on view in the Historical Museum

plans to develop a permanent collection, but at present holds only short-term exhibitions, chiefly of post-1945 American art; these are well worth a visit.

Bayside Marketplace ❸

401 Biscayne Blvd. **Map** 4 F1.
🄲 *(305) 577-3344.* Ⓜ *College/ Bayside.* 🚌 *C, S, 16, 48, 95.* 🄾 *10am–10pm Mon–Thu, 10am–11pm Fri & Sat, 11am–8pm Sun.* ⚫ *Thanksgiving, 25 Dec.* 🄳

BY FAR THE MOST popular spot among tourists Downtown (as well as the best place to park in the area), Bayside Marketplace is an undeniably jolly complex. It curves around Miamarina, where a plethora of boats, some private, some offering trips around Biscayne Bay, lie docked.

With its numerous bars and restaurants – among them a remarkable-looking Hard Rock Café *(see p330)* complete with a guitar erupting from its roof – Bayside is a good place to eat as well as shop. The food court on the first floor does not serve *haute cuisine* but is fine for a meal on the hoof. Bands often play in the waterside forecourt.

The nearby Bayfront Park is austere by comparison. At its centre the Torch of Friendship commemorates President John F Kennedy, surrounded by the coats of arms of Central and South American countries; a plaque from the city's exiled Cuban community thanks the United States for allowing them to settle here.

Boats moored in Miamarina in front of Bayside Marketplace

Biscayne Bay Boat Trips ❹

Bayside Marketplace. **Map** 4 F1.
Ⓜ College/Bayside. 🚍 C, S, 16, 48,
95. **Island Queen Cruises** (305) 379-
5119. **Water Taxi** (954) 467-6677.

THE WORLD'S BUSIEST cruise port and a sprinkling of exclusive private island communities occupy Biscayne Bay between Downtown and Miami Beach. Since racing along MacArthur Causeway in a car provides only an all-too-brief glimpse of this area, cruises from Bayside Market-place offer a better and more leisurely view. "Estates of the Rich and Famous" tours run by Island Queen Cruises and other companies leave regularly throughout the day and last around 90 minutes.

Tours begin by sailing past the port, situated on Dodge and Lummus islands. The port contributes more than $5 billion a year to the local economy, handling over three million cruise passengers annually. The mammoth ships make an impressive sight when they're in dock or heading to or from port (usually at weekends).

Near the eastern end of MacArthur Causeway you pass the US Coastguard's fleet of high-speed craft, used to intercept drug smugglers and illegal aliens. Opposite lies unbridged Fisher Island, separated from South Beach by Government Cut, a deep water channel dredged in 1905. A beach for Negroes in the 1920s, Fisher Island has ironically become a highly exclusive residential enclave,

The Atlantis, the most famous building along Brickell Avenue

**Biscayne Bay
tour boat sign**

with homes costing rarely less than $500,000. The tour continues north around Star, Palm and Hibiscus islands, which were all man-made in the second decade of the 20th century, when real estate lots were sometimes sold "by the gallon". Mansions in every possible architectural style lurk beneath lush tropical foliage, among them the former homes of Frank Sinatra and Al Capone, as well as the present abodes of such celebrities as Gloria Estefan and Julio Iglesias.

Other boat trips from Bayside Marketplace include night-time cruises, deep-sea fishing excursions and even gondola rides. The Water Taxi also provides a shuttle service along the mainland shore, linking Bayside Marketplace with various hotels, as well as a request service between Bayside and Miami Beach Marina, at the eastern end of MacArthur Causeway.

Brickell Avenue ❺

Map 4 E2– E4. Ⓜ various stations.
🚇 Metrorail (Brickell). 🚍 6, 8, 24,
48, B. 🛈 701 Brickell Ave, Suite
2700, (800) 283-2707.

IN THE EARLY 20th century, the building of palatial mansions along Brickell Avenue earned it the name Millionaires' Row. Nowadays, its northern section is Miami's palm-lined version of New York's Wall Street – its international banks enclosed within flash, glass-sided blocks reflecting each other and the blue sky. South of the bend at Southwest 15th Road comes a series of startling apartment blocks glimpsed in the opening credits of television series *Miami Vice*. Created in the early 1980s by an iconoclastic firm of Postmodernist architects called Arquitectonica, the buildings may no longer be strictly *à la mode* but they still manage to impress.

The most memorable is the Atlantis (at No. 2025), for its "skycourt" – a hole high up in its façade containing a palm tree and Jacuzzi. The punched-out hole reappears as an identically-sized cube in the grounds below. Arquitectonica also designed the Palace, at No. 1541, and the Imperial, at No. 1627. Described as "architecture for 55 mph" (that is, best seen when travelling past in a car), these exclusive residences were designed to be admired from a distance; they are out-of-bounds to casual visitors anyway.

One of the lavish mansions seen during a Biscayne Bay boat tour

Little Havana ⑥

Map 3. 🚌 *11 from Downtown, 8, 24 from Coral Gables.*
El Crédito Cigar Factory 1106 SW 8th St. 📞 *(305) 858-4162.* 🕐 *8am–6pm Mon–Fri, 9am–4pm Sat.* 🚫 *public hols.*
Cuban Museum of the Americas 1300 SW 12th Ave. 📞 *(305) 858-8006.* 🕐 *noon–6pm Tue–Fri.* 🚫 *public hols.* ♿

Cubans LIVE all over Greater Miami, however it is the 3.5 sq miles (9 sq km) of Little Havana which, as its name suggests, has been their surrogate homeland since they first started fleeing Cuba in the 1960s *(see p50).* Other Hispanic groups have now settled here too.

Your time in Little Havana is best spent out in the streets, where the bustling workaday atmosphere is vibrant. A salsa beat emanates from every other shop; posters advocate a continuation of the armed struggle against Castro; *bodegas* (canteens) sell Cuban specialities such as *moros y cristianos (see p315),* while wrinkled old men knock back thimblefuls of *café cubano.*

Little Havana's principal commercial thoroughfare and sentimental heart is Southwest 8th Street, better known as **Calle Ocho**. Its liveliest stretch, between 11th and 17th avenues, is best enjoyed on foot, but other points of interest are more easily explored by car.

Founded in Havana in 1907 and moved to Miami in 1968,

El Crédito Cigar Factory, near the corner of Calle Ocho and 11th Avenue, is small but authentic. You are welcome to watch the handful of cigar rollers at work. The leaves are grown in the Dominican Republic – reputedly from Cuban tobacco seeds, the world's best. Local smokers, mainly non-Cuban, come to buy boxes of the wide range of cigars on sale *(see p93).*

Southwest 13th Avenue, south from Calle Ocho, is known as **Cuban Memorial Boulevard** and is the district's nationalistic focal point. The eternal flame of the Brigade 2506 Memorial remembers the Cubans who died in the US-sponsored Bay of Pigs invasion of Cuba in 1961. Every year people gather here on 17 April to remember the disastrous attempt to overthrow Fidel Castro's regime. Beyond, other memorials recall Cuban heroes Antonio Maceo and José Martí, who fought against Cuba's Spanish colonialists in the 1800s *(see pp46–7).*

At intervals along Calle Ocho between 12th and 17th avenues, more recent Latin celebrities such as Julio Iglesias and Gloria Estefan are honoured with stars on the pavement in Little Havana's version of Hollywood's Walk of Fame.

At the corner of 14th Avenue, male Cubans above the age of 55 pit their wits over dominoes in tiny **Máximo Gómez Park** – also known as Domino Park. According to

The eternal flame commemorating the Bay of Pigs invasion

a list of rules, players can be banned from the park for spitting, shouting or foul language.

North of Calle Ocho at West Flagler Street and Southwest 17th Avenue, **Plaza de la Cubanidad** has a map of Cuba sculpted in bronze; José Martí's enigmatic words alongside translate as "the palm trees are sweethearts that wait". Behind, a flourish of flags and banners advertises the headquarters of Alpha 66, Miami's most hardline grouping of anti-Castro Cubans, whose supporters take part in military exercises in the Everglades – although most realize an armed invasion of Cuba will never happen.

The **Cuban Museum of the Americas**, south of Calle Ocho, has a permanent collection of works by local Cuban artists and stages changing exhibitions too; these cover aspects of Cuban culture, such as music and religion.

Much further west, at 3260 Calle Ocho, lies **Woodlawn Cemetery**. You can ask for directions to the memorials to the unknown Cuban freedom fighter in plot 31, with Cuban and US flags flying alongside, or to the unheralded tomb of Gerardo Machado, an infamous Cuban dictator of the 1930s.

Finish off a tour of Little Havana with a snack or full meal at the nearby **Versailles** restaurant *(see p318)*; always buzzing, this is a cultural and culinary bastion of Miami's Cuban community.

Waitress at the Versailles

Cubans enjoying a game of dominoes in Máximo Gómez Park

Miami's Cuban Community

THE CUBAN COMMUNITY in Miami is unusually cohesive, thanks both to a shared passion for its homeland and to a common hatred for Fidel Castro and his dictatorship. The exiles, as they often call themselves, come from all walks of life. Early immigrants were largely wealthy white (and right-wing) professionals, who now sit on the boards of some of Miami's biggest companies and live in the city's smart suburbs. The so-called Marielitos, who came in 1980 (see p50),

Gloria Estefan

were mostly working class, like many of those who have arrived since. Some second-generation Cubans, such as pop star Gloria Estefan, now have very successful careers. Nowadays these professionals are often dubbed "yucas", or Young, Up-and-coming Cuban-Americans.

The Cuban presence is felt in every layer of Miami society – seen in everything from the food to the Spanish spoken on the street, and visible everywhere from Little Havana to elite Coral Gables.

Images of Old Cuba
Murals, such as this one of the Cuban resort of Varadero, symbolize the nostalgia and love for the homeland felt by Cubans of all generations. Many hope to return to the island one day.

Political Action
Cubans in Miami follow events in Cuba keenly. They often take to the streets to wave the Cuban flag and protest against the Castro regime or the US government's Cuban policy.

Salsa music, recorded by Cubans in Miami and popular in the city

CUBAN CULTURE IN MIAMI

The Cubans have brought their music, their religion, their whole way of life to Miami. They are nominally Catholic, but many Cubans adhere to Santería, an unusual blend of Catholic beliefs and the animist cults taken to Cuba by African slaves during the colonial period.

A Cuban-style hole in the wall café, where coffee, snacks and conversation are enjoyed on the hoof

A religious shop or *botánica* in Little Havana selling the paraphernalia of Santería

CORAL GABLES AND COCONUT GROVE

ORAL GABLES, one of the USA's richest neighbourhoods, is a separate city within Greater Miami, and feels it. Aptly named the City Beautiful, its elegant homes line winding avenues shaded by banyans and live oaks; backing on to hidden canals, many have their own jetties and boats. Strict regulations ensure that new buildings use the same architectural vocabulary as that advocated by George Merrick when he planned Coral Gables in the 1920s *(see p80)*. As well as exploring Merrick's legacy, you can peer into some of Miami's most stylish shops.

Fireman's head, Salzedo Street

Coconut Grove is Miami's oldest community. Wreckers *(see p289)* lived here from the mid-1800s, but the area attracted few people until the 1880s, when Ralph Munroe *(see p82)* persuaded some friends to open a hotel. It was staffed by Bahamians and frequented by Monroe's intellectual friends. Ever since, the area has had a mixed flavour, with posh homes just a stone's throw from the blighted, so-called Black Coconut Grove. Affordable restaurants and shops draw weekend and evening crowds, making Coconut Grove the liveliest district in Miami after South Beach.

SIGHTS AT A GLANCE

Museums and Galleries
Lowe Art Museum **6**
Museum of Science and Space Transit Planetarium **11**

Streets and Neighbourhoods
Coconut Grove Village **7**
Miracle Mile **1**

Historic Buildings
The Barnacle **8**
Biltmore Hotel **5**
Coral Gables City Hall **2**
Coral Gables Merrick House **3**
Venetian Pool **4**
Vizcaya pp84–5 **12**

Churches
Ermita de la Caridad **10**

Marinas
Dinner Key **9**

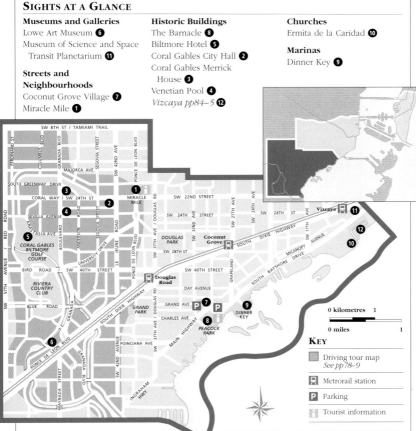

KEY

Driving tour map *See pp78–9*

Metrorail station

P Parking

Tourist information

0 kilometres   1
0 miles   1

◁ **Tower of the Biltmore Hotel, an unmistakable landmark in Coral Gables**

Coral Gables Driving Tour

THIS DRIVING TOUR wends its way along Coral Gables' lush and peaceful lanes connecting the major landmarks of George Merrick's 1920s planned city *(see pp80–81)*. As well as much-admired public buildings such as the Biltmore Hotel, it takes in two of the original four grand entrances and six of Merrick's Disneyesque international "villages".

It is quite possible to visit all the sights on the tour in one busy day. Allow time to get lost: Coral Gables is very confusing for a planned city. Signs for streets, named after Spanish places which Merrick allegedly pulled out of a dictionary, are often hard to spot, lurking on white stone blocks in the grass.

Alhambra Water Tower ③
This folly, built in 1925, was the work of Denman Fink (see p80).

Coral Gables Congregational Church ⑦
Coral Gables' first church, built by Merrick in Spanish Baroque style, has an elaborate bell tower and portal.

Venetian Pool ⑥ is a beautiful public swimming pool embellished with Venetian-style buildings.

Biltmore Hotel ⑧
One of the most stunning hotels in the country, the Biltmore has been beautifully restored to its 1920s' grandeur.

The Lowe Art Museum ⑩
boasts an excellent collection, including some fine European and Native American art.

French City Village ⑪
This is one of seven international villages that were built to add variety to the chiefly Mediterranean-style city.

0 metres   500
0 yards   500

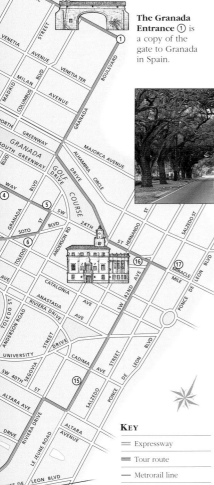

The Granada Entrance ① is a copy of the gate to Granada in Spain.

The Country Club Prado Entrance ②, complete with ornamental pillars, is the most elegant of the grand entrances.

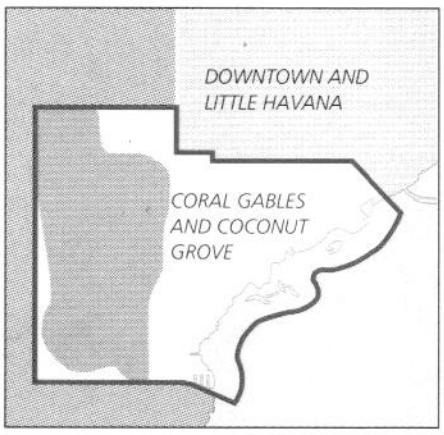

LOCATOR MAP
See Street Finder, map 5

Coral Way ④
Live oaks and Spanish-style houses line one of Coral Gables' loveliest and oldest streets.

Coral Gables Merrick House ⑤ was once the home of George Merrick and is now a museum.

Coral Gables City Hall ⑯ has a decorative interior, featuring murals painted in the 1920s and '50s.

KEY

- Expressway
- Tour route
- Metrorail line

Miracle Mile ⑰
Conservative bridal, fashion and jewellers' stores set the tone along the district's most important shopping street.

TIPS FOR DRIVERS

Tour length: *14 miles (23 km).*
Starting point: *Anywhere, but the route is best done in an anti-clockwise direction.*
Stopping-off points: *There are some highly-rated restaurants off Miracle Mile (see p80), and you can enjoy an English-style tea at the Biltmore if you book 24 hours in advance. Alternatively, take a dip at the Venetian Pool.*
When to go: *Wednesday and Sunday are the best days to visit due to the hours of the Coral Gables Merrick House, Lowe Art Museum and the Biltmore tours (see pp80–81). Avoid the rush hours (7–9:30am, 4:30–6:30pm).*

A private boat moored on one of Coral Gables' tranquil waterways

FINDING THE SIGHTS

① Granada Entrance
② Country Club Prado Entrance
③ Alhambra Water Tower
④ Coral Way
⑤ Coral Gables Merrick House
⑥ Venetian Pool
⑦ Coral Gables Congregational Church
⑧ Biltmore Hotel
⑨ Colonial Village
⑩ Lowe Art Museum
⑪ French City Village
⑫ Dutch South African Village
⑬ French Country Village
⑭ Chinese Village
⑮ French Normandy Village
⑯ Coral Gables City Hall
⑰ Miracle Mile

Galleried rotunda inside the Colonnade Building on Miracle Mile

Miracle Mile ❶

Coral Way between Douglas and Le Jeune roads. **Map** 5 C1. 🚇 *Metrorail (Douglas Rd) then bus J or 40.*

I N 1940, A DEVELOPER hyped Coral Gables' main shopping street by naming it Miracle Mile (the walk along one side and down the other being the mile in question). Along its length, colourful canopies adorn shops as prim and proper as their clientele *(see p92)*. High prices and competition from out-of-town malls mean the street is rarely busy.

The Colonnade Building, at No. 169, was built in 1926 by George Merrick as the sales headquarters for his real estate business. Its superb rotunda is now a lobby for the deceptively modern and very impressive Colonnade Hotel. The Doc Dammers' Saloon *(see p330)* contains evocative photographs of Coral Gables' heyday. Nearby, at Salzedo Street and Aragon Avenue, the Old Police and Fire Station Building, erected in 1939, features a wonderful pair of sculpted firemen.

Coral Gables City Hall ❷

405 Biltmore Way. **Map** 5 C1. 📞 *(305) 446-6800.* 🚇 *Metrorail (Douglas Rd).* 🚌 *24.* 🕐 *8am–5pm Mon–Fri.* ⬤ *public hols.* ♿

B UILT IN 1928, Coral Gables City Hall epitomizes the Spanish Renaissance style favoured by Merrick and his colleagues. Its semi-circular

façade even has a Spanish-style coat of arms, which was designed for the new city of Coral Gables by Denman Fink, George Merrick's uncle. Fink was also responsible for the mural of the four seasons which decorates the dome of the bell tower: winter is represented as an old man, the other seasons as young women. Above the stairs, a mural that illustrates Coral Gables' early days, *Landmarks of the Twenties*, was the work of John St John in the 1950s; he artificially aged it by chain smoking and exhaling onto the paint as it dried.

Coat of arms on Coral Gables City Hall

Coral Gables Merrick House ❸

907 Coral Way. **Map** 5 B1. 📞 *(305) 460-5361.* 🚌 *24.* 🕐 *1–4pm Wed & Sun.* 🌐 🚫 ♿ ▢

M AKE THE EFFORT to tie in with the limited opening hours of the Merrick family home to appreciate the comparatively modest background of Coral Gables' creator.

When Reverend Solomon Merrick brought his family to Florida from New England in 1899, they settled in a wooden cabin south of the growing city of Miami. They later added a much grander extension and named the house Coral Gables, thinking the local oolitic limestone used to build it was coral because of the fossilized marine life it contained.

Now a museum, the emphasis is as much on the family as on Solomon's famous son, George. Some of the furniture was owned by the Merricks, and there are family portraits and paintings by George's mother and his uncle. The grounds have been much reduced in size, but the small garden is awash with tropical trees and plants.

GEORGE MERRICK'S DREAM CITY

The dream of George Merrick was to build a new city. With the help of Denman Fink as artistic advisor, Frank Button as landscaper and Phineas Paist as architectural director, he conjured up a wholly planned aesthetic wonderland. Its architecture was to be part-Spanish, part-Italian – in Merrick's words "a combination of what seemed best in each, with an added touch of gaiety to suit the Florida mood". The dream spawned the biggest real estate venture of the 1920s, costing around $100 million. Some $3 million a year was spent on advertising alone, with posters promoting idyllic canal scenes while they were still on the drawing board. The 1926 hurricane *(see p48)* and the Wall Street Crash left Merrick's city incomplete, but what remains – together with subsequent imitations – is a great testament to his imagination.

Portrait of George Merrick, on show in his family home

Venetian Pool, ingeniously created in the 1920s out of an old coral rock quarry

Venetian Pool ❹

2701 De Soto Blvd. **Map** 5 B2.
📞 (305) 460-5356. 🚊 Metrorail (S
Miami) then bus 72. ⏱ mid-Jun–mid-
Aug: 11am–7:30pm Mon–Fri; Apr–
May & Sep–Oct: 11am–5:30pm; Nov–
Mar: 10am–4:30pm; all year: 10am–
4:30pm Sat & Sun. ● Mon Sep–May,
Thanksgiving, 24–25 Dec, 1 Jan. 📷 ♿

T HE BOAST that this is the
most beautiful public
swimming pool in the world
is a fair one. Worth visiting
whether you fancy a swim or
not, it was fashioned from a
coral rock quarry in 1923 by
Denman Fink and Phineas
Paist. Pink stucco towers and
loggias, candystick Venetian
poles, a cobblestone bridge,
caves and waterfalls surround
the clear, spring-fed waters.
The pool was originally one
of the most fashionable social
venues in Coral Gables: see
the photographs in the lobby
of beauty pageants staged
here during the 1920s.

Biltmore Hotel ❺

1200 Anastasia Ave. **Map** 5 A2.
📞 (305) 445-1926. 🚊 Metrorail
(S Miami) then bus 72. ♿ 🎬 Sun pm.

C ORAL GABLES' outstanding
single building was com-
pleted in 1926. In its heyday,
when it hosted celebrities
such as Al Capone (who had a
speakeasy here), Judy Garland
and the Duke and Duchess of
Windsor, guests hunted fox in
the vast grounds (now a golf

course) and were punted
along canals in gondolas. The
Biltmore served as a military
hospital during World War II,
when its marble floors were
covered in linoleum, and it
remained a veterans' hospital
until 1968. Following a $55-
million restoration in 1986 the
hotel went bankrupt in 1990,
but then opened its doors
again two years later.
 A 315-ft (96-m) near
replica of Seville
Cathedral's Giralda
tower, which was
also the model for
Miami's Freedom
Tower (see p72),
rises from the hotel's
imposing façade. In-
side, Herculean pillars
line the immensely
grand lobby, while
from the terrace   **Han dynasty horse,**
behind you can   **Lowe Art Museum**
survey the largest
hotel swimming pool in the
country. The Biltmore's most
famous swimming instructor,
Johnny Weismuller, star of
Tarzan, set a world swim-
ming record here in the
1930s. Weekly tours of the
hotel depart from the con-
cierge desk in the lobby.

Lowe Art Museum ❻

1301 Stanford Drive. **Map** 5 A5.
📞 (305) 284-3535. 🚊 Metrorail
(University). 🚌 52, 56, 72. ⏱ 10am–
5pm Tue–Sat, noon–5pm Sun, noon–
7pm Thu. ● Thanksgiving, 25 Dec,
1 Jan. 📷 ♿

T HIS MUSEUM is located in the
middle of the campus of
the University of Miami,
founded in 1925 thanks to
a $5-million donation from
George Merrick.
Among the 8,000
works of the Lowe's
permanent hoard are
impressive Renaissance
and Baroque works,
and one of the finest
collections of Native
American art in the
US, including some
exquisite textiles and
ceramics. There is also an
excellent array of ancient art
from Latin America and Asia,
with China being particularly
well represented. Temporary
exhibitions cover many and
diverse subjects, from pre-
Columbian ceramics to
20th-century photography.

South view of the Biltmore Hotel, Coral Gables' most famous landmark

Coconut Grove Village ❼

Map 6 E4, F4. 🚉 *Metrorail (Coconut Grove).* 🚌 *42 from Coral Gables, 48 from Downtown.*

A FABLED HIPPY hangout in the 1960s, these days the focal point of Coconut Grove cultivates a more salubrious air. Well-groomed young couples wining and dining beneath old-fashioned streetlamps now typify what is often known simply as "the village". Only the odd snake charmer and neck masseur, plus a few New Age shops, offer glimpses of alternative lifestyles. Come at night or at the weekend to see the Grove at its best.

The village's nerve centre is the junction of Grand Avenue, McFarlane Avenue and Main Highway, where you'll find Johnny Rockets, a wonderful 1950s-style burger bar, and the rather over-hyped **CocoWalk**. This outdoor shopping mall *(see p92)* is Coconut Grove's busiest spot. Its courtyard is full of cafés and souvenir stalls, while on upper floors a band often plays. There are also family restaurants *(see p318)*, a cinema and nightclub.

A short distance east along Grand Avenue, a smarter mall called the **Streets of Mayfair** *(see p92)* is worth visiting as much for its striking ensemble of Spanish tiles, waterfalls and foliage as for its shops. But in order to better appreciate

CocoWalk open-air mall in Coconut Grove Village

Coconut Grove's relaxed café lifestyle, head along the side-streets of Commodore Plaza and Fuller Street.

For a different atmosphere, browse among the food stalls of the colourful **Farmers' Market**, held on Saturdays at McDonald Street and Grand Avenue. Further along Grand Avenue are the simple homes of the local Bahamian community. This neighbourhood comes alive during Coconut Grove's exuberant Goombay Festival *(see p33)*, but at other times take care here.

A five-minute stroll south along Main Highway takes you through a shady, affluent neighbourhood where palms, bougainvillea and hibiscus conceal handsome clapboard villas. At 3400 Devon Road is the picturesque **Plymouth Congregational Church**,

which appears to have been built a lot longer ago than 1916. It is usually locked, but the ivy-covered façade and setting are the main attraction.

Monroe, designer of the Barnacle, painted by Lewis Benton in 1931

The Barnacle ❽

3485 Main Highway, Coconut Grove. **Map** 6 E4. 📞 *(305) 448-9445.* 🚌 *42, 48.* 🕐 *9am–4pm Fri–Sun.* ⬤ *Thanksgiving, 25 Dec, 1 Jan.* 📷 🎫

H IDDEN FROM Main Highway by tropical hardwood trees, the Barnacle is Dade County's oldest home. It was designed and occupied by one Ralph Monroe, a Renaissance man who made his living from boat building and wrecking *(see p289)*. As well as being a botanist and photographer, he was a keen environmentalist and had a strong belief in the importance of self-sufficiency.

When first constructed in 1891 the house was a bunga-low, built of wood salvaged from wrecks and inventively laid out in order to allow air

---

MIAMI: FACT MEETS FICTION

In the 1980s, the public perception of Miami was as the drug and crime capital of the US. Ironically, the popular TV series *Miami Vice (see p51)* played on this reputation, while also glamorizing both the city and the violence. The best novels about Miami in the 1990s have also emanated from its seedier side. Its two most renowned crime writers are Edna Buchanan, winner of a Pulitzer prize for news reporting on the *Miami Herald*, and Carl Hiaasen, a columnist for the same newspaper. However fanciful his plots might seem (building inspectors practising voodoo or talk-show hosts having plastic surgery on air), Carl Hiaasen claims the ideas come straight from the *Herald's* news pages. *Striptease* was the first of his novels to be made into a film.

Hiaasen's bestsellers

to circulate (essential in those pre-air conditioning times). Then in 1908, Monroe jacked the building up and added a new ground floor to make room for his expanding family.

Inside the two-storey house visitors can explore rooms stuffed with old family heirlooms and wonderful dated practical appliances such as an early refrigerator. The hour-long tours of the property also take in Monroe's clapboard boathouse, full of his tools and workbenches. Alongside, you can see the rail track that Monroe used to winch boats out of the bay.

Dinner Key ⑨

S Bayshore Drive. **Map** 6 F4.
⊟ Metrorail (Coconut Grove). ═ 48.

IN THE 1930s, Pan American Airways transformed Dinner Key into the busiest seaplane base in the USA. It was also the point of departure for Amelia Earhart's doomed round-the-world flight in 1937. You can still see the airline's sleek Streamline Moderne-style *(see p59)* terminal, which houses Miami City Hall, while the hangars where seaplanes were once harboured are now boatyards. For a glimpse of how some

Deco detail on Miami City Hall façade, Dinner Key

people enjoy their leisure time, take a walk among the yachts berthed in what is the most prestigious marina in Miami.

Ermita de la Caridad ⑩

3609 S Miami Ave. **Map** 3 C5.
【 (305) 854-2404. ⊟ Metrorail (Vizcaya). ═ 12, 48. ◯ 9am–9pm daily. &

THIS PECULIAR conical church, erected in 1966, is a very holy place for Miami's Cuban exiles – a shrine to their patron saint, the Virgin of Charity. A mural above the altar (which faces Cuba rather than being oriented eastwards) illustrates the history of the Catholic church in Cuba, showing the Virgin and her shrine on the island. (The church is hard to find: take the first turning north of the Mercy Hospital.)

The Space Transit Planetarium, venue for star and laser shows

Museum of Science and Space Transit Planetarium ⑪

3280 S Miami Ave. **Map** 3 C5.
【 (305) 854-4247. ⊟ Metrorail (Vizcaya). ═ 48. ◯ 10am–6pm daily. ● Thanksgiving, 25 Dec. 🎥 &

CHILDREN WITH enquiring minds may not notice or care that the Museum of Science needs smartening up. It's at its best in its many fun, interactive games, which demonstrate aspects of the five senses, gravity, density and so forth. Adults may be more interested in the moving letters written by victims of Hurricane Andrew, which struck in 1992 *(see p24)*, or by the computer terminals set up for visitors to "surf" the Internet.

You can buy a combination ticket to cover admission to the adjacent Space Transit Planetarium, which puts on impressive star shows daily and laser shows on Friday and Saturday evenings.

The Ermita de la Caridad, right on the edge of Biscayne Bay, which attracts many Cuban worshippers

Vizcaya ⑫

FLORIDA'S GRANDEST RESIDENCE was
completed in 1916 as the winter
retreat for millionaire industrialist James
Deering. His vision was to replicate a
16th-century Italian estate, but one that
had been altered by succeeding generations. Hence, Vizcaya and its opulent
rooms come in a blend of styles from
Renaissance to Neo-Classical, furnished
with the fruits of Deering's shopping sprees
around Europe. The formal gardens combine
beautifully the features of Italian and French
gardens with Florida's tropical foliage.

**Light
fitting**

Deering would constantly enquire of his
ambitious architect: "Must we be so grand?",
fearing that Vizcaya would be too costly
to support. After his death in 1925, it
proved to be so until 1952,
when it was bought by
Dade County. The house
and gardens were opened to
the public soon afterwards.

★ Deering Bathroom
*Deering's elaborate bathroom has
marble walls, silver plaques
and a canopied ceiling reminiscent of a Napoleonic
campaign tent.*

**Seahorse
weathervane**

Pulcinella
*The 18th-century
English statue of
Pulcinella, in the
intimate Theater
Garden, is one
of many European
sculptures in the
grounds of the villa.*

The Dining Room recalls a
Renaissance banqueting hall,
complete with tapestries and
a 16th-century refectory table.

The East Loggia, used for informal
entertaining, contains a model
caravel, a favourite Deering motif.

★ Music Room
*This Rococo room is arguably the loveliest
in the house. It is lit by a striking chandelier
of multicoloured glass flowers.*

STAR FEATURES
★ **Music Room**
★ **Deering Bathroom**
★ **Gardens**

★ **Gardens**
Formal gardens like those at Vizcaya are a rarity in Florida. The Mount provides a lovely view down the symmetrical Center Island to the South Terrace of the villa.

VISITORS' CHECKLIST

3251 S Miami Ave. **Map** 3 C5.
(305) 250-9133. Metrorail
(Vizcaya). 48. 9:30am–
5pm, gardens till 5:30pm (last
adm: 4:30pm) daily. 25 Dec.
 limited.

The courtyard, now protected by glass, was once open to the sky.

Entrance

The roof is covered with barrel tiles taken from buildings in Cuba.

Cathay Bedroom
Lorded over by the luxurious canopied bed, the Cathay Bedroom is decorated with chinoiserie, which was immensely popular in Europe in the 18th century.

The Living Room is a grand Renaissance hall with the curious addition of an organ, made especially for Vizcaya.

The Swimming Pool is visible outside but is reached from a grotto beneath the house.

Deering Sitting Room
The ceiling decoration of this Neo-Classical room features a seahorse, one of Vizcaya's recurrent motifs.

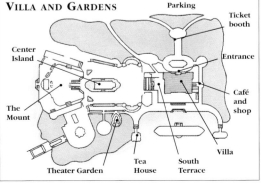

VILLA AND GARDENS

Parking

Ticket booth

Center Island

Entrance

Café and shop

The Mount

Villa

Theater Garden

Tea House

South Terrace

FURTHER AFIELD

THE AREAS north of Miami Beach and Downtown and south of Coral Gables are seldom very scenic, however they are well worth exploring for the great beaches and fun family attractions, as well as some plainly bizarre sights.

Much of northern Miami has a reputation for poverty and danger, in particular Liberty City and Overtown. Avoid these areas, and follow the safety tips on page 362. Be careful, too, when driving through Hialeah or visiting Opa-Locka or Little Haiti – atmospheric neighbourhoods but

Palms in Fairchild Tropical Garden

ones that are likely to appeal mainly to the more adventurous sightseers.

Southern Miami's dull, nondescript suburbs eventually give way to mile after mile of citrus orchards and nurseries. These flatlands were at the epicentre of Hurricane Andrew in 1992 (see p24), and the natural landscape still looks mauled in places. Many of this area's attractions, which consist primarily of zoos, parks and gardens, were very badly damaged. These have mostly reopened, although restoration work continues in many cases.

SIGHTS AT A GLANCE

Historic Buildings
Ancient Spanish Monastery ❷
Coral Castle ⓮

Museums and Galleries
American Police
 Hall of Fame ❺
Weeks Air Museum ⓫

Parks, Gardens and Zoos
Charles Deering Estate ❿
Fairchild Tropical Garden ❽
Miami Metrozoo ⓬
Miami Seaquarium ❻
Monkey Jungle ⓭
Parrot Jungle ❾

Beaches
Key Biscayne ❼
North Beaches ❶

Neighbourhoods
Little Haiti ❹
Opa-Locka ❸

10 miles = 16 km

KEY

▨	Main sightseeing areas
☐	Urban area
═	Expressway
▰	Major highway
═	Secondary route
—	Rail line
🚉	Amtrak station
✈	Airport

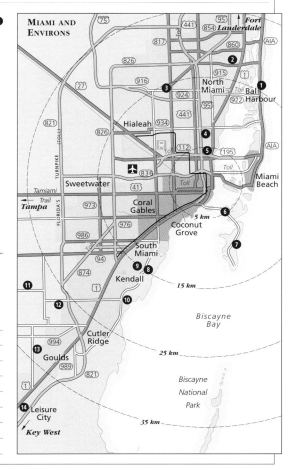

◁ **The 12th-century cloisters of the Ancient Spanish Monastery in northern Miami**

North Beaches **❶**

Collins Avenue. 🚌 *K or S from South Beach or Downtown.*

THE BARRIER ISLANDS north of Miami Beach are occupied mainly by unwelcoming posh residential areas and unlovely resorts, strung out along soulless Collins Avenue. Package tourists often get billeted here when many would probably prefer South Beach. Still, there is lots of cheap accommodation and a long sandy beach.

A peaceful strip of sand between 79th and 87th streets separates Miami Beach from **Surfside**, an unpretentious

Beach at Haulover Park, under the protective eye of a lifeguard

community very popular with French Canadian visitors. At 96th Street Surfside merges with **Bal Harbour**, a smart enclave known for a couple of flash hotels and one of the

swankiest shopping malls around *(see p92)*. Northwards is the pleasant **Haulover Park**, with a marina on the creek side and dune-backed sands facing the ocean.

Ancient Spanish Monastery **❷**

16711 W Dixie Hwy, N Miami Beach. 📞 *(305) 945-1462.* 🚌 *H from South Beach, 3 from Downtown.* 🕙 *10am–4pm daily, noon–4pm Sun.* ⬤ *public hols.* 📷 &

THESE MONASTERY cloisters have an unusual history. Originally built in 1133–41 in Spain, in 1925 they were bought by newspaper tycoon William Randolph Hearst, who had their 35,000 stones packed into crates. An outbreak of foot-and-mouth

disease, however, led to the crates being opened (for the packing straw to be checked), and the stones were repacked incorrectly. Once in New York, they remained there until 1952, when it was decided to

piece together "the world's largest and most expensive jigsaw puzzle" as an attraction in Florida. The cloisters, set in picturesque gardens, resemble the original version, but there is still a pile of unidentified stones in one corner.

Chapterhouse

The Chapel, at one time the dining hall, is still used for worship.

Statue of Alphonso VII, patron of the monastery

The cloister entrance is a carved, early Gothic arch.

The quiet gardens are a popular spot for wedding photos.

The bell outside the chapel door

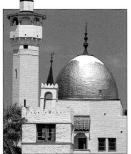

Arabian-style dome of the City Hall in Opa-Locka

Opa-Locka ❸

Junction of NW 27th Ave & NW 135th St, 10 miles (16 km) NW of Downtown. 🚌 E, from Sunny Isles Blvd.

NICKNAMED THE "Baghdad of Dade County", Opa-Locka was the brainchild of aviator Glenn Curtiss. Taking his inspiration from the tales of *The Arabian Nights*, he created his own fantasy city, financing the construction of more than 90 Moorish buildings during the 1920s boom *(see pp48–9).*

Nowadays, Opa-Locka is a depressed area in which you would be unwise to stray far from the restored City Hall (at Opa-Locka and Sharasad boulevards). All in pink with minarets, domes and keyhole arches, this is the best example of the remaining Moorish-style architecture. Otherwise, Opa-Locka's fantasy lives on mainly in shops with names such as Ali Baba Appliances and streets called Caliph or Sultan.

Little Haiti ❹

46th to 79th Streets, E of I-95. 🚌 9 or 10 from Downtown.

EVER SINCE THE 1980s, many Haitian refugees have settled in this part of Miami. It is a visibly impoverished but colourful community, and fairly safe if you stick to the main streets, 54th Street and NE 2nd Avenue.

The **Caribbean Marketplace**, at NE 2nd Avenue and 60th Street, has a few craft stalls, but more interesting are the surrounding shops painted dazzling colours. High-decibel Haitian music blares out of some; others are *botánicas* stocking herb potions and saints' ephemera *(see p75);* more sell "Caribbean-style" chicken and plantains.

American Police Hall of Fame ❺

3801 Biscayne Blvd. 📞 *(305) 573-0070.* 🚌 *3, 16.* 🕐 *10am–5:30pm daily.* ⬤ *25 Dec.* 🎦 ♿

FEW VISITORS are unmoved by the Hall of Fame's vast marble memorial, engraved with the names of over 5,000 American police officers who have died in the line of duty. Yet some of the exhibits, while fascinating, are gory and sensationalist. The *Robo-Cop* mannequin, knuckle-dusters, and weapons disguised as lipstick and an umbrella are innocuous enough. Some

1930s police car, American Police Hall of Fame

visitors, however, may find the prospect of strapping themselves into an electric chair or inspecting the gas chamber harder to stomach.

Miami Seaquarium ❻

4400 Rickenbacker Cswy, Virginia Key. 📞 *(305) 361-5705.* 🚌 *B from Brickell Ave.* 🕐 *9:30am–6pm daily.* 🎦 ♿

IF YOU'RE VISITING Orlando's Sea World *(see pp164–7),* you may not want to bother with the Miami Seaquarium, which is rather run-down by comparison. Nonetheless, the antics in the sea lion, killer whale and two dolphin shows are failproof crowd pleasers; allow a morning or afternoon to see all four shows, which are staged continuously. Other attractions include viewing areas for manatees, sharks, a mangrove swamp full of pelicans, and also a coral reef aquarium.

Key Biscayne ❼

7 miles (11 km) SE of Downtown. 🚌 *B.* **Bill Baggs Cape Florida SRA** 📞 *(305) 361-5811.* 🕐 *daily.*

THE VIEW OF Downtown from Rickenbacker Causeway, connecting the mainland to Virginia Key and Key Biscayne, is one of Miami's best. Views aside, Key Biscayne has some of the city's top beaches. Most impressive is the beach in **Crandon Park** in the upper half of the key, which is 3 miles (5 km) long and enormously wide, with palm trees and picnic areas. At the key's southern end, the **Bill Baggs Cape Florida State Recreation Area** has a shorter beach joined to more picnic areas by boardwalks across dunes. The lighthouse near the tip, built in 1825, is undergoing restoration.

A mix of mini-malls and oceanfront apartments line Crandon Boulevard between the two parks. More scenic are the posh residences around Harbor Drive on the bay side.

Mural advertising a religious shop *(botánica)* in Little Haiti

Fairchild Tropical Garden ❽

10901 Old Cutler Rd. 🗂 *(305) 667-1651.* 🚌 *65 from Coconut Grove.* ⭕ *9:30am–4:30pm daily.* ⬤ *25 Dec.* 🖼 ⬧ **Mattheson Hammock Park** 🗂 *(305) 665-5475.* ⭕ *sunrise to sunset daily.*

T HIS HUGE and dizzyingly beautiful tropical garden, established in 1938, doubles as a major botanical research institution. Around a series of man-made lakes stands one of the largest collections of palm trees in the world (550 of the 2,500 known species) as well as an impressive array of cycads – relatives of palms and ferns – which bear unusual giant red cones. There are countless other wonderful trees and plants, including a comical-looking sausage tree.

During 40-minute tram tours, guides describe how plants are used in the manufacture of medicines, perfumes (the flowers of the ylang-ylang tree, for example, are used in Chanel No. 5) and even golf balls. You should allow another two hours to explore on your own.

Next door to the Fairchild Tropical Garden is the waterfront Mattheson Hammock Park, which has been recovering slowly from the beating it received from Hurricane Andrew. There are walking and cycling trails through mangrove swamps, but most

visitors head for the Atoll Pool, an artificial salt-water swimming pool encircled by sand and palm trees right alongside Biscayne Bay.

Parrot Jungle ❾

11000 SW 57th Ave. 🗂 *(305) 666-7834.* 🚈 *Metrorail (South Miami) then bus 57.* ⭕ *9:30am–6pm daily.* 🖼 ⬧

O VER 1,100 BIRDS populate this beautifully maintained tropical garden. Some are caged, some roam wild, while others perform tricks such as riding roller skates in the ever-popular Trained Bird Show. Other attractions include a jungle trail past ponds infested with alligators and turtles.

A new Parrot Jungle being created on Watson Island in Biscayne Bay will eventually replace the present one.

Charles Deering Estate ❿

16701 SW 72nd Ave. 🗂 *(305) 235-1668.* ⭕ *9am–5pm daily from spring 1998.* 🖼 🖼 ⬧

W HILE HIS BROTHER James enjoyed the splendour of Vizcaya *(see pp84–5),* Charles Deering had his own stylish winter retreat on Biscayne Bay, which he used regularly between 1916 and 1927. His 400-acre (162-ha) estate, including a Mediterranean

The Charles Deering Estate, devastated by Hurricane Andrew

Revival mansion, was acquired by the State in 1985.

Several of the estate's buildings, including the main house and a 19th-century inn called Richmond Cottage, were badly damaged by the passing of Hurricane Andrew. They have since been carefully restored and opened to the public.

It is the grounds, however, that are the main attraction here, although they too were ravaged by Andrew's 160-mph (258-km/h) winds. Included are mangrove and rockland pine forests, a salt marsh, and what is supposed to be the largest virgin coastal tropical hardwood hammock on the US mainland; there is also an extensive fossil site. Interesting guided canoe tours can be taken at the weekends.

The tranquil, palm-fringed lakes of the Fairchild Tropical Garden

A Bengal tiger in front of a mock Khmer temple at Miami Metrozoo

Weeks Air Museum ⓫

14710 SW 128th St, adjacent to Tamiami Airport. ☎ *(305) 233-5197.* ◯ *10am–5pm daily.* ⬤ *Thanksgiving, 25 Dec.* 📷 ♿

Hurricane Andrew damaged all of the aircraft in the Weeks Air Museum, tossing some bombers a mile (1.6 km) from the site. But, appropriately for a museum dedicated to the preservation of old aircraft, most of the planes had been restored by 1997. A new hangar proudly displays the mostly American, German and Russian World War II fighters, along with ejector seats, machine-gun turrets and so forth.

There is also a fascinating section on an American all-black fighter squadron formed in 1941, at a time when the assumption was that African-Americans were incapable of flying combat aircraft.

A new display installed in 1997 recreates a World War II US military encampment in the South Pacific.

Miami Metrozoo ⓬

12400 SW 152nd St, Perrine. ☎ *(305) 251-0400.* 🚇 *Metrorail (Dadeland North) then Zoo Bus.* ◯ *9:30am–5:30pm daily.* 📷 ♿

This GIANT and excellent zoo is considered one of the country's best. Animals are kept in spacious landscaped habitats, separated from humans by moats rather than cages. As well as the many

traditional zoo animals, popular highlights include lowland gorillas, Malayan sun bears and, best of all, white Bengal tigers. The Petting Zoo offers elephant rides, while the Wildlife Show demonstrates the agility of big cats.

The best way to tackle the zoo is first to take the 20-minute ride on the monorail for an overview, and then return to what catches your interest; or take the monorail to Station 4 and then walk back. Hurricane Andrew rid the zoo of much of its foliage, so it can be blisteringly hot – in summer come early or late.

Monkey Jungle ⓭

14805 SW 216th St, Cutler Ridge. ☎ *(305) 235-1611.* 🚇 *Metrorail (Dadeland South) then bus 1, 52 or Busway Max to Cutler Ridge Mall, then taxi.* ◯ *9:30am–5pm daily.* 📷 ♿

This ENDEARING attraction is still run by the family that founded it back in 1933 to study primate behaviour. Both breeding and research

A macaque, one of the most active primates at Monkey Jungle

programmes remain integral to the park's function. Monkey Jungle's best selling point is that human visitors are caged while the animals roam free. You walk through a caged area with Java macaques clambering above you and can observe South American monkeys at close quarters in a simulated rainforest. Other primates, including gorillas, orang-utans, spider monkeys and gibbons, are kept conventionally in cages.

Demonstrations showing the various capabilities of macaques, chimpanzees and other species take place regularly throughout the day.

Crescent moon sculpted from rock at Coral Castle

Coral Castle ⓮

28655 S Dixie Hwy, Homestead. ☎ *(305) 248-6344.* 🚇 *Metrorail (Dadeland South) then bus Busway Max.* ◯ *9am–6pm daily.* ⬤ *25 Dec.* 📷 ♿

This MAY BE NO CASTLE, but it is still one of Miami's most intriguing attractions. From 1920 to 1940 a Latvian called Edward Leedskalnin single-handedly built a series of giant sculptures out of coral rock, using tools assembled from automobile parts. He sculpted most of the stones 10 miles (16 km) away in Florida City, moving them again on his own to their present site. Some, such as a working telescope, represent their creator's great passion for astrology. Others, such as the heart-shaped table, remember a Latvian girl who refused to marry him.

SHOPPING IN MIAMI

MIAMI'S SHOPS range from the ultra chic to the quirky and colourful, reflecting the nature of the city. Being made up of neighbourhoods, Miami offers a choice of districts to shop in. Serious shoppers will probably gravitate towards the malls, which attract visitors from all over Latin America and the Caribbean. Some of these double as entertainment centres *(see p332)*, often staying open until 11pm, though the shops tend to keep normal hours.

**Gucci logo,
Bal Harbour Shops**

If your shopping tastes are more offbeat, head for Coconut Grove or South Beach, where shops are aimed at a totally different market. Here, motorized skateboards, wild leather gear, cardboard art and the like are on offer, and you can pick up fun souvenirs too. Most shops in Coconut Grove stay open late, especially at weekends. Stores in South Beach keep irregular hours, with most opening up late in the day; some don't get going until 11am or even noon.

WHERE TO SHOP

SOUTH BEACH is a fun place to shop, but the most relaxed shopping area is Coconut Grove. It has numerous boutiques concentrated in a small area and boasts two malls *(see p82)*: **CocoWalk**, whose two dozen jewellery, gift and clothes shops play second fiddle to cafés and restaurants, and the **Streets of Mayfair** – where pricey boutiques are suitable mainly for window-shopping.

Bayside Marketplace *(see p72)* aims to entertain but has a wide range of shops too, with all kinds of gift emporia and fashion stores. Otherwise, shop Downtown only if you're after cut-price electronics and jewellery, although **Burdines** department store, founded in 1898, is of more general interest. **Omni International Mall**, to the north, has lost out to Bayside Marketplace but has a good choice of shops as well as its own cinema.

Entirely different in tone is Coral Gables, with its demure stores along Miracle Mile *(see p80)* and its posh art galleries.

Dedicated shoppers head for Miami's famous malls. **Bal Harbour Shops** is a fascinatingly snooty mall in a tropical garden setting, whose tone is set by wealthy old ladies and security staff in uniforms with the tag "Bahamian gendarme". **Aventura Mall**, also in North Miami, is impressive largely for its size: it has over 200 shops including four department stores, one of which is Macy's.

**Typical window-dressing in a
South Beach boutique**

FASHION AND JEWELLERY

MIAMI HAS EVERYTHING, from top designer to discount clothes. In Bal Harbour Shops, jewellers and fashion stores with household names such as Tiffany & Co, Gucci and Cartier stand alongside shops like J W Cooper, specializing in Western gear. By contrast, **Loehmann's Fashion Island,** in nearby

Aventura, deals in cut-price designer clothes. More good deals can be had in the 100 odd discount stores of Downtown's Fashion District – on 5th Avenue between 24th and 29th streets. The **Seybold Building**, also Downtown, is famous for its cut-price gold, diamonds and watches.

In South Beach, stores on Lincoln Road and Washington Avenue deal primarily in leather and "disco dolly" outfits, but there are smarter stores too. The boutiques along Miracle Mile in Coral Gables are more consistently upmarket: **J Bolado**, for made-to-measure clothes, is typical.

GIFTS AND SOUVENIRS

BAYSIDE MARKETPLACE is reliable gift-buying territory, with shops such as the **Warner Brothers Studios Store** and the **Disney Store**, and a gaggle of pushcarts laden with espadrilles, ties

Warner Brothers Studios Store, a kids' favourite at Bayside Marketplace

Cigarmaker in action at El Crédito Factory

a few genuine Art Deco antiques. The shop also maintains an impressive selection of pertinent books.

Ba-Balú on Española Way sells mugs, cigars (some of which are rolled in the shop) and other mementos of Cuban Miami, though nothing is made in Cuba. The best place for cigars, however, is **El Crédito Cigar Factory** in Little Havana (see p74). A mix of tourists and smart businessmen come to buy the cigars which are made by hand at the factory; the best brand is called La Gloria Cubana.

and other items. In Coconut Grove, alongside numerous shops selling T-shirts and sunglasses are shops specializing in anything from oriental crafts to condoms. Have fun browsing around **Easyriders**, which boasts a superb collection of Harley Davidson merchandise, from keyrings to helmets.

Burdines is not a classic hunting-ground for souvenirs, but you can sometimes pick up unusual items, such as genuine artifacts from the wreck of the *Atocha* salvaged by Mel Fisher (see p26).

South Beach is probably the best place for fun mementos and gifts. The **Art Deco Welcome Center** on Ocean Drive has a small but good choice, including T-shirts, posters and models of Ocean Drive buildings, in addition to

A good shop for edible souvenirs, such as Florida jellies and sauces, is **Epicure** in South Beach, although tourists are not targeted by this gourmet supermarket.

Craft stalls are set up in Española Way (see p66) at weekends, but Miami is generally not a good place to buy locally made crafts. Fine art is a much easier proposition. Española Way itself has a few avant-garde galleries, but you'll find a greater concentration

A ceramic Art Deco hotel

of better quality fine art along Lincoln Road. Most of the two dozen or so galleries, including the South Florida Art Center (see p66), feature contemporary paintings, sculpture, ceramics and furniture in provocative or Pop Art style. The art in Coral Gables' galleries is more traditional.

BOOKS AND MUSIC

IF MIAMI gives you a taste for Latin American music, you'll find a good choice at **Casino Records** in Little Havana. For a wider range try **Revolution Records** in South Beach, which sells used CDs and cassettes too.

Books & Books in Coral Gables is everyone's favourite bookshop, with shelves from floor to ceiling and a good selection of travel and arts titles. For books about Florida, don't fail to visit the Indies Company gift shop in the Historical Museum of Southern Florida (see p72), whose stock of books covers every imaginable subject relating to the state. You'll find branches of chain bookstores, such as B Dalton's, in most shopping malls.

ENTERTAINMENT IN MIAMI

A FLEET OF STRETCH LIMOS parked outside the hottest nightclubs attests to the fact that South Beach is one of the trendiest places on the planet: for many people the chance to party in style is one of the city's chief attractions. Most people make for the nightclubs, which are perhaps surprisingly laid-back, but many are also good venues for live music. For anyone not into celebrity-spotting or dancing, Miami offers a good range of cultural and sporting events. The city

Miami Dolphins player in action

used to be thought of as something of a cultural desert, but its performing arts scene is now buoyant. The winter season is the busiest, when Miami attracts many world-famous artists. If you are lucky, your visit may coincide with one of the city's colourful and large-scale festivals (see pp32–5).

The easiest way to purchase tickets for most cultural or sporting events is to call Ticketmaster (see p339). Otherwise, contact the individual sports stadium or theatre direct.

INFORMATION

THE TWO ESSENTIAL sources of information are the Weekend section of Friday's edition of the *Miami Herald*, and the free, and more comprehensive *New Times*, which is published every Wednesday. For hot tips about the latest venues, read Tara Solomon's column in the *Miami Herald*. The vibrant gay nightlife of South Beach is covered in detail in several free, widely available magazines.

PERFORMING ARTS

MAJOR TOURING companies perform at the **Dade County Auditorium**, the **Jackie Gleason Theater of the Performing Arts** (known as TOPA) in South Beach and Downtown's **Gusman Center for the Performing Arts**, a 1920s cinema with a fabulous ornate Moorish interior. The Broadway Series (November to April) in the Jackie Gleason Theater leads Miami's drama scene. More intimate venues include the **Coconut Grove**

Playhouse, which stages a mix of Off-Broadway hits and more avant-garde local work, and the **Actors' Playhouse**, in Coral Gables, for new shows and old favourites.

The much-respected **Miami City Ballet** performs classical and contemporary work, often at the Jackie Gleason Theater, and you can sometimes see the dancers rehearse at the company's base in Lincoln Road. Also in South Beach, the Ballet Flamenco La Rosa, part of the **Performing Arts Network** group of dance companies, is well worth seeing; they often appear at the **Colony Theatre**.

Miami's most acclaimed classical orchestra is Michael Tilson Thomas's New World Symphony, comprised of graduates from the country's most prestigious music schools; it performs at the **Lincoln Theatre** from October to May. The Concert Association of Florida (see p336) organizes most of Miami's top concerts, and keep an eye out for performances by the Florida Philharmonic (see p336).

Hialeah Park, famous for its horse-racing and flock of flamingos

SPECTATOR SPORTS

BOTH THE Miami Dolphins football team and the Florida Marlins baseball squad compete at the **Pro Player Stadium**. The University of Miami's Hurricanes, one of Florida's top college football squads, draws almost equally large crowds; they play at the **Orange Bowl Stadium**. Miami Heat plays basketball and the Florida Panthers ice hockey at the **Miami Arena**, Downtown.

For a more typically Florida scene, catch a game of jai alai (see p31) at the **Miami Jai Alai Fronton** near the airport. Betting is *de rigueur* both here and at the **Hialeah Park** race-track. See pages 30–31 for details of seasons.

LIVE MUSIC

MOST BARS on Ocean Drive offer live music, typically Latin jazz, reggae or salsa, but there are better venues. The MoJazz Café in North Miami

The Coconut Grove Playhouse, which can draw New York shows

The stage show at Club Tropigala, designed to evoke the 1950s

Beach *(see p316)* is a mecca for jazz lovers. Another fine place for live music is **Tobacco Road**, Miami's oldest club, which lays on anything from rock to Latin jazz nightly.

Or try one of Miami's two famous Latin floor shows: both feature Las Vegas-style extravaganzas with sparkling showgirls, a live orchestra and couples of all ages dancing salsa. **Club Tropigala** in the Fontainebleau Hotel is the best known, but **Les Violins**, Downtown, is more kitsch and more evocative of 1950s Havana. At both places you can eat, drink and dance into the early hours.

NIGHTCLUBS

TWO AREAS IN Greater Miami buzz after dark: Coconut Grove, mainly for wining and dining, and South Beach, with its far more hip scene. Here the bars along Ocean Drive and nearby streets are busy all day and the nightclubs get going only after midnight.

As new clubs are opening up all the time, ask around for tips on SoBe's latest hot spots. Favourite venues are: **Bash**, which was started by Sean Penn and Mick Hucknall and is a popular place for celebrity-spotting; **Rezurrection Hall**, where models and men with heavily worked torsos pose among flower arrangements; the ultra-trendy **Liquid**, with a chic crowd strutting to house, funk, soul and hip hop music; and **Amnesia**, a huge, largely open-air venue with outrageous Sunday tea dances.

Many clubs have a gay night. Others advertise themselves as exclusively gay, but the scene is usually mixed. The Deco-era **Warsaw Ballroom**, with stripping go-go dancers most nights, is Miami's oldest and best known gay club. **Twist**, with a Key West-style terrace, is a very popular gay bar and has a dance floor too.

One of the four bars at the Clevelander on Ocean Drive

DIRECTORY

PERFORMING ARTS

Actors' Playhouse
280 Miracle Mile.
Map 5 1C.
(305) 444-9293.

Coconut Grove Playhouse
3500 Main Highway.
Map 6 E4.
(305) 442-2662.

Colony Theatre
1040 Lincoln Rd.
Map 2 D2.
(305) 674-1026.

Dade County Auditorium
2901 W Flagler St.
(305) 545-3395.

Gusman Center for the Performing Arts
174 E Flagler St. **Map** 4 E1.
(305) 372-0925.

Jackie Gleason Theater of the Performing Arts
1700 Washington Ave.
Map 2 E2.
(305) 673-7300.

Lincoln Theatre
555 Lincoln Rd.
Map 2 E2.
(305) 673-3330.

Miami City Ballet
905 Lincoln Rd. **Map** 2 E2.
(305) 532-4880.

Performing Arts Network
555 17th St. **Map** 2 E2.
(305) 672-0552.

SPECTATOR SPORTS

Hialeah Park
2200 E 4th Ave, Hialeah.
(305) 885-8000.

Miami Arena
721 NW 1st Ave.
(305) 530-4400.

Miami Jai Alai Fronton
3500 NW 37th Ave.
(305) 633-6400.

Orange Bowl Stadium
1501 NW 3rd St.
Map 3 1B.
(305) 643-7100.

Pro Player Stadium
2269 NW 199th St.
(305) 620-2578.

LIVE MUSIC

Club Tropigala
Fontainebleau Hilton,
4441 Collins Ave.
(305) 672-7469.

Tobacco Road
626 S Miami Ave.
Map 4. E2.
(305) 374-1198.

Les Violins
1751 Biscayne Blvd.
(305) 371-8668.

NIGHTCLUBS

Amnesia
136 Collins Ave.
Map 2 E5.
(305) 531-5535.

Bash
655 Washington Ave.
Map 2 E4.
(305) 538-2274.

Liquid
1439 Washington Ave.
Map 2 F3.
(305) 532-9154.

Rezurrection Hall
245 22nd St.
Map 2 F1.
(305) 534-1235.

Twist
1057 Washington Ave.
Map 2 E3.
(305) 538-9478.

Warsaw Ballroom
1450 Collins Ave.
Map 2 E3
(305) 531-4555.

MIAMI STREET FINDER

THE MAP REFERENCES given with all sights, shops and entertainment venues described in the Miami chapter refer to the five pages of maps in this section. The key map below shows the area of the city which is covered, with the three major sightseeing districts colour-coded pink. All the principal sights mentioned in the text are marked, as well as useful information, such as transport stations, tourist offices and post offices; a full list is given in the key. Map references are also given for Miami's hotels *(see pp296–9)*, restaurants *(see pp316–19)* and bars and cafés *(see p330)* included in the Travellers' Needs section.

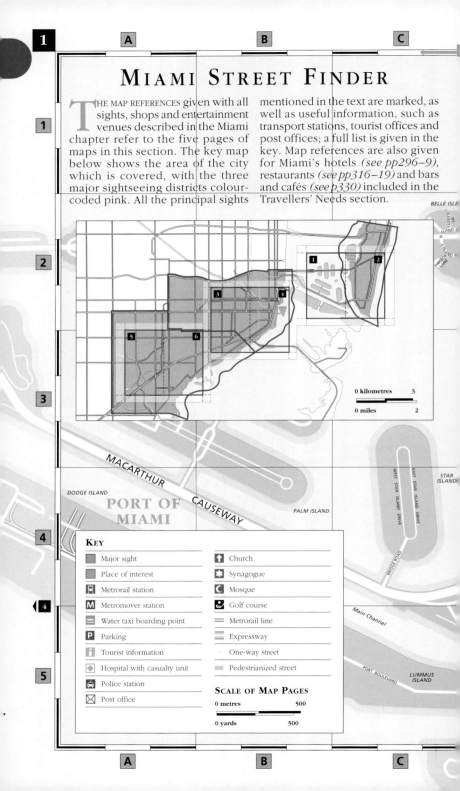

BELLE ISLE

0 kilometres   3

0 miles   2

MACARTHUR CAUSEWAY

DODGE ISLAND

PORT OF MIAMI

PALM ISLAND

WEST STAR ISLAND DRIVE

EAST STAR ISLAND DRIVE

STAR ISLAND

BRIDGE ROAD

Main Channel

PORT BOULEVARD

LUMMUS ISLAND

KEY

▦ Major sight		🕇 Church	
▦ Place of interest		✡ Synagogue	
🚉 Metrorail station		C Mosque	
M Metromover station		⛳ Golf course	
🚤 Water taxi boarding point		= Metrorail line	
P Parking		≡ Expressway	
🛈 Tourist information		— One-way street	
✚ Hospital with casualty unit		▬ Pedestrianized street	
🚓 Police station			
⊠ Post office			

SCALE OF MAP PAGES

0 metres   500

0 yards   500

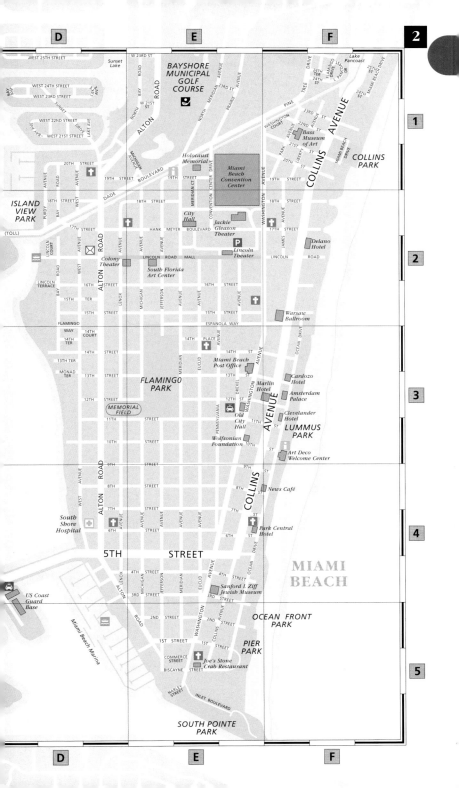

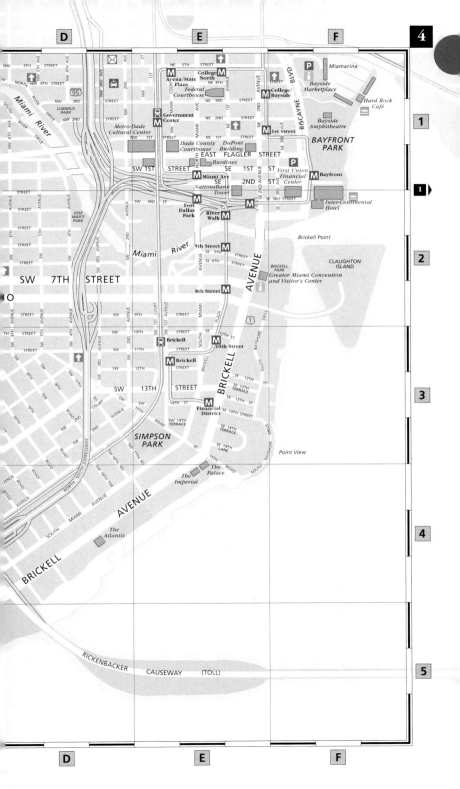

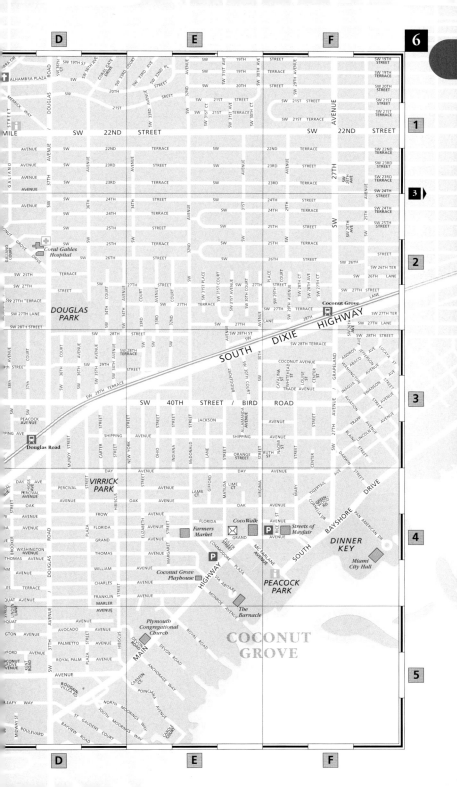

FLORIDA AREA BY AREA

Florida at a Glance

W̶ALT DISNEY WORLD ASIDE, Florida is best known for its
beaches; there are so many of these that everyone
should be able to find one to suit their taste. Most tourist
attractions, from state-of-the-art museums to historic
towns, are also found along the coast. The joy of
Florida, however, is that inland destinations are within
easy reach. It is well worth venturing away from the
hubbub of the coast to explore some of the state's richest
natural landscapes and get the full flavour of Florida.

Canoeing *is very popular i[n]
the Panhandle, where river[s]
such as the Suwannee ar[e]
frequently flanked by lus[h]
vegetation. (See p230.)*

**THE
PANHANDLE**
(see pp210–231)

**THE
NORTHEA[ST]**
(see pp188–2[...])

Beaches *in the
Panhandle boast the
finest sand in Florida,
washed by the warm
waters of the Gulf of
Mexico. Resorts like
Panama City Beach
throng with people
in the summer.*
(See pp222–3.)

**THE
GULF COA[ST]**
(see pp232–2[...])

Busch Gardens*, which
combines a wildlife park
with roller coasters and
other rides, is the top
large-scale family attraction outside Orlando.*
(See pp250–51.)

0 kilometres   75

0 miles   75

The Ringling Museum of Art *boasts one of the
state's top art collections and has a handsome
courtyard filled with copies of Classical statuary,
including this* Lygia and the Bull. *(See pp256–9.)*

Castillo de San Marcos *is a 17th-century Spanish fort in Florida's oldest town, St Augustine. Its well-preserved state is due to both its design and its 13-ft (4-m) thick walls. (See pp200–201.)*

Orlando's theme parks *are Florida's principal attraction away from the coast. Here, you can escape into a man-made fantasy world, where an extraordinary array of shows and rides provide the entertainment. Most famous is Walt Disney World (see pp138–63), but Universal Studios (see pp168–73), pictured here, and Sea World (see pp164–7) draw their own vast crowds.*

Daytona Beach *(see pp203–205)*

Kennedy Space Center *(see pp182–7)*

ORLANDO AND THE SPACE COAST *(see pp134–187)*

The Gold Coast *is full of luxurious homes. In Palm Beach you can visit the 1920s home of Henry Flagler, and marvel at the mansions and yachts along the Intracoastal Waterway. (See pp114–21.)*

THE GOLD AND TREASURE COASTS *(see pp106–133)*

THE EVERGLADES AND THE KEYS *(see pp266–289)*

John Pennekamp Coral Reef State Park *(see pp278–9)*

Everglades National Park, *a vast expanse of prairie, swamp and mangrove that teems with wildlife, is as wild as Florida gets. It is just a short drive from Miami. (See pp272–7.)*

THE GOLD AND TREASURE COASTS

NAMED AFTER BOOTY *found in Spanish galleons wrecked along their shores, the Gold and Treasure coasts today are two of the state's wealthiest regions. The promise of winter sunshine once lured just the well-to-do but now entices millions of holidaymakers.*

Holidays centre on the pencil-thin barrier islands which extend right along the coast, squeezed between prime sands and the Intracoastal Waterway *(see p28)*. The Treasure Coast, stretching from Sebastian Inlet down to Jupiter Inlet, is relatively undeveloped, with great sweeps of wild, sandy beaches and affluent but unshowy communities.

Wedged between the Atlantic and the Everglades, the 60-mile (97-km) Gold Coast extends from just north of West Palm Beach down to Miami. Before being opened up by Flagler's East Coast Railroad in the late 19th century, this part of Florida was a wilderness populated only by Indians and the odd white settler. Today, save for the occasional park and hundreds of golf courses, it is unremittingly built up.

The Gold Coast divides into two counties. In Palm Beach County, rich northerners, most of whom have made their fortunes elsewhere, flaunt their privileged lifestyle in million-dollar homes and on croquet lawns and polo fields.

The winter resorts of Palm Beach and Boca Raton offer the most memorable glimpses of how affluent Americans spend their time, and money. Broward County, synonymous with Greater Fort Lauderdale, is one huge metropolis. Its relentless urbanization is relieved by waterways and beaches: including in Fort Lauderdale itself, one of several local resorts which let their hair down more than their stuffy Palm Beach County counterparts.

Looking out towards the Atlantic Ocean from the top of Jupiter Inlet Lighthouse

◁ One of the verdant alleyways along Worth Avenue, Palm Beach's exclusive shopping street

Exploring the Gold and Treasure Coasts

MOST VISITORS COME here for a stay-put beach holiday. North of Palm Beach you can expect an unspoilt, uncrowded littoral, while to the south you'll find condos, sunbeds and lots of company. Coastal parks rich in bird life provide reminders of how the land looked in its virgin state. Cultural sightseeing comes fairly low on the agenda, but West Palm Beach's superb Norton Museum of Art and the exclusive town of Palm Beach should not be missed. The more active can play golf, shop and fish – the main reason to head inland is for the excellent fishing on Lake Okeechobee. All along the coast, hotel rooms are hard to come by and twice the price from December to April; by contrast, in high summer most of the resorts are very quiet.

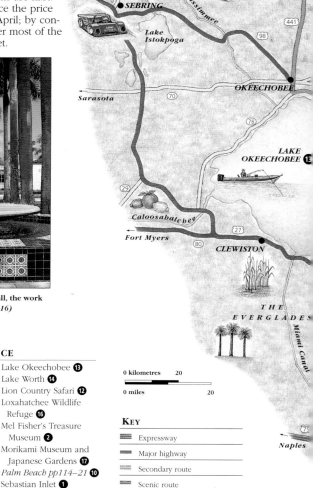

Boca Raton's Old Town Hall, the work of Addison Mizner *(see p116)*

SIGHTS AT A GLANCE

0 kilometres   20

0 miles   20

KEY

≡≡≡	Expressway
▬▬▬	Major highway
≡≡≡	Secondary route
≡≡≡	Scenic route
≋	River
☼	Viewpoint

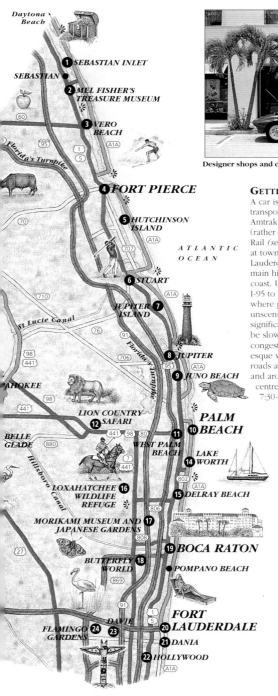

Daytona Beach

1 SEBASTIAN INLET

SEBASTIAN

2 MEL FISHER'S TREASURE MUSEUM

(60)

3 VERO BEACH

(95)
(1)
(5)
(A1A)

Florida's Turnpike

4 FORT PIERCE

(70)

5 HUTCHINSON ISLAND

(707)
(A1A)

ATLANTIC OCEAN

6 STUART

(710)

(A1A)

JUPITER ISLAND 7

St Lucie Canal

(76)
(91)

Florida's Turnpike

(98)
(441)

(706)

8 JUPITER

PAHOKEE

(98)

9 JUNO BEACH

(441)

LION COUNTRY SAFARI 12

PALM BEACH 10

BELLE GLADE

(441)(98)(80)
(880)

11 WEST PALM BEACH

14 LAKE WORTH

(7)
(441)

(802)
(A1A)

Hillsboro Canal

LOXAHATCHEE WILDLIFE REFUGE 16

15 DELRAY BEACH

(806)

MORIKAMI MUSEUM AND 17
JAPANESE GARDENS

(808)

(27)

19 BOCA RATON

BUTTERFLY WORLD 18

POMPANO BEACH

(869)

(91)

DAVIE

(1)
(5)

FORT LAUDERDALE 20

FLAMINGO GARDENS 24 23

21 DANIA

22 HOLLYWOOD

(A1A)

Designer shops and cars in exclusive Palm Beach

GETTING AROUND

A car is absolutely essential, as public transport is either limited or nonexistent. Amtrak basically offers ways to get to (rather than around) the area, but Tri-Rail *(see p360)* has services stopping at towns and airports between Fort Lauderdale and West Palm Beach. Three main highways run the length of the coast. Use the fast-moving, multilaned I-95 to travel any distance. Avoid US 1 where possible: it trawls slowly and unscenically through the centre of every significant conurbation. Route A1A can be slower still but is normally far less congested and often delivers picturesque views. Avoid travelling on major roads anywhere along the Gold Coast and around the Treasure Coast's main centres during rush hours (weekdays 7:30–9:30am and 4:30–7pm).

SEE ALSO

- **Where to Stay** pp299–301
- **Where to Eat** pp319–21 & p330

Fort Lauderdale's popular beach, offering a wealth of water sports

Sebastian Inlet ❶

Road map F3. Indian River Co.
🚊 Sebastian. ℹ️ 1302 US 1, (561)
589-5969.

A T SEBASTIAN INLET, the Atlantic
Ocean mingles with the
brackish waters of the Indian
River section of the Intracoastal Waterway (see p21).
The **Sebastian Inlet State
Recreation Area** spans this
channel and, with its 3 miles
(5 km) of pristine beaches, is
one of the most popular state
parks in Florida.

A tranquil cove on the northern side of the inlet is an ideal
place to swim – avoiding the
waves which make the
southern shores (on
Orchid Island) one of
the best surfing spots
on Florida's east coast.
Competitions take
place on many week-
ends, and there are
boards for hire. The
park is renowned for
its fishing too, and
the inlet's mouth is
invariably chock-a-block with
fishing boats. The two jetties
which jut out into the Atlantic
Ocean on either side are also
crammed with anglers, while
more lines dangle in the limpid
waters of the Indian River.

At the southern end of the
park, the **McLarty Treasure
Museum** takes an in-depth
look at the history surrounding
the loss of a Spanish Plate Fleet
in 1715. On 31 July, a hurricane
wrecked 11 galleons on the
shallow reefs off the coast
between Sebastian Inlet and
Fort Pierce. The ships were
en route from Havana back to

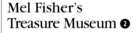

**Spanish plate,
McLarty Museum**

Spain, riding the waters of the
warm Gulf Stream, and laden
with booty from Spain's New
World colonies. About a third
of the 2,100 sailors lost their
lives, while the survivors set
up a camp where the McLarty
Treasure Museum now stands.

Immediately following this
tragedy, some 80 per cent of
the cargo was salvaged by the
survivors, helped by local Ais
Indians. The fleet then lay
undisturbed until 1928, when
one of the wrecks was redis-
covered. Salvaging resumed
in the early 1960s; since then
millions of dollars-worth of
treaures have been recovered.
Finds on display include gold
and silver coins but feature
mostly domestic items,
such as rings,buttons
and cutlery.

🏖️ **Sebastian
Inlet SRA**
9700 S A1A, Melbourne
Beach. 🚗 (407) 984-4852.
⏰ daily. 📷 ♿
🏛️ **McLarty Treasure
Museum**
1380 N Route A1A. 🚗 (561) 589-
2147. ⏰ daily. 📷 ♿

Mel Fisher's Treasure Museum ❷

Road map F3. Indian River Co. 1322
US 1, Sebastian. 🚗 (561) 589-9875.
🚊 Sebastian. ⏰ daily. ● Thanks-
giving, 25 Dec, 1 Jan. 📷 ♿

O FTEN PORTRAYED proudly
displaying his gold and
other treasure, the balding
and bespectacled Mel Fisher
looks more like the big prize
winner on a television game

**Mel Fisher, successful entrepreneur
and treasure hunter**

show than someone who pro-
motes himself as "The World's
Greatest Treasure Hunter".

His museum in downtown
Sebastian contains treasures
from different wrecks, including the 1715 fleet (which his
team has been salvaging for
decades), and goodies from
the Atocha (see p26). There
are dazzling jewels, a gold bar
(with the challenge to lift it), as
well as more everyday items.
In the Bounty Room, you can
buy original Spanish reales or
facsimiles of historic jewellery.

Vero Beach ❸

Road map F3. Indian River Co.
🚶 18,000. 🚉 ℹ️ 1216 21st St,
(561) 567-3491.

T HE MAIN TOWN of Indian
River County, Vero Beach,
and in particular its resort
community on Orchid Island,
is a seductive, well-heeled
place. Mature live oaks line
the residential streets and
buildings are restricted to no
more than four storeys. Pretty
boarded houses along Ocean
Drive contain galleries, boutiques and antique stores.

The **Center for the Arts**
in Riverside Park on Orchid
Island puts on high-profile
exhibitions, but the town is
most famous for its beaches
and two hotels. The Driftwood
Resort, in the heart of oceanfront Vero Beach, began life in
1935 as a beach house. It was
created by a local eccentric
out of reclaimed timbers and
driftwood and filled with an
amazing array of bric-a-brac,
which you can still see today.
Seven miles (11 km) north at

Catching the waves at the Gold Coast's Sebastian Inlet

Wabasso Beach, one of the best of the superb shell-strewn sands all along Orchid Island, is the Vero Beach Resort *(see p301)*. Disney's first Florida hotel outside Orlando, this is a model of measured elegance – with hardly a (Mickey) mouse in sight.

The **Indian River Citrus Museum**, on the mainland, is dedicated to the area's chief crop. All kinds of items to do with the citrus industry are displayed, including some old photographs, harvesting equipment and brand labels.

🏛 **Center for the Arts**
3001 Riverside Park Drive. 📞 *(561) 231-0707.* ⬤ *Thanksgiving, 25 Dec, 1 Jan.* ♿
🏛 **Indian River Citrus Museum**
2140 14th Ave. 📞 *(561) 770-2263.* ◻ *Tue–Fri.* ⬤ *public hols.* 📷 ♿

Fort Pierce ❶

Road map F3. St Lucie Co.
🚶 *37,000.* 🚍 🚌 ℹ *2300 Virginia Ave, (561) 462-1535.*

NAMED AFTER a military post built during the Second Seminole War *(see pp44–5)*, Fort Pierce is nothing to write home about. The town's biggest draw is without doubt its barrier islands, reached via two causeways that sweep across the Intracoastal Waterway.

Take the North Beach Causeway to reach North Hutchinson Island. Its southern tip is occupied by the **Fort Pierce Inlet State Recreation Area**, which includes the town's best beach, backed by dunes and popular with surfers. Just

Vero Beach's Driftwood Resort, built of reclaimed wood

to the north, on the site of a World War II training school, is the **UDT-SEAL Museum**. From 1943 to 1946, more than 3,000 US Navy frogmen of the Underwater Demolition Teams (UDTs) trained here, learning how to disarm sea mines and beach defences. By the '60s, they had become an elite advance fighting force known as SEALs (Sea, Air, Land commandos). This highly patriotic museum explains the frogmen's roles in World War II, Korea, Vietnam and Kuwait. Outside are several SEAL delivery vehicles, which are basically torpedo-like submarines used to carry people rather than bombs and explosives.

Half a mile (0.8 km) away is Jack Island – actually a peninsula on the Indian River. This mangrove-covered reserve teems with bird life, and is crossed by a short trail leading to an observation tower.

Frogman, UDT-SEAL Museum

Situated on the southern causeway linking Fort Pierce to Hutchinson Island is the **St Lucie County Historical Museum**. This has an enjoyable hotchpotch of displays, which include finds from the 1715 wrecks in the Galleon Room, and reconstructions of a Seminole camp and an early 20th-century general store. You can also look around the adjacent "cracker" home *(see p28)*, built in 1907, which was transported lock, stock, and barrel to its present site in 1985.

🏞 **Fort Pierce Inlet SRA**
905 Shorewinds Drive, N Hutchinson Island.
📞 *(561) 468-3985.* 📷 ♿ *limited*
🏛 **UDT-SEAL Museum**
3300 N Route A1A. 📞 *(561) 595-5845.* ◻ *daily.* ⬤ *public hols.* 📷 ♿
🏛 **St Lucie County Historical Museum**
414 Seaway Drive. 📞 *(561) 462-1795.* ◻ *Tue–Sun.* ⬤ *public hols.* 📷 ♿

A 1937 brand label from central Florida using the Indian River name

INDIAN RIVER'S CITRUS INDUSTRY

Citrus fruits were brought to Florida by the Spanish in the 16th century: each ship was purportedly required to leave Spain with 100 citrus seeds for planting in the new colonies. Conditions in Florida proved ideal and the fruit trees flourished, particularly along the Indian River between Daytona and West Palm Beach, which became the state's most important citrus-growing region. In 1931, local farmers created the Indian River Citrus League to stop growers outside the area from describing their fruit as "Indian River". One third of Florida's citrus crop and 75 per cent of its grapefruit yield is produced here. The majority of the oranges are used to make juice; the oranges are especially sweet and juicy because of the warm climate, soil conditions and rainfall.

Gilbert's Bar House of Refuge Museum, on the Atlantic shore of Hutchinson Island

Hutchinson Island **❺**

Road map F3. St Lucie Co/Martin Co. 🏚 *5,000.* ℹ️ *1910 NE Jensen Beach Blvd, (561) 334-3444.*

EXTENDING OVER 20 miles (32 km), this barrier island is most memorable for the cornucopia of breathtaking beaches. In the south of the island, sun-worshippers head for Sea Turtle Beach and the adjacent Jensen Beach Park, close to the junction of routes 707 and A1A. Stuart Beach, at the head of the causeway across the Indian River to Stuart, is well frequented too.

By Stuart Beach is the **Elliott Museum**, created in 1961 in honour of inventor Sterling Elliott, some of whose quirky contraptions are on show. Most space, though, is devoted to a sparkling collection of antique cars, reconstructions of 19th- and early 20th-century rooms and local history displays.

Continuing south for about a mile (1.6 km), you reach **Gilbert's Bar House of Refuge Museum**. Erected in 1875, it is one of ten such

shelters along the east coast, established by the Lifesaving Service (predecessors of the US Coast Guard) for shipwreck victims. The spartan rooms in the charming clapboard house show how hard life was for the early caretakers, who often stayed only a year.

A replica of an 1840s "surf boat" used on rescue missions sits outside. Beyond the refuge is **Bathtub Beach**, the best on the island. The natural pool formed by a sandstone reef offshore makes it a safe and popular bathing spot, especially for families.

🏛 **Elliott Museum**
825 NE Ocean Blvd. ☎ *(561) 225-1961.* ⏱ *daily.* ● *Easter, Thanksgiving, 25 Dec, 1 Jan.* 📷 ♿
🏛 **Gilbert's Bar House of Refuge Museum**
301 SE MacArthur Blvd. ☎ *(561) 225-1875.* ⏱ *Tue–Sun.* ● *Easter, Thanksgiving, 25 Dec, 1 Jan.* 📷 ♿

Stuart **❻**

Road map F3. Martin Co. 🏚 *17,000.* ℹ️ *1650 S Kanner Highway, (561) 287-1088.*

THE MAGNIFICENT causeway across the island-speckled Indian River from Hutchinson Island offers a fine approach to Martin County's main town. Ringed by affluent waterfront enclaves and residential golf developments, Stuart has a fetching, rejuvenated downtown area which is bypassed

by the busy coastal highways. To the south of Roosevelt Bridge, along Flagler Avenue and Osceola Street, there's a short riverside boardwalk, a smattering of pretty 1920s brick and stucco buildings, and a number of art galleries. In the evenings, live music emanates from buzzing and artfully decorated restaurants and bars.

The Florida scrub jay, a resident of Jupiter Island's sand pine scrub

Jupiter Island **❼**

Road map F4. Martin Co. 🏚 *200.* ℹ️ *800 N US 1, (561) 746-7111.*

MUCH OF THIS LONG, thin island is a well-to-do residential neighbourhood, but there are also several excellent public beaches.

Towards Jupiter Island's northern end, **Hobe Sound National Wildlife Refuge** beckons with over 3 miles (5 km) of beach, mangroves and magnificent, unspoilt dunes. The other half of the refuge, a strip of sand pine scrub flanking the Intracoastal Waterway, is a haven for birds, including the Florida scrub jay. There is a nature centre by the junction of US 1 and the A1A.

Blowing Rocks Preserve, a short distance further south, has a picturesque sandy beach. During storms, holes in the shoreline's limestone escarpment shoot water skywards – hence the name.

🦅 **Hobe Sound National Wildlife Refuge**
13640 SE Federal Hwy. ☎ *(561) 546-6141.* 📷 *to the beach.* ♿ *limited.*
Beach ⏱ *daily.* **Nature Center** ⏱ *Mon–Fri.* ● *public hols.*

The brightly painted Riverwalk Café, St Lucie Street, downtown Stuart

ENVIRONS: Named after a man who was shipwrecked nearby in 1696, the vast **Jonathan Dickinson State Park** comprises habitats as diverse as mangrove swamps, pine flatwoods and a cypress-canopied stretch of the Loxahatchee River. As well as walking and horse-riding trails, there are canoes for hire and boat trips along the river; manatees, alligators, ospreys and herons are often sighted along the way.

✖ Jonathan Dickinson State Park
16450 SE Federal Hwy. 【 (561) 546-2771. ◯ daily. ⬛ ⬤ limited.

Jupiter ❽

Road map F4. Palm Beach Co.
🏠 31,000. ⓘ 800 N US 1, (561) 746-7111.

THE SCATTERED settlement of Jupiter is best known for being the home town of the actor Burt Reynolds. Few people can resist a visit to his ranch nearby, but you may prefer the **Florida History Center and Museum**, which has exhibits relating to the area's original inhabitants, the Hobe Indians, and the English settlers who arrived here during the 18th century.

Cut-out of Burt Reynolds

🏛 Florida History Center and Museum
805 N US 1. 【 (561) 747-6639. ◯ Tue–Sun. ⬤ public hols. ⬛ ⬤

Jupiter Inlet Lighthouse as seen from Jupiter Beach Park

ENVIRONS: Close by, on the south side of Jupiter Inlet, is **Jupiter Beach Park**, an easily accessible and superb beach of chocolate-coloured sand; it is also a mecca for anglers and pelicans. There is a fine view across to **Jupiter Inlet Lighthouse**, dating from 1860 and the oldest structure in the county, which you can climb for a wider perspective. The old oil house at its base is now a small museum.

Burt Reynolds' Ranch, 9 miles (14.5 km) inland, is Jupiter's top tourist attraction. It is also America at its strangest. Its museum, a virtual shrine dedicated to the actor, displays copies of the fanzine, *The Reynolds Reporter*, news cuttings on Burt, pictures of Burt posing with presidents, and signed photos of actors dedicated to Burt. Ninety-minute bus tours of the ranch, which has been

turned into unsophisticated film studios, offer the peculiar additional sight of emus and deer wandering peacefully about the grounds. At the studios, you can watch clips of Burt in action and see sets such as those from the movie *Smokey and the Bandit*. You are also shown the chapel he had built for his wedding.

♨ Jupiter Inlet Lighthouse
Beach Rd at US 1. 【 (561) 747-8380. ◯ Sun–Wed. ⬤ public hols. ⬛
🏛 Burt Reynolds' Ranch
16133 Jupiter Farms Rd. 【 (561) 746-0393. ◯ daily. ⬤ public hols. ⬛ ⬤ ⬛

Juno Beach ❾

Road map F4. Palm Beach Co.
🏠 2,700. ⓘ 1555 Palm Beach Lakes Blvd, (561) 471-3995.

THE PRISTINE SANDS by Juno Beach, a small community of high-rise condos, and the beach that stretches north to Jupiter Inlet, amount to one of the world's most productive nesting sites for loggerhead turtles. In Loggerhead Park, which nestles between US 1 and Route A1A, the fascinating **Marinelife Center** exhibits turtle shells and even jars of deformed hatchlings. Live but injured turtles, perhaps cut by boat propellers or snagged on fishing lines, recuperate in tanks. A path leads to through undisturbed coastal vegetation to the beach where turtles nest during the summer.

✖ Marinelife Center
14200 US 1. 【 (561) 627-8280. ◯ Tue–Sun. ⬤ 25 Dec. ⬤

FLORIDA'S SEA TURTLES

Florida's central east coast is the top sea turtle nesting area in the USA. From May to September female turtles lumber up the beaches at night to lay about 100 eggs in the sand. Two months later the hatchlings emerge and dash for the ocean, again under the cover of darkness; sea turtles, including Florida's most common species, the loggerhead, are threatened partly because hatchlings are disorientated by lights from buildings.

The approved way to see a turtle laying eggs is to join an organized turtle watch. These nocturnal expeditions are popular all along the coast: call local chambers of commerce, such as the one in Juno Beach, for details.

A loggerhead hatchling's first encounter with the sea

Palm Beach ⑩

L ITERALLY AND METAPHORICALLY insular, Palm Beach has long provided an eye-opener on serious American wealth. Henry Flagler, pioneer developer of South Florida *(see p121)*, created this winter playground for the rich at the end of the 19th century. In the 1920s, the architect Addison Mizner *(see p116)* gave the resort a further boost and transformed the look of Palm Beach by building lavish Spanish-style mansions for its seasonal residents.

Tiffany & Co's clock

As recently as the 1960s, the town virtually closed down in summer – even traffic lights were dismantled. Nowadays, Palm Beach stays open all year, but it is still essentially a winter resort. In purportedly the richest town in the US, visitors can observe the *beau monde* as they idle away the hours in some of the state's smartest shops and restaurants or make their way to private clubs and glamorous charity balls.

Via Roma's grand entrance belies the charming alleyway beyond

Stylish Worth Avenue, shopping mecca for the very rich

Worth Avenue

For an insight into the Palm Beach lifestyle, Worth Avenue is compulsive viewing. While their employers toy over an Armani dress or an antique Russian icon, chauffeurs keep the air conditioning turning over in the Rolls Royces outside. Stretching four fabulous blocks from Lake Worth to the Atlantic Ocean, it is the town's best known thoroughfare.

Worth Avenue, as well as the architecture of Addison Mizner, first became fashionable with the construction of the exclusive Everglades Club, at the western end, in 1918. This was the result of the collaboration between Mizner and Paris Singer, the heir to the sewing machine fortune, who had first invited the architect down

to Florida. Originally intended as a hospital for officers shell-shocked during World War I, it never housed a single patient, and instead became the town's social hub. Today, the building's loggias and Spanish-style courtyards are still a very up-market, members-only enclave.

Across the street, and in stark contrast to the club's rather plain exterior, are Via Mizner and Via Parigi, lined with colourful shops and restaurants. These interlinking pedestrian alleys were created by Mizner in the 1920s, and are Worth Avenue's aesthetic highlights. Inspired by the backstreets of Spanish villages, the lanes are a riot of

Water fountain, Via Mizner

arches, tiled and twisting flights of steps, bougainvillea, fountains and pretty courtyards. Overlooking the vias' entrances are the office tower and villa that Mizner designed for himself. The tower's first floor originally housed display space for his ceramics business and was the avenue's first commercial unit. Connecting the two buildings is a walkway which forms the entrance to Via Mizner's shopping area. The other vias off Worth Avenue are more modern but, built in the same style and decorated with flowers and attractive window displays, they are nonetheless charming. Don't miss Via Roma or the courtyards joining Via de Lela and Via Flora.

Worth Avenue in 1939, captured by society photographer Bert Morgan

Shopping on Worth Avenue

Necklace by Lindsay Brattan

THE EPITOME of Palm Beach, Worth Avenue and the alleyways that connect with it contain some 250 exquisitely designed clothes boutiques, art galleries and antique shops. The shop fronts, ranging in style from Mizner's signature Spanish look to Art Deco, form an eclectic yet homogenous and pleasing mix. The artful window displays of Florida's most famous shopping street look their best when brightly lit up at night. Some windows flaunt wonderfully ironic symbols of wealth, such as fake caviar on toast or a life-sized model of a butler. In 1979, a Rolls Royce fitted with a bulldozer blade symbolically broke the ground for The Esplanade, an open-air mall at the avenue's eastern end. It is this sort of showy display that typifies Worth Avenue and distinguishes it from other prestigious shopping areas.

WORTH AVENUE'S EXCLUSIVE SHOPS
Worth Avenue boasts a spectacular mix of glitzy shops. Jewellery stores abound, including those specializing in high quality imitations, and you'll also find elegant *prêt à porter* houses, fancy gift shops, designer boutiques and luxury department stores.

Cartier has the ultimate in gifts and souvenirs. Choose from gold jewellery, pens and, of course, their signature watches.

Tiffany & Co is one of the most famous names on Worth Avenue. Best known for its jewellery (including exclusive designs by Paloma Picasso) and silverware, it also sells perfume and leather goods.

Saks Fifth Avenue, located in the elegant Esplanade mall, has two floors of luxury apparel from lingerie to designer menswear.

Greenleaf and Crosby jewellers, in Palm Beach since 1896, has a Deco frontage.

Ungaro's is one of Worth Avenue's designer boutiques. His womenswear is typically classy, chic and bold. The window displays here are changed every week during the winter season.

The Meissen Shop has the world's largest collection of antique Meissen porcelain.

Exploring Palm Beach

THE SPIRIT AND IMAGINATION of Addison Mizner infuses the whole of Palm Beach. As well as those buildings he designed himself, he influenced the look of countless others. Mizner's architecture, described by a biographer as a "Bastard-Spanish-Moorish-Romanesque-Gothic-Renaissance-Bull-Market-Damn-the-Expense Style", gave his contemporaries plenty of ideas to work from. Palm Beach is full of the splendid creations of men such as Marion Wyeth, Maurice Fatio and Howard Major, all active in the 1920s, as well as more recent imitations. Gazing at the luxurious mansions of the rich and famous in the exclusive "suburbs" is an essential activity in Palm Beach.

A panel of the mural at the Society of the Four Arts library

Exploring Palm Beach Town

After the opulence of Worth Avenue, the atmosphere along the mainly residential streets to the north is more restrained. Leafy Cocoanut Row features some luxuriant private homes, but along South County Road, which runs parallel, Mizner's influence is more in evidence – in the street's eclectic architecture, such as the immaculately restored Town Hall, built in 1926. Nearby is the attractive Mizner Memorial Park, where the centrepiece is a fountain and narrow pool flanked by palm trees, and Phipps Plaza – a quiet, shady close containing some delightful buildings with tiled windowsills and flower-decked gates. Mizner himself designed the fine coral house

Mizner Memorial Fountain

at No. 264. Also memorable is Howard Major's tropical cottage (1939), which features delicate Chinese influences.

If you have time to spare, it's worth strolling along some of the streets to the west of South County Road, where you'll find a mix of Mizneresque houses and early 20th-century bungalows set in shady gardens. In contrast, the most imposing street in this area is Royal Palm Way. Its rank of palm trees provides a fine approach to Royal Palm Bridge, which is an excellent platform for gawping at the luxury yachts on Lake Worth. This is particularly worthwhile in December, when they are decked out in coloured lights for the annual boat parade.

⚜ Society of the Four Arts

Four Arts Plaza. [(561) 655-7226.
Library and Gardens ◯ *mid-Apr–Oct: Mon–Fri; Nov–Apr: Mon–Sat.*
Galleries ◯ *Dec–Apr: daily (Sun pm only).* ● *public hols.* ♿
Founded in 1936, the Society of the Four Arts incorporates two libraries, exhibition space and an auditorium for lectures, concerts and films.

The galleries and auditorium were originally part of a private club designed by Mizner, but Maurice Fatio's Italianate Four Arts Library building nearby is far more striking. The Classical murals in its loggia represent art, music, drama and literature. The lovely grounds behind include a formal Chinese garden and a lawn dotted with modern bronze sculptures.

MIZNER'S SPANISH FANTASY

Addison Mizner (1872–1933) came to Palm Beach from New York in 1918 to convalesce after an accident. An architect by profession, he soon began to design houses, and in the process changed the face of Palm Beach and, essentially, Florida *(see p29)*. By adapting the design of old Spanish buildings to suit his environment, Mizner created a new style of architecture. He incorporated features such as loggias and external staircases to accommodate the region's high

Addison Mizner in the mid-1920s

temperatures, and his workmen covered walls in condensed milk and rubbed them with steel wool to fake centuries-old dirt.

Addison Mizner became a multimillionaire, successful because of both his architectural vision and his ability to ingratiate himself into his prospective clients' milieu. He later turned his attention to Boca Raton *(see pp126–7)*, but the collapse of the Florida land boom at the end of the 1920s hit him heavily, and by the end of his life Mizner had to rely on friends to pay his bills.

Via Mizner *(see p114)*, a classic example of Mizner's work

🏛 Hibel Museum of Art

150 Royal Poinciana Plaza. 📞 *(561) 833-6870.* ⭘ *Tue–Sun.* ⬤ *Thanksgiving, 25 Dec, 1 Jan.* ♿

Typical works of Edna Hibel, born in Boston in 1917 and still a resident of neighbouring Singer Island *(see p123)*, are idealized, sugary portraits of mothers and children from around the world. She paints on all manner of surfaces, ranging from wood and silk to crystal and porcelain.

The museum, founded in 1977 by two dedicated Hibel collectors, holds over 1,000 of the artist's creations.

Brittany and Child (1994) by Edna Hibel (oil, gesso and gold on silk)

🏨 The Breakers

1 South County Rd. 📞 *(561) 655-6611.* 🎥 *Wed pm.* ♿

Rising above Florida's oldest golf course, this mammoth Italian Renaissance structure is the third hotel on the site: the first Breakers, built in 1895, burnt down in 1903. Its replacement went the same route in 1925, destroyed by a fire that was supposedly started by a guest's curling iron. Miraculously, the present Breakers was built in less than a year. The hotel has always been a focal point for the town's social life, hosting numerous galas in its magnificent ballrooms.

Palm Beach's grandest hotel is refreshingly welcoming to nonresidents: feel free to watch a game of croquet, have a milkshake in its old-fashioned soda shop, or nose around the lobby (with its hand-painted ceiling) and the palatial public rooms.

For a more in-depth look, take the weekly guided tour with the "resident historian".

Stretch limos waiting for custom outside the Breakers Hotel

Immediately south of the hotel stand three gorgeous 19th-century wooden mansions, all that remain of **Breakers Row**. These oceanfront "cottages" were originally rented out to Palm Beach's wealthier visitors for the winter season.

🏨 Palm Beach suburbs

Palm Beach's high society normally hides away behind appropriately high hedges in multimillion-dollar mansions. Some of these were built by Mizner and his imitators in the 1920s, but since then hundreds of others have proliferated, in all kinds of styles, from Neo-Classical to Art Deco.

The most easily visible ones can be seen sitting on a ridge along South Ocean Boulevard, nicknamed "Mansion Row". At the top end, the Georgian residence at No. 126 belongs to Estée Lauder. No. 720, built by Mizner for himself in 1919, was for a time owned by John Lennon. Eight blocks beyond, Mar-a-Lago (No. 1100) is Palm Beach's grandest residence, with 58 bedrooms, 33 bathrooms and three bomb

shelters. Built by Joseph Urban and Marion Wyeth in 1927, it was bought in 1985 by millionaire Donald Trump, who converted it into a private club with a joining fee of $50,000.

The homes in the northern suburbs are more secluded. North County Road passes Palm Beach's biggest domestic property at No. 513, while No. 548 was reportedly on the market recently for $75 million. Beyond, No. 1095 North Ocean Boulevard was used as a winter retreat by the Kennedy family until 1995.

Glimpsing how the other half lives is discouraged by a minimum speed limit of 25 mph (40 km/h). This makes cycling an attractive option. Bikes are easy to hire *(see p119)* and there are various cycle routes. The most scenic of these is the 3-mile (5-km) Lake Trail, which doubles as an exercise track for the locals. It runs from Worth Avenue virtually to the island's northern tip, hugging Lake Worth and skirting the backs of mansions; its prettiest section is north of Dunbar Road.

Mar-a-Lago, the most extravagant home in the Palm Beach suburbs

A Tour of Palm Beach

ENCIRCLED BY THE MAIN thoroughfares of South County Road and Cocoanut Row, this tour links up all the major sights of central Palm Beach, including Henry Flagler's impressive home, Whitehall. The section of the tour along Lake Drive South forms part of the scenic Palm Beach bicycle trail, which flanks Lake Worth and extends into the suburbs *(see p117)*. Though intended to be followed by car, parts (or all) could equally be done by bicycle, on foot or even on roller-blades. These alternatives get around the problem of Palm Beach's comically zealous traffic wardens who patrol the streets in motorized golf carts.

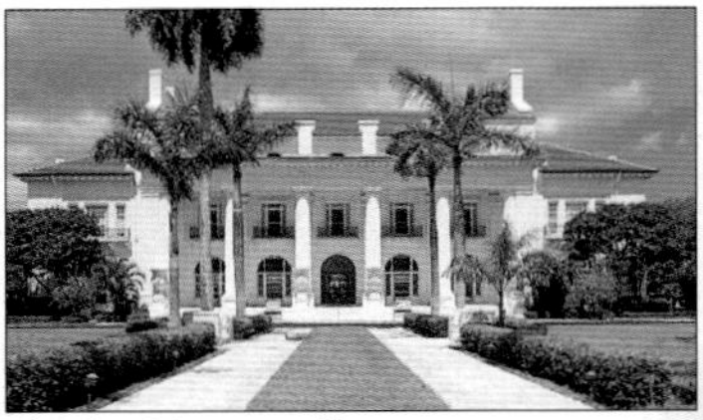

Flagler Museum ①
Formerly Flagler's private winter residence, "Whitehall" opened to the public in 1959. Beautifully restored, most of its furniture is original.

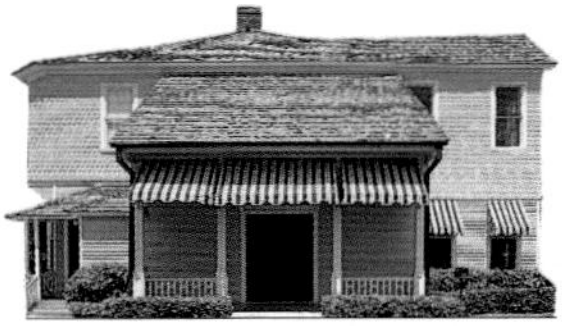

Sea Gull Cottage ②
Built in 1886, this is Palm Beach's oldest building. It was Flagler's first winter home.

Royal Poinciana Chapel ③ was built by Flagler for his guests in 1896.

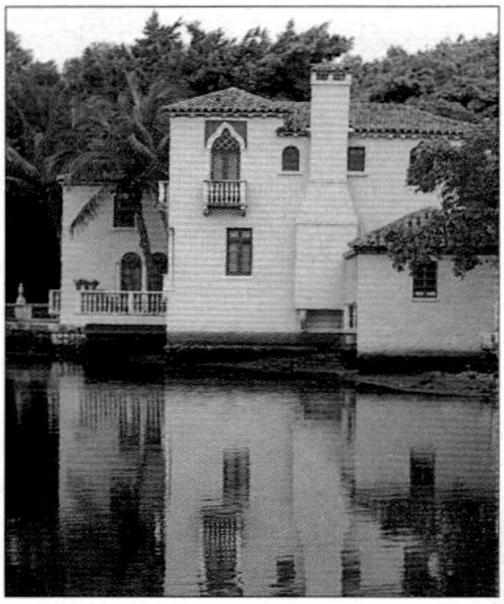

Casa de Leoni ⑤
No. 450 Worth Avenue is one of Mizner's most enchanting buildings. It set a trend for the Venetian Gothic style.

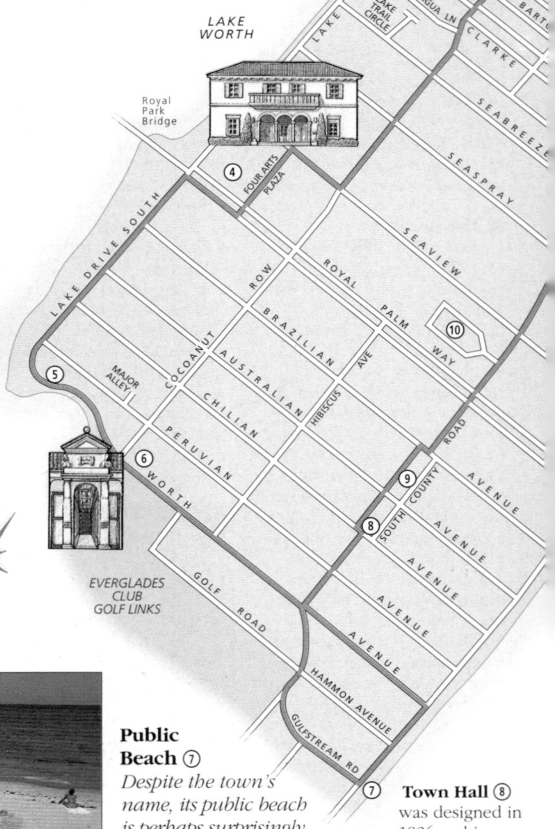

0 metres 250

0 yards 250

KEY

Route of tour

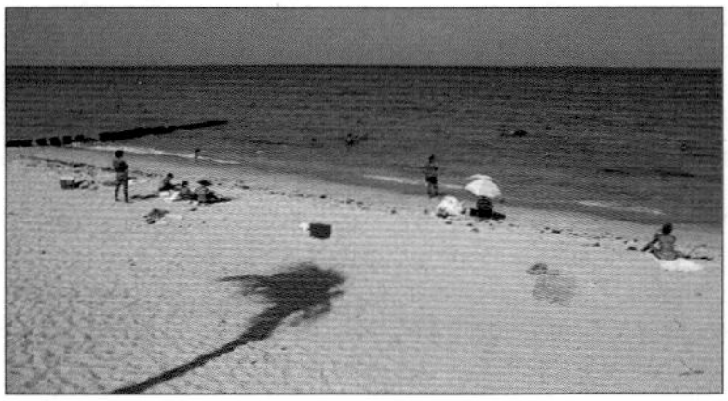

Public Beach ⑦
Despite the town's name, its public beach is perhaps surprisingly unspectacular, but it is free and open to all.

Town Hall ⑧ was designed in 1926 and is a well-known Palm Beach landmark.

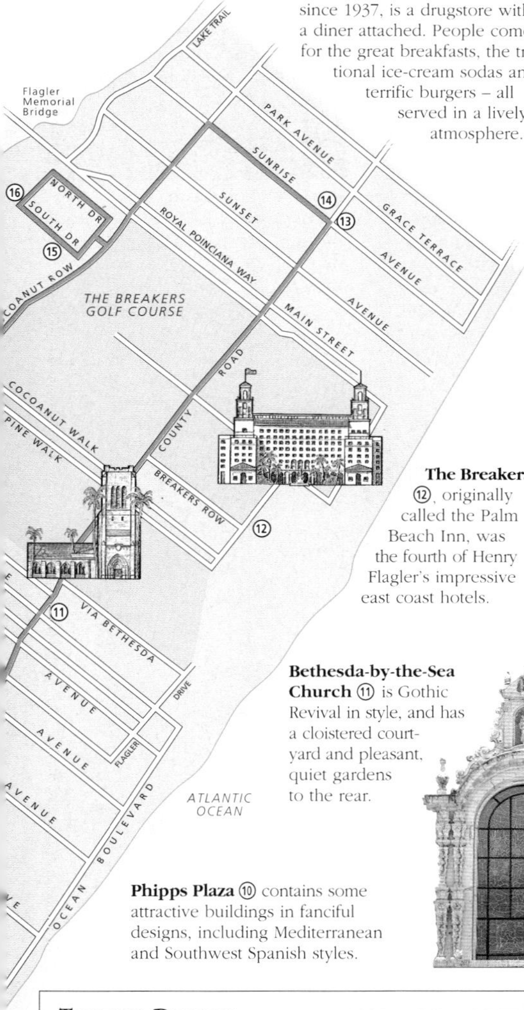

Green's Pharmacy ⑬, open since 1937, is a drugstore with a diner attached. People come for the great breakfasts, the traditional ice-cream sodas and terrific burgers – all served in a lively atmosphere.

The Breakers ⑫, originally called the Palm Beach Inn, was the fourth of Henry Flagler's impressive east coast hotels.

Bethesda-by-the-Sea Church ⑪ is Gothic Revival in style, and has a cloistered courtyard and pleasant, quiet gardens to the rear.

Phipps Plaza ⑩ contains some attractive buildings in fanciful designs, including Mediterranean and Southwest Spanish styles.

Visitors' Checklist

Road map F4. Palm Beach Co. 👥 *10,000.* ✈ *3 miles (5 km) W.* 🚆 *Amtrak and Tri-Rail, 201 S Tamarind Ave, West Palm Beach, (800) 872-7245.* 🚌 *100 Banyan Blvd, West Palm Beach, (800) 231-2222.* 🚍 *4C, 5 from West Palm Beach.* ℹ *45 Cocoanut Row, (561) 655-3282.* 🎉 *Artigras (Feb).*

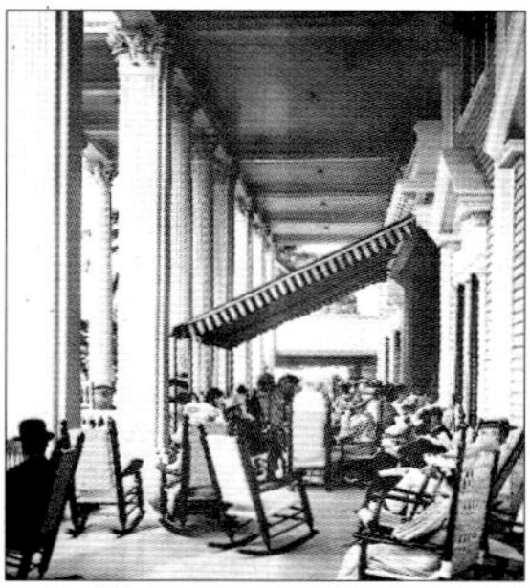

Old Royal Poinciana Hotel ⑮
This lavish 2,000-room, wooden hotel was a winter retreat for the very rich. It burned down in 1935; today only the greenhouse cupola survives.

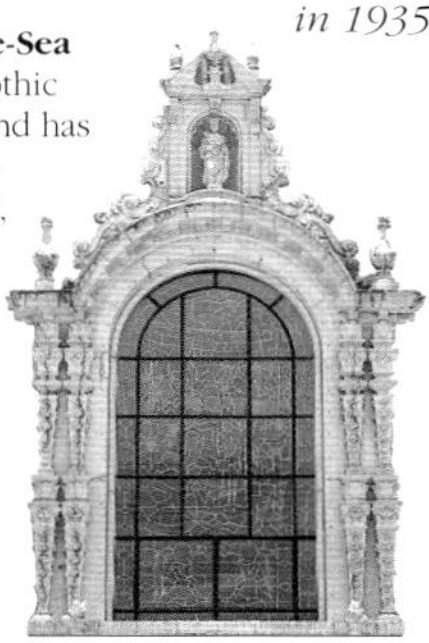

St Edward's Church ⑭
Completed in 1927, St Edward's was built in a Spanish Revival style and features a decorative, cast stone Baroque bell tower and entrance.

Tips for Drivers

Tour length: *4.5 miles (7 km).*
Starting point: *Anywhere. The tour is best followed in a clockwise direction since Worth Avenue is one way, running from east to west. The Palm Beach Bicycle Trail Shop, 223 Sunrise Ave, tel (561) 659-4583 (open daily), is a good starting point if you want to hire a bicycle, tandem or rollerblades.*
Parking: *Stock up on quarters (25c) for parking meters. There are also lots of spaces to park free for an hour, but remember not to overstay.*

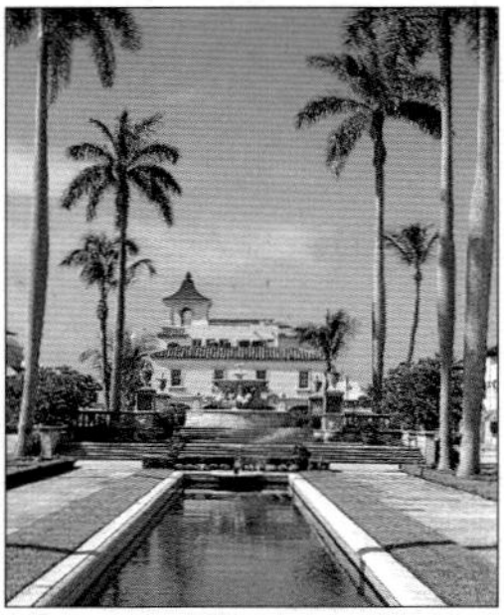

The Memorial Park fountain in downtown Palm Beach ⑨

Finding the Sights

① Flagler Museum *(see pp120–21)*
② Sea Gull Cottage
③ Royal Poinciana Chapel
④ Society of Four Arts *(see p116)*
⑤ Casa de Leoni
⑥ Worth Avenue *(see pp114–5)*
⑦ Public Beach
⑧ Town Hall *(see p116)*
⑨ Memorial Park *(see p116)*
⑩ Phipps Plaza *(see p116)*
⑪ Bethesda-by-the-Sea Church
⑫ The Breakers *(see p117)*
⑬ Green's Pharmacy
⑭ St Edward's Church
⑮ Old Royal Poinciana Hotel
⑯ Hibel Museum of Art *(see p117)*

Flagler Museum

Bronze detail on the front door

THIS 55-ROOM MANSION, known as Whitehall, was called "The Taj Mahal of North America" after it was built in 1902 by Henry Flagler. He gave the $4-million home to his third wife, Mary Lily Kenan, as a wedding present. Incredibly, it was intended just as a winter residence; the Flaglers would travel down every year in one of their private carriages *(see p47)*, now on display on the South Lawn.

In 1925, 12 years after Flagler's death, a ten-storey tower was added to the rear and Whitehall became a hotel. Jean Flagler Matthews bought her grandfather's mansion in 1959 and, after a costly restoration programme which included the removal of the tower, turned it into a museum. Whitehall stands as a monument to the indomitable spirit of America's Gilded Age.

Louis XV Ballroom
Of all the balls held in this sumptuous room, the Bal Poudré *in 1903 was the most lavish.*

The yellow roses bedroom had matching wallpaper and furnishings – an innovation for its time.

Swiss billiard room

★ **Master Bathroom**
Apart from a sunken bath, a lavatory and a wonderful separate shower unit, the Flaglers' private bathroom boasts this gorgeous double washstand made of onyx.

The master bedroom is furnished in yellow silk damask, a faithful copy of the original Rococo-style fabric.

Italian Renaissance Library
Lined with leather-bound books and filled with objects and ornate detailing, this red, wood-panelled room has a rather intimate feel.

STAR FEATURES

★ **Master Bathroom**

★ **Marble Hall**

★ **Best Guest Room**

Courtyard
Whitehall's heart is this lovely open courtyard, with loggias on two sides and a pretty central fountain.

★ Marble Hall
This grand marble entrance hall has a painted ceiling and contains gilded chairs and paintings, including this formal portrait of Jean Flagler Matthews.

The east portico is supported by massive fluted columns. Outsized urns are placed on the steps in front.

Louis XVI salon

★ Best Guest Room
The early 1900s saw a steady flow of guests to Whitehall. The rich and famous stayed in this inviting room, decorated in a colour scheme of cream and Rose de Barry red.

Main entrance

The grand staircase leads off the marble hall and is itself constructed of different marbles and decorated with intricate bronze railings.

FLAGLER'S PALM BEACH

After the Spanish ship *Providencia* was wrecked in 1878, its cargo of coconuts was strewn along the beach near Lake Worth and soon took root. Henry Flagler, busy with his plans to develop Florida's east coast *(see pp46–7)*, spotted the lovely palm-fringed beach around 1890. He was smitten with the area's beauty and immediately bought up land. In 1894, he opened the Royal Poinciana Hotel *(see p119)* and in so doing set the course for the growth of the exclusive resort of Palm Beach.

Henry Flagler and his third wife, Mary Lily, in 1910

High-rise blocks towering over the still waters of Lake Worth in West Palm Beach

West Palm Beach ⑪

Road map F4. Palm Beach Co.
🏚 78,000. ✈ 🚆 Amtrak & Tri-Rail.
🚌 ℹ 1555 Palm Beach Lakes Blvd,
(561) 471-3995.

AT THE END of the 19th century, Henry Flagler *(see p121)* decided to move the unsightly homes of Palm Beach's workers and service businesses to the mainland, out of sight of the tourists. He thus created West Palm Beach, which has been the commercial centre of Palm Beach County ever since.

The city has succeeded in forging a stronger identity for itself in recent decades, but it still plays second fiddle to

its infinitely more glamorous (and considerably smaller) neighbour. The sleek high-rises of downtown West Palm Beach lure only business-people, while to the north lies the historic but depressed Northwest neighbourhood; the outskirts of the city consist mainly of characterless residential and golfing developments.

West Palm Beach may not be the place to spend your entire holiday, but it enjoys a fine setting by scenic Lake Worth, and its small clutch of attractions are well worth making forays to visit – in particular the excellent Norton Museum of Art, rated the top museum in the southeastern US by the *New York Times*.

🏛 South Florida Science Museum
4801 Dreher Trail N. 🛂 (561) 832-1988. ◯ daily. ● Thanksgiving, 25 Dec. 🅿 ♿
This science museum, like many in Florida, is aimed at children. There are plenty of hands-on exhibits to teach visitors about subjects such as light, sound, colour and the weather. You can have a go at creating your own clouds and even touch a mini tornado. The best time to visit is on a Friday evening, when you can also look through a giant telescope in its observatory and watch laser light shows in the planetarium.

🏛 Norton Museum of Art
1451 South Olive Ave. 🛂 (561) 832-5196. ◯ Mon–Sat (Sun pm only). ● public hols. 🅿 ♿
This museum boasts probably the finest art collection in the state; it also attracts high-profile travelling exhibitions.

The museum was established in 1941 with the 100 or so canvases belonging to Ralph Norton, a Chicago steel magnate who had retired to West Palm Beach two years before. He and his wife had wide ranging tastes, which is reflected in the art on display.

The collection falls into three main fields. Foremost among these are the galleries of French Impressionist and Post-Impressionist art, which include paintings by Cézanne, Braque, Picasso, Matisse and Gauguin, whose moving

THE SPORT OF KINGS

Nothing better encapsulates Palm Beach County's upper-class mores than the popularity of polo. From December to April, and especially on Sunday afternoons, you can follow the crowds in their blazers and boaters to clubs in West Palm Beach (the grandest), Boca Raton and Lake Worth; together, they host some of the world's top polo championships. Tickets are cheap, and during the game you may well be treated to a jovial running commentary. Spectators often bring a champagne picnic. For information about dates call the clubs at West Palm Beach, (561) 793-1113; Boca Raton, (561) 994-1876; or Lake Worth, (561) 965-2057.

**Close quarters polo action, popular
entertainment along the Gold Coast**

work *Agony in the Garden* is the most famous painting in the museum. *Night Mist* (1945) by Jackson Pollock is another proud possession, forming part of the Norton's impressive store of 20th-century American art; this also features some fine works by Winslow Homer, Georgia O'Keeffe, Edward Hopper and Andy Warhol.

***Agony in the Garden* by Paul Gauguin (1889)**

The third principal collection comprises an outstanding array of artifacts from China, including tomb jades dating from around 1500 BC and ceramic figures of animals and courtiers from the T'ang Dynasty (4th–11th centuries AD). There is also much fine Buddhist carving, in addition to more modern sculptures by Brancusi, Degas and Rodin.

A rare Florida panther, on view at the Dreher Park Zoo

⚒ Dreher Park Zoo
1301 Summit Blvd. **(f)** *(561) 547-9453.* ◯ *daily.* ● *Thanksgiving.* 🎫 &

This enjoyable little zoo is just as appealing to youngsters as the nearby South Florida Science Museum. Of the 100 or more species represented, the most interesting are the endangered Florida panther and giant tortoises, which can live for up to 200 years. You can visit a recreated South American plain, with llamas, rheas and tapirs wandering about below a viewing platform, follow a boardwalk trail through exotic foliage, or cruise around a lake alive with a huge population of pelicans.

ENVIRONS: A more pleasant alternative to staying in West Palm Beach (and a considerably cheaper option than Palm Beach) is to find accommodation north across the inlet at **Singer Island** or **Palm Beach Shores**. These are relaxing, slow-paced communities, and the wide beach is splendid, though marred by a skyline of apartment blocks.

Boating and fishing are popular activities here. Palm Beach Shores has numerous sport fishing boats for charter, as well as boats offering cruises around Lake Worth. One such is a paddlewheeler, the Star of Palm Beach *(see p338),* which docks by Riviera Bridge.

At the north end of Singer Island is **John D MacArthur Beach State Park**. Here, a dramatic boardwalk bridge meanders across a mangrove-lined inlet of Lake Worth to a hardwood hammock and a lovely beach. Leaflets from the nature centre pick out plants and wading birds, and in the summer, guided night-time walks show you nesting loggerhead turtles *(see p113).*

For alternative entertainment visit **The Gardens** mall, 2 miles (3 km) inland in Palm Beach Gardens. Fragrant walkways and glass elevators link the nearly 200 shops and appetizing food court.

⚒ John D MacArthur Beach State Park
A1A, 2 miles (3 km) N of Riviera Bridge. **(** *(561) 624-6950.* ◯ *daily.* 🎫 &
🏠 The Gardens
3101 PGA Blvd. **(** *(561) 622-2115.* ◯ *daily.* ● *Easter Sun, Thanksgiving, 25 Dec.* &

Lion Country Safari ⓬

Road map F4. Palm Beach Co. Southern Blvd W, Loxahatchee. **(** *(561) 793-1084.* 🚌 *West Palm Beach.* 🚌 *West Palm Beach.* ◯ *daily.* 🎫 &

T WENTY MILES (32 km) inland from West Palm Beach, off US 441, this park is the area's big family attraction.

It comes in two parts. Firstly, you can drive through a 500-acre (200-ha) enclosure and observe lions, giraffes, rhinos and other wildlife at close quarters. (If you have a convertible car you can rent a vehicle with a hard roof.) Secondly, there's a somewhat unsophisticated cross between a zoo and amusement park. Along with aviaries, petting areas and islands inhabited by monkeys, there are fairground rides, boat tours and a park populated by plastic dinosaurs.

Be warned that both sections of the park get very busy at weekends and holiday times.

Antelope resting in the shade at Lion Country Safari

A fisherman enjoying early evening angling on Lake Okeechobee

Lake Okeechobee ⓭

Road map E4, F4. 🚌 *Palm Trans bus to Pahokee & Clewiston, (561) 233-1166.* ℹ️ *115 E Main St, Pahokee, (561) 924-5579.* **Captain JP Boat Cruises** 📞 *(561) 924-2100.*

Meaning "big water" in the Seminole language, Okeechobee is the second largest freshwater lake in the US, covering 750 sq miles (1,942 sq km). The "Big O", as the lake is often called, is famous for its abundance of fish, particularly largemouth bass. Numerous marinas have tackle shops and boats with licensed guides for hire. With three marinas and a choice of decent motels, **Clewiston** offers the best facilities.

If you're not an angler, your time in Florida is better spent elsewhere. The bird life is rich along the shore, but the lake is too big to be scenic and a high, encircling dyke, which protects the countryside from floods, prevents views from the road. **Pahokee** is one of the few places to offer easy lakeside access, and it boasts possibly the best sunsets in Florida after the Gulf Coast. It is also the starting point for five- or six-hour lake trips with Captain JP Boat Cruises.

The grim and hardworking communities at the lake's southern end are dependent on sugar for their prosperity. Half the sugar cane in the US is grown in the plains around Belle Glade and Clewiston

A Lake Okeechobee sugar town proclaims its wealth

("America's Sweetest Town"), where the rich soil is darker than plain chocolate.

The federal government plans to return 100,000 acres (40,500 ha) of sugar cane land south of Lake Okeechobee to marshland, in order to cleanse and increase the water available to the Everglades. Not surprisingly, the scheme is unpopular locally.

Lake Worth ⓮

Road map F4. Palm Beach Co. 🚶 *28,000.* 🚆 ℹ️ *1702 Lake Worth Rd, (561) 582-4401.*

Lake Worth is a civilized, unpretentious community. On its barrier island side there is normally a jolly, down-to-earth beach scene; on the mainland, a dozen or more antique shops set the tone along Lake and Lucerne avenues, the heart of Lake Worth's low-key downtown area. Here, too, you'll find an Art Deco cinema converted into an exciting space for art exhibitions, and the **Museum of the City of Lake Worth**. All

that a local history museum should be, this one is packed full of old photos and every-day items from toasters to cameras. It also has quirky displays about Poland and Finland, reflecting the culture of some local immigrants.

🏛 Museum of the City of Lake Worth
414 Lake Ave. 📞 *(561) 586-1700.* 🕐 *Mon–Fri.* ⚫ *public hols.*

Delray Beach ⓯

Road map F4. Palm Beach Co. 🚶 *50,000.* 🚆 *Amtrak and Tri-Rail.* 🚌 ℹ️ *64 SE 5th Ave, (561) 278-0424.* **Ramblin' Rose** 📞 *(561) 243-0686.*

The most welcoming place between Palm Beach and Boca Raton, Delray Beach has an up-market but unsnobby air. Stars and stripes everywhere celebrate its national award for "civic-mindedness".

The long stretch of sedate beach, with direct access and good facilities, is splendid, and between November and April the Ramblin' Rose riverboat offers daily cruises along the Intracoastal Waterway.

Delray's heart lies inland, along Atlantic Avenue – an inviting street softly lit at night by old-fashioned lamps and lined with palm trees, chic cafés, antique shops and art galleries. Alongside lies Old School Square, with a cluster of handsome 1920s buildings. Nearby, snug **Cason Cottage** has been meticulously restored to the way it might have looked when the house was first built in around 1915.

🚼 Cason Cottage
5 NE 1st St. 📞 *(561) 243-0223.* 🕐 *Tue–Fri.* ⚫ *public hols.* ♿

A peaceful springtime scene by the ocean at Delray Beach

Loxahatchee National Wildlife Refuge **⓰**

Road map F4. Palm Beach Co.
10216 Lee Rd. **📞** *(561) 734-8303.*
🚆 *Delray Beach.* **🚌** *Delray Beach.*
Refuge ⭕ *daily.* ● *25 Dec.* 📷 ♿
🏛 Visitor Center ⭕ *Nov–Apr: daily;*
May–Oct: Wed–Sun. ● *25 Dec.*

THIS 221-SQ MILE (572-sq km)
refuge, which contains the
most northerly remaining part
of the Everglades, has superb
and abundant wildlife. The
best time to visit is early or
late in the day, and ideally in
winter, when many migrating
birds from the north make
their temporary home here.

A blue heron standing alert in the wildlife refuge at Loxahatchee

The visitor centre, off Route
441 on the refuge's eastern
side, 10 miles (16 km) west
of Delray Beach, has a good
information centre explaining
the Everglades' ecology; it is
also the starting point for two
memorable trails. The half-
mile (0.8-km) Cypress Swamp
Boardwalk enters a magical
natural world, with guava and
wax myrtle trees and many
epiphytes *(see p276)* growing beneath the canopy. The
longer Marsh Trail passes by
marshland, whose water levels
are manipulated to produce
the best possible environment
for waders and waterfowl. On
a winter's evening it's a bird-
watcher's paradise, with a
cacophony of sound from

A schoolboy's bedroom, Japanese style, at the Morikami Museum

herons, grebe, ibis, anhingas
and other birds. You may also
spot turtles and alligators.
   Those with their own canoes
can embark on the 5.5-mile
(9-km) canoe trail. There is
also an extensive programme
of guided nature walks.

Morikami Museum and Japanese Gardens **⓱**

Road map F4. Palm Beach Co. 4000
Morikami Park Rd, **📞** *(561) 495-0233.*
🚆 *Delray Beach.* **🚌** *Delray Beach.*
⭕ *Tue –Sun.* ● *public hols.* 📷 ♿

THE COUNTRY'S ONLY museum
that is devoted exclusively
to Japanese culture is located
on land donated by a farmer
named George Morikami; he
was one of a group of Japanese pioneers who established
the Yamato Colony (named
after ancient Japan) on the
northern edge of Boca Raton
in 1905. With the help of
money from a development
company owned
by Henry Flagler
(see pp120–21),
they hoped to grow
rice, tea and silk.
The project never
took off, however,
and the colony
gradually petered
out in the 1920s.
   Displays in the
Yamato-kan villa, on a small
island in a lake, vividly tell the
settlers' story and also delve
into past and present Japanese
culture. There are amusing
reconstructions of a bathroom,
a contemporary schoolboy's

bedroom, and beautiful models
of eel-and-sake restaurants.
Formal Japanese gardens surround the villa, and paths head
off into serene pine woods.
   A new building across the
lake holds stunning exhibitions
on all matters Japanese, a café
serving good Japanese food,
and a traditional tea house
where tea ceremonies are
performed once a month.
There are also classrooms for
origami workshops.

Butterfly World **⓲**

Road map F4. Broward Co.
3600 W Sample Rd, Coconut Creek.
📞 *(954) 977-4400.* **🚆** *Deerfield*
Beach (Amtrak & Tri-Rail). **🚌** *Pompano*
Beach. ⭕ *daily (Sun pm only).*
● *Thanksgiving, 25 Dec.* 📷 ♿

WITHIN GIANT walk-through
aviaries brimming with
tropical flowers, thousands of
dazzling butterflies from all
over the world flit about, often
landing on visitors' shoulders.
Since they're effectively solar
powered, the
butterflies are
most active on
warm, sunny days,
so plan your visit
accordingly. There
are also cabinets
of emerging pupae,
and a collection of
mounted insects as
fascinating as you're
ever likely to see – including
morpho butterflies, with their
incredible metallic blue wings,
and beetles and grasshoppers
the size of an adult hand. Outside, you can wander around
the extensive gardens.

**A blue morpho at
Butterfly World**

Boca Raton ⑲

IN 1925, AN ADVERTISEMENT for Boca Raton announced: "I am the greatest resort in the world". Although the city imagined by the architect Addison Mizner (see p116) did not materialize in his lifetime, Boca Raton has today become one of Florida's most affluent cities. Corporate headquarters and high-tech companies are located here, and executives in a national survey have judged it Florida's most enticing place to live. What must attract them are the country clubs, plush shopping malls and gorgeous beachfront parks, not to mention desirable homes inspired, if not built, by Mizner.

Vivid Spiderman artwork at the Museum of Cartoon Art

Peach-pink Mizner Park, one of Boca's newest shopping malls

Exploring Boca Raton

After initiating the development of Palm Beach, Addison Mizner turned his attention to a sleepy pineapple-growing settlement to the south. However, instead of his envisaged masterpiece of city planning, only a handful of buildings were completed by the time Florida's property bubble burst in 1926 (see p48). Boca, as it is often called today, remained little more than a hamlet until the late 1940s.

The nucleus of Mizner's vision was the ultra-luxurious Cloister Inn, finished in 1926 with his trademark Hispanic details. It stands off the eastern end of Camino Real, which was intended as the city's main thoroughfare, complete with a central canal for gondolas. The hotel is now part of the greatly expanded and very snooty **Boca Raton Resort and Club** (see p299). Non-residents can visit only on a weekly tour arranged by the Boca Raton Historical Society, which is based at the **Town Hall** on

Palmetto Park Road. A couple of rooms here have simple displays concerning local history.

Just opposite, built in a style that apes Mizner's work, is the open-air **Mizner Park**. This is perhaps the most impressive of Boca's dazzling malls that provide the best illustrations of the city's rarefied lifestyle. Even more Mizneresque is the nearby **Royal Palm Plaza**, nicknamed the Pink Plaza, with chic boutiques tucked away in hidden courtyards.

The verdant and historic **Old Floresta** district, about a mile (1.6 km) west of the town hall, contains 29 Mediterranean-style homes built by Mizner for his company directors. It is a pleasant area to explore.

🏛 Boca Raton Museum of Art

801 W Palmetto Park Rd. **[** (561) 392-2500. **○** Tue–Sun. **●** public hols. **⚑ &**

The highlight of this compact art gallery is the small Mayers Collection of late 19th- and early 20th-century art. Work by Modigliani, Léger, Giacometti and Degas, plus a few sensitive charcoal drawings by Picasso and Matisse, form its core.

🏛 International Museum of Cartoon Art

201 Plaza Real. **[** (561) 391-2200. **○** Tue–Sun. **●** 25 Dec, 1 Jan. **⚑ &**

This modern exhibition space in Mizner Park opened in 1996 as home to the International Museum of Cartoon Art. The collection was created in 1974 and numbers some 160,000 pieces dating from the 18th century onwards, gathered from all over the world. The work ranges from political cartoons to comic strip heroes like Peanuts and Spiderman.

There is also a cinema and themed environments such as the Laughter Center, which demonstrates how humour is good for your wellbeing.

🏛 Sports Immortals Museum

6830 N Federal Hwy. **[** (561) 997-2575. **○** Mon–Sat. **●** 25 Dec, 1 Jan. **⚑ &**

Amongst the 10,000 sporting mementos at this museum are Babe Ruth's baseball bat and Muhammad Ali's boxing robes.

Boca's pretty town hall, designed by Addison Mizner and built in 1927

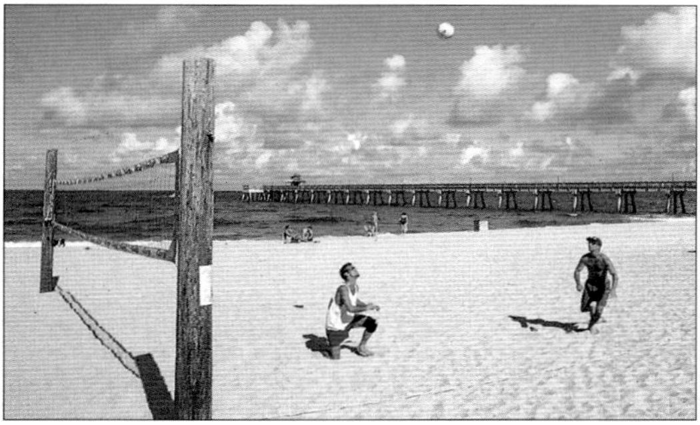

Deerfield Beach, a quiet coastal resort within easy reach of Boca Raton

The most prized item is a rare cigarette card worth an astonishing $600,000: the card was quickly withdrawn as the baseball player depicted objected to any association with tobacco.

🏖 The Beaches

North of Boca Raton's inlet stretches a seductively long, undeveloped, dune-backed beach, reached via beachside parks. The most northerly of these, **Spanish River Park**, is also the most attractive, with pleasant picnic areas shaded by pines and palm trees. Its prettiest spot is a lagoon on the Intracoastal Waterway next to an observation tower. At **Red Reef Park** you can stroll along the boardwalk on top of the dunes and snorkel around an artificial reef *(see p340)* just offshore. Maybe because of the exorbitant parking fees, the sands are usually uncrowded.

🐦 Gumbo Limbo Nature Center

1801 North Ocean Blvd. ☎ *(561) 338-1473.* ○ *daily.* ● *25 Dec.* ♿

This first-rate and highly informative education centre lies next to the Intracoastal, within Red Reef Park. Its boardwalk winds through mangroves and a tropical hardwood hammock to a tower, which pokes above the tree tops and offers sensational panoramic views.

ENVIRONS: High-rise development continues unabated south along Route A1A. Slow-paced **Deerfield Beach** is the area's most inviting community, thanks to its fishing pier and fine, shell-flecked and peaceful beach, backed by a palm-lined promenade. Five miles (8 km) south, **Pompano** is forever tied to its status as "swordfish capital of the world", corroborated by photos of giant catches displayed on its pier.

VISITORS' CHECKLIST

Road map F4. Palm Beach Co. 👥 *67,000.* 🚆 *Tri-Rail, Yamato Rd, (800) 874-7245; Amtrak, 1300 W Hillsboro Blvd, Deerfield Beach, (800) 872-7245.* 🚌 *2190 NE 4th St, Pompano Beach, (800) 231-2222.* ℹ *1555 Palm Beach Lakes Blvd, (561) 471-3995.* **Boca Raton Historical Society**, ☎ *(561) 395-6766 for tours.* 🎉 *Boca Festival (Aug).*

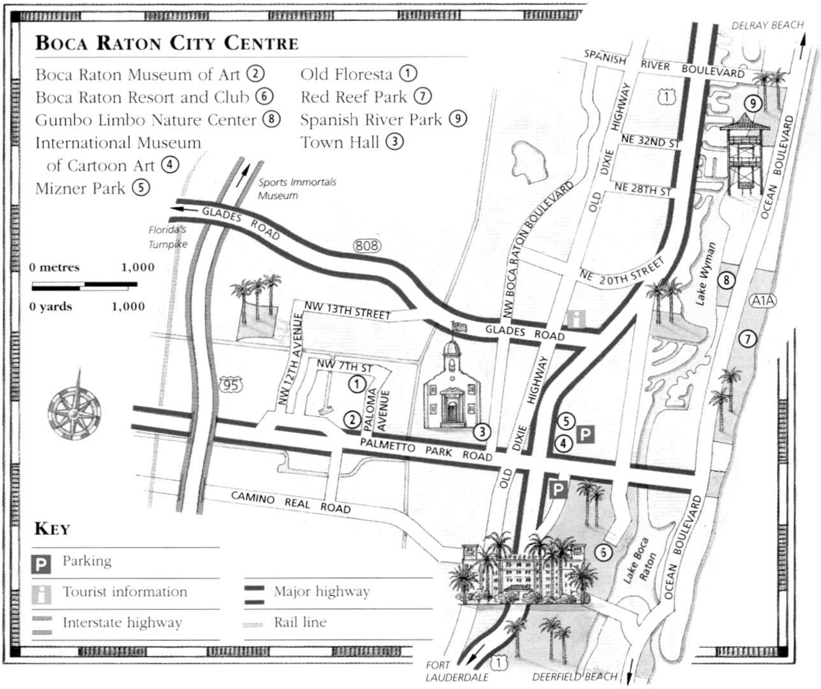
BOCA RATON CITY CENTRE
Boca Raton Museum of Art 2
Boca Raton Resort and Club 6
Gumbo Limbo Nature Center 8
International Museum of Cartoon Art 4
Mizner Park 5
Old Floresta 1
Red Reef Park 7
Spanish River Park 9
Town Hall 3
0 metres 1,000
0 yards 1,000
DELRAY BEACH
SPANISH RIVER BOULEVARD
HIGHWAY
DIXIE
OLD
NE 32ND ST
NE 28TH ST
OCEAN BOULEVARD
NW BOCA RATON BOULEVARD
NE 20TH STREET
Lake Wyman
A1A
Sports Immortals Museum
GLADES ROAD
808
Florida's Turnpike
NW 13TH STREET
NW 12TH AVENUE
NW 7TH ST
PALOMA AVENUE
95
PALMETTO PARK ROAD
CAMINO REAL ROAD
Lake Boca Raton
FORT LAUDERDALE
DEERFIELD BEACH
KEY
Parking
Tourist information
Interstate highway
Major highway
Rail line

Fort Lauderdale ⑳

Appel's *Big Bird with Child*, **Museum of Art**

DURING THE SECOND Seminole War *(see p44)*, Fort Lauderdale consisted of little more than three forts. By 1900, it had become a busy trading post on the New River, which meanders through what has become a sprawling city.

Today, Greater Fort Lauderdale wears many hats: it is an important business and cultural centre, a popular beach resort and a giant cruise port. But it is still the city's waterways *(see p131)* which define its unique character.

Exploring Downtown Fort Lauderdale

Downtown Fort Lauderdale, with its modern, sleek, glass-sided office blocks, presents the city's business face. The **Riverwalk** follows a 1.5-mile (2.4-km) stretch of the New River's north bank and links most of the city's historical landmarks and cultural institutions. This promenade starts near Stranahan House, built on the site of the city's first trading post, and passes through a strip of parkland to end up by the Broward Center for the Performing Arts *(see p336)*.

Old Fort Lauderdale extends along Southwest 2nd Avenue. It is made up of an attractive group of early 1900s' buildings administered by the Fort Lauderdale Historical Society, which is based at the Fort Lauderdale Historical Museum. The King-Cromartie House, built in 1907 on the south bank of the river, was transported by barge to its present site in 1971. Its modest furnishings reflect the basic living conditions of Florida's early settlers. Behind the home is a replica of the city's first schoolhouse, which opened in 1899.

The clutch of cafés and restaurants in old brick buildings along adjacent Southwest 2nd Street are buzzing at lunchtime and in the early evening.

A narrated hop-on hop-off trolley tour is an easy way to get to know the heart of the city. The tour links Fort Lauderdale's downtown area and the beach, taking in all the principal sights.

🏛 Fort Lauderdale Historical Museum

219 SW 2nd Ave.
📞 *(954) 463-4431.*
🕐 *Tue–Fri.*
⬤ *4 Jul , 25 Dec, 1 Jan.* 📷 ♿

The New River Inn in Old Fort Lauderdale was built of concrete in 1905. Now an informative local history museum, it contains various exhibits which chart the area's history and the growth of the city up to the 1940s. A small cinema shows amusing silent films that were made during the 1920s heyday of south Florida's film industry.

The shady Riverwalk, winding along the north bank of the New River

🏛 Museum of Art

1 E Las Olas Blvd. 🗹 *(954) 763-6464.*
⭘ *Tue–Sun.* ⬤ *public hols.* 🈂 🛗
This fine museum, housed in
an impressive postmodern
building, is best known for its
large assemblage of works of
CoBrA art. The name CoBrA
derives from the initial letters
of Copenhagen, Brussels and
Amsterdam, the capitals of the
home countries of a group of
expressionist painters who
experimented with fantastical
imagery from 1948–51. The
museum displays works in a
wide range of media by Karel
Appel, Pierre Alechinsky and
Asger Jorn, the movement's
leading exponents. In addition,
African and South Pacific
art is on show.

🏛 Museum of Discovery and Science

401 SW 2nd St. 🗹 *(954)
467-6637.* ⭘ *daily.*
⬤ *25 Dec.* 🈂 🛗
Boasting the highest
attendance figures for
any museum in the
state, this is one of the
largest and best mus-
eums of its kind in
Florida. Here, all kinds
of creatures appear in
re-created Floridian
"ecoscapes", and you
can take a simulated
ride to the moon or
watch specially trained
rats play basketball.
    In the IMAX theatre,
films like *The Living Sea*
are projected on to a 60-ft
(18-m) high screen. This is
also one of the few places
in the world to show 3-D
IMAX films, in which the
audience uses special glasses
and personal headsets for 360-
degree sound. At weekends,
there are also evening screen-
ings; call the museum for
times and reservations.

🚻 Stranahan House

335 SE 6th Ave. 🗹 *(954) 524-4736.*
⭘ *Wed–Sun.* ⬤ *Jul–Aug; public hols.*
🈂 🛗 *limited.*
The oldest surviving house in
the city is a handsome pine
and oak building, built by the
pioneer Frank Stranahan in
1901. It became the centre of
Fort Lauderdale's community,
serving as a trading post, meeting hall, post office and bank.
Even more evocative of the
early days than the furnishings inside are the old photos
of Stranahan trading with the
local Seminoles *(see p271)*.
Goods such as alligator hides
otter pelts, and egret plumes –
all used in the fashions of the
day and in great demand –
were brought by the Seminoles
from the nearby Everglades in
their dugout canoes.

Las Olas Boulevard

Despite a constant stream of
traffic, the section of Las Olas
Boulevard between 6th and
11th avenues amounts to Fort
Lauderdale's most picturesque
and busiest street. A winning
mix of formal, casual and chic
boutiques and eateries line this
thoroughfare, where you can
pick up anything from a fur
coat to modern Haitian art.
    If you're not a serious shop-
per, visit in the evenings when
the pavements overflow with
drinkers and diners, and you
can take a ride in a horse-
drawn Surrey carriage.
    Heading towards the beach,
the boulevard crosses islands
where you can get a closer
look at a more lavish Fort
Lauderdale lifestyle *(see p131)*.

VISITORS' CHECKLIST

Road map F4. Broward Co.
🚶 150,000. ✈ 5 miles (8 km) S.
🚌 200 SW 21st Terrace, *(800)
872-7245.* 🚆 515 NE 3rd St,
(800) 231-2222. 🚢 1850 Eller
Drive, *(954) 523-3404.* ℹ 1850
Eller Drive *(954) 765-4466.*
Trolley tours 🗹 *(954) 429-3100.*
🛥 *Winter Fest Boat Parade (Dec).*

KEY

🚌 Greyhound bus station

🚢 Boat trip boarding point

🅿 Parking

▬ Major highway

Stranahan House on the New River, Broward County's oldest residence

Exploring Fort Lauderdale: Beyond Downtown

Even if you miss the signs proclaiming "Welcome to Fort Lauderdale – Yachting Capital of the World", it won't take you long to recognize the real focus of the city. For tourists and residents alike, the appeal of Fort Lauderdale lies above all in its attractive and buzzing beaches and in the waterways that branch from the city's historical lifeblood – the New River.

Cyclists and pedestrians enjoying the shady beachfront promenade

The Beach

Until the mid-1980s, when the local authorities began to discourage them, students by the thousand would descend on Fort Lauderdale for the Spring Break. Today, the city's image is restored, and its excellent beach is still the liveliest along the Gold Coast – especially at the end of Las Olas Boulevard, where rollerbladers cruise past a few unsophisticated bars and tacky souvenir shops, faint recollections of more decadent days along "The Strip".

Elsewhere, beachside Fort Lauderdale is more like the family resort it's promoted to be; South Beach Park has the most pleasant strip of sand.

A break in training at the pool, at the Swimming Hall of Fame

🏛 International Swimming Hall of Fame

1 Hall of Fame Drive. 📞 (954) 462-6536. ◯ daily. 🎟 ♿

If you ever wanted to know about the history of Oman's aquatic sports or the evolution of diving positions, this is the place to come. This amazingly detailed museum has an odd but fun mix of exhibits, from ancient woolly swimming costumes to amusing mannequins of stars such as Johnny "Tarzan" Weismuller, holder of 57 world swimming records.

In the famous swimming pools behind, coaches make Olympic hopefuls swim gruelling lengths while attached to one end of the pool by a giant rubber cord. Spectators are welcome to attend these training sessions as well as aquatic competitions and events.

🏠 Bonnet House

900 N Birch Rd. 📞 (954) 563-5393. ◯ Wed–Sun. ● 4 Jul, Thanksgiving, 25 Dec. 🎟 ♿ compulsory, twice daily (phone in advance).

This quirkily furnished house not far from the sea is by far the most enjoyable piece of old Fort Lauderdale. It stands amid idyllic tropical grounds, where the bonnet water lily, from which the house took its name, once grew.

Frederic Bartlett, an artist, built this cosy, plantation-style winter home himself in 1920, and examples of his work, especially murals, are everywhere. He and his wife Evelyn Lilly, also a painter, shared a passion for all things natural: hence the swans and monkeys that inhabit the grounds, the carousel animals in the palm-filled courtyard, the greenhouse full of orchids and the collection of shells.

🦢 Hugh Taylor Birch State Recreation Area

3109 E Sunrise Blvd. 📞 (954) 564-4521. ◯ daily. 🎟 ♿

These 180 acres (73 ha), part of 3 miles (5 km) of barrier island that Chicago lawyer Hugh Taylor Birch bought in 1894, amount to one of the Gold Coast's few undeveloped oases of greenery. Visitors come to hire canoes on the lagoon, wander along a trail through a tropical hammock, and, above all, to exercise along a scenic circular road.

Jewellery stalls and neon lights at the Swap Shop of Fort Lauderdale

Environs: Bargain-hunters will love the **Swap Shop of Fort Lauderdale**, covering an incredible 75 acres (30 ha). This place is an American version of an oriental bazaar, with whole rows devoted to jewellery, sunglasses and other trinkets. Many of the 12 million annual visitors are lured by the funfair and the free circus, complete with clowns and elephants. The car park becomes a huge drive-in movie theatre in the evenings.

🎪 Swap Shop of Fort Lauderdale

3291 W Sunrise Blvd. 📞 (954) 791-7927. ◯ daily. ♿

The Jungle Queen, Fort Lauderdale's most famous cruise boat

The Waterways

Around the mouth of the New River lie dozens of parallel, arrow-straight canals. The area is known as **The Isles**, after the rows of slender peninsular islands created from mud when the canals were dug in the 1920s. This is the most desirable place to live in the city: looming behind lush foliage and luxurious yachts are ostentatious mansions worth millions of dollars. Their residents, such as Wayne Huizenga, owner of the Blockbuster Video empire and local baseball and football teams, are chiefly rich businesspeople.

The islands flank the Intracoastal Waterway, which also crosses **Port Everglades**. Hardly scenic but fascinating nevertheless, this is the world's second-largest cruise port after Miami, as well as a destination for container ships, oil tankers, destroyers and submarines.

The best panorama of the waterways from dry land is from the revolving bar at the top of the tower of the Hyatt Regency Pier 66 Hotel on South East 17th Street. But the mansions, yachts and port can really only be properly viewed from the water. You can take your pick from all kinds of boat trips. The **Jungle Queen** is an old-fashioned riverboat that chugs up the New River to a private island styled as an Indian village; there are daytime trips, taking three hours, and evening cruises that include a vaudeville show and barbecue dinner.

Ninety-minute **Carrie B** riverboat tours depart from the Riverwalk, pass various mansions, browse around the port and then visit the warm waters of a power plant discharge where large numbers of manatees (see p236) gather.

Water Taxis, operating like shared land taxis, go up New River to Downtown and anywhere from the port north to Commercial Boulevard. Call about ten minutes before you want to be picked up, and travel on flat-fee single tickets or better-value day passes. You can hire self-drive boats from the Bahia Mar Yachting Center and Pier 66 Marina.

Finally, day-long trips to the Bahamas and daytime or evening "cruises to nowhere" are big business for **SeaEscape** and other cruise companies (see pp338–9). Entertainment on board comes primarily in the form of casino action and cabaret shows.

A water taxi on the New River

USEFUL ADDRESSES

Carrie B
The Riverwalk at SE 5th Avenue.
[(954) 768-9920.

Jungle Queen
Bahia Mar Yachting Center,
A1A, Fort Lauderdale Beach.
[(954) 462-5596.

SeaEscape
Port Everglades Terminal 1.
[(954) 925-9700.

Water Taxi
651 Seabreeze Boulevard,
A1A, Fort Lauderdale Beach.
[(954) 467-6677.

View over Fort Lauderdale's waterways from the top of the Hyatt Regency Pier 66 Hotel

A garuda statue from Bali, at the
Graves Museum in Dania

Dania ㉑

Road map F4. Broward Co.
🏛 *13,000.* 🚊 *Hollywood.* 🚌 *Hollywood.* ℹ *Dania, (954) 926-2323.*

DANIA BLENDS seamlessly into
the coastal conurbation.
Some locals visit the town only
to watch a game of jai alai,
but the other main attraction
is the **John U Lloyd Beach
State Recreation Area**, a
chunk of virgin barrier island
that contrasts acutely with
nearby Port Everglades *(see
p131).* From the park's northern tip, you can watch ships
come and go, while to the
south stretches one of the
Gold Coast's loveliest beaches:
more than 2 miles (3 km) in
length and backed by pine
trees. You can hire canoes to
explore the scenic, mangrove-
lined creek that runs through
the heart of the park.

The **Graves Museum of
Archaeology and Natural
History**, inland, appeals to all
ages. Overtly educational displays explaining, for example,
the formation of the Keys, are
mixed with more entertaining
exhibits such as models of
dinosaurs and replicas of
Tutankhamun's treasures.

Just a few blocks north lies
an array of some 150 antique
shops. Despite their rather
soulless location running alongside traffic-ridden US 1, they
make entertaining browsing.

♣ **John U Lloyd Beach SRA**
6503 N Ocean Drive. 📞 *(954) 923-
2833.* ◯ *daily.* 🅿 &

🏛 **Graves Museum of
Archaeology and Natural
History**
481 S Federal Highway. 📞 *(954)
925-7770.* ◯ *Tue–Sun.* ● *Easter,
Thanksgiving, 25 Dec, 1 Jan.* 🅿 &

Hollywood ㉒

Road map F4. Broward Co.
🏛 *135,000.* 🚊 *Amtrak and Tri-Rail.*
🚌 ℹ *330 N Federal Highway, (954)
923-4000.*

FOUNDED BY a Californian in
the 1920s, this sizeable and
unpretentious resort is the
destination for the majority of
the 300,000 French Canadians
who migrate to Greater Fort
Lauderdale each winter. Gallic
restaurants and cafés serve
pommes frites and *crêpes* to
customers reading Québecois
newspapers on Hollywood's
seaside Broadwalk.

This pleasant promenade
makes Hollywood unusually
pedestrian-friendly for Florida,
with traffic limited to a steady
stream of rollerbladers and

cyclists. Alongside extend miles
of meticulously maintained
and very popular sands.

Each morning dozens of
Hollywood's predominantly
elderly visitors assemble for
light aerobics at the outdoor
Theater Under the Stars on
the seafront, returning in the
evening for concerts.

ENVIRONS: At the crossroads
of Routes 7 and 448, on the
western edge of Hollywood,
is the **Seminole Indian
Hollywood Reservation**.
Covering 480 acres (194 ha),
it is Florida's smallest Indian
reservation. Like others in the
state it is largely autonomous
(see p271), and hoardings
advertising cut-price tobacco
along the roadside are grim
clues to its exemption from
state cigarette taxes.

You may prefer to avoid
the miserable **Native Indian
Village**, with its craft stalls and
alligator displays laid on for
tourists, in favour of the vast
24-hour **Seminole Indian
Bingo and Poker Casino**

Sunworshippers enjoying the pristine sands of Hollywood Beach

Fortunes being made at the Seminole Indian Bingo near Hollywood

over the road. Reservations are also exempt from gambling laws, and in the cavernous bingo hall as many as 1,400 players compete for five-figure cash prizes. Even if you don't play, the rows of women surrounded by sandwiches, counters and cards make an intriguing spectacle; games begin four times a day. Peer in, too, on the frenetic Lightning Room, where you can watch dabblers in speed bingo lose hundreds of dollars.

Nearby, the small **Ah-Tha-Thi-Ki Museum** explains the life and customs of Seminoles past and present. It is worth a visit, particularly if you have no time to explore its larger, sister museum and park in the Everglades *(see p271)*.

Native Indian Village
3551 N State Rd 7. *(954) 961-4519.* ◯ *daily.* ● *Thanksgiving, 25 Dec.* limited.
Seminole Indian Bingo and Poker Casino
4150 N State Rd 7. *(954) 961-3220.* ◯ *daily.* ● *Easter, 25 Dec.*
Ah-Tha-Thi-Ki Museum
5991 S State Rd 7. *(954) 792-0745.* ◯ *Wed–Sun.* ● *Thanksgiving, 25 Dec, 1 Jan.*

Davie ㉓

Road map F4. Broward Co. 58,000. Fort Lauderdale. Fort Lauderdale. 4185 Davie Rd, (954) 581-0790.

CENTRED ON Orange Drive and Davie Road, and surrounded by paddocks and stables, the bizarre town of Davie adheres to a strictly Old West theme. Cacti grow outside the town hall's wooden huts, and the local McDonald's even has a corral at the back. Drop in on Grif's Western Wear, a cowboy supermarket at 6211 South West 45th Street, to stock up on saddles, cowboy hats and boots. The only way to sample the town's real flavour, however, is to see bronco taming, bull riding and steer wrestling in a rodeo

Stetsons for sale at Grif's Western Wear shop in Davie

at the **Davie Rodeo Arena**. These heart-stopping displays of cowboy skill normally take place on Wednesday nights from around 7:30pm (but call beforehand to check); there are also professional rodeos to be seen every month.

Davie Rodeo Arena
6591 Orange Drive. *(954) 797-1163.* ◯ *for rodeos only.*

Flamingo Gardens ㉔

Road map F4. Broward Co. 3750 Flamingo Rd, Davie. *(954) 473-2955.* Fort Lauderdale. Fort Lauderdale. ◯ *daily.* ● *Thanksgiving, 25 Dec.*

THESE BEAUTIFUL gardens started out in 1927 as a weekend retreat for the Wrays, a citrus-farming family. You can tour their pretty 1930s home, furnished in period style, but the gardens are the attraction here. Tram tours pass groves of lemon and kumquat trees, live oaks, banyan trees and other exotic vegetation.

The gardens are also home and hospital to a mass of Florida birds, including the rare bald eagle *(see p22)* and, of course, flamingos. Many species of ducks, gulls, doves and waders – including the comical roseate spoonbill *(see p275)* – inhabit a splendid walk-through aviary split into habitats such as cypress forest and mangrove swamp.

JAI ALAI – A MERRY SPORT

This curious game originated some 300 years ago in the Basque Country (jai alai means "merry festival" in Basque) and was brought to the USA in the early 1900s via Cuba. Florida has eight of the USA's ten arenas, or "frontons".

Watching a game of jai alai makes for a cheap night out (if you don't bet). The programme explains both the scoring and the intricacies of pari-mutuel betting, in which those who bet on the winners share in the total amount wagered. People yell and cheer loudly during the points since many will have put money on the outcome. Games take place in Dania five times a week: call (954) 927-2841 for details. The rules of the game are explained on page 31.

Jai alai player poised for a hit

ORLANDO AND
THE SPACE COAST

W ITH EVERYTHING *from roller coasters to performing killer whales and a well-known mouse with very big ears, Orlando is a family-oriented fantasyland and the undisputed theme park capital of the world, attracting over 34 million visitors every year.*

Orlando started out as an army post, Fort Gatlin, which was established during the Seminole Wars *(see pp44–5)*. The story goes that the fort was later renamed after a soldier called Orlando Reeves, who was hit by a Seminole arrow in 1835. A town developed, but even through the first half of the 20th century Orlando and neighbouring towns such as Kissimmee were only small, sleepy places dependent on cattle and the citrus crop.

Everything changed in the 1960s. First of all came the job opportunities associated with the space programme at Cape Canaveral. Then Walt Disney World started to take shape: its first theme park, the Magic Kingdom, opened in 1971. Since then, Disney claims that over 500 million visitors have made the pilgrimage to what it modestly calls the world's most popular vacation destination. Its success has generated a booming entertainment industry in Greater Orlando, as more and more attractions appear on the scene, all eager to cash in on the captive market.

Scenically, aside from dozens of lakes, the region is rather dull, with Greater Orlando sprawling gracelessly among the flat agricultural lands. Along the Space Coast, the communities on the mainland shore hold little appeal. However, the barrier islands across the broad Indian River boast 72 miles (116 km) of stunning sandy beaches, and there are two enormous nature reserves rich in bird life. Amid all this, set in a preserved marshy vastness beneath giant skies, in surprising harmony with nature, is the Kennedy Space Center, from where shuttles are launched dramatically out of the earth's atmosphere.

The expansive and unspoilt watery landscape of Merritt Island on the Space Coast

◁ **The imposing entrance to Universal Studios, one of Orlando's top theme parks**

Exploring Orlando and the Space Coast

THE REASON so many holidaymakers come to Orlando is because of its theme parks, the big ones being at Walt Disney World, Sea World and Universal Studios. It is said that in their environs, in Walt Disney World, around International Drive and in Kissimmee, there are over 80,000 hotel rooms, more than in the whole of New York. If you have time to spare, visit Cypress Gardens or Splendid China: elsewhere they would be the leading attractions. At night, experience the razzmatazz at the entertainment complexes of Church Street Station and Disney's Pleasure Island. To see Orlando's more salubrious side, spend some time in the chic suburb of Winter Park.

Just 50 miles (80 km) away, the Space Coast is an easy day trip from Orlando. Here, beaches range from empty, wild sands to the buzzing surfing mecca of brash Cocoa Beach. And Kennedy Space Center competes keenly with Orlando's theme parks for excitement.

KEY

	Interstate highway
	Toll road
	Major highway
	Secondary route
	Scenic route
	River
☆	Viewpoint

0 kilometres   20

0 miles   20

Daytona Beach

Ocala

441

Ocala

Lake Apopka

50

27

33

WINTER PARK 5

ORLANDO 4

UNIVERSAL STUDIOS 3

INTERNATIONAL DRIVE 6

Bee Li

SEA WORLD 2

WALT DISNEY WORLD RESORT 1

GATORLAND 7

4

441

SPLENDID CHINA 10

KISSIMMEE 8

CYPRESS ISLAND 9

Lake Tohopekaliga

POLK CITY

17 92

FANTASY OF FLIGHT 11

17 92

WINTER HAVEN

CYPRESS GARDENS 12

Lake Kissimmee

BOK TOWER GARDENS 13

LAKE WALES

27

64

Bradenton

Kissi

A performing killer whale, a star attraction at Sea World

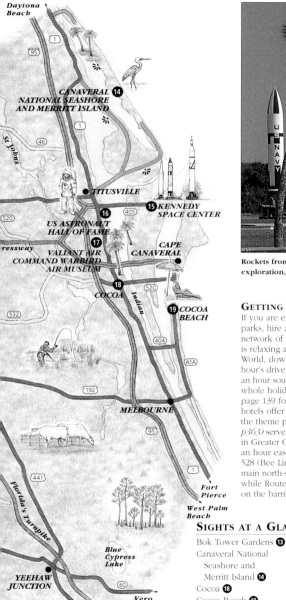

Rockets from the early days of space exploration, at the Kennedy Space Center

GETTING AROUND

If you are exploring beyond the theme parks, hire a car. With an extensive network of dual carriageways, driving is relaxing and fast: from Walt Disney World, downtown Orlando is half an hour's drive north and Cypress Gardens an hour south. If you are spending your whole holiday on Disney property, see page 139 for transport options. Many hotels offer free shuttle bus services to the theme parks, and Lynx buses *(see p363)* serve most tourist destinations in Greater Orlando. The Space Coast is an hour east from Orlando on Route 528 (Bee Line Expressway). I-95 is the main north-south route along the coast, while Route A1A connects the beaches on the barrier islands.

SIGHTS AT A GLANCE

Walt Disney World® Resort ❶

COVERING 43 SQ MILES (69 sq km), Walt Disney World Resort is the largest entertainment complex on earth. Its main draw is its theme parks: presently Epcot, Magic Kingdom and Disney-MGM Studios. But it is also a self-sufficient holiday destination, supplying everything from hotels to golf courses. With under a quarter of its land so far developed, every year some new wonder arrives: Disney's Animal Kingdom is the biggest new attraction.

Peerless in its imagination, attention to detail and, above all, in the Audio-Animatronics® technology – which brings animals and humans to life with extraordinary realism – Walt Disney World is also a hermetic bubble cocooned from the real world. Everything runs like clockwork, and nothing is allowed to shatter the theme parks' illusions: their workings are even secreted in tunnels underground. Unless you're an unreformable cynic, Walt Disney World will amaze you. You needn't be a child to enjoy it: nearly half the visitors come without kids, and it's the most popular honeymoon destination in the US.

When to Visit

YOU NEED TO BE something of a masochist to tackle Walt Disney World at peak times. During the American school holidays, and particularly at Christmas, New Year, Easter, 4 July and Thanksgiving, the theme parks can be very busy, with over 90-minute queues for the top attractions. However, the payoff for going during these periods is that the parks are open for longer hours, and the parades and firework displays are held more frequently. Christmas, when Walt Disney World is glittering with decorations, is the most festive but also the busiest time of year to visit.

During the least busy times, from September to the Christmas holidays and from New Year to mid-February, the parks can be blissfully empty. Another virtue of winter is that the temperature is much more suitable for touring the parks energetically. However, there is less going on at these times, and some rides may even close for maintenance.

Length of Visit

WALT DISNEY WORLD provides at least a week of entertainment; there will be even more once Disney's Animal Kingdom is open *(see p160)*. To enjoy everything, give the Magic Kingdom and Epcot two days each, leaving a day for Disney-MGM Studios. Don't try to see the parks one after the other: intersperse your visits with more leisurely days.

More Information

See page 163 for further information on the following:

- *Types of Passes*
- *Busiest Days*
- *Opening Hours*
- *The Ideal Schedule*
- *Coping with Queues*
- *WDW Dining*
- *Money*
- *WDW with Young Children*
- *Meeting Mickey*

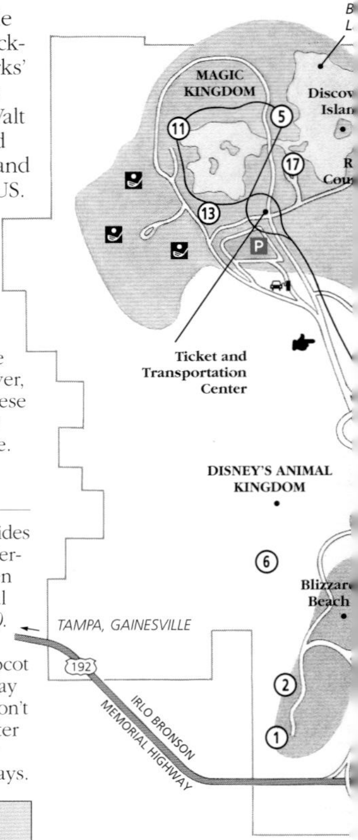

Key

- [P] Parking
- Petrol station
- Golf course
- Monorail
- Major highway
- Interstate highway
- Secondary route
- Theme park entrance

Walt Disney World Resorts

1 All-Star Music	10 Fort Wilderness
2 All-Star Sports	11 Grand Floridian Beach
3 Beach Club	12 Old Key West
4 Caribbean Beach	13 Polynesian
5 Contemporary	14 Port Orleans
6 Coronado Springs	15 WDW Dolphin
7 Disney Institute	16 WDW Swan
8 Disney's BoardWalk	17 Wilderness Lodge
9 Dixie Landings	18 Yacht Club

TICKETS AND PASSES

ELEMENTAL TO THE concept of the theme park is the idea that once you have paid for admission you need not pay any extra for entertainment.

For those on prolonged visits it is uneconomical to buy one-day, one-park tickets. Of better value are the various kinds of passes available, which also offer holders a greater degree of freedom. A complete list of passes can be found on page 163.

Both tickets and passes can be bought at the theme park entrances, but getting them in advance saves time. They are sold at Disney's shop at Orlando International Airport, the Disney resorts, many non-Disney hotels and at the tourist information centre on International Drive *(see p176)*. In addition, Disney Stores around the world sell some passes, which are sometimes included in package deals too.

GETTING AROUND

YOU DON'T NEED a car in Walt Disney World, though it is certainly the quickest and easiest way to travel around.

An extensive and efficient transport system handles an average of 200,000 guests each day. Even if you are staying outside Walt Disney World itself, most nearby hotels offer free shuttle services to and from the theme parks: check before booking. The transport hub of Walt Disney World is the **Ticket and Transportation Center** (TTC). Connecting it to the Magic Kingdom are two monorail services: one clockwise circuit that takes you to the resorts, and another anti-clockwise circuit providing an express (but often more crowded) service. A separate monorail links the TTC to Epcot. Ferries run from the TTC to the Magic Kingdom across the Seven Seas Lagoon (which is useful if there is a queue for the monorail). Other ferry services connect the Magic Kingdom and Epcot with the resorts in their respective areas.

Buses link everything to everything in Walt Disney World. Services include direct links to the Magic Kingdom, cutting out the need to use the monorail or ferry.

Residents and pass holders can use the entire transport system for free, while one-day theme park tickets entitle holders to use the monorails and ferries between the TTC and the Magic Kingdom.

PARKING

VISITORS TO THE Magic Kingdom must park at the TTC and make their way to the theme park by public transport; Epcot and Disney-MGM Studios, on the other hand, have their own car parks.

Parking is free for Disney resort residents. Non-residents must pay, but only once a day (regardless of how many times they move their vehicle). The car parks are very large, so it's a good idea to make a note of where you leave your vehicle.

ADVANTAGES OF STAYING IN WALT DISNEY WORLD RESORT

AROUND 50,000 VISITORS stay in Walt Disney World Resort accommodation each night. Lodgings in the resorts (as the hotels and villa complexes are known) and Walt Disney World Swan and Dolphin (operated independently but Disneyesque in every other respect) are of a very high standard. However, even the cheapest places are more expensive than many hotels outside Walt Disney World. Beyond Disney quality, your money also buys:
• Proximity to attractions and free use of Disney's transport system; the Magic Kingdom resorts on the monorail are the most conveniently situated.
• Early entry into the theme parks. Every day, parts of one theme park open up to 90 minutes early for Disney residents.
• The opportunity to buy passes entitling unlimited admission to Disney attractions; these are valid for two to nine days.
• Guaranteed admission to the theme parks even when the parks are otherwise full.
• The possibility of dining with your favourite Disney character in your hotel.
• The delivery of shopping purchases made anywhere in Walt Disney World.

See pages 303–304 for a list of recommended Disney resorts. Note that the cluster of hotels near Disney Village Marketplace, which are not run by Disney, offer few of the above privileges.

ORLANDO

Downtown Disney

Exit 27

EPCOT

Exit 26B

Typhoon Lagoon

Orlando International Airport

DISNEY-MGM STUDIOS

Disney's Wide World of Sports

Exit 25B

KISSIMMEE, Celebration Florida

TAMPA

| 0 metres | 500 |
| 0 yards | 500 |

☐ Magic Kingdom Resort Area

☐ Disney Village Resort Area

☐ Epcot Resort Area

☐ Studio Resort Area

The Magic Kingdom

REAPPEARING IN SIMILAR form in California, Japan and France, the Magic Kingdom is the essential Disney theme park. Billed as the place where dreams come true, here young children are in seventh heaven and adults can relive their childhood. Cartoon characters and nostalgic visions of how the world and particularly America once was, and how it might be again, fill its relentlessly cheerful 100 acres (40 ha). Made up of seven "lands" – evoking a particular theme or era such as the Wild West, Colonial America, the future – it is effectively seven mini theme parks rolled into one. Binding the park together are stunning parades, musical street performers such as Dixieland bands, and three-dimensional Disney characters ready to greet their guests.

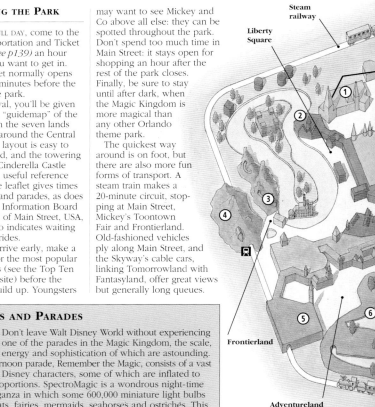

Model riders in a rocket on the roof of Space Mountain

TACKLING THE PARK

FOR A FULL DAY, come to the Transportation and Ticket Center (see p139) an hour before you want to get in. Main Street normally opens about 30 minutes before the rest of the park.

On arrival, you'll be given a detailed "guidemap" of the park. With the seven lands arranged around the Central Plaza, the layout is easy to understand, and the towering spires of Cinderella Castle serve as a useful reference point. The leaflet gives times of shows and parades, as does the Guest Information Board at the end of Main Street, USA, which also indicates waiting times for rides.

If you arrive early, make a beeline for the most popular attractions (see the Top Ten box opposite) before the queues build up. Youngsters may want to see Mickey and Co above all else: they can be spotted throughout the park. Don't spend too much time in Main Street: it stays open for shopping an hour after the rest of the park closes. Finally, be sure to stay until after dark, when the Magic Kingdom is more magical than any other Orlando theme park.

The quickest way around is on foot, but there are also more fun forms of transport. A steam train makes a 20-minute circuit, stopping at Main Street, Mickey's Toontown Fair and Frontierland. Old-fashioned vehicles ply along Main Street, and the Skyway's cable cars, linking Tomorrowland with Fantasyland, offer great views but generally long queues.

SHOWS AND PARADES

Don't leave Walt Disney World without experiencing one of the parades in the Magic Kingdom, the scale, energy and sophistication of which are astounding. The afternoon parade, Remember the Magic, consists of a vast array of Disney characters, some of which are inflated to giant proportions. SpectroMagic is a wondrous night-time extravaganza in which some 600,000 miniature light bulbs coat floats, fairies, mermaids, seahorses and ostriches. This parade happens only if the park stays open late. Usually, the least crowded place to watch any parade is Frontierland.

The best of the shows is an intense fireworks display called Fantasy in the Sky, which is initiated by Tinker Bell, the fairy from *Peter Pan*, flying from Cinderella Castle. On certain nights in December, Mickey's Very Merry Christmas Party takes over the whole park, with special decorations and shows. You need separate tickets for this, which you should book in advance.

Steam railway

Liberty Square

Frontierland

Adventureland

0 metres   100

0 yards   100

◁ **Mickey Mouse and friends performing outside Cinderella Castle**

Main Street, USA

THIS IS A ROMANTICIZED early 20th-century version of a high street and main square in a small American town. Canopies festoon gaudy shopfronts (names displayed in the windows honour important Disney employees), while Stars and Stripes fly from the rooftops; old-fashioned street lamps and barber shop quartets add to the atmosphere.

The only real attraction is a cinema showing classic Disney cartoons. Otherwise, use Main Street to deal with practical matters and for shopping.

ADVENTURELAND

LUSH FOLIAGE, drumbeats, colonial buildings and cool plazas evoke Africa, Polynesia and the Caribbean: Adventureland is a fusion of anywhere exotic and tropical.

Jungle Cruise

Best enjoyed in daylight, this boat ride explores tropical rivers cleverly re-created with waterfalls, lush vegetation, and even a lost temple. Real boatmen tell jokes as they show visitors unreal tigers, crocodiles and elephants.

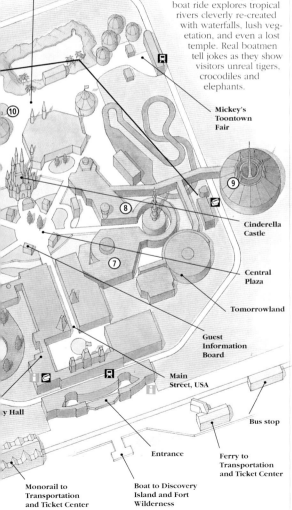

TOP 10 ATTRACTIONS

1. **It's A Small World**
2. **The Haunted Mansion**
3. **Big Thunder Mountain Railroad**
4. **Splash Mountain**
5. **Pirates of the Caribbean**
6. **Jungle Cruise**
7. **The Timekeeper**
8. **ExtraTERRORestrial Alien Encounter**
9. **Space Mountain**
10. **Dumbo the Flying Elephant**

Pirates of the Caribbean

The scale and detail of the Audio-Animatronics on this ten-minute ride – in which a ship fires at a castle and pirates booze and womanize their way around a captured port – surpass anything else in Walt Disney World. Close up, you can see even the pirates' dirty feet and hairy legs.

Tropical Serenade

This lively chorus of 200-plus warbling, whistling, singing birds was Disney's first ever Audio-Animatronics attraction when it opened in California's Disneyland Park in 1963. Seen alongside today's technology the show now seems rather static, but it is entertaining in its own eccentric way.

KEY

▨	Main Street, USA
▨	Adventureland
▨	Frontierland
▨	Liberty Square
▢	Fantasyland
▨	Mickey's Toontown Fair
▨	Tomorrowland
▢	Perimeter area
—	Skyway
🚂	Rail stops
💳	ATM/bank
ℹ	Guest Relations

Labels on map: Fantasyland, Mickey's Toontown Fair, Cinderella Castle, Central Plaza, Tomorrowland, Guest Information Board, Main Street, USA, Bus stop, Entrance, Ferry to Transportation and Ticket Center, Boat to Discovery Island and Fort Wilderness, Monorail to Transportation and Ticket Center, y Hall

FRONTIERLAND

A SALOON with swing doors, a Frontier Trading Post selling shoelace ties and sheriffs' badges, a shooting gallery and cowboys: that's America's Wild West, Disney-style. You can wander in any time to watch the **Diamond Horseshoe Saloon Revue**, during which actors perform energetic slapstick comedy and high-kicking dance routines in a beautiful dance hall saloon. The **Country Bear Jamboree**, "Fun Fur All", features a cast of talking deer, buffalo and moose heads alongside a troupe of lovable singing robotic bears.

Anyone needing to escape the crowds can take a raft to **Tom Sawyer's Island** (which closes at dusk). Complete with a stockade fort, tunnels, swing-and-barrel bridges, a watermill and windmill, this is a dream playground for most children.

Frontierland also has two of the park's most popular and nerve-jangling attractions: Big Thunder Mountain Railroad and Splash Mountain.

Splash Mountain

Many people are discouraged from going on this waterfall-riddled ride by the sight of the terrifying 40-mph (65-km/h) plunge down the mountain. Those who summon up the courage first undergo a number of teasing mini-descents, all the time being entertained by Brer Rabbit and friends from Walt Disney's 1946 film *Song of the South*.

SHOPPING

The shops along Main Street specialize in Disney merchandise, from calculators to Mickey-shaped pasta. The Emporium has the largest selection, with Disney clothes, cuddly toys, autograph books and so forth. Disneyana Collectibles sells posters and story books, along with costly limited-edition animation artwork. Shops in other lands also sell non-Disney items complementing the land's theme, from cowboy boots in Frontierland to Milky Way™ chocolate bars in Tomorrowland. Of particular interest are Traders of Timbuktu (Adventureland) for African musical instruments and animal carvings, and Heritage House (Liberty Square) for books with recipes from the Civil War years and badges from recent US presidential campaigns.

Big Thunder Mountain Railroad

During this tame but highly entertaining roller coaster on a runaway mine train, you pass antique mining equipment, falling rocks, stalactites and stalagmites, waterfalls and a flooded mining town.

LIBERTY SQUARE

COLOURFUL clapboard buildings, a grand live oak (the Liberty Tree) and a replica of a Boston meeting house here represent elements of Colonial America. You'll also find the park's prettiest item here – the **Liberty Square Riverboat**. Taking the paddlesteamer around the Rivers of America, you can spot an Indian settlement, a settler's log cabin ablaze and deer with twitching ears along the way.

The Hall of Presidents

This serious show, which many Americans find very emotive, continues Liberty

---

Square's patriotic theme. Its highlight is a roll call of all 42 US presidents (to date), each looking and moving in such a lifelike manner it is hard to believe they aren't human.

The Haunted Mansion

Complete with artificially created dust and cobwebs, this is one of the park's most enjoyable attractions. Its rattling doors, staring statues, dancing wraiths and flying phantoms entertain rather than scare.

FANTASYLAND

THIS IS THE HEART and soul of the Magic Kingdom. Its landmark Cinderella Castle, an amazing creation of steel and fibreglass, seems straight out of a Germanic fairytale.

Most attractions are geared to younger children. The fairground rides, including the ever-popular **Dumbo the Flying Elephant** and the 1917 carousel, need little explanation. There are also three short rides with sophisticated Audio-Animatronics based on classic children's stories. **Peter Pan's Flight**, in which you can sail over London off to Never Land, is the best; the witch in **Snow White's Adventures** can be scary for some youngsters, while the surreal **Mr Toad's Wild Ride** can be confusing unless you've read Kenneth Grahame's *The Wind in the Willows*.

The only show in Fantasyland is the schmaltzy **Legend of The Lion King**, a low-tech rendition of *The Lion King* with hand-operated puppetry supporting scenes from the film.

EATING AND DRINKING

Food in the Magic Kingdom is fairly unsophisticated: many restaurants serve mainstream American fare, and most are fast-food joints. For a better meal, and alcohol (none is available in the park), take the monorail to restaurants in the nearby resorts *(see pp322–3)*.

Among the park's full-service restaurants, the Liberty Tree Tavern, a re-created colonial inn, has the best reputation, while King Stefan's Banquet Hall in Cinderella Castle is very jolly, with stained-glass windows and medieval-style banners. At both, reserve by calling WDW-DINE or at the restaurants themselves. Of the fast-food places, the most peaceful is Aunt Polly's on Tom Sawyer's Island, but its menu is limited to sandwiches and cold chicken. The Crystal Palace, a Victorian-styled glass house in the Central Plaza serving roasts, pasta and salad dishes, is the most civilized.

It's A Small World

The top ride in Fantasyland is essential viewing, if only to experience Disney at its most folksy and saccharine. A boat trip takes you to meet choirs of dolls in stereotypical scenes from dozens of countries, all singing a song promoting harmony and world peace.

MICKEY'S TOONTOWN FAIR

THIS LAND APPEALS mainly, though not exclusively, to young children. The idea is that Mickey and his gang live here. There's full-size Mickey's House: note Mickey's car and Pluto's kennel outside, while inside a shopping list with seven types of cheese sets the tone. Minnie Mouse has her own mini mansion. The thrills attraction here is **Goofy's Barnstormer**, in which you whizz around a roller coaster in a biplane.

There is a live pantomime for youngsters featuring various Disney characters. Children will also have the opportunity to meet their favourite Disney characters in the Hall of Fame, and Mickey Mouse receives fans in his dressing room at Mickey's Hollywood Theatre.

TOMORROWLAND

OF LATE, Tomorrowland has altered from attempting a serious (and easily outdated) depiction of the future to something less educational and more fantastical. Although its metallic grey buildings make Tomorrowland the least charming part of the park, it still has some of the top attractions in the Magic Kingdom.

Space Mountain

On the most thrilling ride in the Magic Kingdom you fly in a rocket from a launch pad into a space inky black except for shooting stars: it's so dark that you lose any sense that you are travelling along a track. The rockets reach a top speed of only 28 mph (45 km/h), but it seems much faster.

ExtraTERRORestrial Alien Encounter

Here, you can experience what it's like actually to be in a horror movie. Being trapped with a hostile alien on the loose is a recipe for great fun if you enjoy being seriously frightened, though for many children the experience is far too vivid.

Walt Disney's Carousel of Progress

The four tableaux of an Audio-Animatronics American family at home at different times in the 20th century demonstrate technological progress on a domestic scale.

The Timekeeper

With images projected all around, making you feel part of the action, this is the best 360-degree Circle-Vision show in Walt Disney World. First you venture back to the time of the dinosaurs; after picking up Jules Verne (author of *Around the World in 80 Days*) at the Paris Exposition in 1900, you travel with him into the present and future.

RIDES AND SHOWS CHECKLIST

This chart is designed to help you plan your visit to Magic Kingdom. The different rides and shows are listed alphabetically by land.
(R) RIDE   (S) SHOW

		LIKELY TO QUEUE 30 MINS OR MORE	LASTS LESS THAN 15 MINUTES	MAY CAUSE MOTION SICKNESS	SCARY FOR ADULTS	QUALITY AUDIO-ANIMATRONICS	GOOD FOR PRE-SCHOOL KIDS	EDUCATIONAL
JUNGLE CRUISE	(R)	■	●			■	●	
PIRATES OF THE CARIBBEAN	(R)	■	●			■		
TROPICAL SERENADE	(R)					■		
BIG THUNDER MOUNTAIN RAILROAD	(R)	■	●	■				
COUNTRY BEAR JAMBOREE	(S)					■	●	
DIAMOND HORSESHOE SALOON REVUE	(S)							
SPLASH MOUNTAIN	(R)	■	●	■		■		
HALL OF PRESIDENTS	(R)					■		■
HAUNTED MANSION	(R)	■	●			■		
LIBERTY SQUARE RIVERBOAT	(R)					■		
DUMBO THE FLYING ELEPHANT	(R)	■	●				●	
IT'S A SMALL WORLD	(R)	■					●	
LEGEND OF THE LION KING	(S)						●	
MR TOAD'S WILD RIDE	(R)	■	●				●	
PETER PAN'S FLIGHT	(R)	■	●				●	
SNOW WHITE'S ADVENTURES	(R)	■	●			■	●	
GOOFY'S BARNSTORMER	(R)	■	●	■			●	
EXTRATERRORESTRIAL ALIEN ENCOUNTER	(R)	■	●		●			
THE TIMEKEEPER	(S)					■	●	■
SPACE MOUNTAIN	(R)	■	●	■	●			
WALT DISNEY'S CAROUSEL OF PROGRESS	(S)					■		■

Epcot

Epcot is the acronym for the Experimental Prototype Community of Tomorrow, since Walt Disney originally envisioned it as a town of some 20,000 residents, functioning with state-of-the-art technology. It turned out differently, however, opening instead in 1982 as Walt Disney World's most serious, adult-oriented theme park.

Epcot comes in two distinct halves. Future World is a celebration – part educational, part entertaining – of mankind's achievements in science and technology. World Showcase is like a world fair, an architectural, cultural and culinary pastiche of 11 countries where you can circumnavigate the globe without worrying about jet lag, visas or passports.

Replica of China's Temple of Heaven in World Showcase

TACKLING THE PARK

Epcot is enormous – about two and a half times the size of the Magic Kingdom. You need two days to see all of it; allow on average an hour for each of the nine pavilions at Future World and for the six World Showcase countries with attractions; half-an-hour is enough for each of World Showcase's other countries.

If you're visiting only for a day, focus on the Top Ten listed opposite, pop into all the countries of World Showcase, and be sure to dine in one of its restaurants.

In high season, plan your day to avoid the worst of the crowds. Arrive early: some parts of Future World open about 30 minutes before the park's official opening time.

Straight away, experience some of the most popular Future World attractions, such as Body Wars and Honey, I Shrunk the Audience; leave Spaceship Earth and the pavilion's exhibit areas until later. World Showcase opens an hour or so after Future World. By mid-morning, you should head for the two rides in Mexico and Norway, then

wander around other countries while the park is at its busiest. By late afternoon the crowds at the Future World attractions should have lessened. Most of the pavilions at Future World close a couple of hours before World Showcase. When they do, go back to World Showcase for dinner and the Illumi-Nations show.

While adults enjoy everything at Epcot, there's not a great deal geared specifically for young children. Future World has plenty that naturally appeals to teenagers, World Showcase less so: consider buying a passport, which children can have stamped at each country.

The Guest Information Board, located between the Innoventions buildings, displays queuing times for attractions. Also look out for the WorldKey Information Satellite terminals, which provide up-to-date information on everything at Epcot.

The American Adventure

Japan

Italy

Germany

China

Norway

Mexico

World Showcase Lagoon

Test Track

Horizons

Wonders of Life

Universe of Energy

10

9

8

7

6

5

4

ILLUMINATIONS

The one Epcot show which you mustn't miss is IllumiNations. This takes place nightly at the park's advertised closing time around World Showcase Lagoon. It is a rousing *son et lumière* show on an unbelievably extravagant scale – with lasers, fireworks, waterworks, and a panoply of lights that outline each of the 11 countries to the accompaniment of a patriotic tune. Grab a good viewpoint early: most people crowd the lake's Future World side to be nearer the entrance for a quick exit at the end of the show.

0 metres   30
0 yards   30

◁ The unmistakable globe of Spaceship Earth, the focal point of Future World

FUTURE WORLD

THIS HALF OF THE PARK feels rather soulless since all the action takes place inside a series of giant abstract buildings known as pavilions. Each of these focuses on a particular theme of life on this planet, such as energy, transport, communication, the environment and so forth. They are the product of a creative collaboration between Walt Disney World and several major corporations, such as General Motors, Exxon, AT&T, Kodak and Nestlé, and are constantly being updated.

Some pavilions have several attractions under one roof, while others effectively comprise just one big ride or show.

Spaceship Earth

This huge landmark building is often compared to a golf ball. The outer skin of the giant silver sphere is made up of over 14,000 aluminium and plastic-alloy triangles, and the whole building weighs 6,800 tonnes. Ingeniously, rainwater is gradually absorbed by the surface of the ball and is then funnelled into World Showcase Lagoon.

Spaceship Earth contains one long and gentle ride – in which you travel in a "time machine" on a chronological tour through the history of communication. There are some excellent special effects and remarkably detailed tableaux, such as Michelangelo painting the ceiling of the Vatican's Sistine Chapel.

Innoventions

Dozens of state-of-the-art gadgets made by the world's top technology manufacturers, from Sega to Lego, fill the two massive Innoventions buildings. Each of the exhibit areas is sponsored by a different manufacturer. Some of the exhibits are available already, but many won't be on the market yet.

Visit the house of the future and experiment with wrist and video phones. Virtual reality headsets let you walk through cartoons, while the computer software takes you on an interactive trip to far-flung places.

Universe of Energy

Here the attraction is **Ellen's Energy Crisis**, a show with a ride named after television comedienne, Ellen De Generes, who narrates along with Bill Nye (another well-known TV personality in the US).

In between educational but moderately entertaining films on energy sources, the theatre seating divides into segments for a ride through a clammy prehistoric world populated by Audio-Animatronics dinosaurs. Most children enjoy the ride, though young children may be scared by the dinosaurs.

TOP 10 ATTRACTIONS

1. **Honey, I Shrunk the Audience**
2. **The Living Seas**
3. **Spaceship Earth**
4. **Body Wars**
5. **Cranium Command**
6. **Test Track**
7. **Mexico**
8. **Maelstrom**
9. **Wonders of China**
10. **IllumiNations**

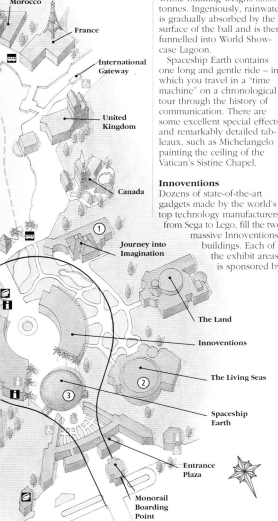

Morocco
France
International Gateway
United Kingdom
Canada
① Journey into Imagination
The Land
Innoventions
② The Living Seas
③ Spaceship Earth
Entrance Plaza
Monorail Boarding Point

KEY

▨	World Showcase
▨	Future World
▢	Perimeter area
— —	Ferry route
——	Monorail
🚌	Bus stop
ℹ	Guest Relations
🛈	WorldKey Information Satellite
🏧	ATM/bank
♿	Wheelchair/pushchair rental

FUTURE WORLD CONT...

Wonders of Life
This lively pavilion, which is particularly appealing to children, deals with the human body. You can ride the latest exercise machines and seek advice on how to strike a baseball better or live more healthily. **The Making of Me** movie describes the facts of life in not too prudish a way.

The **Body Wars** ride is an intense journey in a microscopic craft through the body's bloodstream – a remarkably realistic experience as you judder in time with the action on the screen. There are age, height and health restrictions, and often long queues. Some riders suffer motion sickness.

In **Cranium Command**, the funniest show at Epcot, you sit in the brain of a teenage boy, Bobby, and watch an Audio-Animatronics pilot negotiate parts of the body through a typical school day, in the face of challenges such as love and hunger.

Horizons
The theme here is the 21st century. You board gondolas for an entertaining view of the future as visualized in the works of writers such as Jules Verne and in science fiction movies. An IMAX film follows, and then you move on into the next century for a glimpse at the possible landscapes of the future – including colonies in outer space inhabited by Audio-Animatronics people.

Test Track
This pavilion provides the most exciting ride at Epcot. It is presented by General Motors and offers a first-hand view of how GM cars and trucks are tested.

There are displays of test vehicles and equipment, but the highlight is **Test Track – the Automotive Adventure**.

This is the longest and fastest ride in Walt Disney World; you board six-passenger vehicles to experience every aspect of a road test from the wild skids that test the brakes to the arctic cold and desert heat in the Environmental Chamber Test. In the high-speed test you race along a section of track that loops around the pavilion.

Afterwards, when you've regained your breath, there are interactive displays and a multimedia film showcasing the latest GM models and its cars of the future.

Journey into Imagination
Top billing here goes to the hilarious, amazingly vivid 3-D movie, **Honey, I Shrunk the Audience**. The madcap professor from the films *Honey, I Shrunk The Kids* and *Honey, I Blew Up The Kid* accidentally shrinks the audience. Special effects in the theatre make it seem as though a giant dog is sneezing all over you and that hundreds of mice are actually scurrying beneath your feet.

The amusing **Journey into Imagination** ride is a very upbeat and light-hearted trip in search of ideas in the arts and sciences. However, it is

---

FROM WALT DISNEY TO WALT DISNEY WORLD

Walt Disney wanted Epcot to be far greater than a theme park – a "city of tomorrow, a planned, controlled community, a showcase of American industry and research..." – though the project was abandoned after he died of lung cancer in 1966, aged 65. Following his brother's death, Roy Disney changed the name of Disney World to Walt Disney World "so that people would always know it was Walt's dream". While his dreams for Epcot were never realized, Walt Disney succeeded in revolutionizing the entertainment industry.

Disney prided himself on being an ideas man rather than an artist or animator. His greatest creation must be Mickey Mouse (who first appeared in *Steamboat Willie* in 1928), but with California's Disneyland Park, which opened in 1955, he also invented the concept of the theme park as we know it today. His ambition was to build a place where families could have a good time together – a world of childhood nostalgia which had enormous success in a country recovering from both the Depression and World War II.

Disneyland Park was, and still is, financially constrained, since it is hemmed in by non-Disney developments. Walt Disney avoided making this same mistake in Florida; after choosing a site in the middle of the state, he arranged, throughout 1965, for dummy corporations to buy 27,400 acres (11,100 ha) of land with great secrecy, for a mere $5 million. The result is a self-contained vacation world where Disney enjoys quasi-governmental powers over the land within the boundaries of Walt Disney World.

CELEBRATION FLORIDA

Materializing out of former swampland adjacent to Walt Disney World, Celebration is a new town with old values. Inspired partly by the romantic streets of Charleston in South Carolina, Disney is attempting to re-create the wholesome small-town atmosphere that many middle-aged Americans remember and miss. The residents will experience a cookie-jar world of friendly neighbours and corner grocery stores.

People began moving in in 1996, the first of an expected total of 20,000 inhabitants. The pedestrian-friendly streets, the nostalgic architecture (designed by some respected architects) and the hospital that treats both "wellness" and illness seem tailor-made for fugitives from the fear and drudgery of modern city life – people who aren't daunted by Celebration's strict rules, which set out, for example, that visible curtains must be white or off-white and that streetside shrubbery must be approved by Disney. In some ways, however, Celebration is like any other town: the public is free to visit and have a look around.

overcomplicated and overlong. More successful is **The Image Works**, whose assemblage of high-tech, interactive games, such as painting on a computer screen or activating an orchestra with a sweep of the hand, require creative play.

The Land
The theme of The Land is food and agriculture. Scientists carry out all kinds of research here; in the pavilion's biotechnology laboratory the sustainability of life in space is studied.

Characters from the film *The Lion King* lead the **Circle of Life** – a stirring, partly animated 20-minute film with an environmental message. In the witty musical show **Food Rocks**, fruit, vegetables and kitchen utensils that have come to life as pop stars such as Pita Gabriel and Neil Moussaka belt out well-known hits with altered, nutritional lyrics.

Living with the Land is an instructive 15-minute boat trip that reveals the past, present and future of agriculture. You pass through various environments (such as a re-created rainforest, prairie and desert) into greenhouses, where crops are grown using special

---

DISNEY'S AUDIO-ANIMATRONICS®

Audio-Animatronics is a unique system that brings to life three-dimensional figures from human beings to flowers by using state-of-the-art technology that synchronizes sounds and movement. The electronic and mechanical equipment is hidden beneath a shell of fibreglass that is painted, covered or dressed to suit the designated purpose, and the result is truly lifelike. Abraham Lincoln in the Hall of Presidents at the Magic Kingdom can make 15 separate facial expressions, while in The American Adventure show, in World Showcase, three dozen figures move and speak with remarkable realism. First invented in 1963, Audio-Animatronics is constantly being refined by Disney's California-based "Imagineers" – the creative force behind the Disney theme parks.

---

cultivation techniques – one of these, known as hydroponics, requires no soil. For further information it is well worth joining a walking tour, which lasts about an hour.

The Land, appropriately, is the best place to eat in Future World. There is one sit-down restaurant *(see p153)* and a large fast-food court. People head primarily for the former, which is therefore at its most crowded at lunchtime.

The Living Seas
The most ingenious and integrated experience at Future World is at Sea Base Alpha, a deep-sea research centre which really feels as if it is under the sea. Its centrepiece is a giant, 200-ft (60-m) wide aquarium – said to be the largest in the world – with a man-made reef and some 6,000 inhabitants, including turtles, sharks and dolphins.

Manatees can be observed close-up in a tank, and there are also videos on the oceans' ecosystems. Exhibits include a tube of plankton and robotic instruments for underwater exploration, and there is also a diving suit which you can try to manoeuvre. In addition to this, scientists and divers can sometimes be watched carrying out underwater experiments.

RIDES AND SHOWS CHECKLIST

This chart is designed to help you plan what to visit at Epcot. The rides and shows are listed alphabetically in Future World and World Showcase respectively.
(R) RIDE   (S) SHOW

	LIKELY TO QUEUE 30 MINS OR MORE	LASTS LESS THAN 15 MINUTES	MAY CAUSE MOTION SICKNESS	SCARY FOR ADULTS	QUALITY AUDIO-ANIMATRONICS	GOOD FOR PRE-SCHOOL KIDS	EDUCATIONAL
BODY WARS (R)	■	■					
CIRCLE OF LIFE (S)							■
CRANIUM COMMAND (S)					■		■
ELLEN'S ENERGY CRISIS (S)					■		■
FOOD ROCKS (S)		■			■	■	
HONEY, I SHRUNK THE AUDIENCE (S)	■						
HORIZONS (R)		■			■		■
LIVING WITH THE LAND (R)		■					■
JOURNEY INTO IMAGINATION (R)		■					■
SPACESHIP EARTH (R)	■	■			■		■
THE MAKING OF ME (S)		■					■
TEST TRACK (R)	■		■				■
THE AMERICAN ADVENTURE (S)					■		■
EL RIO DEL TIEMPO (R)					■		■
IMPRESSIONS DE FRANCE (S)		■					■
MAELSTROM (R)	■	■			■		■
O CANADA! (S)							■
WONDERS OF CHINA (S)							■

WORLD SHOWCASE

THE TEMPLES, churches, town halls and castles of these 11 pavilions or countries are sometimes replicas of genuine buildings, sometimes merely in vernacular style. But World Showcase is much more than just a series of architectural set pieces. Every pavilion is staffed by people from the country it represents, selling high-quality local products as well as surprisingly good ethnic cuisine.

At set times (which are given on the guidemap) normally native performers stage live shows in the forecourts of each country: the best are the excellent acrobats at China and the bizarre and comic Living Statues at Italy. Only a couple of pavilions include rides, while a number have stunning giant-screen introductions to their country's history, culture and landscapes. A few even have art galleries, though these often go unnoticed.

Double-decker buses do the rounds of the lake's 1.3-mile (2-km) perimeter, but it is usually quicker to walk. There are also ferries across World Showcase Lagoon, linking Canada to Morocco and Mexico to Germany.

Mexico
A Mayan pyramid conceals the most remarkable interior at World Showcase. Stalls selling sombreros, ponchos and papier-mâché animals (piñatas), a highly-rated restaurant and mariachi players fill a colonial plaza, all bathed in a purple twilight. The backdrop to all this is nothing less than a rumbling volcano.

After such a scene, the tranquil **El Río del Tiempo** ("The River of Time") boat ride is somewhat underwhelming. It passes through Audio-Animatronics and cinematic scenes of Mexico past and present.

Norway
The buildings which comprise the latest addition to World Showcase include replicas of a stave church (a medieval wooden church) and Akershus Castle (a 14th-century fortress above Oslo harbour), arranged attractively around a cobblestone square.

You can buy trolls, sweaters, Lego and other native crafts, however the essential element here is **Maelstrom**, a short but exhilarating journey down fjords in a longboat, into troll country and across an oil rig-flecked North Sea – before docking at a fishing port. The ride is followed by a short film about Norway.

China
In this pavilion the pièce de résistance is the half-size replica of Beijing's well-known landmark, the Temple of Heaven. The peaceful scene here contrasts with the more rowdy atmosphere in some of the nearby pavilions.

For the purposes of entertainment, there is **Wonders of China**, a Circle-Vision film (shown on nine screens all around the audience simultaneously), which makes the most of the country's fabulous, little-seen ancient sites and scenery. Note that you must stand throughout the film.

The pavilion's extensive shopping emporium sells everything from Chinese lanterns and painted screens to tea bags. Unfortunately, the restaurants are disappointing.

Germany
The jolliest country in World Showcase is a hotchpotch of gabled and spired buildings gathered around a central square, St Georgsplatz. They are based on real buildings from all over Germany, including a merchants' hall in the town of Freiburg and a castle on the Rhine. If you have children, try to time your visit so that it coincides with the hourly chime of the impressive glockenspiel in the square

An accordionist sometimes plays, and the shops are full of quirky or clever gifts such as beautifully crafted wooden dolls. However, you really need to dine here to get the full flavour of Germany.

Italy
The bulk of Italy's relatively small pavilion represents Venice: from gondolas moored alongside candystick poles in the lagoon to the tremendous versions of the towering redbrick campanile and the 14th-century Doge's Palace of St Mark's Square; even the fake marble looks authentic. The courtyard buildings behind are Veronese and Florentine in style, and the Neptune statue is a copy of a Bernini work.

The architecture is the big attraction, but you should also stop off to dine in one of the restaurants or browse around the shops where you can pick up pasta, amaretti, wine and so forth.

The American Adventure
The American pavilion is the centrepiece of World Showcase, though it lacks the detail and charm found in most of the other countries. However, Americans usually find **The American Adventure** show, which takes place inside a vast Georgian-style building, very moving. For foreigners it will provide an interesting insight into the American

---

WORLD SHOWCASE: BEHIND THE SCENES

If you'd like more than just a superficial view of Walt Disney World, its behind-the-scenes tours may appeal. In World Showcase, two-hour Hidden Treasures tours provide a closer look at the architecture and traditions of the countries featured in the park, while in the Gardens of the World tours the creation of the World Showcase gardens is explained; you are even given tips on how to create a bit of Disney magic back home. These tours cost around $25 per person. If you have $160 and seven hours to spare, you might want to sign up for the Backstage Magic tour which includes all three theme parks; one of the highlights is the visit to the famous tunnel network beneath the Magic Kingdom. For information on all Disney tours call (407) WDW-TOUR/(407) 939-8687.

psyche. The show is an openly patriotic yet thought-provoking romp through the history of the United States up to the present day. It incorporates tableaux on screen and some excellent Audio-Animatronics figures, particularly of the narrators Mark Twain and the great 18th-century statesman, Benjamin Franklin.

 Japan
This is a restrained, formal place with a traditional Japanese garden, a Samurai castle and a pagoda modelled on a seventh-century temple in Nara – whose five storeys represent earth, water, fire, wind and sky.

The Mitsukoshi department store, a copy of the ceremonial hall of the Imperial Palace in Kyoto, offers kimonos, wind chimes, bonsai trees and the chance to pick a pearl from an oyster. However, Japan really only comes to life in its restaurants.

 Morocco
Morocco's appeal lies in its enamelled tiles, its keyhole-shaped doors, its ruddy fortress walls and the twisting alleys of its *medina* (old city), which is reached via a reproduction of a gate into the city of Fez. The use of native artists gives the show a greater sense of authenticity.

Morocco offers some of the best handmade crafts in World Showcase. The alleys of the old city lead you to a bustling market of little stores selling carpets, brassware, leatherware and shawls, with belly dancing and couscous in the Restaurant Marrakesh.

 France
A Gallic flair infuses everything in France, from its architecture (including a one-tenth scale replica of the Eiffel Tower, Parisian Belle Epoque mansions and a rustic village main street) to its up-market shops (good for perfume, wine and berets). French food can be sampled in a couple of restaurants and a patisserie selling croissants and cakes.

A soothing film entitled **Impressions de France** is the principal entertainment.

EATING AND DRINKING

 Dining well is fundamental to visiting Epcot and particularly World Showcase. Some of the latter's pavilions have decent fast-food places, but the best restaurants (including those listed below unless otherwise stated) require reservations. Call (407) 939-3463 as soon as you know when you'll be at Epcot. Book early in the day, using the TV monitors of the WorldKey Information Satellite (*see p148*). Most restaurants serve lunch and dinner; try unpopular hours such as 11am or 4pm if other times are unavailable. Lunch is usually about two-thirds of the price of dinner, and children's menus are available at even the smartest restaurants.

Recommended in World Showcase are:
Mexico: the San Angel Inn serves interesting and pricey Mexican cuisine. It is the most romantic place to dine at Epcot.
Norway: Akershus offers a good-value *koldtbord* (buffet) of unfamiliar Norwegian dishes in a castle setting.
Germany: the Biergarten has a beer hall atmosphere, with a cheap and hearty buffet and hearty oompah-pah music.
Italy: L'Originale Alfredo di Roma restaurant is enormously popular and engagingly chaotic, with sophisticated dishes.
Japan: you can eat communally, either in the Teppanyaki Dining Rooms around a grilling, stir-frying chef, or at the bar of Tempura Kiku for sushi and tempura (no reservations).
France: there are three top-notch restaurants here: the up-market Bistro de Paris (dinner only); Chefs de France, the smartest and priciest restaurant in Epcot, with *haute cuisine* by acclaimed French chefs; and the terraced Au Petit Café (no reservations possible) for steaks, escargots and crêpes.

Recommended in Future World are:
The Land: the revolving Garden Grill passes a re-created rainforest, prairie and desert while Disney characters entertain.
The Living Seas: at the expensive Coral Reef you can both eat fish and watch fish – the latter in the pavilion's aquarium.

The film, which is shown on five adjacent screens, offers a whirlwind tour through the country's most beautiful regions set to the sounds of French classical music.

 **United Kingdom**
The Rose and Crown Pub is the appropriate focal point in the United Kingdom. It serves traditional English fare such as Cornish pasties, fish and chips and even draught bitter – though this is chilled to suit American tastes. Pleasant gardens surround the pub, as well as a medley of buildings of various historic architectural styles. These include a castle based on Hampton Court, an imitation Regency terrace and a thatched cottage (where the roof is in fact made from plastic broom bristles).

There is not much to do in the United Kingdom other than browse around the

shops, which sell everything from quality tea and china to sweaters, tartan ties, teddy bears and toy soldiers.

 Canada
Thirty-ft (9-m) high totem poles, a log cabin, a replica of Ottawa's Victorian-style Château Laurier Hotel, a rocky chasm and ornamental gardens make up the large but rather staid Canadian pavilion.

The country in all its diversity, and particularly its grand scenery, comes to life much better in the Circle-Vision film **O Canada!** (though China's Circle-Vision film is even better). The audience stands in the middle of the theatre and turns around to follow the film as it unfolds on no less than nine screens.

Shops at Canada sell a range of Indian and Inuit crafts, as well as various edible specialities, including wine.

Disney-MGM Studios

DISNEY-MGM STUDIOS opened in 1989, not only as the third and smallest theme park in Walt Disney World, but also as a fully-fledged working film and TV production facility. The park combines top-notch shows and rides, based on Disney and Metro-Goldwyn-Mayer films (to which Disney bought the rights), with educational and entertaining shows and tours that allow visitors to glimpse and experience "inside the magic" – that is, how films and TV shows are made. A number of the varied attractions change every year as each new Disney blockbuster is adapted into a show or parade. Tours are the only way to see the working parts of the studios, which take up about half the park. Like Universal Studios, Disney-MGM Studios gears itself primarily towards adults and teenagers, but it is rather more nostalgic and only about half the size.

Mann's Chinese Theatre

TACKLING THE PARK

VISITORS TO Disney-MGM Studios should realize two things: firstly, everything can be seen in a single day, particularly when the park closes late; secondly, the park is relatively small and has few attractions, so it can be very crowded. The Guest Information Board at the junction of Hollywood and Sunset Boulevards gives details of queuing times.

It is best to arrive early and to deal with as many of the most popular rides and shows as possible straight away: see the Top Five list opposite.

The best time for the educational tours – Disney-MGM Studios Backlot Tour and The Magic of Disney Animation – is during office hours, when there's more work going on. In the evening, enjoy the outdoor shows and the rest of the park: lasers and neon make Disney-MGM Studios enchanting after dark.

The layout at Disney-MGM Studios can be confusing. The theme park, with open access, occupies the map's bottom half, covering Hollywood and Sunset Boulevards, Echo Lake and New York Street (which double as potential filming sets). The studios' working areas lie in the map's top half, in the area marked as Sound Stages.

There's a fair chance, particularly in winter, that TV shows will be taping in the Sound Stages. Details are posted and tickets given out (always on a first-come first-served basis) at the Production Information Window by the turnstiles outside the park.

Many young children find the thrill rides at Disney-MGM Studios too intense and the educational tours too long and technical. Most popular among kids are the Voyage of The Little Mermaid and the two outdoor musical shows based on recent animated Disney films, staged in New York Street and on Sunset Boulevard.

Jim Henson's Muppet™ Vision 3-D

Honey, I Shrunk the Kids

Disney-MGM Studios Backlot Tour

Star Tours

Monster Sound Show

Indian Jones™ Epic Stunt Spectacular!

0 metres   100

0 yards   100

PARADES AND FIREWORKS

One spectacle that should not be missed is the joyous Disney-MGM Studios parade, which is based on any of the major Disney films (for example *Toy Story* or *101 Dalmatians*). This occurs twice a day in high season, once in low season: the exact times are provided on the guidemap. Sorcery in the Sky, arguably the best fireworks display in all of Walt Disney World, takes place ten minutes before closing when the park stays open until 9pm or later. The sky is illuminated to the music from *Fantasia*, one of Walt Disney's earliest and best-loved animated films.

◁ **Hollywood Boulevard, the main street of Disney-MGM Studios**

Hollywood Boulevard

Garish, neon-decked buildings, some sleek Art Deco creations, others in fanciful mock oriental or Spanish styles, make the main street of Disney-MGM Studios like a utopian vision of Hollywood's 1930s and '40s Golden Age. Hollywood doesn't and never did look like this.

So-called Streetsmosphere Characters (a lively crew of starlets, policemen, cabbies and reporters) pester guests for autographs, or chase an exclusive story or photo. The air is filled with the sound of piped music or tunes played by roving entertainers.

There are shops to explore *(see p158)*, but you can linger over these later. Head first for The Great Movie Ride.

The Great Movie Ride
Dominating the central plaza is a full-scale reproduction of Mann's Chinese Theatre, with hand and footprints of celebrities embedded in the pavement – just as at the real theatre on the real Hollywood Boulevard. Inside, guests board vehicles for the unmissable, fast-moving Great Movie Ride.

The tour takes a long and fond look at scenes from films as diverse as *Casablanca, Singin' in the Rain, Raiders of the Lost Ark, The Wizard of Oz* and *Alien*, with remarkably realistic Audio-Animatronics personifications of the likes of James Cagney, Clint Eastwood and John Wayne. Some real live action (by humans) is thrown in too.

Sunset Boulevard

Like Hollywood Boulevard, Sunset Boulevard is a rose-tinted evocation of the famous Hollywood street in the 1940s. Beneath an avenue of palm trees, theatres and shopfronts (some real, some merely façades) have been re-created with Disney's characteristic attention to detail; dominating one end is the Hollywood Tower Hotel.

Mickey is usually signing autographs at the Beverly Sunset Theater, and when you visit, the tea cups and candles may still be dancing in the long-running **"Beauty and the Beast" Live on Stage** show at the Theater of the Stars.

The Twilight Zone Tower of Terror™
The lightning-ravaged, decrepit Hollywood Tower Hotel is the venue for Orlando's scariest ride – in which you're strapped into the service elevator for a voyage inspired by the 1950s TV show *The Twilight Zone™*.

The elevator doors open to allow glimpses of ghostly corridors, but it's hard to concentrate on anything other than the ghastly 13-storey plunge that everyone knows will come – but not exactly when. If you aren't into big thrills, the special effects are superb; and you can also enjoy the fleeting view over the whole park before you begin the descent.

Top 5 Attractions

- [4] **Jim Henson's Muppet™ Vision 3d**
- [2] **Star Tours**
- [3] **The Great Movie Ride**
- [4] **Voyage of The Little Mermaid**
- [5] **Twilight Zone Tower of Terror™**

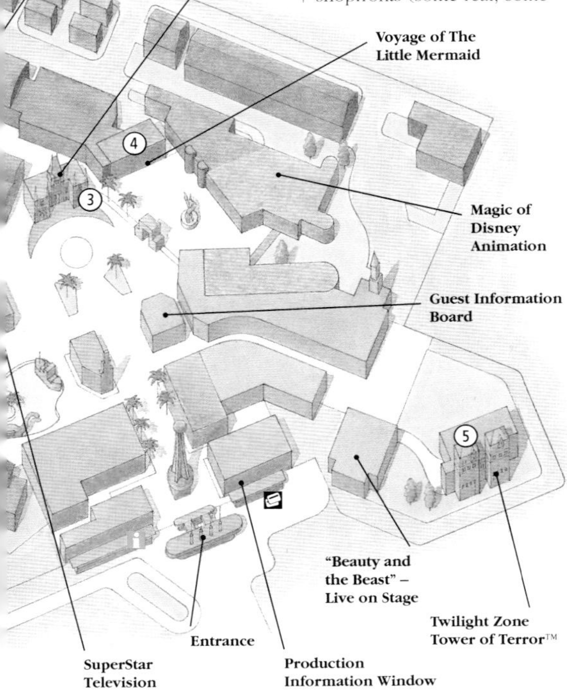
Backstage Pass to "101 Dalmatians"
The Great Movie Ride
Voyage of The Little Mermaid
Magic of Disney Animation
Guest Information Board
"Beauty and the Beast" – Live on Stage
Twilight Zone Tower of Terror™
Entrance
SuperStar Television
Production Information Window
4
3
5

Key

- Hollywood Boulevard
- Sunset Boulevard
- Animation Courtyard
- Sound Stages
- New York Street
- Echo Lake
- Perimeter area
- Guest Relations
- ATM/bank

Animation Courtyard

THE BIG APPEAL of Animation Courtyard is the chance to have a glimpse behind the scenes during the creation of Disney's Audio-Animatronics.

Magic of Disney Animation
The most fascinating tour at Disney-MGM Studios begins with a display of Walt Disney's many Oscar® awards and original "cels" – drawings that each represent a frame in an animated film. After a film in which actor Robin Williams introduces you to how cartoons are created, you enter the working studios. Here, you are separated from the Disney animators by windows, but video monitors explain what you are seeing at each stage – such as the development of the story line in the Story Room or the refining of the cartoon images in the Ink and Paint departments.

Voyage of The Little Mermaid
Inspired by the animated feature film *The Little Mermaid*, this is a song and dance show enacted by cartoon, live and Audio-Animatronics characters. Lasers and water effects are used to create the feel of an underwater grotto. It helps if you know the film, but the

show remains one of the most popular in the park. It appeals to all ages, although young children sometimes find the lightning storm scary.

Sound Stages

LIKE THE Magic of Disney Animation tour, the Sound Stages provide an opportunity to see how things are done in the working part of the studios. Films called *The Making of...*, which explain how the latest Disney releases were created, are often technically complex but fascinating. If time is short, you should concentrate on the Studios Backlot Tour.

Backstage Pass to "101 Dalmatians"
This 25-minute tour devoted to the film *101 Dalmatians* starts with the chance for you to meet several puppy dalmatians with their trainer. Further in, you're shown how the puppet puppies are made and operated. A number of props used in the film are also on display.

Disney-MGM Studios Backlot Tour
Although it never fails to be entertaining, this half-hour tour best comes to life when a film is actually being shot.
A tram ride takes you for a peek at the wardrobe, camera,

props and lighting departments as well as the suburban homes used as outdoor sets for TV shows. The scene everyone remembers is just-for-fun Catastrophe Canyon, where the tram ends up in the midst of a flood and explosions.
The walking part of the tour is more informative. With audience participation, it demonstrates some of the special effects used in making films; battle scenes at sea are re-created using just models in a water tank. You also get to look in on three sound stages, where, if you're lucky, a TV show, commercial or movie might be being filmed.

New York Street

THE BRICKS AND STONE in this version of New York are in fact just painted on plastic and fibreglass, the buildings' façades simply propped up with girders. Washing on the line outside a brownstone, a Chinese laundry and the Empire State Building (painted in forced perspective to make it appear tall) add authenticity to the Big Apple. The streets were once closed to visitors, but you can now wander around freely – even though the set is still used for filming.

The Hunchback of Notre Dame: A Musical Adventure
This musical is based on the animated film *The Hunchback of Notre Dame*, released by Disney in 1996.

Honey, I Shrunk the Kids Movie Set Adventure
If you've got young children, don't miss this imaginative playground with 30-ft (9-m) high blades of grass, a slide made from a roll of film and an ant the size of a pony. The tunnels, slides and other props keep children amused for hours. Being small, the play area can get very crowded, so it's best to go early.

Jim Henson's Muppet™ Vision 3-D
In this highly enjoyable, slapstick 3-D movie (starring the Muppets), trombones, cars and rocks launch themselves

---

Eating and Drinking

It is definitely worth going to the trouble of making a reservation for three of the full-service restaurants at Disney-MGM Studios, though more for their atmosphere than their food. You can reserve a table by calling (407) 939-3463/WDW-DINE, or by going directly to the Dining Reservation Booth (at the crossroads of Hollywood and Sunset boulevards) or to the restaurants themselves.
The civilized, costly Hollywood Brown Derby replicates the Original Brown Derby in Hollywood, where the stars met in the 1930s – right down to the celebrities' caricatures on the walls and the house specialities of Cobb Salad and grapefruit cake. Kids usually prefer the Sci-Fi Dine-In Theater Restaurant, a 1950s drive-in where customers sit in mini Cadillacs under a starry sky to watch old science-fiction movies, while munching on popcorn and burgers. In the '50's Prime Time Café you are served by maternal waitresses in 1950s kitchens with the TV tuned to period sitcoms; the food, such as meatloaf and pot roast, is homely.
The best place to eat without a reservation is the self-service Art Deco-themed cafeteria Hollywood & Vine, where you can choose from a varied menu that includes pasta, salads, seafood, ribs and steaks.

at you out of the screen; they are so realistic that children often grasp the air expecting to touch something.

Audio-Animatronics characters and special effects, such as cannon blowing holes in the walls of the theatre, provide the fourth dimension.

ECHO LAKE

THE INTEREST here focuses on three shows and one thrill ride, though children will also enjoy the sight of a great green dinosaur. The shows reveal a few tricks of the trade used in making movies and TV shows. While educational, the aim is above all to entertain.

Monster Sound Show
In this show, selected members of the audience act as audio or "Foley" artists – Foley being the name of the sound effects system used in Hollywood. They add thunder, lightning and other sounds to a short mystery-comedy film, which is then played back to the rest of the audience. The degree of entertainment depends on the skill of the amateurs.

SoundWorks
In this play area, as enjoyable as the Monster Sound Show, you can experience amazingly realistic noises in a Sound-sensations booth.

SHOPPING

Shops at Disney-MGM Studios specialize in film-orientated merchandise as well as the usual Disney gifts and souvenirs. Most of the best shops are on Hollywood Boulevard, which stays open half an hour after the rest of the theme park has closed. Mickey's of Hollywood is the big emporium for general Disney merchandise. Celebrity 5 & 10 has a plethora of affordable movie souvenirs, such as clapper boards and Oscars®, as well as books and posters. Much pricier is Sid Cahuenga's One-Of-A-Kind, where you can buy rare film and TV memorabilia such as genuine autographed photos (of Boris Karloff and Greta Garbo, for example), or famous actors' clothes. Limited-edition "cels" in Animation Gallery in Animation Courtyard will make an even bigger dent in your wallet; the same shop sells good Disney posters and books too.

SuperStar Television
A few lucky guests are chosen to be filmed on a popular chat show and in celebrated American sitcoms such as *I Love Lucy* and *Cheers*. The rest of the audience can sit back and laugh at their efforts as they appear on the television monitors. Thanks to the special effects, it seems as though the novices are actually on screen with the real actors.

You should be at the front of the queue at least half an hour in advance to have a chance of being filmed.

Star Tours
The storyline of this sensational ride is based on the *Star Wars* films. Your spaceship, a flight simulator akin to those used to train astronauts, takes a wrong turn and has to evade meteors and cope in an inter-galactic battle. What you see on screen seems unbelievably real since your craft jolts in synchronicity with the action.

Indiana Jones™ Epic Stunt Spectacular!
This large-scale show re-creates well-known scenes from the Indiana Jones movies to deliver lots of big bangs and daredevil feats to thrill the audience. Death-defying stuntmen leap between buildings as they avoid sniper fire and sudden explosions. As an educational sideline, the stunt director and real stunt doubles demonstrate how some action sequences are realized. Try to arrive early if you want to take part as an extra in the show.

RIDES, SHOWS AND TOURS CHECKLIST

This chart is designed to help you plan your visit to Disney-MGM Studios. The rides, shows and tours are listed alphabetically by area.

(R) RIDE   (S) SHOW   (T) TOUR

	LIKELY TO QUEUE 30 MINS OR MORE	LASTS LESS THAN 15 MINUTES	MAY CAUSE MOTION SICKNESS	SCARY FOR ADULTS	QUALITY AUDIO-ANIMATRONICS	GOOD FOR PRE-SCHOOL KIDS	EDUCATIONAL
GREAT MOVIE RIDE (R)	●				●		●
"BEAUTY AND THE BEAST" LIVE ON STAGE (S)						●	
TWILIGHT ZONE TOWER OF TERROR™ (R)	●		●	■			
MAGIC OF DISNEY ANIMATION (T)							●
VOYAGE OF THE LITTLE MERMAID (S)	●				●	●	
BACKSTAGE PASS TO "101 DALMATIANS" (T)						●	●
DISNEY-MGM STUDIOS BACKLOT TOUR (T)						●	●
THE HUNCHBACK OF NOTRE DAME (S)						●	
JIM HENSON'S MUPPET™ VISION 3-D (S)	●					●	
INDIANA JONES™ EPIC STUNT SPECTACULAR! (S)							●
MONSTER SOUND SHOW (S)							●
STAR TOURS (R)	●	■	●				
SUPERSTAR TELEVISION (S)							

The Rest of the Walt Disney World® Resort

THERE IS A LOT MORE to Walt Disney World than just its theme parks. At the last count, it also included 18 gigantic resorts, a camp ground, three water parks, nearly 200 places to eat, a variety of nightclubs, a nature reserve, a shopping village and half a dozen golf courses. There are also many opportunities for water sports and fishing trips on its network of lakes. As with the rest of Walt Disney World, opening hours can vary according to the time of year, and outdoor attractions may be affected by changes due to the weather.

DISNEY'S ANIMAL KINGDOM

OPEN FROM spring 1998, Disney's Animal Kingdom is the largest of the Disney theme parks, being five times the size of the Magic Kingdom. Here, exhilarating rides are combined with a rich variety of exotic landscapes, flora and fauna – some genuine, some make-believe.

The park consists of three sections: the real, the mythical and the extinct. The first is a re-created African savannah, where visitors go on safari and get a close-up view of herds of giraffe, elephant and zebra. Dragons, unicorns and other fanciful creatures are brought to life in the mythical section with the help of magic, story-telling and the latest Audio-Animatronics technology.

Using similar techniques, the spotlight is then turned on the extinct, giving you the chance to witness the ferocious Tyrannosaurus rex and other dinosaurs live and die before your very eyes.

THE WATER PARKS

THE MOST POPULAR places in which to recuperate after a day in a theme park are the three beautifully designed and well-supervised water parks. Each has beaches and pools, plus slides for the more energetic. Once you have bought an admission ticket, all rides are free. One-day hopper passes provide admission to any of the three water parks as well as to Discovery Island.

In summer, the water parks can get very crowded and may close their car parks by noon; visit early to minimize queuing for rides. Most parks open at 9 or 10am and in summer close at around 7pm. The parks may close for periods of renovation in winter, so call ahead to avoid disappointment.

Blizzard Beach
((407) 560-3400.
The improbable theme for the newest, biggest and most imaginative of Disney's water parks is an Alpine ski resort. Icicles hang from roofs while shops request that you leave your skis outside. Cable cars take you up Mount Gushmore, topped by a snowy ski jump, from where you can take dare-devil rides such as Summit Plummet and Slush Gusher. At a height of 120 ft (37 m), Summit Plummet is claimed to be the tallest speed slide in the world. At Melt Away Bay there's sand and a large wave pool, as well as two excellent pre-teen play areas.

Typhoon Lagoon
((407) 560-4141.
Complete with a shipwrecked fishing boat stranded on top of a mountain, Typhoon Lagoon re-creates a tropical resort in the aftermath of a major storm.

In addition to its thrill rides, this vast watery playground is beautifully landscaped, with lush gardens, a long circular river for floating in inner tubes through caves and a make-believe rainforest, and (best of all) a huge lagoon with waves. You can go white-water rafting and snorkel amid a man-made reef alongside real exotic fish and harmless small sharks.

An exhilarating slide down Summit Plummet at Blizzard Beach

ROMANCE DISNEY STYLE

Already the most popular honeymoon destination in the United States, Walt Disney World is also putting in its bid to become the top place in the country in which to get married. Should you decide on a Disney wedding, you and your spouse-to-be could arrive at the wedding pavilion in Cinderella's glass coach to be greeted by Alice and the Mad Hatter; later, your nuptials over, you could then be whisked away in a limousine chauffeured by Mickey Mouse, to prepare for your honeymoon at one of the nearby Disney resorts. If this doesn't appeal to you, more traditional and elegant ceremonies are also available.

You can wed at any of the theme parks and at many of the resorts, most of which offer honeymoon packages too; the Polynesian Resort is considered the most romantic. Special wedding co-ordinators can arrange everything from gown design to bachelor parties. The cost of the ceremony ranges from $950 to over $1,200, depending on how many frills you require. Everything else is extra, including hotel costs (you have to stay at least four nights in Walt Disney World). Call (407) 363-6333 for Disney wedding information, and (407) 934-7639 for honeymoon packages.

River Country

C *(407) 824-2760.*

The oldest water park in Walt Disney World is also by far the smallest, and, like everything in and around Fort Wilderness, can be quite awkward to get to. Nevertheless, situated right alongside Bay Lake, the park is delightfully pretty. It has been designed to resemble a back woods swimming hole and is equipped with rope swings and water flumes.

The centrepiece is a naturalistic cove, crossed by wooden bridges and fed by chutes of water gushing like waterfalls from pine trees and rocks. Consider visiting in conjunction with Discovery Island, whose ferry is just yards away.

FORT WILDERNESS AND DISCOVERY ISLAND

FIRST AND FOREMOST, the 700 acres (285 ha) of woods in Fort Wilderness are a camp ground. However, its facilities for horse riding and bike and canoe hire are available to everyone.

To reach Fort Wilderness you must park your car at its entrance and take a bus, or you can arrive by boat from the Magic Kingdom *(see p143)*.

Discovery Island, only a short ferry ride from the Fort Wilderness marina (or a longer boat trip from the Magic Kingdom) is a magical 11-acre (4-ha) nature reserve, home to over 100 species. A path winds through dense (imported) tropical foliage and takes you to see exotic animals such as Galapagos tortoises. There are numerous colourful birds to see, many of which reside in a gigantic aviary.

Fort Wilderness and Discovery Island

C *(407) 824-3784.*

WDW RESORTS

NON-RESIDENTS can dine and shop in any of the Disney resorts. The ones located on the monorail can be reached easily from the Magic Kingdom and Epcot and provide the option of taking a break from the theme parks during the day; they are also a popular place to eat and make merry in the evening.

Most of the resorts follow a theme and are sights in their own right. At the **Polynesian Resort** coconut palms and tropical plants help re-create a South Pacific island, while the Victorian-styled **Grand Floridian Beach Resort** provides a convincing imitation of a grand 19th-century railway hotel. These two resorts, both near the Magic Kingdom, are more popular than most.

Opened in 1996, **Disney's BoardWalk Resort** goes out of its way to provide entertainment for all, not just for its guests. Modelled after a 1920s-style waterfront village, it features a boardwalk and a green, with shops, restaurants, old-fashioned dance halls and nightclubs – as well as a hotel and villas *(see pp303–304)*.

The **Disney Institute** *(see p304)* adopts a totally different approach, promoting the idea that you can combine a theme park holiday with the opportunity for self-improvement. Its hotel-cum-campus is aimed at adults and families with older children, and courses cover 60 activities from film production to rock climbing. Any resident of Walt Disney World is welcome to sample a day at the Institute, which costs about $50 and also enables you to use its entertainment and sports facilities.

Individual Disney resorts are described in the hotels listings on pages 303–304, their restaurants on pages 322–23.

WALT DISNEY WORLD AFLOAT

Ever keen to expand, Disney is now getting involved in the lucrative cruise business. *Disney Magic* and *Disney Wonder*, which set sail in 1998, are at the cutting edge of cruise ship design, being 25 per cent bigger than the average ocean liner. The usual Disney abundance of facilities and entertainment is provided, from restaurants and adult-only nightclubs to game shows and fitness programmes; each ship has almost an entire deck dedicated to children.

The ships' course follows a route from Port Canaveral in Florida to Nassau in the Bahamas, and from there to Disney's private island, known as Castaway Cay. Three- to seven-day package deals cost from $700 to over $3,500, and usually comprise half a week at Walt Disney World and half a week at sea. For further details or bookings call (407) 566-7000.

EATING AND DRINKING

The best Disney restaurants are in the resorts, but there are others at some of the attractions. The ones listed here do not require reservations.

Fort Wilderness: *Trail's End Buffeteria* serves good-value, hearty breakfast, lunch and dinner buffets (roasts, pastas, pizzas) in the rustic Pioneer Hall close to River Country; the adjacent *Crockett's Tavern* dishes up sides of beef, spare ribs and fried chicken for dinner.

Disney Village Marketplace: *Cap'n Jack's* is best known for its steamed or baked garlic oysters and peel-and-eat prawns. Local cuisine, including seafood, is also served at the more expensive *Fulton's Crabhouse*, inside a four-storey ship. Try the pan-fried oysters and crab cakes.

Pleasure Island: *Planet Hollywood*, a gigantic restaurant in a purple neon globe by the entrance to Pleasure Island, is the most visually startling of the international chain of Planet Hollywoods. Come for the loud music, video screens, movie memorabilia and ships, cars and planes suspended from the ceiling. *Portobello Yacht Club* serves fine freshly made pasta, a range of gourmet pizzas and other northern Italian cuisine. The *Fireworks Factory*, in a similarly expensive price range, offers explosive cocktails at the crowded bar and serves great barbecue meals, smoked specialities, hearty steaks and fresh seafood.

SPORTING ACTIVITIES

AT FORT WILDERNESS, Disney Village Marketplace and at all the lakeside resorts, you can rent jet skis and all kinds of boats. You can water-ski on the Seven Seas Lagoon and Bay Lake, and fishing trips are also available. Every resort has sports and fitness facilities but these are for residents only.

Known also as the "Magic Linkdom", Walt Disney World has six golf courses, five of which are championship level; reservations are recommended.

Motor racing fans can see professional races at the Walt Disney World Speedway, just south of the Magic Kingdom.

Golf Reservations
(407) 824 2270.

Disney's Wide World of Sports
(407) 824-4321.
This massive sports complex, which occupies over 200 acres (80 ha) of Walt Disney World, was opened in 1997. There are facilities for over 30 sports ranging from basketball and American football to sumo wrestling. It has its own football pitches and a 7,500-seat baseball stadium, which are both used for professional

competitions as well as training programmes. The Harlem Globetrotters and the Atlanta Braves baseball squad now have their training sites here. There is also a track-and-field complex, a golf driving range and 12 tennis courts.

WDW AFTER DARK

AFTER THE THEME PARKS close, as well as relaxing at the resorts you should consider checking out Disney's prime after-dark entertainment area or taking in a dinner show.

Downtown Disney
(407) 828-3058.
Downtown Disney divides into three distinct but neighbouring areas: Pleasure Island, Disney Village Marketplace and Disney's West Side.

Keen nightclubbers will like **Pleasure Island** the most, although every visitor should experience its sheer size and slick razzle-dazzle. The wide range of clubs offer music to suit all tastes. There is a disco devoted to 1970s music and a trendy club (for over 21s) with a revolving dance floor. An improvised comedy club, the Comedy Warehouse, is hugely popular, and at the eccentric Adventurers Club the offbeat

paraphernalia on the walls sometimes comes to life. "A full-blown New Year's Eve celebration every night" takes the form of fireworks and a rousing song and dance performance outdoors. Allow a whole evening to do justice to Pleasure Island; a single admission ticket allows entry to all the clubs.

Disney Village Marketplace is a very pretty outdoor mall. It doesn't deserve your valuable Disney time during the day, but it is a pleasant place to browse around in the evening. Located by a lake, the marketplace is dotted with topiaries and fountains (which children love playing in). There are over a dozen shops, including The World of Disney, which is the largest emporium selling Disney merchandise in Walt Disney World – and that's saying something.

The most recent addition to Downtown Disney is **Disney's West Side**. The attractions here include the House of Blues, serving up live blues and jazz, and Bongo's Cuban Café, a restaurant and club created by Gloria Estefan. There is also a 24-screen cinema and a circus, where the famous Cirque du Soleil will eventually perform.

Dinner shows
(407) 939-3463.
These shows shouldn't tempt you to leave the theme parks early, but they are still good fun. You need to book about three months in advance to secure seats at the Hoop-Dee-Doo Musical Revue, a Western comedy in Fort Wilderness's Pioneer Hall. It's easier to get tickets to see the Polynesian Luau's South Seas dancing, at the Polynesian Resort. For both shows, you can reserve up to two years in advance.

Electrical Water Pageant
Every night a set of illuminated sea creatures appears briefly on a flotilla of barges in front of the hotels around the Seven Seas Lagoon and in Bay Lake in a little-publicized but charming spectacle. The pageant usually begins outside the Polynesian Resort at 9pm and ends at the Contemporary Resort about an hour later.

WALT DISNEY WORLD TIPS

TYPES OF PASSES

Y OU CAN BUY one-day, one-park tickets, but if you're staying for more than three days buy one of the following passes, arranged here in ascending order of cost:
Four-Day Value Pass: entitles one-day admission to each theme park, plus a second day in one park, on any four days.
Four-Day Park-Hopper Pass: offers unlimited access to the theme parks on any four days.
Five-Day World-Hopper Pass: gives unlimited access to the theme parks on any five days, and to Pleasure Island and the water parks within seven days of the first use of the pass. If you're staying a whole week, this is the best pass to buy.
Annual Pass: great value for repeat visitors; unused days on passes never expire.

Note that these passes may change once Disney's Animal Kingdom is open.

Regarding prices, adulthood starts at age 10 at Walt Disney World. Three- to nine-year-olds get a reduction of 20 per cent; under threes enter free.

BUSIEST DAYS

D ISNEY MAINTAINS that each of the theme parks is consistently busy on certain days, but crowding will also depend on the day on which each park offers early entry to Disney resort guests. The busiest days are as follows:
Magic Kingdom: Monday, Thursday and Saturday.
Epcot: Tuesday, Friday and Saturday.
Disney-MGM Studios: Wednesday and Sunday.

OPENING HOURS

W HEN THE theme parks are busiest, opening hours are the longest, typically 9am to 10/11pm or midnight. Days are shorter in less busy periods, usually 9am to 6/7/8pm. Call in advance to check.

At any time of year, the theme parks usually open at least 30 minutes ahead of schedule. Attractions close at the official closing time, but many shops stay open longer.

THE IDEAL SCHEDULE

T O AVOID the worst of the crowds and the heat:
• Arrive as early as possible and visit the most popular attractions straightaway.
• Take a break in the early afternoon, when it's hottest and the parks are busiest.
• Return to the parks in the cool of the evening, when you can often see parades and fireworks displays.

COPING WITH QUEUES

Q UEUES TEND TO BE shortest at the beginning and end of the day, diminishing a bit at parade and meal times.
• Queues for the rides move slowly. Shows, by contrast, can absorb as many as 1,000 spectators at a time; most of them run continuously, and the wait is rarely longer than the length of the show.
• Normally, signs along the queue indicate the length of wait. Ask a Disney "cast member" if in doubt.

WDW DINING

Y OU SHOULD MAKE reservations in advance for any full-service restaurant in Walt Disney World, especially in the theme parks and above all in Epcot. Whether or not you are staying at one of the resorts, reservations can be made 60 days in advance, though tables are also kept back for same-day reservations: make bookings as early in the morning as possible. For restaurant recommendations, see pages 322–3.

MONEY

M ASTERCARD, American Express and VISA credit cards are accepted for all purchases except fast food.

WDW WITH YOUNG CHILDREN

I F YOU'VE COME with pre-school-age kids:
• Focus mainly on the Magic Kingdom.
• Realize that Walt Disney World can be both physically and emotionally tiring for young children. You should try to adapt your schedule accordingly.
• Hire a pushchair ("stroller"), available at all the theme parks: trudging around is very tiring for short legs.
• Forewarn the children that for some of the theme parks' top attractions you must be over a certain height, typically 4 ft (1.25 m).
• In a system called "switching off", parents can enjoy a ride one at a time while the other childminds – without having to queue twice.

MEETING MICKEY

F OR MANY YOUNGSTERS, the most exciting moment at Walt Disney World is meeting Mickey, Minnie, Donald and other Disney characters. You will spot them in all the theme parks and it is worth buying a Disney autograph book for them to sign.

You can have more relaxed encounters in a number of restaurants, when Disney characters turn up to liven up the proceedings (usually at breakfast time). Each theme park and many of the resorts also offer "character dining", though to dine in the company of Mickey Mouse you must ring ahead of time to make a reservation.

USEFUL NUMBERS

General information
(407) 824-4321. Or write to Guest Letters Dept, PO Box 10040, Lake Buena Vista, FL 32830-0040.
Accommodation information and reservations
(407) 934-7639/(407) W-DISNEY.
Dining reservations and character dining
(407) 939-3463/(407) WDW-DINE.

Sea World ❷

IN SCALE AND SOPHISTICATION, the world's most popular marine-life park, opened in 1973, is a match for any of Orlando's other theme parks. While keen to promote its educational, research and conservation endeavours, the park delivers out-and-out entertainment too. A big-eared mouse may help Walt Disney World to pull the crowds; Sea World's answer is Shamu, a lovable killer whale, and the Shamu show tops the bill. The park's shows are complemented by attractions that are open throughout the day, some of which allow you to touch or feed the marine life. Interactive displays and knowledgeable and enthusiastic staff add an educational angle.

Penguin Encounter
Swimming, preening, or simply standing around, hundreds of penguins entertain visitors with their antics.

Manatees: The Last Generation?
This exhibit offers the chance to get face-to-face with the remarkable manatee and explains why it is now an endangered species.

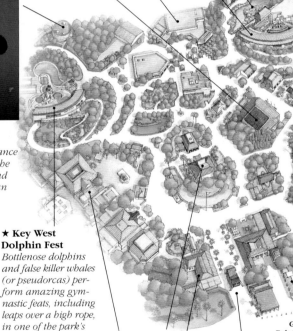

Sea World Theatre

Sea Lion and Otter Stadium

Pacific Point Preserve

Tropical Reef

Information

Entrance

Gue
Relation

★ **Key West Dolphin Fest**
Bottlenose dolphins and false killer whales (or pseudorcas) perform amazing gymnastic feats, including leaps over a high rope, in one of the park's most stunning shows.

Key West at Sea World
Visitors can actually touch the dolphins and stingrays at this attraction, which also seeks to re-create the atmosphere of Key West.

STAR ATTRACTIONS

★ **Key West Dolphin Fest**

★ **Shamu: World Focus**

★ **Wild Arctic**

★ **Shamu: World Focus**
Dramatic stunts by the park's star, Shamu the killer whale, and action on a giant video screen provide the excitement at Sea World's top show.

VISITORS' CHECKLIST

Road map E2. Orange Co. 7007 Sea World Drive, intersection of I-4 and Bee Line Expressway. (407) 351-3600. 8, 42 from Orlando. *minimum hours 9am–7pm daily; until 10pm in summer and extended hours in holiday periods.*

Shamu: Close Up!

Terrors of the Deep   Sky Tower   Nautilus Theatre

★ **Wild Arctic**
At this attraction a thrilling simulated helicopter ride transports you to a realistic arctic habitat.

0 metres   50
0 yards   50

Atlantis Bayside Stadium

SEA WORLD'S SERIOUS SIDE

The buzz words at the non-profit-making Sea World Research Institute are Research, Rescue and Rehabilitation – the "three Rs". Florida's Sea World has helped thousands of whales, dolphins, turtles and manatees in difficulty. The animals are nursed and, if necessary, operated on in the park's rehabilitation centre. Those that recover sufficiently are released back into the wild. Sea World runs three cheap and popular tours, which offer a glimpse of this work. The Sharks! tour, for example, takes you behind the scenes at Terrors of the Deep. Enquire at Guest Relations when you enter the park.

A green turtle, one of the animals rehabilitated at Sea World

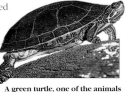

Baywatch at Sea World
Based on the hugely popular Baywatch *TV series, this show features no animals but plenty of jet skis, boats and water-skiing action.*

Exploring Sea World

ALLOW EIGHT HOURS TO SEE all of Sea World's shows and attractions. In holiday periods, when the park closes as late as 11pm, you could come at lunch time and still see everything by the end of the day. Plan your day by choosing Baywatch at Sea World and specific performances of the live animal shows, and fitting in the continuous attractions in between. The main shows happen at least two or three times a day: on arrival, you are given a schedule and a map. Leave shows that do not feature wildlife until last since they are generally the least impressive aspects of the park.

Sea lions basking on the rocks at Pacific Point Preserve

TACKLING THE PARK

SEA WORLD is usually less crowded than Orlando's other theme parks and rarely has their long queues. The stadia are so big that finding a seat is seldom a problem, though for a good seat try to arrive 15 minutes before the show starts; bear in mind that if you sit near the front you are liable to get wet. In peak periods, find a seat in good time for the Hotel Clyde and Seamore show (this is performed in the smallest stadium), and see Wild Arctic and Terrors of the Deep either early or during the Shamu or water-skiing shows.

Children should enjoy meeting the actors in furry suits who play the parts of Shamu and Crew – a killer whale accompanied by a penguin, pelican, dolphin and an otter. You can normally find them near Sea World's exit at around closing time.

For an overview of the park and everything else within a 25-mile (40-km) radius, take the six-minute ride up the 400-ft (122-m) Sky Tower.

If you have any problems or queries, go to Guest Relations, close to the exit gate.

ATTRACTIONS

THREE METICULOUSLY land- scaped outdoor habitats, including two that allow you to feed and pet the marine life, are incorporated in **Key West at Sea World**. Dolphin Cove, a wave pool in the style of a Caribbean beach,

offers underwater viewing of bottlenose dolphins and the chance to pat their noses and even feed them. You can also touch magnificent stingrays, of which there are around 200 in Stingray Lagoon; stroking them is more enjoyable than it sounds. Lastly, Turtle Point is home to rescued logger- head, hawksbill and green sea turtles which are too injured to survive on their own in the wild.

Pacific Point Preserve re-creates the rugged north Pacific coast in the form of a large, rocky pool. Here, you can watch harbour seals, South American fur seals and California sea lions (the ones making the noise) basking on the rocks and gliding elegantly through the water.

Shamu, the park's official mascot

Most of the other wildlife at Sea World is viewed through glass. **Manatees: The Last Generation?** offers a splendid

underwater view of the tiny heads and bloated bodies of these ungainly, doleful and irresistibly appealing herbi- vores *(see p236)*. The exhibit is strongly educational and includes a film show.

In the altogether more upbeat **Penguin Encounter**, a moving walkway takes you past a frozen landscape where a large colony of king, rock- hopper and other penguins demonstrate their comical waddling and elegant swim- ming. The gawky puffins are also a delight to watch.

Billed as the world's largest collection of dangerous sea creatures, **Terrors of the Deep** is understandably pop- ular. Moray eels, barracuda and pufferfish are the hors d'oeuvre before a main course of sharks, whose toothy grim- aces are just a short distance away from your head as you walk through a plastic tunnel inside their aquarium.

Dolphin Cove, where everyone can touch and feed the dolphins

Shamu: Close Up!, located alongside Shamu Stadium, is a research and breeding facility where you can study killer whales behaving more or less as they would in the wild; ten of them have actually been born in the park so far.

Wild Arctic is the park's most exciting attraction. Its first half (which the timorous can skip) is a thrilling, high-tech ride simulating a helicopter flight through blizzards and avalanches. Then you arrive at Base Station Wild Arctic, created around a 150-year-old expedition ship and kitted out with scientists' trunks, survival food and bunk beds. Most attention, however, is focussed on the engrossing antics of polar bears, walruses and beluga whales, from which you are separated by mere plates of glass.

Two adult killer whales with Baby Shamu in Shamu: World Focus

SHOWS

THE EXCITEMENT of seeing a killer whale erupt out of the water carrying one the Sea World trainers on its nose is hard to overstate. In **Shamu: World Focus** stunts such as this are supplemented by a giant video screen, which provides both close-ups of the action and footage of the beasts in the wild. The show also features the killer whales performing an amazing "underwater ballet". There are, in fact, five Shamus, which take turns to perform, as well as a Baby Shamu.

Key West Dolphin Fest is remarkable due to the speed and agility of its performing bottlenose dolphins and false killer whales. During the show, the mammals play with their trainers and also interact with members of the audience, although the highlight is the dolphins' synchronized leaps over a high rope.

The slapstick **Hotel Clyde and Seamore** show, in the Sea Lion and Otter Stadium, features two sea lions (Clyde and Seamore) which take on the roles of managers of a hotel. Along with an otter and a walrus, they mimic human movements, sounds and emotions to hilarious effect – they are even able to appear frightened or smug.

The best of the shows which do not involve live animals is **Baywatch at Sea World**. While less impressive than the water-ski extravaganza at Cypress Gardens *(see p179),*

the show incorporates speed boats, jet skis and impressive water-skiing stunts, including skiing in pyramid formation. All of this is combined with plenty of clowning around as Los Angeles County lifeguards involved in mock sea rescues, in the style of the hit television series, *Baywatch.*

Jumping between moving speed boats at Baywatch at Sea World

In **Mermaids, Myths and Monsters**, which rounds off the park's entertainment each evening, stunning images of mythical creatures are projected onto misty screens of water rising out of the lake; the accompanying laser and fireworks displays, however, are not especially spectacular.

As for the indoor shows at Sea World, **Golden Dragons Acrobats** combines beautifully choreographed juggling and balancing with oriental dance and comedy acts, enhanced by clever laser effects. Meanwhile, the **Mickey Finn Show** is Sea World's newest extravaganza – a foot-stomping Dixieland comedy show, with pianos, banjos and plenty of audience participation.

EATING, DRINKING AND SHOPPING

Bimini Bay Café, by the lake, is the park's only full-service restaurant and offers steaks, grilled fish and seafood dishes. The Smokehouse Chicken & Ribs and Waterfront Sandwich Grill, for fast food, are also pleasantly located at the lakeside. The best place for sandwiches is the Deli in the Anheuser-Busch Hospitality Center, and Florida-style finger food is available in Key West at Sea World. For entertainment while you eat, try the Polynesian Luau dinner show; it is not as good as dinner shows elsewhere but you still need to book. Souvenirs are mainly soft toys and Shamu memorabilia: Shamu's Emporium has the largest selection. Coconut Traders, at Key West at Sea World, has items made in Key West and Florida food.

Cuddly versions of Sea World's stars

Universal Studios ❸

LIKE UNIVERSAL STUDIOS in Hollywood and Disney-MGM Studios (see pp156–9), this theme park, which opened in 1990, doubles as a film and TV production centre. Here, the production centre and sound stages (where most filming takes place) are basically out-of-bounds to visitors. The theme park occupies the studios' Backlot, where painstakingly replicated Hollywood, New York and San Francisco streets serve both as film sets and as colourful backdrops for the park. The millions of visitors, though, come mainly for the thrilling rides and entertaining, educational shows on how movies are made. Most attractions appeal more to adults and teenagers than to young children. Universal is bigger and brasher than Disney-MGM Studios: visit both if time allows.

Universal Studios Globe
This enormous globe is the trademark of Universal Studios, the biggest film and TV studios in the US apart from Hollywood.

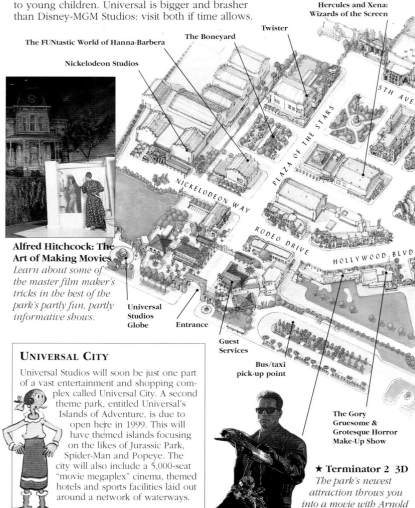

The FUNtastic World of Hanna-Barbera

Nickelodeon Studios

The Boneyard

Twister

Hercules and Xena: Wizards of the Screen

NICKELODEON WAY

PLAZA OF THE STARS

5TH AVENU

RODEO DRIVE

HOLLYWOOD BLVD

Alfred Hitchcock: The Art of Making Movies
Learn about some of the master film maker's tricks in the best of the park's partly fun, partly informative shows.

Universal Studios Globe

Entrance

Guest Services

Bus/taxi pick-up point

UNIVERSAL CITY

Universal Studios will soon be just one part of a vast entertainment and shopping complex called Universal City. A second theme park, entitled Universal's Islands of Adventure, is due to open here in 1999. This will have themed islands focusing on the likes of Jurassic Park, Spider-Man and Popeye. The city will also include a 5,000-seat "movie megaplex" cinema, themed hotels and sports facilities laid out around a network of waterways.

Olive Oyl, featured in the new park

The Gory Gruesome & Grotesque Horror Make-Up Show

★ Terminator 2 3D
The park's newest attraction throws you into a movie with Arnold Schwarzenegger, using the latest 3-D technology.

★ Kongfrontation
Board an aerial tram for a ride over Manhattan with King Kong in hot pursuit. This ride is great fun and less terrifying than some of the others.

VISITORS' CHECKLIST

Road map E2. Orange Co. 1000 Universal Plaza, exits 29 or 30B on I-4. (407) 363-8000. 21, 37, 40 from Orlando. minimum opening hours 9am–6pm daily; extended evening opening in summer and on public hols.

Beetlejuice's Graveyard Revue is a lively stage show with excellent special effects.

★ Earthquake – The Big One
Here you can learn about special-effects photography and play an extra on a train in the film Earthquake.

THE EMBARCADERO

Jaws
You can pose inside a shark's mouth or go on the Jaws ride – in a boat hounded by a great white shark.

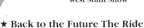
The Wild, Wild, Wild West Stunt Show

★ Back to the Future The Ride
Four minutes of simulated time-travel offer the most thrilling experience at Universal Studios, if not in the whole of Orlando.

0 metres   25
0 yards   25

Animal Actors Stage

A Day in the Park with Barney

Fievel's Playland

★ ET Adventure
This is the best ride for the whole family: an airborne bicycle adventure on which you meet dozens of animated ETs.

STAR ATTRACTIONS

★ **Kongfrontation**

★ **Earthquake – The Big One**

★ **Back to the Future The Ride**

★ **ET Adventure**

★ **Terminator 2 3D**

Exploring Universal Studios

YOU WILL NEED about 14 hours to see everything at Universal Studios. When the park is open until late, one very full day is just about long enough. When the park closes early – the only disadvantage of visiting Universal Studios in low season – you really need two days. Buy a day pass initially. Later, if you decide you want to come back, you can make a considerable saving by upgrading this to a two-day pass: just visit Guest Services, the place for all queries, as you leave. At off-peak times, you can often redeem your pass at the end of the day for one entitling you to a second day free.

Fievel's Playland, a favourite with young visitors to the park

TACKLING THE PARK

THE BUSIEST times of the year at Universal Studios are the same as at Walt Disney World *(see p138)*; weekends are normally quieter than weekdays.

Queues at Universal can if anything be longer and slower moving than at Walt Disney World: up to two hours for the best rides. At peak times, combat the queues by arriving early (the gates open up to an hour before the official opening time) and by doing as many of the popular rides *(see p169)* as possible straight away. You won't be able to do them all before the crowds arrive, so ride the others just before the park closes. When the park is busy, waiting times are posted on a notice board opposite Mel's Drive-In on Hollywood Boulevard.

You are unlikely to have to queue so long for shows. Certain shows take place at specific times, details of which are provided on the map you are given on entering the park.

Arrive 15 minutes early in high season to be sure of getting a seat. Those with no displayed schedule run continuously, and you will rarely have to wait longer than the show's duration. Queues for rides close to big shows swell considerably when the performances end.

Most rides are likely to be too intense for young children, and some have minimum height restrictions; the exception is ET Adventure. The attractions specifically designed to appeal to youngsters are A Day in the Park with Barney, Fievel's Playland and the Nickelodeon Studios.

On a very busy day, consider indulging in the four-hour VIP Tour. This provides priority admission to six attractions and a walk around the back lot and a few sound stages; phone in advance to book.

FRONT LOT

THE ENTRANCE AREA for the theme park is made to look like the front lot of a working Holly-wood film studios from the 1940s. The shooting schedule notice

Board showing the shooting schedule

LIVE FILMING

While there is no guarantee that you will be able to see live filming on the day that you visit Universal Studios, there is just a slim chance that cameras may be rolling on the backlot (within the theme park itself).

It is more probable, especially from September to December, that you could be in the audience for the taping of a TV show. You are most likely to be able to see one of Nickelodeon's kids' programmes being recorded: call (407) 363-8500 for the production schedule. Tickets for shows are issued on a first come first served basis (on the day of filming) at the booth located near Guest Services. Go there as soon as you enter the park to pick some up.

board near the turnstiles, with details of shows being filmed, is real enough, however. The park's two signature landmarks are also here: the grandiose entrance archway and, just to the left of it, the dramatic Universal Studios Globe.

Immediately inside the park, the palm-lined Plaza of the Stars has several shops *(see p173)*, but do not dally here on arrival: instead you should head off straight away to the main attractions, before the queues reach their peak.

The imposing entrance archway to Universal Studios

New York's Fifth Street, lined with impressive replica buildings

PRODUCTION CENTRAL

EXCEPT FOR The Boneyard, a repository of interesting old film props such as a pram from *The Flintstones* and fake plastic topiary from *Edward Scissorhands*, this is the least aesthetic section of the park. Maps show the studios' main sound stages here, but these are actually off limits to those not on a VIP Tour.

Production Central's one ride, **The FUNtastic World of Hanna-Barbera**, is great fun. Messrs Hanna and Barbera are the creators of such world-famous cartoon characters as the Flintstones, Yogi Bear and Scooby Doo. In the ride, you seem to chase Dick Dastardly and the others right into the cartoons as your seat judders violently in time with the action on the screen.

There are two educational shows. **Alfred Hitchcock: The Art of Making Movies** begins with a collage of his 53 movies, including 3-D clips of *Dial M for Murder* and *The Birds*. It then reveals various cinematic tricks, such as how the famous shower scene from *Psycho* was created by using selective camera angles.

In **Hercules and Xena: Wizards of the Screen** you can see how the popular TV shows *Xena: Warrior Princess* and *Hercules: The Legendary Journeys* are made. The highlight is the use of live action and special effects to give you the chance to fight gods and other mythical creatures as if in a real episode.

The **Nickelodeon Studios Tour** visits the production centre of Nickelodeon, a very popular American TV network exclusively for young people. Also pitched at children, the tour lets you have a peek at a couple of sound studios (but be warned that there is no assurance that anything will be happening), and finishes with several messy party games in the Game Lab. Children will enjoy the Slime Geyser outside, which erupts in a shower of green slime approximately every ten minutes or so.

The Slime Geyser erupting outside Nickelodeon Studios

NEW YORK

THIS BACKLOT AREA has more than 60 façades, some of which replicate real buildings, others which reproduce those which have only ever appeared on screen. There are cut-outs of the Guggenheim Museum and New York Public Library, cleverly creating an illusion of depth and distance. Macy's, the famous department store, is there, as is Louie's Italian Restaurant, where a shootout took place in the original *Godfather* movie. The shop-fronts, warehouses and even the cobblestones have been painted to appear old in a process called "distressing".

Behind the front façade of Pennsylvania Station (which appears as it was in *Strangers on a Train*) is New York's top attraction, **Kongfrontation**. On this ride, you enter a subway station to take an aerial tramway across the East River. Below are the streets of 1970s Manhattan, pulverized by King Kong. Soon the largest ever computer-animated figure – with an arm span of over 50 ft (15 m) – is shaking the tramway, swatting helicopters and breathing his banana breath all over you. In truth, most passengers find the ride more fun than scary.

Twister, new for 1998, pits visitors against Mother Nature at her most ferocious inside a huge compound containing a simulated tornado: you will experience the terrifying power of the elements as you stand within 20 ft (6 m) of the five storey-high funnel of winds.

MEETING THE STARS

Actors in wonderful costumes wander the streets playing the likes of Ghostbusters, Jake and Elwood from *The Blues Brothers*, Frankenstein, the Flintstones and legends of the silver screen such as Marilyn Monroe and the Marx Brothers; they tend to congregate in the Front Lot.

Daily during the high season, and twice a week in low season, you can eat with the stars at a Character Breakfast in the park an hour prior to the scheduled opening time. Reservations are required: call (407) 354-6339 to book.

Actress playing screen star Marilyn Monroe

HOLLYWOOD

H OLLYWOOD BOULEVARD and
Rodeo Drive are the most
attractive streets in Universal
Studios. While ignoring actual
geography, these sets pay tribute to Hollywood's golden
age from the 1920s to the
1950s – in the famous Ciro's
and Mocambo nightclubs, the
luxurious Beverly Wilshire
Hotel, the top beauty salon,
Max Factor, and the movie
palace, Pantages Theater.

The Brown Derby was a
restaurant shaped like a hat
where the film glitterati once
congregated; Universal's own
version is a fun hat shop.
Schwab's Pharmacy, where
hopefuls hung out sipping
sodas and waiting to be discovered, is brought back to
life as an old-fashioned ice-
cream parlour. Notice too the
Hollywood Walk of Fame, with
the names of stars embedded
in the pavement, just as in the
real Hollywood Boulevard.

Hollywood Boulevard, a fine example of the park's superbly created sets

The Gory, Gruesome & Grotesque
Horror Make-Up Show

The top attraction in Hollywood is **Terminator 2 3D**.
This ride uses the latest in 3-D
film technology and robotics,
together with explosive live
stunts, to catapult the audience
into the action alongside the
star of the *Terminator* films,
Arnold Schwarzenegger. A
typical sequence, combining
film and live action, has a
Harley-Davidson "Fat Boy"
dramatically bursting off the
screen and on to the stage.

**The Gory, Gruesome &
Grotesque Horror Make-Up
Show** is the funniest of the
semi-educational attractions
at Universal Studios. The audience is shown scenes from
films such as *The Exorcist, The
Fly* and *An American Werewolf*

in London, and then bloodied
and automated masks are
used to demonstrate how the
special effects are realized.

EXPO CENTER

T HE INSPIRATION behind Expo
Center's architecture is the
Los Angeles 1984 Olympics
and Expo '86 in Vancouver.
The emphasis here is on the
rides and shows.

**Back to the Future The
Ride** is the most popular ride
at Universal, and the most
intense in Orlando; note all
the health warnings before
queueing. No knowledge of
the *Back to the Future* films
is needed to enjoy this journey
in a time-travelling sports car.
The car's movements are synchronized to the action on a
mammoth wraparound screen,
making it seem as though you
really are plunging over a flow
of molten lava, skimming ice
fields and flying right into the
mouth of a dinosaur.

In contrast, everyone should
ride the enchanting, tame **ET
Adventure**, based on Steven

Spielberg's 1982 movie. You
are off to ET's home planet on
a flying bicycle, soaring over
a twinkling cityscape before
arriving at a world inhabited
by ET lookalikes.

In the **Animal Actors Stage**
show, animal lookalikes take
the parts of canine superstars
such as Lassie and Beethoven
and demonstrate how they are
trained for film work. Among
other creatures, a skunk, a cat,
a horse, a chimp and birds
also perform tricks.

**A Day in the Park with
Barney** appeals only to young
children. A musical show set
in a magical park, it features
a lovable Tyrannosaurus Rex
called Barney – hero of *Barney
& Friends*, a top pre-school
American TV show.

Fievel's Playland is inspired
by the popular animated films
An American Tail and *An
American Tail: Fievel Goes
West*. Fievel is a mouse, and
the playground's props, such
as a cowboy hat, boots, glasses
and a tea cup, are giant – just
as they would seem to the
films' star rodent.

Back to the Future The Ride – Universal's most thrilling ride

SAN FRANCISCO/AMITY

HALF OF THIS AREA is based on San Francisco, notably the city's Fisherman's Wharf district. Chez Alcatraz, for instance, is a snack bar closely modelled on the ticket kiosks for tours to Alcatraz Island.

San Francisco's big draw is **Earthquake – The Big One**, a ride with an educational angle. First, the audience is shown how earthquakes can be simulated using detailed models, and how actors can be superimposed onto dramatic scenes. Then you find yourself riding a subway train in the movie *Earthquake*. An earthquake measuring 8.3 on the Richter scale hits, a tidal wave descends, an oil tanker erupts and trains collide. After it's all over, you can watch as the set rights itself again.

Of more limited appeal is **Beetlejuice's Graveyard Revue**. Derived from the 1988 comedy horror film *Beetlejuice*, this is a song-and-dance, rock-and-roll show starring the likes of Dracula and Frankenstein.

Amity, the other half of this corner of the park, is named after the fictional village in New England which was the setting for the 1975 film *Jaws*, where a killer shark terrorizes a resort. Huts festooned with lobster buoys set the tone, added to which is a boardwalk fairground based on the one in the film *Big*. A "Jaws" is strung up on a gallows: people stick

Beetlejuice show's sign

EATING, DRINKING AND SHOPPING

The food in Universal Studios is generally good. The Hard Rock Café is the largest in the world, but there are plenty of other options. Advance reservations are advisable for Lombard's Landing, specializing in fish dishes, and the Studio Stars Restaurant, which serves Californian and Italian cuisine and has a good-value buffet. Mel's Drive-In is the place to go for fast food and shakes; the wonderful 1950s diner is straight out of the 1973 film *American Graffiti*.

Leave your shopping until last: shops in the Front Lot stay open after the park's official closing time. Here you'll find Universal Studios Store, with everything from fake Oscars to oven gloves with the Universal logo, and On Location, where a signed photo of your favourite film star costs hundreds of dollars. Most of the attractions have their own shop: in Hitchcock's 3-D theatre you can buy Bates Motel soap.

Gleaming Cadillacs outside Mel's Drive-In

their heads into its mouth for a photo. The **Jaws** ride starts off as a serene cruise around Amity Harbor, but soon you catch your first glimpse of the deadly dorsal fin, and then the giant great white shark is lunging relentlessly at your boat as it tears through the water at terrifying but realistic speeds. At one point your vessel is encircled by a wall of flame. All in all, it is an exhausting, exhilarating and also somewhat wet six minutes. Finally, there are two stunt shows. **The Wild, Wild, Wild West Stunt Show** is a largely slapstick affair involving lots of fake punches and plenty of high dives. During the finale the whole set blows up, but in general the show does not really live up to its title.

The **Dynamite Nights Stuntacular** is on a much bigger scale. Once a day, just before the park closes, riders perform high-speed daredevil feats in motor boats on The Lagoon. Its highlight is a 60-ft (18-m) boat jump through a three-storey wall of fire. The show is undoubtedly spectacular, but good viewing can be a problem: the best (and most crowded) spots are on either side of the lagoon, rather than at its ends, so you are advised to arrive early.

The dramatic Dynamite Nights Stuntacular, which lights up The Lagoon every night before the park closes

Downtown Orlando, dominated by the SunTrust Center

Orlando ❶

Road map E2. Orange Co.
👥 *170,000.* 🚌 🚆 🚍 🛈 *75 S
Ivanhoe Blvd, (407) 425-1234.*

UNTIL THE 1950s, Orlando was not much more than a sleepy provincial town. Its proximity to Cape Canaveral and the theme parks, however, helped change all that.

Downtown Orlando, where glass-sided high-rises mark a burgeoning business district, beckons only really at night. This is when tourists and locals flock to Church Street Station and, to a lesser degree, to the bars and restaurants on Church Street and Orange Avenue, Orlando's main street.

During the daytime, a stroll in the park around **Lake Eola**, three blocks east of Orange Avenue, is a pleasant way to while away some time. This is

Fountain at the centre of the rose garden, Harry P Leu Gardens

one of the few places where you'll get a taste of Orlando's (comparatively) early history. Overlooking the lake are a few of the wood-built homes of the town's earliest white settlers; some of these have been converted into B & Bs.

Anyone in need of a more serious antidote to the theme parks should head into the quieter residential areas just north of Downtown, where there are a number of parks and museums. If you are short of time, Winter Park should be your priority.

❦ Loch Haven Park
N Mills Avenue at Rollins St.
Orlando Museum of Art 📞 *(407) 896-4231.* ◯ *Tue–Sun.* ● *public hols.*
Loch Haven Park, 2 miles (3 km) north of Downtown, is rather nondescript but has a trio of small museums. The most highly regarded of these is the Orlando Museum of Art, which has three collections on permanent show: memorable pre-Columbian artifacts, including animal figurines from Nazca in Peru, African art, and American paintings of the 19th and 20th centuries. The museum also hosts major international exhibitions.

❦ Harry P Leu Gardens
1920 N Forest Ave. 📞 *(407) 246-2620.* ◯ *daily.* ● *25 Dec.* ♿ &
The Harry P Leu Gardens offer 50 acres (20 ha) of serenely beautiful gardens in which to stroll. Elements such as Florida's largest rose garden

are formal, while elsewhere you find mature woods of spectacular live oaks, maples and bald cypresses, festooned with Spanish moss; in winter, seek out the mass of blooming camellias. Of less interest are the early 20th-century **Leu House** and its gardens, which a local businessman, called Harry P Leu, donated to the city in 1961 – perhaps as a tax write-off it is suggested.

🏛 Maitland Art Center
231 W Packwood Ave, 6 miles (9 km) N of Downtown. 📞 *(407) 539-2181.* ◯ *daily.* ● *public hols.* ♿ &
This art centre in the leafy suburb of Maitland occupies studios and living quarters designed in the 1930s by artist André Smith as a winter retreat for fellow artists. Set around courtyards and gardens, the buildings are delightful, with abundant use made of Mayan and Aztec motifs. The studios are still used, and changing exhibitions of contemporary American arts and crafts are shown in a gallery.

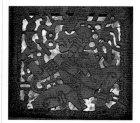
Decoration inspired by the Aztecs, at the Maitland Art Center

🎵 Church Street Station
129 W Church St. 📞 *(407) 422-2434.* ◯ *daily.* 🎫 *one fee for all shows.*
Created in the 1970s from an area of dilapidated hotels and shops, this entertaining nightlife complex pulls a big crowd. Top of the bill are three live musical shows performed from about 7pm until after midnight; each one re-creates a different era with appropriate antique furnishings. A Dixieland jazz band plays in **Rosie O'Grady's Good Time Emporium**, decked out with etched glass mirrors from British pubs; can-can girls dance on the bartops and slick, waistcoated bartenders join in the songs. The triple-tiered, golden oak

Cheyenne Saloon and Opera House *(see p330)* recalls the Wild West, with barmen in stetsons, a country and western band and line dancing; while the Victorian-style, wrought-iron palace of the **Orchid Garden Ballroom** presents live rock and roll, with music from the 1950s to the 1990s. A single fee provides admission to all the live shows.

The rest of the complex, including street entertainment by acrobats and jugglers, can be enjoyed for free. There's **Phineas Phogg's**, a good dance club with a ballooning theme (restricted to those of 21 years of age and over), and also 50 one-of-a-kind shops selling anything from hats to Gothic statuary in the **Exchange Shopping Emporium**. The Buffalo Trading Co nearby keeps an excellent stock of western gear.

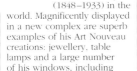
Detail from Tiffany's *Four Seasons* window

The best place to eat is Lili Marlene's *(see p321)*, which boasts a dining table that once belonged to Al Capone.

Winter Park 5

Road map E2. Orange Co.
🏃 *25,000*. 🚆 🚌 ℹ️ *150 N New York Ave, (407) 644-8281*. **Scenic Boat Tour** 📞 *(407) 644-4056*.

GREATER ORLANDO'S most refined neighbourhood took off in the 1880s, when wealthy northerners began to build winter retreats here. The aroma of expensive perfume and coffee emanates from classy stores and cafés along its main street, Park Avenue, while at the country club up the road members all in white enjoy a game of croquet. At the northern end of Park Avenue, the **Charles Hosmer Morse Museum of American Art** holds probably the finest collection of works by Louis Comfort Tiffany (1848–1933) in the world. Magnificently displayed in a new complex are superb examples of his Art Nouveau creations: jewellery, table lamps and a large number of his windows, including

Main door of Knowles Memorial Chapel, Rollins College

The Four Seasons, dated 1899. This, like all his windows, is a staggering fusion of glass, gold leaf, enamel, paint, lead and copper. The galleries also exhibit pieces from the same period by luminaries such as Frank Lloyd Wright.

At the southern end of Park Avenue is prestigious **Rollins College**, with a delightful arboreal campus dotted with Spanish-style buildings erected in the 1930s. Most noteworthy is the Knowles Memorial Chapel, whose main entrance features a relief of a meeting between the Seminoles and the Spanish conquistadors. The college's **Cornell Fine Arts Museum** has over 6,000 works of art, including an impressive collection of Italian Renaissance paintings.

To see where the wealthy Winter Park residents live, take the narrated **Scenic Boat Tour**. Between 10am and 4pm, boats depart hourly from the east end of Morse Boulevard and chug around nearby lakes and along their interconnecting canals. The canals are overhung with hibiscus, bamboo and papaya, while the lakes are surrounded by magnificent live oaks and cypress trees as well as grand mansions with sweeping lawns.

🏛 **Charles Hosmer Morse Museum of American Art**
445 Park Ave N. 📞 *(407) 645-5311*.
◯ *Tue–Sun*. ⬤ *public hols*. 🚫 ♿
🏛 **Cornell Fine Arts Museum**
1000 Holt Ave. 📞 *(407) 646-2526*.
◯ *Tue–Sun*. ⬤ *public hols*. ♿

Crowds enjoying the street entertainment at Church Street Station

One of the gentler rides at Wet 'n Wild on International Drive

International Drive ❻

Road map E2. Orange Co.
🚌 Orlando. 🚌 Orlando. ℹ️ Gala
Center, 8723 S International Drive,
(407) 363-5872.

ONLY A STONE'S THROW from Walt Disney World, and anchored by Universal Studios and Sea World at either end, International Drive is here solely because of the theme parks. "I Drive", as everyone knows it, is a tawdry, 3-mile (5-km) ribbon of restaurants, hotels, shops and theatres, many of which scream out some discounted deal. In the daytime, when everyone is at the theme parks, I Drive is deserted; after dark, however, it becomes a lively neon strip with everything open late.

I Drive's biggest and most popular attraction is **Wet 'n Wild**, billed as the world's first water park when it opened in 1977. Unlike Disney's water parks *(see pp160–61)*, Wet 'n Wild doesn't worry about making itself pretty. Where it excels is in its eight big-thrill rides such as Bomb Bay and Der Stuka – terrifyingly fast descents down near-vertical slides. Water-skiing on your knees or trying to stay on the bucking, automated Robo Surfer requires more skill. There is also the watery Kid's Playground and a couple of gentle rides, but Disney's water parks better serve families with young children. In the

summer Wet 'n Wild is open as late as 11pm, offering half-price admission to those who visit just for the evening.

Filled with fantastical objects, illusions and film footage of strange feats, **Ripley's Believe It or Not!** is I Drive's other quality attraction. It is one of a worldwide chain of museums that was born out of the 1933 Chicago World Fair's so-called Odditorium – the creation of a famous American broadcaster and cartoonist, Robert Ripley, who travelled the globe in search of the weird and wonderful. You can't miss Orlando's Ripley's Believe It or Not! – it is housed in a building that appears to be falling into one of Florida's infamous sinkholes *(see p20)*. Inside await all kinds of eccentricities: a Rolls Royce made of 1,016,711 matchsticks, a Mona Lisa fashioned from pieces of toast, a three-legged man, a two-headed kitten, and a man who can smoke through his eye.

On sale at Gatorland

Close by, **The Mercado** is a Spanish-style outdoor shopping mall, with pleasant courtyards and fountains, some four dozen gift shops, several restaurants and free entertainment (usually a band) in the evenings. Two blocks from the mall you'll find Orlando's excellent Official Visitor Information Center, which has coupons for many of Orlando's attractions, hotels and restaurants; you can save money by stopping off here *(see p346)*.

🌊 **Wet 'n Wild**
6200 International Drive. 📞 *(407) 351-3200.* ⭘ *daily.* 🔲 ♿
🏛 **Ripley's Believe It or Not!**
8201 International Drive. 📞 *(407) 363-4418.* ⭘ *daily.* 🔲 ♿
🎭 **The Mercado**
8445 S International Drive. 📞 *(407) 345-9337.* ⭘ *daily.* ⬤ *25 Dec.* ♿

Gatorland ❼

Road map E3. Orange Co. 14501 S Orange Blossom Trail, Kissimmee. 📞 *(800) 777-9044.* 🚌 *Kissimmee.* 🚌 *Kissimmee.* ⭘ *daily.* 🔲 ♿

THIS GIANT WORKING farm, open since the 1950s, has a licence to rear alligators for their hides and meat. Gatorland's breeding pens, nurseries and rearing ponds hold thousands of alligators of every size, from infants that would fit into the palm of your hand to 12-ft (4-m) monsters. The animals can be most enjoyably observed from a boardwalk and tower as they bask undisturbed in the shallows of a cypress swamp. Gatorland's other attractions are more contrived: they include

The unmistakable sinking home of Ripley's Believe It or Not!

The gaping jaws of an alligator mark the entrance to Gatorland

a few depressed animals in cages, an alligator wrestling show and a Gator Jumparoo, in which the animals leap out of the water to grab chunks of chicken; there are also handling demonstrations of Florida's poisonous snakes.

You can try 'gator nuggets or ribs at the restaurant or buy a tin of 'gator chowder.

One of the typically offbeat shops in Kissimmee's Old Town

Kissimmee ⓭

Road map E3. Osceola Co.
⚶ *35,000.* 🚃 🚌 🚶 *1925 E Irlo Bronson Memorial Hwy, (407) 847-5000.*

IN THE EARLY 1900s, cows freely roamed the streets of this cattle boom town. Now, the only livestock you are likely to see is that appearing in the twice-yearly rodeo at Kissimmee's Silver Spurs Arena *(see p31)*, or at the more down-to-earth rodeos held every Friday night at the **Kissimmee Arena**.

Kissimmee means "Heaven's Place" in the language of the Calusa Indians *(see pp38–9)*, but the reason most people visit is to make use of the glut of cheap motels located so close to Walt Disney World. They are strung out along the traffic-ridden US 192, amid chain restaurants and countless billboards advertising the latest attractions, shopping malls and dinner shows. The latter are the chief appeal of Kissimmee after dark.

After a day in a theme park, however, you might prefer to visit Kissimmee's **Old Town**. This recreated pedestrian street of early 20th-century buildings has eccentric shops offering psychic readings, tattoos, Irish linen, candles and so forth. There is also a moderately entertaining haunted house and a small fairground with antique equipment.

The **Flying Tigers Warbird Restoration Museum**, by Kissimmee municipal airport, is also enjoyably quirky. It is visited by old timers who remember piloting the mainly World War II aircraft which undergo meticulous repair here. For a small fee you can take a guided tour of the hangar to hear about the finer points involved in wing and rivet reconstruction. For a sizeable fee you can take a spin in a 1934 biplane.

▼ Kissimmee Arena
1010 Suhls Lane. 📞 *(407) 933-0020.* ◻ *for shows.* 📷 &
🏛 Flying Tigers Warbird Restoration Museum
231 Hoagland Blvd. 📞 *(407) 933-1942.* ◻ *daily.* ● *25 Dec.* 📷 &

DINNER SHOWS

For rumbustious family fun (if you still have the energy after the theme parks have closed), consider going to a dinner show *(see p337)*. Orlando boasts around a dozen – excluding Disney's two shows *(see p162)* – strung along I Drive or off US 192 near Kissimmee. Tickets cost $30–35 for an adult and about $20 for children, but discounts are available with coupons from the Orlando Visitor Center. The following are the best of the bunch.

American Gladiators: Stars of the TV show take part in a live sporting competition. 📞 *(800) 228-8534.*

Arabian Nights: A gaudy equestrian extravaganza in a giant indoor arena. 📞 *(407) 239-9223.*

Colossal Studios Pirate's Dinner Adventure: A lavish show set around a pirates' ship, with boat races, acrobatics and a tour of the studios beforehand. 📞 *(407) 248-0590.*

King Henry's Feast: Fun and games in a recreation of King Henry VIII's banqueting hall. 📞 *(407) 351-5151.*

Medieval Times: Jousting knights get top billing at this colourful and dramatic show. 📞 *(407) 396-1518.*

Wild Bill's Wild West Dinner Extravaganza: Indian and can-can dancers entertain in a stockade fort. 📞 *(407) 351-5151.*

A star of Wild Bill's Wild West Dinner Extravaganza

Cypress Island 𝟵

Road map E3. Osceola Co. 3 miles (5 km) S of Kissimmee. ⓕ *(407) 935-0087.* ▣ *Kissimmee.* ▣ *Kissimmee.* ▤ *from downtown Kissimmee marina on Lakeshore Drive.* ◯ *Wed–Sun.* ● *Thanksgiving, 25 Dec.* ♿ *limited.*

A FERRY MAKES the ten-minute journey every hour to this wonderfully unspoilt 200-acre (80-ha) retreat on Lake Toho-pekaliga. The island was once a Seminole settlement and later became a cattle ranch. Now, most of it is given over to a nature reserve for exotic animals such as emus, llamas and the Patagonian cavy (an unusual hybrid of dog, deer and rabbit). Follow the 2-mile (3-km) track around the island amid orange groves and palm and cypress woods, or take a tour on a safari cart (in reality just a golf buggy). There are also boat trips and horseback rides.

Terracotta warrior at Splendid China

Splendid China 𝟭𝟬

Road map E3. Osceola Co. 3000 Splendid China Blvd, Kissimmee. ⓕ *(407) 396-7111.* ▣ *Kissimmee.* ▣ *Kissimmee.* ◯ *daily.* 🖾 ♿

O RLANDO'S MOST cultural, adult-oriented theme park is wonderfully peaceful (do not expect any crowds), but some may find it rather too sedate. Opened in 1993 at a cost of $100 million, its 76 acres (30 ha) are a virtual

duplication of a similar park in Shenzhen, China. Allow half a day for a thorough visit.

There are no thrills or rides, but you can walk or take a tram to scaled-down replicas of China's most famous land-marks, each of which is dec-orated with hundreds of toy people and animals. The Great Wall reappears half-a-mile (1-km) long, made from 6.5 million bricks; the Leshan Grand Buddha Statue, 236 ft (72 m) tall in China, is still magnificent in its 35-ft (11-m) version. A sizeable portion of the army of 8,000 terracotta warriors discovered in China in the 1970s is re-created at a third of its original size, while Beijing's enormous Forbidden City is reduced by a factor of 15.

Once you tire of the models – and 55 can indeed be a little overwhelming – you can take a seat in one of the theatres for a display of traditional Chinese skills such as martial arts and the imitation of bird-songs; the Chongqing Acrobats are the most entertaining.

Suzhou Gardens, at the park's entrance, is a full-scale reconstruction of the eastern Chinese town of Suzhou as it would have looked 700 years ago; its latticework buildings and pagoda were constructed using period techniques, with-out nuts and bolts. There are up-market shops selling bonsai trees and Chinese tea. The Suzhou Pearl Restaurant, like most of the others in the park, serves good Chinese food.

Amateur pilot in simulated combat at Fantasy of Flight

Fantasy of Flight 𝟭𝟭

Road map E3. Polk Co. 1400 Broadway Blvd SE, Polk City. ⓕ *(941) 984-3500.* ▣ *Winter Haven.* ▣ *Winter Haven.* ◯ *daily.* 🖾 ♿

W HERE FANTASY OF FLIGHT thinks it has the edge over Florida's many other aviation attractions is that it provides the very sensations of flying. A series of vivid walk-through exhibits takes you into a World War II B-17 Flying Fortress during a bomb-ing mission, and into World War I trenches in the middle of an air raid.

For a few extra dollars you can ride a World War II fighter aircraft simulator in a dogfight over the Pacific. In the cockpit, you will be given a pre-flight personal briefing and receive advice from the control tower about takeoff, landing and the presence of enemy aircraft. A hangar full of mint antique aeroplanes contains the USA's

Beijing's Forbidden City, reduced to more manageable dimensions at Splendid China

first widely used airliner – the 1929 Ford Tri-Motor, which made an appearance in the film *Indiana Jones and the Temple of Doom* – and the Roadair 1, a combined plane and car that flew just once, in 1959.

Cypress Gardens ⑫

Road map E3. Polk Co. 2641 South Lake Summit Drive, Winter Haven. 🅲 *(941) 324-2111.* 🅿 *Winter Haven.* 🚌 *Winter Haven.* ⭘ *daily.* 🖻 🖆

F LORIDA'S FIRST theme park, opened in 1936, Cypress Gardens relies on the unlikely twin elements of flowers and water-skiing to attract the crowds. Set beside a massive cypress-fringed lake, 8,000 varieties of plants make the park a floral wonderland and unquestionably romantic. It is especially popular with the older generation.

Resplendent Southern Belles adding colour to Cypress Gardens

A water-ski pyramid, climax of the show at Cypress Gardens

A luscious botanical garden makes up about a third of the grounds. Plants, all painstakingly labelled, range from a 1,600-year-old cypress tree to numerous epiphytes *(see p276)*, a very rare double-headed palm and a gigantic banyan tree. You can either explore on foot or take the scenic Botanical Boat Cruise, which weaves along the garden's waterways. It stops for visitors to take photographs of the park's most famous view: "Southern Belles" in garish hooped dresses, usually posing beside a lilied lagoon, a tumbling waterfall or the sugary Neo-Classical "Love Chapel".

Other sections of the park are devoted to impressive large-scale floral displays. Around two-and-a-half million chrysanthemum blooms appear in November, and the following month hordes of poinsettias burst into colour.

Splendid topiaries can be seen during much of the year. For the Spring Flower Festival these include butterflies, fish, birds and an Easter bunny. During the summer Victorian Garden Party you will see a horse and cart, a steamship, a carousel, and ladies and gentlemen in elegant attire. In the formal, plantation-style gardens, amusing topiaries of the gardeners themselves "work" amid the heady scents of rose, herb and fruit and vegetable allotments.

Cypress Gardens calls itself the water-ski capital of the world. Its water-ski shows, which originated from revues put on during World War II for soldiers stationed in the area, take place at least three times a day. The sometimes graceful, sometimes dramatic stunts involve barefoot skiing, jumps and somersaults off ramps. Do not miss the highlight of the show, a gravity-defying pyramid of ten or more skiers that undoubtedly justifies the hype.

If you have set aside an entire day to see everything, you will also have time for the butterfly conservatory and for a ride on the park's intriguing hydraulically lifted aerial viewing platform. If you have still got the energy, there are also reptiles, exotic birds and Russian circus acts.

Bok Tower Gardens ⑬

Road map E3. Polk Co. 1151 Tower Blvd, Lake Wales. 🅲 *(941) 676-9412.* 🅿 *Winter Haven.* 🚌 *Lake Wales.* ⭘ *daily.* 🖻 🖆

E DWARD W BOK arrived in the US from Holland in 1870, at the age of six, and subsequently became an influential publisher. Shortly before his death in 1930, he presented these 128 acres (52 ha) of lovely woodland gardens to the American public "for the success they had given him".

Sitting at the highest spot in peninsular Florida – a dizzying 298 ft (91 m) above sea level – they centre on the Singing Tower, which soars above the tree-tops and shelters Bok's grave at its base. You cannot climb the tower, but try to attend its 45-minute live carillon service, rung daily at 3pm.

The striking, pink marble Singing Tower at Bok Tower Gardens

Canaveral National Seashore and Merritt Island ⓮

Road map F2. Brevard Co.
🚇 *Titusville.*

THESE ADJACENT reserves on the Space Coast share an astounding variety of fauna and a wide range of habitats, including saltwater estuaries, marshes, pine flatwoods and hardwood hammocks. This proliferation is due to the meeting of temperate and sub-tropical climates here. You can often see alligators, as well as endangered species such as manatees, but it is the bird life that makes the greatest visual impact.

Many visitors simply head straight for the beach. The **Canaveral National Seashore** incorporates Florida's largest undeveloped barrier island beach – a magnificent 24-mile (39-km) strip of sand backed by dunes strewn with sea oats and sea grapes. Apollo Beach, at the northern end, is accessible along Route A1A, while Playalinda Beach is reached from the south, along Route 402; no road connects the two. The beaches are fine for sunbathing, but swimming conditions can be hazardous and there are no lifeguards.

Behind Apollo Beach, Turtle Mound is a 40-ft (12-m) high rubbish dump of oyster shells created by Timucua Indians *(see pp38–9)* between AD 800 and 1400. Climb the boardwalk

An alligator in the wild

to the top for a view over Mosquito Lagoon, flecked with a myriad mangrove islets.

Route 402 to Playalinda Beach provides memorable views too – of the Kennedy Space Center's shuttle launch pads, rising eerily out of the watery vastness. This route also crosses **Merritt Island National Wildlife Refuge**, which covers an area of 220 sq miles (570 sq km). Most of the refuge lies within Kennedy Space Center and is out of bounds, but there is plenty to explore in the area immediately to the north.

By far the best way to experience the local wildlife at first hand is to follow the 6-mile (10-km) Black Point Wildlife Drive. An excellent leaflet, available at the track's start near the junction of routes 402 and 406, explains such matters as how dykes control local mosquito populations (though you should still come armed with insect repellent in summer). Halfway along the drive you can stretch your legs by following the 5-mile (8-km) Cruickshank Trail, which starts nearby and has an observation tower.

East along Route 402 towards Playalinda, the Merritt Island Visitor Information Center has excellent displays on the habitats and wildlife within the refuge. A mile (1.5 km) further east, the Oak Hammock and Palm Hammock trails have short boardwalks across marshland.

✕ Canaveral National Seashore
Route A1A, 20 miles (32 km) N of Titusville or Route 402, 10 miles (16 km) E of Titusville. 📞 *(407) 267-1110.* ☐ *daily.* ● *for shuttle launches.* 📷
✕ Merritt Island National Wildlife Refuge
Route 406, 4 miles (6.5 km) E of Titusville. 📞 *(407) 861-0667.* ☐ *daily.* ● *for shuttle launches.*

SPACE COAST BIRD LIFE

The magnificent and abundant bird life of the Space Coast is best viewed early in the morning or shortly before dusk. Between November and March, in particular, the marshes and lagoons teem with migratory ducks and waders, as up to 100,000 arrive from colder northern climes.

Sandhill crane

Brown pelican

Royal tern

Black skimmer

View from Black Point Drive, Merritt Island National Wildife Refuge

Kennedy Space Center ⓯

See pp182–7.

US Astronaut Hall of Fame ⑯

Road map E2. Brevard Co. Junction of Route 405 and US 1. 【 *(407) 269-6100.* 🚌 *Titusville.* ◯ *daily.* ● *25 Dec.* 📷 ⛟

THIS HALL OF FAME is both educational and entertaining. It eulogizes the USA's early astronauts and has many of their personal items on display. A full-size mock shuttle orbiter serves as a cinema showing a film of a shuttle's journey into space, while in the flight simulator riders undergo G-forces equal to those experienced by fighter pilots.

The US Space Camp, on the same site, runs courses for youngsters, with activities such as trying out weightlessness.

"Tico Belle", the prize exhibit at the Warbird Air Museum

Valiant Air Command Warbird Air Museum ⑰

Road map E2. Brevard Co. 6600 Tico Road, Titusville. 【 *(407) 268-1941.* 🚌 *Titusville.* ◯ *daily.* ● *Thanksgiving, 25 Dec, 1 Jan.* 📷 ⛟

AT THIS MUSEUM an enormous hangar houses military planes from World War II and later, all lovingly restored to flying condition. The pride of the collection is a working

Porcher House, on the edge of Cocoa's leafy historic district

Douglas C-47 called Tico Belle: the aircraft saw service during World War II before becoming the official carrier for the Danish royal family.

Every March there is an air show, with strafing runs and dog-fight demonstrations.

Cocoa ⑱

Road map E3. Brevard Co. 🚶 *18,000.* 🚌 ℹ *Cocoa Beach, (407) 459-2200.*

COCOA IS THE most appealing community among the sprawling conurbations along the Space Coast mainland. Its historic district, near where Route 520 crosses the Indian River to Cocoa Beach, is an attractive enclave known as Cocoa Village – with buildings dating from the 1880s (some of which house unpretentious boutiques), replica gas street lamps and brick pavements.

In Delannoy Avenue, on the eastern edge of the village, is the Classical Revival Porcher House, built of coquina stone *(see p201)* in 1916 by a leading citrus plantation owner. The

interior is unexciting, but note the spade, heart, diamond and club carvings on its portico wall: Mrs Porcher was an extremely keen bridge player.

Cocoa Beach ⑲

Road map F3. Brevard Co. 🚶 *13,000.* 🚌 *Cocoa.* ℹ *400 Fortenberry Rd, (407) 459-2200.*

THE SPACE COAST'S big, no-frills resort calls itself the east coast's surfing capital. Surfing festivals and bikini contests set the tone, along with win-your-weight-in-beer competitions on the pier. Motels, chain restaurants and the odd strip joint characterize the main thoroughfare.

These are all eclipsed by the **Ron Jon Surf Shop**. This neon palace has surf boards galore (for sale and for hire) and a huge T-shirt collection. In front of its flashing towers, beach bum sportspeople are frozen in modern sculpture.

🏄 **Ron Jon Surf Shop**
4151 N Atlantic Ave. 【 *(407) 799-8888.* ◯ *daily: 24 hours.* ⛟

The Ron Jon Surf Shop in Cocoa Beach, with everything for the surfing or beach enthusiast

Kennedy Space Center ⑮

NASA insignia

SITUATED ON MERRITT ISLAND, just an hour's drive east of Orlando, the Kennedy Space Center is the only place in the western hemisphere where humans are launched into space. It was from here, with the launch of Apollo 11 in July 1969, that President JF Kennedy's dream of landing a man on the moon was realized. The centre is the home of NASA (National Aeronautics and Space Administration), whose manned Space Shuttle *(see pp186–7)* can regularly be seen lifting off from one of the launch pads. Comparable to Orlando's theme parks in its scale and ambition, the recently revamped Space Center aims to both inform and entertain.

★ Apollo/Saturn V Center
A Saturn V rocket, of the kind used by the Apollo missions, is the showpiece here. There is also a reconstructed control room where visitors experience a simulated launch (see p185).

Spacemen
Staff dressed up as spacemen may put in a surprise appearance at any time, providing ideal photo opportunities for children.

The Gallery of Spaceflight is a showcase of space vehicles and equipment.

Children's Play Dome

★ Rocket Garden
You can walk through a group of towering rockets, each of which represents a different period of space flight's history. There is also a lunar module of the kind used by the Apollo missions.

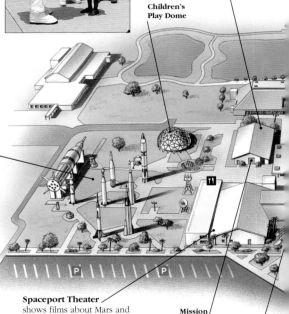

Spaceport Theater shows films about Mars and the rescue of Apollo 13.

Mission to Mars

Entrance

STAR FEATURES

★ Apollo/Saturn V Center

★ Rocket Garden

★ Bus Tours

★ IMAX Films

VISITOR CENTER
Part of an evolving facility to cater for the Space Center's numerous visitors, the Visitor Center was established in 1966 to offer bus tours of the area. It is now an extensive museum with several places to eat and a souvenir shop. Public access is provided by US 405 from Titusville and Route 3 from Cocoa.

★ Bus Tours
Bus tours make a circuit of the centre's launch pads, passing the Vehicle Assembly Building and the "crawlerway", along which the shuttle is slowly manoeuvred into position.

★ IMAX Films
At the Galaxy Center, huge IMAX cinemas run films about satellites and space exploration. Footage from the shuttle missions offers some breathtaking views of Earth from space (see p184).

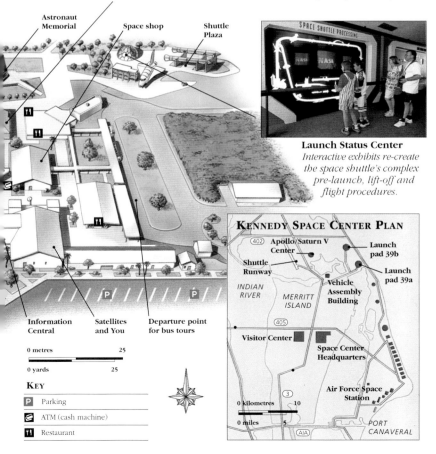

Launch Status Center
Interactive exhibits re-create the space shuttle's complex pre-launch, lift-off and flight procedures.

Astronaut Memorial

Space shop

Shuttle Plaza

Information Central

Satellites and You

Departure point for bus tours

0 metres 25

0 yards 25

KEY

P	Parking
@	ATM (cash machine)
🍴	Restaurant

KENNEDY SPACE CENTER PLAN

(402) Apollo/Saturn V Center

Shuttle Runway

Launch pad 39b

Launch pad 39a

INDIAN RIVER

MERRITT ISLAND

Vehicle Assembly Building

(405)

Visitor Center

Space Center Headquarters

Air Force Space Station

0 kilometres 10

0 miles 5

(3)

(A1A)

PORT CANAVERAL

Exploring the Kennedy Space Center

YOU SHOULD DIVIDE your time equally between the Visitor Center and the rest of the 131-sq mile (340-sq km) facility, which can be explored on two separate bus tours. Together with the excellent IMAX films at the Visitor Center, the other unmissable sight is the Apollo/Saturn V Center – the climax of one of the bus tours. You will need a whole day to see everything. If you have less time, cut out the tour to the Cape Canaveral Air Station, which concentrates on the early missions and is of more limited interest – especially to children. Everything at the Space Center is free except for the IMAX films and the bus tours; buy tickets for these as soon as you arrive.

An unearthly photo opportunity at the Lunar Surface Theater

VISITOR CENTER

THE PLACE where everyone wants to head first is the **Galaxy Center**, where the IMAX cinemas put on three stunning films on screens more than five storeys high. For some people this is the highlight of their visit.

Top of the bill is *Destiny in Space*, narrated by *Star Trek* star, Leonard Nimoy, which contains footage from nine Space Shuttle flights – among them the launch of the Hubble telescope in 1990, and its subsequent repair in 1993. You can also enjoy a number of magnificent views of Earth, Mars and Venus. A second film, the *Dream is Alive*, provides the insider's view,

with in-flight footage gathered during a number of space missions; the thrills and basics of everyday life in space are narrated by Walter Cronkite. The third film, *L5: First City in Space*, combines real film footage with 3-D computer graphics to transport you to an imaginary city in outer space; highlights from this film include a flight past Mars and a landing on a comet.

For a glimpse of NASA's most up-to-date technology, the Galaxy Center also shows a model of one of the space vehicles designed for the proposed International Space Station, but children will probably prefer the latest planetary explorer

robots revealed in **Mission to Mars**. This exhibition also includes models of the Viking probes sent to Mars in the 1970s. These paved the way for the Mars Pathfinder probe, launched in 1995, and for the proposed first manned expedition to Mars.

In Shuttle Plaza you can enjoy a close-up view of the **Explorer** – a replica of the Space Shuttle – but it's rather frustrating not being able to go inside. The **Launch Status Center** alongside has displays of genuine flight hardware and rocket boosters, plus a number of shows illustrating various space-related topics. Nearby, a "Space Mirror" tracks the movement of the sun, reflecting its light onto the names inscribed on the **Astronaut Memorial**. This honours the 16 astronauts, from Apollo 1 to the Space Shuttle Challenger, who have died for space exploration.

If you are at all short of time, skip **Satellites and You**, which offers a 45-minute film explaining the importance of satellite technology.

The *Explorer*, a life-size replica of the Space Shuttle

TIMELINE OF SPACE EXPLORATION

1958 First American satellite, the *Explorer 1*, is launched (31 Jan)	**1962** John Glenn orbits the earth in *Mercury* spacecraft	**1969** Neil Armstrong and Buzz Aldrin *(Apollo 11)* walk on the moon (24 Jul) **1966** *Gemini 8* makes first space docking (16 Mar)	*Buzz Aldrin*	**1977** Th Space Shutt *Enterprise* tested aboar a Boeing 7 (18 Feb
1955	**1960**	**1965**	**1970**	**1975**
1961 On 5 May Alan Shepherd becomes the first American in space. Kennedy commits nation to moon landing *John Glenn*		**1968** *Apollo 8* orbits the moon (24 Dec) **1965** Edward White is the first American to walk in space (3 Jun)	**1975** American *Apollo* and Russian *Soyuz* vehicles dock in orbit (17 Jul)	

BUS TOURS

BUSES LEAVE continuously from the Visitor Center, providing two separate tours of the centre's major facilities; each lasts over two hours.

The first tour, to the Cape Canaveral Air Station, will really only appeal to visitors interested in the history of rocketry. The station was set up in the 1940s as a missile testing range and went on to launch the first missions into space. The US space administration was moved from here to today's more spacious site on Merritt Island in the 1960s, but it is still a satellite launch facility; a museum and rocket garden commemorate such past glories as the Gemini and Mercury projects.

More interesting – especially in the run-up to a launch – is the tour of Launch Complex 39, where NASA prepares and launches the Space Shuttle. The first stop is at the huge Vehicle Assembly Building, where the shuttles are built or "stacked". Enclosing over 130 million cu ft (3.5 million cu m),

The Vehicle Assembly Building, dwarfing the surrounding Space Center

it is one of the world's largest structures. Equally daunting are the Crawler Transporters, which move the shuttle to the launch pad; half the size of a football field, they move along the 3.5-mile (5-km) Crawler-way at 1 mph (1.6 km/h). The bus pauses for a view of the launch pads (dull if there's no shuttle) and moves on to the Launch Control Center, where the final tests are done before the signal to "go for launch". The final stop is the Apollo/Saturn V Center.

APOLLO/SATURN V CENTER

THIS COMPLEX, opened in 1996, pays tribute to Project Apollo, the space programme which landed the first human beings on the moon.

First of all, you are given the background to the space race between the US and the Soviet Union, leading to the creation in the 1960s of Saturn V, the most powerful rocket of its time. You are then ushered into the Firing Room Theater, where you'll see a launch

control room arranged as it was when Apollo 8, the first manned mission to the moon, was launched in 1968. Much of the display is original, and there are even notes from the test supervisor's log book. A film show re-creates the awe-inspiring moment when Apollo 8 was launched, during which the whole auditorium trembles with the violence of the lift-off.

Outside the theatre is one of only three Saturn V rockets still in existence. Now lying on its side, the 363-ft (110-m) monster is separated into its various sections.

The Lunar Surface Theater focuses on the first moon landing itself and re-creates the nail-biting final stages of Apollo 11's descent in July 1969. The climax shows the historic footage of Buzz Aldrin and Neil Armstrong taking their first steps on the moon.

You should allow about three hours to do justice to the Apollo/Saturn V Center. You'll find all the facilities you need here, including shops and cafés.

Rockets on display at the Cape Canaveral Air Station

1981 Columbia is the first shuttle in space (12 Apr)	**1983** The first American woman goes into space, aboard Space Shuttle *Challenger* (18 Jun)	**1988** *Discovery*, the first shuttle since the *Challenger* disaster, is launched (29 Sep)	*Atlantis – Mir* insignia (Jun 1995)	
1980	**1985**	**1990**	**1995**	
 Space Shuttle Columbia	**1986** The *Challenger* explodes, killing all its crew (28 Jan) **1984** First American woman, Kathryn Sullivan, walks in space (11 Oct)	**1990** Hubble telescope is launched (24 Apr) **1995** The *Atlantis* docks with Russian *Mir* space station (29 Jun)	**1996** *Mars Pathfinder* is sent to gather data from the surface of Mars (4 Dec)	

The Space Shuttle

Shuttle mission insignia

B Y THE LATE 1970s, the cost of sending astronauts into space had become too much for the American space budget; hundreds of millions of dollars were spent lifting the Apollo missions into space, with little more than a scorched command module ever returning to Earth. The time had come to develop reusable spacecraft made for years of service, whose main cost after production would lie in maintenance. The answer was the Space Shuttle *Columbia*, which was launched into space on 12 April 1981 *(see pp50–51)*. The shuttle's large cargo capacity allows it to take all kinds of satellites and probes into space, and it will be used to lift materials for the construction of the International Space Station.

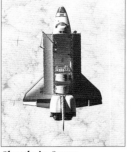

Shuttle in Space
In orbit, the shuttle's cargo doors are opened. The Hubble telescope was one of its payloads.

Flight Deck
The shuttle is built like an aircraft, but its flight deck is even more complex. You can get some idea of how it is navigated at the Launch Status Center (see p183).

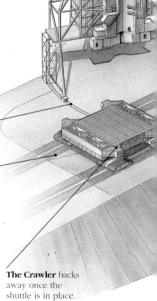

Tracks enable the tower to be moved away before lift-off.

Crawlerway
This double pathway, 100 ft (30 m) wide, is specially designed to withstand the weight of the shuttle as it is taken to the launch pad by gigantic crawlers. The rock surface overlies a layer of asphalt and a 7 ft (2 m) bed of crushed stone.

The Crawler backs away once the shuttle is in place.

SHUTTLE CYCLE

The Space Shuttle has three principal elements: the main Orbiter spacecraft (with its three engines), an external tank of liquid hydrogen and oxygen fuel, and two solid-fuel booster rockets, which provide the extra thrust needed for lift-off. Like earlier rockets, the shuttle reaches orbit in stages.

1 Pre-launch
The external tank and rocket boosters are fitted to the Orbiter in the Vehicle Assembly Building. Then it is moved to the launch pad.

2 Launch
After a final check, the shuttle blasts off using its own three engines and its two booster rockets.

The service tower gives access for fuelling and cargo installation.

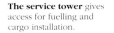

The access arm is a corridor through which the astronauts board the shuttle.

Orbiter

Solid Rocket Booster

The flame trench channels the burning gases away from the vehicle.

THE SHUTTLE LAUNCHES

Since the shuttle made its maiden voyage in 1981, there have been many missions shared between the *Columbia, Challenger, Discovery, Atlantis* and *Endeavour* vehicles. Though the programme was severely crippled when the *Challenger* exploded shortly after lift-off in 1986, there are now up to eight launches a year. To view the launches within the Space Center you will need to apply to NASA for a complimentary car pass a good three months in advance. Outside the centre, there are prime, free viewing sites on the US 1 at Titusville and the A1A at Cocoa Beach and Cape Canaveral.

Shuttle clearing the launch tower

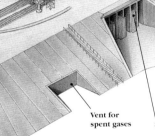

Shuttle Landing
Once it has re-entered the atmosphere, the shuttle glides with its engines off on its way back to the Space Center. It lands on the runway at 220 mph (360 km/h).

PLAN OF THE LAUNCH PAD

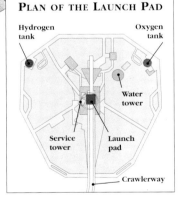

Hydrogen tank

Oxygen tank

Water tower

Vent for spent gases

Steel pedestals

Service tower

Launch pad

Crawlerway

SHUTTLE LAUNCH
The launch pad is made of 2 million cu ft (56,000 cu m) of reinforced concrete, supported by six steel pedestals. The flame trench is flooded with cooling water when the engines ignite, producing an immense cloud of steam.

3 Separation
Two minutes later, the boosters separate and are parachuted back to earth. At eight minutes, the external tank detaches.

4 Orbital Operations
Using its own engines, the shuttle manoeuvres itself into orbit and begins its operations. The mission may last between 7 and 18 days, flying at an altitude of 115–690 miles (185–1,110 km).

5 Re-entry
The shuttle re-enters the atmosphere backwards, using its engines to decelerate. It turns nose-first as it descends into the stratosphere and uses parachutes to stop.

THE NORTHEAST

THE CHARMS OF THE NORTHEAST *are more discreet than the glitz of Miami or the thrills of Orlando. Just a few miles from busy interstate highways, salty fishing villages, overgrown plantations and quaint country towns recall old-time Florida. Fabulous beaches lure sun-worshippers, while the historic town of St Augustine can claim to be the longest inhabited European settlement in the US.*

The state's recorded history begins in the Northeast, on the aptly named First Coast. Juan Ponce de León first stepped ashore here in 1513 *(see p40)* and Spanish colonists established St Augustine, now a well-preserved town guarded by the mighty San Marcos fortress – one of the region's highlights.

The Northeast also saw the first influx of pioneers and tourists during the 19th-century steamboat era *(see p46)*. At this time, Jacksonville was the gateway to Florida, with steamboats plying the broad St Johns River and its tributaries. In the 1880s, Henry Flagler's railway opened up the east coast and wealthy visitors flocked to his grand hotels in St Augustine and Ormond Beach. Those in search of the winter sun headed further south too.

Broad sandy beaches flank the popular resort of Daytona, which has been synonymous with motor-racing ever since the likes of Henry Ford and Louis Chevrolet raced automobiles on the beach during their winter vacations. Daytona is also the favourite place for students to spend the Spring Break: this is as lively as it gets in the Northeast.

Venturing inland, west of the St Johns is the wooded expanse of the Ocala National Forest; the woods then thin out to reveal the rolling pastures of Marion County's billion-dollar thoroughbred horse industry. Nearby, charming country towns and villages such as Micanopy have been virtually bypassed by the 20th century.

St Augustine's splendid Lightner Museum, occupying the former exclusive Alcazar Hotel

◁ The boardwalk trail at Blue Spring State Park, located next to the mighty St Johns River

Exploring the Northeast

T HE FIRST COAST is a well-travelled route, unfurling along the Atlantic shore in a 120-mile (193-km) string of beaches and resorts, interrupted by dunes and marshland popular with bird-watchers. Resorts run the gamut from decorous Fernandina Beach to action-packed Daytona Beach. Between these two extremes lies the historic jewel of St Augustine. Strike inland, and the Ocala National Forest offers dozens of hiking trails, boating and fishing on spring-fed lakes. Snorkelling and diving are also popular pursuits in crystal-clear springs. Many of the region's Victorian homes have become bed-and-breakfast inns, which make a pleasant change from hotels, and provide a more homely base for exploring.

SIGHTS AT A GLANCE

Blue Spring State Park ⑮
Bulow Plantation State
  Historic Site ⑩
Daytona Beach ⑫
Daytona International Speedway ⑬
Fernandina Beach ❶
Fort Caroline National Memorial ❹
Gainesville ㉓
Jacksonville pp194–5 ❺
Jacksonville Beaches ❻
Kingsley Plantation ❸
Little Talbot Island ❷
Marineland Ocean Resort ❽
Marjorie Kinnan Rawlings State
  Historic Site ㉑
Micanopy ㉒
Mount Dora ⑰
Ocala ⑳
Ocala National Forest ⑱
Ormond Beach ⑪
Ponce de Leon Inlet Lighthouse ⑭
St Augustine pp196–201 ❼
Sanford ⑯
Silver Springs ⑲
Washington Oaks State Gardens ❾

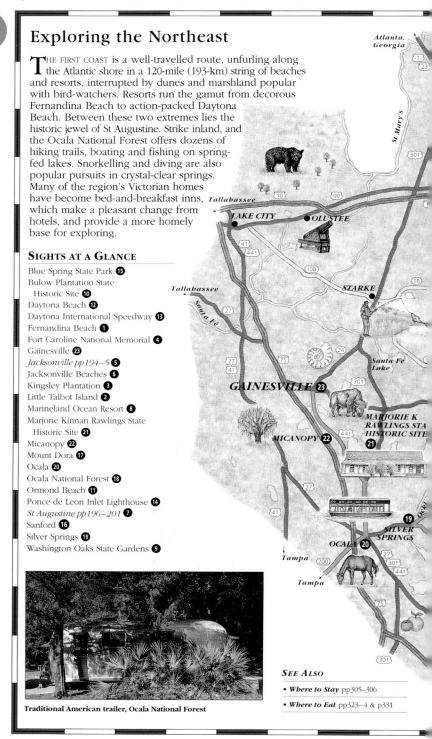

Traditional American trailer, Ocala National Forest

SEE ALSO

- *Where to Stay* pp305–306
- *Where to Eat* pp323–4 & p331

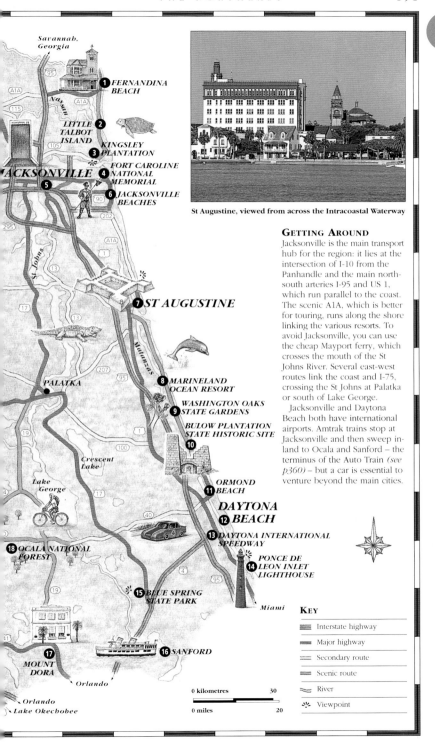

St Augustine, viewed from across the Intracoastal Waterway

Savannah, Georgia

1 **FERNANDINA BEACH**

LITTLE TALBOT ISLAND 2

KINGSLEY PLANTATION 3

FORT CAROLINE NATIONAL MEMORIAL 4

JACKSONVILLE 5

6 **JACKSONVILLE BEACHES**

7 **ST AUGUSTINE**

St Johns

PALATKA

Matanzas

8 **MARINELAND OCEAN RESORT**

9 **WASHINGTON OAKS STATE GARDENS**

BULOW PLANTATION STATE HISTORIC SITE 10

Crescent Lake

Lake George

11 **ORMOND BEACH**

DAYTONA BEACH 12

13 **DAYTONA INTERNATIONAL SPEEDWAY**

18 **OCALA NATIONAL FOREST**

14 **PONCE DE LEON INLET LIGHTHOUSE**

15 **BLUE SPRING STATE PARK**

Miami

16 **SANFORD**

17 **MOUNT DORA**

Orlando

Orlando
Lake Okeechobee

GETTING AROUND

Jacksonville is the main transport hub for the region: it lies at the intersection of I-10 from the Panhandle and the main north-south arteries I-95 and US 1, which run parallel to the coast. The scenic A1A, which is better for touring, runs along the shore linking the various resorts. To avoid Jacksonville, you can use the cheap Mayport ferry, which crosses the mouth of the St Johns River. Several east-west routes link the coast and I-75, crossing the St Johns at Palatka or south of Lake George.

Jacksonville and Daytona Beach both have international airports. Amtrak trains stop at Jacksonville and then sweep in-land to Ocala and Sanford – the terminus of the Auto Train (see *p360*) – but a car is essential to venture beyond the main cities.

KEY

▬▬	Interstate highway
▬▬	Major highway
▬▬	Secondary route
▬▬	Scenic route
～～	River
⚹	Viewpoint

0 kilometres 30

0 miles 20

Fernandina's Beech Street Grill with Chinese Chippendale motifs

Fernandina Beach ①

Road map E1. Nassau Co. 🏛 *47,000.*
🚉 *Jacksonville.* ✈ *Jacksonville.*
ℹ *102 Centre St, (904) 261-3248.*

THE TOWN OF Fernandina Beach on Amelia Island, just across the St Mary's River from Georgia, was renowned as a pirates' den until the early 1800s. Its deep-water harbour attracted a motley crew of foreign armies and adventurers, whose various allegiances earned Amelia Island its soubriquet, the Isle of Eight Flags. Today, Fernandina is better known as a charming Victorian resort and Florida's primary source of sweet Atlantic white shrimp: more than two million pounds (900,000 kilos) are caught by the shrimping fleet each year.

The original Spanish settlement was established at Old Fernandina, a sleepy backwater just north of the present town. In the 1850s the whole town moved south to the eastern terminus of Senator David Yulee's cross-Florida railroad. The move, coupled with the dawn of Florida tourism in the 1870s *(see pp46–7),* prompted the building boom that created the much-admired heart of today's Fernandina, the 50-block **Historic District**.

The legacy of Fernandina's golden age is best seen in the Silk Stocking District, which occupies more than half of the Historic District and is so-named for the affluence of its original residents. Sea captains and timber barons built homes here in a variety of styles: Queen Anne houses decorated with fancy gingerbread detailing and turrets jostle graceful Italianate residences and fine examples of Chinese Chippendale, such as the Beech Street Grill *(see p323).*

Watching the shrimp boats put into harbour at sunset is a local ritual; the fleet is commemorated by a monument at the foot of downtown Centre Street, where chandleries and naval stores once held sway. These weathered brick buildings now house antique shops and up-market gift emporiums. The 1878 Palace Saloon, however, still serves a wicked Pirate's Punch at the long mahogany bar adorned with hand-carved caryatids.

Down on 3rd Street, the 1857 Florida House Inn *(see p323)* is the state's oldest tourist hotel, and a couple of blocks further south, the **Amelia Island Museum of History** occupies the former jail. Guides bring local history to life by talking visitors through the island's turbulent past – from the time of the first Indian inhabitants to the early 1900s. Period items and archaeological finds are used to illustrate the 90-minute tours. Guided tours of the town are also offered (book ahead).

🏛 **Amelia Island Museum of History**
233 S 3rd St. ☎ *(904) 261-7378.*
◻ *Mon–Sat.* ● *public hols.* 🎫 ♿
🎥 *compulsory; two tours daily.*

ENVIRONS: Thirteen miles (21 km) long and only 2 miles (3 km) wide at its broadest point, **Amelia Island** was first settled by the Timucua tribe in the second century BC. The rich fishing grounds and abundant hunting suggest that the island may have supported around 30,000 Indians, though few signs remain of their presence.

There's still excellent fishing, and the island also offers five golf courses and one of Florida's rare opportunities to ride horses along the beach. The splendid sands are backed by dunes that can reach 40 ft (12 m) high in places.

The northern tip of the island is occupied by the 1,121-acre (453-ha) **Fort Clinch State Park**, with trails, beaches and camp sites, as well as a 19th-century fort built to guard the Cumberland Sound at the mouth of the St Mary's River. Construction of the fort, an irregular brick pentagon with massive earthworks, 4.5-ft (1.5-m) thick walls and a battery of Civil War era cannons, took from 1847 until the 1860s.

Today, the park's rangers wear Civil War uniforms. They are joined by volunteers on the first full weekend of each month in re-enactments, when a wide variety of duties are re-created; candlelit tours are given on the Saturday.

Peg Leg, of Fernandina Beach

Amelia Island's Atlantic shore, in easy reach of Fernandina Beach

⚓ **Fort Clinch State Park**
2601 Atlantic Ave. ☎ *(904) 277-7274.*
◻ *daily.* 🎫 ♿ *limited.* 🅰

Little Talbot Island State Park ❷

Road map E1. Duval Co. 12157 Heckscher Drive, Jacksonville. ☎ (904) 251-2320. ⊟ Jacksonville. ⊟ Jacksonville. ◯ daily. ▨ ♿ limited. △

M UCH OF AMELIA ISLAND and the neighbouring islands of Big Talbot, Little Talbot and Fort George to the south remains undeveloped and a natural haven for wildlife.

Little Talbot Island State Park has a good family camp ground, trails through coastal hammocks and marshlands, and great fishing. Expect to see anything from otters and marsh rabbits to fiddler crabs, herons and laughing gulls. Bobcats hide out in the woods, manatees bob about in the intracoastal waters, while in summer, turtles lay their eggs on the beach *(see p113)*. In autumn, northern right whales travel here to calve offshore.

View along a trail through marshland on Little Talbot Island

Kingsley Plantation ❸

Road map E1. Duval Co. 11676 Palmetto Ave, Fort George. ☎ (904) 251-3537. ⊟ Jacksonville. ⊟ Jacksonville. ◯ daily. ● 25 Dec. ♿

L OCATED IN THE Timucuan Ecological and Historic Preserve, Kingsley Plantation is the oldest plantation house in Florida. Built in 1798 at the northern end of Fort George Island, it takes its name from Zephaniah Kingsley, who moved here in 1814. He amassed 32,000 acres (12,950

Ruins of the original slave cabins unique to the Kingsley Plantation

ha) of land, stretching from Lake George near the Ocala National Forest north to the St Mary's River. This area used to encompass four major plantations; the Kingsley plantation itself had as many as 100 slaves working in the fields where cotton, sugar cane and corn were cultivated.

Kingsley was a rather liberal thinker for his time, supporting slavery while also advocating a more lenient "task-system" for his slaves. He married a freed slave, Anna Jai, and they lived in the clapboard plantation house *(see p43)* until 1839.

Described at the time as "a very nice commodious house", Kingsley's relatively simple home has been restored and now contains a visitor centre. The building is topped by a small rooftop parapet called a "widow's walk", once used to survey the surrounding fields. Nearby are the barn and separate kitchen house, but the plantation is best known for the 23 slave cabins located in woods near the entrance gate. Built of durable tabby *(see p282)*, these basic dwellings have survived the years, and one has been restored.

Fort Caroline National Memorial ❹

Road map E1. Duval Co. 12713 Fort Caroline Rd, Jacksonville. ☎ (904) 641-7155. ⊟ Jacksonville. ⊟ Jacksonville. ◯ daily. ● 25 Dec. ♿

T HE ACTUAL SITE of Fort Caroline was washed away when the St Johns River was dredged in the 1880s. At Fort Caroline National Memorial, a reconstruction of the original 16th-century defences clearly illustrates the style of the first European forts in the New World. Information panels around the site explain the citadel's violent history, which began shortly after French settlers arrived in June 1564.

In the attempt to stake a claim to North America, three small French vessels carrying 300 men sailed up the St Johns and made camp 5 miles (8 km) inland. René de Goulaine de Laudonnière led the French, who were helped by local Timucua Indians to build a triangular wooden fort, named La Caroline in honour of Charles IX of France *(see p40)*. A year later, with the settlers close to starvation, reinforcements under Jean Ribault arrived. The Spanish, however, took the fort, crushing the French land claims.

In the park, there is a replica of the stone column erected by Jean Ribault, as well as several short hiking trails.

Fort Caroline in 1564 by Theodore de Bry

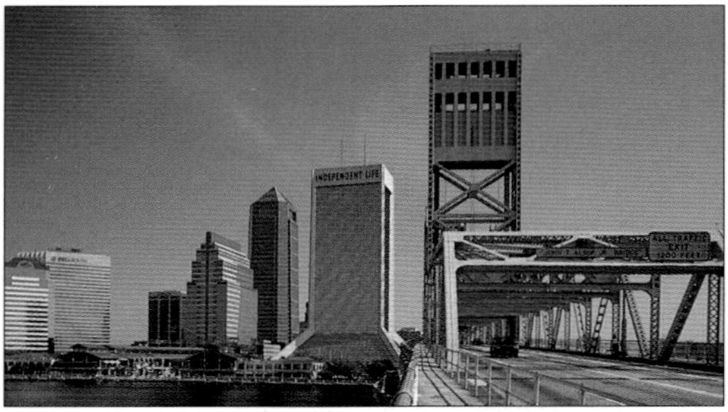

The glass and steel skyline which dominates Jacksonville's north bank

Jacksonville 5

Road map E1. Duval Co.
👥 *1,000,000.* ✈ 🚆 🚌 ℹ *3 Independent Drive, (904) 798-9148.*

JACKSONVILLE, the capital of the First Coast of Florida, was founded in 1822. Named after General Jackson *(see p43)*, the town boomed as a port and rail terminus in the late 1800s. Today, the more sedentary but just as lucrative financial businesses fuel the impressive downtown commercial district, which you can view from the Skyway or ASE *(see p363)*.

This, Florida's largest city in area, spans the St Johns River, which flows through it and provides a welcome focus for visitors. Most people head for the pedestrian areas that flank the river banks and are connected by water taxi services *(see p363)*, though other sights are dotted around the city.

The **Jacksonville Landing** shopping and dining complex is located on the north bank of the St Johns, whilst on the south, the pleasant 1.2-mile (2-km) long **Riverwalk** connects the Jacksonville Historic Center and the impressive Museum of Science and History.

Riverside, on the opposite bank, is home to the renowned Cummer Museum of Art. This large residential district, which contains a wonderful array of Revival-style architecture popular up to the 1920s, is best explored by car.

🏛 Museum of Science and History

1025 Museum Circle Drive. ☎ *(904) 396-7062.* 🕒 *daily.* 📷 ♿

This ever-expanding museum houses an eclectic collection of exhibits and provides a user-friendly guide to local history. The 12,000 year-old material culture of the local Timucua Indians *(see pp38–9)* and their predecessors is illustrated with tools, arrowheads, pottery and other archaeological finds.

There are sections dealing with the ecology and history of the St Johns and the *Maple Leaf*, a Civil War steamship

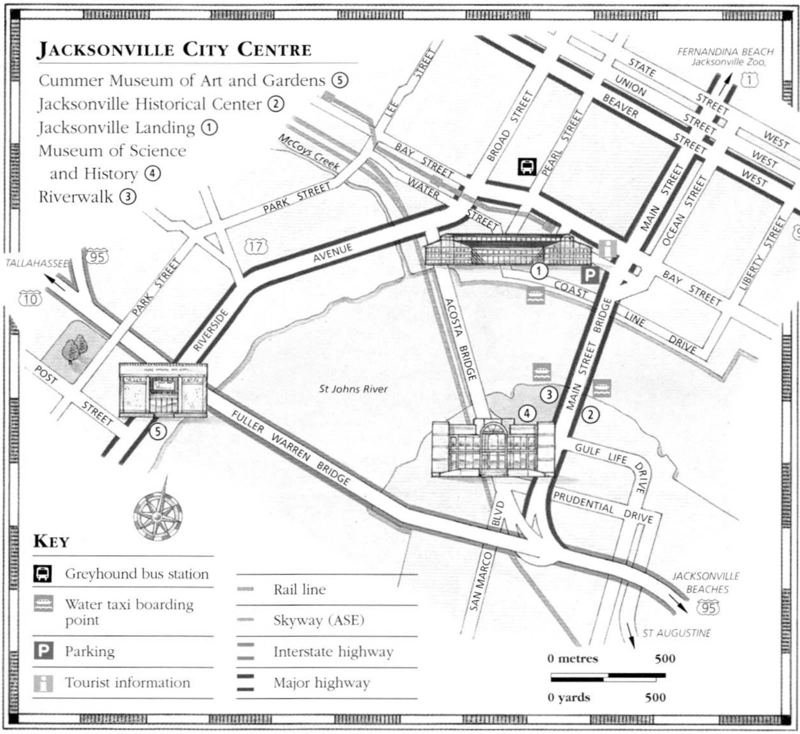
JACKSONVILLE CITY CENTRE
Cummer Museum of Art and Gardens 5
Jacksonville Historical Center 2
Jacksonville Landing 1
Museum of Science and History 4
Riverwalk 3
FERNANDINA BEACH Jacksonville Zoo
STATE STREET
UNION STREET
BEAVER STREET
WEST
LEE STREET
BROAD STREET
PEARL STREET
McCoys Creek
BAY STREET
WATER STREET
PARK STREET
AVENUE
MAIN STREET
OCEAN STREET
LIBERTY STREET
BAY STREET
COAST LINE DRIVE
TALLAHASSEE
RIVERSIDE
ACOSTA BRIDGE
MAIN STREET BRIDGE
St Johns River
POST STREET
FULLER WARREN BRIDGE
GULF LIFE DRIVE
PRUDENTIAL DRIVE
SAN MARCO BLVD
JACKSONVILLE BEACHES
ST AUGUSTINE
KEY
Greyhound bus station
Water taxi boarding point
Parking
Tourist information
Rail line
Skyway (ASE)
Interstate highway
Major highway
0 metres 500
0 yards 500

which sank in 1864, a host of entertaining hands-on gadgets in the exhibition hall, and the Alexander Brest Planetarium. This also runs state-of-the-art 3-D laser shows.

🏛 Jacksonville Historical Center

Southbank Riverwalk. [(904) 398-4301. ◯ daily. ● Thanksgiving, 25 Dec, 1 Jan. ⟨&⟩
At the foot of the Main Street Bridge, the Jacksonville Historical Center is a modest museum that charts local history using information panels, artifacts, old photographs and video footage. One section of the centre salutes the silent movie era, when the city was the world's Winter Film Capital and a rotund movie projectionist from the state of Georgia named Oliver Hardy got his first acting break in 1913.

Ostriches and rare white rhinos at the famous Jacksonville Zoo

🐾 Jacksonville Zoo

8605 Zoo Parkway. [(904) 757-4462. ◯ daily. ● Thanksgiving, 25 Dec. ⟨⟩ ⟨&⟩
Opened in 1914, Jacksonville Zoo lies north of the city, off I-95. Its outmoded cages have recently been replaced with natural habitats where some 600 animals, from anteaters to zebras, are on view. Lions, elephants and kudu roam the African veldt, while diminutive dik-dik deer, African crocodiles and porcupines can be found along the zoo's Okavango Trail. Other attractions include an aviary, a petting zoo and a Florida wetlands area.
For a broader picture, take the 15-minute miniature train journey which loops around half of the 73-acre (30-ha) site.

🏛 Cummer Museum of Art and Gardens

829 Riverside Ave. [(904) 356-6857. ◯ Tue–Sun. ● Thanksgiving, 25 Dec, 1 Jan. ⟨⟩ ⟨&⟩
This excellent museum stands in exquisite formal gardens which lead down to the St Johns River. Its twelve galleries exhibit a small but satisfying collection of both decorative and fine arts. These range from Classical and pre-Columbian sculpture and ceramics through Renaissance paintings to the Wark Collection of jewel-like early Meissen porcelain.
Other notable pieces include the tiny *Entombment of Christ* (c.1605) by Rubens, and a striking collection of Japanese netsuke. There's also work by American Impressionists and 19th- and 20th-century artists such as John James Audubon.

Jacksonville Beaches ❻

Road map E1. Duval Co, St Johns Co. ▣ Jacksonville. ▣ Jacksonville ▥ BH1, BH2, BH3. ▯ Jacksonville Beach, (904) 249-3868.

SOME 12 MILES (19 km) east of downtown Jacksonville, half a dozen beaches stretch 28 miles (45 km) north and south along the Atlantic shore linked by the A1A. In the south, Ponte Vedra Beach is known for its sports facilities, particularly golf. Jacksonville Beach itself is the busiest and brashest spot and is home to **Adventure Landing**, a year-round entertainment complex and summer

Swimmers enjoy the freshwater lakes of Kathryn Abbey Hanna Park

season water park. Heading north, Neptune Beach and Atlantic Beach are both quieter and are popular with families.
By far the nicest spot is the **Kathryn Abbey Hanna Park**, with its 1.5 miles (2.5 km) of unspoilt fine white sand beach, woodland trails, freshwater lake fishing and swimming, picnic and camping facilities. The park lies just south of the quaint town of **Mayport**, one of the oldest fishing villages in the US, which still has its own shrimping fleet. The St Johns ferry *(see p191)* links the town to the north bank of the mighty St Johns river.

🎢 Adventure Landing

1944 Beach Blvd. [(904) 246-4386. ◯ daily. ⟨⟩ ⟨&⟩
🌿 Kathryn Abbey Hanna Park

500 Wonderwood Drive. [(904) 249-4700. ◯ daily. ● Thanksgiving, 25 Dec, 1 Jan. ⟨⟩ ⟨&⟩ ⟨⚠⟩

Shrimp boats moored at the picturesque docks of Mayport on the St Johns

Street-by-Street: St Augustine ❼

Aᴍᴇʀɪᴄᴀ's ᴏʟᴅᴇsᴛ continuously-occupied European settlement was founded by Pedro Menéndez de Avilés *(see p40)* on the feast day of St Augustine in 1565. The town burned down in 1702 but was soon rebuilt in the lee of the mighty Castillo de San Marcos; many of the picturesque, narrow streets of the old town, lined by attractive stone buildings, date from this early period.

When Henry Flagler *(see p121)* honeymooned in St Augustine in 1883, he was so taken by the place that he returned the following year to found the Ponce de Leon Hotel, now Flagler College, and soon the gentle trickle of visitors became a flood. St Augustine has been a major stop on the tourist trail ever since.

★ Flagler College
Tiles and other Spanish touches were used in the architecture of this former Flagler hotel.

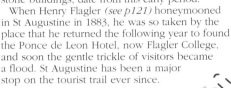

Zorayda Castle
This house contains artifacts such as this 2,300-year old Egyptian sacred cat rug.

★ Lightner Museum
Cleopatra *(c.1890)* by Romanelli is one of the exhibits from Florida's Gilded Age on display here.

The Cordoba Hotel became Flagler's third hotel in town in 1888.

Oldest Store Museum
Groceries, domestic appliances and hardware crowd this re-created 19th-century store.

To Oldest House

★ Ximenez-Fatio House
This was built as a private house in 1797. Later, a second floor with an airy veranda was added, and in the mid-1800s it became a boarding house.

Sᴛᴀʀ Sɪɢʜᴛs

★ **Flagler College**

★ **Lightner Museum**

★ **Ximenez-Fatio House**

Plaza de la Constitution

The heart of the Spanish settlement is this leafy square flanked by Government House and the Basilica Cathedral.

VISITORS' CHECKLIST

Road map E1. St Johns Co.
🏠 16,000. ☐ 100 Malaga St,
(904) 829-6401. 🛈 10 Castillo
Drive, (904) 825-1000. ⚑ Arts
& Crafts Spring Festival (late Mar),
Cross & Sword Play (Jul–Aug).

To City Gate

City Gate

Dating from the 18th century, this city entrance leads to the Old Town via historic George Street.

The Peña-Peck House, dating from the 1740s, is the finest First Spanish Period home in the city.

Bridge of Lions

Marble lions guard the bridge built across Matanzas Bay in 1926.

0 metres   50

0 yards   50

KEY

 — — — Suggested route

Spanish Military Hospital

This reconstruction of a ward re-creates the spartan hospital conditions available to Spanish settlers in the late 1700s.

Exploring St Augustine

THE HISTORIC HEART of St Augustine is compact and easy to explore on foot. Part of the fun is escaping off the busy main streets and wandering down shady side turnings, peering into courtyards, and discovering quiet corners where cats bask in the sunshine and ancient live oaks trail curtains of grey-green Spanish moss. Horsedrawn carriage tours are a popular way to get around and depart from Avenida Menendez, north of the Bridge of Lions. Miniature tourist trains follow a more extensive route around the main sights while their drivers narrate an anecdotal history of St Augustine.

St George Street, the historic district's main thoroughfare

A Tour of St Augustine

Pedestrianized St George Street is the focus of the historic district, with a collection of shops and some of St Augustine's main attractions, including the excellent Spanish Quarter Museum. Set back two blocks from the waterfront, the street leads from the old City Gate to the town square, the Plaza de la Constitution. Attractive, cobbled Aviles Street, which runs south from this square, also has several interesting colonial buildings.

There is a very different feel along King Street, west of the plaza. Here, the Lightner Museum and Flagler College are housed in hotels built by Henry Flagler (see pp46–7) during St Augustine's heyday, in the late 19th century.

⚱ The Oldest Wooden Schoolhouse

14 St George St. ((904) 824-0192
○ daily. ● 25 Dec. 🎨 &
Built some time before 1788, this is purportedly America's oldest wooden schoolhouse. Walls made of rough planks

of cypress and red cedar are held together by wooden pins and cast-iron spikes, and the house is encircled by a massive chain designed to anchor it to the ground in high winds.

🏛 Spanish Quarter Museum

33 St George St. ((904) 825-6830.
○ daily. ● 25 Dec. 🎨 &
This entertaining and informative museum offers a fascinating step back in time to the simple lifestyles of the mid-18th century garrison town. It is housed in seven reconstructed buildings, laid out in a grassy compound planted with citrus trees and vegetable gardens.

Staff in period costume explain the purpose of essential household items in the spartan homes, and various craft demonstrations reveal the intricacies and sheer hard work needed to produce even basics such as clothing. Sparks fly in the blacksmith's shop, one of the best shows in town, and a taverna is set up with hand-blown glasses, earthenware pitchers and casks of Cuban rum, along with games such as dominoes and dice.

The blacksmith at work in the Spanish Quarter Museum

⚱ Peña-Peck House

143 St George St. ((904) 829-5064.
○ daily. 🎨 &
This graciously restored house was built in the 1740s for the Spanish Royal Treasurer, Juan de Peña. In 1837 it became the home and office of Dr Seth Peck, and the Peck family continued to live here for almost 100 years. The house is furnished in mid-19th century style and many of the objects displayed are family heirlooms.

🏛 Government House Museum

48 King St. ((904) 825-5033.
○ daily. ● 25 Dec. 🎨 &
Government House, which overlooks the Plaza de la Constitution, is adorned with Spanish-style loggias copied from a 17th-century painting of the original building. Inside, a small local history museum displays archaeological and colonial artifacts including silver and gold coins salvaged from Spanish treasure ships.

The Oldest Wooden Schoolhouse, built in the 1700s

⚕ Spanish Military Hospital
3 Aviles St. ☎ *(904) 825-6808.*
◯ *daily.* ● *25 Dec.*
The Spanish Military Hospital offers a rare glimpse into the care afforded soldiers in the late 1700s. Rooms include an apothecary's and a simple cot-lined ward. On display is a list of surprisingly patient-friendly hospital rules, medical instruments and suitably gory accounts of medical practices.

🏛 Oldest Store Museum
4 Artillery Lane. ☎ *(904) 829-9729.*
◯ *daily.* ● *25 Dec.* 📷 &
Arranged as an early 1900s general store, this unashamedly nostalgic museum houses a veritable cornucopia of antique hardware and foodstuffs. The collection's 100,000 odd items include box cameras, chewing tobacco and eccentric-looking apple-peelers.

⚕ Ximenez-Fatio House
20 Aviles St. ☎ *(904) 829-3575.*
◯ *Oct–Aug: Thu–Mon.* ● *Thanks-giving, 25 Dec.* & *limited.*
The attractive Ximenez-Fatio House was originally built in 1797 as the home and store of a Spanish mer-chant. Today, run by the National Society of Colonial Dames, this museum recreates the genteel boarding house that it became in the 1830s, when invalids, developers and adventurers first began to visit Florida to escape the harsh northern winters.
Using antique furnish-ings, each room is decorated as if for a particular lodger.

⚕ Oldest House
14 St Francis St. ☎ *(904) 824-2872.*
◯ *daily.* ● *25 Dec.* 📷 &
The well-documented history of this house has enabled its development to be traced through almost 300 years. There is even evidence that the site was first occupied in the early 1600s, though the existing structure post-dates the English raid of 1702 *(see p41).*
   The coquina walls *(see p201)* were part of the original one-storey home of a Spanish artilleryman, Tomas Gonzalez, who lived here with his family.

The Gonzalez Room, named after the first residents of the Oldest House

A second storey was added during the English occupation of 1763–83, and additional changes were made later. Each room has been restored and furnished in a style relevant to the different periods of the house's long history.

🏛 Lightner Museum
75 King St. ☎ *(904) 824-2874.*
◯ *daily.* ● *25 Dec.* 📷 &
Formerly the Alcazar Hotel, set up by Henry Flagler, this Hispano-Moorish building was an inspired choice for a museum devoted to the country's Gilded Age. The setting was selected by the Chicago pub-lisher Otto C Lightner, who transferred his extensive collections of Victorian fine and decorative arts to St Augustine, prior to opening the museum in 1948. Elegantly exhibited over three floors, there's a glitter-ing display of superb glass (including work by Louis Tiffany), furnishings, sculpture and paintings, plus mechanical musical instruments and toys. In the basement, the Alcazar's former indoor swimming pool now houses an antiques mall.

Tiffany stained-glass window

⚕ Flagler College
King St at Cordova St. ☎ *(904) 829-6481.* ◯ *daily.* &
This building started out as the Ponce de Leon Hotel, another of Henry Flagler's splendid endeavours. When it opened in 1888 it was heralded as "the world's finest hotel". A rather dapper statue of Flagler him-self still greets visitors, but only the college dining room

and the elegant marble-clad foyer in the rotunda are open to the public. Here, the gilded and stuccoed cupola is deco-rated with symbolic motifs representing Spain and Florida: notably the golden mask of the Timucuan *(see pp38–9)* sun god, and the lamb symbolizing Spanish knighthood. During the college's summer break you can also visit the Flagler Room with its odd illusionary paintings executed circa 1887.

🏛 Zorayda Castle
83 King St. ☎ *(904) 824-3097.*
◯ *daily.* ● *25 Dec.* 📷 &
This former private residence is a one-tenth scale replica of part of the Alhambra palace in Granada, Spain. Built in 1883, with 40 windows differ-ing in size, shape and colour, it is home to a collection of oriental curiosities. Amongst the exhibits is a Persian tear vase used to collect the tears of mourners at weddings and funerals. The tears were saved: the greater the quantity, the greater the family's importance.

Moorish tracery and Arabic motifs decorating the Zorayda Castle

Castillo de San Marcos

D ESPITE ITS ROLE as protector of the Spanish
fleets en route back to Europe, St Augustine
was guarded for over a century only by a suc-
cession of wooden forts. The Spanish colonizers finally began to build a stone fortification
in 1672, after suffering repeated pirate attacks
and the attentions of Sir Francis Drake *(see p41)*.

The resulting Castillo de San Marcos, which
took 23 years to finish, is the largest and most
complete Spanish fort in the US. Constructed
of coquina, it is a textbook example of 17th-
century military architecture, with layers of outer
defences and walls up to 19 ft (6 m) thick.

After the US gained Florida in 1821, the castillo
was renamed Fort Marion. It was used chiefly
as a military prison and storage depot for the
rest of the 19th century.

Mortars
*Often highly decorated and bear-
ing the royal coat of arms, these
short-barrelled weapons fired
large, heavy projectiles on a
curved trajectory. Bombs
could thus clear obstacles
or land on ships' decks.*

The Plaza de Armas is
ringed by rooms which
were used to contain
stockpiles of food and
weapons.

★ Guard Rooms
*No Spanish soldiers actually lived in
the fort. During guard duty
(usually 24-hour shifts),
they would cook, eat
and shelter in these
reinforced vaults.*

The moat, which
once encircled the
entire fort, was
usually kept dry.
During sieges
livestock was
kept there.

★ Glacis and Covered Way
*Across the moat, a walled area known as the
"covered way" shielded soldiers firing on the
enemy. Leading up to the wall, a slope (the
"glacis") protected the fort from cannon fire.*

The ravelin
guarded the
entrance from
enemy attack.

**The inner drawbridge
and portcullis**, built of
iron-clad pine beams,
were the fort's final
defences.

COQUINA

This sedimentary limestone rock, formed by billions of compacted seashells and corals, had the consistency of hard cheese when waterlogged and was easy to quarry. It hardened as it dried, but could still absorb the impact of a cannon ball without shattering. During the siege of 1740, the English attackers fired projectiles which buried themselves in the fort's coquina walls. Legend has it that they were then dug out and fired back.

The thick coquina walls of the powder magazine

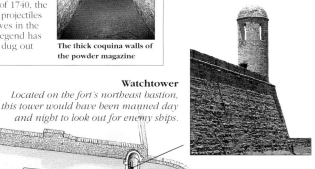

Watchtower
Located on the fort's northeast bastion, this tower would have been manned day and night to look out for enemy ships.

British room

Chapel

Powder magazine

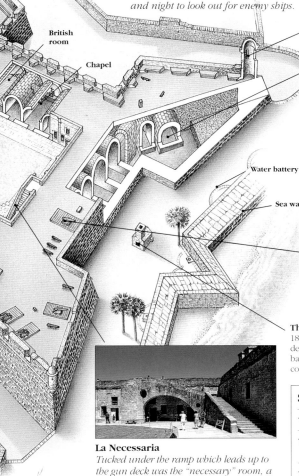

Water battery

Sea wall

★ Gun Deck
From here, cannons could reach targets up to 3 miles (5 km) away. Strategic positioning made a deadly crossfire.

The shot furnace, built in 1844 by the US Army, was designed to heat up cannon balls. The red-hot "shot" could set enemy ships alight.

La Necessaria
Tucked under the ramp which leads up to the gun deck was the "necessary" room, a tidal-flush sewage system.

STAR FEATURES

★ **Guard Rooms**

★ **Glacis and Covered Way**

★ **Gun Deck**

Marineland Ocean Resort ⑧

Road map E2. Flagler Co. 9507 Ocean Shore Blvd, Marineland. ☎ (904) 471-1111. 🚌 St Augustine. ⭘ daily. 🅿️ ♿

A POPULAR ATTRACTION and resort, Marineland started life as a film facility in the late 1930s and can claim to be the original Florida marine park. Perennial favourites – the sea lion and dolphin shows – are scheduled regularly, and you can see divers feed sharks and moray eels in the Oceanarium.

The "Wonders of the Spring" exhibit recreates life in one of Florida's artesian springs (see p206), while the "Secrets of the Reef" teems with exotic tropical fish. A half-hour 3-D film, Sea Dream, is shown all day and has the audience gripping their seats as toothy denizens of the deep appear to swim right out of the screen.

The 1938 Marineland complex, a pleasing blend of old and new

Washington Oaks State Gardens ⑨

Road map E2. Flagler Co. 6400 N Ocean Shore Blvd, 2 miles (3 km) S of Marineland. ☎ (904) 446-6780. 🚌 St Augustine. ⭘ daily. 🅿️ ♿

B ENEATH A SHADY canopy of oaks and palms, 400 acres (162 ha) of former plantation land have been transformed into lovely gardens planted with hydrangeas, azaleas and luxuriant ferns. There is also a rose garden, and trails loop through a coastal hammock

Ruins of the 19th-century sugar mill at Bulow Plantation

to the Matanzas River. Across the A1A a boardwalk leads down to the beach, which is strewn with coquina boulders (see p201) and tidal pools that over time have been eroded out of the soft stone.

Bulow Plantation Ruins State Historic Site ⑩

Road map E2. Flagler Co. Old Kings Rd, 3 miles (5 km) S of SR 100. ☎ (904) 517-2084. 🚌 Daytona Beach. ⭘ daily. 🅿️ ♿

S OMEWHAT OFF the beaten track west of Flagler Beach, the ruins of this 19th-century plantation stand in a dense hammock where sugar cane once grew. The site is part of the 4,675 acres (1,890 ha) of land adjacent to a creek that Major Charles Bulow bought in 1821. His slaves cleared half this area and planted rice and cotton as well as sugar cane. The plantation, known as Bulowville, was abandoned after Indian attacks during the Seminole Wars (see pp44–5).

Today, Bulow Creek is a state canoe trail, and you can hire canoes to explore this pretty backwater. On its banks are the foundations of the plantation house, and from here it's a ten-minute stroll through the forest to a clearing where the ruins of the old sugar mill still stand. These resemble the mysterious remains of some long-lost ancient South American temple.

Ormond Beach ⑪

Road map E2. Volusia Co. 🏠 50,000. 🚌 Daytona Beach. ℹ️ 126 E Orange Ave, Daytona Beach (904) 255-0415.

O RMOND BEACH was one of the earliest winter resorts on Henry Flagler's railway (see pp46–7). No longer standing, his fashionable Ormond Hotel boasted a star-studded guest list including the likes of Henry Ford and John D Rockefeller.

Rockefeller bought a house just across the street from the hotel in 1918 – prompted, so the story goes, by overhearing that another guest was paying less; despite his immense

The Rockefeller Room in The Casements, Ormond Beach

wealth, the millionaire chief of Standard Oil guarded his nickels and dimes closely. This winter home, **The Casements**, has been restored and today functions as a museum and cultural centre. Inside are examples of Rockefeller-era memorabilia, which include the great man's high-sided wicker beach chair with glazed portholes. There's also a period-style room and a rather incongruous Hungarian arts and crafts display.

A short walk from The Casements, the **Ormond Memorial Art Museum** is set in a small but charming tropical garden. Shady paths wind around lily ponds inhabited by basking turtles and flanked by stands of bamboo and lush tropical vegetation. The museum itself hosts frequently changing exhibitions, mainly of works by contemporary Florida artists.

Old Flagler engine, Ormond Beach

🚂 **The Casements**
25 Riverside Drive. 📞 *(904) 676-3216.* ⏰ *Mon–Sat.* 🔴 *public hols.* ♿ 📷
🏛 **Ormond Memorial Art Museum**
78 E Granada Blvd. 📞 *(904) 676-3347.* ⏰ *daily.* 🔴 *public hols.* 📷 ♿

Daytona Beach ⓬

Road map E2. Volusia Co. 🏠 *64,000.* ✈ 🚉 ℹ *126 E Orange Ave, (904) 255-0415.*

EXTENDING SOUTH from Ormond Beach is brash and boisterous Daytona Beach. As many as 200,000 students descend on the resort for the Spring Break *(see p32)*, even though Daytona has tried to discourage them. Its famous 23-mile (37-km) beach is one of the few in Florida where cars are allowed on the sands, a hangover from the days when motor enthusiasts raced on the beaches *(see p205)*.

Daytona is still a mecca for motorsports enthusiasts. The nearby speedway *(see p204)* draws huge crowds, especially during the Speedweeks in February and the Motorcycle Weeks in March and October.

Downtown Daytona, known simply as "Mainland", lies across the Halifax River from the beach. Most of the action, though, takes place on the seafront, which is lined with a concrete barrier of hotels. The old-fashioned Boardwalk is both nostalgic and tacky, with concerts in the open-air bandstand, arcades, go-karts, candy floss and fast food. The gondola skyride glides above Ocean Pier, while down on the beach itself, jet skis, windsurfers, buggies and beach bicycles can be hired. Across the Halifax River, in the restored downtown area, the **Halifax Historical Society Museum** occupies a grand 1910 bank building decorated with fancy pilasters and murals. Local history displays include a model of the Boardwalk circa 1938, with chicken feather palm trees, a ferris wheel and scores of miniature people.

West of downtown, exhibits at the excellent **Museum of Arts and Sciences** cover a broad range of subjects. The Florida prehistory section is dominated by the 13-ft (4-m) skeleton of a giant sloth, while Arts in America features fine and decorative arts from 1640–1920. Additionally, there are notable Cuban and African collections and a planetarium.

Miss Perkins **(c.1840) by J Whiting Stock, Museum of Arts and Sciences**

Gamble Place is run by the same museum. Built in 1907 for James N Gamble, of Procter & Gamble, this Cracker-style backwoods hunting lodge sits on a bluff above Spruce Creek, surrounded by open porches. The furnishings inside are all period pieces. Tours are by reservation only through the museum; these also take in the Snow White House, which was built in 1938 for Gamble's great-grandchildren, and is an exact copy of the one in the 1937 Disney classic.

🏛 **Halifax Historical Society Museum**
252 S Beach St. 📞 *(904) 255-6976.* ⏰ *Tue–Sat.* 🔴 *public hols.* 📷 ♿
🏛 **Museum of Arts and Sciences**
1040 Museum Blvd. 📞 *(904) 255-0285.* ⏰ *Tue–Sun.* 🔴 *public hols.* 📷 ♿ **Gamble Place** ⏰ *Wed & Sat.* 📷 🎟 *compulsory.*

Cars cruising the hard-packed sands of Daytona Beach

Daytona International Speedway ⓭

Road map E2. Volusia Co. 1801 W International Speedway Blvd. **☎** *(904) 254-2700.* 🚌 *Daytona.* 🚎 *9 from bus terminal at 209 Bethune Blvd.* 🕐 *daily.* ● *25 Dec.* 🈂️ ♿

D AYTONA'S VERY OWN "World Center of Racing", the Daytona International Speedway, attracts thousands of race fans and visitors every year. People come from around the world to attend the eight major racing weekends held annually at the track – which can hold over 110,000 spectators. The Speedway is host to NASCAR (National Association for Stock Car Auto Racing) meets – the Daytona 500 being the most famous – and sports car, motorcycle and go-karting races. In between, there is a full programme of events such as charity bike-a-thons, vintage car rallies, superbike spectaculars and production car tests.

1953 red Corvette in the Klassix Auto Museum

Tickets for each Daytona 500 are sold out a year in advance, but visitors can relive the experience at DAYTONA USA, the ultimate motorsports attraction in the visitor centre. A film featuring behind-the-scenes action and spectacular in-car camera shots filmed during a recent Daytona 500 is just one of the state-of-the-art exhibits on offer. Visitors can also test their own stock car using the latest computer technology, design and take part in a simulated interactive pit stop, and try their skill at race commentary. You can go on half-hour tram tours around the speedway track itself on days when no races take place.

ENVIRONS: The nearby Klassix Auto Museum has an impressive collection of Corvettes, one for each year since 1953. There are also stock cars, vintage motorcycles and racing memorabilia on display.

🏛 **Klassix Auto Museum**
2909 W International Speedway Blvd. **☎** *(904) 252-3800.* 🕐 *daily.* 🈂️ ♿

The Daytona 500, held each February at Daytona International Speedway

Ponce de Leon Inlet Lighthouse ⓮

Road map E2. Volusia Co. 4931 S Peninsula Drive. **☎** *(904) 761-1821.* 🕐 *daily.* ● *25 Dec.* 🈂️ ♿

T HIS IMPOSING red brick lighthouse dates from 1887 and guards the entrance to a hazardous inlet at the tip of the Daytona peninsula. Tapering skywards for 175 ft (53 m), its beacon is visible 19 miles (30 km) out to sea, and there are far-reaching views from the wind-swept observation deck reached by a 203-step spiral staircase. One of the former keepers' cottages at its base has been restored to its 1890s appearance, another is home to the small Museum of the Sea, while a third contains a magnificent 17-ft (5-m) high first order Fresnel lens.

DAYTONA INTERNATIONAL SPEEDWAY

LAKE LLOYD

ℹ️

🅿️

DAYTONA BEACH

Williamson Beltway

W International Speedway Blvd (92)

I-4
I-95

KEY

☐	Visitor centre
☐	Track
☐	Grandstand
◼	Winton tower

0 metres   500
0 yards   500

The striking Ponce de Leon Inlet lighthouse south of Daytona Beach

The Birthplace of Speed

DAYTONA'S LOVE AFFAIR with the car started in 1903, when the first timed automobile runs took place on the sands at Ormond Beach, the official "Birthplace of Speed". That year, Alexander Winton achieved a land speed record of 68 mph (109 km/h). The speed trials were enormously popular and attracted large crowds. Rich motor enthusiasts gathered at Henry Flagler's Ormond Hotel *(see p202)*, and included the likes of Harvey Firestone and Henry Ford. Speed trials continued until 1935, when Malcolm Campbell set the last world record on the beach. Stock cars began racing at Ormond Beach in 1936, and the first Daytona 200 motorcycle race took place there the following year. Development forced the racetrack to be moved in 1948; in 1959 Daytona International Speedway opened and racing on the beach was abandoned altogether.

1936 Harley-Davidson

RACING ON THE BEACH
In 1902, a guest at the Ormond Hotel noticed just how easy it was to drive his car on the hard sandy beach. He organized the first speed trials, which continued for the next 32 years.

*Ransom E Olds' **Pirate** was the first car to race on Ormond Beach in 1902. The first official race was held in 1903, when Olds challenged Alexander Winton and Oscar Hedstrom on a motorcycle. Winton won in his car,* Bullet No 1.

*The **Bluebird Streamliner** was driven to a new world record for the measured mile by Malcolm Campbell at Ormond Beach in 1935. Powered by a Rolls-Royce engine, the car reached speeds of just over 276 mph (444 km/h).*

THE "WORLD CENTER OF RACING"
In 1953 Bill France, who had entered the inaugural stock car race, saw that the growth of Daytona Beach would soon put an end to the beach races. He proposed the construction of Daytona International Speedway, today one of the world's leading race tracks.

Go-karts look like the fun machines that you can race on holiday, but the karts that compete at Daytona manage speeds of over 81 mph (130 km/h).

Lee Petty won the first Daytona 500 at Daytona International Speedway in 1959, beating Johnny Beauchamp, his fellow competitor, by a mere 2 ft (50 cm). The 500-mile (800-km) competition was watched by a crowd of 41,000 and involved 59 cars.

Blue Spring State Park ⓯

Road map E2. Volusia Co. 2100 W French Ave, Orange City. 📞 *(904) 775-3663*. ◯ *daily.* 🅿 ♿ **Boat Rides** 📞 *(904) 734-2474*.

ONE OF THE USA's largest first-magnitude artesian springs, Blue Spring pours out around 100 million gal (450 million litres) of water a day. As this is at a constant 20° C (68° F), the park is a favourite winter refuge for manatees *(see p236)*. Between November and March, when the manatees escape the cooler waters of the St Johns River, you can see them from the park's elevated boardwalks.

You can snorkel or scuba dive in the turquoise waters of the spring head, or canoe on the St Johns. Two-hour return boat trips to Hontoon Island also depart from here.

Thursby House, which sits atop one of the park's ancient shell mounds, was built in the late 19th century.

ENVIRONS: About 2 miles (3 km) north as the crow flies is wooded **Hontoon Island State Park**. Reached by a free passenger ferry from Hontoon Landing, the island has an 80-ft (24-m) observation tower, camping and picnic areas, and a nature trail. Canoes and fishing skiffs can also be rented.

In 1955 a rare wooden owl totem made by the ancient local Timucua Indians *(see pp38–9)* was found here.

🛶 Hontoon Island State Park

2309 River Ridge Rd, De Land. 📞 *(904) 736-5309*. ◯ *daily.* 🅿

FLORIDA'S BUBBLING SPRINGS

Most of Florida's 320 known springs are located in the upper half of the state. The majority are artesian springs, formed by waters forced up often deep fissures from underground aquifers (rock deposits containing water). Those which gush over 100 cu ft (3 cu m) per second are known as first-magnitude springs.

Filtered through the rock, the water is extremely pure and sometimes high in salts and minerals. These properties, plus the sheer beauty of the springs, have long attracted visitors for recreational and health purposes.

Juniper Springs in Ocala National Forest, adapted for swimmers in the 1930s

Sanford ⓰

Road map E2. Seminole Co. 🏠 *35,000.* ℹ *400 E 1st St, (407) 322-2212.* 🚆 *inc Auto Train.* 🚌 *Lynx buses from Orlando (see p363).*

BUILT DURING the Seminole Wars *(see pp43–5)*, Fort Mellon was the first permanent settlement on Lake Monroe. Sanford was founded nearby in the 1870s. It became a major inland port thanks to the commercial steamboat services, which eventually also brought Florida's adventurous early tourists *(see p46)*.

Restored downtown Sanford dates from the 1880s, the height of this Steamboat era. Several of the lovely old red brick buildings (a rarity in Florida) house antique shops, and the area can easily be explored on foot in a couple of hours. Today's

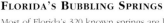

Sanford town sign

visitors are more likely to arrive on the Auto Train *(see p360)* than by river, but short pleasure cruises are still available.

Mount Dora ⓱

Road map E2. Lake Co. 🏠 *8,000.* 🚆 *Sanford.* ℹ *341 Alexander St, (352) 383-2165.*

SET AMONG THE citrus groves of Lake County, this town is one of the prettiest Victorian settlements left in the state. Its name comes from both the relatively high local elevation of 184 ft (56 m) and the small lake on which it sits. The town was originally known as Royellou, after Roy, Ella and Louis, the children of the first postmaster.

Mount Dora's attractive tree-lined streets are laid out on a bluff above the lakeshore, and a 3-mile (5-km) historic tour map is available from the chamber of commerce. The tour takes a scenic route around quiet neighbourhoods of late 19th-century clapboard homes and the sympathetically restored downtown historic district, with its tempting array of stores and antique shops.

On Donnelly Street, the splendid Donnelly House, now a Masonic Hall, is a notable example of ornate Steamboat architecture, adorned with pinnacles and a cupola.

Children playing in front of Thursby House, Blue Spring State Park

Shingles and gingerbread decoration on Donnelly House, Mount Dora

Nearby, the small Royellou Museum depicts local history in the old fire station which later became the town jail. Down on Lake Dora, fishing and water sports are available.

🏛 Royellou Museum

450 Royellou Lane. **[** *(352) 383-0006.* ☐ *Thu–Sun.* ● *Thanksgiving, 25 Dec, 1 Jan.* **ᵫ** *limited.*

Ocala National Forest ⑱

Road map E2. Lake Co/Marion Co. ☐ *daily.* 🅿 *to camp site & swimming areas.* **ᵫ** 🅰 **Visitor Center** *10863 E Hwy 40, (352) 625-7470.* **Juniper Springs canoe hire** *(352) 625-2808.*

BETWEEN OCALA and the St Johns River, the world's largest sand pine forest covers 366,000 acres (148,000 ha), criss-crossed by spring-fed rivers and numerous hiking trails. It is one of the last refuges of the endangered Florida black bear and also home to many more common animals such as deer and otter. Birds, including bald eagles, ospreys, barred owls, the non-native wild turkey and many species of waders (which frequent the river swamp areas), can all be spotted here.

Dozens of hiking trails vary in length from boardwalks and short loop trails of under a mile (1.5 km) to a 66-mile (106-km) stretch of the cross-state National Scenic Trail (*see p343*). Bass-fishing is popular on the many lakes scattered through the forest, and there are swimming holes, picnic areas and camp grounds at recreation areas such as Salt Springs, Alexander Springs and Fore Lake.

Canoe hire is widely available; the 7-mile (11-km) canoe run down Juniper Creek from the Juniper Springs Recreation Area is one of the finest in the state, but book in advance. Bird-watching for waders is particularly good along the Salt Springs Trail, and wood ducks with their colourful faces congregate on Lake Dorr.

You can pick up information and guides at the main visitor centre on the western edge of the forest, or at the smaller centres at Salt Springs and Lake Dorr, both on Route 19.

Silver Springs ⑲

Road map E2. Marion Co. *5656 E Silver Springs Blvd.* **[** *(352) 236-2121.* ☐ *daily.* 🅿 **ᵫ** *limited.*

GLASS-BOTTOMED boat trips at Silver Springs have been revealing the natural wonders of the world's largest artesian spring since 1878.

Today, Florida's oldest commercial tourist attraction offers a range of family activities, although the glass-bottomed boat rides remain the firm favourite. Jeep safaris and "Jungle Cruises" travel through the Florida outback, where the original Tarzan movies starring Johnny Weismuller were filmed. Wild Waters, located next to the springs, is a lively family-oriented water park.

ENVIRONS: On a quieter note, at **Silver River State Park**, 2 miles (3 km) southeast, you can do a lovely 15-minute walk along a trail through a hardwood hammock and a cypress swamp area, leading to a swimming hole in a bend of the crystal clear river.

🛶 Silver River State Park

7165 NE 7th St, Ocala. **[** *(352) 236-1827.* ☐ *daily.* 🅿 **ᵫ**

The Jungle Cruise, one of many attractions at Silver Springs

The Young Shepherdess (1868) by
Bougereau, Appleton Museum

Ocala ❷⓿

Road map D2. Marion Co.
🚶 *65,000.* 🚍 🚌 🛈 *Chamber of
Commerce, 110 E Silver Springs Blvd,
(352) 629-8051.*

Surrounded by undulating
pastures neatly edged by
mile upon mile of white wood-
en fences, Ocala is the seat of
Marion County and centre of
Florida's thoroughbred horse
industry. The grass hereabouts
is enriched by the subterranean
limestone aquifer *(see p206),*
and the calcium-rich grazing
helps to contribute to the light,
strong bones of championship
horses. Florida's equine industry has produced more than
37 champions, including five
Kentucky Derby winners.

There are over 400 thoroughbred farms and specialized
breeding centres around Ocala.
Many are open for visits, which
are usually free of charge.
Expect to see Arabians, Paso
Finos and miniature ponies on
the farms; contact the Ocala
Chamber of Commerce for
up-to-date information regarding farm visits.

The only other reason to stop
off in this area is to visit the
Appleton Museum of Art,
east of Ocala. Built in 1984 of
Italian marble by the industrialist and horsebreeder Arthur I
Appleton, the museum houses
stunning art from around the
world. His eclectic collection
includes pre-Columbian and
European antiquities, Oriental
and African pieces and Meissen
porcelain, and is known for
its strong core of mainstream
19th-century European art.

🏛 **Appleton Museum of Art**
4333 E Silver Springs Blvd. 📞 *(352)
236-7100.* 🕐 *daily.* ⬤ *public hols.*
♿ &

Marjorie Kinnan Rawlings State Historic Site ❷⓵

Road map D2. Alachua Co. S CR 325,
Cross Creek. 📞 *(352) 466-3672.*
🚍 *Ocala.* 🕐 *grounds daily; house
Thu–Sun.* ⬤ *Aug–Sep.* ♿ & 🎫

The author Marjorie Kinnan
Rawlings arrived in the tiny
settlement of Cross Creek,
which she was later
to describe fondly as
"a bend in a country
road", in 1928. Her
rambling farmhouse
remains largely un-
changed, nestling in
a well-tended citrus
grove where chickens
peck and ducks waddle
up from the banks of
Orange Lake.

The writer remained
here through the 1930s,
and then visited on and off
until her death in 1953. The
local scenery and characters
fill her autobiographical novel,

**Herlong Inn,
stick collection**

Cross Creek (1942), while the
big scrub country to the south
inspired her Pulitzer prize-
winning novel, *The Yearling*
(1938), a coming-of-age story
about a boy and his fawn.

Guided tours around the
site explore the Cracker-style
homestead, built in the 1880s,
which has been imaginatively
preserved and contains original
Rawlings' furnishings: book-
cases full of contemporary
writings by authors such as
John Steinbeck and Ernest
Hemingway, a secret liquor
cabinet, and a typewriter and
sunhat on the veranda. Lived-
in touches like fresh flowers
make it look as though the
owner has just popped out for
a stroll around the garden.

Micanopy ❷❷

Road map D2. Alachua Co. 🚶 *650.*
🛈 *30 East University Ave, Gainesville,
(352) 374-5260.*

Established in 1821, Florida's
second oldest permanent
white settlement was a trading
post on Indian lands, originally
known as Wanton. Renamed
Micanopy in 1826,
after an Indian chief,
this attractive, time-
warp village is now as
decorous as they come,
and a haven for film
makers and antiques
lovers. Planted with live
oaks trailing Spanish
moss, the main street,
Cholokka Boulevard,
is lined with Victorian
homes and a strip of
historic, brick-fronted
shops stuffed with bric-a-brac
and craft galleries. Here, too,
is the grandest building in
Micanopy, the imposing redbrick antebellum **Herlong
Mansion**, supported by four
massive corinthian columns.
Built by a 19th-century timber
baron, today it serves as a
bed and breakfast *(see p306).*

Micanopy's picturesque
cemetery, established in 1825,
is located on a canopied street
off Seminary Road, en route
to I-75. Shaded by spreading
live oaks and majestic cedars,
and covered with a carpet of
velvety moss, it is a tranquil
oasis well worth seeking out.

The airy porch where author Marjorie Kinnan Rawlings once wrote

Lichen-stained gravestones in Micanopy's atmospheric cemetery

ENVIRONS: During the 17th century one of the largest and most sucessful Spanish cattle ranches in Florida was located to the north of present-day Micanopy. Cattle, horses and hogs once grazed on the lush grass of **Payne's Prairie State Preserve**, where today a small herd of wild American bison can sometimes be seen, as well as over 200 species of local and migratory birds.

Passing through the preserve is the pleasant 17-mile (27-km) **Gainesville–Hawthorne State Trail**, which follows a former railway line and is used by hikers, horseriders and cyclists.

Paynes Prairie State Preserve
US 441, 1 mile (0.5 km) N of Micanopy.
(352) 466-3397. daily.

Gainesville ㉓

Road map D2. Alachua Co.
95,000. 300 East University Avenue, (352) 334-7100.

A UNIVERSITY TOWN, the cultural capital of north central Florida, and also home of the Gators football team, Gainesville is a comfortable blend of town and gown. In the restored downtown historic district are brick buildings which date from the 1880s to the 1920s, several of which house cafés and restaurants. The large, leafy university campus is dotted with several fraternity houses and boasts two important museums.

Leave plenty of time for the first of these, the excellent **Florida Museum of Natural History**. The natural science collections contain over 10 million fossil specimens, plus superb butterfly and shell collections. There are displays dedicated to the various Florida environments and an illuminating anthropological journey through the state's history right up to the 19th century. Also on campus, the sleek, modern **Samuel P Harn Museum of Art** is one of the largest and best-equipped university art museums in the country. Its permanent collection of fine

Gainesville's own "pop"

art and crafts includes Asian ceramics, African ceremonial objects, examples of Japanese woodcuts, and European and American paintings.

Florida Museum of Natural History
Museum Rd at Newell Drive. (352) 392-1721. daily. 25 Dec.
Samuel P Harn Museum of Art
Hull Road (off SW 34th St). (352) 392-9826. Tue–Sun. public hols.

ENVIRONS: Just southwest of town, the lovely **Kanapaha Botanical Gardens** are at the height of their beauty from June to September, though visitors in springtime are rewarded by masses of azaleas in bloom. A trail encircles the sloping 62-acre (25-ha) site, whose beauty was first noted by the naturalist William Bartram (see p43) in the late 1800s. The paths meander beneath vine-covered arches and through bamboo groves. Other distinct areas include a desert garden, a lakeside bog garden, and a colourful hummingbird garden.

Kanapaha Botanical Gardens
4625 SW 63rd Blvd (off Route 24).
(352) 372-4981. Fri–Wed 25 Dec.

Giant Amazonian water lilies, the late summer highlight of the bog garden in Kanapaha Botanical Gardens

THE PANHANDLE

THERE IS A SAYING IN FLORIDA *that "the farther north you go, the farther south you get". Certainly, the Panhandle has a history and sensibility closer to that of the Deep South than to the lower part of the state. Not only geography and history but climate and even time (the western Panhandle is one hour behind the rest of the state) distinguish this intriguing region from other parts of Florida.*

The Panhandle was the site of the first attempt by the Spanish at colonizing Florida and much subsequent fighting by colonial powers. A community was set up near present-day Pensacola in 1559, predating St Augustine, but was abandoned after a hurricane. It later re-emerged and was the main settlement in the region until the 1820s, when Tallahassee was chosen as the capital of the new Territory of Florida *(see p44)*. The site of the new city, equidistant from St Augustine and Pensacola, was a compromise – the precise location reputedly being the meeting point of two scouts sent out on horseback from the two cities. Today, Tallahassee is a dignified state capital with elegant architecture but a small-town air. Thanks to the timber and cotton trade, the 1800s saw spells of prosperity, but the region was bypassed by the influx of wealth that came to other parts of Florida with the laying of the railways.

Tourism in the Panhandle is a more recent development, even though its fine white-sand beaches are unparalleled in the state. This stretch of coast has become increasingly popular with holiday-makers from the Southern states, but it is still often overlooked by overseas visitors. At the eastern end of the Panhandle, in the area known as the "Big Bend", the family resorts give way to quaint historic coastal towns like Cedar Key – a laid-back fishing village reminiscent of old-time Key West. Inland, parks incorporating forests, springs and navigable rivers provide the main attraction.

One of the Panhandle's many dazzling quartz sand beaches, near Pensacola

◁ Tallahassee's Old Capitol Building, in the shadow of its modern replacement

Exploring the Panhandle

MOST VISITORS TO THE Panhandle head straight for the famous beach resorts which stretch in an arc between Pensacola and Panama City Beach. Ideal for family holidays, resorts such as Fort Walton Beach and Destin offer all kinds of accommodation as well as activities ranging from water sports and deep-sea fishing to golf and tennis. While most attention is focused on the coast, the rest of the Panhandle should not be ignored – the resorts can be used as a good base for forays into the hilly, pine-forested interior, where it is possible to escape the crowds. Excellent canoeing can be enjoyed on the Blackwater and the Suwannee rivers, while near Tallahassee you will find some of Florida's prettiest countryside, crossed by unspoilt canopy roads.

Quietwater Beach, near Pensacola on Santa Rosa Island

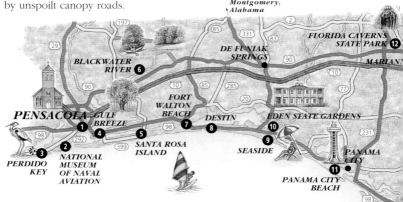

SIGHTS AT A GLANCE

The elegant, plantation-style mansion at Eden State Gardens

GETTING AROUND

Though the Amtrak line runs through the region, following the line of I-10, a car is essential for exploring the Panhandle. There are two main driving routes: the fast but dull I-10, which streaks from Pensacola to Tallahassee, and then on to the Atlantic Coast; and US 98, which parallels the coast all the way from Pensacola to the so-called "Big Bend", where it links up with the main north-south Gulf Coast highway, US 19. Country roads in the Panhandle are generally quiet, but be on the alert for logging trucks pulling out of concealed forest exits.

Waterfront buildings at the popular harbour of Destin

0 kilometres   30

0 miles   30

TORREYA STATE PARK

13

AB MACLAY STATE GARDENS

19

COTTON TRAIL

21

20

MONTICELLO

Albany, Georgia

319

19

Macon, Georgia

SUWANNEE RIVER STATE PARK

22

75

Jacksonville

LIVE OAK

18

TALLAHASSEE

10

221

Gainesville

12

65

17

WAKULA SPRINGS STATE PARK

59

19

27

PERRY

51

129

98

27

319

19

98

51

65

98

●CARRABELLE

APALACHICOLA

15

16 ST GEORGE, ST VINCENT AND DOG ISLANDS

STEINHATCHEE

23

349

CHIEFLAND ● Ocala

345

Tampa

24

24

CEDAR KEY

SEE ALSO

KEY

▬	Interstate highway
▬	Major highway
▬	Secondary route
▬	Scenic route
～	River
☀	Viewpoint

Pelicans enjoying the peace and quiet of Apalachicola

Street-by-Street: Pensacola ❶

T HE CITY'S FIRST SETTLERS were a party of Spanish colonists, led by Tristan de Luna *(see p41),* who sailed into Pensacola Bay in 1559. Their settlement survived only two years before being wiped out by a hurricane. The Spanish returned, but Pensacola changed hands frequently: in the space of just over 300 years the Spanish, French, English, Confederate and US flags all flew over the city. Pensacola took off in the 1880s, when much of the present down-town district was built. This area features a diverse collection of architectural styles, ranging from quaint colonial cottages to elegant Classical-Revival homes built during the late 19th-century timber boom. The route shown here focuses on the area known as Historic Pensacola Village *(see p216).*

Lavalle House
The simple plan and bright colour scheme of this early 19th-century two-room cottage was designed to appeal to its French Creole immigrant tenants.

Civil War Soldiers Museum
Exhibits here focus on the life of the ordinary soldier and include medical equipment, antique weaponry and contemporary accounts of the Battle of Gettysburg.

The Museum of Industry recalls Pensacola's timber and maritime trades using a reconstructed sawmill and ship's chandlery.

★ **TT Wentworth Museum**
A broad collection of Florida memorabilia, such as this 1870s' bed, fill this unusual museum.

Pensacola Museum of Art
The old city jail, dating from 1908, was converted into a museum in the 1950s. This William Nell landscape is among the broad array of art on show.

A British officers' compound has been excavated in this car park. The exposed foundations form part of the city's Colonial Archaeological Trail *(see p216).*

Steamboat House
Dating from the mid-19th-century steamboat era (see p46), *this delightful house echoes the shape of a riverboat. It comes complete with veranda "decks".*

★ **Seville Square**
Shaded by live oaks and magnolia trees, Seville Square lies at the heart of the Seville District, which was laid out by the British in the 1770s.

Fountain Square
centres around a fountain decorated with plaques showing local features.

0 metres	200
0 yards	200

Dorr House, a fine Greek-Revival mansion, is the last of its kind in western Florida.

KEY

– – – Suggested route

★ **Museum of Commerce**
A fully equipped print workshop is one of the many interesting exhibits in the museum's cleverly constructed late-Victorian streetscape.

STAR SIGHTS

★ **TT Wentworth Museum**

★ **Seville Square**

★ **Museum of Commerce**

Exploring Pensacola

S EVERAL HISTORIC DISTRICTS provide the most interesting areas to explore in Pensacola. Foremost is the old downtown district, Historic Pensacola Village, centered on pretty Zaragoza Street. Further north, in the North Hill Preservation District, you can stroll past the homes built by prominent local professionals and merchants during the 19th-century timber boom. Between the two, Palafox Street is a busy commercial district with a number of distinctive buildings dating from 1900–20.

Downtown Pensacola is linked by two bridges to its barrier island resort satellite, Pensacola Beach *(see p222)*. While sightseeing is focused on the mainland, visitors often stay in hotels by the beach, now largely recovered from the onslaught of 1995's Hurricane Opal.

Cell doors now standing open, Pensacola Museum of Art

Guides in 19th-century costume in Historic Pensacola Village

🏛 Historic Pensacola Village
Tivoli House, 205 E Zaragoza St.
📞 *(904) 444-8905.* ⏰ *Mon–Sat.*
● *public hols.* 📷 ♿ 🛍
This collection of museums and historic houses is located in Pensacola's oldest quarter, called the Seville District. You can enjoy an unhurried stroll through the village's streets which offer a taste of the city as it was in the 19th century.

For a more in-depth look, you should take one of the guided tours which depart twice daily from Tivoli House on Zaragoza Street; in high season, tour guides liven up the proceedings by dressing in period costume. The tours visit the simply furnished French Creole Lavalle House (1805) and the gracious Dorr House (1871). Other properties, while not included on the tour, are open to visitors. A single ticket, available from Tivoli House, covers the tour and entrance to all village properties over two days. You

will need this ticket to visit the Museum of Industry and Museum of Commerce. Housed in a late 19th-century warehouse, the Museum of Industry on Church Street provides an informative introduction to Pensacola's early development. Exhibits cover brick-making, fishing, transportation and the timber trade.

Forming a backdrop to Zaragoza Street's Museum of Commerce is a Victorian street scene complete with reconstructed stores including a printer's shop with a working press, a pharmacy, a saddlery and an old-time music store.

Overlooking leafy Seville Square is Old Christ Church, built in 1832 and the oldest church building in Florida still standing on its original site. It is currently being restored.

🏛 TT Wentworth Florida State Museum
330 Jefferson St. 📞 *(904) 444-8586.*
⏰ *Mon–Sat.* ● *public hols.* 📷 ♿
This museum is laid out in the former City Hall, an imposing Spanish Renaissance Revival building. The founder's eclectic collections include West Florida memorabilia and

weird and wonderful oddities from all over the world. These run the gamut from arrowheads and a shrunken head from pre-Columbian times to a 1930s telephone exchange and old Coca-Cola bottles.

The museum contains well thought-out historical displays and dioramas illustrating points along Pensacola's Colonial Archaeological Trail, which links remains of fortifications dating from 1752–1821; you can pick up a leaflet explaining the trail's sites.

A ticket to Historic Pensacola Village includes admission to the TT Wentworth too.

🏛 Pensacola Museum of Art
407 S Jefferson St. 📞 *(904) 432-6247.*
⏰ *Tue–Sun.* ● *4 Jul, Thanksgiving, 25 Dec, 1 Jan.* 📷 ♿
The cells of the old city jail, complete with steel-barred doors, have taken on a new lease of life as whitewashed galleries for the Pensacola Museum of Art. Frequently changing exhibitions draw on the museum's broad-based collections, which include pre-Columbian pottery, 19th-century satinware glass and Roy Lichtenstein's Pop Art.

The Spanish Renaissance-style home of the TT Wentworth Museum

🏛 Civil War Soldiers Museum

108 S Palafox Place. 📞 *(904) 469-1900.* 🕐 *Mon–Sat.* ⬤ *Thanksgiving, 25 Dec, 1 Jan.* 📷 ♿

Designed to appeal both to experts of the Civil War and to the amateur enthusiast (but perhaps a little biased towards the former), this museum is devoted to the main characters and campaigns of the Civil War *(see pp44–5).*

With an appropriate soundtrack of marching songs, period weaponry, uniforms and field kit illustrate different aspects of what, in the Panhandle as well as other southern states, is sometimes still called the War of Northern Aggression. Among the exhibits are an officer's liquor chest, snipers' glasses, and even a gruesome medical section.

🌲 North Hill Preservation District

This historic district (stretching for about ten blocks from Wright Street, north of Pensacola Historic Village) features elegant late 19th- and early

McCreary House in the North Hill Preservation District

The extensive, unspoilt sands at Johnson Beach on Perdido Key

20th-century houses. They were built on the site of former British and Spanish forts and even now cannon balls are occasionally dug up in their tree-shaded gardens. All the houses are privately owned. Among the most striking is the veranda-fronted McCreary House *(see p28)* on North Baylen Street, close to the junction with De Soto Street.

National Museum of Naval Aviation ❷

See pp218–19.

Perdido Key ❸

Road map A1. Escambia Co. Route 292, 12 miles (19 km) W of Pensacola. 🚉 *Pensacola.* 🚌 *Pensacola.* ℹ️ *1401 E Gregory St, Pensacola, (904) 434-1234.*

A 30-MINUTE DRIVE southwest from Pensacola are the pristine shores of Perdido Key, which regularly feature in the list of the top 20 US beaches. There are bars and

restaurants and facilities for water sports, fishing and diving, or you can simply swim or soak up the sun.

The whole eastern end of the island is accessible only by foot. The road runs as far as the **Johnson Beach Day Use Area**, just east of the bridge from the mainland, from where a boardwalk leads down to the main beach. The sands extend for some 6 miles (10 km) on both gulf and bay sides, and there are facilities for visitors and a ranger station.

On the mainland opposite Perdido Key, **Big Lagoon State Recreation Area** combines stretches of sandy beach with salt-marsh areas offering excellent bird-watching and hiking. You can enjoy sweeping views of the coast from an observation tower.

🏖 Johnson Beach Day Use Area

Johnson Beach Rd, off Route 292. 📞 *(904) 492-0912.* 🕐 *daily.* ⬤ *25 Dec.* 📷 ♿
🏖 Big Lagoon SRA
12301 Gulf Beach Highway. 📞 *(904) 492-1595.* 🕐 *daily.* 📷 ♿

FLORIDA'S TIMBER BOOM

In the 19th century, the demand for timber and naval stores including tar and turpentine played an important part in northern Florida's development. Its vast stands of live oaks were particularly popular with shipbuilders for their disease- and decay-resistant wood. Flourishing timber towns such as Cedar Key *(see p231)* were established, and the fortunes made during the timber boom of the 1870s–80s were transformed into Pensacola's elegant homes, including Eden Mansion *(see p223).*

By the 1930s, most of Florida's mature hardwood forest had been destroyed, and other building materials and forms of fuel had begun to replace wood. The timber mills closed, leaving thousands unemployed.

Loggers in the 19th century, who worked long hours of hard manual labour

National Museum of Naval Aviation ❷

Beechcraft GB-2 insignia

THIS VAST MUSEUM is set among the runways and hangars of the country's oldest naval air station, founded in 1914. More than 150 aircraft and spacecraft, as well as models, artifacts, technological displays and works of aviation-related art trace the history of flight – from early wing-and-a-prayer wood and fabric biplanes to the latest state-of-the-art rocketry. Even those who are not great aviation fans will enjoy flying with the Blue Angels display team in the IMAX cinema or testing themselves in the training cockpits. Veteran pilots at the information desk field questions and lend first-hand authenticity to guided tours.

★ Blue Angels
Four former Blue Angels A-4 Sky-hawks are suspended in a dramatic diamond formation from the ceiling of the seven-storey glass atrium.

The USS Cabot Flight Deck is a life-sized reconstruction of an aircraft carrier deck, complete with a line-up of famous World War II fighter planes.

Sunken Treasures displays two aircraft recovered from Lake Michigan, where they sank during training in World War II.

Flying Tigers
The painted jaws of these World War II fighters were the trademark of the Volunteer Flying Tiger pilots who fought in the skies over China and Burma.

Spirit of Naval Aviation Monument

GALLERY GUIDE

The museum occupies two floors, or "decks", which are divided into two wings joined by an atrium. The west wing is devoted almost entirely to World War II carrier aircraft, while the south wing is more broadly historical. More aircraft can be found on the lawns surrounding the museum.

F14 Tomcat

Entrance

The IMAX cinema shows dramatic in-flight footage seven times daily.

Biplane
Early aircraft include World War I training planes and biplanes once favoured by circus barnstormers.

STAR FEATURES

- ★ **Blue Angels**
- ★ **Flight Simulator**

K47 Airship
America's "K"-type airships performed vital maritime patrol duties during World War II.

VISITORS' CHECKLIST

Road map 1A. 1750 Radford Blvd, Pensacola. 🕻 *(904) 453-2389.* 🚍 *Pensacola.* 🚌 *Pensacola.* ⬜ *9am–5pm daily.* ⬤ *Thanksgiving, 25 Dec, 1 Jan.* ♿ ✔ 🎦 🍴

The Space Capsule Display has a Skylab Command Module as its centrepiece, alongside several tons of gadgetry and some moon rock.

★ **Flight Simulator**
The motion-based flight simulator is just one of more than 100 interactive displays designed to convey the complexity and wonder of avionics.

Cockpit trainers provide hands-on tuition on how to fly an aircraft.

Coast Guard Helicopter
A fully equipped rescue helicopter pays tribute to the contribution made by the Coast Guard services to the story of naval aviation.

FORT BARRANCAS

Enclosed by water on three sides, the strategic Naval Air Station site was fortified by Spanish colonists in 1698. The original ramparts, built on a bluff *(barranca* in Spanish) overlooking Pensacola Bay, were replaced by a more substantial fort in 1781, and major additions were made by the US Army in the 1840s. The remains of the Spanish and US forts, concealed behind formidable defensive earthworks, are linked by a tunnel. The fort is a few minutes' walk from the museum, where you can arrange to go on a guided tour of the area.

View of the earthworks surrounding Fort Barrancas

KEY TO FLOORPLAN

- ⬜ WWII/Korean War aircraft
- ⬜ Early aircraft
- ⬜ Modern aircraft
- ▨ Cinema
- ▨ Interactive exhibits
- ⬜ Displays
- ⬜ Art gallery
- ▨ Non-exhibition space

Gulf Breeze 4

Road map A1. Santa Rosa Co.
🏛 *6,300.* 🚆 *Pensacola.*
🚌 *Pensacola.* ℹ *1170 Gulf Breeze Parkway, (904) 932-7888.*

THE AFFLUENT community of Gulf Breeze lies at the western end of a promontory reaching out into Pensacola Bay. The area east of the town is heavily wooded and once formed part of the huge swathes of southern woodlands which were earmarked in the 1820s to provide timber for shipbuilding *(see p217).*

The **Naval Live Oaks Reservation**, off US 98, was originally a government-owned tree farm, and now protects some of the remaining woodland. Visitors can follow trails through 1,300 acres (500 ha) of oak hammock woodlands, sand-hill areas and wetlands, where wading birds feast off an abundance of marine life. A visitor centre dispenses maps and information on local flora and fauna, and also has historical exhibits.

Ten miles (16 km) east of Gulf Breeze, **The Zoo** is a favourite family excursion, with more than 700 animals in residence. You can take a ride on the Safari Line train through 30 acres (12 ha) of land where animals roam freely, catch a show by Ellie the elephant or stroll through

The Safari Line train, on its tour around The Zoo, Gulf Breeze

the botanical gardens. Visitors even get the chance to look a giraffe in the eye from the high-rise feeding platform.

🦌 **Naval Live Oaks Reservation**
1801 Gulf Breeze Parkway. 📞 *(904) 934-2600.* ⭕ *daily.* ● *25 Dec.* ♿
🦌 **The Zoo**
5701 Gulf Breeze Parkway. 📞 *(904) 932-2229.* ⭕ *daily.* ● *Thanksgiving, 25 Dec.* 🅿 ♿

Santa Rosa Island 5

Road map A1. Escambia Co, Okaloosa Co, Santa Rosa Co. 🚆 *Pensacola.*
🚌 *Pensacola or Fort Walton Beach.*
ℹ *8543 Navarre Parkway, Navarre, (904) 939-2691.*

ALONG, THIN STREAK of sand, Santa Rosa stretches all the way from Pensacola Bay to Fort Walton Beach, a distance of 45 miles (70 km). At its western tip **Fort Pickens**, completed in 1834, is the largest of four US forts constructed in the early 19th century to defend Pensacola Bay.

The Apache chieftain Geronimo was imprisoned here from 1886–8, during which time people came from far and wide to see him; the authorities supposedly encouraged his transformation into a tourist attraction. The fort remained in use by the US army until 1947. Now, you are free to explore

the brick fort's dark and atmospheric passageways, and there is also a small museum.

Santa Rosa boasts several fine sugar-white beaches. Pensacola Beach and Navarre Beach are both popular, each having a fishing pier and plenty of opportunities for water sports. Between the two is a beautiful, undeveloped stretch of sand, where you can relax away from the main crowds. There is a camp ground at the western end of the island, near Fort Pickens.

⚓ **Fort Pickens**
1400 Fort Pickens Rd (Route 399).
🎫 *(904) 934-2621.* ⭕ *daily.* 🅿 ♿

Boardwalk leading onto Pensacola Beach on Santa Rosa Island

Blackwater River 6

Road map A1. Santa Rosa Co.
🚆 *Pensacola.* 🚌 *Pensacola.* ℹ *5247 Stewart St, Milton, (904) 623-2339.*

THE BLACKWATER RIVER rises in Alabama and flows for 60 miles (95 km) south to the Gulf of Mexico. One of the purest sand-bottomed rivers in the world, its dark, tannin-stained waters meander prettily through the forest, creating oxbow lakes, natural levees and sand beaches.

The river's big attraction is its canoeing: one of the state's finest canoe trails runs for 31 miles (50 km) along its course. Canoe and kayak trips can be arranged through several operators in Milton, the self-styled "Canoeing Capital of Florida". These trips range from half-day paddles to three-day marathons, with the option of tackling the more

The nature trail, Naval Live Oaks Reservation

The Blackwater River, well known for its canoeing trail

challenging Sweetwater and Juniper creeks to the north.

The small **Blackwater River State Park**, located at the end of the canoe trail, offers swimming, picnicking areas and the Chain of Lakes Trail. This 1-mile (1.5-km) nature trail runs through woodlands thick with oak, hickory, southern magnolia and red maple trees, and ends up at a clutch of oxbow lakes.

🏕 Blackwater River State Park
Off US 90, 15 miles (24 km) NE of Milton. **(904) 983-5363.** *daily.*

Fort Walton Beach ❼

Road map A1. Okaloosa Co.
🏛 22,000. ✕ 🚉 *Crestview.* 🚌
🛈 *34 Miracle Strip Parkway SE, (904) 244-8191.*

FORT WALTON BEACH lies at the western tip of the so-called Emerald Coast, a 24-mile (40-km) strip of dazzling beach stretching east to Destin

and beyond. Diving shops and marinas line US 98, which skirts the coast and links Fort Walton to Santa Rosa Island. Known locally as Okaloosa Island, this is where most local people and visitors end up. The gin-clear sea offers superb swimming as well as pier and deep-sea fishing, and this is a prime location for water sports too.

You can also swim or try your hand at sailing or wind-surfing off the island's north shore, on sheltered Chocta-whatchee Bay. And all kinds of boat trips can be arranged at the numerous marinas. For those who prefer dry land, the Emerald Coast boasts a dozen golf courses.

Performing dolphins and sea lions star in daily shows at the popular **Gulfarium** marine park. The glass walls of the Living Sea aquarium reveal sharks, rays and huge sea turtles. There are also seal and otter enclosures, as well as alligators and exotic birds.

Indian pot, Temple Mound Museum

There's not a great deal to lure you downtown except for the informative **Indian Temple Mound Museum**, which stands in the shadow of an ancient Indian earthwork. This former ceremonial and burial site of the Apalachee Indians *(see pp38–9)* dates from around AD 1400. The museum exhibits artifacts recovered from the mound and other Indian sites nearby, while well-illustrated displays trace more than 10,000 years of human habitation in the Choctawhatchee Bay area.

Three miles (5 km) north of town at Shalimar is the vast Eglin Air Force Base, the largest air force base in the world. Here, the **US Air Force Armament Museum** displays aircraft, missiles and bombs dating from World War II to the present day. Visitors can snoop around a SR-71 "Blackbird" spy plane and inspect antique side arms and high-tech laser equipment. Tours of the 720-sq mile (1,865-sq km) base can be arranged in advance.

✈ Gulfarium
1010 Miracle Strip Parkway. **(904) 243-9046.** *daily.* 🅿 ♿
🏛 Indian Temple Mound Museum
139 Miracle Strip Parkway. **(904) 833-9595.** *daily.* ● *public hols.* 🅿 ♿
🏛 US Air Force Armament Museum
100 Museum Drive (Route 85). **(904) 882-4062.** *daily.* ● *Thanksgiving, 25 Dec, 1 Jan.* ♿

People strolling along the Gulf of Mexico's white powder sands at Fort Walton Beach

Destin ➑

Road map A1. Walton Co. 🏚 *13,000.*
☒ 🚌 *Fort Walton Beach.* ℹ️ *1021
Highway 98 E, (904) 837-6241.*

Situated between the Gulf of
Mexico and Choctawhatchee
Bay, Destin is a narrow strip of
a town which runs parallel to
the coastal highway, US 98. It
started out in 1845 as a fishing
camp but has since grown
into what is claimed to be the
"most prolific fishing village"
in the US. Deep-sea fishing is

**Fisherman at work on his catches
at the harbour, Destin**

the big draw, and a steady
flow of charter boats buzzes
in and out of the harbour. The
waters near Destin are particularly rich due to a 100-ft (30-m)
drop in the continental shelf
only 10 miles (16 km) from the
shore; prime catches include
amberjack, tarpon and blue
marlin. There is a busy calendar of fishing tournaments, the
most notable being October's
month-long Fishing Rodeo,
and in early October people
flock to Destin for the annual
Seafood Festival.

For a close-up look at some
of the Gulf of Mexico's smaller
marine residents, call in at the
shrimp-sized **Destin Fishing
Museum** and peer into the
aquarium-lined walls.

With its stunning beaches
and clear waters typical of the
Emerald Coast, Destin is also
a very popular resort. There
are good opportunities for
diving and snorkelling too.

🏛 **Destin Fishing Museum**
20009 Emerald Coast Parkway.
📞 (904) 654-1011. 🔲 Mon, Wed.
🔴 Thanksgiving, 25 Dec, 1 Jan. 🈲 ♿

**A wooden tower characteristic of
Seaside's gulfshore homes**

Seaside ➒

Road map B1. Walton Co. 🏚 *200.*
ℹ️ *(904) 231-4224.*

When Robert Davis decided
to develop Seaside in the
mid-1980s, the vanished resorts
of his childhood provided his
inspiration. Davis's vision was
of a nostalgic holiday town of
traditional northwest Florida-
style wooden cottages, with
wraparound verandas, steeply
pitched roofs and white picket
fences. The original style was
rapidly hijacked, however, by

The Beaches of the Panhandle

Between Perdido Key and Panama City Beach lie
some of the most beautiful beaches in Florida. The
finely ground sand – 90 per cent quartz, washed down
from the Appalachian mountains – sweeps into broad
beaches and can be nearly blinding in the sunlight.
The hordes descend in June and July, but the Gulf
waters are still pleasantly warm as late as November.
You can choose between quiet, undeveloped
beaches and more dynamic resorts, and
there is also plenty of opportunity
for diving and other water sports.

Pensacola Beach ③ has
miles of pristine sand overlooked by a string of shops,
hotels and bars. A large
crowd gathers at the
weekend. *(See p220.)*

Perdido Key ①
Some of the state's most
westerly shores, on Perdido
Key, are inaccessible by car
and are therefore quieter
than most. *(See p217.)*

Quietwater Beach ② is on the inland
shore of Santa Rosa Island. While not
the Panhandle's finest beach it is at
least an easy hop from Pensacola.

Navarre Beach ④ is one of
the quieter of the island's beaches.
It has good facilities, including a
pier for fishing. *(See p220.)*

0 kilometres   15

0 miles   10

whimsy gingerbread detailing, turrets and towers *(see p29)*.

The town's pastel-painted, Neo-Victorian charms have an unreal, Disneyesque quality and if you're driving along US 98, it's hard to resist stopping for a quick peek. And then of course there is the additional appeal of the beach.

Environs: Just 1 mile (1.5 km) west of Seaside, the **Grayton Beach State Recreation Area** boasts another magnificent stretch of Panhandle shoreline, and one which regularly features high in the rankings of the nation's top beaches.

In addition to its broad strand of pristine quartz-white sand, the park offers good surf fishing, boating facilities, a nature trail and also a camp ground. During the summer, campers can take part in ranger-led programmes, which are suitable for all the family.

🏞 Grayton Beach SRA
County Rd 30-A , off US 98, (1 mile) 1.5 km W of Seaside. ☎ *(904) 231-4210.* 🕐 *daily.* 🎟 ♿

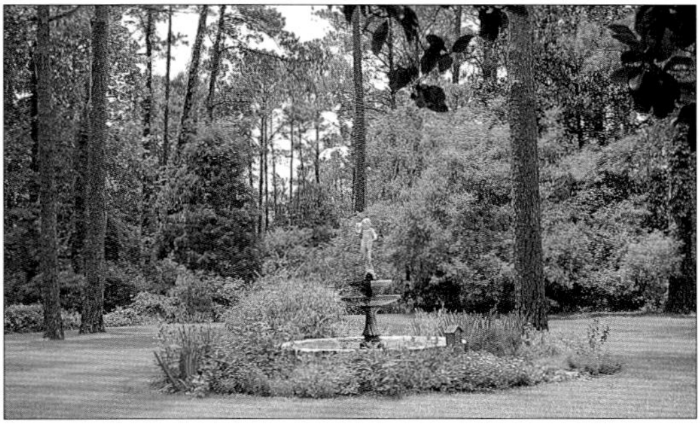

Statue amid the lush surroundings of the Eden State Gardens

Eden State Gardens and Mansion [10]

Road map B1. Walton Co. Point Washington. ☎ *(904) 231-4214.* 🚌 *Fort Walton Beach.* **Gardens** 🕐 *daily.* **House** 🕐 *Thu–Mon.* 🎟

Timber baron William H Wesley built this fine Greek Revival mansion overlooking the Choctawhatchee River in 1897. The gracious two-storey wooden building, styled after an antebellum mansion, with high-ceilinged rooms and broad verandas, is furnished with antiques. Equally appealing are the gardens, planted with camellias and azaleas, and shaded by southern magnolia trees and live oaks; these lead to picnic tables by the river, near where the old timber mill once stood. Whole trees were once floated from inland forests downriver to the mill, where they were sawn into logs. From there they were sent by barge along the Intracoastal Waterway to Pensacola.

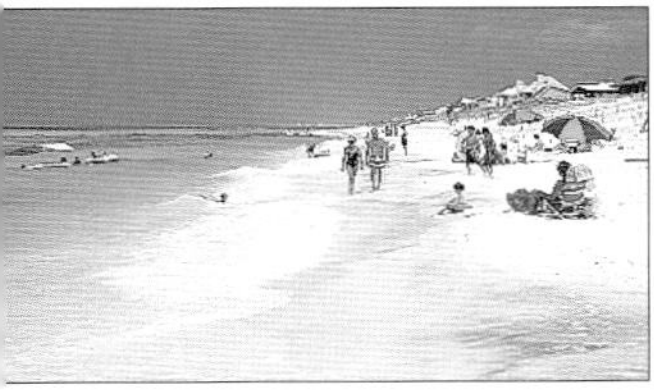

Santa Rosa Beach [7]
This undeveloped sandy beach is backed by dunes and marshlands teeming with birds and other wildlife.

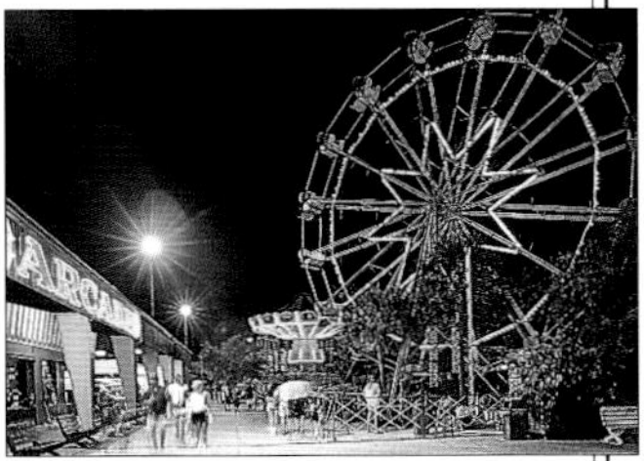

Panama City Beach [9]
Condos, hotels and amusement and water parks line buzzing Panama City Beach. Diving and water sports are popular pastimes. *(See p224.)*

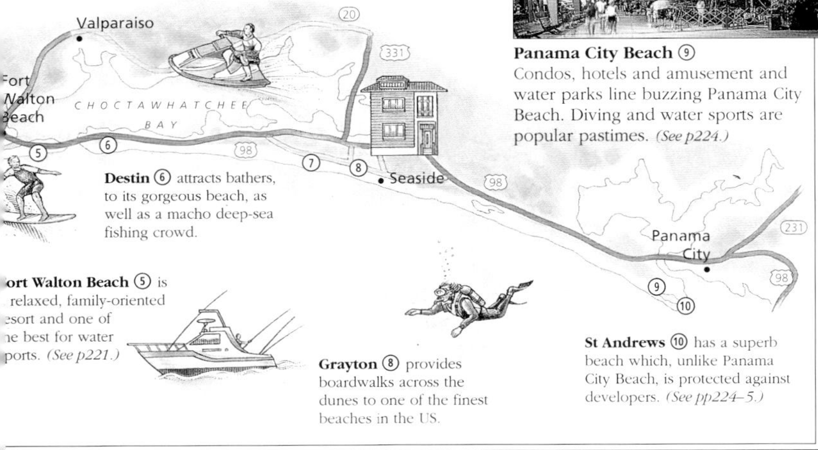

Destin [6] attracts bathers, to its gorgeous beach, as well as a macho deep-sea fishing crowd.

Fort Walton Beach [5] is relaxed, family-oriented resort and one of the best for water sports. *(See p221.)*

Grayton [8] provides boardwalks across the dunes to one of the finest beaches in the US.

St Andrews [10] has a superb beach which, unlike Panama City Beach, is protected against developers. *(See pp224–5.)*

Panama City Beach, the liveliest seaside resort in the Panhandle

Panama City Beach ⓫

Road map B1. Bay Co. 🏠 6,000.
✖ 🚆 ℹ️ *12015 Front Beach Rd,
(904) 233-5070.* **Captain Anderson's**
📞 *(904) 234-3435.* **Treasure Island
Marina** 📞 *(904) 234-8944.*

A BRASH, CHEEKY postcard sort
of a place, Panama City
Beach is a 27-mile (43-km)
"Miracle Strip" of hotels,
amusement parks and arcades
bordered by a gleaming quartz
sand beach. The Panhandle's
biggest resort, it caters both to
the young crowds that swamp
the place at Spring Break *(see
p32)* and to families, who
dominate in summer. The
sports facilities are excellent.
   Panama City Beach, nicknamed the "wreck capital of
the south", is renowned for its
diving. Besides natural coral
reefs, it has more than 50
artificial diving sites created by
scuppered boats – providing
some of the best diving in the
Gulf. Dive operators offer
scuba and snorkelling trips,
and tuition too. For the less
energetic, Captain Anderson's
and Treasure Island Marina
offer dolphin feeding trips
and glass-bottomed boat tours.

🐦 Gulf World
15412 Front Beach Rd. ℹ️ *(904) 234-
5271.* ⏰ *Feb–Oct: daily; Thanksgiving, 25 Dec–1 Jan.* 🈺 ♿
Dolphin and sea lion shows
are the highlights of a visit to
Gulf World marine park. Other
attractions, including aquariums and a walk-through shark
tank, are set in lush tropical
gardens with a resident troupe
of performing parrots.

🏛 Museum of Man in the Sea
17314 Panama City Beach Parkway.
📞 *(904) 235-4101.* ⏰ *daily.*
● *Thanksgiving, 25 Dec, 1 Jan.* 🈺 ♿
The Museum of Man in the
Sea provides a homespun but
educational look at the history
of diving and marine salvage.
It has amassed exhibits ranging
from ancient diving helmets
to salvaged treasures from the
17th-century Spanish galleon
Atocha (see p26), and there is
a car park full of submarines.
A favourite among the latter
is Moby Dick, a whale rescue
vessel painted to resemble a
killer whale.

🦒 ZooWorld
9008 Front Beach Rd. 📞 *(904) 230-
1243.* ⏰ *daily.* ● *25 Dec.* 🈺 ♿
ZooWorld is home to over
350 animals, including bears,
big cats, alligators, camels,
giraffes and orang-utans, and
has more than 15 endangered
species among its charges.
   The Gentle Jungle Petting
Zoo, which offers plenty of
opportunity to come face to
face with and touch the wildlife, is particularly popular
with young children.

An orang-utan, one of ZooWorld's more entertaining residents

🎢 Shipwreck Island Water Park
12000 Front Beach Rd. 🎟 *(904) 234-
0368.* ⏰ *Apr–Sep: daily.* 🈺 ♿
This water park, next to the
Miracle Strip Amusement Park,
will have no trouble keeping
the family entertained for the
entire day. The 1,600-ft (490-m)
Lazy River tube ride is a firm
favourite, but there are also
higher-energy options for the
more adventurous: try the
35-mph (55-km/h) Speed Slide,
the Rapid River or the 370-ft
(110-m) White Water Tube.
There are gentler rides for
youngsters too, as well as a
kids' swimming pool. Other
attractions include a wave pool
and sunbathing areas. Lifeguards keep a watchful eye.

Fun on the Lazy River ride at Shipwreck Island Water Park

🎢 Miracle Strip Amuse-ment Park
12000 Front Beach Rd. 🎟 *(904)
234-5810.* ⏰ *Mar–Jun: Fri & Sat;
Jun–Aug: daily.* 🈺 ♿
The beach by night is about
as vibrant and gaudy as you
would expect, with snack bars
and discos galore. Top of the
bill is the Miracle Strip Amusement Park, a fun fair boasting
a world-class 2,000-ft (600-m)
roller coaster, a ferris wheel
and dozens of other rides,
games and sideshows.

ENVIRONS: An easy 3-mile
(5-km) hop southeast of the
main Strip, **St Andrews State
Recreation Area** is a good
antidote to Panama City Beach,
even though it can get very
busy in summer. The reserve

A replica of a turpentine still in St Andrews State Recreation Area

has a fabulous white sand beach which was named the USA's best beach in 1995. The swimming is good, and there is excellent snorkelling around the rock jetties. Behind the dunes, marshland areas and lagoons are home to alligators and a variety of wading birds.

Also within the park, not far from the fishing pier, is a modern recreation of a Cracker turpentine still, similar to those found throughout the state in the early 1900s *(see p217)*; a woodland trail starts nearby.

✗ St Andrews SRA
4415 Thomas Drive. **(** *(904) 233-5140.* ◻ *daily.* 🏖 🕭 🅰

Florida Caverns State Park ⓬

Road map B1. Jackson Co. 3345 Caverns Rd, off Route 166, (5 km) N of Marianna. 🚌 *Marianna.* **(** *(904) 482-9598.* ◻ *daily.* 🏖 🕭 🗶 🅰

T HE LIMESTONE that underpins Florida is laid bare in this series of underground caves hollowed out of the soft rock and drained by the Chipola River. The filtering of rainwater through the limestone rock over thousands of years has created a breathtaking subterranean cavescape of stalactites, stalagmites, columns and glittering rivulets of crystals. Wrap up warm for the guided tours, since the caverns maintain a cool 61–66 °F (16–19 °C).

The park also offers hiking trails and horse-riding, and you can swim and fish in the Chipola River. A 52-mile (84-km) canoe trail slips

through the high limestone cliffs along the river's route south to Dead Lake, just west of Apalachicola National Forest *(see p226)*.

Torreya State Park ⓭

Road map C1. Liberty Co. Route CC 1641, 13 miles (21 km) N of Bristol. 🚌 *Bloomtown.* **(** *(904) 643-2674.* ◻ *daily.* 🏖 🕭 *limited.*

M ORE OFF THE beaten track than most other parks in Florida, Torreya State Park is well worth seeking out. Named after the torreya, a rare type of yew tree that once grew here in abundance, the park abuts a beautiful forested bend in the Apalachicola River. High limestone bluffs, into which Confederate soldiers dug gun pits to repel Union gun boats during the Civil War, flank the river, offering one of the few high natural vantage points in Florida.

Gregory House, a fine 19th-century Classical Revival mansion, stands atop the

150-ft (45-m) high bluff. It was moved here from its first site downriver by conservationists in 1935 and has since been restored. Inside, it is simply furnished with period antiques.

It is a 25-minute walk from Gregory House down to the river and back, or you can take the 7-mile (11-km) Weeping Ridge Trail. Both paths run through woodland and offer a chance to spot all kinds of birds, deer, beavers and the unusual Barbours map turtle (so-called for the map-like lines etched on its shell).

St Joseph Peninsula State Park ⓮

Road map B1. Gulf Co. Route 30E. 🚌 *Bloomtown.* **(** *(904) 227-1327.* ◻ *daily.* 🏖 🕭 🅰 *open all year.*

A T THE TIP OF the slender sand spit which extends north from Cape San Blas to enclose St Joseph's Bay, this beautifully unspoilt beach park is ideal for those in search of a little peace and quiet. The swimming is excellent, and snorkelling and surf fishing are also popular activities. Bird-watchers should pack their binoculars, since the bird life is prolific along the shoreline: over 200 species of birds have been recorded here. You can stay in cabins overlooking the bay, and there are basic camping facilities too.

The only reason to venture away from the beach is to explore the saw palmetto and pine woodlands, where you may see deer, racoons, bobcats and even coyotes.

The forested course of the Apalachicola River in Torreya State Park

Restored houses on the water's edge in Water Street, Apalachicola

Apalachicola **⑮**

Road Map B1. Franklin Co.
🏠 *2700.* 🚌 *Tallahassee.* ℹ️ *99 Market Street, (904) 653-9419.*

A RIVERSIDE CUSTOMS post established in 1823, Apalachicola saw its grandest days during the first 100 years of its existence. It boomed first with the cotton trade then, later on, sponge divers and timber barons made their fortunes here. Today, a swathe of pines and hardwoods still stands as the Apalachicola National Forest, extending from 12 miles (19 km) north of Apalachicola right to the outskirts of Tallahassee.

At the end of the timber boom in the 1920s, the town turned to oystering and fishing in the waters at the mouth of the Apalachicola River. Oyster and other fishing boats still dock at the quayside, which is lined with refrigerated seafood houses and old brick-built cotton warehouses. Among the seafood houses on Water Street there are several places to sample fresh oysters.

The old town is laid out in a neat grid with many fine historic buildings dating from the cotton boom era. A walking map, available from the chamber of commerce, takes in such privately owned treasures as the 1838 Greek Revival Raney House.

Devoted to the town's most notable resident, the **John Gorrie State Museum** has a model of Gorrie's patent ice-making machine. Designed to cool the sickrooms of yellow fever sufferers, Dr Gorrie's 1851 invention was the vanguard of modern refrigeration and air conditioning.

🏛 John Gorrie State Museum
6th Street (Gorrie Square). 📞 *(904) 653-9347.* ⏰ *Thu–Mon.* 🔴 *Thanksgiving, 25 Dec, 1 Jan.* 📷

St Vincent, St George and Dog Islands **⑯**

Road Map B2, C2, C1. Franklin Co. 🚌 *Tallahassee.* ℹ️ *99 Market St, Apalachicola, (904) 653-9419.* **Jeannie's Journeys** 📞 *(904) 927-3259.*

T HIS STRING of barrier islands separates the waters of Apalachicola Bay from the Gulf of Mexico. St George, linked by a bridge to Apalachicola is developing fast and has a growing number of holiday homes. However, a 9-mile (14-km) stretch of beautiful dunes at its eastern end is preserved as the **St George Island State Park**; the main expanse of beach is on the island's gulf shore.

To the west, the **St Vincent National Wildlife Refuge** is uninhabited and accessible

Surf fishing, a popular activity on the quiet sands of St George Island

only by boat from St George Island: Jeannie's Journeys on East Gorey Drive run tours. You can watch nesting ospreys in spring, sea turtles laying their eggs in summer and migrating waterfowl in winter.

To the east, little Dog Island must be reached by boat from Carrabelle on the mainland. It has a small inn, big dunes, and a shoreline which is excellent for shell hunting.

🦎 St George Island State Park
📞 *(904) 927-2111.* ⏰ *daily.*
🦎 St Vincent National Wildlife Refuge
📞 *(904) 653-8808.* ⏰ *daily.*

Fun in the pool at Wakulla Springs

Wakulla Springs State Park **⑰**

Road map C1. Wakulla Co. 550. Wakulla Park Drive, Wakulla Springs. 📞 *(904) 922-3633.* 🚌 *Tallahassee.* ⏰ *daily.* 📷 ♿

O NE OF THE WORLD'S largest freshwater springs, the Wakulla pumps 700,000 gal (2.6 million litres) of water a minute into the large pool which is the big appeal of this park.

You can swim or snorkel in the beautifully clear, limestone-filtered water, or take a ride in a glass-bottomed boat. There are also trips on the Wakulla River, with a good chance of seeing alligators, ospreys and wading birds, and you can follow woodland trails.

Do not leave without visiting the Spanish-style Wakulla Springs Lodge hotel and restaurant, built in the 1930s.

Fishing for Shellfish in Apalachicola Bay

APALACHICOLA BAY is one of the most productive estuarine systems in the world. Fed by the nutrient-rich Apalachicola River, the bay is a valuable nursery, breeding and feeding ground for many marine species. The warm, shallow waters of the salt marshes between Apalachicola Bay and Cedar Key *(see p231)* are important feeding grounds too, and the fishing tradition extends all along the coast.

A blue crab

Oysters, blue crab, prawns (known as shrimp in the US) and other crustaceans, as well as fish, all contribute to the local fishing industry, which is worth about $15 million a year. Apalachicola Bay is most famous for its oysters, which account for 90 per cent of the state's total catch. The oysters grow rapidly in the bay's ideal conditions and reach a marketable size of 3 inches (8 cm) in under two years.

"Tongs", a pair of rakes joined like scissors, are used to lift the oysters from the sea.

A "culler" separates the oysters by size, throwing back any that are too small.

OYSTER FISHING
Oystermen, known locally as "tongers" after the tools they use, fish from small wooden boats, primarily in public grounds called oyster bars. The oysters can be harvested all year round, but there is usually a lull in the summer and autumn, when fishermen focus on other species.

Fishing for oysters in Apalachicola Bay

Fresh oysters, best served on ice

Fresh seafood is sold throughout the year around Apalachicola. On the first weekend of November, seafood enthusiasts converge on the town for the annual Florida Seafood Festival.

White, brown and pink shrimps are fished both inshore, from small boats in the bay, and offshore in the Gulf of Mexico, from larger vessels which may be away for a week or more. The catch is brought back to seafood houses on land for sorting and distribution.

Blue crabs, both the hard-shell and soft-shell varieties (the latter known as "peelers"), are caught in baited wire traps, which are dropped and collected by small boats. The crabs appear in warm weather, sometimes as early as February.

Tallahassee ⓲

JUST 14 MILES (23 KM) FROM the Georgia border, encircled by rolling hills and canopy roads, Tallahassee is the epitome of "The Other Florida" – gracious, hospitable and uncompromisingly Southern. The former site of an Apalachee Indian settlement and a Franciscan mission, this remote spot was an unlikely place to found the new capital of Territorial Florida in 1824 *(see p211)*. However, from its simple beginnings, Tallahassee grew dramatically during the plantation era and after Florida's elevation to full statehood in 1845. The elegant town houses built by politicians, plantation owners and businessmen during that period can still be enjoyed today.

Exploring Tallahassee

The historic district, where you'll find the city's fine 19th-century homes, is focused around Park Avenue and Calhoun Street, both quiet, shady streets planted with century-old live oak trees and southern magnolias. The Brokaw-McDougall House on Meridian Street is a splendid Classical Revival building. Similar influences are evident in The Columns, an 1830 mansion on Duval Street. The city's oldest building, it now houses the Chamber of Commerce, where you can pick up walking-tour maps. The Capitol Complex is at the very heart of downtown Tallahassee. Here, the venerable Old Capitol building has been beautifully restored to its 1902 state, with a pristine white dome and striped awnings. Inside, you can visit the Supreme Court chamber, the old cabinet meeting room and also the Senate. The 22-floor New Capitol building behind, where the March–May legislative sessions take place, casts a shadow over its predecessor. But although it is a grim 1970s structure, it does at least offer a lovely view of Tallahassee from its top floor.

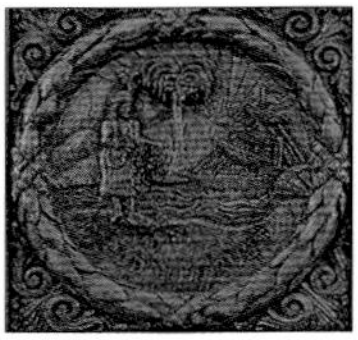

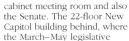

Wood carving in the Old Capitol Senate

VISITORS' CHECKLIST

Road map C1. Leon Co. 👥 *137,000.* ✈ *8 miles (13 km) S.* 🚆 *918 Railroad Avenue, (800) 872-7245.* 🚌 *112 W Tennessee Street, (904) 222-4240.* ℹ *New Capitol Building (first floor), Duval Street, (904) 413-9200, (800) 628-2866.* 🎉 *Springtime Tallahassee (Mar–Apr).*

🏛 Knott House Museum

301 East Park Ave. ☎ *(904) 922-2459.* ◯ *Wed–Sat.* ● *Thanksgiving, 25 Dec, 1 Jan.* $ ♿

This house is unusual for the claim that it was built by a free black in 1843 – 20 years prior to the emancipation of Florida's slaves. Now one of the most beautifully restored Victorian homes in Tallahassee, it is named after the Knotts, who moved here in 1928 and completely refurbished the house. The lovely interior is evocative of the former owners. Poems

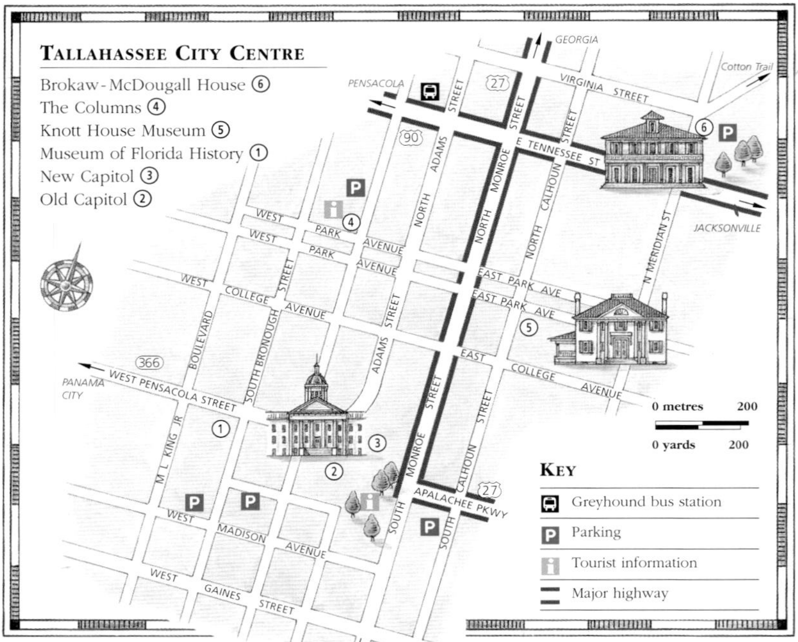
TALLAHASSEE CITY CENTRE
Brokaw-McDougall House (6)
The Columns (4)
Knott House Museum (5)
Museum of Florida History (1)
New Capitol (3)
Old Capitol (2)
GEORGIA
PENSACOLA
VIRGINIA STREET
Cotton Trail
E TENNESSEE ST
NORTH ADAMS STREET
NORTH MONROE STREET
NORTH CALHOUN STREET
N MERIDIAN ST
JACKSONVILLE
WEST PARK AVENUE
EAST PARK AVE
WEST COLLEGE AVENUE
EAST COLLEGE AVENUE
SOUTH BRONOUGH STREET
ADAMS STREET
BOULEVARD
M L KING JR
WEST PENSACOLA STREET
PANAMA CITY
SOUTH MONROE STREET
SOUTH CALHOUN STREET
APALACHEE PKWY
WEST MADISON AVENUE
WEST GAINES STREET
WAKULLA
27
90
366
0 metres 200
0 yards 200
KEY
Greyhound bus station
Parking
Tourist information
Major highway

that Luella Knott composed for and tied to her favourite antique furnishings are still in place to this day.

🏛 Museum of Florida History

500 S Bronough St. 【 *(904) 488-1484.* ☐ *daily.* ● *Thanksgiving, 25 Dec.* ♿

The museum tackles 12,000 years of the region's history in entertaining style. Varied dioramas feature elements of paleo-Indian culture, massive armadillos and a mastodon skeleton made of bones found in Wakulla Springs *(see p226).* Numerous artifacts and succinct storyboards provide an excellent potted history from the colonial era up to the "tin can" tourists of the 1920s *(see p49).*

Boardwalk in the Museum of History and Natural Science

ENVIRONS: Three miles (5 km) southwest of the city, Lake Bradford Road leads to the **Tallahassee Museum of History and Natural Science,** which is very popular with children. The centrepiece is the Big Bend Farm – a superb recreation of late 19th-century rural life, where staff dressed as farmhands tend goats and geese among authentic 1880s farm buildings. Bellevue, a small plantation home built in the 1830s, is among the other attractions. On the shores of Lake Bradford, this woodland area provides natural habitat enclosures for black bears and bobcats, while alligators lurk amidst the water lillies and cypress swamp areas.

Goodwood Plantation, on the northeastern edge of Tallahassee, was a major producer of cotton and corn in the 19th century *(see pp44–5).* The main house, built in the 1830s, retains many original features inside, including a mahogany staircase and marble fireplaces from Europe. After years of neglect, the plantation buildings are being restored. Visitors can already explore the grounds, as well as some of the outbuildings.

🏛 Tallahassee Museum of History and Natural Science

3945 Museum Drive. 【 *(904) 576-1636.* ☐ *daily.* ● *Thanksgiving, 24–25 Dec, 1 Jan.* 📷 ♿

🏛 Goodwood Plantation

1600 Miccosukee Rd. 【 *(904) 877-4202.* ☐ *Mon–Fri (gardens and outbuildings only).*

A B Maclay State Gardens ⑲

Road map C1. 3540 Thomasville Rd, Leon Co. 【 *(904) 487-4556.* 🚌 *Tallahassee.* 🚌 *Tallahassee.* ☐ *daily.* 📷 ♿

THESE GORGEOUS GARDENS, 4 miles (6 km) north of Tallahassee, were originally laid out around Killearn, the 1930s winter home of New York financier Alfred B Maclay. More than 200 varieties of plants are featured in the landscaped gardens that surround the shores of Lake Hall. They remain eye-catching even in winter, when the magnificent camellias and azaleas are in full

A B Maclay State Gardens near Tallahassee, at their best in the spring

bloom (from January to April). Visitors can also swim, fish, go boating, or enjoy a stroll along the woodland Big Pine Nature Trail.

Monticello ⑳

Road map C1. Jefferson Co.
👥 *2,800.* 🚌 *Tallahassee.* 🚌 *Tallahassee.* ⓘ *420 W Washington St, (904) 997-5552.*

FOUNDED IN 1827, Monticello (pronounced "Montisello") was named after the Virginia home of former President Thomas Jefferson. Lying at the heart of northern Florida's cotton-growing country, the town prospered and funded the building of elegant homes. Some of these are now bed-and-breakfasts, making the town a good base for exploring the Tallahassee area.

Monticello radiates from the imposing courthouse on US 90. The historic district lies to the north, where you'll find tree-canopied streets and a wealth of lovely old buildings, ranging from 1850s antebellum mansions to Queen Anne homes with decorative woodwork and Gothic features. Every year at the end of June, the town hosts its Watermelon Festival to celebrate a mainstay of the local agricultural economy. Pageants, dancing, rodeos and the traditional watermelon seed spitting contest are among the festival's many attractions.

Unadorned Presbyterian church, Monticello

Suwannee River State Park ㉒

Road map D2. Suwannee Co.
8 miles (13 km) NW of Live Oak.
🚉 Live Oak. ☎ (904) 362-2746.
⏱ daily. 🅿 ♿ ⛺

MADE FAMOUS the world over by the song *Old Folks at Home*, written by Stephen C Foster in 1851, the Suwannee has its sources in Georgia, from where it runs 265 miles (425 km) to the Gulf of Mexico.
Suwannee River State Park offers some of the best back-country canoeing in Florida. The river is easy flowing here and its low banks support a high forest of hickory, oak, southern magnolia and some cypress trees. Canoeists have a good chance of encountering a broad range of wildlife, including herons, American coots, hawks and also turtles. Canoe-hire is available and there is a boat ramp and a shady camp site.

Enjoying the sun at a wharf in Suwannee River State Park

Steinhatchee ㉓

Road map D2. Taylor Co. 🏠 7,000.
🚉 Chiefland. 🛈 428 N Jefferson, (904) 584-5366.

SET BACK FROM THE mouth of the Steinhatchee River, this is a sleepy old fishing town, strung out along the riverbank. To get a flavour of the place, ignore the trailer parks and stroll among the jumble of fish camps, bait shops and boats tied up to the cypress wood docks. Trout fishing is big here, and you may also find people crabbing along the coast.
About 26 miles (42 km) northwest of Steinhatchee is **Keaton Beach**, a tiny but popular coastal resort surrounded by woodlands and marshes.

Cedar Key ㉔

Road map D2. Levy Co. 🏠 750.
🚉 Chiefland. 🛈 2nd Street, (352) 543-5600.

AT THE FOOT of a chain of little bridge-linked keys jutting out into the Gulf of Mexico, Cedar Key is a picturesque, weathered Victorian fishing village. In the 19th century it flourished as the gulf terminal of Florida's first cross-state railway and from the burgeoning timber trade. However, within a few decades

Cotton Trail Tour ㉑

IN THE 1820S AND '30S, the area around Tallahassee was the most important cotton-growing region in Florida. From the outlying plantations, horse-drawn wagons creaked along red clay roads to market in the capital. Today, these old roads pass through one of the last corners of unspoilt rural Florida.
This tour follows the old Cotton Trail, along canopied roads and past cattle pastures and paddocks carved out of deep green woodlands. It takes about 3.5 hours, or it could be done en route between Tallahassee and Monticello (*see p229*).

Bradley's Country Store ④
Famous for its home-made sausages, this traditional country store is still run by the Bradleys, who established the business in 1927.

Old Pisgah United Methodist Church ③
This unadorned Greek Revival church, built in 1858, is the oldest Methodist building in Leon County.

Miccosukee Road ②
Originally an Indian trail, this canopy road was used by 30 local plantations in the 1850s.

Goodwood Plantation ①
This former cotton plantation (*see p229*) retains its lovely 1840s mansion shaded by live oak trees.

KEY

▬▬ Tour route

══ Other roads

its namesake stands of cedar forest had been transformed into pencils and the logging boom ended. A few of the old timber warehouses have been turned into shops and restaurants, but the Cedar Key of today is blissfully quiet.

You can take a boat from the docks to an offshore island beach in the Cedar Keys National Wildlife Refuge, or take a bird-watching trip along the saltmarsh coast. Various boats run trips from the docks.

Alternatively, visit the entertaining **Cedar Key Historical Society Museum**, in which eclectic exhibits include some fossilized tapir teeth, Indian pottery shards and crab traps. At the museum you can also pick up a map for touring the town's historic buildings.

🏛 Cedar Key Historical Society Museum

Corner of D and 2nd Streets. ☎ *(352) 543-5549.* ○ *daily.* ● *Thanksgiving, 25 Dec, 1 Jan.* 🎟 ♿

Environs: Thirty miles (50 km) to the north of Cedar Key is **Manatee Springs State Park**, where a spring gushes from a cave mouth more than 30 ft (9 m) below the surface of an azure pool. The swift-running spring water, which feeds the Suwannee River, is as clear as glass and is very popular with divers and snorkellers. Sightings of manatees, which occasionally winter here, are unreliable, but it is easy to spot dozens of turtles, fish and egrets feeding in the shallows, and the ubiquitous turkey eagles hovering overhead. You can also swim, hire a canoe, take a boat tour, or follow one of the many walking trails; you may be lucky enough to catch an armadillo in the undergrowth.

✂ Manatee Springs State Park

Route 320, 6 miles (10 km) W of Chiefland. ☎ *(352) 493-6072.* ○ *daily.* ⛺

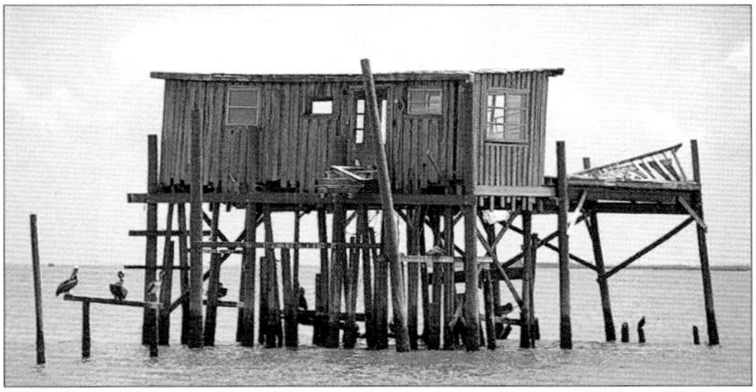

Weather-beaten hut on stilts off the coast of Cedar Key

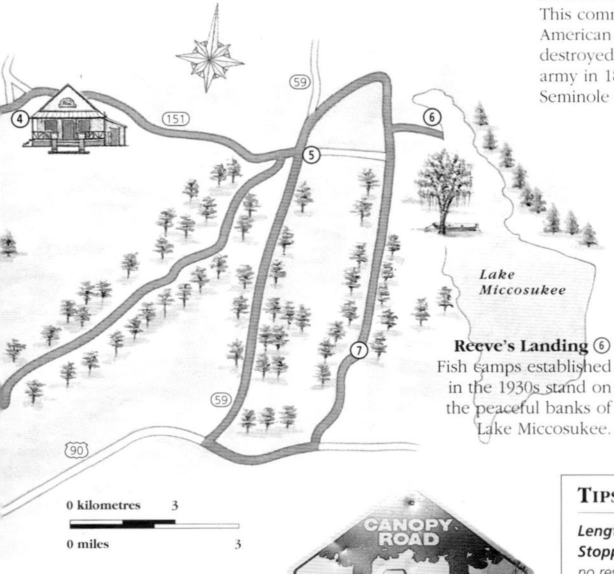

Miccosukee 5
This community was a Native American village until it was destroyed by Andrew Jackson's army in 1818, during the First Seminole War *(see pp44–5).*

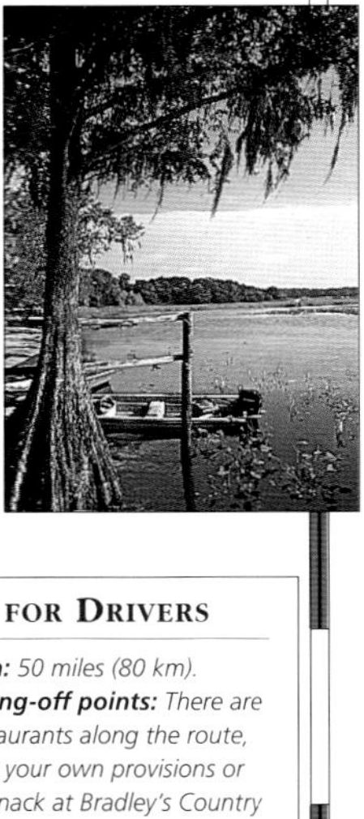

Reeve's Landing 6
Fish camps established in the 1930s stand on the peaceful banks of Lake Miccosukee.

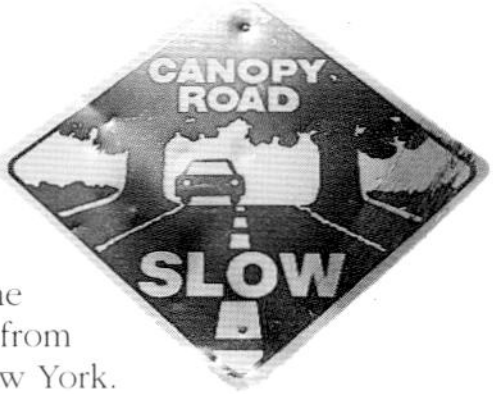

Magnolia Road 7
One of Florida's last unpaved canopy roads, this track led to the now-vanished port of Magnolia, from which cotton was shipped to New York.

Tips for Drivers

Length: *50 miles (80 km).*
Stopping-off points: *There are no restaurants along the route, so take your own provisions or buy a snack at Bradley's Country Store, and enjoy a picnic on the banks of Lake Miccosukee.*

THE GULF COAST

OR MANY VISITORS *the Gulf Coast begins and ends with its fabulous beaches, bathed by the warm, calm waters of the Gulf of Mexico, and their accompanying resorts. However, with only a little effort you can kick the sand from your shoes and visit some of Florida's most interesting cities or explore wilderness areas that have been left virtually untouched by the vagaries of time.*

Ever since the Spanish colonization, the focus of activity along the Gulf Coast has been around Tampa Bay, the large inlet in Florida's west coast. Pánfilo de Narváez anchored in the bay in 1528, and Hernando de Soto *(see p41)* landed nearby in 1539. The bay was a perfect natural port and became a magnet to pioneers in the 19th century. The favourable climate even drew the odd sugar-grower: Gamble Plantation near Bradenton is the southernmost plantation house in the US *(see p252)*.

After the Civil War, the Gulf Coast became a significant centre for trade between the US and the Caribbean. This was due in part to Henry Plant, whose rail line from Virginia, laid in the 1880s, helped to fuel both Tampa's and the region's greatest period of prosperity. Pioneers flooded in, from ethnic groups such as the Greek sponge fishermen who settled in Tarpon Springs, to wealthier American immigrants – chief among whom was circus king John Ringling, whose splendid Italianate home and impressive European art collection is the city of Sarasota's top attraction.

Henry Plant, like Flagler in eastern Florida *(see pp46–7)*, used the promise of winter sunshine to lure wealthy travellers from the north. The west coast's much-advertised average of 361 days of sunshine a year still helps attract great hordes of package tourists to the generous scattering of beaches. Throbbing beach scenes are the norm around St Petersburg and Clearwater, but you can easily escape the cosmopolitan holiday atmosphere: only a short distance inland are quirky cattle towns, rivers perfect for canoeing, and swamps and forests where wild animals reside undisturbed.

The high-rise downtown skyline of Tampa, the most important city along the Gulf Coast

◁ The boardwalk giving access to the broad beach at Sand Key, near Clearwater Beach

Exploring the Gulf Coast

THE BEACHES THAT RUN in an almost continuous line along the Gulf Coast, interrupted only by a series of bays and inlets, are hard to resist. But the joy of this region is that it is easy to spice up a seaside holiday with some sightseeing. The abundant accommodation by the sea, from quaint cottages to no-expense-spared resorts, makes this the natural place to base yourself, and all the main cities and inland sights are within easy reach. You'll find some of Florida's best museums in St Petersburg, Tampa and Sarasota, as well as high-profile attractions like Busch Gardens and the Florida Aquarium in Tampa. There are also plenty more quirky sights: from the world's largest concentration of Frank Lloyd Wright buildings at Florida Southern College to the weird and wonderful mermaids of Weeki Wachee Spring.

The glistening towers and dome of the old
Tampa Bay Hotel *(see p244)*

SEE ALSO

- *Where to Stay* pp308–310
- *Where to Eat* pp326–8 & p331

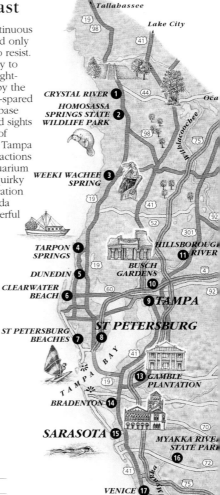

Tallahassee

Lake City

CRYSTAL RIVER **1**

HOMOSASSA
SPRINGS STATE **2**
WILDLIFE PARK

Ocala

WEEKI WACHEE **3**
SPRING

TARPON **4**
SPRINGS

HILLSBOROUGH **11**
RIVER

DUNEDIN **5**

BUSCH
GARDENS

CLEARWATER
BEACH **6**

10

9 TAMPA

ST PETERSBURG
BEACHES **7**

8

ST PETERSBURG

TAMPA BAY

13 GAMBLE
PLANTATION

BRADENTON **14**

SARASOTA **15**

MYAKKA RIVER
STATE PARK
16

VENICE **17**

PORT
CHARLOTTE

GASPARILLA **18**
ISLAND

LEE ISLAND
COAST **23**

SANIBEL

Exploring the pristine landscapes of Myakka River State Park

GETTING AROUND

The region is easy to get around by car. US 19 runs
along the coast north of Tampa Bay, crossing the
mouth of the bay over the magnificent Sunshine
Skyway Bridge, while US 41 links the coastal communities south of Tampa. If speed is of the essence
you'll want to use I-75, which runs further inland.
As in every other region of Florida, life is hard without a car. Greyhound buses link the main towns, but
rail services are more limited; Amtrak trains run only
as far as Tampa, although its connecting "Thruway"
buses (see p360) provide a link to St Petersburg and
south along the coast as far as Fort Myers.

Deserted Clearwater Beach at sunset

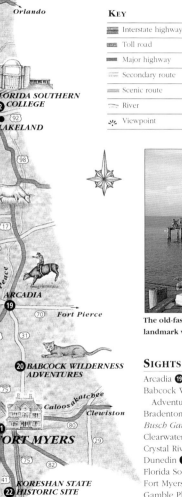

KEY

  Interstate highway

Toll road

Major highway

Secondary route

Scenic route

River

Viewpoint

0 kilometres   30

0 miles   25

**The old-fashioned pier on Anna Maria Island, a well-known local
landmark west of Bradenton**

SIGHTS AT A GLANCE

Crystal River ➊

Road map D2. Citrus Co. 👤 *5,000.*
🚌 ℹ *28 NW US 19, (352) 795-3149.*

Crystal river has two main attractions. In winter people come to watch the manatees, which gather in herds of up to 300 to bask in the warm local springs, particularly between January and March. You can go on boat trips around the **Crystal River National Wildlife Refuge**, which incorporates the springs and inlets of nearby Kings Bay and was set up specifically to protect the manatees. The clear water, after which Crystal River was named, makes spotting the animals easy.

A year-round attraction is the **Crystal River State Archaeological Site**, a complex of six Indian mounds 2 miles (3 km) west of the town. The site is thought to have been occupied for 1,600 years, from 200 BC to AD 1400, one of the longest continually occupied sites in Florida. An estimated 7,500 Native Americans visited the complex every year for ceremonial purposes, frequently travelling large distances to do so. Excavation of 400 of the possible 1,000 graves at the site has also revealed that local tribes had trade links with peoples north of Florida.

Climb up to the observation deck for a bird's-eye view of the site. Just below is the main temple mound, built in around AD 600. Beyond, two carved

Pottery at Crystal River

ceremonial stones, or stelae, erected in around AD 440 can be seen flanking two of the site's three burial mounds. This style of stone is typical of the pre-Columbian cultures of Mesoamerica, but there is no evidence that they had links with Crystal River. On the western edge of the site is a large village area marked by two midden mounds *(see p38)* on a midden ridge. There is a model of the site in the visitor centre, as well as examples of the pottery found.

🦋 **Crystal River National Wildlife Refuge**
1502 SE Kings Bay Drive. 📞 *(352) 563-2088.* ⬜ *Mon–Fri.*
⛰ **Crystal River State Archaeological Site**
3400 N Museum Point. ℹ *(352) 795-3817.* ⬜ *daily.* 🅿 ♿

THE MANATEE IN FLORIDA

You cannot go far in Florida without hearing about the sea cow, or manatee, an animal in serious risk of extinction. It is believed that there are only about 2,500 manatees left in the US, concentrated in the warm waters of Florida. Once plentiful, the animals were extensively hunted for meat and sport until the beginning of the 20th century, since when habitat destruction and boat accidents have done most of the damage.

The manatee, which grows to an average length of 10 ft (3 m), is a huge but gentle creature. It lives in shallow coastal waters, rivers and springs, spending about five hours a day feeding; seagrass is its favourite food.

The manatee, an inhabitant of both salt and fresh water

Homosassa Springs State Wildlife Park ➋

Road map D2. Citrus Co. *9225 West Fishbowl Drive, Homosassa.*
🚌 *Crystal River.* ℹ *(352) 628-2311.* ⬜ *daily.* 🅿 ♿

One of the best places to see manatees in the wild is at Homosassa Springs State Wildlife Park, where a floating observatory enables visitors to get close up to the animals.

Injured manatees, usually the victims of boat propellers, are treated and rehabilitated here before being released into the wild. There are often half a dozen in the recovery pool, and in winter more gather outside the park fence: as at Crystal River, in cold weather the manatees are attracted by the warm spring water.

Weeki Wachee Spring ➌

Road map D2. Hernando Co. *Junction of US 19 & SR 50.* 📞 *(352) 596-2062.* 🚌 *Brooksville.* ⬜ *daily.* 🅿 ♿

This long-standing theme park is built on one of Florida's largest freshwater springs. In the 1940s, ex-Navy frogman Newton Perry hit on the idea of using women swimmers to take the part of "live mermaids" performing a kind of underwater ballet.

A performing "mermaid" at Weeki Wachee Spring

A theatre was built 15 ft (5 m) underwater with strategically placed air pipes. Nowadays, the shows change regularly, and each one has a plot.

Other attractions include Buccaneer Bay water park, a children's zoo and a popular wilderness river cruise.

Tarpon Springs ❹

Road map D3. Pinellas Co.
🚶 20,000. 🚆 Clearwater. ℹ️ 11 E Orange St, (813) 937-6109.

THIS LIVELY TOWN on the Anclote River is most famous as a centre of Greek culture – the legacy of the immigrant fishermen lured here at the start of the 20th century by the prolific local sponge beds. You'll find restaurants specializing in Greek food, an Athens Street, a Poseidon gift shop, a Parthenon bakery and so on.

Alongside Dodecanese Boulevard are the Sponge Docks, which are busy once more thanks to the recovery of the nearby sponge beds, decimated by bacterial blight in the 1940s. Boat trips organized by local sponge fishermen include a demonstration of sponge diving by a diver kitted out in a traditional suit.

The other main attraction along Dodecanese Boulevard is **Spongeorama**, a combined museum and shopping village housed in former dockside sheds. Also popular is the Sponge Exchange, a modern complex housing up-market boutiques, galleries and cafés.

Trimming natural sponges before sale in Tarpon Springs

The nature trail through unspoilt woodland on Caladesi Island

Two miles (3 km) south rises **St Nicholas Greek Orthodox Cathedral**, the most striking symbol of Tarpon Springs' Greek heritage. The Byzantine Revival church, a replica of St Sophia in Istanbul, was erected in 1943 using marble transported all the way from Greece. It is the starting point for the Epiphany Festival, the most important date in the local calendar (see p35).

🏠 Spongeorama
510 Dodecanese Blvd. 📞 (813) 943-9509. 🕐 daily. ♿

⛪ St Nicholas Greek Orthodox Cathedral
36 N Pinellas Ave at Orange St. 📞 (813) 937-3540. 🕐 daily. ♿

Dunedin ❺

Road map D3. Pinellas Co.
🚶 36,000. 🚆 Clearwater. ℹ️ 301 Main St, (813) 733-3197.

DUNEDIN WAS founded by a Scotsman, John L Branch, who in 1870 opened a store to supply ships on their way down the Gulf Coast to Key West. Passing sea and rail routes brought trade and prosperity, and this soon attracted a number of his compatriots. Dunedin's Scottish heritage is still expressed in its annual Highland Games festival held in late March or early April.

The renovated properties on and around Main Street impart the authentic flavour of early 20th-century small-town Florida. The **Historical Museum**, which occupies Dunedin's former railway

station, has a fine collection of photographs and artifacts from the town's early days. Nearby Railroad Avenue is now part of the Pinellas Trail, a paved walking and cycling path running for 47 miles (76 km) from Tarpon Springs to St Petersburg, along the route of the former railroad.

🏛️ Historical Museum
349 Main St. 📞 (813) 736-1176. 🕐 Tue –Sat. ● public hols. ♿

ENVIRONS: Three miles (5 km) north of Dunedin, a causeway crosses to **Honeymoon Island State Recreation Area**. You can swim and fish there, but this barrier island is largely undeveloped, in order to preserve its status as an important osprey nesting site. It is also the departure point for the passenger ferry to the even more alluring **Caladesi Island State Park**, which can alternatively be reached from Clearwater Beach (see p238).

Caladesi's 3-mile (5-km) beach, fronting the Gulf of Mexico, was rated in 1995 as the second best in the US. The glorious beach gives way to dunes fringed by sea oats, which lead in turn to pine, cypress and mangrove woods traversed by a 3-mile (5-km) nature trail. Maps are available from the visitor centre.

🏊 Honeymoon Island SRA
Route 586, 3 miles (5 km) NW of Dunedin. 📞 (813) 469-5942. 🕐 daily. 🅿️ ♿ limited.
🏊 Caladesi Island State Park
1 Causeway Blvd. 📞 (813) 469-5918. 🕐 daily. 🅿️ ♿ limited.

Interior of the McMullen Log House, Pinellas County Heritage Village

Clearwater Beach **6**

Road map D3. Pinellas Co. 🏛 *20,000.*
🔹 🚌 *Clearwater.* 🚋 *tourist trolley
from Cleveland St.* ℹ *1130 Cleveland
St, Clearwater, (813) 461-0011.*

THE SATELLITE of Clearwater
city, this lively resort marks
the start of the holiday
strip that extends as far
as Tampa Bay. Hotels
and bars, often filled
with European pack-
age tourists, dom-
inate the seafront,
but Clearwater Beach
manages to retain some
character. If you can't
afford to stay on the
Gulf side, there are
cheaper hotels by the
Intracoastal Waterway.

**Screech owls
in the Suncoast
Sanctuary**

The broad sandy beach is
very impressive, and the water
sports facilities are excellent.
Boat trips of all kinds depart
from the marina: from diving
or sports fishing expeditions
to sunset cruises on the Gulf.

ENVIRONS: Across Clearwater
Pass is Sand Key, which runs
south for 12 miles (19 km).
Sand Key Park, near the top,
has a popular palm-fringed
beach ranked in the top 20 in
the country, and offers a more
down-to-earth scene than
throbbing Clearwater Beach.

About 7 miles (11 km) to
the south – beyond the chic
residential district of Belleair,
complete with a hotel built by
Henry Plant *(see pp46–7)* – is
the much-visited **Suncoast
Seabird Sanctuary**. Up to
500 injured birds live at this
sanctuary in Indian Shores.

Pelicans, owls, herons, egrets
and other species are all on
view, while Ralph Heath, who
runs the sanctuary, and his
helpers offer guided tours.

It is well worth making the
diversion inland to Largo, 8
miles (12 km) southeast of
Clearwater Beach, to visit the
**Pinellas County Heritage
Village**. This consists of 16
historic buildings, brought
here from various sites
and restored. The
highlights include
the McMullen Log
House *(see p28)* and
the Seven Gables
Home (1907), which
offers a taste of the
lifestyle of a wealthy
Victorian family.
Spinning, weaving and
other skills typical of
Florida's pioneers are
demonstrated in the museum
at the centre of the park.

**🏛 Pinellas County
Heritage Village**
11909 125th Street N. ℹ *(813) 582-
2123.* ◯ *Tue–Sun.* ● *public hols.* ♿
**🦅 Suncoast Seabird
Sanctuary**
18328 Gulf Blvd, Indian Shores.
ℹ *(813) 391-6211.* ◯ *daily.* ♿ 📷

St Petersburg Beaches **7**

Road map D3. Pinellas Co. ✈️
🚗 *Tampa.* 🚌 *St Petersburg.* 🚌 *many
services from St Petersburg.* ℹ *St Pete
Beach Chamber of Commerce, 6990
Gulf Blvd, (813) 360-6957 .*

SOUTH OF Clearwater you
enter the orbit of the St
Petersburg Beaches. Until you
reach Madeira Beach the
seafront scenes are rather disappointing. **Madeira Beach**,
however, is a good place to
stay if you prefer a laid-back
atmosphere to the buzzing
scenes of the bigger resorts.
Johns Pass Village, a re-created
fishing village nearby, also
offers a quirkier-than-average
choice of restaurants and
shops. There is also a fishing
pier and a marina, where fishing and other boats gather.

Further south, monotonous
ranks of hotels characterize
Treasure Island. Next in line,
St Pete Beach (St Petersburg
was officially shortened to St
Pete as it was considered more
evocative of a fun-filled resort),
has a 7-mile (11-km) strip of
white sand and a buzzing
scene along the seafront. At
its southern end towers the
Don CeSar Resort *(see p309).*
Built in the 1920s, the hotel's
scale and roll call of celebrity
guests are typical of the grand
hotels of that era.

At the southern tip of the
barrier island group, **Pass-a-
Grille** is a breath of fresh air
after crowded St Pete Beach.
Skirted by the main coastal
road, this sleepy community
has some lovely homes from
the early 1900s and beaches
still in their natural state. A
word of warning: take lots of
change for the parking meters.

The extravagant Don CeSar Resort overlooking St Pete Beach

Gulf Coast Beaches

With an average of 361 days of sunshine a year and just two hours' drive from Orlando, the coast between St Petersburg and Clearwater is the busiest resort area along the Gulf Coast, attracting hordes of overseas visitors. Known variously as the Holiday Isles, the Pinellas Coast or the Suncoast, the strip encompasses 28 miles (45 km) of superb barrier island beaches. Due to the high quality of the sand and water, plus the relative scarcity of pests, litter and crime, the Suncoast regularly appears in lists of the nation's top beaches. Further south, Sarasota's barrier island beaches are of an equally high standard; they attract more Floridians than package tourists. Wherever you are, expect a more laid-back mood than on the east coast.

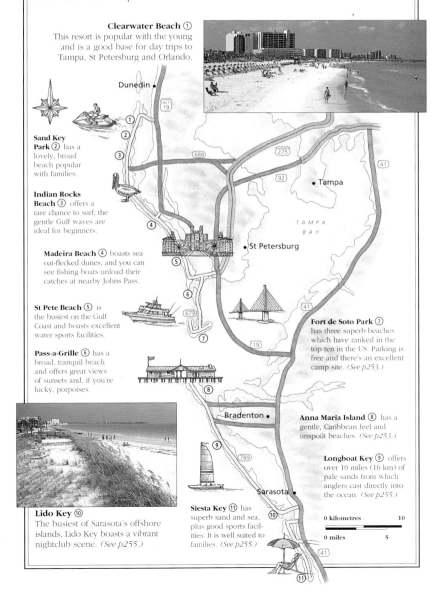

Clearwater Beach (1)
This resort is popular with the young and is a good base for day trips to Tampa, St Petersburg and Orlando.

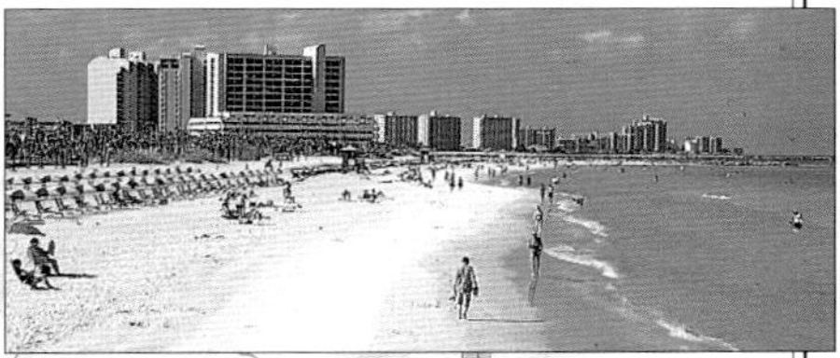

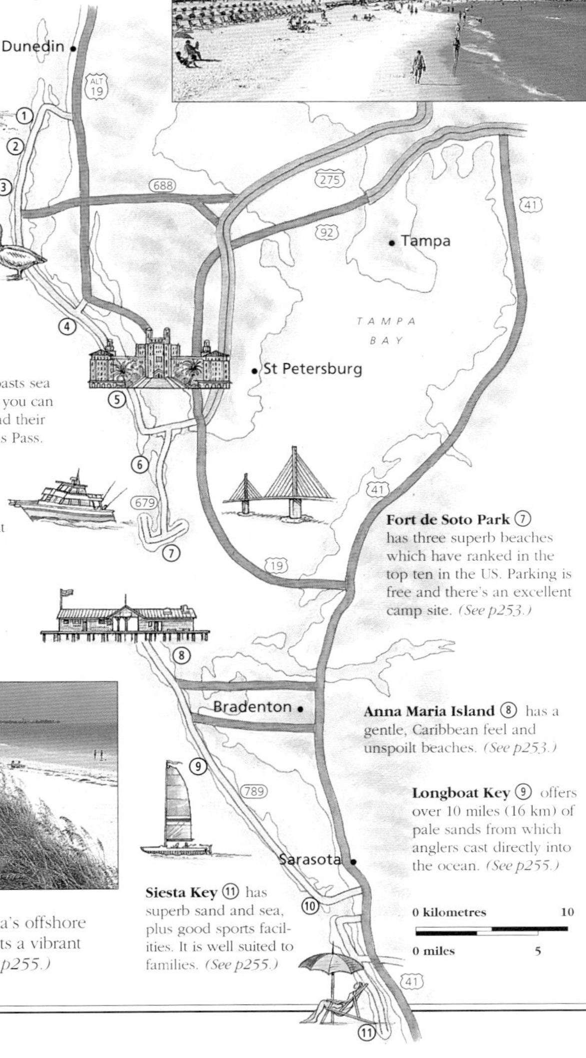
Dunedin
ALT 19
688
275
92
41
Tampa
TAMPA BAY
St Petersburg
679
19
41
Bradenton
789
Sarasota
41
0 kilometres 10
0 miles 5

Sand Key Park (2) has a lovely, broad beach popular with families.

Indian Rocks Beach (3) offers a rare chance to surf; the gentle Gulf waves are ideal for beginners.

Madeira Beach (4) boasts sea oat-flecked dunes, and you can see fishing boats unload their catches at nearby Johns Pass.

St Pete Beach (5) is the busiest on the Gulf Coast and boasts excellent water sports facilities.

Pass-a-Grille (6) has a broad, tranquil beach and offers great views of sunsets and, if you're lucky, porpoises.

Fort de Soto Park (7) has three superb beaches which have ranked in the top ten in the US. Parking is free and there's an excellent camp site. *(See p253.)*

Anna Maria Island (8) has a gentle, Caribbean feel and unspoilt beaches. *(See p253.)*

Longboat Key (9) offers over 10 miles (16 km) of pale sands from which anglers cast directly into the ocean. *(See p255.)*

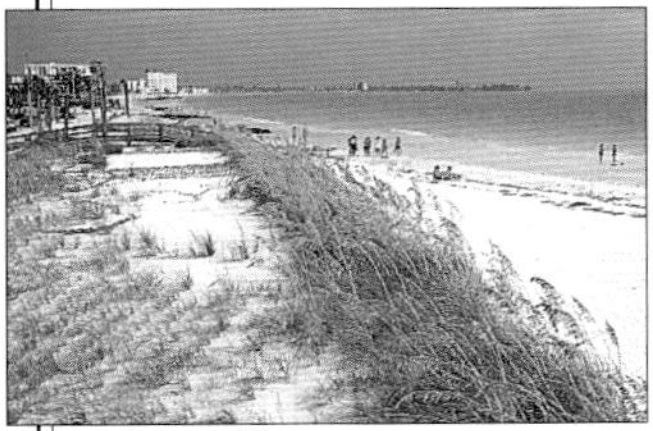

Lido Key (10)
The busiest of Sarasota's offshore islands, Lido Key boasts a vibrant nightclub scene. *(See p255.)*

Siesta Key (11) has superb sand and sea, plus good sports facilities. It is well suited to families. *(See p255.)*

St Petersburg [8]

THIS CITY of broad avenues grew up in the great era of 19th-century land speculation. In 1875, Michigan farmer John Williams bought a plot of land beside Tampa Bay, with a dream of building a grand city. An exiled Russian nobleman called Peter Demens soon provided St Petersburg with both a railroad and its name – the latter in honour of his birthplace.

"St Pete", as it is often called, used to be best known for its ageing population. But times have changed and the city now has a much more vibrant image. Extensive renovation has brought new life to the waterfront area downtown, and St Petersburg's claim to be a lively cultural centre is greatly boosted by the presence of the prestigious Salvador Dali Museum *(see pp242–3).*

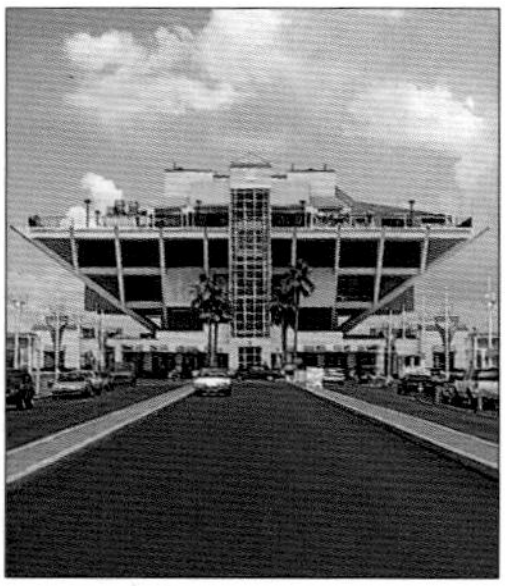

St Petersburg's eye-catching Pier, its best known landmark

Exploring St Petersburg

The landmark that appears in every tourist brochure about the city is **The Pier**. Its distinctive upside-down pyramid contains shops, restaurants, a disco, an aquarium and an observation deck, and acts as a magnet for visitors heading for the downtown area. A tourist trolley service runs from the pier down to Great Explorations, stopping at all the major attractions en route.

Looking north from the pier, the handsome **Renaissance Vinoy Resort** *(see p309)*, built in the 1920s as the Vinoy Hotel and much modernized, dominates the downtown skyline. Away from the waterfront is the massive **Tropicana Field**, St Petersburg's other main landmark. This is a popular venue for large-scale events ranging from rock concerts to sports events *(see p339).*

🏛 St Petersburg Museum of History

335 2nd Avenue NE. ☎ *(813) 894-1052.* ○ *daily.* ● *Thanksgiving, 25 Dec, 1 Jan.* 📷 ♿

This museum tells the story of St Petersburg from prehistoric times to the present. Exhibits range from mastodon bones, fossils and native pottery to an entertaining mirror gallery, which gives visitors a comic taste of how they would have looked in Victorian fashions.

A special pavilion houses a replica of a sea plane called the Benoist, which marks St Petersburg's status as the birthplace of commercial aviation. It was in this aircraft that the first flight with a paying passenger was made across Tampa Bay in 1914.

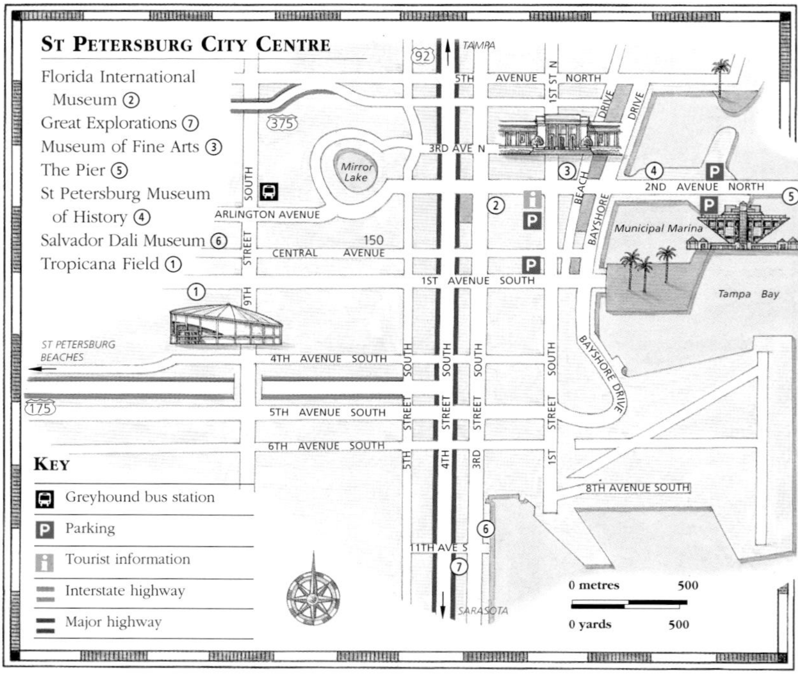
ST PETERSBURG CITY CENTRE
Florida International Museum ②
Great Explorations ⑦
Museum of Fine Arts ③
The Pier ⑤
St Petersburg Museum of History ④
Salvador Dali Museum ⑥
Tropicana Field ①
TAMPA
92
375
175
5TH AVENUE NORTH
3RD AVE N
2ND AVENUE NORTH
ARLINGTON AVENUE
CENTRAL AVENUE
150
1ST AVENUE SOUTH
4TH AVENUE SOUTH
5TH AVENUE SOUTH
6TH AVENUE SOUTH
8TH AVENUE SOUTH
11TH AVE S
9TH STREET SOUTH
5TH STREET SOUTH
4TH STREET SOUTH
3RD STREET SOUTH
1ST STREET SOUTH
1ST ST N
BEACH DRIVE
BAYSHORE DRIVE
Mirror Lake
Municipal Marina
Tampa Bay
ST PETERSBURG BEACHES
SARASOTA
KEY
Greyhound bus station
Parking
Tourist information
Interstate highway
Major highway
0 metres 500
0 yards 500

Poppy, one of Georgia O'Keeffe's acclaimed flower paintings, in the Museum of Fine Arts

🏛 Museum of Fine Arts

255 Beach Drive NE. 📞 *(813) 896-2667.* ⭕ *Tue –Sun.* ● *Thanksgiving, 25 Dec, 1 Jan.* 🏷 ♿ ☑

Housed in a striking modern Palladian-style building overlooking the bay, the Museum of Fine Arts is renowned for its wide-ranging collection of European, American, pre-Columbian and Asian works. Supreme among the French Impressionist paintings are *A Corner of the Woods* (1877) by Cézanne and Monet's classic *Parliament, Effect of Fog, London* (1904). Other prominent works are the vivid *Poppy* (1927) by Georgia O'Keeffe, *La Lecture* (1888) by Berthe Morisot and Auguste Rodin's *Invocation* (1886) which stands in the sculpture garden.

Selections from the largest collection of photographs in the southeast US, dating from the early 1900s to the present, round off the collection.

🏛 Florida International Museum

100 2nd Street N. 🆔 *(813) 821-1448.* ⭕ *daily.* ● *24 & 25 Dec.* 🏷 ♿

Two blocks inland from St Petersburg's pier, this museum occupies the former Maas Brothers department store, built in the 1950s. Behind an unprepossessing façade, the spacious interior provides excellent exhibition space. The museum has no permanent collection, but instead hosts a couple of large exhibitions each year, featuring items from some of the world's top museums. It opened in 1995 with "Treasures of the Czars" from the Kremlin; call ahead to check what is on display during your visit.

🏛 Great Explorations

1120 4th Street S. 🆔 *(813) 821-8885.* ⭕ *daily.* ● *Thanksgiving, 25 Dec, 1 Jan.* 🏷 ♿

"Hands on" is the ethos at this museum, which is aimed at children, but is equally fascinating to adults. It has six exhibit areas, focusing on the arts, sciences and health.

Highlights include the Body Shop, where visitors can measure their strength and flexibility through a series of physical tests including a climbing wall, and the Think Tank, with brain-teasers and problem-solving games. In the Touch Tunnel, you can check your reactions as you clamber and slide through a 90-ft (27-m) pitch-black maze.

🌵 Sunken Gardens

1825 4th Street N. 📞 *(813) 896-3187.* ⭕ *daily.* 🏷 ♿

Thousands of tropical plants and flowers flourish in this large walled garden, which descends to 10 ft (3 m) below the street outside. The site was

once a water-filled sinkhole *(see p20)*; its soil is kept dry by a network of hidden pipes.

Wander among the bougainvillea and hibiscus, and visit the extensive orchid garden. Other features include bird and alligator shows, and a walk-through aviary full of parrots and macaws.

Lush tropical plants flanking a stream at the Sunken Gardens

ENVIRONS: Five islands in Boca Ciega Bay south of St Petersburg make up **Fort De Soto Park**. The park offers great views of the Sunshine Skyway Bridge and superb beaches, especially along the southern and western coasts. The islands are thick with vegetation and bird colonies, and are popular with campers.

History fans should head for the chief island, Mullet Key, where massive gun emplacements concealed by high concrete walls mark the remains of Fort De Soto. The fort was begun during the Spanish-American War *(see p47)*, but was never finished.

🦌 Fort De Soto Park

Pinellas Bayway, off Route 682, 9 miles (14 km) S of St Petersburg. 📞 *(813) 866-2484.* ⭕ *daily.* ♿

The Sunshine Skyway Bridge, which spans the mouth of Tampa Bay

Salvador Dali Museum

Although a long way from the native country of Spanish artist Salvador Dali (1904–89), this museum boasts the most comprehensive collection of his work in the world, spanning the years 1914–70. The museum opened in 1982, 40 years after Ohio businessman Reynolds Morse first met the young artist and began collecting his works. As well as 95 original oil paintings, the museum has more than 100 watercolours and drawings, along with 1,300 graphics, sculptures and other objects. The works range from Salvador Dali's early figurative paintings through to his first experiments in Surrealism and the mature, large-scale compositions described as his "masterworks".

Masterworks Gallery
This focal point of the museum contains six of Dali's 18 masterworks, such as the Hallucinogenic Toreador, *which he painted in the years 1969–70.*

Nature Morte Vivante
This 1956 work is an example of Salvador Dali's use of a mathematical grid and the DNA spiral (as shown in the cauliflower) as the basis of a composition.

Museum Shop

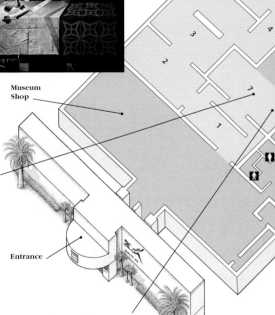

★ The Sick Child
This is the earliest painting by Dali in the museum. It was composed in 1914, when he was just ten years of age and already showing huge talent.

Entrance

STAR PAINTINGS

★ The Sick Child

★ The Discovery of America

★ Daddy Longlegs of the Evening–Hope!

View of Cadaques
Impressionist influences are evident in this view, painted in 1917, of the shadow of Mount Pani stretching towards Dali's family home and other houses around the bay.

Don Quixote and Sancho
This 1968 etching is just one of over 1,000 drawings and other illustrations produced during Dali's Classic Period. Examples from the museum's collection appear in temporary exhibitions.

VISITORS' CHECKLIST

1000 3rd St S, St Petersburg.
(813) 823-3767. 4, 32, or the tourist trolley from the Pier.
9:30am–5:30pm Mon–Sat; noon–5:30pm Sun. Thanksgiving, 25 Dec.

Raymond James Room

★ **The Discovery of America**
Inspired by a "cosmic dream", this work (1958–9) pays homage to the Spanish painter Velázquez while predicting man's first step on the moon.

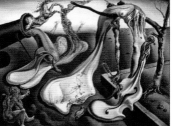

★ **Daddy Longlegs of the Evening–Hope!**
This bizarre image was the foundation stone of the collection. Painted in 1940, it shows a daddy longlegs crawling over the face of a hideously distorted violinist.

KEY TO FLOORPLAN

- Introductory Gallery
- Early Works 1914–28
- Surrealism 1929–40
- Classic Period 1943–89
- Masterworks 1948–70
- Temporary exhibitions
- Non-exhibition space

GALLERY GUIDE

The collection is divided into five main galleries, ordered chronologically, with an introductory room. Temporary displays of Dali's many other works normally occupy the Raymond James Room.

HOW DALI'S ART CAME TO ST PETERSBURG

Reynolds Morse and his fiancée Eleanor were fascinated by Salvador Dali from the time they saw an exhibition of his art in 1941. They bought their first Dali work, *Daddy Longlegs of the Evening–Hope!*, two years later and met the artist soon after. Thus began the Morses' life-long friendship with Dali and his wife, Gala. Over the next 40 years the Morses amassed the largest private collection of Dali's art in the world. After a nationwide search, Morse chose the present waterfront site for the collection because of its resemblance to the artist's home town of Cadaques. The collection, bought by the Morses for about $5 million, is now worth in excess of $350 million.

Tampa ⑨

**Greek vase,
Museum
of Art**

Tampa is one of the fastest-growing cities in Florida. Modern skyscrapers have replaced many original buildings, but vestiges of a colourful history remain – mainly in the old Cuban quarter, Ybor City *(see pp246–7)*, where Tampa's famous cigar industry took root in the 1880s, and in some quirky architecture downtown. The Spanish arrived here in 1539, but Tampa was just a small town until the late 1800s, when Henry Plant *(see pp46–7)* extended his railway here. Today, Tampa's big attraction is nearby Busch Gardens *(see pp250–51)*, but the sleek Florida Aquarium in the new Garrison Seaport Center is drawing more and more people downtown.

View across Tampa with the university in the foreground

Exploring Downtown

You can easily explore Tampa's compact downtown area on foot. The main thoroughfare is the partly pedestrianized Franklin Street, where you'll find the historic Tampa Theatre and several examples of the public art on which the city justifiably prides itself.

Situated at the mouth of the Hillsborough River, Tampa can also be enjoyed from the water. The old paddlewheeler Starlite Princess *(see p339)* runs daytime and evening trips, while the Tampa Town Ferry, anchored near the Florida Aquarium, has regular hour-long tours, costing about $10. A water taxi covers a similar route, providing a view of the city's chief sights, including the old Tampa Bay Hotel and the Museum of Art.

For another view of downtown, take the free "People-mover" monorail from near the Hyatt Regency Hotel on Franklin Street across the water to Harbour Island.

🚰 Henry B Plant Museum

401 W Kennedy Blvd. 📞 *(813) 254-1891.* ⚪ *Tue–Sun.* ⚫ *Thanksgiving, 25 Dec, 1 Jan.* ♿

The luxurious Tampa Bay Hotel, which houses the Henry B Plant Museum, is Tampa's most famous historic landmark, its Moorish minarets visible from all over the city.

Henry Plant commissioned the building in 1891 as a hotel for the well-to-do passengers of his newly built railway.

The construction alone cost $3 million, with an additional $500,000 spent on furnishings. The hotel was not the success that he'd hoped, however, and it fell into disrepair soon after Plant's death in 1899. The hotel was bought by the city in 1905 and became part of the University of Tampa in 1933. The south wing of the ground floor was set aside and preserved as a museum.

Complete with a solarium, the museum is splendidly furnished and equipped, with 90 per cent of the exhibits on display original to the hotel. Wedgwood china, Venetian mirrors and 18th-century French furniture effortlessly evoke a lost age. Visitors are also welcome to walk around what is now the university campus to appreciate the sheer size of the building.

🏛 Tampa Museum of Art

600 N Ashley Drive. 📞 *(813) 274-8130.* ⚪ *daily.* ⚫ *Easter, Thanksgiving, 25 Dec, 1 Jan.* 🎟 ♿

This museum enjoys a good reputation for its wide variety of exhibits, which range from classical Greek, Roman and Etruscan antiquities to 20th-century American fine art. The collection is too extensive to be displayed all at once, so the pieces are shown in rotation; the ancient pottery stands out among the antiquities. A large outdoor sculpture garden is the museum's most recent addition, and there is also a gallery devoted to local artists.

On the second Saturday of each month, the museum conducts free walking tours of the city's sculptures and other works of public art.

The elegant solarium at the Henry B Plant Museum

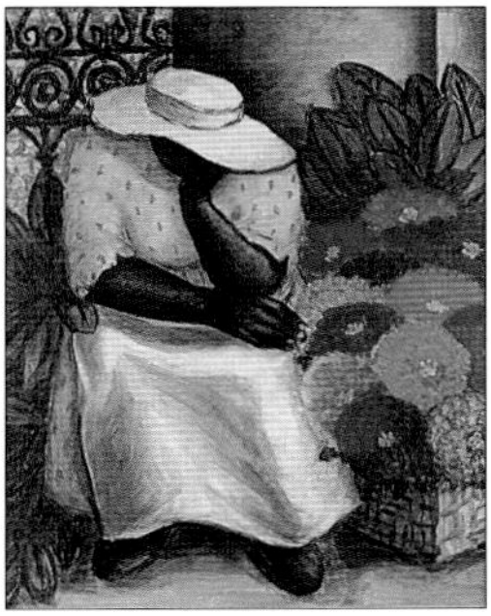

Ellis Wilson's *Flower Vendor*, Museum of African-American Art

🏛 Museum of African-American Art

1305 N Florida Ave. ☎ *(813) 272-2466.* ○ *Tue–Sat.* ● *public hols.* 🎟 ♿

This small museum has one of the most important collections of African-American art in the United States. The works date from the 1800s to the present day and cover a wide range of art including paintings, sculpture and drawings. Particular highlights among the museum's major works are *Negro Boy* (1941), in oil on masonite, by Hale Woodruff; *Flower Vendor* (1945), an oil on canvas by Ellis Wilson; and *War* (1955), a lithograph by Romare Bearden.

There are also displays of traditional African art, with West African statuary forming the bulk of the collection.

🏛 Tampa Theatre

711 Franklin St. ☎ *(813) 274-8981.* ○ *daily.* ● *25 Dec.* 🎟 ♿ 👉 *phone in advance to check.*

In its day, the Tampa Theatre was one of the most elaborate cinemas in America. The building was designed in 1926 by the architect John Eberson in an architectural style known as Florida-Mediterranean. The lavish result was described by the historian Ben Hall as an "Andalusian bonbon".

In an attempt to create the illusion of an outdoor location, Eberson fitted the ceiling with lights designed to twinkle like stars. Other effects included artificial clouds, produced by a smoke machine, and lighting designed to simulate the rising sun. There is also Greek and Roman sculpture galore.

The simplest way to visit the theatre, now beautifully restored, is to go and see a film there *(see p339)*. Film festivals are held regularly and the theatre is also used for special events.

Guided tours, which are organized just twice a month, include a 20-minute film about the theatre and a mini-concert on a traditional 1,000-pipe theatre organ.

Visitors' Checklist

Road map D3. Hillsborough Co. 👥 *285,000.* ✈ *5 miles (8 km) NW.* 🚆 *601 Nebraska Ave, (800) 872-7245.* 🚌 *610 Polk St, (800) 231-2222.* ⛴ *Channelside Drive, (813) 272-0555.* 🚌 *HARTline buses, (813) 254-4278.* ⛴ *Tampa Town Ferry and water taxi, (813) 223-1522.* ℹ *400 N Tampa St, (813) 223-1522.* 🎉 *Gasparilla Festival (early Feb).*

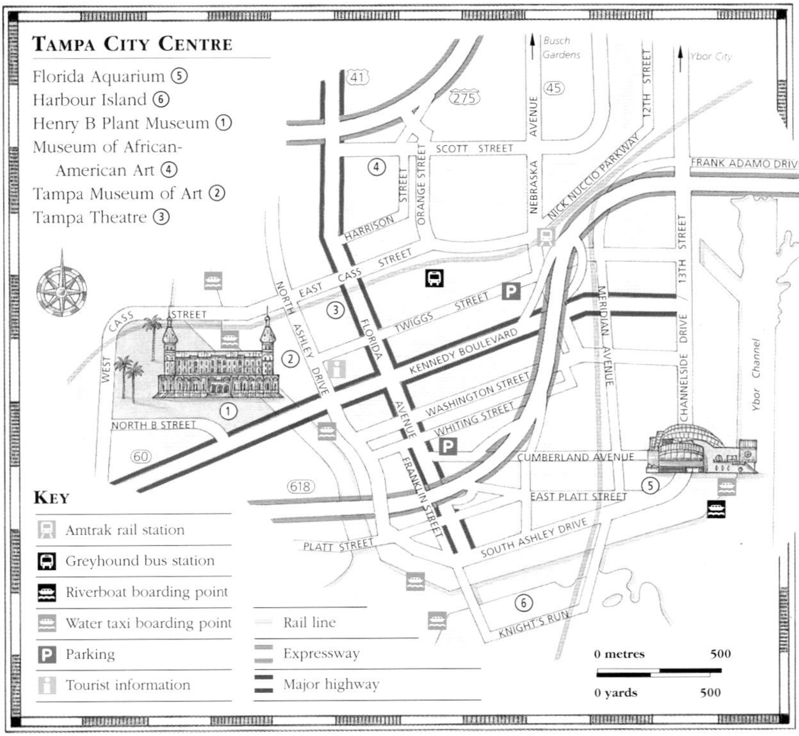
TAMPA CITY CENTRE
Florida Aquarium 5
Harbour Island 6
Henry B Plant Museum 1
Museum of African-American Art 4
Tampa Museum of Art 2
Tampa Theatre 3
KEY
Amtrak rail station
Greyhound bus station
Riverboat boarding point
Water taxi boarding point
Parking
Tourist information
Rail line
Expressway
Major highway
0 metres 500
0 yards 500
Busch Gardens
Ybor City
SCOTT STREET
HARRISON STREET
ORANGE STREET
NEBRASKA AVENUE
12TH STREET
13TH STREET
NICK NUCCIO PARKWAY
FRANK ADAMO DRIVE
EAST CASS STREET
CASS STREET
WEST
NORTH ASHLEY DRIVE
FLORIDA AVENUE
TWIGGS STREET
KENNEDY BOULEVARD
WASHINGTON STREET
WHITING STREET
MERIDIAN AVENUE
CHANNELSIDE DRIVE
Ybor Channel
NORTH B STREET
CUMBERLAND AVENUE
EAST PLATT STREET
FRANKLIN STREET
PLATT STREET
SOUTH ASHLEY DRIVE
KNIGHT'S RUN
41
275
45
60
618

Street-by-Street: Ybor City

A CUBAN CALLED Don Vicente Martinez Ybor moved his cigar business from Key West to Tampa in 1886. About 20,000 migrant workers, mostly from Cuba and Spain, eventually joined him. The legacy of the cigar boom years of the late 1800s and early 1900s is still visible in Ybor City. Its main street, 7th Avenue, with its Spanish-style tiles and wrought-iron balconies, looks much as it did then. The district is today enjoying a new lease of life. What were once cigar factories and workers' cottages now house shops, restaurants and clubs. Though quiet during the day, Ybor City comes to life in the evening.

★ Ybor Square

The three enormous brick buildings of VM Ybor's original cigar factory, once the largest in the world, are now occupied by a shopping mall, where you can buy quirky antiques, crafts and gifts.

The Pleasuredome has a tapas bar and three dance rooms playing everything from jazz to high energy dance music.

Café Creole and Oyster Bar

You can enjoy excellent Cajun food here, and eat alfresco in the courtyard. Jazz musicians entertain diners at weekends.

9TH AVENUE

13TH STREET

AVENIDA / REPUBLICA DE CUBA

8TH AVENUE

15TH STREET

7TH AVENUE

Masquerade at the Ritz, a stunning 1917 movie theatre, now houses one of Ybor's top nightclubs.

José Martí Park

A statue commemorates José Martí, the Cuban freedom fighter who made several visits to Ybor City to rally support for Cuba's independence campaign (see p47).

STAR SIGHTS
★ Ybor Square
★ Cigar Worker's House

0 metres	100
0 yards	100

KEY

– – – Suggested route

★ **Cigar Worker's House**
This tiny house (attached to Ybor City State Museum) is furnished to look like a cigar worker's home. "La Casita" is a fine example of the shotgun houses (see p287) built for the flood of immigrants who came to work in Ybor city in the late 1800s.

VISITORS' CHECKLIST

3 miles (5 km) E of Downtown. ⬛ *Tampa–Ybor trolley from Fort Brook Station.* 🛈 *1800 E 9th Avenue, (813) 248-3712.* **Ybor Square** 📞 *(813) 247-4497.* ⬜ *daily (Sun pm only).* **Ybor City State Museum** 📞 *(813) 247-6323.* ⬜ *Tue–Sat.* 🚫 ✔ ♿

Ybor City State Museum, housed in a former bakery, explores the history of Ybor City and also organizes walking tours of the district. There is a small ornamental garden attached.

Little Sicily, an Italian-style deli, is a good place for lunch-time snacks.

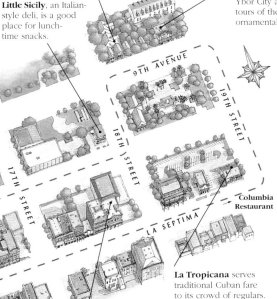

Columbia Restaurant

Columbia Restaurant
Florida's oldest restaurant takes up a whole block on 7th Avenue. The Hispanic food and lively flamenco dancing make it popular with tourists (see p327).

La Tropicana serves traditional Cuban fare to its crowd of regulars.

El Sol Cigars
Although Ybor's oldest cigar store (opened in 1929) no longer rolls its cigars by hand, it is a good place to buy them.

THE CIGAR INDUSTRY IN TAMPA

With ships able to bring a regular supply of tobacco from Cuba to its port, Tampa was ideally located for cigar-making. Several huge cigar factories sprang up soon after VM Ybor moved here, and by 1900 Ybor City was producing over 111 million cigars annually. Each cigar was skilfully rolled by hand, by workers who were often entertained by a lector reading aloud to them. Automation and the growing popularity of cigarettes changed all this. Cigars are still made in Tampa (mostly with leaves grown in Honduras), but now usually by machine. The Tampa Rico Company in Ybor Square is one of the few companies to hand roll cigars.

Workers in an Ybor City cigar factory, 1929

A diver amid reefs and exotic fish at the Florida Aquarium

🐟 Florida Aquarium

701 Channelside Drive. 📞 *(813) 273-4000.* ⭕ *daily.* ● *Thanksgiving, 25 Dec.* 🏷 ♿

No expense was spared in the creation of this enormous aquarium, which opened in 1995 at a cost of $84 million. Located on the waterfront, it is unmissable with its blue shell-shaped dome, it is a state-of-the-art interpretation of a modern aquarium. Inside, visitors will not only find tanks of fish but will also come face to face with baby alligators, birds, otters and all kinds of other creatures living in their authentic habitats.

The purpose of the Florida Aquarium is to enable visitors to follow the passage of a drop of water from its first appearance in an underground spring to its arrival in the sea, passing through various habitats along the way.

The conditions of each habitat are re-created in separate galleries. The Florida Coral Reefs Gallery, for instance, takes visitors underwater for a panoramic view of a coral colony and its schools of colourful tropical fish. You can hire recorded commentaries by experts at different stages of the tour, and there are regular "hands-on labs", with special projects and activities, and biologists and botanists standing by to explain them.

⚜ Hyde Park

Across the river, southwest of Downtown off Bayshore Boulevard, Hyde Park is a rare historic area in Tampa. Dating from the late 19th century, its houses display a striking mix of architectural styles from Colonial to Gothic Revival.

The quiet, residential streets of Hyde Park are best explored by car. The one part to tempt people out of their vehicles is Old Hyde Park Village, off Snow Avenue, where you'll find several up-market shops and restaurants. On some days, musicians come out to entertain the shoppers.

An open-air concert for visitors to Old Hyde Park Village

🏛 Museum of Science and Industry

4801 E Fowler Ave. 📞 *(813) 987-6100.* ⭕ *daily.* 🏷 ♿

This excellent museum, commonly referred to as MOSI, is another distinctive addition to the Tampa skyline; its Art Nouveau-style dome houses an IMAX giant-screen cinema. The museum features all kinds of interactive displays. The Amazing You is an exploration of the human body and how it works, while in the hurricane room visitors can create their own tropical storm. The GTE Challenger Learning Centre is a living memorial to the crew of the space shuttle Challenger *(see p185)*, with simulators of a space station and a mission control room. Another major attraction is the Focus Gallery, which houses visiting exhibits.

MOSI is also home to the Saunders Planetarium, which hosts regular astronomical shows. On every Friday and Saturday evening, there are special star-viewing sessions at which, weather permitting, telescopes are set up in the car park so that visitors can observe the night sky.

🦒 Lowry Park Zoo

7530 N Blvd. 📞 *(813) 932-0245.* ⭕ *daily.* ● *Thanksgiving, 25 Dec.* 🏷 ♿

This zoo, 6 miles (10 km) north of downtown Tampa, is one of the best in North America. One of the main attractions is the manatee centre, which has up to 20 animals in residence at any one time and a rehabilitation pool. You can learn more about this endangered species by taking part in the "Manatee Sleepover", a special programme which offers the chance to explore the zoo after closing time, learn about the rehabilitation programme and spend the night at the manatee centre.

The zoo's Florida Wildlife Center, a special sanctuary for native animals such as alligators and the Florida panther, is another highlight. Other areas to visit are Primate World, the Asian Domain, home to Sumatran tigers and

The eye-catching dome of the Museum of Science and Industry

THE LEGEND OF GASPAR

José Gaspar was a legendary pirate who preyed on ships and communities between Tampa and Fort Myers in the 19th century. His stronghold was among the isles of the Lee Island Coast *(see pp264–5)*, many of whose modern names recall the association – including Gasparilla and Captiva, where Gaspar is said to have kept his female captives. The story goes that the pirate was eventually cornered by a US warship, and that he drowned himself in anchor chains rather than be taken prisoner.

Tampa suffered from several of Gaspar's raids, and now holds a Gasparilla Festival each February *(see p35)*. The highlight of this celebration is a mock invasion of the city by hundreds of rowdy villains aboard the world's only fully-rigged "pirate ship".

"Pirates" celebrating Tampa's Gasparilla Festival in the 1950s

A Sumatran tiger lounges at Asian Domain, Lowry Park Zoo

an extremely rare Indian rhino, and a free-flight aviary. There is also a children's museum, an amusement centre, and a pleasant picnic area.

Busch Gardens ⑩

See pp250–51.

Hillsborough River ⑪

Road map D3. Hillsborough Co. 🚉 *Tampa.* 🚌 *Tampa.*

EXTENDING THROUGH the countryside northeast of Tampa, the Hillsborough River provides a pleasant respite from the hustle and bustle of the city. It is flanked on both sides by dense backwoods of live oak, cypress, magnolia and mangrove trees, which once covered great swathes of Florida's terrain.

One of the best ways to experience the Hillsborough River is by canoe: **Canoe Escape** organizes trips along a stretch of the river about 15 minutes' drive from downtown Tampa. Although only just beyond the city boundary the area is surprisingly wild, and you have a good chance of spotting a great variety of wildlife, including herons, egrets, alligators, turtles and otters. Canoeing conditions are ideal for beginners. You can choose from three main itineraries, each of which covers about 5 miles (8 km) – involving roughly two hours' paddling and allowing you plenty of time to absorb the surroundings; longer day trips are also available.

A section of the river is protected as **Hillsborough River State Park**. Canoeing is a popular way to explore here too; there are also walking trails, and you can swim and fish. The park has a large and popular camp ground,

which is open all year round, and there are also numerous picnic sites.

Developed in 1936, the Hillsborough River State Park became one of Florida's earliest state parks partly due to the historic significance of Fort Foster, built during the Second Seminole War *(see p44)* to guard a bridge at the confluence of the Hillsborough River and Blackwater Creek. The fort and bridge have been reconstructed and a battle is re-enacted here annually in March. Tours visit the fort every weekend and on holidays; a shuttle bus runs to it from the park's entrance.

Canoe Escape
9335 E Fowler Ave, Thonotosassa, 12 miles (19 km) NE of Tampa. 📞 *(813) 986-2067.* ⏰ *daily.* ⬤ *Thanksgiving, 24 & 25 Dec.* ♿

Hillsborough River State Park
15402 US 301, 12 miles (19 km) NE of Tampa. 📞 *(813) 987-6771.* ⏰ *daily.* ♿ 🅿 ⛺

Re-created buildings at Fort Foster in Hillsborough River State Park

Busch Gardens ➓

BUSCH GARDENS is one-of-a-kind – a theme park which incorporates one of America's top zoos. To fulfil its unusual aim of re-creating life in colonial-era Africa, the park supports over 3,000 animals, with giraffe, buffalo and zebra roaming freely over the "Serengeti Plain". Elsewhere, specially built habitats are home to elephants, gorillas and Bengal tigers. Among the park's outdoor venues, Timbuktu's Dolphin Theater stages a popular dolphin show, while World of Birds features resident macaws, cockatoos and birds of prey. Although the animals are the main attraction, roller coasters and other rides also draw enthusiasts from far and wide. The newest creation at Busch Gardens is the 7-acre (3-ha) park called Egypt.

Congo River Rapids
Rapids, geysers, waterfalls and a dark cave await rafters set adrift on a swift river current.

★ **Kumba**
The largest and fastest roller coaster in Florida, Kumba is Busch Gardens' top thrill ride. Participants plunge for 140 ft (43 m) at speeds of more than 60 mph (100 km/h).

Dolphin Theater

Timbuktu

Land of the Dragons
This children's play area has scaled-down rides for young visitors and a three-storey tree-house, complete with bridges and a winding staircase.

Mystic Sheiks of Morocco
A marching band called the Mystic Sheiks gives impromptu performances at a variety of locations throughout the day.

STAR ATTRACTIONS
★ **Kumba**
★ **Edge of Africa**
★ **Egypt**

World of Birds

0 metres   100

0 yards   100

KEY

🚉 Train station

🏧 ATM (cash machine)

★ Edge of Africa
This safari experience, on the southern edge of the Serengeti Plain, offers visitors a chance to have a close-up view of lions, hippos, hyenas and other African animals.

VISITORS' CHECKLIST

Road map 3D. Busch Boulevard, Tampa. **☎** *(813) 987 5082.* **🚂** *Tampa.* **🚌** *Tampa.* **🚐** *5, 14 & 18 from Marion St, downtown Tampa.* **🕐** *9:30am–6pm daily, extended hours for summer and holidays.* ♿ 🅿 🍴 🎁

Serengeti Plain

★ Egypt
The largest addition to Busch Gardens, Egypt includes a replica of Tutankhamun's tomb, a museum, a roller coaster and a bazaar.

A train can be taken around all the major areas within the park.

A monorail circles the Serengeti Plain.

Entrance

Guest Relations

Myombe Reserve
This simulated rain-forest is the habitat of six western lowland gorillas and seven chimpanzees, both of which are endangered species.

Hollywood Live on Ice
Tinseltown is the inspiration for this 35-minute ice-skating spectacular, which pays tribute to decades of film-making. Skaters and singers sketch Hollywood history from the original silent films to today's blockbusters.

Florida Southern College ⓬

Road map E3. Polk Co. 111 Lake Hollingsworth Drive, Lakeland. ☎ *(941) 680-4110.* 🚆 *Lakeland.* 🚌 *Lakeland.* ○ *Mon–Fri.* ● *4 Jul, Thanksgiving, 25 Dec, 1 Jan.* **Visitor Center** ○ *Tue–Sat, Sun (pm only).* ♿

THIS PROVINCIAL COLLEGE has the world's largest collection of buildings designed by Frank Lloyd Wright. Amazingly, the college president managed to persuade Wright (probably the most eminent architect of his day) to design the campus at Lakeland with the promise of little more than the opportunity to express his ideas – and payment when the money could be raised.

The light and spacious interior of the Annie Pfeiffer Chapel

Work began in 1938 on what Wright, already famous as the founder of organic architecture, termed his "child of the sun". His aim of blending buildings with their natural surroundings made special use of glass to bring the outdoor light into the interiors. The original plan was for 18 buildings, but only seven had been completed by the time Wright died in 1959; five were finished or added later.

The Annie Pfeiffer Chapel is a particularly fine expression of his ideas. Windows of stained glass break the monotony of the building blocks, and the entire edifice is topped by a spectacular tower in place of the traditional steeple; Wright called it a "jewel box".

As a whole, the campus has the light and airy feel which Wright sought to achieve. The buildings are linked to each other by the Esplanades – a covered walkway, stretching for 1.5-miles (2 km), in which light, shade and variations in height draw attention from one building to the next.

You can wander around the campus at any time, but the interiors can be explored only during the week. The Thad Buckner Building, complete with clerestory windows, now houses a visitor centre, where you can see drawings and furniture by Wright and photographs of the building work.

The antebellum Gamble Mansion

Gamble Plantation ⓭

Road map D3. Manatee Co. 3708 Patten Ave, Ellenton. ☎ *(941) 723-4536.* 🚆 *Tampa.* 🚌 *Bradenton.* ○ *Thu–Mon.* ● *Thanksgiving, 25 Dec, 1 Jan.* 💲 ♿ *limited.* 🎫

THE ONLY ANTEBELLUM home left in southern Florida, this whitewashed mansion stands a little incongruously behind a picket fence on the main road into Bradenton.

It was built in 1845–50 by Major Robert Gamble, one of the most successful of the sugar planters who settled along the fertile Manatee River after the Second Seminole War *(see p44)*. Gamble built up his holding to cover 3,500 acres (1,416 ha), but only a fraction of this remains. The

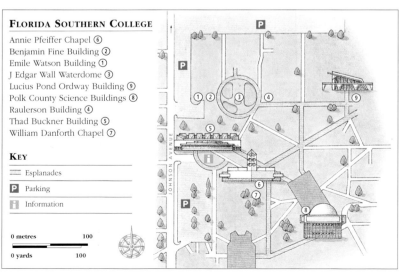

FLORIDA SOUTHERN COLLEGE

Annie Pfeiffer Chapel ⑥
Benjamin Fine Building ②
Emile Watson Building ①
J Edgar Wall Waterdome ③
Lucius Pond Ordway Building ⑨
Polk County Science Buildings ⑧
Raulerson Building ④
Thad Buckner Building ⑤
William Danforth Chapel ⑦

KEY

Esplanades
[P] Parking
[i] Information

0 metres 100
0 yards 100

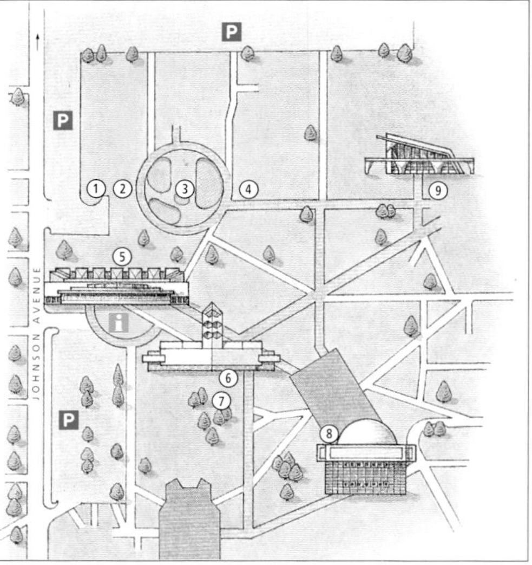
P
P
P
JOHNSON AVENUE
1
2
3
4
5
6
7
8
9

site of the old slave quarters, for instance, is now a school. The house is furnished just as it was in its heyday, and the garden, flourishing with live oak trees draped with Spanish moss, is pure Deep South.

However, romantic notions about Gamble's life are swept away in the small museum in the visitor centre. Gamble got into financial difficulties and was forced to sell the house to pay his debts; among the artifacts on display in the museum is a document showing that the plantation, along with the grounds and 191 slaves, was sold in 1856 for the sum of $190,000.

Bradenton 🄸

Road map D3. Manatee Co.
🏛 48,000. ✈ 🚌 *including Amtrak Thruway bus.* 🛈 *5030 Highway 301 N, (941) 729-7040.*

THE SEAT of Manatee County, Bradenton is best known as the home of the Nick Bollettieri Tennis Academy *(see p343)*, the school which has nurtured the early promise of world tennis stars such as Andre Agassi and Pete Sampras.

The local beaches are a big attraction, but a couple of sights deserve a visit before you head off to the seaside. **Manatee Village Historical Park** recounts the story of the Florida frontier a century ago through a fascinating collection of restored buildings. These include a boat house, a general store and an early settler's house, and all have been furnished to look as they would have done originally.

The **South Florida Museum** is both educational and fun. "Florida from Stone Age to Space Age" is the theme, with exhibits ranging from dinosaur dioramas to life-size replicas of 16th-century Spanish-style buildings and early cars. Laser shows add excitement to the Bishop Planetarium programme, while the Parker Aquarium gives a lively overview of local marine life.

The kitchen of an early settler's house at Manatee Village Historical Park

🏯 **Manatee Village Historical Park**
604 15th St E. 📞 *(941) 749-7165.*
⭕ *Mon–Fri (additionally Sep–Jun: Sun pm).* ⬤ *public hols.* ♿

🏛 **South Florida Museum**
201 10th St W. 📞 *(941) 746-4131.*
⭕ *daily.* ⬤ *Thanksgiving, 25 Dec, 1 Jan.* 🏷 ♿

ENVIRONS: Five miles (8 km) west of central Bradenton, the **De Soto National Memorial** commemorates the landing near here in 1539 of Hernando de Soto *(see pp40–41).* He and his 600 men set out on an epic four-year 4,000-mile (6,500-km) trek into the southeastern US in search of gold. They discovered the Mississippi, but the trek was disastrous and de Soto and half his army died. A monument recalls the luckless explorers and marks the start of the De Soto Trail, which follows part of the route they took. The park also has a replica of de Soto's

Stone monument to explorer De Soto

base camp; this is staffed at peak times by costumed volunteers, who give a memorable insight into the daily routines of the Spanish conquistadors. A visitor centre has examples of 16th-century weapons and armour, and there is also a half-mile (1-km) nature trail through mangrove thickets.

Two bridges link Bradenton to **Anna Maria Island**, whose sandy shoreline, backed by dunes, is largely undeveloped but is washed by breakers big enough to attract a handful of surfers. There is a scattering of small resorts based around the three main communities of Anna Maria in the north, Holmes Beach in the middle and Bradenton Beach in the south. In the north stands the picturesque Anna Maria Pier, which was built in 1910. It has a small restaurant, snack bar and shop at its seaward end.

⚓ **De Soto National Memorial**
75th Street NW. 📞 *(941) 792-0458.*
⭕ *daily.* ⬤ *Thanksgiving, 25 Dec, 1 Jan.* ♿

Sunset on Anna Maria Island's beautiful, unspoilt beach

Sarasota ⑮

Hibiscus in the Selby Gardens

THIS CITY IS KNOWN AS Florida's cultural centre, a fact often credited to John Ringling *(see p255)*, who was one of many influential people attracted to the up-and-coming town in the early 1900s. Ringling poured money into the area, and his legacy is all around, nowhere more so than in his house and fine art collection, the city's biggest attraction *(see pp256–9)*. Sarasota's other great asset is that it seems to have escaped the worst excesses of the state's other cities. Promoted as "Florida's Mild Side", Sarasota is an attractive and clean community, with the bonus of a waterfront setting. You can join its affluent and conservative inhabitants browsing around its smart shops or lying on the beach. Fabulous barrier island beaches are just a short drive from downtown Sarasota and are the best place to stay.

Exploring Sarasota

The most pleasant area of downtown Sarasota focuses on Palm Avenue and Main Street, where restored shopfronts dating from the early 20th century house antique shops, bars and restaurants. Shopping and eating are also the main activities at nearby Sarasota Quay, and you can sign up for dinner cruises and other boat trips at the adjacent marina.

Dominating the waterfront to the north is the striking Van Wezel Performing Arts Hall *(see p29)*. Opened in 1970, this distinctive pink and lavender building is worth a visit both to admire its sweeping, seashell-inspired lines, and to attend one of the many events, including concerts and Broadway shows, which are staged here *(see p339)*.

🏛 Bellm's Cars and Music of Yesterday

5500 N Tamiami Trail. **[** *(941) 355-6228.* ◯ *daily.* 🅿 ⚙ ⚙

This museum is a strange mixture of enthusiasms, with 120 old cars and over 1,000 music boxes, organs and other musical novelties all under one roof.

An 1890s carousel organ at Bellm's

Highlights of the car collection, charmingly described by expert guides, are a rare 1954 Packard Model 120 convertible, a 1955 Rolls-Royce Silver Wraith and a 1981 De Lorean, all in mint condition. The Great Music Hall, which contains pianos, phonographs and a musical chair (which plays when you sit on it), must be visited on a guided tour.

A favourite among young visitors is the antique amusement arcade with dozens of working slot machines.

Flamingos gather at a small lake at Sarasota Jungle Gardens

🌺 Sarasota Jungle Gardens

3701 Bayshore Rd. **[f]** *(941) 355-5305.* ◯ *daily.* ● *25 Dec.* 🅿 ⚙

Originally developed as a botanical garden, this 10-acre (4-ha) former banana grove offers an oasis of tropical plants, trees and flowers from around the world, with palm forests and gardens of hibiscus, ferns, roses, gardenias and bougainvillea. The flamingo lagoon is a big attraction.

Other attractions, including a children's zoo and butterfly museum, place an emphasis on education and conservation. Simple and unsophisticated entertainment, however, is more the point of the exotic bird shows, in which macaws and cockatoos ride bicycles and rollerskates.

🌺 Marie Selby Botanical Gardens

811 S Palm Ave. **[f]** *(941) 366-5730.* ◯ *daily.* ● *25 Dec.* 🅿 ⚙

You needn't be a gardener to appreciate the former home of wealthy Sarasota residents William and Marie Selby. Set among laurel and banyan trees overlooking Sarasota Bay, the estate was designed by Marie during the early 1920s as an escape from the modern world: you can still see the bamboo curtain she had planted to obscure the growing Sarasota skyline.

The gardens have more than 20,000 tropical plants and are particularly famous for their collection of orchids and epiphytes *(see p276)*. There are also display areas devoted to all kinds of exotic plants, from tropical foods and herbs to

Christy Payne House in the Marie Selby Botanical Gardens

colourful hibiscus plants. The Tropical Display House brings together an impressive array of jungle vegetation.

The Selbys' Spanish-style house, now a gift shop, is of less interest than the 1930s Christy Payne House. Once part of a neighbouring estate, this delightful plantation-style mansion contains a Museum of Botany and Arts.

St Armands Circle

This up-market shopping and dining complex on St Armands Key was one of John Ringling's creations. He purchased the island in 1917 and produced an adventurous plan for a housing development, which centred on a circular shopping mall featuring gardens and classical statues. The area flourished briefly before being caught up in the Depression, but was revived in the 1950s. It now looks much as Ringling planned, with shady avenues radiating from a central point.

St Armands Circle, well placed between Downtown and the beaches, is popular both during the day and at night. The shops are mostly expensive but anyone can enjoy the street entertainers, who often congregate here.

Mote Marine Aquarium

1600 Ken Thompson Parkway. *(941) 388-2451.* daily. Easter, Thanksgiving, 25 Dec.
This aquarium is located on City Island, between Lido and Longboat keys. It features a bay walk, which gives an excellent view of the Sarasota skyline, but the real attractions

Young visitors observe tropical fish at the Mote Marine Aquarium

are to be found inside. Among the most popular exhibits is a huge shark tank, complete with underwater observation windows, and a "touch tank", where you can get to grips with all kinds of marine creatures, from comical horseshoe crabs and whelks to stingrays. More than 30 other aquariums are stocked with local fish and plants, and there is an illuminating display on the rivers, bays and estuaries of the surrounding area.

Explanatory leaflets provide a useful insight into every exhibit, while guides explain how the aquarium ties in with the work of the attached laboratory, prominent in the study of sharks and pollution.

Pelican Man's Bird Sanctuary

1708 Ken Thompson Parkway. *(941) 388-4444.* daily. public hols.
Also on City Island, Pelican Man's Bird Sanctuary treats more than 5,000 injured birds annually in its hospital. Most

VISITORS' CHECKLIST

Road map D3. Sarasota Co.
58,000. 2 miles (3 km) N.
575 N Washington Blvd, (941) 955-5735; also Amtrak Thruway bus, (800) 872-7245.
655 N Tamiami Trail, (941) 957-1877. Circus Festival (Jan).

of the birds are returned to the wild once they have been rehabilitated, while those too badly hurt to fend for themselves join the permanent residents; these can be seen in the sanctuary's many pens.

The "Pelican Man" himself is Dale Shields, a self-taught bird expert who is more than happy to share his knowledge with inquisitive visitors.

Dale Shields, alias "Pelican Man", at his sanctuary

Sarasota Beaches

The nearby barrier islands, Longboat Key, Lido Key and Siesta Key boast superb sandy beaches facing the Gulf of Mexico, and they are understandably popular *(see p239)*. Development has been intense, with condos along the shore in places, but there are several quieter areas too. The beach in South Lido Park, on Lido Key, is peaceful during the week and has a pleasant woodland trail too.

On Siesta Key the main residential area is in the north, focused around a network of canals. The broad Siesta Key Beach nearby is lively at any time. You'll find a quieter scene at Turtle Beach, which also has the only camp ground on the keys. Longboat Key is well known for its golf courses. Wherever you are, the water sports are excellent.

South Lido Park beach, with a view south of nearby Siesta Key

Ringling Museum of Art

JOHN RINGLING was an Ohio-born circus manager whose phenomenally successful show *(see p258)* made him a multimillionaire. His money and his regular trips abroad gave him many opportunities to purchase European art, and when he moved his winter home to Sarasota in 1910 he built a museum to house his vast collection. He and his wife Mable had a particular affection for Italy and their magnificent Italian Baroque paintings are the cornerstone of the collection. Their estate, which includes the palatial Ca' d'Zan *(see pp258–9)*, was bequeathed to the state following John Ringling's death in 1936.

Majolica jar (c.1550)

Statuary
The courtyard is dotted with copies of Classical sculpture, such as this bronze chariot.

A replica of Michelangelo's David

West Galleries
Built in the 1960s, these rooms contain temporary exhibits of mostly contemporary art; photography, painting and sculpture are all represented. John Chamberlain's Car Parts stands at the entrance to the galleries.

12
13
14
15
16
17
18

GALLERY GUIDE

The galleries are arranged around a sculpture garden, with the West Galleries and Asolo Theater dominating one end of the courtyard. Starting with the galleries to the right of the entrance hall, the rooms roughly follow a chronological order anticlockwise, ranging from late medieval European painting to 18th-century American art. Each gallery covers a particular period, the best represented being 16th- and 17th-century Italian painting. Modern art and special exhibitions are displayed in the West Galleries.

★ Astor Rooms
These lavish 19th-century interiors came from a New York mansion. Displays include a series of exquisite majolica jars from the early 16th century.

PLAN OF RINGLING MUSEUM

Ca' d'Zan

P

Circus Museum

Entrance

P

Sarasota Bay

P

Rose Garden

Exit

Museum of Art

P

41

STAR FEATURES
★ **Astor Rooms**
★ **Courtyard**
★ **Rubens Gallery**

🦅 Key West Cemetery

701 Passover Lane. ⬛ (305) 292-8177. ◯ daily. ♿

Due to the proximity of the limestone bedrock and water table, most of the tombs here are above ground. Laid out on a grid system, the cemetery holds the remains of many of Key West's earliest residents. Within the compound there are separate areas for Jews and Roman Catholics, while many of the Cuban crypts are crowned with a statue of a chicken, probably associated with the Santería religion *(see p75)*. There is even a special burial area devoted to pets.

A statue of a single sailor commemorates the loss of 252 crewmen on the battleship *USS Maine*, which was sunk in Havana's harbour at the onset of the Spanish-American War in 1898 *(see p47)*. Stroll around to read the often amusing inscriptions and epitaphs, "I told you I was sick" among others. Many of the town's early settlers were known simply by their first or nicknames, and this Key West informality followed them to their graves. There are references to Bunny, Shorty, Bean and so forth. Dismissive of this tradition, Ernest Hemingway is reported to have said "I'd rather eat monkey manure than die in Key West."

Statue of the Lone Sailor

THE BUSINESS OF WRECKING

From the late 1700s, the waters off the Keys were fished mainly by Bahamians of British descent, who also patrolled the reef in order to salvage shipwrecks. Lookouts at their vantage points would shout "Wreck ashore!" to send salvage vessels racing towards the reef to be the first to claim a grounded ship. In this way, goods from around the world ended up in the Keys; these ranged from basics such as timber to luxury goods like lace, wine and silver. This opportunistic scavenging came to be known as "wrecking". It grew so popular that in 1825 an act of the US Congress legislated for much tighter control and decreed that only US residents could have such salvage rights. Key West boomed and in the years that followed it became the richest city in Florida.

Facsimile of a wrecker's licence

Dry Tortugas National Park ⑱

Road map D5. Monroe Co.
🚤 Key West. 🛈 402 Wall St, (305) 294-2587.

THE DRY TORTUGAS consist of seven reef islands lying 68 miles (109 km) west of Key West. Of these, Garden Key is the most visited, being the site of **Fort Jefferson**, the largest brick fortification in the US. The hexagonal design included a moat 70 ft (21 m) wide, and walls up to 8 ft (2.5 m) thick and 50 ft (15 m) high. It was originally envisaged that the fort would control the Florida Straits with a garrison of 1,500 men and 450 cannons. Beginning in 1845, construction continued for the next 30 years, but the fort was never completed or involved in any battle. During the Civil War, after being occupied by Union forces it was downgraded to a prison for captured deserters.

The only access is by boat or seaplane. Most people come on organized trips from Key West, which often include an opportunity to snorkel in the crystal-clear sea. The bird-watching is especially good between March and October, when the islands are home to migrant and nesting birds, such as boobies, sooty terns, and magnificent frigatebirds with their 7-ft (2-m) wingspan.

Remote Garden Key in Dry Tortugas National Park, occupied by the imposing 19th-century Fort Jefferson

TRAVELLERS' NEEDS

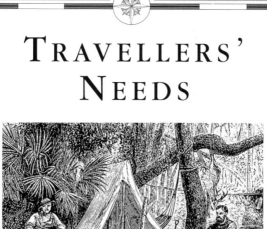

WHERE TO STAY

LORIDA HAS a huge variety of places to stay suitable for all budgets and tastes – from rustic wooden cabins with minimal facilities to luxurious resort hotels that cater to their guests' every need. In between, you can choose from ordinary hotels, more characterful bed and breakfasts, convenient motels, or fully equipped apartments. Camp sites, where you can pitch a tent or hook up an RV, or camper van, are also plentiful. On the whole you get good value for

Sign outside the Coombs House Inn *(see p306)*

money in Florida, though prices fluctuate greatly according to the season and location. The listings on pages 296–311 recommend more than 200 places around the state, all representing the best of their kind and in all price ranges. The *Florida Accommodation Directory*, available from the tourist board, lists hotels, motels and other lodgings all over the state, and local tourist offices can provide more detailed information about places in their particular area.

The lobby of the stylish Eden Roc Hotel in Miami *(see p297)*

HOTELS AND RESORTS

UNLESS YOU STAY in one of Miami Beach's superb Art Deco establishments, you'll find that most hotels in the state are large, modern affairs, with excellent facilities and a swimming pool but minimal atmosphere and often rather impersonal service.

Chain hotels are common and extremely popular in the US, and have the advantage of at least being predictable – although prices vary depending on the location. They range from the up-market Marriott and Inter-Continental hotels through the mid-range Holiday Inns and Howard Johnsons (HoJo's) to the budget Days Inn chain.

Resorts are large hotel complexes generally located by the sea and often set in immaculately kept grounds. Prices are high, but these resorts provide all manner of amenities, from swimming

pools (sometimes Olympic-size) to shops and usually a choice of restaurants. Many have excellent sports facilities, including golf courses and tennis courts, and may provide instructors for individual tuition. Health programmes are increasingly popular, with daily fitness classes and special spa diets often available.

The shady gardens and pool at Key West's Marquesa Hotel *(see p311)*

With their well-equipped games rooms, special children's programmes and other facilities, these resorts can be a good option for families.

BED AND BREAKFASTS

ANYONE IN SEARCH of a more traditional sense of hospitality should stay in a bed and breakfast (B & B). Sometimes referred to as "homestays", these are private homes where the owner is your host. Breakfast is usually excellent with home-made breads and so on, and guests often eat together in an informal atmosphere. The ambience and personal touch usually make up for the absence of traditional hotel facilities – though some B & Bs are quite luxurious.

Anywhere called an "inn" tends to be bigger and pricier than the average B & B, and may even have a restaurant, but it is still likely to be more friendly than a chain hotel.

Rural areas and historic towns have the best choice of bed and breakfasts. In Key West and St Augustine, for example, you can stay in beautiful old homes with antique furnishings.

The main drawbacks with B & Bs are that they may have restrictions on children, and may require a minimum stay in high season; since most have just a few rooms, you also need to book well in advance.

Several agencies specialize in arranging B & B accommodation. They include **B & B Scenic Florida**, which covers

Cedar Key Bed and Breakfast *(see p306)* in the Panhandle

primarily Orlando and the Gulf Coast; **A & A Bed and Breakfast of Florida**, which focuses on Orlando; and **Bed & Breakfast Co – Tropical Florida**, with properties all over the state. The southeast edition of the *Bed and Breakfast USA* guide, a list of B & Bs affiliated to the **Tourist House Association of America**, is also a useful source.

How to Book

To secure a room in the hotel of your choice in the high season, particularly in Miami or Orlando, book several months in advance; in the off season, you can usually get a room at short notice. At any time of year you should always be able to find a room, even if the hotel is not your ideal choice.

You can book by phone with a credit card (a deposit may be required), and should give advance notice if you plan to arrive after 5pm; otherwise you may lose your reservation.

Facilities

Competition in Florida's hotel trade is fierce so facilities are generally good. Rooms without a TV, en suite bathroom and air conditioning are rare, even in B & Bs, and most have a refrigerator and desk; some hotels also provide kitchen facilities *(see p294)*. Bedrooms usually have two queen-size beds.

People with disabilities will be best provided for in a conventional hotel or resort. In addition to lifts and ramps, quite a few hotels have rooms especially designed for people in wheelchairs. If you have special needs, inform the hotel when you reserve your room.

Prices

Room rates vary enormously depending on the time of year, with prices in high season often 30–50 per cent more than in low season. In South Florida the high season runs from mid-November to Easter, while in the Panhandle and the Northeast, where it is cooler in winter, hotels charge their highest rates in summer. Wherever you are, however, expect to pay peak rates at Christmas, Easter and Thanksgiving. At any time of year, you can pay up to 25 per cent more for a room facing the sea, so it's worth asking for the full range of prices.

Rooms that cost less than about $70 tend to offer similar facilities, and it is only above $70 (less in rural areas) that the standard is noticeably different. Rates are usually calculated per room rather

than per person. This means that only a small reduction is made on the cost of a double room when calculating the price of a single.

It is always worth enquiring about any special deals. For example, you may get a lower price on your room if you eat in the hotel (ask about meal plans), or if you plan to stay for a week or more. Many hotels also offer discounts for senior citizens and families.

The fashionable Delano Hotel in South Beach, Miami *(see p297)*

Hidden Extras

Room rates are generally quoted exclusive of both sales tax *(see p332)* and the so-called resort tax, which is 2–5 per cent of the price of the room (depending on the area). So taxes can add as much as 11 per cent to the rate quoted.

The cost of making phone calls from a hotel room is extortionate. A few places offer free local calls from rooms, but as a rule using a pay phone in the lobby is much cheaper. You are often charged for receiving faxes too.

Many hotels charge for valet parking: a fee of anything from $2 to a shocking $17 a day (as at the Delano Hotel) is not unusual, not counting the optional tip for the attendant.

Given the inflated price of most hotel breakfasts, you'd do well to go out to a nearby café or diner. Be warned too that you must pay for watching certain in-room movies: read the screen before pressing your remote control button.

A Deco room in the Brigham Gardens Guest House, Miami *(see p296)*

Cabins for rent by the ocean at Bahia Honda in the Keys *(see p283)*

MOTELS

FEW HOLIDAYMAKERS are likely to go out of their way to stay in a motel. But motels are a good last-minute option, particularly during the high season. The outskirts of towns and cities are classic motel territory, but in Florida they are also common in seaside resorts, where they provide a good alternative to conventional hotels, especially at the busiest times of year.

Motels are cheaper than many hotels and more convenient too. You can park your car (for free) near your room, unload your bags and be off to the beach or out sightseeing in minutes. Rooms are usually simple but adequate. Try to inspect the room before checking in, however, since some motels can be squalid.

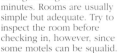

Colourful neon sign for a motel in Orlando

ACCOMMODATION IN ORLANDO

FOR ANYONE PLANNING to visit Walt Disney World, proximity to the theme parks is a major consideration: arriving early is the best way to avoid the worst queues *(see p163)*. Waiting in traffic for an hour or more to get into the park can take up precious time. Furthermore, you will have the option to return to your hotel if you need a break during the day, or while you wait for queues to die down.

Rooms in Walt Disney World are expensive, often $150 plus per night, but there are two cheaper hotels – the All-Star Sports Resort and the All-Star Music Resort *(see p303)*, which charge under $100 per day including tax. Disney also has some excellent camp sites, costing around $40 per night.

Disney lodgings are in big demand and must be booked well in advance: six months is ideal, a year if you wish to visit at Easter or Christmas. However, there are so many hotels in Greater Orlando that you need never worry about finding a room. When choosing where to stay it is worth asking how long it takes to get to Walt Disney World and to the other theme parks, whether shuttle buses are available and, if so, how often they run.

SELF-CATERING ACCOMMODATION

WITH FLORIDA being such a big family destination, self-catering accommodation is very popular. Rooms with cooking facilities, known as "efficiencies", are provided in some hotels and motels. These may cost more than standard rooms but enable families to avoid expensive restaurant meals. In rural areas you find self-catering cabins attached to camp sites.

Condominiums ("condos"), consisting of apartments, are found mainly in beach resorts. They may seem expensive ($1,200 per week is cheap), but can be good value if you have a large family. **Overseas Connection** and **Vacation Home Rentals Worldwide** are among the many agencies to arrange condo rental, and they can normally organize rental of a private apartment or house too. Abroad, tour operators that specialize in Florida can sometimes provide the same service.

Finally, you can stay in a private home for free by doing a house swap. To arrange this, you should enrol as a member of a home-exchange organization: **HomeLink**, for example, has members worldwide.

CAMPING

FLORIDA HAS A HUGE number of camp sites. These range from the basic, where there may be no running water, to the luxurious, with swimming pools, restaurants, shops and

A camper enjoying privacy and quiet in Torreya State Park *(see p225)*

boat rental outlets. People more often stay in mobile homes or RVs than camp in tents, but even RV parks have space for tents; some rent out trailers and cabins too. State parks charge $10–25 per site, while private camp ground charges go up to about $40 per night. Most sites take advance bookings, but state parks hold back some spaces for people who arrive on the day.

The **Florida Association of RV Parks and Campgrounds** (ARVC) produces the annual *Florida Camping Directory,* listing its licensed members; copies can be ordered direct from the ARVC, and you can sometimes get the directory free from the tourist board. Contact the **Department of Environmental Protection,**

The well-kept gardens and pool at the youth hostel in Kissimmee

Parks and Recreation for a list of camp sites in the state parks. You may also want to contact **KOA Kampgrounds of America**, which runs about 30 good quality sites in Florida and issues its own directory.

YOUTH HOSTELS

FLORIDA HAS several youth hostels, including ones in South Beach, Orlando and Fort Lauderdale. The parent organization, **Hostelling International – American Youth Hostels**, issues a list of its members, and the UK's **Youth Hostel Association** can provide addresses too.

Facilities are often excellent, with a swimming pool and games room for example, but rates are very cheap: around $15 per night, slightly more for non-members. You should book ahead in high season.

TRAVELLING WITH CHILDREN

MOST HOTELS provide basic facilities for families, such as cots; a babysitting service may also be available. Some places, however, particularly in Orlando and popular sea-side locations, put children higher on their list of priorities and provide kids' swimming pools and play areas; some have children's programmes too, with organized activities and day trips (for which you may have to pay extra).

Most hotels do not charge for children under 12 sharing a room with their parents; in some cases (at Walt Disney World, for example) this is extended to those under 18. Rooms sometimes have a sofa that folds out into a bed; otherwise, an extra bed may be set up for a small additional fee.

A trailer in a tranquil spot in a Panhandle park

DIRECTORY

BED AND BREAKFASTS

A & A Bed and Breakfast of Florida
PO Box 1316,
Winter Park, FL 32790.
(*(407) 628-0322.*

Bed & Breakfast Co – Tropical Florida
PO Box 262,
South Miami, FL 33243.
(*(305) 661-3270.*

B & B Scenic Florida
Box 3385,
Tallahassee, FL 32315.
(*(904) 386-8196.*

Tourist House Association of America
PO Box 12A, Greentown,
PA 18426.
(*(717) 676-3222.*

SELF-CATERING ACCOMMODATION

Overseas Connection
PO Box 1800,
Sag Harbour,
NY 11963.
(*(516) 725-9308.*

HomeLink
PO Box 650,
Key West, FL 33041.
(*(800) 638-3841.*

Vacation Home Rentals Worldwide
235 Kensington Ave,
Norwood, NJ 07648.
(*(201) 767-9393.*

CAMPING

Department of Environmental Protection, Parks and Recreation
3900 Commonwealth Blvd,
Tallahassee, FL 32399.
(*(904) 488-9872.*

Florida Association of RV Parks and Campgrounds
1340 Vickers Drive,
Tallahassee, FL 32303.
(*(904) 562-7151.*

KOA Kampgrounds of America
PO Box 30558,
Billings, MT 59114.
(*(406) 248-7444.*
(*(0990) 143610 for bookings in the UK.*

YOUTH HOSTELS

Hostelling International
PO Box 37613,
Washington DC 20013-7613.
(*(202) 783-6161.*

Youth Hostel Association
14 Southampton St,
London WC2.
(*(0171) 836-1036.*

Choosing a Hotel

THE HOTELS IN THIS GUIDE have been selected across a wide price range for their good value, facilities and location. This chart highlights some of the factors which may influence your choice. Entries are listed by region, beginning with Miami. For Miami map references see pages 96–101; for road map references see pages 12–13.

	CREDIT CARDS	CHILDREN'S FACILITIES	SWIMMING POOL	GOOD RESTAURANT	KITCHEN FACILITIES
MIAMI					
MIAMI BEACH: *Clay Hotel and International Youth Hostel* $ 1438 Washington Ave, FL 33139. **Map** 2 E3. **(** *(305) 534-2988.* **FAX** *(305) 673-0346.* Booking is essential for this youth hostel, housed in a lovely Spanish Revival building. Unbeatably cheap for such a prime location. *Beds: 220*	MC V				▬
MIAMI BEACH: *Brigham Gardens Guest House* $$ 1411 Collins Ave, FL 33139. **Map** 2 F3. **(** *(305) 531-1331.* **FAX** *(305) 538-9898.* Two 1930s buildings and a gorgeous garden with caged singing birds nestle peacefully in the heart of buzzing South Beach. The rooms are individually decorated with a Deco mix of colour and art. 🏠 🖊 *Rooms: 20*	AE MC V				▬
MIAMI BEACH: *The Governor* $$ 435 21st St, FL 33139. **Map** 2 F1. **(** *(305) 532-2100.* **FAX** *(305) 532-9139.* Secluded but well situated on a side street, this is an undiscovered Deco gem. Rooms are comfortable and the decor unfussy. ⚡ 🖊 *Rooms: 125*	AE DC MC V		▬		
MIAMI BEACH: *Kenmore* $$ 1050 Washington Ave, FL 33139. **Map** 2 E3. **(** *(305) 674-1930.* **FAX** *(305) 534-6591.* Jointly run with the Park Washington and popular with a gay crowd, the Kenmore is distinctively Deco, both inside and out. 🖊 *Rooms: 60*	AE MC V		▬		
MIAMI BEACH: *Lido Spa* $$ 40 Island Ave, FL 33139. **Map** 1 C1. **(** *(305) 538-4621.* **FAX** *(305) 534-3680.* A favourite spa for locals who know a bargain, the Lido is located on Belle Isle close to South Beach. ⚡ 🖊 🍴 🅿 🖊 ⬤ *May–Oct.* **Rooms:** *120*	AE MC V		▬		▬
MIAMI BEACH: *Park Washington* $$ 1020 Washington Ave, FL 33139. **Map** 2 E3. **(** *(305) 532-1930.* **FAX** *(305) 672-6706.* One of a trio of Deco hostelries (with neighbours Kenmore and Bel Air). Lemon-toned rooms house original 1930s furnishings. 🖊 *Rooms: 50*	AE MC V		▬		▬
MIAMI BEACH: *Avalon* $$$ 700 Ocean Drive, FL 33139. **Map** 2 F3. **(** *(305) 538-0133.* **FAX** *(305) 534-0258.* You're right at the heart of the action at this trendy 1930s hotel. Rooms are Deco-style, the restaurant lively *(see p316).* 🖊 🅿 *Rooms: 106*	AE DC MC V			⬤	
MIAMI BEACH: *Betsy Ross* $$$ 1440 Ocean Drive, FL 33139. **Map** 2 F3. **(** *(305) 531-3934.* **FAX** *(305) 531-5282.* A cocktail of Deco and Colonial styles, this hotel has very comfortable rooms with great views of the beach and ocean. 🅿 🖊 *Rooms: 78*	AE DC MC V		▬	⬤	▬
MIAMI BEACH: *Dorchester* $$$ 1850 Collins Ave, FL 33139. **Map** 2 F2. **(** *(305) 531-5745.* **FAX** *(305) 673-1006.* A big pool, a tropical garden and better than average service are among the attractions of the Dorchester. ⚡ 🖊 *Rooms: 100*	AE DC MC V		▬		▬
MIAMI BEACH: *Indian Creek* $$$ 2727 Indian Creek Drive, FL 33139. **(** *(305) 531-2727.* **FAX** *(305) 531-5651.* This small, friendly hotel retains its 1936 look, with sepia photos, period furniture and period features. There is a delightful tropical garden and a tiny Asian-Caribbean restaurant. ⚡ 🖊 🍴 🖊 *Rooms: 61*	AE DC MC V		▬		
MIAMI BEACH: *Marseilles* $$$ 1741 Collins Ave, FL 33139. **Map** 2 F2. **(** *(305) 538-5711.* **FAX** *(305) 673-1006.* The family-run Marseilles isn't fancy but is well located in SoBe. Thanks to the unusual design, most rooms have a dual aspect. ⚡ 🖊 *Rooms: 111*	AE DC MC V		▬		
MIAMI BEACH: *Mermaid Guest House* $$$ 909 Collins Ave, FL 33139. **Map** 2 E4. **(** *(305) 538-5324.* **FAX** *(305) 538-2822.* Flowering banana trees hide this South Beach hang-out, popular with models and actors. Each room has unique decor. 🖊 🏠 🖊 *Rooms: 10*	AE MC V				▬

Price categories for a standard double room per night in high season, including tax and service charges:

$ under $60
$$ $60-$100
$$$ $100-$150
$$$$ $150-$200
$$$$$ over $200

CHILDREN'S FACILITIES
A child-friendly hotel, with cots, high chairs and other facilities which may include a baby-sitting service and special children's programmes.

SWIMMING POOL
The hotel has a swimming pool for use by residents.

GOOD RESTAURANT
There is a particularly good restaurant, which is normally also accessible to non-residents.

KITCHEN FACILITIES
The hotel has rooms with cooking and other kitchen facilities, usually known as "efficiencies".

	CREDIT CARDS	CHILDREN'S FACILITIES	SWIMMING POOL	GOOD RESTAURANT	KITCHEN FACILITIES
MIAMI BEACH: *Ramada Resort Deauville* $$$ 6701 Collins Ave, FL 33141. 📞 *(305) 865-8511.* FAX *(305) 865-0154.* Between SoBe and Bal Harbour, this oceanfront hotel is well-equipped with a huge pool, tennis courts and solarium. *Rooms: 554*	AE DC MC V		▪		
MIAMI BEACH: *Shore Club* $$$ 1901 Collins Ave, FL 33139. Map 2 F1. 📞 *(305) 672-0303.* FAX *(305) 672-6287.* This is a showpiece hotel in the Art Deco district. It has an expansive lobby with terrazzo floors and soft lighting. *Rooms: 205*	AE DC MC V	●	▪		
MIAMI BEACH: *Astor* $$$$ 956 Washington Ave, FL 33139. Map 2 E3. 📞 *(305) 531-4056.* FAX *(305) 531-3193.* This is an Art Deco showpiece with marble bathrooms, VCRs in the rooms and a very stylish clientele. *Rooms: 41*	AE MC V			●	
MIAMI BEACH: *Breakwater* $$$$ 940 Ocean Drive, FL 33139. Map 2 F3. 📞 *(305) 532-1220.* FAX *(305) 532-4451.* Guests get a gracious welcome at this oceanfront hotel. The colourful rooms reflect the hotel's original Deco charm. *Rooms: 59*	AE DC MC V		▪		▪
MIAMI BEACH: *Pelican* $$$$ 826 Ocean Drive, FL 33139. Map 2 F4. 📞 *(305) 673-3373.* FAX *(305) 673-3255.* Designer-kitsch in the extreme, this hip hostelry has theme rooms ranging from a pink satin brothel chamber to one filled with church art and furnishings. No expense is spared on the details. *Rooms: 26*	AE DC MC V				
MIAMI BEACH: *Shelborne Beach Resort* $$$$ 1801 Collins Ave, FL 33139. Map 2 F2. 📞 *(305) 531-1271.* FAX *(305) 531-2206.* Directly on the ocean in South Beach, the Shelborne has an impressive marble lobby and rooftop fitness centre. *Rooms: 225*	AE DC MC V		▪		▪
MIAMI BEACH: *Casa Grande* $$$$$ 834 Ocean Drive, FL 33139. Map 2 F4. 📞 *(305) 672-7003.* FAX *(305) 673-3669.* Elegantly furnished, this hotel is one of the best in South Beach. Every room has a VCR and CD-player. *Rooms: 33*	AE DC MC V				▪
MIAMI BEACH: *Delano* $$$$$ 1685 Collins Ave, FL 33139. Map 2 F2. 📞 *(305) 672-2000.* FAX *(305) 532-0099.* SoBe's most chic hotel – where staff dress all in white and match the gorgeous, if stark, rooms. *Rooms: 238*	AE DC MC V	●	▪	●	
MIAMI BEACH: *Eden Roc Resort and Spa* $$$$$ 4525 Collins Ave, FL 33140. 📞 *(305) 531-0000.* FAX *(305) 531-6955.* Built to look like a beached cruise liner, this star of 1950s flamboyance has since been overhauled. It now has contemporary rooms and myriad facilities, including a stylish spa. *Rooms: 350*	AE DC MC V	●	▪		
MIAMI BEACH: *Fontainebleau Hilton Resort and Towers* $$$$$ 4441 Collins Ave, FL 33140. 📞 *(305) 538-2000.* FAX *(305) 673-5351.* The most prestigious resort in Miami Beach *(see p67)*, the Fontainebleau has every amenity imaginable, from children's activities to the famous Tropigala floor show *(see p95)*. *Rooms: 1,206*	AE DC MC V	●	▪	●	
MIAMI BEACH: *Impala* $$$$$ 1228 Collins Ave, FL 33139. Map 2 F3. 📞 *(305) 673-2021.* FAX *(305) 673-5984.* You'll see plenty of limos pull up at this busy Deco hotel. The restrained but exquisite sandy-toned rooms house beautiful wooden and wrought-iron furniture, majestic beds and original artworks. *Rooms: 17*	AE DC MC V				
MIAMI BEACH: *Raleigh* $$$$$ 1775 Collins Ave, FL 33139. Map 2 F2. 📞 *(305) 534-6300.* FAX *(305) 538-8140.* The Raleigh boasts classy, minimalist rooms, some with ocean views, a trendy pool area and a hip restaurant. *Rooms: 107*	AE DC MC V	●	▪		

For key to symbols see back flap

Price categories for a standard double room per night in high season, including tax and service charges:
[$] under $60
[$][$] $60-$100
[$][$][$] $100-$150
[$][$][$][$] $150-$200
[$][$][$][$][$] over $200

CHILDREN'S FACILITIES
A child-friendly hotel, with cots, high chairs and other facilities which may include a baby-sitting service and special children's programmes.

SWIMMING POOL
The hotel has a swimming pool for use by residents.

GOOD RESTAURANT
There is a particularly good restaurant, which is normally also accessible to non-residents.

KITCHEN FACILITIES
The hotel has rooms with cooking and other kitchen facilities, usually known as "efficiencies".

Hotel	Credit Cards	Children's Facilities	Swimming Pool	Good Restaurant	Kitchen Facilities
MIAMI BEACH: *Westin Resort* [$][$][$][$][$] 4833 Collins Ave, FL 33140. ☎ *(305) 532-3600.* [FAX] *(305) 534-7409.* This big but relatively quiet hotel offers proximity to the exclusive shops in Bal Harbour plus countless water sports and children's activities. [24] 🚭 ❄ 🏋 🛗 [P] 🍴 **Rooms:** *420*	AE DC MC V	●	■		
DOWNTOWN: *Hampton* [$][$] 2500 Brickell Ave, FL 33129. **Map** 4 D4. ☎ *(305) 854-2070.* [FAX] *(305) 856-5055.* The Hampton offers easy access to Downtown, Coconut Grove and Coral Gables. Rooms are bright and breakfast is included. 🚭 🛗 🐕 🍴 **Rooms:** *69*	AE DC MC V		■		
DOWNTOWN: *Miami River Inn* [$][$][$] 118 SW South River Drive, FL 33130. **Map** 4 D1. ☎ *(305) 325-0045.* [FAX] *(305) 325-9227.* Built in 1906 and restored to its early Miami charm, the building features period decor and airy rooms. 🚭 ❄ 🛗 🍴 **Rooms:** *40*	AE DC MC V		■		■
DOWNTOWN: *Crowne Plaza Miami* [$][$][$] 1601 Biscayne Blvd, FL 33132. ☎ *(305) 374-0000.* [FAX] *(305) 374-0020.* Rising high above the 125-store Omni shopping mall, this central hotel is near Bayside and offers panoramic views. 🚭 ❄ 🏋 🛗 [P] **Rooms:** *528*	AE DC MC V	●	■	●	
DOWNTOWN: *Doubletree Grand* [$][$][$] 1717 N Bayshore Drive, FL 33132. ☎ *(305) 372-0313.* [FAX] *(305) 372-9455.* Here you get great views of Biscayne Bay and many amenities, including a marina, a health club and boats for hire. 🚭 ❄ 🏋 🛗 [P] 🍴 **Rooms:** *178*	AE DC MC V		■		■
DOWNTOWN: *Doral Golf Resort and Spa* [$][$][$][$][$] 4400 NW 87th Ave, FL 33178. ☎ *(305) 592-2000.* [FAX] *(305) 594-4682.* Located on a championship golf course, this hotel is beautifully landscaped and has a world class spa. 🚭 ❄ 🏋 🛗 [P] 🍴 **Rooms:** *694*	AE DC MC V	●	■	●	
DOWNTOWN: *Inter-Continental Miami* [$][$][$][$][$] 100 Chopin Plaza, FL 33131. **Map** 4 F1. ☎ *(305) 577-1000.* [FAX] *(305) 577-0384.* A short walk from Bayside Marketplace, this luxury hotel has city views and a gourmet restaurant *(see p317).* [24] 🚭 ❄ 🏋 🛗 [P] **Rooms:** *644*	AE DC MC V	●	■	●	
CORAL GABLES: *Riviera Court Motel* [$][$] 5100 Riviera Drive, FL 33146. **Map** 6 F3. ☎ *(305) 665-3528.* This cheap and cheerful 1950s-style hotel is on Dixie Highway, with easy access to area attractions. Rooms are pleasant and homely. **Rooms:** *31*	AE DC MC V		■		■
CORAL GABLES: *Omni Colonnade* [$][$][$][$] 180 Aragon Ave, FL 33134. **Map** 6 D1. ☎ *(305) 441-2600.* [FAX] *(305) 445-3929.* This plush hotel just off Miracle Mile incorporates a 1920s George Merrick rotunda *(see p80).* The period theme echoes throughout, with mahogany furniture and marble floors. [24] 🚭 ❄ 🏋 🛗 [P] 🍴 **Rooms:** *157*	AE DC MC V	●	■		
CORAL GABLES: *Place St Michel* [$][$][$][$] 162 Alcazar Ave, FL 33134. **Map** 5 C1. ☎ *(305) 444-1666.* [FAX] *(305) 529-0074.* This romantic 1926 hotel, a short walk from Miracle Mile, is evocative of Paris: dark wood panelling, 1930s French furniture and Deco fittings create the illusion. It also boasts a fine French restaurant. 🚭 🛗 **Rooms:** *27*	AE DC MC V			●	
CORAL GABLES: *The Biltmore* [$][$][$][$][$] 1200 Anastasia Ave, FL 33134. **Map** 5 A2. ☎ *(305) 445-1926.* [FAX] *(305) 913-3159.* Rich in history (Al Capone gambled here in the 1920s), the grande dame of Miami's hotels will pamper you with every modern amenity in opulent, antique-filled suites. [24] 🚭 ❄ 🏋 🛗 [P] 🍴 **Rooms:** *279*	AE DC MC V	●	■	●	
COCONUT GROVE: *Hampton Inn* [$][$][$] 2800 SW 28th Terrace, FL 33133. **Map** 6 F3. ☎ *(305) 448-2800.* [FAX] *(305) 442-8655.* Located under a mile (1.5 km) from Coconut Grove's cafés and nightlife. Continental breakfast is included. 🚭 🏋 🛗 **Rooms:** *137*	AE DC MC V		■		

COCONUT GROVE: *Doubletree* $$$$
2649 S Bayshore Drive, FL 33133. **Map** 6 F4. **C** *(305) 858-2500.*
FAX *(305) 858-5776.* A stroll from the cafés and boutiques of "the village",
this sleek hotel offers beautiful views of Biscayne Bay marina. There's
marble and modern art throughout. **24** 🏊 🖼 🍴 🍷 💆 *Rooms:* 192

| | AE DC MC V | • | ▦ | |

COCONUT GROVE: *Grand Bay* $$$$$
2669 S Bayshore Drive, FL 33133. **Map** 6 F4. **C** *(305) 858-9600.*
FAX *(305) 858-1532.* Amongst the world's finest hotels, Grand Bay has crystal
chandeliers, designer furnishings and original art. Pavarotti's suite can be
rented when he's not in residence. **24** 🏊 🍴 🖼 🍷 **P** 💆 *Rooms:* 178

COCONUT GROVE: *Mayfair House* $$$$$
3000 Florida Ave, FL 33133. **Map** 6 E4. **C** *(305) 441-0000.* **FAX** *(305) 447-9173.*
Perched on top of an exclusive shopping mall, Mayfair House provides
opulent lodgings. Large rooms have rich mahogany furniture and private
balconies; some even have antique pianos. **24** 🏊 🍴 🍷 **P** 💆 *Rooms:* 183

FURTHER AFIELD: *Paradise Inn Motel* $$
8520 Harding Ave, Surfside, FL 33141. **C** *(305) 865-6216.* **FAX** *(305) 865-9028.*
This budget motel isn't fancy but it's clean and located just a block
from the beach and the huge North Shore Park. *Rooms:* 92

FURTHER AFIELD: *Suez Oceanfront Resort* $$
18215 Collins Ave, Sunny Isles, FL 33160. **C** *(305) 932-0661.* **FAX** *(305) 937-0058.*
Located on the beach, and with good amenities, the Suez is child-friendly
with a kids' pool and playground. 🏊 🍴 🍷 💆 *Rooms:* 196

FURTHER AFIELD: *Riu Pan American Ocean Resort* $$$
17875 Collins Ave, Sunny Isles, FL 33160. **C** *(305) 932-1100.* **FAX** *(305) 935-2769.*
The service is friendly, for a resort, and guests are offered complimentary
afternoon tea. Good sports facilities include a putting green and
tennis and volleyball courts. 🏊 🖼 🍴 🍷 **P** 💆 *Rooms:* 146

FURTHER AFIELD: *Newport Beachside Crowne Plaza Resort* $$$
16701 Collins Ave, Sunny Isles, FL 33160. **C** *(305) 949-1300.* **FAX** *(305) 947-5873.*
Best known for its entertainment, from comedy shows to Las Vegas-style
revues, the Newport offers huge rooms, many with balconies, and its
own fishing pier. 🏊 🖼 🍴 🍷 **P** *Rooms:* 355

FURTHER AFIELD: *Sheraton Bal Harbour Resort* $$$$
9701 Collins Ave, Bal Harbour, FL 33154. **C** *(305) 865-7511.* **FAX** *(305) 864-2610.*
If you want proximity to the Bal Harbour shops, deluxe rooms overlooking the ocean and a 10-acre (4 ha) tropical garden, then this
is the place to stay. **24** 🏊 🖼 🍴 🍷 **P** 💆 *Rooms:* 668

FURTHER AFIELD: *Sonesta Beach* $$$$
350 Ocean Drive, Key Biscayne, FL 33149. **C** *(305) 361-2021.* **FAX** *(305) 361-3096.*
Stylish but casual, this resort has kids' activities, tennis courts and a
health club. The hallmarks of the rooms are soft colours and often
tremendous ocean views. **24** 🏊 🖼 🍴 🍷 💆 *Rooms:* 292

THE GOLD AND TREASURE COASTS

BOCA RATON: *Ocean Lodge* $$
531 N Ocean Blvd, FL 33432. **Road map** F4. **C** *(561) 395-7772.* **FAX** *(561) 395-0554.*
No more than a shell's throw from the beach, this motel is also close to
restaurants and shops. It has a shady barbecue area. 🏊 💆 *Rooms:* 18

BOCA RATON: *Shore Edge Motel* $$
425 N Ocean Blvd, FL 33432. **Road map** F4. **C** *(561) 395-4491.*
At this quaint, cosy motel across the street from the ocean the rooms
are small but tidy and the proprietors very friendly. *Rooms:* 16

BOCA RATON: *Boca Raton Resort and Club* $$$$$
501 E Camino Real, FL 33431. **Road map** F4. **C** *(561) 395-3000.* **FAX** *(561) 391-3183.*
The smartest and most pretentious place in town *(see p126),* this Spanish-
style hotel boasts rooms in a choice of decor, from dark woods to
Oriental rugs and sleek marble. **24** 🏊 🖼 🍴 🍷 **P** 💆 *Rooms:* 963

CLEWISTON: *Clewiston Inn* $$
108 Royal Palm Ave, FL 33440. **Road map** E4. **C** *(941) 983-8151.*
FAX *(941) 983-4602.* This traditional inn with the look of a colonial mansion
provides comfortable lodging and good Southern cooking. *Rooms:* 53

Price categories for a standard double room per night in high season, including tax and service charges:

$ under $60
$$ $60-$100
$$$ $100-$150
$$$$ $150-$200
$$$$$ over $200

CHILDREN'S FACILITIES
A child-friendly hotel, with cots, high chairs and other facilities which may include a baby-sitting service and special children's programmes.

SWIMMING POOL
The hotel has a swimming pool for use by residents.

GOOD RESTAURANT
There is a particularly good restaurant, which is normally also accessible to non-residents.

KITCHEN FACILITIES
The hotel has rooms with cooking and other kitchen facilities, usually known as "efficiencies".

	CREDIT CARDS	CHILDREN'S FACILITIES	SWIMMING POOL	GOOD RESTAURANT	KITCHEN FACILITIES
DELRAY BEACH: *Seagate Hotel and Beach Club* $$$ 400 S Ocean Blvd, FL 33483. **Road map** F4. ((561) 276-2421. FAX (561) 243-4714 This friendly oceanfront hotel with private beach offers well-furnished rooms in earthy tones, and fresh- and saltwater pools. ☒ ☒ ☒ **P** *Rooms: 70*	AE DC MC V	●	■		■
FORT LAUDERDALE: *Venetian Court* $$ 71 Isle of Venice, FL 33301. **Road map** F4. ((954) 525-2223. FAX (954) 524-2520. Hidden beside a canal, this pleasant hotel offers views of luxury yachts and local mansions. The rooms are well furnished. ☒ ☒ ☒ ☒ *Rooms: 16*	DC MC V		■		■
FORT LAUDERDALE: *A Little Inn by the Sea* $$$ 4546 El Mar Drive, FL 33308. **Road map** F4. ((954) 772-2450. FAX (954) 938-9354. Swiss-run and popular with Europeans, this beachfront inn north of downtown has a relaxed family feel. Fine fabrics, quality wicker furniture and canopy beds adorn the attractive rooms. ☒ ☒ ☒ *Rooms: 29*	AE DC MC V		■		
FORT LAUDERDALE: *Holiday Inn Lauderdale-By-The-Sea* $$$ 4116 N Ocean Drive, FL 33308. **Road map** F4. ((954) 776-1212. FAX (954) 776-1212 ext 600. In a quiet spot just across the street from the beach, this hotel is perfect for families. ☒ ☒ ☒ ☒ *Rooms: 187*	AE DC MC V	●	■		■
FORT LAUDERDALE: *Riverside* $$$$ 620 E Las Olas Blvd, FL 33301. **Road map** F4. ((954) 467-0671. FAX (954) 462-2148. Built in 1936 in a now-trendy area of restaurants and shops, this hotel has ceiling fans, terracotta floors and a tasteful mix of wicker and oak. ☒ ☒ **P** *Rooms: 109*	AE DC MC V		■		
FORT LAUDERDALE: *Hyatt Regency Pier 66 Marina* $$$$$ 2301 SE 17th St Causeway, FL 33316. **Road map** F4. ((954) 525-6666. FAX (954) 728-3541. This high-rise hotel offers great views and a smart fitness centre and spa. ☒ ☒ ☒ ☒ ☒ **P** ☒ *Rooms: 388*	AE DC MC V		■	●	
FORT PIERCE: *Harbor Light Inn* $$ 1160 Seaway Drive, FL 34949. **Road map** F3. ((561) 468-3555. On the Intracoastal Waterway and with two private piers, this inn is good for boating and fishing. Inside, nautical themes dominate. ☒ ☒ *Rooms: 21*	AE DC MC V		■		■
HOLLYWOOD: *Holiday Inn Sunspree Resort* $$$ 2711 S Ocean Drive, FL 33019. **Road map** F4. ((954) 923-8700. FAX (954) 923-7059. Located by the beach, this family-oriented resort has a kids-eat-free policy. ☒ ☒ ☒ ☒ **P** ☒ *Rooms: 201*	AE DC MC V	●	■		
HUTCHINSON ISLAND: *Indian River Plantation Beach Resort* $$$$$ 555 NE Ocean Blvd, FL 34996. **Road map** F3. ((561) 225-3700. FAX (561) 225-0003. A good family resort with lots going on, such as children's activities, tennis and golf lessons and nature walks. ☒ ☒ ☒ ☒ **P** ☒ *Rooms: 298*	AE DC MC V	●	■	●	■
JUPITER: *Innisfail* $$ 134 Timber Lane, FL 33458. **Road map** F4. ((561) 744-5905. FAX (561) 744-5902. A pair of sculptors own Innisfail, and their work is on display at this small and peaceful ranch-cum-B & B. ☒ ☒ ☒ *Rooms: 2*			■		
JUPITER: *Jupiter Beach Resort* $$$$$ 5 North A1A, FL 33477. **Road map** F4. ((561) 746-2511. FAX (561) 747-3304. This plush but unpretentious resort has relatively simple rooms with marble baths and colourful furnishings. Private balconies afford grand ocean and sunset views. ☒ ☒ ☒ ☒ **P** ☒ *Rooms: 186*	AE DC MC V	●	■		■
PALM BEACH: *Beachcomber Apartment Motel* $$$ 3024 S Ocean Blvd, FL 33480. **Road map** F4. ((561) 585-4646. FAX (561) 547-9438. This basic but very comfortable motel is only a couple of steps from its own private beach. ☒ ☒ *Rooms: 46*	AE MC V		■		■

PALM BEACH: *Palm Beach Hawaiian Ocean Inn* $$$
3550 S Ocean Blvd, FL 33480. **Road map** F4. (*(561) 582-5631.*
FAX *(561) 582-5631 ext 165.* About 7 miles (11 km) south of downtown, this inn is good value, with large, bright rooms. **Rooms:** 58
AE DC MC V

PALM BEACH: *Heart of Palm Beach* $$$$
160 Royal Palm Way, FL 33480. **Road map** F4. (*(561) 655-5600.*
FAX *(561) 832-1201.* The best thing here is the plum site a few blocks from Worth Avenue. Ample suites but small rooms. **Rooms:** 84
AE DC MC V

PALM BEACH: *Plaza Inn* $$$$
215 Brazilian Ave, FL 33480. **Road map** F4. (*(561) 832-8666.*
FAX *(561) 835-8776.* This Deco gem has four-poster beds, hand-crocheted spreads and cooked-to-order breakfasts. **Rooms:** 50
AE MC V

PALM BEACH: *The Breakers* $$$$$
1 South County Rd, FL 33480. **Road map** F4. (*(561) 655-6611.*
FAX *(561) 659-8403.* Sumptuous and classy, this "Italian palace" is Palm Beach's finest hotel *(see p117).* Not a classic family establishment, but the children's facilities are great. **Rooms:** 572
AE DC MC V

PALM BEACH: *Four Seasons Palm Beach* $$$$$
2800 S Ocean Blvd, FL 33480. **Road map** F4. (*(561) 582-2800.* FAX *(561) 547-1557.*
The elegant lobby filled with antiques and tapestries gives way to huge, beautifully furnished rooms with every modern amenity. The balconies enjoy fine sea views. **Rooms:** 210
AE DC MC V

PALM BEACH GARDENS: *Heron Cay* $$$
15106 Palmwood Rd, FL 33410. **Road map** F4. (*(561) 744-6315.*
FAX *(561) 744-0943.* This Key West-style B & B lazes beside the Intracoastal Waterway. Guests take trips on the owners' fishing boat. **Rooms:** 9
MC V

PALM BEACH GARDENS: *PGA National Resort and Spa* $$$$$
400 Avenue of the Champions, FL 33418. **Road map** F4. (*(561) 627-2000.*
FAX *(561) 622-0261.* Here, the fabulous spa boasts mineral-rich pools; tennis and golf instruction is also available. **Rooms:** 339
AE DC MC V

POMPANO BEACH: *Ronny Dee Motel* $$
717 S Ocean Blvd, FL 33062. **Road map** F4. (*(954) 943-3020.* FAX *(954) 783-5112.*
Nothing fancy here, but Ronny Dee is clean and convenient for the beach. A coffee and doughnut breakfast is included. **Rooms:** 35
AE DC MC V

STUART: *Harborfront Inn Bed & Breakfast* $$
310 Atlanta Ave, FL 34994. **Road map** F3. (*(561) 288-7289.* FAX *(561) 221-0474.*
Harborfront's blue-trimmed cottages on the riverside are within walking distance of downtown. Enjoy the home-cooked breakfast. **Rooms:** 6
AE MC V

VERO BEACH: *Islander Motel* $$
3101 Ocean Drive, FL 32963. **Road map** F3. (*(561) 231-4431.* FAX *(561) 589-5100.*
Here you're just 300 ft (100 m) from the beach, near restaurants and shops, and can barbecue your own food by the pool. Each room has its own unique decor. **Rooms:** 16
AE MC V

VERO BEACH: *Disney's Vero Beach Resort* $$$$$
9250 Island Grove Terrace, FL 32963. **Road map** F3. (*(561) 234-2000.*
FAX *(561) 234-2030.* Hallmark Disney quality abounds in luxury bedrooms and timeshare cottages; the pool is centred around a Spanish galleon and activities include campfire sing-alongs. **Rooms:** 204
AE MC V

WEST PALM BEACH: *Comfort Inn* $$
5981 Okeechobee Blvd, FL 33417. **Road map** F4. (*(561) 697-3388.*
FAX *(561) 697-2834.* Beyond the airport, adjacent to Florida's Turnpike, this is a clean, comfortable inn. Breakfast is included. **Rooms:** 113
AE DC MC V

WEST PALM BEACH: *Hibiscus House* $$$
501 30th St, FL 33407. **Road map** F4. (*(561) 863-5633.* FAX *same as telephone.*
Built in 1922, this historic home has been lovingly restored. Decor is Victorian and breakfast arrives on beautiful china and crystal. There is a free shuttle bus into town. **Rooms:** 8
AE DC MC V

WEST PALM BEACH: *Palm Beach Polo and Country Club* $$$$$
11809 Polo Club Rd, FL 33414. **Road map** F4. (*(561) 798-7000.*
FAX *(561) 798-7340.* This exclusive resort has condos, villas or studios, but the main attraction is the tennis, golf and polo. **Rooms:** 60
AE MC V

For key to symbols see back flap

<table>
<tr><td>

Price categories for a standard double room per night in high season, including tax and service charges:

$Ⓢ$ under $60
$ⓈⓈ$ $60–100
$ⓈⓈⓈ$ $100–150
$ⓈⓈⓈⓈ$ $150–200
$ⓈⓈⓈⓈⓈ$ over $200

</td><td>

CHILDREN'S FACILITIES
A child-friendly hotel, with cots, high chairs and other facilities which may include a baby-sitting service and special children's programmes.

SWIMMING POOL
The hotel has a swimming pool for use by residents.

GOOD RESTAURANT
There is a particularly good restaurant, which is normally also accessible to non-residents.

KITCHEN FACILITIES
The hotel has rooms with cooking and other kitchen facilities, usually known as "efficiencies".

</td></tr>
</table>

ORLANDO AND THE SPACE COAST

	CREDIT CARDS	CHILDREN'S FACILITIES	SWIMMING POOL	GOOD RESTAURANT	KITCHEN FACILITIES
CAPE CANAVERAL: *Radisson Resort* $ⓈⓈⓈ$ 8701 Astronaut Blvd, FL 32920. **Road map** F2. 【 (407) 784-0000. **FAX** (407) 784-3737. Ceiling fans and wicker give this resort a Caribbean feel. Ten minutes' drive from Kennedy Space Center. ✈ 📷 🍴 🛏 🅿 *Rooms: 199*	AE DC MC V	●	▬		
COCOA: *Econo Lodge* $ⓈⓈ$ 3220 N Cocoa Blvd, FL 32926. **Road map** E3. 【 (407) 632-4561. **FAX** (407) 631-3756. Nothing spectacular, but adequate, clean and well located just 8 miles (13 km) from the Kennedy Space Center. ✈ *Rooms: 142*	AE DC MC V		▬		
COCOA BEACH: *Comfort Inn* $ⓈⓈ$ 3901 N Atlantic Ave, FL 32931. **Road map** E3. 【 (407) 783-2221. **FAX** (407) 783-0461. A hop, skip and jump from the beach, this inn opens onto a palm-shaded pool-side area with barbecue grills. ✈ 📷 🛏 🅿 *Rooms: 144*	AE DC MC V		▬		▬
COCOA BEACH: *Inn at Cocoa Beach* $ⓈⓈⓈⓈ$ 4300 Ocean Beach Blvd, FL 32931. **Road map** E3. 【 (407) 799-3460. **FAX** (407) 784-8632. Patios and balconies give sea views at this B & B, where room decor ranges from modern to traditional. 📷 🛏 🅿 *Rooms: 50*	AE MC V		▬		
CYPRESS GARDENS: *Best Western Inn* $ⓈⓈ$ 5665 Cypress Gardens Blvd, FL 33884. **Road map** E3. 【 (941) 324-5950. **FAX** (941) 324-2376. Just steps from the beautiful Cypress Gardens, this inn has comfortable (though not fancy) rooms. 🍴 🛏 🛏 *Rooms: 156*	AE DC MC V		▬		
DOWNTOWN ORLANDO: *Harley* $ⓈⓈ$ 151 E Washington St, FL 32801. **Road map** E2. 【 (407) 841-3220. **FAX** (407) 849-1839. The Harley is in easy walking distance of Church Street Station and offers guests an inclusive all-you-can-eat breakfast. ✈ 📷 🍴 🛏 🅿 *Rooms: 281*	AE DC MC V		▬		
DOWNTOWN ORLANDO: *Courtyard at Lake Lucerne* $ⓈⓈⓈ$ 211 N Lucerne Circle E, FL 32801. **Road map** E2. 【 (407) 648-5188. **FAX** (407) 246-1368. This well-run B & B in a quiet garden beside Lake Lucerne comprises three historic houses, one of which is the oldest in town. The decor ranges from Victorian to Deco. ✈ 🛏 🅿 *Rooms: 24*	AE DC MC V				▬
DOWNTOWN ORLANDO: *The Veranda Bed & Breakfast* $ⓈⓈⓈ$ 115 N Summerlin Ave, FL 32801. **Road map** E2. 【 (407) 849-0321. **FAX** (407) 872-7512. Two 1920s wooden homes nestled in a pretty garden in the old district. Verandas, hardwood floors and ceiling fans create a Key West look. Period furnishings add charm to the rooms. ✈ 🛏 🛏 🅿 *Rooms: 10*	MC V		▬		▬
INTERNATIONAL DRIVE: *La Quinta Inn* $ⓈⓈ$ 8300 Jamaican Ct, FL 32819. **Road map** E2. 【 (407) 351-1660. **FAX** (407) 351-9264. This low-price inn 9 miles (14 km) from Walt Disney World offers well-kept rooms and a free continental breakfast. ✈ 🛏 🛏 *Rooms: 200*	AE DC MC V		▬		▬
INTERNATIONAL DRIVE: *Best Western Plaza International* $ⓈⓈ$ 8738 International Drive, FL 32819. **Road map** E2. 【 (407) 345-8195. **FAX** (407) 352-8196. Walt Disney World is ten minutes' drive away and Sea World is even closer. Family suites are good for kids. ✈ 🛏 *Rooms: 672*	AE DC MC V	●	▬		▬
INTERNATIONAL DRIVE: *Ramada Inn* $ⓈⓈ$ 4855 S Orange Blossom Trail, FL 32839. **Road map** E2. 【 (407) 851-3000. **FAX** (407) 859-8972. Within reach of downtown Orlando and busy "I Drive", this inn has large suites and a tropical pool area. ✈ 📷 🛏 🅿 *Rooms: 132*	AE DC MC V		▬		▬
INTERNATIONAL DRIVE: *Clarion Plaza Hotel* $ⓈⓈⓈ$ 9700 International Drive, FL 32819. **Road map** E2. 【 (407) 352-9700. **FAX** (407) 352-9710. An expansive marble lobby welcomes you to this efficiently-run hotel with airy rooms. ✈ 📷 🍴 🛏 🅿 🅿 *Rooms: 810*	AE DC MC V	●	▬		

INTERNATIONAL DRIVE: *Country Hearth Inn* $$$ AE DC MC V
9861 International Drive, FL 32819. **Road map** E2. (*(407) 352-0008.*
FAX *(407) 352-5449.* This mansion-style inn has a lovely front porch lounge and quiet rooms with balconies. Breakfast is included. **Rooms:** 150

INTERNATIONAL DRIVE: *Holiday Inn Express* $$$ AE DC MC V
6323 International Drive, FL 32819. **Road map** E2. (*(407) 351-4430.*
FAX *(407) 345-0742.* Close to Walt Disney World, the Inn is geared to children. They stay and eat for free and enjoy a special "comedy zone". **Rooms:** 217

INTERNATIONAL DRIVE: *Renaissance Orlando Resort* $$$$
6677 Sea Harbor Drive, FL 32821. **Road map** E2. (*(407) 351-5555.*
FAX *(407) 351-9991.* Across the street from Sea World, this resort has an outstanding children's programme. The marble bathrooms and golf privileges are there to please the adults. **Rooms:** 780

LAKE WALES: *Chalet Suzanne* $$$$ AE DC MC V
3800 Chalet Suzanne Drive, FL 33853. **Road map** E3. (*(941) 676-6011.*
FAX *(941) 676-1814.* A local institution, this pleasant hotel set in orange groves has quirky rooms decorated with an eclectic choice of souvenirs. The in-house restaurant is superb. **Rooms:** 30

WALT DISNEY WORLD: *Comfort Inn Maingate* $ AE DC MC V
7571 W Irlo Bronson Hwy, FL 34747. **Road map** E3. (*(407) 396-7500.*
FAX *(407) 396-7497.* This clean and comfortable hotel is located one mile (1.5 km) west of Walt Disney World. **Rooms:** 281

WALT DISNEY WORLD: *Disney's All-Star Music Resort* $$ AE MC V
1801 W Buena Vista Drive, FL 32830. **Road map** E3. (*(407) 939-6000.*
FAX *(407) 939-7222.* Musically themed throughout, from the bedspreads to walk-through jukebox. The rooms are pleasant. **Rooms:** 1,920

WALT DISNEY WORLD: *Disney's All-Star Sports Resort* $$ AE MC V
1701 W Buena Vista Drive, FL 32830. **Road map** E3. (*(407) 939-5000.*
FAX *(407) 939-7333.* Fans will enjoy the sports decor. Facilities, including huge pools, are shared with the adjacent Music Resort. **Rooms:** 1,920

WALT DISNEY WORLD: *Perri House* $$ AE MC V
10417 State Rd 535, FL 32836. **Road map** E3. (*(407) 876-4830.*
FAX *(407) 876-0241.* Perfect for families, this is a quiet country inn secluded on a 20-acre (8-ha) nature reserve adjacent to Walt Disney World. Comfortable rooms feature cherry and oak furnishings. **Rooms:** 8

WALT DISNEY WORLD: *Days Inn, Days Suites* $$$ AE DC MC V
5820 W Irlo Bronson Hwy, FL 34746. **Road map** E3. (*(407) 396-7900.*
FAX *(407) 396-1789.* Here you can enjoy four pools, a children's playground and a picnic area. Just 2 miles (3 km) from Walt Disney World. **Rooms:** 604

WALT DISNEY WORLD: *Disney's Caribbean Beach Resort* $$$ AE MC V
900 Cayman Way, FL 32830. **Road map** E3. (*(407) 934-3400.* **FAX** *(407) 934-3288.*
Five cheerful "villages" with attractive rooms are situated around a lake where water birds congregate. Pools and artificial white sand beaches dot the property, and contribute to a tropical feel. **Rooms:** 2,112

WALT DISNEY WORLD: *Grosvenor Resort* $$$ AE DC MC V
1850 Hotel Plaza Blvd, FL 32830. **Road map** E3. (*(407) 828-4444.*
FAX *(407) 828-8192.* This elegant, colonial-theme hotel features pleasant rooms and a wide range of facilities. **Rooms:** 626

WALT DISNEY WORLD: *Holiday Inn Hotel and Suites* $$$ AE DC MC V
5678 W Irlo Bronson Hwy, FL 34746. **Road map** E3. (*(407) 396-4488.*
FAX *(407) 396-8915.* Children are made a fuss of here – there is even a kids' check-in desk. Clowns make up the rooms and lead activities at a children's camp. Just 3 miles (5 km) outside Walt Disney World. **Rooms:** 614

WALT DISNEY WORLD: *Buena Vista Palace* $$$$ AE DC MC V
1900 Buena Vista Drive, FL 32830. **Road map** E3. (*(407) 827-2727.*
FAX *(407) 827-6034.* This resort features a host of restaurants and facilities. Room decor is in earthy tones. **Rooms:** 1,014

WALT DISNEY WORLD: *Disney's BoardWalk Villas* $$$$$ AE MC V
2101 N Epcot Resorts Blvd, FL 32830. **Road map** E3. (*(407) 939-5100.*
FAX *(407) 939-5150.* Opened in 1996, these New England-style "seaside" cottages offer comfy family lodgings. **Rooms:** 532

For key to symbols see back flap

	CREDIT CARDS	CHILDREN'S FACILITIES	SWIMMING POOL	GOOD RESTAURANT	KITCHEN FACILITIES
WALT DISNEY WORLD: *Disney's Vacation Club Resort* ⓈⓈⓈ 1510 N Cove Rd, FL 32830. **Road map** E3. **☎** *(407) 827-7700.* **FAX** *(407) 827-7710.* Ceiling fans, picket fences and palm trees re-create the atmosphere of old Key West. Recreational facilities abound. 🛗 📺 🍴 ♿ *Rooms: 709*	AE MC V	●	▪	●	▪
WALT DISNEY WORLD: *Disney's Wilderness Lodge* ⓈⓈⓈ 901 W Timberline Drive, FL 32830. **Road map** E3. **☎** *(407) 824-3200.* **FAX** *(407) 824-3232.* Wind down at this isolated but romantic "mountain retreat" with wooden floors and crackling fires. 🛗 📺 **P** *Rooms: 728*	AE MC V	●	▪	●	
WALT DISNEY WORLD: *Disney's Beach Club Resort* ⓈⓈⓈⓈ 1800 Epcot Resorts Blvd, FL 32830. **Road map** E3. **☎** *(407) 934-8000.* **FAX** *(407) 934-3850.* Echoing the style of New England's grand hotels of the 1870s, this resort has exquisite rooms, extensive facilities and one of the best restaurants in Walt Disney World. 24 🛗 📺 🍴 ♿ **P** *Rooms: 538*	AE MC V	●	▪	●	
WALT DISNEY WORLD: *Disney's BoardWalk Inn* ⓈⓈⓈⓈⓈ 2101 N Epcot Resorts Blvd, FL 32830. **Road map** E3. **☎** *(407) 939-5100.* **FAX** *(407) 939-5150.* This elegant inn, with its floral rugs and hardwood floors, evokes an old-world B & B. 24 🛗 📺 🍴 ♿ **P** *Rooms: 378*	AE MC V	●	▪		
WALT DISNEY WORLD: *Disney's Contemporary Resort* ⓈⓈⓈⓈⓈ 4600 N World Drive, FL 32830. **Road map** E3. **☎** *(407) 824-1000.* **FAX** *(407) 824-3539.* A monorail ride from Epcot and the Magic Kingdom, this slick, lively resort has Deco-style rooms. 24 🛗 📺 🍴 ♿ **P** *Rooms: 1,041*	AE MC V	●	▪	●	
WALT DISNEY WORLD: *Disney's Grand Floridian Resort* ⓈⓈⓈⓈⓈ 4401 Grand Floridian Way, FL 32830. **Road map** E3. **☎** *(407) 824-3000.* **FAX** *(407) 824-3186.* Verandas, oak beds and Victorian-style opulence offer a taste of old Florida just next door to the Magic Kingdom. Enjoy total indulgence, with the host of facilities on offer. 24 🛗 📺 🍴 ♿ **P** *Rooms: 900*	AE MC V	●	▪	●	
WALT DISNEY WORLD: *Disney's Yacht Club Resort* ⓈⓈⓈⓈⓈ 1700 Epcot Resorts Blvd, FL 32830. **Road map** E3. **☎** *(407) 934-7000.* **FAX** *(407) 934-3450.* Styled like a swanky Cape Cod yacht club, with brass fittings and charts on the walls, this lavish resort shares its wide range of facilities with the adjacent Beach Club. 24 🛗 📺 🍴 ♿ **P** *Rooms: 631*	AE MC V	●	▪		
WALT DISNEY WORLD: *Walt Disney World Dolphin* ⓈⓈⓈⓈⓈ 1500 Epcot Resorts Blvd, FL 32830. **Road map** E3. **☎** *(407) 934-4000.* **FAX** *(407) 934-4099.* Architecturally arresting and close to Epcot, the urbane Dolphin caters to a business crowd. 24 🛗 📺 🍴 ♿ **P** *Rooms: 1,510*	AE DC MC V	●	▪	●	
WALT DISNEY WORLD: *Walt Disney World Swan* ⓈⓈⓈⓈⓈ 1200 Epcot Resorts Blvd, FL 32830. **Road map** E3. **☎** *(407) 934-3000.* **FAX** *(407) 934-4499.* Topped by two swans, five-storeys high, and with the swan theme found throughout, this hotel offers colourful rooms and some of the best dining in the park. 24 🛗 📺 🍴 ♿ **P** *Rooms: 758*	AE DC MC V	●	▪	●	
WALT DISNEY WORLD: *The Villas at the Disney Institute* ⓈⓈⓈⓈⓈ 1901 N Magnolia Way, FL 32830. **Road map** E3. **☎** *(407) 827-1100.* **FAX** *(407) 827-4100.* Ideal for families, this resort-cum-campus *(see p161)* has great sports and entertainment facilities. 🛗 📺 🍴 ♿ **P** *Rooms: 585*	AE MC V	●	▪	●	▪
WINTER PARK: *The Fortnightly Inn* ⓈⓈ 377 E Fairbanks Ave, FL 32789. **Road map** E2. **☎** *(407) 645-4440.* Built in 1922, this prim B & B is furnished with handsome antiques. A delicious breakfast of fresh fruit and pastries is served. 🛗 *Rooms: 5*	MC V				
WINTER PARK: *Park Plaza* ⓈⓈⓈ 307 Park Ave S, FL 32789. **Road map** E2. **☎** *(407) 647-1072.* **FAX** *(407) 647-4081.* Wooden floors and oriental rugs set the tone at this delightful hotel. Unique rooms are furnished with antique beds and wicker. 🛗 📺 **P** *Rooms: 27*	AE DC MC V			●	

THE NORTHEAST

DAYTONA BEACH: *Coquina Inn Bed & Breakfast* $$ — AE MC V
544 S Palmetto Ave, FL 32114. **Road map** E2. ((904) 254-4969.
FAX *same as telephone.* This 1912 home, on a quiet tree-lined street in the historic district, has beautifully furnished rooms with oak floors and ceiling fans. The bountiful breakfast is a delight. *Rooms: 4*

DAYTONA BEACH: *Quality Inn* $$ — AE DC MC V
1615 S Atlantic Ave, FL 32118. **Road map** E2. ((904) 255-0921. FAX (904) 255-3849.
This budget oceanfront hotel has spacious efficiencies, a sundeck, and both full-sized and kids' swimming pools. *Rooms: 195*

DAYTONA BEACH: *Bahama House* $$$ — AE DC MC V
2001 S Atlantic Ave, FL 32118. **Road map** E2. ((904) 248-2001.
FAX (904) 248-0991. This friendly Bahamas-themed establishment offers efficiencies with bleached-wood furnishings. There are daily children's activities and some units have Jacuzzis. *Rooms: 95*

DAYTONA BEACH: *Adam's Mark* $$$$ — AE DC MC V
100 N Atlantic Ave, FL 32118. **Road map** E2. ((904) 254-8200.
FAX (904) 253-0275. Overlooking the beach boardwalk, this is Daytona's most stylish resort. It has several restaurants, a health club, disco and children's playground. *Rooms: 437*

FERNANDINA BEACH: *The Bailey House* $$$ — AE MC V
28 S 7th St, FL 32034. **Road map** E1. ((904) 261-5390. FAX (904) 321-0103.
Stained glass, antique beds and fireplaces evoke a Victorian ambience at this 1895 home. A veranda complete with porch swing and rocking chairs encircles the house. Bikes are provided for exploring. *Rooms: 5*

FERNANDINA BEACH: *Amelia Island Plantation* $$$ — AE DC MC V
3000 First Coast Hwy, FL 32034. **Road map** E1. ((904) 261-6161.
FAX (904) 277-5159. At the southern end of Amelia Island, surrounded by live oak forests and towering dunes, this golf resort offers spacious rooms, condos and villas. Facilities are extensive. *Rooms: 550*

FERNANDINA BEACH: *The Amelia Island Williams House* $$$ — MC V
103 S 9th St, FL 32034. **Road map** E1. ((904) 277-2328. FAX (904) 321-1325
Rated one of the South's best B & Bs, this 1856 mansion has exquisite rooms with clawfoot baths. Priceless antiques range from 16th-century Japanese prints to a carpet owned by Napoleon. *Rooms: 8*

GAINESVILLE: *Magnolia Plantation* $$ — AE MC V
309 SE 7th St, FL 32601. **Road map** D2. ((352) 375-6653. FAX (352) 338-0303.
Decked with verandas and countless windows, this charming, antique-filled 1880s mansion offers a warm welcome. Imaginative breakfasts are served indoors or alfresco under the magnolias. *Rooms: 6*

GAINESVILLE: *Residence Inn by Marriott* $$ — AE DC MC V
4001 SW 13th St, FL 32608. **Road map** D2. ((352) 371-2101. FAX (352) 371-2101.
This centrally located inn offers airy suites with well-equipped kitchens and living areas. Some have Jacuzzis. *Rooms: 80*

JACKSONVILLE: *House on Cherry Street* $$ — AE MC V
1844 Cherry St, FL 32205. **Road map** E1. ((904) 384-1999. FAX (904) 384-5013.
This early 20th-century clapboard house provides an attractive, relaxed alternative to staying downtown (15 minutes' drive away). A porch overlooks a croquet lawn leading down to the river. *Rooms: 4*

JACKSONVILLE: *Radisson Riverwalk Hotel* $$ — AE DC MC V
1515 Prudential Drive, FL 32207. **Road map** E1. ((904) 396-5100.
FAX (904) 396-7154. Enjoy an awesome view of the St Johns River and city skyline from rooms with cheerful decor. *Rooms: 321*

JACKSONVILLE: *Omni Jacksonville Hotel* $$$ — AE DC MC V
245 Water St, FL 32202. **Road map** E1. ((904) 355-6664. FAX (904) 791-4812.
Located in the heart of downtown, this stylish hotel features good, friendly service and an excellent restaurant. *Rooms: 354*

JACKSONVILLE BEACH: *Sea Turtle Inn* $$ — AE MC V
1 Ocean Blvd, FL 32233. **Road map** E1. ((904) 249-7402. FAX (904) 247-1517.
This oceanfront inn offers great sea views from private balconies. Wake up to coffee and newspapers brought to your room. *Rooms: 194*

For key to symbols see back flap

Price categories for a standard double room per night in high season, including tax and service charges:

$ under $60
$$ $60-$100
$$$ $100-$150
$$$$ $150-$200
$$$$$ over $200

CHILDREN'S FACILITIES
A child-friendly hotel, with cots, high chairs and other facilities which may include a baby-sitting service and special children's programmes.
SWIMMING POOL
The hotel has a swimming pool for use by residents.
GOOD RESTAURANT
There is a particularly good restaurant, which is normally also accessible to non-residents.
KITCHEN FACILITIES
The hotel has rooms with cooking and other kitchen facilities, usually known as "efficiencies".

	CREDIT CARDS	CHILDREN'S FACILITIES	SWIMMING POOL	GOOD RESTAURANT	KITCHEN FACILITIES
MICANOPY: *The Herlong Mansion* $$ 402 NE Cholokka Blvd, FL 32667. **Road map** D2. (352) 466-3322. FAX *same as telephone.* Imposing columns front this splendid 1845 house set in beautiful gardens. Breakfasts are served *en famille.* **Rooms:** 12	MC V				
MOUNT DORA: *Lakeside Inn* $$$ 100 N Alexande St, FL 32757. **Road map** E2. (352) 383-4101. FAX (352) 735-2642. Built in 1883 and refurbished a century later, the tranquil Lakeside Inn is popular with anglers, bird-watchers and antique hunters. **Rooms:** 88	AE DC MC V		■	●	
OCALA: *Holiday Inn* $$ 3621 W Silver Springs Blvd, FL 34478. **Road map** D2. (352) 629-0381. FAX (352) 629-0381. Clean and comfortable, this budget inn has a heated pool, tennis courts and an exercise centre. **Rooms:** 273	AE DC MC V		■		
ORMOND BEACH: *Comfort Inn on the Beach* $$ 507 S Atlantic Ave, FL 32176. **Road map** E2. (904) 677-8550. FAX (904) 673-6260. At this beachside inn, close to restaurants and shops, the rooms are light and airy and all have ocean views. **Rooms:** 50	AE MC V		■		■
ST AUGUSTINE: *Howard Johnson Lodge* $$ 137 San Marco Ave, Fl 32084. **Road map** E1. (904) 824-6181. FAX (904) 825-2774. Close to the historic district, this hotel has spacious units, all with kitchenettes. There is a free tram to local attractions. **Rooms:** 77	AE DC MC V		■		■
ST AUGUSTINE: *Alexander Homestead* $$$ 14 Sevilla St, FL 32084. **Road map** E1. (904) 826-4147. FAX (904) 823-9503. Lace curtains and wooden floors are the motif at this 1880s home turned B & B. Guests are treated to after-dinner liqueurs. **Rooms:** 4	AE DC MC V				
ST AUGUSTINE: *Casablanca Inn Bed & Breakfast* $$$ 24 Avenida Menendez, FL 32084. **Road map** E1. (904) 829-0928. FAX (904) 824-2240. Elegantly furnished throughout, this classy B & B provides stunning bay views from private balconies, two of which are equipped with hammocks. Breakfast is unforgettable. **Rooms:** 12	AE MC V				■
ST AUGUSTINE: *Kenwood Inn Bed & Breakfast* $$$ 38 Marine St, FL 32084. **Road map** E1. (904) 824-2116. FAX (904) 824-1689. Built in the 1880s, this charming inn in the historic district has a secluded courtyard and individually decorated rooms with period features. A tasty continental breakfast is served indoors or out. **Rooms:** 12	MC V		■		
ST AUGUSTINE: *Southern Wind East* $$$ 18 Cordova St, FL 32084. **Road map** E1. (904) 825-3623. FAX (904) 825-0360. This colonnaded house has rooms decorated with period pieces and Flagler-era antiques. Breakfast is served on vintage china. **Rooms:** 10	AE MC V				

THE PANHANDLE

	CREDIT CARDS	CHILDREN'S FACILITIES	SWIMMING POOL	GOOD RESTAURANT	KITCHEN FACILITIES
APALACHICOLA: *Coombs House Inn* $$ 80 6th St, FL 32320. **Road map** B1. (904) 653-9199. FAX (352) 653-2785. In a 1905 clapboard home, this B & B comes complete with a traditional veranda and antiques. Some rooms have four-poster beds. **Rooms:** 17	AE MC V				
CEDAR KEY: *Cedar Key Bed & Breakfast* $$ 3rd and F St, FL 32625. **Road map** D2. (352) 543-9000. FAX (352) 543-8070. Gingerbread woodwork adorns this pretty 1880 home by the sea. Antiques please the eye and hearty breakfasts fill the stomach. **Rooms:** 7	MC V				
CEDAR KEY: *Island* $$ Main St, FL 32625. **Road map** D2. (352) 543-5111. FAX (352) 543-6949. This 1859 hotel has thick tabby walls (*see p282*), original wooden floors and nautical murals. Dine on the veranda in good weather. **Rooms:** 13	MC V			●	

DESTIN: *Village Inn* $$
215 Hwy 98 E, FL 32541. **Road map** A1. **(** *(904) 837-7413.* **FAX** *(904) 654-3394.*
Just over the street from Destin harbour and its fishing boats, this family-oriented motel has spacious rooms. The beaches, restaurants and shops are all within ten minutes' drive. **Rooms:** 100
Credit cards: AE DC MC V

DESTIN: *Holiday Inn* $$$
1020 Hwy 98 E, FL 32541. **Road map** A1. **(** *(904) 837-6181.* **FAX** *(904) 837-1523.*
This circular hotel gives some rooms a grand view of the Gulf. It has children's activities and a friendly staff. **Rooms:** 233
Credit cards: AE DC MC V

DESTIN: *Henderson Park Inn Bed & Breakfast* $$$$
2700 Hwy 98 E, FL 32541. **Road map** A1. **(** *(904) 654-0400.* **FAX** *(904) 654-0405.*
Pricey and quite large for a B & B, the rooms in this New England-style inn are beautiful and the breakfast is a treat. Private balconies afford views of the Gulf and the uncluttered white beach. **Rooms:** 35
Credit cards: AE MC V

FORT WALTON BEACH: *Howard Johnson Lodge* $$
314 Miracle Strip Parkway, FL 32548. **Road map** A1. **(** *(904) 243-6162.*
FAX *(904) 664-2735.* Stately oak trees fill the courtyard of this friendly lodge, 2 miles (3 km) from downtown and the beach. **Rooms:** 140
Credit cards: AE MC V

FORT WALTON BEACH: *Sheraton Inn* $$$
1325 Miracle Strip Parkway, FL 32548. **Road map** A1. **(** *(904) 243-8116.*
FAX *(904) 244-3064.* The Sheraton has large, brightly decorated rooms, many with sea views and some right on the beach. **Rooms:** 138
Credit cards: AE DC MC V

GULF BREEZE: *Holiday Inn Bay Beach* $$
51 Gulf Breeze Parkway, FL 32561. **Road map** A1. **(** *(904) 932-2214.*
FAX *(904) 932-0932.* Overlooking Pensacola Bay, this hotel offers spacious rooms and a waterfront eatery with great pastries. **Rooms:** 168
Credit cards: AE DC MC V

NAVARRE: *Comfort Inn* $$$
8680 Navarre Parkway, FL 32566. **Road map** A1. **(** *(904) 939-1761.*
FAX *(904) 939-2084.* A small, comfortable B & B inn, conveniently located across the bridge from uncrowded white beaches. **Rooms:** 63
Credit cards: AE DC MC V

PANAMA CITY BEACH: *Best Western Del Coronado* $$
11815 Front Beach Rd, FL 32407. **Road map** B1. **(** *(904) 234-1600.*
FAX *(904) 235-1645.* Smack on the Gulf, this small complex is a delight, with its friendly staff and well-furnished lodgings. **Rooms:** 100
Credit cards: AE DC MC V

PANAMA CITY BEACH: *Marriott's Bay Point Resort* $$$
4200 Marriott Drive, FL 32408. **Road map** B1. **(** *(904) 234-3307.*
FAX *(904) 233-1308.* Nestled in a quiet wildlife reserve away from the beach, the Bay Point is considered one of the country's top golf and tennis resorts. The rooms are elegantly furnished. **Rooms:** 355
Credit cards: AE DC MC V

PANAMA CITY BEACH: *Edgewater Beach Resort* $$$
11212 Front Beach Rd, FL 32407. **Road map** B1. **(** *(904) 235-4044.*
FAX *(904) 233-7529.* Tropically-themed both inside and out, this lavish sea-side resort offers condos with one, two or three bedrooms. Sports and recreational facilities are extensive. **Rooms:** 520
Credit cards: AE MC V

PENSACOLA: *Bay Breeze Bed and Breakfast* $$
1326 E Jackson St, FL 32501. **Road map** A1. **(** *(904) 470-0316.* **FAX** *(904) 470-0488.*
A white picket fence and wicker swing greet you at this immaculate B & B. The rooms, filled with period pieces and homely touches, conjure up early 20th-century charm. **Rooms:** 4
Credit cards: MC V

PENSACOLA: *Residence Inn by Marriott* $$$
7320 Plantation Rd, FL 32504. **Road map** A1. **(** *(904) 479-1000.* **FAX** *(904) 477-3399.*
This pleasant inn with spacious rooms is in a quiet area 7 miles (11 km) from downtown. Breakfast is included. **Rooms:** 64
Credit cards: AE DC MC V

PENSACOLA BEACH: *Five Flags Inn* $$
299 Fort Pickens Rd, FL 32561. **Road map** A1. **(** *(904) 932-3586.*
FAX *(904) 934-0257.* Right on the beach with all rooms overlooking the Gulf, the Five Flags is friendly and well furnished. **Rooms:** 50
Credit cards: AE MC V

PENSACOLA BEACH: *Best Western Pensacola Beach* $$$
16 Via de Luna, FL 32561. **Road map** A1. **(** *(904) 934-3300.* **FAX** *(904) 934-9780.*
This relaxed, Gulf-side hostelry has bright, airy rooms, some with marine views. A continental breakfast is included. **Rooms:** 122
Credit cards: AE DC MC V

For key to symbols see back flap

			CREDIT CARDS	**CHILDREN'S FACILITIES**	**SWIMMING POOL**	**GOOD RESTAURANT**	**KITCHEN FACILITIES**

Price categories for a standard double room per night in high season, including tax and service charges:

$ under $60
$$ $60-$100
$$$ $100-$150
$$$$ $150-$200
$$$$$ over $200

CHILDREN'S FACILITIES
A child-friendly hotel, with cots, high chairs and other facilities which may include a baby-sitting service and special children's programmes.

SWIMMING POOL
The hotel has a swimming pool for use by residents.

GOOD RESTAURANT
There is a particularly good restaurant, which is normally also accessible to non-residents.

KITCHEN FACILITIES
The hotel has rooms with cooking and other kitchen facilities, usually known as "efficiencies".

	CC	CF	SP	GR	KF
SEASIDE: *Josephine's French Country Inn* $$$$ 101 Seaside Ave, FL 32459. **Road map** B1. ☎ *(904) 231-1940.* FAX *(904) 231-2446.* Visit the unique town and stay at this 1990s, antebellum-style mansion. Antiques and lace blend imperceptibly with modern conveniences. The restaurant is a local favourite. 🔹🔹🔹🔹 *Rooms: 11*	AE MC V			●	■
TALLAHASSEE: *Ramada Inn* $$ 2900 N Monroe St, FL 32302. **Road map** C1. ☎ *(904) 386-1027.* FAX *(904) 422-1025.* Just a short drive from downtown, this efficiently-run hotel provides spacious rooms and friendly service. 🔹🔹🔹🔹 *Rooms: 200*	AE DC MC V		■		
TALLAHASSEE: *The Riedel House* $$ 1412 Fairway Drive, FL 32301. **Road map** C1. ☎ *(904) 222-8569.* This 1937 Federal-style home is within striking distance of downtown. A spiral staircase leads to an art gallery and the refined rooms. 🔹🔹 *Rooms: 3*					
TALLAHASSEE: *Governors Inn* $$$ 209 S Adams St, FL 32301. **Road map** C1. ☎ *(904) 681-6855.* FAX *(904) 222-3105.* Beams from a stable that once stood here are built into this modern inn. Some rooms have open fireplaces, all feature antiques. 🔹🔹🔹 *Rooms: 40*	AE DC MC V				

THE GULF COAST

	CC	CF	SP	GR	KF
ANNA MARIA ISLAND: *Haley's Motel and Resort Complex* $$ 8102 Gulf Drive, FL 34217. **Road map** D3. ☎ *(941) 778-5405.* FAX *(941) 778-1991.* Just a short stroll from the beach, Haley's offers either simple, comfortable one-bed efficiencies or two-bed apartments. 🔹🔹 *Rooms: 16*	AE DC MC V		■		■
CAPTIVA ISLAND: *South Seas Plantation Resort* $$$$$ 5400 Plantation Rd, FL 33924. **Road map** D4. ☎ *(941) 472-5111.* FAX *(941) 481-4947.* Once a coconut plantation, the 330 acres (130 ha) at this lavish resort contain villas, cottages, condos and hotel rooms. Countless sports facilities are also on site. 🔹🔹🔹🔹🔹 *Rooms: 600*	AE DC MC V	●	■	●	■
CLEARWATER BEACH: *Howard Johnson Express Inn* $$ 656 Bayway Blvd, FL 34630. **Road map** D3. ☎ *(813) 442-6606.* FAX *(813) 461-0809.* This small hotel is set back from the beach but overlooks the bay. It has a fishing deck, unfussy rooms and shops nearby. 🔹🔹🔹 *Rooms: 40*	AE DC MC V		■		
CLEARWATER BEACH: *Clearwater Beach* $$$ 500 Mandalay Ave, FL 34630. **Road map** D3. ☎ *(813) 441-2425.* FAX *(813) 449-2083.* Run by the same family for 40 years, this grand hotel on the Gulf offers an old-fashioned, homely atmosphere. 🔹🔹🔹🔹P 🔹 *Rooms: 210*	AE DC MC V	●	■		■
CLEARWATER BEACH: *Holiday Inn SunSpree Resort* $$$$ 715 S Gulfview Blvd, FL 34630. **Road map** D3. ☎ *(813) 447-9566.* FAX *(813) 443-7908.* At this modern, family-oriented resort, the under 12s eat free and there are activities for teenagers. 🔹🔹🔹🔹🔹 *Rooms: 205*	AE DC MC V	●	■		
DUNEDIN: *Inn on the Bay* $$ 1420 Bayshore Blvd, FL 34698. **Road map** D3. ☎ *(813) 734-7689.* FAX *(813) 734-0972.* Clean and comfortable, the accommodation here offers sweeping bay views. Breakfast is included. 🔹🔹🔹 *Rooms: 43*	AE MC V		■		■
FORT MYERS: *Sheraton Harbor Place* $$$ 2500 Edwards Drive, FL 33901. **Road map** E4. ☎ *(941) 337-0300.* FAX *(941) 337-7528.* This swish high-rise has fine views of the yacht basin and river. Downtown sights are just a walk away. 🔹🔹🔹🔹🔹 *Rooms: 419*	AE DC MC V		■		
LONGBOAT KEY: *The Resort at Longboat Key Club* $$$$$ 301 Gulf of Mexico Drive, FL 34228. **Road map** D3. ☎ *(941) 383-8821.* FAX *(941) 383-0359.* Ideal for golf and tennis, this luxurious resort has large suites with balconies overlooking the Gulf. 🔹🔹🔹🔹 *Rooms: 232*	AE DC MC V	●	■		■

ST PETERSBURG: *Beach Park Motel* $$
300 Beach Drive, FL 33701. Road map D3. 📞 *(813) 898-6325.* FAX *(813) 894-4226.*
Located downtown, with a view of the pier, this motel is ideally placed
for sightseeing. The rooms have small balconies. 🏊 ⛱ 🅿 **Rooms:** *26*
AE MC V

ST PETERSBURG: *Bayboro House* $$$
1719 Beach Drive SE, FL 33701. Road map D3. 📞 *(813) 823-4955.*
FAX *(813) 823-4955.* This gracious Queen Anne home, built in 1907 and filled
with lace and antiques, is only 2 miles (3 km) south of downtown. There's a
panoramic view of Tampa Bay from the veranda. 🏊 ⛱ **Rooms:** *4*
MC V

ST PETERSBURG: *Renaissance Vinoy Resort* $$$$$
501 5th Ave NE, FL 33701. Road map D3. 📞 *(813) 894-1000.* FAX *(813) 822-2785.*
Dating from 1925, this elegantly restored hotel offers lovely bay views
and imaginatively furnished rooms. Most downtown attractions are within
walking distance. 24 🏊 ⛱ 🍴 🅱 🅿 🅰 **Rooms:** *360*
AE DC MC V

ST PETE BEACH: *Colonial Gateway Inn* $$
6300 Gulf Blvd, FL 33706. Road map D3. 📞 *(813) 367-2711.* FAX *(813) 367-7068.*
Popular with families and right on the beach, this inn offers rooms and
efficiencies decorated with floral prints. ⛱ 🅱 🅰 **Rooms:** *200*
AE DC MC V

ST PETE BEACH: *Dolphin Beach Resort* $$$
4900 Gulf Blvd, FL 33706. Road map D3. 📞 *(813) 360-7011.* FAX *(813) 367-5909.*
Located on the ocean, the Dolphin offers sailing boats for rent, bus tours
to attractions, nightly entertainment and free parking. ⛱ 🅱 🅰 **Rooms:** *173*
AE DC MC V

ST PETE BEACH: *Don CeSar Resort and Spa* $$$$$
3400 Gulf Blvd, FL 33706. Road map D3. 📞 *(813) 360-1881.* FAX *(813) 367-7597.*
Once the haunt of the likes of Scott Fitzgerald, this 1928 Mediterranean-style
"pink palace" is breathtaking. Each room is different and the walls are
hung with original art. 24 🏊 ⛱ 🍴 🅱 🅿 🅰 **Rooms:** *277*
AE DC MC V

SANIBEL ISLAND: *Island Inn* $$$$
3111 W Gulf Drive, FL 33957. Road map E4. 📞 *(941) 472-1561.*
FAX *(941) 472-0051.* Built around 100 years ago, this inn has a genteel, old-
world air. Comfy, wicker-filled cottages and rooms overlook the Gulf.
Guests return year after year, so book well ahead. ⛱ 🅰 **Rooms:** *57*
AE MC V

SANIBEL ISLAND: *Sanibel Inn* $$$$
937 E Gulf Drive, FL 33957. Road map E4. 📞 *(941) 472-3181.* FAX *(941) 472-5234.*
With a choice of rooms or condos, this beachside inn has accommodation
to suit most needs, and offers sports facilities aplenty. 🏊 ⛱ 🅱 🅰 **Rooms:** *96*
AE DC MC V

SANIBEL ISLAND: *Sanibel's Seaside Inn* $$$$$
541 E Gulf Drive, FL 33957. Road map E4. 📞 *(941) 472-1400.* FAX *(941) 481-4947.*
In a peaceful location, right on the shell-strewn beach, this "olde Florida"
inn has a choice of brightly decorated accommodation from rooms to
cottages. Bicycles are available for island exploration. ⛱ 🅰 **Rooms:** *32*
AE DC MC V

SARASOTA: *Best Western Golden Host Resort* $$
4675 N Tamiami Trail, FL 34234. Road map D3. 📞 *(941) 355-5141.*
FAX *(941) 355-9286.* The resort is set in lovely tropical grounds, close to local
attractions and the beach. Breakfast is included. 🏊 ⛱ 🅰 **Rooms:** *80*
AE DC MC V

SARASOTA: *Wellesley Inn* $$
1803 N Tamiami Trail, FL 34234. Road map D3. 📞 *(941) 366-5128.*
FAX *(941) 953-4322.* This friendly inn just north of downtown overlooks
a marina. The rooms are colourful and airy. 🏊 ⛱ 🅱 🏈 **Rooms:** *106*
AE DC MC V

SARASOTA: *Hyatt Sarasota* $$$$
1000 Blvd of the Arts, FL 34236. Road map D3. 📞 *(941) 953-1234.*
FAX *(813) 952-1987.* This bayfront hotel is convenient for downtown
Sarasota. Most rooms have balconies. 🏊 ⛱ 🍴 🅱 🅿 🅰 **Rooms:** *297*
AE DC MC V

TAMPA: *Days Inn* $$
2522 N Dale Mabry Hwy, FL 33607. Road map D3. 📞 *(813) 877-6181.*
FAX *(813) 875-6171.* Situated between downtown and the airport, this motel
offers comfortable rooms. Breakfast is included. 🏊 🅱 🏈 🅰 **Rooms:** *285*
AE DC MC V

TAMPA: *Gram's Place* $$
3109 N Ola Ave, FL 33603. Road map D3. 📞 *(813) 221-0596.* FAX *same as telephone.*
Basically a pub with rooms, this music-filled B & B is promoted as an artists'
retreat. It attracts a bohemian gay and straight crowd. 24 🏈 🅰 **Rooms:** *6*
AE MC V

Price categories for a standard double room per night in high season, including tax and service charges:

$ under $60
$$ $60-$100
$$$ $100-$150
$$$$ $150-$200
$$$$$ over $200

CHILDREN'S FACILITIES
A child-friendly hotel, with cots, high chairs and other facilities which may include a baby-sitting service and special children's programmes.

SWIMMING POOL
The hotel has a swimming pool for use by residents.

GOOD RESTAURANT
There is a particularly good restaurant, which is normally also accessible to non-residents.

KITCHEN FACILITIES
The hotel has rooms with cooking and other kitchen facilities, usually known as "efficiencies".

	CREDIT CARDS	CHILDREN'S FACILITIES	SWIMMING POOL	GOOD RESTAURANT	KITCHEN FACILITIES
TAMPA: *Holiday Inn Select Downtown* $$$ 111 W Fortune St, FL 33602. **Road map** D3. **(** (813) 223-1351. **FAX** (813) 221-2000. On the Hillsborough River downtown, within walking distance of most attractions, this is a modern hotel with large rooms. 🔲 🔲 🔲 *Rooms: 311*	AE DC MC V		▦		
TAMPA: *Hyatt Regency Westshore* $$$$ 6200 Courtney Campbell Causeway, FL 33607. **Road map** D3. **(** (813) 874-1234. **FAX** (813) 281-9168. Secluded on a bayside nature reserve, this slick hotel has airy rooms overlooking the sea. 🔲 🔲 🔲 🔲 🔲 *Rooms: 445*	AE DC MC V	●	▦	●	
TAMPA: *Wyndham Harbour Island Hotel* $$$$$ 725 S Harbour Island Blvd, FL 33602. **Road map** D3. **(** (813) 229-5000. **FAX** (813) 229-5322. On an island overlooking the river mouth, this exclusive hotel is linked to downtown Tampa by the Peoplemover *(see p244)*. Dark wood and floral fabrics in the rooms. 24 🔲 🔲 🔲 🔲 🔲 *Rooms: 300*	AE DC MC V	●	▦		
TARPON SPRINGS: *Spring Bayou Inn* $$ 34 W Tarpon Ave, FL 34689. **Road map** D3. **(** (813) 938-9333. Built in 1905, this homely B & B has wooden floors and an eclectic mix of furnishings, which includes antiques. 🔲 🔲 *Rooms: 5*					
VENICE: *The Banyan House* $$ 519 S Harbor Drive, FL 34285. **Road map** D4. **(** (941) 484-1385. **FAX** (941) 484-8032. A grand old Mediterranean-style home, this B & B has splendid Victorian furnishings and high, beamed ceilings. 🔲 🔲 🔲 🔲 *Rooms: 9*			▦		▦
VENICE: *Best Western Venice Resort* $$$ 455 US 41 Bypass N, FL 34292. **Road map** D4. **(** (941) 485-5411. **FAX** (941) 484-6193. A buffet dinner, Broadway-style show and relaxed atmosphere put this Best Western a cut above the rest. 🔲 🔲 *Rooms: 160*	AE DC MC V		▦		
THE EVERGLADES AND THE KEYS					
BIG PINE KEY: *Barnacle Bed and Breakfast* $$$ 1557 Long Beach Drive, FL 33043. **Road map** E5. **(** (305) 872-3298. **FAX** (305) 872-3863. Swamped by lush foliage, this architectural delight has a rooftop sundeck. One room faces the private beach. 🔲 🔲 🔲 *Rooms: 4*	MC V				▦
ISLAMORADA: *Breezy Palms Resort* $$ MM 80, Overseas Hwy, FL 33036. **Road map** F5. **(** (305) 664-2361. **FAX** (305) 664-2572. Sunny rooms and apartments are dotted around the grounds of this resort, which has its own moorings. 🔲 🔲 🔲 *Rooms: 40*	AE MC V		▦		▦
ISLAMORADA: *Cheeca Lodge* $$$$$ MM 82, Overseas Hwy, FL 33036. **Road map** F5. **(** (305) 664-4651. **FAX** (305) 664-2893. This tranquil low-rise resort offers a plethora of seaside activities for both kids and adults. Bamboo-furnished rooms include subtle touches such as hand-painted mirror frames. 🔲 🔲 🔲 🔲 🔲 🔲 *Rooms: 203*	AE DC MC V	●	▦		▦
KEY LARGO: *Holiday Inn* $$$$ MM 100, Overseas Hwy, FL 33037. **Road map** F5. **(** (305) 451-2121. **FAX** (305) 451-5592. Located close to fishing boats and maritime attractions, this pretty resort has bright, modern rooms. 🔲 🔲 🔲 🔲 🔲 *Rooms: 132*	AE DC MC V	●	▦		·
KEY LARGO: *Sheraton Key Largo Resort* $$$$ MM 97, Overseas Hwy, FL 33037. **Road map** F5. **(** (305) 852-5553. **FAX** (305) 852-8669. Hidden in a grove of trees crossed by nature trails, this resort has rooms with private balconies. 24 🔲 🔲 🔲 🔲 🔲 🔲 *Rooms: 200*	AE DC MC V	●	▦		
KEY WEST: *Key West International Youth Hostel* $ 718 South St, FL 33040. **Road map** E5. **(** (305) 296-5719. **FAX** (305) 296-0672. At this simple but well-maintained hostel, the cosmopolitan backpacking crowd have the use of pool tables and rented bicycles. *Beds: 80*	MC V				▦

KEY WEST: *Wicker Guesthouse* $$$ AE DC MC V
913 Duval St, FL 33040. **Road map** E5. ☎ (305) 296-4275. FAX (305) 294-7240.
This friendly complex of new and restored houses in the historic district has a range of rooms and spacious suites. 🌣 🛈 *Rooms: 19*

KEY WEST: *La Pensione* $$$ AE DC MC V
809 Truman Ave, FL 33040. **Road map** E5. ☎ (305) 292-9923. FAX (305) 296-6509.
Built in 1891 by a local cigar family, this gracious house has unfussy rooms with firm beds and no phone or TV; for some an added bonus. 🛈 *Rooms: 9*

KEY WEST: *La Te Da (La Terraza)* $$$ AE MC V
1125 Duval St, FL 33040. **Road map** E5. ☎ (305) 296-6706. FAX (305) 296-0438.
Famous for its drag shows and Sunday tea dance, centrally located La Te Da provides plush lodgings for its largely gay clientele. 🛁 🛈 *Rooms: 16*

KEY WEST: *Nancy's William Street Guesthouse* $$$ AE DC MC V
329 William St, FL 33040. **Road map** E5. ☎ (305) 292-3334. FAX (305) 296-1740.
Beautifully renovated, this Key West home is furnished with wicker and antiques. The two rooms and four apartments have outside access and descendants of Hemingway's cats frequent the garden. 🌣 🛈 *Rooms: 6*

KEY WEST: *Southernmost Motel* $$$ AE MC V
1319 Duval St, FL 33040. **Road map** E5. ☎ (305) 296-6577. FAX (305) 294-8272.
Within walking distance of the Old Town, this motel is always busy. It has beautiful tropical rooms with balconies. 🌣 🛁 🛈 *Rooms: 127*

KEY WEST: *Curry Mansion Inn* $$$$$ AE DC MC V
511 Caroline St, FL 33040. **Road map** E5. ☎ (305) 294-5349. FAX (305) 294-4093.
This historic house, just off Duval Street, is also a museum *(see p284)*. Most rooms are in a lovely annexe and very comfortable. 🌣 🛁 🛏 🛈 *Rooms: 28*

KEY WEST: *Holiday Inn La Concha* $$$$$ AE DC MC V
430 Duval St, FL 33040. **Road map** E5. ☎ (305) 296-2991. FAX (305) 294-3283.
Mentioned by Hemingway and once home to Tennessee Williams, this 1925 hotel is a local landmark. The rooms have original features and the rooftop affords some of the best views in town. 🌣 🖼 🛁 🛈 *Rooms: 160*

KEY WEST: *Marriott's Casa Marina Resort* $$$$$ AE DC MC V
1500 Reynolds St, FL 33040. **Road map** E5. ☎ (305) 296-3535. FAX (305) 296-4633.
Built in the 1920s by Henry Flagler, Key West's first grand hotel is set in beautiful grounds. Opulent public areas lead to relatively simple rooms, many with balconies facing the sea. 🌣 🖼 🍴 🛁 P 🛈 *Rooms: 311*

MARATHON: *Faro Blanco Marine Resort* $$$ AE MC V
MM 48.5, Overseas Hwy, FL 33050. **Road map** E5. ☎ (305) 743-9018.
FAX (305) 743-2918. Choose from 1950s garden cottages, houseboats, as well as lighthouse apartments and condos at this relaxing resort. 🖼 🛏 *Rooms: 144*

MARCO ISLAND: *Boat House Motel* $$$ AE MC V
1180 Edington Place, FL 34145. **Road map** E4. ☎ (941) 642-2400.
FAX (941) 642-2435. Situated in the old town, beside the river, this comfortable motel has a variety of rooms and a two-bedroom cottage. There are picnic tables and barbecue grills. 🖼 🛏 🛈 *Rooms: 20*

NAPLES: *Beachcomber Club* $$ AE MC V
290 5th Ave S, FL 34102. **Road map** E4. ☎ (941) 262-8112. FAX (941) 263-2299.
This quiet motel is just a stone's throw from both the old town and the beach. It offers one- and two-bedroom apartments. *Rooms: 69*

NAPLES: *Inn By The Sea* $$$ AE MC V
287 11th Ave S, FL 34102. **Road map** E4. ☎ (941) 649-4124.
Patchwork quilts, pine floors and wicker fill this 1937 clapboard home, two blocks from the beach in the heart of Old Naples. 🌣 🛈 *Rooms: 5*

NAPLES: *Vanderbilt Beach Motel* $$$ AE MC V
9225 Gulfshore Drive N, FL 34108. **Road map** E4. ☎ (941) 597-3144.
FAX (941) 597-2199. The Vanderbilt is a small, friendly inn on the beach with both rooms and suites. Breakfast is complimentary. 🖼 🛈 *Rooms: 66*

NAPLES: *The Registry Resort* $$$$$ AE DC MC V
475 Seagate Drive, FL 34103. **Road map** E4. ☎ (941) 597-3232.
FAX (941) 597-3147. This deluxe resort caters to families and has an excellent children's programme and the best Sunday brunch in town. The beach is a stroll away through the mangroves. 🕘 🌣 🖼 🍴 🛁 P 🛈 *Rooms: 474*

WHERE TO EAT

FAST FOOD IS as much a staple here as anywhere in the US, but the joy of Florida is the abundant fresh produce, from tropical fruit to seafood, which restaurants of every description use to great effect. Fierce competition also helps to ensure that food is usually of both excellent quality and good value. Restaurants cater to every palate and budget, from the trendy establishments in Miami, which set or follow the latest

Sign of the Green Turtle Inn *(see p328)*

culinary fashions, to simpler places in the interior, where the food tends to be more homely and traditional. Wherever you are, the most enjoyable meals are often to be had in the most down-to-earth local restaurants. The restaurants listed on pages 316–29 are recommended for their quality of food, service and value for money. Cafés and bars, for drinking and more informal eating, are listed separately on pages 330–31.

The restaurant at South Beach's Art Deco Cardozo Hotel *(see p61)*

TYPES OF RESTAURANTS

FLORIDA'S SMARTEST restaurants, mostly located in cities or attached to resort hotels, tend to serve European (often French) or elaborate regional cuisine. A breed of innovative chefs has combined Florida's fine local produce with zesty Caribbean flavours to create what people call New Florida or "Floribbean" cuisine. This kind of food is also served in smaller, more casual bistro-style restaurants, which are very popular and whose menus often change daily.

Miami and the cities of the Gold and Gulf coasts have a good reputation for their restaurants. The quality of the food in Walt Disney World is also well regarded.

Miami is home to the state's greatest concentration of ethnic restaurants and cafés. Here, you can eat your way around

the world from Asia to Europe and the Caribbean. Florida has the United States' best choice of Hispanic food, which you can eat anywhere from a cheap diner to a formal supper club.

Restaurants of every size and shape serve seafood. In one Florida institution, the "raw bar", you can enjoy deliciously fresh raw oysters or clams and steamed shrimp.

EATING HOURS

URBAN DWELLERS like to eat out, even for breakfast. This is an especially popular tradition on Sundays, when a leisurely brunch, often served buffet-style, can be taken from around 10am to 2pm.

On weekdays lunch is eaten from noon to 2:30pm and supper from 6pm onwards. Away from the resorts and buzzing districts like South Beach in Miami, where many people prefer to dine at around 11pm, Floridians tend to eat early – usually between 7 and 9pm.

RESERVATIONS

TO AVOID disappointment, it is wise to reserve a table, especially at weekends or at the more up-market or popular restaurants. At some places, like Joe's Stone Crab in South Beach *(see p316)*, you cannot book ahead and instead must wait in line for a table.

TIPS ON EATING OUT

DINING OUT in Florida is mostly an informal affair. Very few restaurants require a jacket and tie, and those that do normally provide jackets for diners without. "Casual but neat" is the general rule.

All restaurants have separate areas for smokers and non-smokers. If you book ahead, you will often be asked which section you'd prefer; if not, be sure to specify.

Tips range from 15 to 20 per cent. At sophisticated places, diners frequently tip the higher amount if the service has

The informal surroundings of the Blue Desert Café, Cedar Key *(see p325)*

been exceptionally good. The state sales tax of 6 per cent will be added to your bill automatically.

Dollar travellers' cheques and credit cards are accepted in most restaurants, but neighbourhood diners, fast food chains, coffee shops and delis tend to accept only cash.

VEGETARIAN FOOD

VEGETARIANS WHO eat fish and seafood will have no problem at all in Florida. The rest, however, will often scour menus in vain for meat- and fish-free dishes. Unless you encounter one of the few truly vegetarian restaurants, prepare yourself for a diet in which salads, pasta dishes and pizzas will feature strongly.

McGuire's Irish Pub in Pensacola, serving food as well as beer (*see p326*)

Cheap eats at a picnic site in one of Florida's state parks

DINING ON A BUDGET

THERE ARE SEVERAL easy ways to cut your food budget. Firstly, as a rule, helpings in America are huge, so order less than you would normally; an appetizer is often enough for a light meal. Diners can also share dishes, though there is usually a small charge for this.

All-you-can eat buffets are good value, and some restaurants have cheaper meals on a "prix-fixe" menu. In addition, "early bird" menus or specials feature set meals at a reduced price for those who eat early, usually from 5 to 6pm: these are a great boon for families. In this way, a full meal can be discounted by up to 35 per cent. Check the listings for restaurants which offer early bird specials: call ahead for

details since the times and conditions usually vary.

It is cheaper to eat out at lunchtime than in the evening if you want to do so in a smart restaurant. Hotel dining, however, is always pricey. For breakfast, for example, you'd do well to join the locals in a nearby deli or diner for what is likely to be a much livelier and probably superior meal.

Bars often serve reasonably priced food, and during happy hour many serve tapas-style snacks – enough for a meal if you aren't feeling ravenous.

Some restaurants, especially in the Keys, will cook your own fish for a reduced price. Also, many state parks have barbecues where you can grill your catch or whatever food you care to bring along. Delis and supermarkets are good for picnic provisions; delis also have great cooked dishes and sandwiches which you can eat on or off the premises.

MENUS

MENUS IN FLORIDA, as in other US restaurants, list appetizers (starters), followed by entrées (main courses) and then desserts. Some of the ingredients or preparations listed may be unfamiliar. "Aged" beef, for example, is tender prime meat with a distinctive nutty flavour, while "surf 'n' turf" describes a combination of seafood and meat, usually steak and lobster. "Dolphin" refers to *mahi-mahi*, a white-fleshed fish, not the mammal, and note that in the United States prawns are known as

shrimps. Fish or any other food that is "blackened" has been covered with cajun-style spices and cooked in a smoking-hot pan. "Broiled" food, most often meat, has been grilled.

If you're unsure of what anything is, staff will be pleased to help: it's all part of the service.

CHILDREN

MOST RESTAURANTS are happy to accommodate the needs of younger diners. Some places provide small portions at about half the regular price, while others have special menus featuring child-sized meals of things kids like to eat such as hot dogs and fries. Some also provide highchairs or booster chairs; call ahead to check what is available.

Children are not allowed in bars, but if food is served on the premises they can accompany adults and have a meal in an area away from the bar.

Jaws hot dog stand at Keaton Beach in the Panhandle

What to Eat in Florida

Hot sauce

THE FOOD IN FLORIDA is more culturally diverse than in any other US state – above all in south Florida, where the Latin American and Caribbean influence is strong. In the north, where links to the Southern states run deep, more homely meals feature staples such as cornbread and black-eyed beans. Thanks to the state's long coastline you can enjoy fine fresh fish and seafood wherever you are, and Florida's benign climate means that fresh fruit and vegetables are available all year. For tips on interpreting a Florida menu see page 313.

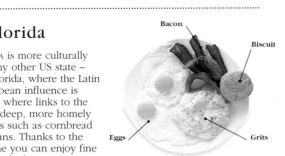

Bacon

Biscuit

Eggs

Grits

Southern Breakfast
A classic breakfast includes grits, a corn porridge best served with lots of butter and black pepper.

Crab cakes

Spicy "red" sauce

Conch fritters

Gator bites

Fritters
Anything from shrimp to alligator can be fried in batter, ready for dipping in a spicy sauce.

Conch Chowder
This creamy soup is made with a giant sea snail, or conch – a popular ingredient in Florida. Other seafood may also be used.

Melted butter

Mustard sauce

Stone Crab Claws
Served chilled, usually as a starter, the claws are the only part of the stone crab to be eaten. They are harvested from October to April.

U-Peel Shrimp
This simple dish consists of prawns cooked in a spicy broth. They are peeled and eaten with the fingers, ideally with a glass of cold beer.

Hush puppies

Black-eyed bean salad

Fish fried in batter

Sweet potato

Ribs
Spicy, barbecued ribs, usually served with fries, are best when gnawed directly off the bone.

Heart of palm salad

Hush Puppies
Southern-style cornmeal fritters are eaten primarily in the Panhandle, traditionally with fried catfish.

Seared Tuna
Tuna is served here New Florida style, with a mango salsa and grilled chayote, a kind of squash.

Chicken Tropicana
This sautéed chicken dish comes with a tropical fruit sauce, coconut and cashews.

Jerk Pork
Marinaded pork served with roasted corn on the cob is a classic Caribbean meal.

Key Lime Pie
Filled with a tangy custard flavoured with Florida's own tiny key lime, this is the most famous dessert in the state.

FLORIDA FRUITS

Tropical and citrus fruits are grown in lush abundance in Florida. They are used in both sweet and savoury dishes, but are perhaps best when served unadorned in fruit salads or when whipped up with ice to make shakes.

Star fruit

Kiwi fruit

Rice Pudding
Sweet, creamy and enriched with nutmeg and lemon, this homely dessert is popular in city diners and cafés.

Kumquat

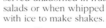

Lime

Orange   Papaya   Fruit shake

HISPANIC FOOD

Menus in all kinds of establishments, from smart restaurants to no-frills diners, reflect the spread of Latin American dishes, above all those of Cuban origin, into Florida's mainstream cuisine: the Cuban sandwich, filled with generous amounts of cheese, ham and pork, and *moros y cristianos* ("Moors and Christians", after the white rice and black beans) are seen everywhere; more unusual combinations such as the guava and cheese dessert are found only in the most authentic restaurants.

Cuban sandwich

Strong, sweet café cubano

Flan, crème caramel Hispanic style

Moros y cristianos (rice and beans)

Vaca frita (fried beef)

Fried plantains

Tomato relish

Moros y cristianos, *vaca frita* (literally "fried cow") and fried plantains – a classic Cuban combination

Guava paste with white cheese, an acquired taste

Choosing a Restaurant

THE RESTAURANTS in this guide have been selected for their good value or exceptional food. This chart highlights some of the factors which may influence your choice, such as the style of food and whether you can opt to eat outdoors. Entries are alphabetical within each price category. Information on cafés and bars is given on pages 330–31.

	CREDIT CARDS	CHILDREN'S FACILITIES	EARLY BIRD SPECIALS	GOOD REGIONAL CUISINE	BAR
MIAMI					
MIAMI BEACH: *Charlotte's Chinese Kitchen* $ 1403 Washington Ave. **Map** 2 E3. **(** *(305) 672-8338.* A small storefront Chinese restaurant offering the best Chinese food in the area at budget prices. Try the sesame chicken. ● *Sun L.*	MC V				
MIAMI BEACH: *11th Street Diner* $ 1065 Washington Ave. **Map** 2 E3. **(** *(305) 534-6373.* This top-notch 24-hour diner occupies a 1948 steel dining car. Dynamic staff serve both traditional food (try the key lime pie) and more modern dishes.	AE MC V	●	▬		▬
MIAMI BEACH: *MoJazz Café* $ 928 71st St. **(** *(305) 867-0950.* The grill in the MoJazz Club *(see p94)* serves tasty Southwestern food including great appetizers for sharing. **V �️ ♫** ● *Mon, Tue; public hols.*	MC V				▬
MIAMI BEACH: *Puerta Sagua* $ 700 Collins Ave. **Map** 2 E4. **(** *(305) 673-1115.* Serving staples like black beans, rice and plantain, this diner is nothing fancy but offers tasty Cuban cuisine in an informal atmosphere.	AE DC MC V				
MIAMI BEACH: *Woolfies* $ 2038 Collins Ave. **Map** 2 E4. **(** *(305) 538-6626.* A well-known deli, in business since 1947, where characterful waitresses dispense good-sized portions of New York Jewish food 24 hours a day.	DC MC V	●	▬		
MIAMI BEACH: *Stephan's Gourmet Market and Café* $$ 1430 Washington Ave. **Map** 2 E3. **(** *(305) 674-1760.* Downstairs, a glorious Italian deli has delicious food to take away or to eat at sidewalk tables; upstairs is a tiny, simple restaurant frequented by locals.	AE DC MC V		▬		
MIAMI BEACH: *Tap Tap* $$ 819 5th St. **Map** 2 E4. **(** *(305) 672-2898.* Serving real Haitian food such as grilled conch with manioc and prawns in coconut sauce, this unusual restaurant attracts a vibrant, multicultural crowd. Inside are stunning murals and sculpture. **�️ 🚃 ♫** ● *Aug–Sep.*	AE DC MC V				▬
MIAMI BEACH: *Astor Place Bar and Grill* $$$ 956 Washington Ave. **Map** 2 E3. **(** *(305) 672-7217.* One of the in-places of South Beach, this up-and-coming restaurant features modern dishes such as corn-crusted yellowtail snapper. **P �️ 🚃 ♫** *Sun.*	AE DC MC V			●	▬
MIAMI BEACH: *Bang* $$$ 1516 Washington Ave. **Map** 2 E2. **(** *(305) 531-2361.* This bistro throngs with a trendy, youthful clientele and offers candle-light dining and contemporary dishes with ethnic flavours. **V �️**	AE DC MC V			●	
MIAMI BEACH: *A Fish Called Avalon* $$$ Avalon Hotel, 700 Ocean Drive. **Map** 2 E4. **(** *(305) 532-1727.* In the heart of the Art Deco district, this seafood grill is known for its delicious Floribbean cuisine and lively atmosphere. **P �️ 🚃 ♫** ● *L.*	AE DC MC V		▬	●	▬ ·
MIAMI BEACH: *The Forge* $$$ 432 Arthur Godfrey Rd. **(** *(305) 538-8533.* Celebrities abound at this Miami Beach landmark. Its glitzy decor has opulent American food to match; the desserts are sublime and The Forge boasts the longest wine list in the city. **P V �️ 🚃 ♫** ● *Mon–Sat L.*	AE MC V			●	▬
MIAMI BEACH: *Joe's Stone Crab* $$$ 227 Biscayne St. **Map** 2 E5. **(** *(305) 673-0365.* This Miami institution is a must. There's lobster, prawns and fish as well as the signature stone crab claws. **P V �️** ● *Sun & Mon L; May–Aug L; Sep–mid-Oct.*	AE DC MC V			●	▬

<table>
<tr><td rowspan="2">

Price categories include a three-course meal for one, a glass of house wine and all unavoidable extras including service and tax.
$ under $20
$$ $20–30
$$$ $30–45
$$$$ $45–60
$$$$$ over $60

</td><td rowspan="2">

CREDIT CARDS
Indicates which credit cards are accepted: AE American Express; DC Diners Club; MC MasterCard; V VISA.
CHILDREN'S FACILITIES
Small portions and highchairs available, and there may also be a special children's menu.
EARLY BIRD SPECIALS
Meals offered at a discounted price if you eat early, usually before 7pm.
GOOD REGIONAL CUISINE
Florida specialities, such as seafood or dishes with Hispanic or Caribbean influence.

</td></tr>
</table>

	CREDIT CARDS	CHILDREN'S FACILITIES	EARLY BIRD SPECIALS	GOOD REGIONAL CUISINE	BAR
MIAMI BEACH: *Osteria del Teatro* $$$ 1443 Washington Ave. **Map** 2 F3. **(** *(305) 538-7850.* This Italian restaurant serves traditional and more modern dishes, such as crab-stuffed ravioli with lobster sauce. Book ahead. **P V Y ●** *L.*	AE DC MC V			●	
MIAMI BEACH: *The Raleigh Restaurant* $$$ Raleigh Hotel, 1775 Collins Ave. **Map** 2 F2. **(** *(305) 534-1775.* Meals here range from spa food for the diet conscious through Floribbean dishes to simpler supper fare of old family favourites. Eat in the elegant dining room or on the terrace overlooking the pool. **P Y 📻 ●** *Mon & Tue D.*	AE DC MC V			●	▦
MIAMI BEACH: *YUCA* $$$ 501 Lincoln Rd. **Map** 2 E2. **(** *(305) 532-9822.* YUCA, an acronym for "young upwardly mobile Cuban Americans" earns rave reviews for its Nuevo Cubano cuisine. Traditional dishes with new twists include sweet plantain stuffed with dried, cured beef. **Y 📻 ♫**	AE MC V			●	▦
MIAMI BEACH: *Blue Door* $$$$ Delano Hotel, 1685 Collins Ave. **Map** 2 F2. **(** *(305) 674-6400.* A highly sophisticated and expensive restaurant co-owned by Madonna, where deft waiters in cream uniforms serve daring, modern cuisine. **P 📻**	AE DC MC V	●		●	▦
MIAMI BEACH: *China Grill* $$$$ 404 Washington Ave. **Map** 2 E4. **(** *(305) 534-2211.* Gathering flavours and techniques from around the globe, this place serves world cuisine in a futuristic setting. Sake and vodka bar. **P Y ●** *Sat & Sun L.*	AE DC MC V			●	▦
MIAMI BEACH: *Pacific Time* $$$$ 915 Lincoln Rd. **Map** 2 E2. **(** *(305) 534-5979.* The menu changes daily at this pleasant eatery. Recipes use inspired combinations of Pacific Rim and Caribbean flavours for a unique cuisine. Vegetarians are well catered for. **V Y 📻 ●** *L; 25 Dec.*	AE DC MC V		▦	●	▦
MIAMI BEACH: *Steak House at the Fontainebleau Hilton* $$$$ 4441 Collins Ave. **(** *(305) 538-2000.* Perfect for a romantic dinner, this up-market steakhouse produces out-standing seafood and pasta. Candlelight, soft music, superb service. **P Y**	AE DC MC V			●	▦
DOWNTOWN: *S & S Restaurant* $ 1757 NE 2nd Ave. **Map** 4 E1. **(** *(305) 373-4291.* A no-frills diner serving a good selection of staple American dishes around a counter. Specials include pot roast and meat loaf. **●** *Sun.*					
DOWNTOWN: *East Coast Fisheries* $$ 360 W Flagler St. **Map** 4 D1. **(** *(305) 372-1300.* This riverside restaurant has a huge choice of fresh fish and seafood, cooked any way you like. It's very popular, so book ahead. **P 📻**	AE MC V	●			
DOWNTOWN: *Las Tapas* $$ Bayside Marketplace, 401 Biscayne Blvd. **Map** 4 F1. **(** *(305) 372-2737.* A large Spanish restaurant featuring traditional tapas (and some with a Florida twist), as well as more substantial meals such as paella and roast pork with black beans. Attractive decor, laid-back atmosphere. **Y 📻 ♫**	AE DC MC V	●			▦
DOWNTOWN: *The Fish Market* $$$ Crowne Plaza Hotel, 1601 Biscayne Blvd. **(** *(305) 374-0000.* One of Miami's best kept secrets, this seafood restaurant, decorated with mirrors and marble, serves excellent Floribbean seafood. **P Y ●** *Sat L; Sun.*	AE DC MC V			●	▦
DOWNTOWN: *The Royal Palm Court* $$$ Inter-Continental Hotel, 100 Chopin Plaza. **Map** 4 F2. **(** *(305) 577-1000.* Try the value-for-money buffets served at lunch and dinner, or one of the filling pasta dishes. Popular with the locals. **P Y**	AE DC MC V	●		●	▦

Price categories include a three-course meal for one, a glass of house wine and all unavoidable extras including service and tax.
[$] under $20
[$][$] $20–30
[$][$][$] $30–45
[$][$][$][$] $45–60
[$][$][$][$][$] over $60

Credit Cards
Indicates which credit cards are accepted: AE American Express; DC Diners Club; MC MasterCard; V VISA.

Children's Facilities
Small portions and highchairs available, and there may also be a special children's menu.

Early Bird Specials
Meals offered at a discounted price if you eat early, usually before 7pm.

Good Regional Cuisine
Florida specialities, such as seafood or dishes with Hispanic or Caribbean influence.

Restaurant	Credit Cards	Children's Facilities	Early Bird Specials	Good Regional Cuisine	Bar
Little Havana: *La Carreta I* [$] 3632 SW 8th St. ☎ *(305) 444-7501.* From its menu to its clientele, this popular family restaurant is thoroughly Cuban. Come for good food and good fun: La Carreta draws a fine crowd on weekend nights. Open 24 hours a day. 🍷	AE DC MC V	●		●	●
Little Havana: *Versailles* [$] 3555 SW 8th St. ☎ *(305) 445-7614.* Little Havana's most famous restaurant is as vast as its menu and portions. You'll find every Cuban speciality imaginable, though some dishes are a bit stodgy. The atmosphere is informal and welcoming to non-Cubans. 🍷	AE DC MC V	●			
Little Havana: *Casa Juancho* [$][$] 2436 SW 8th St. ☎ *(305) 642-2452.* Deservedly famous for its superlative Spanish cuisine, this restaurant is very popular with Miami's Hispanic community. The decor evokes rural Spain and troubadours entertain in the evenings. [P] 🍷 ⛱ ♫	AE MC V	●			●
Coral Gables: *John Martin's* [$] 253 Miracle Mile. **Map** 6 C1. ☎ *(305) 445-3777.* A lovely dining room, charming hospitality and good food (including a few Irish dishes) make this a local favourite. 🍷 ♫ *Tue, Sat & Sun.* ⬤ *25 Dec.*	AE DC MC V	●			●
Coral Gables: *La Bussola Ristorante* [$][$][$] 264 Giralda Ave. **Map** 6 C1. ☎ *(305) 445-8783.* A gracious restaurant serving Italian fare such as gnocchi and pasta. The fabulous desserts are recommended. [P] 🍷 ♫ *Tue–Sat.* ⬤ *Sat & Sun L; 25 Dec.*	AE DC MC V				●
Coral Gables: *Caffè Abbracci* [$][$][$] 318 Aragon Ave. **Map** 6 C1. ☎ *(305) 441-0700.* This café serves tempting north Italian dishes. Innovative pastas, grilled goose liver and fried calamari are house specialities. 🍷 [P] ⬤ *Sat & Sun L.*	AE DC MC V	●			●
Coral Gables: *Christy's* [$][$][$] 3101 Ponce de Leon Blvd. **Map** 6 C2. ☎ *(305) 446-1400.* A very popular steak house featuring succulent beef and seafood in a club-like setting. A tasty Caesar salad accompanies each entrée. 🍷 ⬤ *Sat–Sun L.*	AE DC MC V				●
Coral Gables: *Restaurant St Michel* [$][$][$] Hotel St Michel, 162 Alcazar Ave. **Map** 6 C1. ☎ *(305) 446-6572.* New American cuisine with a Caribbean zing is dished up in this delightfully French environment. Specialities include sesame-coated tuna. [V] 🍷 ⛱ ♫	AE DC MC V		●	●	●
Coral Gables: *Il Ristorante* [$][$][$][$] 1200 Anastasia Ave. **Map** 6 A2. ☎ *(305) 445-1926.* Located in the Biltmore Hotel, this restaurant has a tempting array of dishes. Great for Sunday brunch or a romantic dinner. [V] 🍷 [P] ♫ ⬤ *L.*	AE DC MC V			●	●
Coconut Grove: *Café Tu Tu Tango* [$][$] CocoWalk, 3015 Grand Ave. **Map** 6 E4. ☎ *(305) 529-2222.* This lively informal café has a tapas-style menu; order a few light snacks or one more substantial dish. Great for people-watching. [V] 🍷 ⛱ ♫	AE DC MC V	●		●	●
Coconut Grove: *Cheesecake Factory* [$][$] CocoWalk, 3015 Grand Ave. **Map** 6 E4. ☎ *(305) 447-9898.* A taste of California in Miami, offering a vast menu from burgers to pasta and over 30 types of cheesecake. Special Sunday brunch menu. [V] 🍷 ⬤ *25 Dec.*	AE DC MC V	●			●
Coconut Grove: *Señor Frog's* [$][$] 3008 Grand Ave. **Map** 6 E4. ☎ *(305) 448-0999.* Expect traditional food at this Mexican eatery. Only fresh produce is used and sauces are prepared daily. Try the sizzling *fajitas*, stuffed *enchiladas* or one of the unusual savoury chocolate *mole* dishes. [V] 🍷 ⛱ ♫ *Fri & Sat.*	AE DC MC V				●

Coconut Grove: *The Grand Café* $$$
Grand Bay Hotel, 2669 S Bayshore Drive. **Map** 6 F4. ((305) 858-9600.
Setting a new trend in Floribbean cuisine, this unashamedly up-market
restaurant also boasts impeccable service and elegant decor. P ♟ 🍴 🎵
AE DC MC V

Further Afield: *Here Comes the Sun* $
2188 NE 123rd St, North Miami Beach. ((305) 893-5711.
This bistro is biased towards vegetarian dishes, but a choice of fish is also
available. Vegetables are organic and there are daily specials. V ♟ ● *Sun.*
AE DC MC V

Further Afield: *Rusty Pelican* $$$
3201 Rickenbacker Causeway, Key Biscayne. ((305) 361-3818.
You'll get the best view of the Miami skyline from this elegant waterfront
bistro. Local seafood dishes are recommended. P ♟ 🍴 🎵 *Wed–Sat.*
AE DC MC V

Further Afield: *Sunday's On The Bay* $$$
5420 Crandon Blvd, Key Biscayne. ((305) 361-6777.
A good family restaurant which offers seafood and sea views. There
is a huge and varied choice for Sunday brunch. ♟ 🍴 🎵 *Sun.*
AE MC V

Further Afield: *Chef Allen's* $$$$
19088 NE 29th Ave, North Miami Beach. ((305) 935-2900.
Sleek and chic, this Miami landmark is known for its high quality,
daring New Florida cuisine. The activity in the kitchen, framed by
a huge picture window, is fascinating. P ♟ ● *L.*
AE DC MC V

THE GOLD AND TREASURE COASTS

Boca Raton: *TooJay's* $
5030 Champion Blvd. **Road map** F4. ((561) 241-5903.
There's usually a queue outside this deli but it's worth the wait. Choose
from overstuffed pastrami and corned beef sandwiches, salmon bagels
and massive portions of cheesecake. Not for weight-watchers. ● *25 Dec.*
AE DC MC V

Boca Raton: *Max's Grille* $$
404 Plaza Real, Mizner Park. **Road map** F4. ((561) 368-0080.
A place to see and be seen at Mizner Park, where you can enjoy some
excellent regional cuisine in classy surroundings. P V ♟ 🍴
AE DC MC V

Boca Raton: *La Vieille Maison* $$$$
770 E Palmetto Park Rd. **Road map** F4. ((561) 391-6701.
Built by Addison Mizner *(see p116)*, this home is now an intimate
French restaurant, ideal for romantic dinners. P ♟ 🍴 ● *L; 4 Jul.*
AE DC MC V

Dania: *Martha's Supper Club* $$$
6024 N Ocean Drive. **Road map** F4. ((954) 923-5444.
Known for its superb seafood (the coconut fried prawns are very good),
Martha's also enjoys great views of the Intracoastal Waterway. ♟ P 🎵
AE DC MC V

Davie: *Armadillo Café* $$
4630 SW 64th Ave. **Road map** F4. ((954) 791-4866.
Southwestern food at its best with delicious dishes from smoked duck
to tacos, served up in a casual atmosphere. ♟ 🍴 ● *L; public hols.*
AE DC MC V

Deerfield: *Pal's Charley's Crab* $$
1755 SE 3rd St. **Road map** F4. ((954) 427-4000.
Located on the Intracoastal Waterway, this restaurant has different
menus for lunch and dinner with the emphasis on seafood. A special
sunset menu is available from 4–6pm. ♟ P 🍴
AE DC MC V

Deerfield Beach: *Brooks* $$$
500 S Federal Hwy. **Road map** F4. ((954) 427-9302.
Brooks tempts you with Floribbean dishes created from wonderfully fresh
ingredients. Prix fixe or à la carte. A local favourite. P ♟ ● *L; 25 Dec.*
AE DC MC V

Delray Beach: *Erny's* $$
1010 E Atlantic Ave. **Road map** F4. ((561) 276-9191.
Delray's most popular saloon offers the best drinks and food in town. Fresh
seafood, steaks and home-made desserts. ♟ 🎵 ● *Sun L; public hols.*
AE MC V

Fort Lauderdale: *Café Europa* $
726 E Las Olas Blvd. **Road map** F4. ((954) 763-6600.
This buzzing self-service café serves excellent pizzas, salads and sand-
wiches, plus cappuccinos in 52 regular and unusual flavours. 🍴

Price categories include a three-course meal for one, a glass of house wine and all unavoidable extras including service and tax.
$ under $20
$$ $20–30
$$$ $30–45
$$$$ $45–60
$$$$$ over $60

CREDIT CARDS
Indicates which credit cards are accepted: AE American Express; DC Diners Club; MC MasterCard; V VISA.

CHILDREN'S FACILITIES
Small portions and highchairs available, and there may also be a special children's menu.

EARLY BIRD SPECIALS
Meals offered at a discounted price if you eat early, usually before 7pm.

GOOD REGIONAL CUISINE
Florida specialities, such as seafood or dishes with Hispanic or Caribbean influence.

	CREDIT CARDS	CHILDREN'S FACILITIES	EARLY BIRD SPECIALS	GOOD REGIONAL CUISINE	BAR
FORT LAUDERDALE: *The Floridian Restaurant* $ 1410 E Las Olas Blvd. **Road map** F4. ((954) 463-4041. Sunday mornings are especially busy at this trendy neighbourhood meeting place, when devotees enjoy three-egg omelettes, buttermilk pancakes and steak. Lunches and dinners are also very reasonable.					
FORT LAUDERDALE: *Bobby Rubino's* $$ 4100 N Federal Hwy. **Road map** F4. ((954) 561-5305. One of Florida's first rib restaurants; you can't beat their onion loaf and special recipe barbecue sauce. Fabulous ribs and grills. P ▮ ● *Sat–Sun L.*	AE DC MC V	●			■
FORT LAUDERDALE: *California Café* $$ 2301 SE 17th St Causeway. **Road map** F4. ((954) 728-3500. Sweet potato crusted-salmon is one of the dishes offered at this restaurant, which uses the flavours of California and Florida. The innovative seasonal menu also includes pizza and pasta dishes. P V ▮ ▦ ♫ *Thu-Sat.*	AE DC MC V			●	■
FORT LAUDERDALE: *Mango's* $$ 904 E Las Olas Blvd. **Road map** F4. ((954) 523-5001. Mango's has a wide choice of dishes from tasty appetizers to pastas and specialities such as the prawn pepperpot. ▮ ▦ ♫ ● *Thanksgiving, 25 Dec.*	AE MC V			●	■
FORT LAUDERDALE: *Burt & Jacks* $$$ Berth 23, Port Everglades. **Road map** F4. ((954) 522-5225. Hidden away in Port Everglades, this formal restaurant offers panoramic views as you chew on man-sized portions of steak and seafood. The wine list and service are excellent. P T ▮ ▦ ♫ ● *L; 25 Dec.*	AE DC MC V			●	■
FORT PIERCE: *Mangrove Mattie's* $$ 1640 Seaway Drive. **Road map** F3. ((561) 466-1044. Delectable seafood, including pasta sauces, is the mainstay at this pleasant restaurant. Meaty steaks and ribs are also available. ▮ ▦ ● *25 Dec.*	AE DC MC V		■	●	■
HOLLYWOOD: *Bavarian Village* $$ 1401 N Federal Hwy. **Road map** F4. ((954) 922-7321. This welcoming restaurant is definitely for those with a hearty appetite and a yen for German food. Traditional American dishes (steak and fish) are also on the menu and it's very family-friendly. ▮ ♫ ● *Mon–Sat L.*	AE DC MC V	●			■
HUTCHINSON ISLAND: *Scalawags* $$ 555 NE Ocean Blvd. **Road map** F3. ((561) 225-3700. Ceiling fans and wicker furniture give Scalawags a tropical flavour which complements its Floribbean dishes. Seafood buffets on Wednesdays. ▦ ♫	AE DC MC V	●	■	●	■
JUPITER: *Charley's Crab* $$ 1000 N US 1. **Road map** F4. ((561) 744-4710. Overlooking Jupiter River, this is one in the chain of Charley's Crab eateries and prides itself on expertly prepared Floribbean seafood. P ▮ ▦	AE DC MC V	●	■	●	■
PALM BEACH: *Chuck & Harold's* $$ 207 Royal Poinciana Way. **Road map** F4. ((561) 659-1440. The porch tables are the best for celebrity-spotting while you enjoy dishes such as conch chowder or one of the blackboard specials. P ▮ ▦ ♫	AE DC MC V	●	■	●	■
PALM BEACH: *Bice Ristorante* $$$$ 313½ Worth Ave. **Road map** F4. ((561) 835-1600. Seriously good Italian food is served in this formal restaurant. The dress-code matches the elegant decor. P T ▮ ● *25 Dec, 1 Jan.*	AE DC MC V				■
PALM BEACH: *Florentine Dining Room* $$$$ Breakers Hotel, 1 South County Rd. **Road map** F4. ((561) 655-6611. For a truly memorable experience, try the refined setting of this restaurant and the lavish New Florida cuisine served here. P T ▮ ♫	AE DC MC V	●		●	■

PALM BEACH: *Renato's* $ $ $ $
87 Via Mizner. **Road map** F4. **📞** *(561) 655-9752.*
Tucked away in one of Palm Beach's alleys, Renato's offers European
dishes, carefully prepared and faultlessly served. **P** **T** **Y** **🏠** **🎵** **●** *Sun L.*

| | AE | | | | ⊕ | ▥ |
| DC |
| MC |
| V |

POMPANO BEACH: *Flaming Pit* $
1150 N Federal Hwy. **Road map** F4. **📞** *(954) 943-3484.*
Locals flock here for the prime rib and steak, great chicken and the salad
bar, which comes with all the fixings. Low prices and friendly service.

| | AE | ⊕ | ▤ | | | ▥ |
| MC |
| V |

STUART: *The Ashley* $ $
61 SW Osceola St. **Road map** F3. **📞** *(561) 221-9476.*
A varied breakfast menu is available and, later on, dishes like coco-mango
prawns, salads, fresh fish and pasta are served. **V** **🎵** *Wed–Sat.* **●** *Sat–Mon D.*

| | AE | ⊕ | ▤ | | | ▥ |
| MC |
| V |

VERO BEACH: *Ocean Grill* $ $
1050 Sexton Plaza. **Road map** F3. **📞** *(561) 231-5409.*
Decorated with antiques, this 1940s waterfront restaurant offers flavour-
some seafood and meat dishes such as Indian River crab cakes and roast
duckling. **●** *Sat & Sun L; Super Bowl Sunday, first 2 weeks in Sep, Thanksgiving.*

| | AE | | | | ⊕ | ▥ |
| DC |
| MC |
| V |

WEST PALM BEACH: *Randy's Bageland* $
911 Village Blvd, Village Commons. **Road map** F4. **📞** *(561) 640-0203.*
Randy's Jewish deli-style cooking produces mouth-watering *knishes* (stuffed
dumplings), *pierogies* (pies) and, of course, bagels. Also a few fish dishes. **V**

| | MC | ⊕ |
| V |

WEST PALM BEACH: *Aleyda's Tex Mex* $ $
1890 S Military Trail. **Road map** F4. **📞** *(561) 642-2500.*
Sink your teeth into good old-fashioned Tex-Mex food at this popular
joint. You'll find *tacos, fajitas, tamales* and much, much more. **V** **●** *L.*

| | AE | ⊕ | | | | ▥ |
| DC |
| MC |
| V |

ORLANDO AND THE SPACE COAST

COCOA BEACH: *Herbie K's* $
2080 N Atlantic Ave. **Road map** F3. **📞** *(407) 783-6740.*
In this jolly, family-oriented '50s-style diner, complete with jukebox,
effervescent waitresses serve meaty burgers with a sherbet cup and bring the
bill with a piece of bubblegum. There's a dance club at the rear. **●** *25 Dec.*

| | AE | ⊕ | | | | ▥ |
| DC |
| MC |
| V |

DOWNTOWN ORLANDO: *Crackers Seafood Restaurant* $ $
Church Street Station, 129 W Church St. **Road map** E2. **📞** *(407) 422-2434.*
A Victorian saloon-style restaurant serving creole food with the emphasis
on seafood. Try the gumbo, oysters or the blackened gator tail. **Y**

| | AE | | | | | |
| DC |
| MC |
| V |

DOWNTOWN ORLANDO: *Le Coq au Vin* $ $
4800 S Orange Ave. **Road map** E2. **📞** *(407) 851-6980.*
Welcoming surroundings and consistently fine rustic French cuisine are
the draw at this popular restaurant. **Y** **●** *Mon; Sat & Sun L; most public hols.*

| | AE | | | | | |
| DC |
| MC |
| V |

DOWNTOWN ORLANDO: *Lili Marlene's* $ $ $
Church Street Station, 129 W Church St. **Road map** E2. **📞** *(407) 422-2434.*
Brass, stained glass and antique fittings from around the world set the
mood at this brasserie, which serves meat, fish and pasta dishes. **Y**

| | AE | ⊕ | | | | ▥ |
| DC |
| MC |
| V |

INTERNATIONAL DRIVE: *The Crabhouse* $ $
8291 International Drive. **Road map** E2. **📞** *(407) 352-6140.*
Choose from no less than nine crab dishes at this informal restaurant. The
seafood salad bar is loaded with freshly shucked oysters, prawns, marinated
mussels and crayfish, and there's a whole range of other seafood dishes. **🏠**

| | AE | ⊕ | | | ⊕ | ▥ |
| DC |
| MC |
| V |

INTERNATIONAL DRIVE: *Damon's The Place For Ribs* $ $
Mercado, 8445 International Drive. **Road map** E2. **📞** *(407) 352-5984.*
Just follow your nose to some of the best ribs in town at this no-frills eatery
which also serves steak, seafood and monster sandwiches. **●** *25 Dec.*

| | AE | ⊕ | | | | ▥ |
| DC |
| MC |
| V |

INTERNATIONAL DRIVE: *Bergamo's Italian Restaurant* $ $ $
Mercado, 8445 International Drive. **Road map** E2. **📞** *(407) 352-3805.*
This Italian trattoria serves better than average mall food. Try the osso bucco
with risotto or one of the heavenly pasta dishes. **V** **Y** **🎵** **●** *L; 25 Dec.*

| | AE | ⊕ | | | | ▥ |
| DC |
| MC |
| V |

INTERNATIONAL DRIVE: *The Butcher Shop Steakhouse* $ $ $
Mercado, 8445 International Drive. **Road map** E2. **📞** *(407) 363-9727.*
Here, you'll get the biggest and best steaks along I Drive, and you
can even cook your own at the grill if you like. **Y** **●** *L; 25 Dec.*

| | AE | ⊕ | | | | ▥ |
| DC |
| MC |
| V |

For key to symbols see back flap

<table>
<tr><td colspan="2">

Price categories include a three-course meal for one, a glass of house wine and all unavoidable extras including service and tax.
$ under $20
$$ $20–30
$$$ $30–45
$$$$ $45–60
$$$$$ over $60

</td><td>

CREDIT CARDS
Indicates which credit cards are accepted: AE American Express; DC Diners Club; MC MasterCard; V VISA.
CHILDREN'S FACILITIES
Small portions and highchairs available, and there may also be a special children's menu.
EARLY BIRD SPECIALS
Meals offered at a discounted price if you eat early, usually before 7pm.
GOOD REGIONAL CUISINE
Florida specialities, such as seafood or dishes with Hispanic or Caribbean influence.

</td></tr>
</table>

	CREDIT CARDS	CHILDREN'S FACILITIES	EARLY BIRD SPECIALS	GOOD REGIONAL CUISINE	BAR
INTERNATIONAL DRIVE: *Hard Rock Café* $$ 5800 Kirkman Rd, Universal Studios. **Road map** E2. **(** *(407) 351-7625.* This guitar-shaped building is festooned with pop memorabilia and murals on a musical theme. The music is deafening but the burgers, sandwiches and sundaes go down a treat. **P**	AE MC V				■
INTERNATIONAL DRIVE: *Dux* $$$ Peabody Hotel, 9801 International Drive. **Road map** E2. **(** *(407) 345-4550.* This glitzy restaurant produces creative gourmet dishes inspired by world cuisine but with a distinctly American twist. Wonderful service. **P** *L.*	AE DC MC V				■
KISSIMMEE: *Pacino's Italian Restorant* $$ 5795 W Highway 192. **Road map** E3. **(** *(407) 396-8022.* Char-broiled food is the focus of this comfortable and friendly family restaurant. If you prefer, there's a free delivery service to any nearby hotel. *L.*	AE DC MC V				■
WALT DISNEY WORLD: *California Grill* $$ Disney's Contemporary Resort. **Road map** E3. **(** *(407) 939-3463.* A stylish restaurant with great views and an open-plan kitchen, serving creative West Coast fare like smoked salmon pizza and pork and polenta. **P**	AE MC V				■
WALT DISNEY WORLD: *Cape May Café* $$ Disney's Beach Club Resort. **Road map** E3. **(** *(407) 939-3463.* The buffet breakfast proceedings here are conducted by Admiral Goofy. At dinner, a bell announces the start of the clam bake buffet, laden with a great array of food to choose from. **P** *L.*		●		●	
WALT DISNEY WORLD: *Chef Mickey's* $$ Disney's Contemporary Resort. **Road map** E3. **(** *(407) 939-3463.* Very much a family-oriented place offering breakfast and dinner buffets. Enjoy the antics of your favourite Disney characters as you eat. **P** *L.*	AE MC V	●			
WALT DISNEY WORLD: *Coral Café* $$ Walt Disney World Dolphin Hotel. **Road map** E3. **(** *(407) 934-4000.* One for all the (health conscious) family – the menu here even counts the calories and fat content of each dish. Themed dinner buffets nightly. **P V**	AE MC V	●		●	
WALT DISNEY WORLD: *Narcoossee's* $$ Disney's Grand Floridian Resort. **Road map** E3. **(** *(407) 939-3463.* The fun, informal restaurant in an octagonal chalet right alongside the Seven Seas lagoon specializes in shellfish and Surf 'n Turf dishes. **P**	AE MC V	●			
WALT DISNEY WORLD: *Ohana* $$ Disney's Polynesian Resort. **Road map** E3. **(** *(407) 939-3463.* This buzzing, open-plan dining room is the setting for Polynesian-style cuisine. Set-price dinners include meat and shellfish roasted over a fire pit and served on 3-ft (1-m) long skewers. **P** *L.*	AE MC V	●			
WALT DISNEY WORLD: *Planet Hollywood* $$ 1506 E Buena Vista Drive. **Road map** E3. **(** *(407) 827-7827.* Located within a purple neon globe, you'll find video screens and masses of movie memorabilia to gaze at while you munch on mainstream fare such as meaty burgers and tasty pizzas.	AE MC V	●			■
WALT DISNEY WORLD: *Olivia's Café* $$ Disney Old Key West. **Road map** E3. **(** *(407) 939-3463.* You'll think you're in old Key West at this café serving conch-style meals. Check out the Florida paella, conch chowder and mojo chicken. **P**	AE MC V	●		●	
WALT DISNEY WORLD: *Whispering Canyon Café* $$ Disney Wilderness Lodge. **Road map** E3. **(** *(407) 939-3463.* Snap on your six-guns and settle in for an all-you-can-eat campfire cookout buffet in a Wild West setting. Also open for frontier-style breakfasts. **P V**	AE MC V	●			■

WALT DISNEY WORLD: *Yacht Club Galley* $$
Disney Yacht Club Resort. **Road map** E3. ((407) 939-3463.
Open all day for "down home" favourites including fish, steak and pasta
in nautical surroundings. The dinner buffet has scrumptious desserts. **P**

AE
MC
V

WALT DISNEY WORLD: *Gulliver's Grill* $$$
Walt Disney World Swan Hotel. **Road map** E3. ((407) 934-3000.
Try the tastes of *Brobdingnag*, the legendary land of giants, at this
lovely plant-filled restaurant. It serves well-prepared American cuisine,
and vegetarian dishes are available upon request. **P V ♥ ♬**

AE
DC
MC
V

WALT DISNEY WORLD: *The Outback* $$$
Buena Vista Palace, 1900 Buena Vista Drive. **Road map** E3. ((407) 827-3430.
An indoor waterfall creates a soothing atmosphere at this down-under
bistro. Feast on jumbo stuffed prawns and steaks. **P V ♥ ●** *L.*

AE
DC
MC
V

WALT DISNEY WORLD: *Season's Dining Room* $$
The Disney Institute. **Road map** E3. (939-3463.
With its park-like setting, Season's is ideal for a quieter meal. The good value
set-price menu is usually themed and changes each day. **P V ♥ ♬ ●** *L.*

AE
MC
V

WALT DISNEY WORLD: *Arthur's 27* $$$$
Buena Vista Palace, 1900 Buena Vista Drive. **Road map** E3. ((407) 827-3450.
There's a fabulous view and a meal to match at this 27th-floor restaurant.
Probably some of Orlando's finest Floribbean cuisine. **P ♥ ♬ ●** *L.*

AE
DC
MC
V

WALT DISNEY WORLD: *Victoria & Albert's* $$$$$
Disney's Grand Floridian Beach Resort. **Road map** E3. ((407) 939-3463.
Reservations are a must at this lavish restaurant. The six-course fixed-price
menu is superlative and you're waited on by a butler and a maid. Ask for
the chef's table, the most exclusive one in the house. **P ♥ V ♥ ♬ ●** *L.*

AE
MC
V

WINTER PARK: *Café de France* $$$
526 Park Ave S. **Road map** E2. ((407) 647-1869.
A cozy French bistro serving lighter meals such as crêpes at lunchtime; at
dinner try the rack of lamb or the daily special. **♥ ▦ ●** *Sun–Mon; public hols.*

AE
DC
MC
V

WINTER PARK: *Park Plaza Gardens* $$$
319 Park Ave S. **Road map** E2. ((407) 645-2475.
An airy courtyard in a plant-filled atrium provides the setting for your meal
at this elegant restaurant. The consistently delicious and award-winning
American cuisine is served with panache. **♥ ♬** *Fri & Sat.* **●** *25 Dec, 1 Jan.*

AE
DC
MC
V

THE NORTHEAST

DAYTONA BEACH: *Hog Heaven* $
37 N Atlantic Ave. **Road map** E2. ((904) 257-1212.
The inviting aroma of meat cooking on a traditional pit barbecue pervades
this friendly, casual dining spot. Bring a hearty appetite. **●** *25 Dec.*

MC
V

DAYTONA BEACH: *Aunt Catfish's* $$
4009 Halifax Drive. **Road map** E2. ((904) 767-4768.
This popular eatery located on the Intracoastal Waterway is especially
renowned for its fried catfish and other Southern-style dishes such as crab
cakes and clam strips. Also open for Sunday brunch. **▦ ●** *25 Dec.*

AE
MC
V

DAYTONA BEACH: *Down the Hatch* $$
4894 Front St, Ponce Inlet. **Road map** E2. ((904) 761-4831.
A homely, family-oriented restaurant serving beautifully fresh fish and a
few meat dishes. Set right on the water, you can watch the boats unload
their catch at the end of the day. **▦ ♬** *Wed–Sun.* **●** *Thanksgiving, 25 Dec.*

AE
MC
V

FERNANDINA BEACH: *Florida House Inn* $
20–22 S 3rd St. **Road map** E1. ((904) 261-3300.
At this lovely gingerbread house (Florida's oldest surviving hotel), diners
sit at long trestle tables laden with generous servings of good American
home cooking. Genuinely friendly service. **●** *Sun–Mon D; 24 Dec D.*

MC
V

FERNANDINA BEACH: *Beech Street Grill* $$$
801 Beech St. **Road map** E1. ((904) 277-3662.
Occupying a gorgeous 1889 building, the Grill offers a progressive
menu of contemporary Florida cuisine and an excellent wine list.
Daily specials showcase the innovative seafood dishes. **♥ ♬** *Thu–Sat.*
● *L; 25 Dec, Super Bowl Sunday.*

AE
DC
MC
V

<table>
<tr><td colspan="2">

Price categories include a three-course meal for one, a glass of house wine and all unavoidable extras including service and tax.
$Ⓢ$ under $20
$ⓈⓈ$ $20–30
$ⓈⓈⓈ$ $30–45
$ⓈⓈⓈⓈ$ $45–60
$ⓈⓈⓈⓈⓈ$ over $60

CREDIT CARDS
Indicates which credit cards are accepted: AE American Express; DC Diners Club; MC MasterCard; V VISA.
CHILDREN'S FACILITIES
Small portions and highchairs available, and there may also be a special children's menu.
EARLY BIRD SPECIALS
Meals offered at a discounted price if you eat early, usually before 7pm.
GOOD REGIONAL CUISINE
Florida specialities, such as seafood or dishes with Hispanic or Caribbean influence.

</td></tr>
</table>

	CREDIT CARDS	CHILDREN'S FACILITIES	EARLY BIRD SPECIALS	GOOD REGIONAL CUISINE	BAR
FERNANDINA BEACH: *The Grill* $ⓈⓈⓈ$ 4750 Amelia Island Parkway. **Road map** E1. ☎ *(904) 277-1100.* An up-market restaurant which offers a minimum three-course menu. This includes meat and seafood and changes daily. 🅿 🍴 🍷 🏧 🎵 ● *L; Sun D.*	AE DC MC V	●		●	▬
GAINESVILLE: *The Chuck Wagon* $Ⓢ$ 3483 Williston Rd. **Road map** D2. ☎ *(352) 336-5677.* This country-style eatery, complete with rocking chairs, offers dishes like honey-glazed ham and catfish fillets. No alcohol. 🆅 ● *Thanksgiving, 25 Dec.*	AE MC V				
JACKSONVILLE: *Café Carmon* $ⓈⓈ$ 1986 San Marco Blvd. **Road map** E1. ☎ *(904) 399-4488.* This bistro tempts diners with excellently prepared foods from tomato and basil pasta to grilled or blackened fresh catch of the day. 🆅 🍷 🏧	AE DC MC V	●		●	▬
JACKSONVILLE: *Juliette's, A Florida Bistro* $ⓈⓈ$ Omni Jacksonville Hotel, 245 Water St. **Road map** E1. ☎ *(904) 355-6664.* The menu here promises treats such as grilled swordfish with banana ginger butter. Make the most of the excellent service, the gourmet desserts and a popular and generous Sunday brunch. 🅿 🍷 🎵	AE DC MC V	●		●	▬
JACKSONVILLE: *The Wine Cellar* $ⓈⓈⓈ$ 1314 Prudential Drive. **Road map** E1. ☎ *(904) 398-8989.* One of Jacksonville's top restaurants, the Wine Cellar features 200 wines and dishes like grilled salmon with dill sauce. 🍷 🏧 ● *Sat L; Sun; public hols.*	AE DC MC V	●		●	
JACKSONVILLE BEACH: *Dolphin Depot* $ⓈⓈ$ 704 N 1st St. **Road map** E1. ☎ *(904) 270-1424.* Once a railroad store, this Art Deco building contains one of the Northeast's best restaurants. Its small size ensures a quieter meal and the blackboard menu changes daily. Reservations are advised. 🍷 ● *L; Thanksgiving, 25 Dec.*	AE DC MC V	●		●	▬
OCALA: *Arthur's* $ⓈⓈ$ Ocala/Silver Springs Hilton, 3600 SW 36th Ave. **Road map** E2. ☎ *(352) 854-1400.* Arthur's is known for its weekend buffets: seafood on Friday nights, ribs on Saturdays, and a lavish brunch on Sundays. 🅿 🍷 🏧 🎵 *Fri & Sat.*	AE DC MC V	●	▬	●	▬
ORMOND BEACH: *Barnacle's Restaurant & Lounge* $ⓈⓈ$ 869 S Atlantic Ave. **Road map** E2. ☎ *(904) 673-1070.* This beachside eatery is always packed; the casual atmosphere, seafood, succulent ribs and splendid views make it a popular choice. ● *L.*	AE MC V	●	▬	●	▬
ORMOND BEACH: *La Crepe en Haut Restaurant* $ⓈⓈⓈⓈ$ 142 E Granada Blvd. **Road map** E2. ☎ *(904) 673-1999.* This elegant French restaurant with crisp white tablecloths, ornate crystal and fine cuisine is off the beaten path but worth the trip. 🍷 ● *Sat & Sun L; Mon; most public hols.*	AE MC V			●	▬
ST AUGUSTINE: *Salt Water Cowboy's* $Ⓢ$ 299 Dondanville Rd. **Road map** E1. ☎ *(904) 471-2332.* Set in a reconstructed fish camp, this informal restaurant serves local dishes such as alligator tail, oysters and jambalaya. ● *L; Super Bowl Sunday; 24 & 25 Dec.*	AE MC V	●		●	▬
ST AUGUSTINE: *Santa Maria* $ⓈⓈ$ 135 Avenida Menedez. ☎ *(904) 829-6578.* **Road map** E1. Seafood is the speciality here, but dishes such as black bean soup, steaks and ribs are also recommended. Located on a pier in the marina. 🍷	AE DC MC V	●		●	
ST AUGUSTINE: *Raintree* $ⓈⓈ$ 102 San Marco Ave. **Road map** E1. ☎ *(904) 824-7211.* Occupying one of the street's remaining historic buildings, Raintree is renowned for its award-winning food. Round off a meal of superb seafood or traditional meat dishes with a crêpe at the dessert bar. 🍷 ● *L; 25 Dec.*	AE DC MC V	●	▬	●	▬

THE PANHANDLE

APALACHICOLA: *Seafood Grill & Steakhouse* $$
100 Market St. **Road map** B1. 📞 *(904) 653-9510.*
Located downtown, this friendly grill features a good range of meals. Tuck
into the "world's largest" fried fish sandwich, the area's famous oysters, or
one of the fancier chef's specials. 🔲 ● *Sun; Thanksgiving, 25 Dec.*
AE MC V

CEDAR KEY: *Blue Desert Café* $
12518 Hwy 24. **Road map** D2. 📞 *(352) 543-9111.*
In this shotgun home, efficient staff serve an eclectic mix of Tex-Mex,
Cajun and Asian dishes. The decor is western kitsch, the ambience fun
and friendly and it's the only place in town open late. 🔲 V ● *L; Sun & Mon.*

DESTIN: *The Donut Hole* $
635 Hwy 98. **Road map** A1. 📞 *(904) 837-8824.*
Good, hearty basic food at modest prices make this eatery a great bargain.
There's a different menu for each day of the week. V ● *Nov–Dec.*

DESTIN: *The Back Porch* $$
1740 Old Hwy 98. **Road map** A1. 📞 *(904) 837-2022.*
This seafood and oyster house dishes up succulent char-grilled, broiled and
fried fish and shellfish. The views are sensational. 🔲 ● *Thanksgiving, 25 Dec.*
AE DC MC V

DESTIN: *Marina Café* $$$
404 E Highway 98. **Road map** A1. 📞 *(904) 837-7960.*
A jewel on the Emerald Coast, this restaurant combines excellent service,
a spectacular location and creative, internationally inspired cuisine. Early
diners benefit from two-for-one dinners. 🔲 🔲 ● *L; 25 Dec, Jan.*
AE DC MC V

FORT WALTON BEACH: *Harpoon Hanna's* $$
1450 Miracle Strip Parkway. **Road map** A1. 📞 *(904) 243-5500.*
Right on the beach, this family restaurant serves burgers, seafood
baskets and fish dishes. Lunch specials are good value. 🔲 ♫
AE DC MC V

FORT WALTON BEACH: *Staff's Seafood Restaurant* $$
24 Miracle Strip Parkway. **Road map** A1. 📞 *(904) 243-3526.*
Opened in 1931, Staff's has been well-known for its fine local recipes ever
since. The menu also offers meat dishes. 🔲 ♫ ● *L; Thanksgiving, 25 Dec.*
AE MC V

GRAYTON BEACH: *Criolla's* $$$
170 E County Rd. 30 A. **Road map** A2. 📞 *(904) 267-1267.*
Criolla's signature is an enterprising menu of elaborately concocted dishes.
The Creole set meal is unusual and very reasonable. 🔲 ● *L; Sun; Dec & Jan.*
MC V

GULF BREEZE: *Bon Appetit Waterfront Café* $$
Holiday Inn, 51 Gulf Breeze Parkway. **Road map** A1. 📞 *(904) 932-2214.*
This waterfront café offers appetizing Floribbean food. Choose one
of the mouth-watering desserts to round off your meal. 🔲
AE DC MC V

NAVARRE: *Cap'n Bubbas Seafood Restaurant* $$
8487 Navarre Parkway. **Road map** A1. 📞 *(904) 939-2800.*
A gulfside brasserie, Cap'n Bubbas is child-friendly and has a good value
all-you-can-eat seafood buffet at weekends. 🔲 ● *Thanksgiving, 25 Dec.*
AE MC V

PANAMA CITY BEACH: *Capt. Anderson's* $$$
5551 N Lagoon Drive. **Road map** B1. 📞 *(904) 234-2225.*
Great for seafood, the menu at this huge dockside restaurant also
includes meat dishes and Greek specialities. 🔲 ● *L; Nov–Jan.*
AE DC MC V

PANAMA CITY BEACH: *The Treasure Ship* $$$
3605 S Thomas Drive. **Road map** B1. 📞 *(904) 234-8881.*
Housed in a replica of a 16th-century galleon, this three-level restaurant has
open-air decks, water views and tasty fresh seafood. 🔲 🔲 ♫ ● *Nov–Jan.*
AE DC MC V

PANAMA CITY BEACH: *Fiddler's Green* $$$$
Marriott's Bay Point Resort, 4200 Marriott Drive. **Road map** B1.
📞 *(904) 234-3307.* The city's most elegant restaurant tempts
.customers with top-notch contemporary gourmet cuisine. 🔲 🔲
AE DC MC V

PENSACOLA: *Cock of the Walk* $
550 Scenic Hwy. **Road map** A1. 📞 *(904) 432-6766.*
A family restaurant serving local fare and Southern dishes. Try grain-fed
catfish, corn bread and fried dill pickles. 🔲 V ● *Sat–Mon L; most public hols.*
AE MC V

Price categories include a three-course meal for one, a glass of house wine and all unavoidable extras including service and tax.
$ under $20
$$ $20–30
$$$ $30–45
$$$$ $45–60
$$$$$ over $60

CREDIT CARDS
Indicates which credit cards are accepted: AE American Express; DC Diners Club; MC MasterCard; V VISA.

CHILDREN'S FACILITIES
Small portions and highchairs available, and there may also be a special children's menu.

EARLY BIRD SPECIALS
Meals offered at a discounted price if you eat early, usually before 7pm.

GOOD REGIONAL CUISINE
Florida specialities, such as seafood or dishes with Hispanic or Caribbean influence.

	CREDIT CARDS	CHILDREN'S FACILITIES	EARLY BIRD SPECIALS	GOOD REGIONAL CUISINE	BAR
PENSACOLA: *Landry's Seafood House* $$ 905 E Gregory St. **Road map** A1. (*(904) 434-3600.* Here, tasty Cajun-style meals with a hint of the Caribbean include gumbos and freshly cooked seafood with a variety of sauces. 🍷 🏠 🎵 ● *25 Dec.*	AE DC MC V	●		●	■
PENSACOLA: *McGuire's Irish Pub & Brewery* $$ 600 E Gregory St. **Road map** A1. (*(904) 433-6789.* A visit to Pensacola isn't complete without a stop at McGuire's, where huge portions of steak, pasta, pizza and pub fare are served. Wash it down with one of their home-brewed beers. V 🍷 🎵 ● *Thanksgiving, 25 Dec.*	AE DC MC V	●			■
PENSACOLA: *Skopelos on the Bay* $$$ 670 Scenic Hwy. **Road map** A1. (*(904) 432-6565.* Famous for award-winning food, this restaurant serves seafood and meat dishes with a European twist. The Greek appetizers such as *dolmades* are delicious. 🍷 🏠 ● *Mon–Thu, Sat L; Sun; 25 Dec, 1 Jan.*	AE MC V				■
PENSACOLA BEACH: *Chan's Florida Cuisine* $$$ 2½ Via De Luna. **Road map** A1. (*(904) 932-3525.* Inspired Floribbean dishes such as sauteed herb trigger fish in a tomato pesto are served upstairs in a formal setting or in a more casual eatery downstairs. 🍷 🏠 🎵 ● *24 Dec.*	AE DC MC V	●	■	■	
SEASIDE: *Bud & Alley's* $$$ County Rd 30 A. **Road map** B1. (*(904) 231-5900.* This unpretentious, friendly meeting place offers an innovative menu of regional food which changes seasonally. The open-air rooftop bar has spectacular Gulf views. 🍷 🏠 🎵 ● *Tue; Nov 1–20.*	MC V		■		■
TALLAHASSEE: *Chez Pierre* $$ 1215 Thomasville Rd. **Road map** C1. (*(904) 222-0936.* Southern hospitality plus good French food make this bistro a local favourite. Delicious pastries too. 🍷 🎵 ● *Sun; 25 Dec, 1 Jan.*	AE DC MC V		■		■
TALLAHASSEE: *Andrew's 2nd Act* $$$ 228 South Adams St. **Road map** C1. (*(904) 222-3444.* This gourmet restaurant has an excellent set menu, or else you can choose from perennial favourites and contemporary seasonal dishes. Service is attentive. P T 🍷 🏠 🎵 ● *Sat & Sun L.*	AE DC MC V		■		■

THE GULF COAST

	CREDIT CARDS	CHILDREN'S FACILITIES	EARLY BIRD SPECIALS	GOOD REGIONAL CUISINE	BAR
ANNA MARIA ISLAND: *Sign of the Mermaid* $$ 9707 Gulf Drive. **Road map** D3. (*(941) 778-9399.* A good spot for Sunday brunch, the Mermaid is always busy so book ahead. The seafood gumbo is recommended. No licence so BYO. 🍷 ● *Mon–Sat L.*			■	●	
CAPTIVA ISLAND: *The Bubble Room* $$ 15001 Captiva Rd. **Road map** D4. (*(941) 472-5558.* Here, gigantic portions of seafood and steaks and outrageous desserts are served by high-energy staff. The fun activity and funky decor make it popular with children. ● *25 Dec.*	AE DC MC V	●		●	■
CAPTIVA ISLAND: *Chadwick's at South Seas Plantation* $$$ 5400 South Seas Plantation Rd. **Road map** D4. (*(941) 472-5111.* This place is open all day and laid out on several levels, with special areas for family dining. It serves an excellent Sunday brunch and buffet-style set meals are offered from Thursday to Sunday. 🍷 🎵	AE DC MC V	●		●	■
CAPTIVA ISLAND: *The Old Captiva House at 'Tween Waters Inn* $$$ 15951 Captiva Rd. **Road map** D4. (*(941) 472-5161.* Regional cuisine is served in fine old Florida style, in a casual atmosphere. There's a choice of four price bands for dinner entrées. 🍷 🏠 🎵 ● *L.*	AE MC V	●		●	

CLEARWATER BEACH: *Alley Cat's Café* $$
2475 McMullen Booth Rd. **Road map** D3. (*(813) 797-5555.*
The fish here is either cooked to a special house recipe, such as swordfish with ancho-chilli and avocado salsa, or according to taste, for example pan-roasted or blackened. 🍴 ▦ 🎵 *Wed, Fri & Sat.* ● *Easter, Thanksgiving, 25 Dec.*

	AE				
	MC				
	V				

CLEARWATER BEACH: *Seafood & Sunsets at Julie's Café* $$
351 S Gulfview Blvd. **Road map** D3. (*(813) 441-2548.*
This casual café across the street from the beach is a great place to enjoy the sunsets and the good, reasonably priced local cuisine. ▦ ● *Thanksgiving.*

	AE
	MC
	V

DUNEDIN: *Bon Appetit* $$
148 Marina Plaza. **Road map** D3. (*(813) 733-2151.*
Consistently good food with an American flavour is dished up here and accompanied by breathtaking views of St Joseph's Sound. 🅿 🍷 ▦

	AE
	DC
	MC
	V

FORT MYERS: *The Veranda* $$$
2122 2nd St. **Road map** E4. (*(941) 332-2065.*
This charming restaurant housed in a 1902 building offers original culinary creations like artichoke fritters stuffed with blue crab. The decor is Deep South and the service attentive. 🅿 🍷 ▦ 🎵 ● *Sat L; Sun; 4 Jul, 25 Dec & 1 Jan.*

	AE
	DC
	MC
	V

ST PETERSBURG: *Columbia Restaurant* $$
800 2nd Ave NE. **Road map** D3. (*(813) 822-8000.*
One in a chain of Columbia restaurants in Florida offering fine Spanish cuisine, this one also has spectacular views of Tampa Bay. 🅿 🍷

	AE
	DC
	MC
	V

ST PETERSBURG: *Keystone Club* $$
320 4th St N. **Road map** D3. (*(813) 822-6600.*
This eatery has an informal atmosphere, is popular with locals and serves the best prime rib steak for miles around. 🍷 ● *Sat & Sun L; some public hols.*

	AE
	DC
	MC
	V

ST PETERSBURG: *Merchand's Bar & Grill and Terrace Room* $$$
Renaissance Vinoy Resort, 501 5th Ave. **Road map** D3. (*(813) 894-1000.*
Located in a beautiful 1920s hotel, this elegant restaurant features largely Mediterranean-style food. The bouillabaisse is recommended. 🅿 🍷 🎵

	AE
	DC
	MC
	V

ST PETE BEACH: *Hurricane Seafood Restaurant* $
807 Gulf Way. **Road map** D3. (*(813) 360-9558.*
Set right on the beach, this restaurant prides itself on its crab cakes and fresh Florida grouper, which comes blackened, grilled, broiled or in a sandwich. The cocktail deck is especially popular at sunset. 🍷 ▦

	MC
	V

ST PETE BEACH: *Maritana Grille* $$$$
Don CeSar Beach Resort, 3400 Gulf Blvd. **Road map** D3. (*(813) 360-1882.*
A winner of several culinary awards, the Maritana Grille boasts elaborate dishes using local and organic produce. The atmosphere is relaxed and the decor is tropical. 🅿 🍷 ● *L.*

	AE
	DC
	MC
	V

SANIBEL ISLAND: *Windows On The Water* $$$
Sundial Beach Resort, 1451 Middle Gulf Drive. **Road map** D4. (*(941) 395-6014.*
In a beautiful location overlooking the Gulf of Mexico, this rather elegant restaurant features delicious Floribbean cuisine. 🍷

	AE
	DC
	MC
	V

SARASOTA: *Nick's On The Water* $$$
230 Sarasota Quay. **Road map** D3. (*(941) 954-3839.*
Choose traditional Italian food or tasty seafood such as stuffed lobster. Dine indoors or on the terrace overlooking the bay. 🅿 🍷 ▦ 🎵 *Fri & Sat.*

	AE
	MC
	V

SARASOTA: *Chez Sylvie* $$$
1526 Main St. **Road map** D3. (*(941) 953-3232.*
Located downtown, this café-style restaurant specializes in French cuisine. Open for breakfast at weekends. ▦ ● *Sun D, Mon; Thanksgiving, 25 Dec, 1 Jan.*

	MC
	V

SARASOTA: *Michael's On East* $$$
1212 E Avenue S. **Road map** D3. (*(941) 366-0007.*
One of Sarasota's premier restaurants, Michael's has innovative regional cuisine and a large selection of micro-beers. 🍷 🅿 🎵 *Fri & Sat.* ● *Sat & Sun L.*

	AE
	DC
	MC
	V

TAMPA: *Columbia Restaurant* $$
2117 E 7th Ave, Ybor City. **Road map** D3. (*(813) 248-4961*
This is the original Columbia restaurant and has been serving Spanish and Cuban food since 1905. There are several dining rooms with beautiful tiled floors and a nightly flamenco show. 🍷 🅿 🎵

	AE
	DC
	MC
	V

Price categories include a three-course meal for one, a glass of house wine and all unavoidable extras including service and tax.

$ under $20
$$ $20–30
$$$ $30–45
$$$$ $45–60
$$$$$ over $60

CREDIT CARDS
Indicates which credit cards are accepted: AE American Express; DC Diners Club; MC MasterCard; V VISA.

CHILDREN'S FACILITIES
Small portions and highchairs available, and there may also be a special children's menu.

EARLY BIRD SPECIALS
Meals offered at a discounted price if you eat early, usually before 7pm..

GOOD REGIONAL CUISINE
Florida specialities, such as seafood or dishes with Hispanic or Caribbean influence.

	CREDIT CARDS	CHILDREN'S FACILITIES	EARLY BIRD SPECIALS	GOOD REGIONAL CUISINE	BAR
TAMPA: *Lauro Ristorante Italiano* $$ 3915 Henderson Blvd. **Road map** D3. (813) 281-2100. This restaurant offers delicious traditional Italian food in pleasant surroundings with good service, all for moderate prices. 🍴 ● *Sat L; Sun.*	AE DC MC V				▬
TAMPA: *Mis en Place* $$ 442 W Kennedy Blvd. **Road map** D3. (813) 254-5373. The innovative menu of this busy bistro changes daily but never fails to please. Locals love this place so reserve ahead. 🍴 ● *Sat L, Mon D; Sun*	AE DC MC V			●	▬
TAMPA: *Bern's Steak House* $$$ 1208 S Howard Ave. **Road map** D3. (813) 251-2421. A must for meat-lovers, Bern's has made steak cuisine a fine art. Each order is prepared to your specifications, and accompanied by organic vegetables. It is very popular and reservations are essential. P 🍴 🎵 ● *L; 25 Dec.*	AE DC MC V				▬
TAMPA: *Oystercatchers* $$$ 6200 Courtney Campbell Causeway. **Road map** D3. (813) 281-9116. Next to the Hyatt Regency Westshore hotel, this place specializes in seafood. Choose from the menu or from what is on display. P 🍴 🎵 ● *Sat L; 25 Dec.*	AE DC MC V	●		●	▬
VENICE: *Sharky's on the Pier* $$ 1600 S. Harbor Drive. **Road map** D4. (941) 488-1456. Fish cooked in a variety of styles are the house speciality; your choice can be broiled, blackened, char-grilled or fried. 🍴 ▦ 🎵 ● *Thanksgiving, 25 Dec.*	AE MC V	●		●	▬

THE EVERGLADES AND THE KEYS

	CREDIT CARDS	CHILDREN'S FACILITIES	EARLY BIRD SPECIALS	GOOD REGIONAL CUISINE	BAR
ISLAMORADA: *Manny and Isa's Kitchen* $ MM 81.6, Overseas Hwy. **Road map** F5. (305) 664-5019. Nothing fancy, but this place serves authentic Cuban dishes and tasty fried lobster at budget prices. ● *Tue; Oct; Thanksgiving, 25 Dec, 1 Jan.*	AE DC MC V	●		●	
ISLAMORADA: *Marker 88* $$ MM 88, Overseas Hwy. **Road map** F5. (305) 852-9315. This gourmet restaurant overlooking Florida Bay offers creative Keys seafood as well as classic European cuisine. 🍴 ● *L; Mon; Thanksgiving, 25 Dec.*	AE DC MC V	●		●	▬
ISLAMORADA: *Green Turtle Inn* $$$ MM 81.5, Overseas Hwy. **Road map** F5. (305) 664-9031. A Keys tradition since 1947; locals flock to eat the famous turtle chowder and alligator steak. A pianist entertains in the evenings. 🍴 🎵 ● *Mon.*	AE DC MC V	●		●	▬
KEY LARGO: *The Italian Fisherman* $$ MM 104, Overseas Hwy. **Road map** F5. (305) 451-4471. Tasty pastas, Italian dishes and fresh seafood are on the menu here. Or bring your own fish and the staff will cook it for you. 🍴 ▦ ● *25 Dec.*	AE MC V	●	▬	●	▬
KEY LARGO: *Mrs Mac's Kitchen* $$ MM 99.4, Overseas Hwy. **Road map** F5. (305) 451-3722. A local institution, this unpretentious diner serving overstuffed sandwiches, bowls of chilli and nightly specials is great. ● *Sun; most public hols.*		●			
KEY WEST: *Blue Heaven* $$ 729 Thomas St. **Road map** E5. (305) 296-8666. Housed in a wonderful old Key West building, this friendly restaurant offers delicious conch food in a laid-back atmosphere. The seating at painted wooden tables is basic. V 🍴 ▦ 🎵 ● *Thanksgiving, 25 Dec.*	MC V	●		●	▬
KEY WEST: *Mangia Mangia Pasta Café* $$ 900 Southard St. **Road map** E5. (305) 294-2469. Superb freshly-made pasta and the tasty accompanying sauces have earned this centrally located café an enviable reputation. 🍴 ● *L; most public hols.*	AE MC V				▬

KEY WEST: *Godfrey's Restaurant at the La-Te-Da Hotel* $$$
1125 Duval St. **Road map** E5. (*(305) 296-6706.*
Inspired by the flavours of California, the Caribbean, the Mediterranean and
the Middle East, a meal here is a memorable experience. 🍴 🚬 🎵 ● *Sun D.*
AE DC MC V

KEY WEST: *Louie's Back Yard* $$$
700 Waddell Ave. **Road map** E5. (*(305) 294-1061.*
The interesting menu at this beautifully restored conch house restaurant
features dishes which use Cuban, Caribbean and Thai flavours. Set amidst
tropical vegetation, the restaurant's location is very inviting. 🚬 ● *25 Dec.*
AE DC MC V

KEY WEST: *Mangoes* $$$
700 Duval St. **Road map** E5. (*(305) 292-4606.*
Choose from fabulous salads (most of which are suitable for vegetarians)
and innovative Floribbean dishes at this Duval Street bistro. Sidewalk
tables are perfect for people-watching. 🚬 🅥
MC V

KEY WEST: *Pier House Restaurant* $$$$
Pier House Resort, 1 Duval St. **Road map** E5. (*(305) 296-4600.*
This exclusive waterfront restaurant, one of the best in the Keys, serves
fancy Florida cuisine such as lobster with marinated plantain. Reserve an
outside table for the best sunset views *(see p284)*. 🍴 🚬 🎵 ● *Mon–Sat L.*
AE MC V

MARATHON: *Brian's in Paradise* $
MM 52, Overseas Hwy. **Road map** E5. (*(305) 743-3183.*
Family-style dining with a long menu and many specials under $10. Choose
from burgers, fish dishes and home-style meals. ● *Thanksgiving, 25 Dec.*
AE DC MC V

MARATHON: *Kelsey's Fine Dining* $$$
MM 48.5, Overseas Hwy. **Road map** E5. (*(305) 743-9018.*
Located on the docks of Faro Blanco Resort, Kelsey's offers seafood and
steaks and will also prepare your own catch for you. 🍴 🚬 🎵 ● *L; Mon.*
AE MC V

MARCO ISLAND: *Konrad's* $$
Mission San Marco. **Road map** E4. (*(941) 642-3332.*
Konrad's boasts stylish decor and one of the best salad bars on the island.
The early bird dinners and the scampi are very popular. 🅿 🚬 🎵 ● *25 Dec.*
AE DC MC V

MARCO ISLAND: *Snook Inn* $$
1215 Bald Eagle Drive. **Road map** E4. (*(941) 394-3313.*
Seafood is the speciality at this waterfront eatery and they'll also cook your
own fish for you. Great sunset views from the separate bar. 🚬 🎵 ● *25 Dec.*
AE DC MC V

MARCO ISLAND: *Olde Marco Inn* $$$
100 Palm St. **Road map** E4. (*(941) 394-3131.*
This up-market restaurant, built as a lodge in 1896, features an eclectic
international menu. The German dishes are popular. 🍴 🎵 ● *L.*
AE DC MC V

NAPLES: *First Watch* $
1400 Gulf Shore Blvd N. **Road map** E4. (*(941) 434-0005.*
The best place in town for breakfast, this family-orientated country kitchen
just opposite Lowdermilk Park is always busy. 🚬 ● *D; Thanksgiving, 25 Dec.*
AE MC V

NAPLES: *Chart House* $$
1193 8th St S. **Road map** E4. (*(941) 649-0033.*
Overlooking the bay, this cosy restaurant serves excellent food including a few
vegetarian dishes and their famous mud pie dessert. 🅿 🅥 🍴 🚬 ● *L.*
AE DC MC V

NAPLES: *The Dock at Crayton Cove* $$
12th Ave S, on Naples Bay. **Road map** E4. (*(941) 263-9940.*
Fish and shellfish dishes predominate at this restaurant next to the marina.
Try the generous sandwiches or something from the raw bar. 🚬 ● *25 Dec.*
AE MC V

NAPLES: *Bistro 821* $$$
821 5th Ave. **Road map** E4. (*(941) 261-5821.*
Try this stylish bistro for creative Floribbean cuisine. Choose from the menu
or from a selection of daily specials featuring recipes such as lemon sole
stuffed with scallop and lobster mousse. 🍴 🚬 ● *L; Thanksgiving, 25 Dec, 1 Jan.*
AE DC MC V

NAPLES: *Savannah* $$$
5200 Tamiami Trail N, Suite 103. **Road map** E4. (*(941) 261-2555.*
The influences of America's Deep South are found both in the decor and in
the cuisine of this traditional restaurant, with Southern-style dishes such as
pan-fried spicy blue cornmeal catfish. 🅿 🍴 ● *June–Oct L.*
AE DC MC V

Bars and Cafés

FLORIDA'S EASY-GOING LIFESTYLE helps to ensure an abundance of bars and cafés. The term café often denotes an informal, bistro-style restaurant but can also refer to a coffee house or, indeed, a bar. Sports bars are very popular and usually have several television sets, each tuned to a different station – though frequently the sound is turned off while loud music plays in the background. Many bars and cafés have a happy hour, generally from 4 to 7pm, when drinks are cheaper and snacks are often served free of charge; those included here are good for just a drink as well as a meal, or a coffee and a snack.

MIAMI

Miami Beach: *Abbey Brewing Company*
1115 16th St. **Map** 2 D2.
((305) 538-8110.
With its wood panelling and pew-style seats, this bar has a good try at looking like a pub. Popular with locals, it is ideal for anyone needing a break from the SoBe scene. It serves its own microbrewed beers, as well as other draft and bottled beers. The bar is open from 1pm to 5am, and snacks are available at all times. 🍴

Miami Beach: *News Café*
800 Ocean Drive. **Map** 2 F4.
((305) 538-6397.
With ample pavement tables, this laid-back café is the top meeting place in South Beach and is open 24 hours a day. People gather to drink, eat and take in the Ocean Drive scene. The eclectic menu features good breakfasts and huge bowls of pasta as well as light, healthy meals. There are a dozen kinds of coffee, and the pastry list is equally long. 🍽 🍴 *AE DC MC V*

Miami Beach: *Van Dyke Café*
846 Lincoln Rd. **Map** 2 E2.
((305) 534-3600.
This popular SoBe hangout, with tables inside and out, occupies a lovely restored Mediterranean-style building. House specialities are bread pudding and zabaglione with fresh berries. There is a good choice of coffees and herbal teas, and a jazz trio performs in the evenings. 🍽 🍴 🎵 *AE DC MC V*

Downtown: *Hard Rock Café*
401 Biscayne Blvd. **Map** 4 F1.
((305) 377-3110.
Tourists and locals alike fill the Hard Rock Café, which is festooned with rock memorabilia and throbs with loud music. There's a bar for those intent on drinking and soaking up the atmosphere, but book ahead if you want to eat. The food is American, from juicy burgers to hot apple pie, and the portions are generous. 🍴 🎵 *AE DC MC V*

Coral Gables: *Doc Dammers Saloon*
180 Aragon Ave. **Map** 5 C1.
((305) 441-2600.
Inside the Omni Colonnade Hotel, this well-stocked, mahogany Deco bar is frequented by a sophisticated, 30-plus set. Tasty food is served, the Latin American and Caribbean specialities being the highlights. 🍴 *AE DC MC V*

Coconut Grove: *Dan Marino's American Sports Bar and Grill*
CocoWalk, 3015 Grand Ave. **Map** 6 E4.
((305) 567-0013.
Owned by Miami Dolphins super-star Dan Marino this busy sports bar has three satellite dishes, 51 TVs and three pool tables, and is full of Marino's personal memorabilia. US and imported beer and wines are available, and the menu includes light meals and snacks, such as buffalo wings, veggie pizza, fajita burgers and Mississippi mud pie. 🍴 *AE DC MC V*

THE GOLD AND TREASURE COASTS

Boca Raton: *Pete Rose's Ballpark Café*
8144 W Glades Rd. **Road map** F4.
((561) 488-7383.
There's plenty of Cincinnati Reds memorabilia at the Ballpark Café, as well as the usual videos and bar games. You can also shoot a game of pool or watch TV at your table. A live sports radio show is broadcast from 6 to 8 pm, when the place is packed with people on their way home from work. 🍴 *AE DC MC V*

Fort Lauderdale: *Pier Top Lounge*
Pier 66, 2301 SE 17th St.
Road map F4.
((954) 525-6666.
It takes one hour for the revolving lounge on the rooftop of the Hyatt Regency Pier 66 Hotel to rotate a full 360-degree turn. Customers are treated to some breathtaking views of Fort Lauderdale's skyline and its waterways – a spectacular sight at sunset. There's live music and dancing, but no cover charge. 🎵 *AE DC MC V*

Fort Lauderdale: *Shooters*
3033 NE 32nd Ave. **Road map** F4.
((954) 566-2855.
This waterfront bar and restaurant is a people-watcher's paradise. It is always packed with a casual crowd eating, drinking and watching the boats sail by. The menu is quite extensive and reasonably priced. You can nibble on dishes such as prawn and crab cakes, or tuck into more substantial food, such as seared tuna salad or a Florida grouper sandwich. 🍽 🍴 *AE DC MC V*

Palm Beach: *The Leopard Lounge*
363 Cocoanut Row. **Road map** F4.
((561) 659-5800.
Located in the Chesterfield Hotel, the Leopard Lounge is strikingly decorated with scarlet and black drapes, and the leopard theme is picked out in the plush carpeting and tablecloths. At weekends the place is jammed with locals who dance to the sounds of the "big band" era, performed live. A full menu is served. 🍴 🎵 *AE DC MC V*

ORLANDO AND THE SPACE COAST

Orlando: *Blazing Pianos*
8445 International Drive.
Road map E2.
((407) 363-5104.
One of Orlando's most popular night spots, this large piano bar offers musical entertainment every night, drawing a steady crowd of mixed ages. The stage has three Yamaha grand pianos and musicians play requests and conduct a sing-along. Food is served, and the full bar offers imported and local beers, but the real attraction here is the music. 🍴 🎵 *AE DC MC V*

Orlando: *Cheyenne Saloon and Opera House*
Church Street Station, 129 W Church St.
Road map E2.
((407) 422-2434.
This is downtown Orlando's best country and western music venue. The tri-level saloon has balcony seating in restored church pews that overlook the stage. The entertainment ranges from country music to demonstrations of clog dancing. You can snack on the excellent appetizers or feast on barbecued ribs, grilled chicken and steaks. 🍴 🎵 *AE DC MC V*

THE NORTHEAST

JACKSONVILLE: *River City Brewing Company*
835 Museum Circle. **Road map** E1.
[*(904) 398-2299.*
Home-brewed beer and a varied selection of food at reasonable prices make this a popular spot with the locals. On Friday and Saturday nights there is a live band that plays chart music; there is no cover charge. 🏠 🍴 🎵 AE MC V

St Augustine: *A1A Ale Works*
1 King St. **Road map** E1.
[*(904) 829-2977.*
Situated at the foot of the Bridge of Lions, this friendly pub and restaurant has a microbrewery on site. Ale aficionados come for the seven varieties of home-brewed ale that are available. Live bands play at weekends. 🏠 🍴 🎵 AE DC MC V

St Augustine: *OC White's Seafood and Spirits*
118 Avenida Menendez. **Road map** E1.
[*(904) 824-0808.*
In an 18th-century building found across the street from St Augustine's marina, OC White's offers a great view and live entertainment nightly. The interior is decorated with wax figures of pirates, and a full menu of seafood, steaks and burgers is served. 🏠 🍴 🎵 AE MC V

Daytona Beach: *Oyster Pub*
555 Seabreeze Blvd. **Road map** E2.
[*(904) 255-6348.*
Just one block from the beach, this pub has a raw bar serving fresh oysters, prawn and other seafood. During happy hour prices are cut for both drinks and seafood. There is sports coverage on 27 TVs, a pool room and a disc jockey at weekends. 🍴 🎵 AE MC V

Gainesville: *Purple Porpoise Oyster Pub*
1728 W University Ave. **Road map** D2.
[*(352) 376-1667.*
This is a long-established college bar for students at Gainesville's University of Florida. What it lacks in sophistication it makes up for in atmosphere and the staff are very friendly. A band plays on Thursday evenings. 🍴 🎵 AE DC MC V

THE PANHANDLE

Panama City Beach: *Shuckum's Oyster Pub*
15614 Front Beach Rd. **Road map** B1.
[*(850) 235-3214.*
The bar at this unpretentious and popular watering hole is covered with signed dollar bills left by satisfied customers. Shuckum's is

best known for its local oysters, which are served raw, baked, steamed or fried in a sandwich. Other seafood dishes are also available. 🏠 🍴 🎵 MC V

Pensacola Beach: *Sidelines Sports Bar and Restaurant*
2 Via de Luna Drive. **Road map** A1.
[*(904) 934-3660.*
This informal meeting place in Pensacola Beach has a different special for each night of the week; on "Cajun Night", for example, they serve up Cajun Bloody Marys. There's seating in booths, and the ubiquitous sports memorabilia and giant-screen televisions adorn the walls. 🍴 🎵 AE MC V

Tallahassee: *The Mill Brewery, Eatery and Bakery*
2329 Apalachee Pkwy. **Road map** C1.
[*(904) 656-2867.*
The Mill produces some of the best pastries and beer in the city, all made on the premises; the beers are brewed in small batches without chemicals or preservatives. You can enjoy delicious homemade soups and pizzas, and there's live entertainment on Monday nights. 🏠 🍴 🎵 AE DC MC V

THE GULF COAST

Lee Island Coast: *The Mucky Duck*
11546 Andy Rosse Lane, Captiva Island. **Road map** D4.
[*(941) 472-3434.*
This British-style pub occupies a charming 1930s building in Captiva town. Its creator, a former British policeman, named it after his favourite pub back home. You can play darts, enjoy a beer and watch the sunset. The eclectic menu has English meals such as fish and chips and vegetarian platters. 🏠 🍴 🎵 AE DC MC V

Tampa: *Elmer's Sports Café*
2003 E 7th Ave, Ybor City. **Road map** D3.
[*(813) 248-5855.*
Ybor City's original sports bar is renowned for its thick and chewy pizzas and great beers. Elmer's has giant-screen TVs scattered all around the café, and there's also a pool table. This place is far from fancy, but the homemade food is tasty and the atmosphere pleasant. 🍴 AE MC V

Tampa: *Ovo Café*
1901 E 7th Ave, Ybor City. **Road map** D3.
[*(813) 248-6979.*
With freshly cut flowers on every table, fine art on the walls and cabinets displaying jewellery, this informal bistro offers food for the

eyes as well as the stomach. One of the house specialities is potato-stuffed pasta shells, but the salads and puddings, such as Belgian waffles, are also recommended. There's a separate bar too. 🍴 AE MC V

THE EVERGLADES
AND THE KEYS

Naples: *HB's On The Gulf*
851 Gulf Shore Blvd N.
Road map E4.
[*(941) 261-9100.*
Sophisticated HB's On The Gulf, opened in 1946, is located in the Naples Beach Hotel on Naples Pier. It is a fine place for watching the sun go down, although you need to arrive early to get a seat. After sunset, the huge outside bar is packed with people and a live band provides musical entertainment. HB's serves a full menu but the food is not the highlight here. 🏠 🍴 🎵 AE DC MC V

Key West: *Hog's Breath Saloon*
400 Front St. **Road map** E5.
[*(305) 292-2032.*
The original Hog's Breath Saloon was established by an Alabama expatriate in Fort Walton Beach in 1976, but it moved down to Key West in 1988. It is now a local favourite, offering a raw bar, local seafood dishes and tasty desserts (including a fine version of the famous key lime pie). There is live music every day from 1pm until 2am. 🏠 🍴 🎵 AE MC V

Key West: *Jimmy Buffet's Margaritaville Café*
500 Duval St. **Road map** E5.
[*(305) 292-1435.*
There are plenty of Jimmy Buffet trinkets here, both on display and for sale *(see p285)*, though the local singer-songwriter is rarely seen. Frosty Margaritas are the house speciality, and light meals, sandwiches, burgers and local seafood such as conch fritters are also available. 🍴 🎵 AE MC V

Key West: *Sloppy Joe's*
201 Duval St. **Road map** E5.
[*(305) 294-5717.*
Formerly Ernest Hemingway's favourite drinking place *(see p284)*, Sloppy Joe's is more commercial than in the novelist's day, attracting mainly tourists. However, it retains its Key West character, and when bands play it can be hard to get a seat. The menu includes typical bar fare, with jalapeño or conch fritters, chicken fingers and fries, and the renowned "original Sloppy Joe" burger. 🍴 🎵 MC V

For key to symbols see back flap

SHOPPING IN FLORIDA

Hammock shop sign
in Cedar Key

SHOPPING IS probably the most popular pastime in Florida, and Miami in particular attracts many overseas shoppers. The state is known for its discount stores, but at the other end of the scale also boasts some extraordinarily up-market shops, usually clustered in smart shopping districts or malls.

For first-time visitors to the US, the shopping culture may take some getting used to. Rather than do their shopping in town centres, Floridians generally gravitate towards the huge out-of-town shopping malls, where department stores and all kinds of other shops sell everything from clothes to computers. If you're after souvenirs and gifts, the small speciality shops are your best bet.

For a taste of Florida's souvenirs and other good buys, see pages 334–5. If you're looking for something specific, local tourist offices can provide listings of stores in their area. Shops in Miami are described on pages 92–3.

Mizner Park in Boca Raton, with shops as elegant as its architecture

WHEN TO SHOP

MOST STORES open from 10am to 6pm Monday to Saturday, often staying open late once a week. Shopping mall stores may keep longer hours. Some shops open on Sundays too, typically noon to 6pm, while some (mainly in cities) never close.

SALES TAX

FLORIDA LEVIES a sales tax on all goods except children's clothes and pharmacy drugs. This is usually about 6 per cent but varies from county to county. Tax is not included in displayed prices, but is automatically added to the bill.

SHOPPING MALLS

SHOPPING MALLS are a quintessential feature of the shopping scene in the US. As well as shops, they provide all kinds of facilities from cinemas to restaurants, so in theory you can spend a whole day in the mall and want for nothing. Parking is easy, and out-of-town malls can normally be reached by public bus.

As well as department stores, there is often a daunting array of smaller one-of-a-kind shops and chains, from bookstores such as Barnes & Noble to clothes shops like The Gap.

Miami is well known for its malls, such as the posh Bal Harbour Shops (see p92), and affluent Gold Coast towns like Boca Raton and Palm Beach also have a good selection. Malls, however, are part of the scenery all over Florida.

SHOPPING DISTRICTS

FOR THOSE horrified by the idea of shopping malls, Florida's open-air shopping districts are a fine alternative. Some of these have breathed new life into historic districts, such as St Armands Circle in Sarasota (see p255) and Hyde Park Village in Tampa (see p248). Palm Beach's Worth Avenue (see pp114–15), one of the world's most exclusive shopping streets, has been fashionable since the 1920s. By contrast, pristine Mizner Park in Boca Raton (see p126) is new but built in an old style.

Shops in these districts are predominantly up-market, but you find more down-to-earth places too, particularly those geared to the tourist market – such as the quaint Johns Pass Village near Madeira Beach on the Gulf Coast (see p238).

DEPARTMENT STORES

MOST SHOPPING MALLS include at least one department store. These are often huge affairs, offering an amazing range of goods and services, from complimentary gift-

A stylish fashion boutique in Bal Harbour Shops in Miami

wrapping to assistants to help you with your shopping.

Most of the department stores are found throughout the country, and all have a particular reputation for their quality or merchandise. For example, Bloomingdale's has a good name for its stock of new fashions and also its gourmet food. Some stores deal just in fashion, such as the elegant Saks Fifth Avenue, most famous for its designer clothes, Neiman Marcus and the conservative Lord and Taylor. Florida's own, long-established Burdines chain has branches throughout the state, but it has lost out to the nationwide chains.

For essentials, from pencils to toothpaste, you need look no further than the no-frills supermarkets such as Target, K-Mart and Wal-Mart, which you'll find everywhere. Sears and JC Penney also deal in general merchandise.

SHOPPING FOR BARGAINS

FOR SOME PEOPLE, the chief appeal of Florida's shops are their cut-price goods. Discount stores carry all kinds of general merchandise, but electronic equipment, household goods and cheap clothes are the biggest draw. Some stores specialize in inexpensive designer clothes, chief among them being Loehman's, TJ Maxx and Marshalls, with branches in all major cities.

Particularly popular among bargain-hunters are the factory outlet malls, where slightly imperfect or discontinued merchandise is sold at 50 to 75 per cent below the retail price. At most of these you

One among Micanopy's collection of quaint antique shops

find brand-name stores selling household items and all types of clothing, such as Levi jeans and Benetton jumpers.

Orlando's International Drive (*see p176*) is lined with a multitude of discount stores and factory outlet malls. You can even find cut-price Disney souvenirs here, but be warned that the quality may not be up to that found in the theme parks themselves.

Flea markets, usually large, lively affairs that function at weekends, are popular territory for bargains. Used goods may not interest you, but at most markets you'll find crafts, antiques and other things you might consider taking home, and plenty of food stalls. Some markets are equally good for their entertainment value, such as the Fort Lauderdale Swap Shop (*see p130*), the state's largest flea market and allegedly its most popular attraction after Walt Disney World.

GIFTS AND SOUVENIRS

FRESH ORANGES are a popular buy among US visitors. The best quality fruit is grown by the Indian River on the east coast (*see p111*), where shops and stalls sell oranges by the sackful. Shops can normally send the fruit home for you if you live within the US.

Seashells have wider appeal, but always check the origins of these. The Lee Island Coast (*see pp264–5*) is most famous for its shells, and you can buy legally harvested specimens in the Shell Factory near Fort Myers (*see p263*). The shells and coral touted by roadside stalls along US 1 in the Keys are mostly imported. The same stalls often sell natural sponges, but the classic place for these is Tarpon Springs (*see p237*).

Sponges for sale in Key West

Native Americans sell crafts made on their reservations at Miccosukee Indian Village (*see p271*) and in Hollywood (*see p132*), but Florida is not a great place for crafts. Antiques are more plentiful. Several towns are famous for their antique stores, including Micanopy (*see p208*) and Dania (*see p132*).

Disney has turned merchandising into a fine art, and shopping is a major activity at Walt Disney World and at Orlando's other theme parks. More mundane museum stores are a good source of souvenirs too, from reproductions of artifacts to educational games.

One of Florida's many factory outlets, advertising its bargain prices

What to Buy in Florida

Chocolate
sea shells

PEOPLE WILL PROBABLY TELL YOU that you can buy just about anything you could ever want in Florida, from a designer bikini to a state-of-the art CD player – or even a new home. Indeed some overseas visitors go to Florida specifically to shop. Even if you are searching for more humble souvenirs or gifts, you will be spoilt for choice in the state's theme parks and seaside tourist centres. You may have to search around if you want to avoid kitsch memorabilia – though, in fact, this is what Florida probably does best and is what evokes more than anything else the flavour of the Sunshine State.

Miami Dolphins baseball cap

Unmistakably Florida

All over Florida you can buy fun (and tacky) souvenirs from towels to ashtrays, often at reasonable prices. They are frequently emblazoned with "Florida", a palm tree, alligator or some other characteristic image.

Keyring

Dried meal from the
Kennedy Space Center

Theme Park Fare

All the theme parks, from Universal Studios to Busch Gardens, produce their own merchandise, designed to appeal to all ages.

Fake Oscar from
Universal Studios

Tile with flamingos –
a favourite motif

Alligator
money bank

Seminole Crafts

Crafts made by Florida's Seminole Indians are available in a few places (see p333). You can pick up dolls and jewellery for just a few dollars, and brightly coloured clothes, bags and blankets can be a good buy too.

Hand-Rolled Cigars

The Cuban tradition of hand-rolling cigars survives in Ybor City in Tampa (see pp246–7) and in Miami's Little Havana (see p93), though many are now made by machine. They make a fine gift for cigar-smoking friends.

Books

Books about Miami's Art Deco district often feature superb photos and make a lasting souvenir of the city. Or take home the flavours of Florida in the form of a recipe book.

Latin Music

If you get a taste for the Latin rhythms of Miami's Hispanic community, there is plenty of locally-produced music to buy.

CHEAP GOODS

Many overseas visitors to the US will find that because of lower taxes a whole range of goods are cheaper than they are at home, including jeans, sunglasses, running shoes, CDs, cameras, books and so on. Florida also has many discount stores *(see p333)* which offer lower prices still; small electrical appliances are often a good buy. Downtown Miami is famous for its bargain shops *(see pp92–3)*, which sell primarily cheap gold, jewellery and electronic equipment. Feel free to bargain if you have the nerve. Note that if you buy electronic equipment you will need to get a transformer for it to work outside the US. Most shops are used to foreign visitors and can send bulky purchases back home for you.

T-Shirts
Sold everywhere from gift shops to ordinary discount stores, T-shirts can be very cheap – but you should check the quality before buying.

Authentic cowboy boots

Leather belt

Western Gear
The leather goods sold in stores such as JW Cooper are not necessarily made in Florida, and may not appeal to visitors from Texas. However, they are often good value by international standards.

THE FLAVOURS OF FLORIDA

Florida is famous worldwide for its citrus fruits, which you can buy either fresh (all year round in the case of some varieties) or preserved – as colourful sweets, jams or jellies, or as tasty marinades and oils for cooking. For those with a sweet tooth there are all sorts of sugary goodies, from sticky coconut patties to chewy sweets such as "salt water taffy". Locally made chocolate is not of great quality, but often comes in fun shapes.

Coconut patties

A basket of jellied citrus fruit, a favourite edible souvenir

Florida-grown oranges, sold by the sack

Colourful salt water taffy, popular among US visitors

Lime marmalade

Tangerine jam or "butter"

Hot jalapeño pepper jelly

Mango marinade

Key lime oil for cooking

ENTERTAINMENT IN FLORIDA

WHETHER YOUR preference is for a Broadway drama, a lavish Las Vegas-style floorshow, a night in a disco or a spot of gambling, Florida has something for everyone. You'll find the greatest range of entertainment in South Florida, particularly along the Gold Coast and in Miami (see pp94–5), but Sarasota and Tampa are also big cultural centres. Walt Disney World and Orlando offer the best choice as far as family entertainment is concerned, with theme parks galore to thrill the children during the day and

Performer at Wild Bill's dinner show

dinner shows at night. In the Northeast and the Panhandle the entertainment is more limited, being best in resorts like Panama City Beach and university cities such as Gainesville and Tallahassee.

Wherever you are, in cities with distinct mainland and beach areas, such as Fort Lauderdale, you'll find the liveliest nightlife along the seafront. As far as the performing arts are concerned, most high-quality shows take place between October and April, though there is a good choice of events all year round.

The Raymond F Kravis Center for the Performing Arts, West Palm Beach

SOURCES OF INFORMATION

MOST REGIONAL newspapers in Florida have a special weekend section that lists all local attractions and events, as well as details of venues. Local Convention and Visitors' Bureaux and chambers of commerce are also chock-a-block with brochures.

MAKING RESERVATIONS

THE EASIEST WAY to buy tickets for a concert, play, football game or other event is to call the relevant box office and pay by credit card. Some venues, however, will require you to make your reservation through **Ticketmaster**. This company runs an extensive pay-by-phone operation and also has outlets in music and discount stores. It charges a commission of $2–8 per ticket above the ticket's face value, depending on the event.

MAJOR VENUES

FLORIDA'S LARGEST venues, some of which are known as performing arts centers, are used for a whole range of performances, from operas to rock concerts, as well as for special events including, in some cases, sports fixtures. This is where major national touring companies or artists usually perform, though you can sometimes see local productions here too.

The following are among the most important venues in Florida: the **Raymond F Kravis Center for the Performing Arts** in West Palm Beach; Fort Lauderdale's **Broward Center for the Performing Arts**; the huge **Tampa Bay Performing Arts Center** in Tampa; and the **Van Wezel Performing Arts Hall** in

Emblem of the Saenger Theater, Pensacola

Sarasota. Other major theatres with large arenas include St Petersburg's **Tropicana Field**, Florida's only domed stadium, and the **Florida Citrus Bowl** in Orlando, a 70,000-seat arena where stars from Paul McCartney to George Michael perform. The huge **Gator Bowl** in Jacksonville hosts major rock concerts too.

THEATRE

ROAD SHOWS, often lavish productions with extravagant sets and big casts, which originate on Broadway in New York, are the highest quality productions you are likely to see in Florida. But the state boasts several good quality theatre companies of its own, whose shows are performed in smaller, more atmospheric venues such as the **Saenger Theater** in Pensacola or Key West's **Red Barn Theater**. The **Florida State University Center for the Performing Arts** is home to Sarasota's Asolo Theatre Company. The building, originally the opera house of Dunfermline in Scotland, was brought to Sarasota in the 1980s. The **Players of Sarasota** is the city's longest established theatre company, where a number of famous actors, such as Montgomery Clift, launched their careers. Its performances of musicals and plays usually earn high praise.

CLASSICAL MUSIC, OPERA AND DANCE

MOST MAJOR cities have their own symphony orchestra. The **Florida Philharmonic Orchestra**, which performs mainly in Miami and in the cities along the Gold Coast, is the best in the state – though Miami's New World Symphony *(see p94)* is better known internationally. Also keep an eye open for perfomances by the **Concert Association of Florida** (in Fort Lauderdale and Miami), and the Jacksonville Symphony Orchestra, which is based at the city's **Times-Union Center for the Performing Arts**.

The state's largest opera company is the **Florida Grand Opera**, the fruit of a merger in 1994 of Miami's and Fort Lauderdale's own opera companies. It puts on around five major productions every year in Broward and Dade counties. **Gold Coast Opera** presents classical opera at four locations in southeast Florida. For a more intimate experience, visit a small venue such as the **Monticello Opera House**, which hosts opera between September and May.

The best ballet company is the Miami City Ballet *(see p94)*, whose choreographer is Edward Villela, a protegé of the late George Balanchine.

CINEMA

FOR ARTS MOVIES you'll do better in New York or Los Angeles, but Florida has plenty of multi-screen cinemas showing blockbuster films. The state's most famous cinema is the historic **Tampa Theatre** *(see p245)*, which hosts a variety of live acts but serves up mainly a mixture of classic and foreign films.

Also keep a look out for annual film festivals: Sarasota has one in November, and the Miami International Film Festival takes place in February, when films are shown at the Gusman Center for the Performing Arts *(see p94)*.

DINNER SHOWS

DINNER SHOWS are a popular form of family entertainment in Florida, especially in Orlando *(see p177)*. Here, diners sit at communal tables and are served huge meals which are generally themed to the show that you are watching. Audience participation is normally *de rigueur*.

Outside Orlando, the dinner shows tend to be less raucous but still provide varied entertainment, from conventional plays to comedies and musicals. The **Mystery Dinner Theater** in Clearwater Beach invites diners to solve a murder mystery as the drama is acted out on stage; whereas the **Mai Kai** in Fort Lauderdale, a long-running and superbly tacky Polynesian revue, entertains with dancers dressed in grass skirts, fire eaters and the like. Jacksonville's **Alhambra Dinner Theater** puts on ambitious musicals of the *Oklahoma* and *South Pacific* school.

A singer entertains at Miami's Latin Carnival *(see p.32)*

LIVE MUSIC AND NIGHTCLUBS

SOME OF THE MOST entertaining places to dance are clubs where you can dance to live instead of piped music. The best are often clubs where the music is provided by a big band or orchestra; "supper clubs" offer food as well as a band. The music can be varied: the **Coliseum Ballroom**, a Moorish-style gem in St Petersburg, draws a crowd for both ballroom and country dancing. South Beach has the greatest choice of conventional discos *(see p95)*, but you'll find good clubs in popular holiday spots. The **Coliseum** in Daytona Beach offers impressive laser shows, while the **Baja Beach Club** in Fort Lauderdale and Jacksonville's **Club Carousel** impress as much for their size as anything else. Note that nightclubs require you to show ID to prove that you are over 18 or, in some cases, 21.

Festivals are fertile territory for live music, and there are also countless places where dancing to the music isn't compulsory. Key West has several well-established venues, like the Hog's Breath Café *(see p331)*, and Ybor City also has a good choice, its **Jazz Cellar** drawing a loyal crowd. Country and western music is popular, for which Panama City Beach's **Ocean Opry Theater** is a major venue. Some of the bars listed on pages 330–31 also offer live entertainment.

Sign for Hog's Breath Café in Key West

The lavish interior of the Tampa Theatre, an historic cinema

Street performers in Mallory Square, providing nightly entertainment at sunset

CRUISE AND BOAT TRIPS

FLORIDA IS THE world's leading departure point for cruises to the Caribbean, and ships set off regularly from Miami, Port Everglades and other, smaller ports. But you can also go on mini cruises, for a day or just an evening – the cost of which starts at around $40.

Evening cruises usually entail dinner and dancing, but for some they are just an excuse to gamble. **Europa SeaKruz**, which has ships in Miami, Tampa and Fort Myers, and the **Discovery Cruise Line**, operating out of Miami and Port Everglades, both have casinos on board.

If you are happy with a more modest cruise, pleasure boat trips are available all over Florida. The Jungle Queen in Fort Lauderdale *(see p131)*, Tampa's **Starlite Princess** and the **Star of Palm Beach** *(see p123)* are old-fashioned boats particularly popular with tourists. The **Rivership Romance** offers trips on the St Johns River starting from Sanford *(see p206)*.

The Rivership Romance on the St Johns River

GAMBLING

GAMBLING ON cruise ships is popular because conventional casinos are illegal on the mainland: once a ship is in international waters, about 3 miles (5 km) from shore, the law no longer applies. On land, you can visit one of the state's legal **Seminole Indian Casinos**, of which there are three: one is in Hollywood *(see p133)*, another in Immokalee near Naples, and a third near Tampa. You can play poker, and there are slot machines, but the main activity is bingo. Poker is also played at race courses, where you can also bet on the horses.

CHILDREN'S ENTERTAINMENT

KIDS ARE WELL CATERED to all over Florida, not just at the theme parks. Museums often have excellent hands-on exhibits, and in many zoos and some parks you find "petting zoos", where children can enjoy direct contact with the animals. Kids can also have fun at the water parks *(see p341)*, found all over the state. With **Walt Disney World**, **Sea World** and the area's other big attractions, Orlando is not short of family entertainment. Keep an eye out for what's on at the **Orlando Arena**, which hosts everything from circuses to ice skating shows.

There is also plenty of free entertainment. Kids often enjoy street entertainers, who perform in Mallory Square in Key West, for example, and there are festivals to choose from all year round *(see pp32–5)*.

GAY ENTERTAINMENT

SOUTH BEACH in Miami is well known for its vibrant gay scene *(see p95)*, which is attracting more and more gay visitors from both home and abroad. Key West has been a gay mecca for many years, as has Fort Lauderdale, where **The Copa** club is the most popular gay stomping ground. You'll find a less developed scene in Tampa, however there are a number of well established gay venues in Ybor City, including the justifiably popular **Mecca** club.

For further information, buy *The Out Pages*, which is an excellent book listing gay venues and businesses in Florida. Alternatively, listings information is provided in the Southern edition of the US *Gay Yellow Pages*, and in selected books published by the **Damron Company**.

Festivities during the Gay Pride celebration in Fort Lauderdale

DIRECTORY

TICKETMASTER OUTLETS

Central Florida
(407) 839-3900.

Fort Lauderdale
(954) 523-3309.

Fort Myers
(941) 334-3309.

Miami
(305) 358-5885.

North Florida
(904) 353-3309.

St Petersburg
(813) 898-2100.

Tampa
(813) 287-8844.

West Palm Beach
(561) 966-3309.

MAJOR VENUES

Broward Center for the Performing Arts
201 SW Fifth Ave,
Fort Lauderdale.
(954) 462-0222.

Florida Citrus Bowl
1610 W Church St,
Downtown Orlando.
(407) 849-2020.

Gator Bowl
1 Gator Bowl Blvd,
Jacksonville.
(904) 630-3900.

Raymond F Kravis Center for the Performing Arts
701 Okeechobee Blvd,
West Palm Beach.
(561) 832-7469.

Tropicana Field
1 Tropicana Drive,
St Petersburg.
(813) 825-3120.

Tampa Bay Performing Arts Center
1010 N MacInnes Place,
Tampa.
(800) 955-1045.

Van Wezel Performing Arts Hall
777 N Tamiami Trail,
Sarasota.
(941) 953-3366.

THEATRE

Florida State University Center for the Performing Arts
5555 N Tamiami Trail,
Sarasota.
(941) 351-8000.

Players of Sarasota
838 N Tamiami Trail,
Sarasota.
(941) 365-2494.

Red Barn Theater
319 Duval St, Key West.
(305) 296-9911.

Saenger Theater
118 S Palafox St,
Pensacola.
(904) 444-7686.

CLASSICAL MUSIC, OPERA AND DANCE

Times-Union Center for the Performing Arts
300 W Water St,
Jacksonville.
(904) 633-6110.

Concert Association of Florida
555 17th St, Miami Beach.
(305) 532-3491.

Florida Grand Opera
1200 Coral Way, Miami.
(305) 854-7890.

Florida Philharmonic Orchestra
3401 NW 9th Ave,
Fort Lauderdale.
(954) 561-2997.

Gold Coast Opera
1000 Coconut Creek Blvd,
Pompano Beach.
(954) 973-2323.

Monticello Opera House
West Washington St,
Monticello.
(904) 997-4242.

CINEMA

Tampa Theatre
711 Franklin St,
Tampa.
(813) 274-8981.

DINNER SHOWS

Alhambra Dinner Theater
12000 Beach Blvd,
Jacksonville.
(904) 641-1212.

Mai Kai
3599 N Federal Highway,
Fort Lauderdale.
(954) 563-3272 or
(800) 262-4524.

Mystery Dinner Theater
25 Belleview Blvd,
Clearwater Beach.
(813) 584-3490.

LIVE MUSIC AND NIGHTCLUBS

Baja Beach Club
3200 N Federal Highway,
Fort Lauderdale.
(954) 561-2432.

Coliseum
176 N Beach St,
Daytona Beach.
(904) 257-9982.

Coliseum Ballroom
535 4th Ave North,
St Petersburg.
(813) 892-5202.

Club Carousel
8550 Arlington Expressway,
Jacksonville.
(904) 725-2582.

Jazz Cellar
1311 E 9th Ave,
Ybor City, Tampa.
(813) 248-1862.

Ocean Opry Theater
8400 Front Beach Rd,
Panama City Beach.
(904) 234-5464.

CRUISE AND BOAT TRIPS

Discovery Cruise Line
1850 Eller Drive,
Port Everglades,
Fort Lauderdale
(954) 525-7800.

Europa SeaKruz
Miami Beach Marina,
1280 5th St, Miami Beach.
(800) 688-7529 for
information on all cruises.

Rivership Romance
433 N Palmetto Ave,
Sanford.
(407) 321-5091.

Starlite Princess Cruises
Garrison Seaport Center,
651 Channelside Drive,
Tampa.
(813) 229-1200.

Star of Palm Beach
900 E Blue Heron Blvd,
Singer Island.
(561) 848-7827.

GAMBLING

Seminole Indian Casino
5223 N Orient Rd,
I-4 Exit 5, Tampa.
(800) 282-7016.

Seminole Indian Casino
506 South 1st St,
Immokalee.
(800) 218-0007.

CHILDREN'S ENTERTAINMENT

Orlando Arena
600 W Amelia St,
Orlando.
(407) 849-2020.

Sea World
7007 Sea World Drive,
Orlando.
(407) 363-2613.

Walt Disney World
Guest Letters Dept,
PO Box 10040,
Lake Buesna Vista,
FL 32830-0040.
(407) 849-2020.

GAY ENTERTAINMENT

The Copa
624 SE 28th St,
Fort Lauderdale.
(954) 463-1507.

Damron Company
PO Box 422458,
San Francisco, CA 94142.
(415) 255-0404.

Mecca
2004 N 16th St,
Ybor City, Tampa.
(813) 248-3053.

Sports and Outdoor Activities

THANKS TO FLORIDA'S CLIMATE, you can take part in many sports and outdoor activities all year round, making the state a top destination for all sports enthusiasts, from golfers and tennis players to canoeists and deep-sea divers; some people even base their entire holiday around the sporting opportunities available. Water sports of all kinds are well catered for, with wonderful beaches on both the Atlantic and Gulf coasts. Florida also boasts approximately 10 million acres (4 million ha) of protected land, which can be explored on foot, horseback, bicycle or boat. For those who prefer to watch rather than take part, Florida has a wide range of spectator sports on offer; these are described on pages 30–31.

A seaside golf course at Boca Raton on the Gold Coast

SOURCES OF INFORMATION

THE TWO BEST sources of general information are the **Florida Sports Foundation** and the **Department of Environmental Protection (DEP)**, which can provide information on most outdoor activities. The *Florida Vacation Guide*, available from Florida tourist board offices abroad, gives useful addresses, or you can contact local tourist offices for information about specific areas. Further sources are given in individual sections.

GOLF

FLORIDA IS A GOLFER'S paradise; with over 1,100 public and private courses, it is the country's top golfing destination. Palm Beach offers so many courses (150 in total) it claims to be the "golfing capital of the world", though Naples boasts the greatest concentration.

Courses in Florida are flat by most standards, but landscaping provides some relief. Many of the most challenging courses are attached to resort hotels along the coast (some of which offer special golf holiday packages), though you'll find courses inland too, including at Walt Disney World *(see p162)*. About two-thirds of Florida's courses are open to the public.

Golf is a year-round sport, but winter is the busiest season. If you play in summer, start early in the day to avoid late afternoon thunderstorms and lightning. Green fees vary from under $20 to over $75 per person, and are highest in the peak winter season.

The *Fairways in the Sunshine* golf guide, from the Florida Sports Foundation, lists all public and private courses.

TENNIS

TENNIS, LIKE GOLF, is very popular in Florida. Many hotels have courts, and some resorts offer holiday packages that include tuition. Contact the **United States Tennis Association (Florida Section)** for information on coaching, clubs and competitions. The state's most famous tennis school is the **Nick Bollettieri Tennis Academy** *(see p253)*, which offers weekly training programmes for $800 and up, as well as one-day sessions.

DIVING AND SNORKELLING

FLORIDA IS SUPERB diving and snorkelling territory. The country's only living coral reef skirts the state's southeast coast, stretching the length of the Keys, where there is a magnificent variety of coral and fish *(see pp278–9)*. The reef lies 3–5 miles (5–8 km) offshore and is easily accessible to amateur snorkellers. Guided snorkelling trips are available throughout the Keys and are generally excellent.

The state's estimated 4,000 diving sites have increased thanks to the artificial reefs programme. All over Florida, from Panama City Beach to Fort Lauderdale, everything from bridge spans to freighters have been used to create a habitat for coral and colourful fish; there is even a Rolls Royce in the waters off Palm Beach. Sunken Spanish galleons also provide fascinating dive sites, mainly in south Florida.

If you don't have a Certified Divers Card you'll need to do a course. Recognized NAUI or PADI courses are widely available, and novices can learn in just four days for $300–400.

For further information, the Florida Sports Foundation's *Florida Boating and Diving Guide* is helpful, or you can call the **Florida Association of Dive Operators**.

Freshwater swimming at Wakulla Springs in the Panhandle

Colourful jet ski and boat rental outlet in the Panhandle

SWIMMING AND WATER SPORTS

SWIMMING is as natural as breathing to most Floridians. Many hotels have pools, but the joy of Florida is the chance to swim in the ocean or in the many lakes, springs and rivers.

The Atlantic provides the best waves and Florida's only surfing beaches, including Cocoa Beach (see p181). The warm, gentle swells of the Gulf of Mexico are better for kids. These western beaches are beautiful, with whiter-than-white sands in the Panhandle, though the waters can be less clear than on the Atlantic side. Coastal erosion means that the southeastern beaches are often quite narrow, while there are only a couple of sandy beaches in the Florida Keys.

Beach access is sometimes controlled: many lie within parks, which charge admission. Some hotels like to give the impression that their beach is for guests only, but they can't stop public access. Lifeguards monitor the most popular beaches in high season.

Many inland parks have freshwater swimming areas, including some beautifully clear spring water holes, such as in Blue Spring State Park (see p206). Another fun alternative for families are the water parks, found throughout the state, which have all kinds of rides and pools.

The full range of water sports, from windsurfing to jet skiing, is on offer at Florida's resorts, while water-skiing can also be enjoyed on freshwater lakes and inland waterways.

FISHING

FLORIDA'S NUMEROUS lakes and rivers are overflowing with fish, and fishing is not so much a sport as a way of life for a great many Floridians. The opportunities are endless both inland and all along the coast.

The Atlantic and Gulf shores are both dotted with the haunts of dedicated fishermen. Fishing right off the pier is popular at many coastal spots, but for those who enjoy angling on a different scale there is plenty of sport fishing, for which the state is probably best known.

Deep-sea fishing boats can be chartered at many seaside resorts. The biggest fleets are in the Panhandle, especially around Fort Walton Beach and Destin, and in the Keys. With the Gulf Stream nearby, the waters off the Keys offer the most varied fishing in the state (see p281). Organized group excursions are an excellent option for novices. If you want to take your big fish home, a taxidermist will preserve it for you, though the more eco-conscious alternative these days is to have a model made of your catch. Bait and tackle shops should be able to give you the names of local taxidermists; another possibility is to contact the **Florida State Taxidermy Association**.

Florida has thousands of lakes, as well as rivers and canals for freshwater fishing. Boat rentals and fishing guides are available along the larger rivers, such as the St Johns, and in other popular fishing areas like Lake Okeechobee (see p124). Fishing is also permitted in many state and other parks. In rural parts, fish camps offer simple accommodation and basic supplies, though some are open only during the summer.

Licences, costing from $12 to $30, are required for both freshwater and saltwater fishing. The Fishing Handbook, available from the **Florida Game and Fresh Water Fish Commission**, gives information on locations and licensing. It also gives details of the entry dates, fees, regulations and prizes of Florida's fishing tournaments; one of the best known is Destin's Fishing Rodeo (see p34).

For further information on fishing contact the Department of Environmental Protection, which publishes a helpful brochure, Fishing Lines, aimed primarily at saltwater anglers.

Fishing fleet sign, Destin

Pelicans observing anglers on a pier on Cedar Key

The Intracoastal Waterway at Boca Raton, on the Gold Coast

BOATING

Florida's waterways attract boats of every description, from state-of-the-art yachts to wooden skiffs. With over 8,000 miles (12,870 km) of tidal coastline and 4,500 sq miles (11,655 sq km) of inland waters, the state is a paradise for boaters. Having a boat is as normal as having a car for some Floridians; the state has over 700,000 registered boats, and this doesn't include the 300,000 brought in annually from outside Florida.

The Intracoastal Waterway, extending 500 miles (800 km) down the east coast to the tip of the Keys (see pp20–21), is very popular. Often sheltered from the Atlantic Ocean by barrier islands, the route runs through rivers, creeks and dredged canals. Though most of the west coast is open, the most interesting territory for boaters is where the Intra-coastal Waterway resumes among the islands of the Lee Island Coast (see pp264–5).

The 135-mile (217-km) Okeechobee Waterway, which cuts through the state, is ano-ther popular route, becoming positively busy during the summer. It runs along the St Lucie Canal from Stuart, across Lake Okeechobee and then on to Sanibel Island via the Caloosahatchee River.

These inland waterways, like many of the state's 166 rivers, are suitable for small boats or houseboats. Many of the latter are more like float-ing apartments, often being equipped with air conditioning, microwave ovens and even television. Houseboats can be rented from several marinas, in Sanford on the St Johns River for example (see p206), while small to medium-sized boats are available at many fish camps or marinas.

Florida has an astonishing 1,250 marinas. Those along the coast usually have excellent facilities, with accommodation and rental outlets for boats and fishing tackle; inland marinas tend to be more basic. *Florida Boating and Diving*, a brochure available from the **Florida Sports Foundation**, lists most marinas in the state, with details of their facilities.

BACKCOUNTRY PURSUITS

Florida's protected areas vary from popular beaches to much wilder areas like the Everglades. The provision of facilities varies too, but most parks have some kind of visitors' centre, dispensing maps and other information.

Some also organize ranger-led tours. Winter is the best time to explore, when the summer rains and mosquitos are over.

Over 110 areas are protected by the state, classified variously as State Parks, State Recreation Areas and State Preserves. They all charge admission and usually open from 8am to sunset daily. The Department of Environmental Protection (DEP) issues a free guide, *Florida State Parks*, which lists them all plus their facilities.

Information on the fewer federally run national parks is available from the **National Park Service** in Georgia. Many other parks are private, in-cluding sanctuaries run by the **Florida Audubon Society**; these are particularly good for bird life. The *Florida Trails* guide, issued by the national tourist board (see p347), has a com plete list of private, state and national parks.

Florida state park emblem

As a result of the Florida Rails-to-Trails Programme, old rail way tracks have been turned into trails, suitable for hiking, cycling, rollerblading and horse riding. Best are the 16-mile (26-km) Tallahassee–St Marks Historic Railroad State Trail, south of Tallahassee, and the Gainesville–Hawthorne State Trail (see p209) in the Northeast. The DEP's Office of Greenways and Trails has information on these and many other trails.

Outdoor adventure tours are organized by a few companies. One is **Florida Outback Safaris**, which arranges trips all over the state including in the Everglades and the Keys.

Visitors on a boardwalk in the Everglades National Park

CYCLING

THERE IS PLENTY of scope for both on-road and off-road cycling in Florida, where the flatness of the land makes for easy cycling territory – though keen cyclists may find it rather dull. The rolling countryside of the Panhandle is the most rewarding area to explore, while the Northeast has some good trails too, for example in Paynes Prairie *(see p209)*.

If you don't bring your own, bicycles can usually be rented on site or from a local source. For general cycling information, contact the **State Bicycle Office** or the Department of Environmental Protection.

Canoeing in the Blackwater River State Park

WALKING

FLORIDA MIGHT not seem ideal walking country, but the variety of habitats makes up for the flat landscape. Most state parks have hiking trails, and there is a project currently underway to create the National Scenic Trail – starting at the Big Cypress National Preserve *(see p270)* in south Florida and ending near Pensacola. So far, 550 miles (880 km) of the planned 1,292-mile (2,080-km) route have been completed.

The **Florida Trail Association** is the best place to get information on hiking trails.

CANOEING

THERE IS ample opportunity for canoeing in Florida, with the Florida Canoe Trail System comprising 36 routes along creeks and rivers totalling 950 miles (1,520 km). Several parks are renowned for their canoe runs, the most famous being the exhilarating, 99-mile (160-km) Wilderness Waterway in the Everglades National Park *(see pp272–7)*. Some of the best rivers, such as the Blackwater River *(see p220)*, can be found in the north, though the Hillsborough River on the Gulf Coast is also popular *(see p249)*. Always

Enjoying the countryside near Ocala on horseback

check the water level before setting off, as both high and low levels can be dangerous.

HORSE RIDING

THE OCALA NATIONAL FOREST in the Northeast *(see p207)* has over 100 miles (160 km) of trails suited to horse riding. There are 15 state parks with riding trails, including Myakka River *(see p260)*, Jonathan Dickinson *(see p113)* and the Florida Caverns *(see p225)*; about half the parks have facilities for overnight stays.

Information is available from the *Florida Horse Trail Directory*, issued by the **Department of Agriculture and Consumer Services**, or from the Department of Environmental Protection.

DIRECTORY

SOURCES OF INFORMATION

Department of Environmental Protection (DEP)
3900 Commonwealth Blvd,
Tallahassee, FL 32399.
☏ *(904) 488-3701.*

Florida Sports Foundation
1319 Thomaswood Drive,
Tallahassee, FL 32312.
☏ *(904) 488-8347.*

TENNIS

Nick Bollettieri Tennis Academy
5500 34th St West,
Bradenton, FL 34210.
☏ *(941) 755-1000.*

United States Tennis Association (Florida Section)
1280 SW 36th Ave,
Pompano Beach, FL 33069.
☏ *(954) 968-3434.*

DIVING AND SNORKELLING

Florida Association of Dive Operators
PO Box 12393,
Tallahassee, FL 32317.
☏ *(904) 552-1063.*

FISHING

Florida Game and Fresh Water Fish Commission
620 S Meridian St,
Tallahassee, FL 32399.
☏ *(904) 488-6411.*

Florida State Taxidermy Association
Box 7995, Starke,
FL 32091.
☏ *(904) 964-3337.*

BACKCOUNTRY PURSUITS

Florida Audubon Society
1331 Palmetto, Suite 110,
Winter Park, FL 32789.
☏ *(407) 539-5700.*

Florida Outback Safaris
17490 SW 58th St, Fort
Lauderdale, FL 33331.
☏ *(954) 680-4009.*

National Park Service (Southeast)
100 Alabama St SW,
Atlanta, GA 30303.
☏ *(404) 562-3123.*

CYCLING

State Bicycle Office
Dept of Transportation,
605 Suwannee St,
Tallahassee, FL 32399.
☏ *(904) 487-1200.*

WALKING

Florida Trail Association
PO Box 13708,
Gainesville, FL 32604.
☏ *(352) 378-8823 or
(800) 343-1882.*

HORSE RIDING

Department of Agriculture and Consumer Services
Room 416, Mayo Building,
Tallahassee, FL 32399.
☏ *(904) 488-5100.*

SURVIVAL
GUIDE

PRACTICAL INFORMATION

WITH MORE THAN 40 million visitors a year, Florida is very well geared to catering to tourists' needs. It is the ultimate family holiday destination. A strong emphasis is placed on entertaining children, and the informal lifestyle and excellent facilities make travelling with youngsters a real pleasure. The only complaint a child is likely to have is if the queue to see Mickey Mouse is too

The state seal of Florida

long or the sun too hot. Given its warm climate, for most North Americans Florida is a winter destination. The peak season runs from December to April, when rates for flights and hotels are at their height, while the beaches and attractions are at their busiest. Anyone visiting Walt Disney World or the other theme parks should be prepared for long waiting times during any holiday period.

A roadside tourist information centre in Kissimmee

VISAS

BRITISH CITIZENS, members of many EU countries, and citizens of Australia and New Zealand do not need a visa provided they have a return ticket and their stay in the US does not exceed 90 days. All that is required is a completed "visa waiver" form, issued by flight attendants either before or during the flight.

Other citizens must apply for a non-immigrant visa from a US consulate, while Canadians need only proof of residence.

US immigration officers are known for their stringency. On entering the country it is quite possible that you may be asked to prove that you have sufficient funds to cover your stay.

CUSTOMS ALLOWANCES

CUSTOMS ALLOWANCES for visitors over 21 years of age entering the US are: 1 litre (2 pints) of alcohol, gifts worth up to $100 and 200 cigarettes, 100 cigars (as long as they're not made in Cuba) or 3 pounds (1.4 kilograms) of tobacco. A number of goods are prohibited, including cheese, fresh fruit, meat products and, of course, illegal drugs.

TOURIST INFORMATION

MOST LARGE CITIES in Florida have a Convention and Visitors' Bureau (CVB), where you'll find a daunting array of free brochures. In smaller places go to the Chamber of Commerce, though since these offices cater mainly to the business community, some can be of only limited help.

For information before you leave home, phone or write off for a special vacation pack, distributed by the Florida Tourism Corporation both in the US and abroad. This will include a list of all the tourist offices in Florida, which can then be contacted directly. In some countries, including the UK, individual regions and even the top theme parks have their own information offices.

ADMISSION CHARGES

MOST MUSEUMS, parks and other attractions charge an admission fee. This can vary enormously, from $2 at a small museum to over $40 for a day pass into Walt Disney World's Magic Kingdom.

Children and card-carrying students and senior citizens can often claim a discount, and

anyone can use the coupons found in brochures available at tourist offices. These can cut the price of admission fees and also buy cheap meals in local restaurants. Coupons from the information centre on International Drive near Orlando *(see p176),* can save you hundreds of dollars.

OPENING TIMES

SOME ATTRACTIONS close once a week, often on Monday, yet the majority open daily. State parks are usually open every day from sunrise to sunset, though attached visitor centres may close earlier. The theme parks have extended opening hours during the high season. Most sights close on major national holidays: typically New Year, Thanksgiving and Christmas *(see p35).*

TRAVELLING WITH CHILDREN

AS A TOP FAMILY destination, Florida places the needs of children high on its list of priorities. You can rent pushchairs ("strollers" in the US) at

A boy enjoying a ride in a dolphin pushchair, for hire at Sea World

the major theme parks; car hire firms are obliged to supply children's seats; and many restaurants offer special menus *(see p313)*. On planes, buses and trains, children under 12 usually pay only half the standard fare, less if they are very young.

The main thing to worry about if you have children is the sun. Just a few minutes' exposure to the midday sun can burn young skin; apply sunblock and encourage them to wear a hat.

Florida's theme parks are vast and it is well worth agreeing on a place to meet in the event that someone gets lost; most parks also have a special "lost kids area".

For information on hotel facilities for children, see page 295; for entertainment for children, see page 338.

SENIOR CITIZENS

FLORIDA IS A MECCA for senior citizens, both to visit and to settle. Anyone over 65 (less in some instances) is eligible for all kinds of discounts – at attractions, hotels, restaurants, and also on public transport.

The **American Association of Retired Persons** can help members plan their holiday and offers discounts on air fares, car rental and rooms.

ETIQUETTE

DRESS IN FLORIDA is casual, except in a few top restaurants *(see p312)*. Shorts and T-shirts are acceptable in most beachside bars. On the beach itself it is illegal for women to go topless, except in a few places, such as Miami's South Beach. Drinking alcohol on beaches and in other public places is also illegal.

It is against the law to smoke in buses, trains, taxis and in most public buildings; there are usually separate areas for smokers and non-smokers in restaurants and cafés.

Unless a service charge is imposed, in restaurants you should tip 15 to 20 per cent of the bill. Taxi drivers expect a similar bonus. For hotel porters, $1 per bag is usual.

TRAVELLERS WITH DISABILITIES

AMERICA IS WAY AHEAD of most nations in the help it gives people with disabilities. Federal law demands that all public buildings be accessible to people in wheelchairs, although some old buildings have remained exempt. This guide specifies whether or not a sight is accessible, but you are advised to call ahead for details. For example, in nature reserves wheelchair-friendly boardwalks may make some areas accessible, while others remain out of bounds.

Accessible to wheelchairs

A few rental companies have cars adapted for people with disabilities, and some buses have wheelchair access – look for a sticker on the windscreen or by the door. Amtrak and Greyhound offer reduced fares.

Mobility International offers general advice for travellers with disabilities. The Florida Tourism Corporation issues a useful services directory and Walt Disney World has its own special guide too.

ELECTRICAL APPLIANCES

YOU WILL NEED a voltage converter and an adaptor to use the American 110–120 volts AC system; adaptors for the two-prong plugs used in the US can be bought abroad or locally. Many hotels, however, have plugs that power both 110- and 220-volt electric shavers, and often supply wall-mounted hair dryers.

Customers in casual dress at the bar in the Columbia Restaurant, Tampa

Personal Security and Health

PUBLICITY ABOUT ATTACKS on tourists in the early 1990s was considered exaggerated by the Florida authorities given the small number of assaults relative to the vast number of visitors. Even so, the police responded quickly, introducing extra security measures and offering new safety guidelines to visitors. Crimes against tourists have since fallen. You must still be alert in urban areas, above all in Miami or if you are driving, but anyone who takes precautions should enjoy a trouble-free trip.

Police officers on patrol, Florida-style, in St Augustine

LAW ENFORCEMENT

ENFORCEMENT OF THE LAW is shared by three agencies: the city police forces, sheriffs (who police country areas) and the Florida Highway Patrol, which deals with traffic accidents and offences outside the cities. Major tourist centres are well policed, and Miami and Orlando also have a special Tourist Oriented Police (TOP), a recent arrival on the scene, and one which may well be copied elsewhere.

Given Florida's eagerness to both attract and protect tourists, police officers are friendly and helpful to visitors.

GUIDELINES ON SAFETY

MOST CITIES IN FLORIDA, like elsewhere in the world, have "no-go" areas that should be avoided. The staff at the local tourist office or in your hotel should be able to advise. Note that downtown areas are generally unlike city centres elsewhere; they are first and foremost business districts, which are dead at night and often unsafe. If in doubt, take a taxi rather than walk.

Burglaries within hotels are not unheard of. Leave your best jewellery at home and lock other valuables in the safe in your room, or hand them in at the reception desk; few hotels will guarantee the security of any belongings kept in your

room. If someone knocks on your door claiming to be hotel staff, you may want to check with reception before letting the person in.

Carry as little money as possible when you go out, keep your passport separate from your travellers' cheques and leave your room key with the desk clerk. If you are unlucky enough to be attacked, hand your wallet over immediately. Do not try to resist.

STAYING SAFE IN MIAMI

ALTHOUGH VISITORS are rarely the victim, Miami has one of the highest crime rates in the US. Certain districts are to be avoided at all costs. These include Liberty City and Overtown, both located between the airport and Downtown. Further north, Little Haiti and Opa-Locka are interesting areas to visit, but they should be treated with caution (see pp87–9). Avoid all deserted areas at night, including the transport terminals and Downtown. Lively night spots such as Coconut Grove and South Beach are the safest areas to hang out in after dark, but even here you should not venture into quiet back streets (such as south of 5th Street in South Beach). Whatever time of day you go out, be sure to carry a decent map with you.

In addition to the regular police patrols, Miami's Tourist Oriented Police provides extra

cover in the area around the airport, especially around car hire outlets. Rental staff should be able to advise motorists on the best route into town and will also supply drivers with a map. See page 358 for safety tips for drivers.

In an emergency dial 911, or contact **Metro-Dade Police Information** if you don't need immediate help.

LOST PROPERTY

EVEN THOUGH you have only a slim chance of retrieving stolen property, you should report all lost or stolen items to the police. Keep a copy of the police report carefully if you are planning to make an insurance claim.

Most credit card companies have toll-free numbers for reporting a loss, as do Thomas Cook and American Express for lost travellers' cheques. If you lose your passport, contact your embassy or consulate immediately (see p347).

TRAVEL INSURANCE

TRAVEL INSURANCE COVER of a minimum of $1 million is highly recommended, mainly because of the high cost of medical care. Prices depend on the length of your trip, but make sure the policy covers accidental death, emergency medical care, trip cancellation and baggage or document loss. Your insurance company or travel agent should be able to recommend a suitable policy, but it's worth shopping around for the optimum deal.

A county sheriff, in the regulation dark uniform, and his patrol car

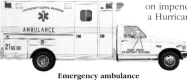
Emergency ambulance

Orange County fire engine

MEDICAL TREATMENT

LARGER CITES IN THE STATE, and some smaller towns, have 24-hour walk-in medical and dental clinics, where minor casualties and ailments can be treated. For less serious complaints, drugstores (many of which stay open late or for 24 hours), should be sufficient.

If you have a serious accident or illness, you can rely on high-quality treatment at a hospital. Stories of medics making accident victims wait while they haggle over money are largely apocryphal; even so, guard your insurance documents with your life. Nothing comes for free: a straightforward visit to the doctor can cost about $50. Hospitals accept most credit cards, but doctors and dentists will usually want cash. Those without insurance may need to pay in advance.

Anyone on prescribed medication should take a supply with them and ask their doctor to provide a copy of the prescription in case of loss or the need for more.

NATURAL HAZARDS

HURRICANES are infrequent but devastating when they do strike *(see pp24–5)*. There are tried and tested emergency procedures, and if the worst should happen follow the announcements on local television and radio. You can call the **National Hurricane Center** in Miami, which gives out information

on impending hurricanes, and a Hurricane Hotline may also be established.

The climatic hazard to affect most visitors is the sun. Use high-factor sun screen lotions and try to wear a hat; and make sure that your children are well protected too. Remember that heat can be as big a problem as sunlight; drink plenty of fluids to prevent dehydration.

Florida may be famous for its man-made attractions, but there are places where the natural world still dominates. While the Everglades holds potentially more danger than other areas, you should be careful wherever you go. Alligators are a thrilling sight but they can and do kill – so treat them with respect. There are also several venomous snakes native to Florida, including the water moccasin, whose bite can be fatal. It is best not to touch unfamiliar vegetation, and steer clear of Spanish moss, which hangs from many trees in northern Florida; it houses the red mite, which can cause a rather nasty skin irritation.

Road sign indicating alligators are nearby

Biting and stinging insects, including mosquitos, are a real nuisance between June and November, particularly in areas close to fresh water.

A lifeguard keeps watch over a beach in the Panhandle

Visits to parks and reserves can be uncomfortable if you don't wear insect repellent.

Florida's beaches are usually well supervised by lifeguards, but still keep a close eye on young children. Riptides are a danger in some places.

EMERGENCIES

IN AN EMERGENCY, the police, ambulance or fire services can be reached by dialling 911. The call is free from public phones, and on expressways there are emergency call boxes roughly every half-mile (1 km). If you are robbed in the street, go directly to the closest police station – dial 911 should you need help in locating it.

If you need emergency cash, ask someone to transfer this from your bank at home to a specified bank in Florida; or use the **Moneygram** service, a more tourist-friendly option offered by American Express.

Banking and Currency

GIVEN THE DOLLAR'S STATUS in the world, it is perhaps no surprise that the US doesn't cater particularly well to the needs of visitors from abroad. Foreign currency can be exchanged in comparatively few places, and exchange rates tend to be poorer than at home. The best rule is to take plenty of US dollar travellers' cheques and, ideally, a credit card or two.

Automatic teller machine (ATM)

BANKING

BANKS ARE GENERALLY open from 9am to 3 or 4pm on weekdays, though some keep slightly longer hours. **Barnett Bank**, one of Florida's major banks, offers foreign exchange in all its branches. The other main banks include Sun Bank, First Union National Bank and NationsBank of Florida, all of which have branches throughout the state.

TRAVELLERS' CHEQUES

TRAVELLERS' CHEQUES are the best way to carry money around, both for ease of use and security (lost or stolen cheques can be refunded). In many instances you can use them as if they were cash: US dollar travellers' cheques are commonly accepted in shops, restaurants and hotels; those issued by American Express or Thomas Cook are the most widely recognized. Change will be given in cash; if your cheques are in large denominations, be sure to ask the assistant if there is enough money in the till before you countersign on the dotted line.

To exchange your travellers' cheques into cash directly, go to a bank or exchange bureau. Remember to enquire about

commission fees before starting your transaction. All banks cash dollar travellers' cheques, but you'll get the best rates in a big city bank or at a private exchange office. The latter are not common, but **American Express** and **Thomas Cook**, for example, both have a branch in Miami and Orlando, as well as in a number of other cities around the state.

Travellers' cheques in other currencies, including sterling, will be no use in shops, and only some banks and hotels will exchange them. Personal cheques drawn on overseas banks, such as Eurocheques, cannot be used in Florida.

AUTOMATIC TELLER MACHINES

MOST BANKS in Florida have ATMs (Automatic Teller Machines) in their lobbies or in an external wall. These machines enable you to withdraw US banknotes, usually $20 bills, from your bank or credit card account at home.

Before leaving home, ask your credit card company or bank which American ATM systems or banks will accept your bank card, and check the cost of each transaction. Make sure, too, that you have (and know) your PIN number.

The largest ATM systems are **Plus** and **Cirrus**, which accept VISA and MasterCard as well as various US bank cards.

ATMs allow you 24-hour access to cash, but take care when using them in deserted areas, especially after dark; robberies are not unheard of.

CREDIT CARDS

CREDIT CARDS are so much a part of everyday life in Florida, as in other parts of the country, that anyone not carrying one may feel like a social outcast. The most widely accepted credit cards are VISA, American Express, MasterCard, Diners Club and Japanese Credit Bureau.

Credit cards enable you to avoid having to carry around large amounts of cash and can be used to pay for everything from admission fees to hotel bills. It is also standard practice for car hire companies to take an imprint of your card as security; often the only alternative is to pay a hefty deposit in cash. Some hotels adopt the same practice: a "phantom" sum of $200–300 may be debited even for one night in a hotel. This should be automatically restored to your credit when you check out, but it's as well to remind the clerk when you leave; any delay could result in your having less credit available on your card than you think.

Credit cards are useful in emergencies – hospitals will accept most major cards. With MasterCard and VISA you can withdraw cash at some banks too, as well as from an ATM.

One of many drive-in banks, for fast, user-friendly banking

Coins

American coins (actual size shown) come in denominations of 1, 5, 10 and 25 cents. There are also 50-cent and $1-dollar coins, but these are rarely seen. Each value of coin has a popular name: copper-coloured 1-cent coins are known as "pennies", 5-cent coins as "nickels", 10 cents as "dimes" and 25 cents as "quarters". If anyone refers to "two bits", this means a quarter.

**25-cent coin
(a quarter)**

**10-cent coin
(a dime)**

**5-cent coin
(a nickel)**

**1-cent coin
(a penny)**

Bank Notes

There are 100 cents to the dollar, known as a "buck" in popular slang. Dollar notes, called "bills", come in 1, 2, 5, 10, 20, 50 and 100 denominations; the $2 bill is rarely seen. It is helpful to have some low denomination bills for tips, and coins for phone calls or parking meters. The bills at a glance look very similar, so check what you are handing over, especially when tipping.

**The American eagle
on a $1 bill**

1-dollar bill ($1)

5-dollar bill ($5)

20-dollar bill ($20)

50-dollar bill ($50)

100-dollar bill ($100)

Communications

US stamp

COMMUNICATING WITH PEOPLE both within and outside Florida, whether by post or telephone, rarely causes problems – though no one claims that the United States' postal system is the world's fastest (at least as far as domestic mail is concerned). There is more competition in the field of telecommunications: Southern Bell, for example, operates the majority of public telephones, but since there are a number of companies in the field it is often worth shopping around. An easy way to save money is to avoid making telephone calls direct from your hotel room, for which often exorbitant surcharges are imposed.

USING A COIN-OPERATED TELEPHONE

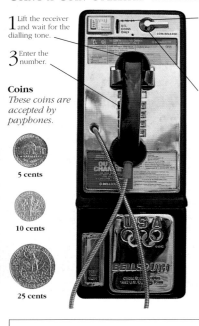

1 Lift the receiver and wait for the dialling tone.

3 Enter the number.

Coins
These coins are accepted by payphones.

5 cents

10 cents

25 cents

2 Insert the correct coin or coins.

4 If you decide not to make a connection, or if the call does not get through, you can retrieve your money by pressing the coin return.

5 If the call is answered and you talk for longer than the allotted time, the operator will interrupt and ask you to deposit some more coins into the phone. Payphones do not give change.

PUBLIC TELEPHONES

PUBLIC PAYHONES ARE everywhere in cities; elsewhere, you will find them mainly in petrol stations and shops.

Most public telephones take coins only – you'll need about $8 worth of quarters to make an international call. However, there is a growing number of card-operated phones. Some of these take special pre-paid debit cards, which involve dialling a toll-free number to gain access to your required number. Alternatively, you can use your credit card from any phone. You must simply dial (800) CALLATT, key in your credit card number and then wait to be connected; you will be charged at normal rates.

Telephone directories are supplied at most public phones and give details of rates.

Phone cards that can be used in selected public telephones

TELEPHONE CHARGES

TOLL FREE NUMBERS (which are prefixed by 800 or 888) are common in the US and are well worth taking advantage of – though some hotels have the gall to impose an access charge for these calls. While you can dial 800 or 888 numbers from abroad, note that they are not toll free.

When making a local call from a public telephone, the minimum charge, 25 cents, will buy you about three minutes. For long-distance domestic calls the cheapest rate (which is 60 per cent less than the standard rate) runs from 11pm to 8am on weekdays and at weekends (except 5 to 11pm on Sunday). These discounts also apply to calls to Canada but they take effect an hour later. International rates vary depending on which country you are contacting: the cheapest rate for the UK is from 6pm to 7am.

Most telephone calls are possible without the aid of an

REACHING THE RIGHT NUMBER

- Direct-dial calls to another area code: dial **1** followed by the area code and the 7-digit number. Since the 3-digit area codes can cover large areas, some "zone calls" (those within the same area) also require you to dial 1 first.
- International direct-dial calls: dial **011**, then the code of the country (Australia 61, New Zealand 64, UK 44), followed by the local area/city code (minus the first 0) and the number.
- International operator assistance: dial **01**.
- International directory enquiries: dial **00**.
- Local operator assistance: dial **0**.
- Local directory enquiries: dial **411**.
- Long-distance information: dial **1**, then the appropriate area code, followed by **555-1212**.
- An **800** or **888** prefix means the call will be free.
- For the police, fire or ambulance service, dial **911**.

operator: this increases the price of a normal call. Collect or reversed charge calls can be made only via the operator and so can be very expensive.

TELEGRAMS AND FAXES

VARIOUS COMPANIES provide a telegram service, principally Western Union, whose offices are listed in the *Yellow Pages*; or you can send a telegram by dialling their toll free number (800) 325-6000 and paying for it with a credit card.

Public fax machines can be found at major airports and in some stores and public buildings. Many hotels accept faxes on their guests' behalf but the charge to receive one is often high *(see p293)*.

POSTAL SERVICES

POST OFFICE opening hours vary but are usually 9am to 5pm on weekdays, with some offices opening on Saturday mornings too. Drugstores and hotels often sell stamps, and some department stores and big transport terminals have stamp vending machines; but note that stamps not bought from a post office cost extra.

Surface mail sent overseas from the US takes weeks, so you'd do better to send letters air mail, which should take five to ten working days.

All domestic mail goes "first class" and takes one to five days – longer if you forget to include the zip code. You can

A rank of newspaper-dispensing machines in a Palm Beach street

pay extra for **Priority Mail**, for a delivery in two to three days, or **Express Mail**, which offers next-day delivery in the US and within two to three days to many foreign countries. Be sure to use the right postbox for the required service. Postboxes are painted blue, while Express and Priority boxes are silver and blue.

Many Americans use private courier services, such as UPS and Federal Express, for both domestic and international mail; they can offer next-day delivery to most destinations.

Many shops can mail purchases home for you; posting a parcel yourself involves the use of approved materials available from post offices.

TELEVISION AND RADIO

TELEVISION IN FLORIDA is the same as anywhere else in the US: that is, dominated by game shows, sit-coms, chat shows and soaps. The cable channels offer more variety: ESPN is devoted to sport, CNN to news, for example. Hotel rooms usually have cable TV, but you may have to pay to see a movie *(see p293)*.

Most radio stations pump out pop and easy listening music, but if you hunt around (especially on the FM band) you can often pick up entertaining local stations, including Spanish-language ones in south Florida. More serious broadcasting is left to the likes of NBC, ABC and PBS (Public Broadcasting System), which serve up a diet of documentaries, talk shows and classical music.

NEWSPAPERS

EVERY LARGE CITY publishes its own daily newspaper. Most widely read is the *Miami Herald*, which provides good coverage of national and international news; it also has a widely read Spanish-language edition, *El Heraldo*.

You can usually pick up a national paper such as *USA Today* from street dispensers, but most of these are given over to local papers. For other national US dailies, such as the *New York Times*, and foreign newspapers you will normally have to rely on bookshops and good newsstands.

Two of the most widely read daily newspapers in the state of Florida

FLORIDA TIME

MOST OF FLORIDA runs on Eastern Standard Time (EST). The Panhandle west of the Apalachicola River, however, is on Central Standard Time (CST), which is one hour behind the rest of the state.

EST is five hours and CST six hours behind Greenwich Mean Time (GMT). If you are making an international telephone call, add five hours for the United Kingdom, 15 hours for Australia and 17 hours for New Zealand.

Standard postbox

TRAVEL INFORMATION

United Airlines flies to Florida from around the world

Florida is the top tourist destination in the US and is well served by flights from all over the world. The state's chief gateways are Miami, Orlando and Tampa, while the growing number of charter flights is raising the profile of other airports. Flying is also worth considering if you plan to travel any distance within Florida. The hop between Miami and Key West, for example, takes 40 minutes, compared with four hours by car. However, when it comes to getting around the state, the car reigns supreme, with fast interstates, major highways and quieter county roads to choose from. Trains and buses provide an alternative for those willing to plan their routes carefully.

Clean and orderly interior of Orlando International Airport

ARRIVING BY AIR

All the main US carriers, including **Continental**, **American Airlines**, **United Airlines** and **Delta Air Lines**, have many scheduled domestic services to Orlando and Miami, as well as to Florida's other main airports. Most offer direct flights from abroad too, but this will normally entail a stop at a US airport en route.

From the UK, **British Airways** and **Virgin Atlantic** have scheduled direct flights to Miami and Orlando; BA also has a service between London and Tampa. American Airlines runs daily flights to Miami from London's Gatwick and Heathrow airports. Delta Air Lines flies to Florida from Ireland via Atlanta, Georgia or New York.

European carriers such as Air France, KLM and Iberia also offer a range of flights. Qantas and several US airlines offer one- or two-stop flights from Australia and New Zealand.

For flights into one of Florida's smaller gateways, you'll often have to fly to another US state and then use the national airlines' extensive domestic networks to reach Florida.

Increasingly, charter flights are offering direct access to some of Florida's smaller resorts such as Palm Beach and Fort Myers. Most charter flights emanate from Canada, the Caribbean and Latin America, but there is a growing number from Europe too. **Laker Airways**, for example, offers a service to Orlando and Fort Lauderdale (an alternative gateway to Miami) from Gatwick, Manchester and Prestwick in the UK. The choice of charter flights to Orlando has been further boosted by the upgrading of nearby Sanford airport.

AIR FARES

The cheapest return fares to Florida are generally economy or APEX tickets on a scheduled flight (which must be booked in advance). The competition between travel agencies and between

AIRPORT	INFORMATION	DISTANCE FROM CITY	TAXI FARE TO CITY (APPROX)	SHUTTLE BUS FARE TO CITY (APPROX)
Miami	((305) 876-7000	10 miles (16 km) to Miami Beach	$20 to Miami Beach	$8–15 to Miami Beach
Orlando	((407) 825-2352	18 miles (28 km) to Walt Disney World	$40–45 to Walt Disney World	$15 to Walt Disney World, or 75c by Lynx bus
Sanford	((407) 322-7771	40 miles (64 km) to Walt Disney World	$45–50 to Walt Disney World	$50 to Walt Disney World
Tampa	((813) 870-8700	6 miles (9 km) to Downtown	$12–15 to Downtown	$13 to Downtown
Fort Lauderdale	((954) 359-1200	8 miles (13 km) to Fort Lauderdale, 30 miles (48 km) to Miami	$12–15 to Fort Lauderdale, $45 to Miami	$6 to Fort Lauderdale, $12 to Miami

A shuttle bus serving Miami airport

the numerous airlines serving Florida means that it is worth shopping around. Keep an eye out for promotional fares, and some specialist operators offer good deals on charter flights.

Fares can be surprisingly cheap in low season, and you'll often get a better deal if you fly midweek. During holiday periods, by contrast, seats are in big demand and air fares can rocket to more than double their normal rates, being highest in December. Note that US airlines sometimes offer discounted seats on domestic flights if you buy an inbound ticket from them.

PACKAGE DEALS

THE CHEAPEST holiday deal to Florida is a package that throws in car hire and/or accommodation with the cost of the flight. Fly-drive deals offer a rental car "free" or at a vast discount, but be warned: there are heavy surcharges to pay (see p357).

Flight and accommodation packages are common and often good value. What you lose out in terms of flexibility, you may gain in peace of mind. Twin centre deals are very popular – combining, for example, a week in Orlando with a week at a Gulf Coast resort. Package deals to Walt Disney World are worth considering if you're spending the whole time there; these are available direct from Disney or from tour operators.

FLORIDA AIRPORTS

FLORIDA'S TOP international airports are reasonably well equipped with information desks, banks, car rental desks and other facilities. If you're collecting a rental car, you may be taken by bus to a pick-up point nearby. If you are heading into town, check out the shuttle buses (or "limos"), which offer a door-to-door

service to and from the airport; they operate like shared taxis but are cheaper than regular cabs. Major hotels usually offer a courtesy bus service to their guests.

MIAMI AIRPORT

MIAMI INTERNATIONAL AIRPORT is one of the busiest in the world, which can mean long queues at immigration. The walk between concourses and gates is often long too.

Tourist information desks are found outside all Customs exits, and car rental counters, taxis, private limos and shuttle buses are on the lower level concourse. Companies such as **SuperShuttle** run 24-hour shuttle bus services to all the main districts of Miami. City buses in theory serve the airport, but these services should not be relied upon.

ORLANDO AND SANFORD AIRPORTS

A RECENT SURVEY rated Orlando International Airport the USA's number one airport for overall customer convenience. Moving walkways and the automated monorail system make moving around the two terminals easy. Multilingual tourist information centres by the security checkpoints are open from 7am to 11pm.

Many hotels have their own courtesy buses but there are also shuttle buses; the **Mears Transportation Group** serves most destinations in the area.

A much cheaper way to travel to International Drive or downtown Orlando is by Lynx bus (see p363). Services leave from outside the "A Side" terminal every half hour. Both journeys take about 50 minutes.

The newly revamped airport at Sanford is much quieter than the main Orlando airport. Facilities are still being developed, but there are taxis and several car rental outlets, which are conveniently located right outside the terminal building.

DIRECTORY

AIRLINE NUMBERS

American Airlines
((800) 433-7300 (US).

British Airways
((800) 247-9297 (US).
((0345) 222111 (UK).

Continental
((800) 231-0856 (US).

Laker Airways
((01293) 789000 (UK).

Delta Air Lines
((800) 241-4141 (US).

United Airlines
((800) 241-6522 (US).

Virgin Atlantic
((800) 862-8621 (US).
((01293) 747747 (UK).

SHUTTLE BUSES

SuperShuttle
((305) 871-2000.

Mears Transportation Group
((407) 423-5566.

The People Mover monorail at Orlando International Airport

Driving in Florida

**Interstate
Highway 4**

**US Highway 1,
heading south**

D RIVING IN FLORIDA is a delight. Most highways are uncrowded, and Floridians are generally courteous and considerate road-users. Petrol ("gas") is cheap and car hire rates are the lowest in the United States.

You can get by without a car in Orlando *(see p363)*, but wherever you are life is much easier with one. Incidents of foreign motorists being victims of crime on the road have deterred some from driving, but safety measures are improving. Many rest areas on interstate highways are now covered by 24-hour armed security patrols and direction signs have been improved in Miami *(see p358)*.

**Overhead signs at the junction
of two routes**

ARRIVING BY CAR

T HERE IS A GOOD choice of routes into Florida from the neighbouring states of Georgia and Alabama. The advantage of using the main highways is that you will find welcome centres just over the border dispensing fresh orange juice and general information. They are located on the Florida side of the state line along I-95, I-75, I-10 and US 231.

ROADS IN FLORIDA

F LORIDA HAS AN excellent road network. The fastest and smoothest routes are the interstate highways, referred to as I-10, I-75 and so on. These usually have at least six lanes, with rest areas located every 60 miles (100 km) or so.

Interstates form part of the expressway system of roads (sometimes called "freeways"), to which access is permitted only at specified junctions or exits. Among other expressways are turnpikes and toll roads. Chief among the latter are the Bee Line Expressway (between Orlando and the Space Coast) and Florida's

Turnpike, which runs from I-75, northwest of Orlando, to Florida City south of Miami. The toll you have to pay is dependent, logically, on the distance covered; if you travel the entire 329 miles (530 km) of the Turnpike, for example, the trip will cost around $17. Tolls can be paid to a collector in a booth or, if you have the right change and don't need a receipt, dropped into a collecting bin, where the money is counted automatically.

Be warned that local drivers change lanes frequently on expressways. Stick to the right to stay out of trouble and take care when approaching exits, which can be on both sides of the carriageway; most accidents occur during left turns.

Other routes include the US highways, which are usually (but not always) multi-laned, but slower than expressways and often less scenic, lined with motels and gas stations. State Roads and County Roads are smaller and better for touring. Unpaved routes exist in some of Florida's more rural areas; note that some car hire companies may not permit you to drive on these.

**City parking
restrictions**

**Mile
marker in
the Keys**

**Speed limit
(in mph)**

**Rest area,
indicated off
an interstate**

ROAD SIGNS

M OST ROAD SIGNS are clear and self-explanatory. If you are caught disregarding instructions you may be fined.

Generally, road numbers or names rather than destinations are signposted, and different types of roads are indicated by signs of different shapes and colours. Directional signs are usually green.

NAVIGATING

A GOOD ROAD MAP is vital for touring Florida by car. The *Florida Transportation Map*, available free from most Convention and Visitors' Bureaux and Florida tourist

The toll plaza on Florida's Turnpike at Boca Raton

offices abroad is adequate for general purposes; it gives the location of rest areas on interstate highways and includes maps of the main cities. If you plan to spend any length of time in a city, however, you should try to pick up a detailed local map. The city maps in tourist offices are often inadequate for driving – in which case a good bookshop would be the best source.

Navigating your way around Florida is comparatively easy. East-west routes have even numbers and north-south routes odd numbers. Signs at the roadside, including mile markers in the Keys (see p269), tell you which road you are on; while the name hanging over junctions is not the road you are on but the one you are crossing. Some roads have two numbers – for example when through routes follow the same course for a time.

SPEED LIMITS

SPEED LIMITS in the US are set by individual states. The limits in Florida are as follows:
• 55–70 mph (90–105 km/h) on highways.
• 20–30 mph (32–48 km/h) in residential areas.
• 15 mph (24 km/h) near schools.

Speed limits can vary every few miles, so keep a close eye out for the signs. On an interstate you can be fined for driving slower than 40 mph (64 km/h). Speed limits are

A typical Florida road intersection, in Tallahassee

rigorously enforced by the Florida Highway Patrol, whose representatives issue tickets on the spot. A fine can set you back as much as $150.

CAR HIRE

CAR RENTAL COSTS in Florida are already cheap by most standards, and you can save even more by booking and paying before leaving home. Fly-drive deals can knock more than 50 per cent off the cost, but don't be fooled by offers of so-called "free" car hire. Hidden extras like state tax and insurance will not be included in these offers.

If you wait until you arrive to organize your car rental, it is usually cheaper to hire one at the airport rather than from a downtown outlet.

Highway Patrol insignia

All you need to hire a car is your driver's licence, passport and a credit card. If you don't have the latter, you'll have to pay the deposit in cash. The minimum age for car hire is 21, but drivers under 25 may need to pay a surcharge.

Make sure your car rental agreement includes Collision Damage Waiver (CDW) – also known as Loss Damage Waiver (LDW) – or you'll be liable for any damage to the car, even if it was not your fault. Rental agreements include third party insurance, but this is rarely adequate: you are advised to purchase "top up" insurance (called additional or supplementary Liability Insurance), which should provide cover of up to $1 million. These extras, plus taxes, can add $35–40 to each day's rental.

Some companies impose a premium if you want to drop the car off in another city, and all charge a lot for petrol: if you return the car with less fuel than it had initially, the difference can cost you as much as $3 per gallon.

The majority of international car rental agencies (see p359) offer a reasonable range of vehicles, from "economy" models to convertibles. All rental cars are automatic and come equipped with power steering and air-conditioning.

TIPS FOR DRIVERS

• Traffic travels on the right-hand side of the road.
• Seat belts are compulsory for both drivers and passengers and children under three must sit in a child seat.
• You can turn right on a red light unless there are signs to the contrary, but you must come to a stop first.
• A flashing amber light at intersections means slow down, check for oncoming traffic and then proceed with caution.
• Overtaking is allowed on both sides on any multi-lane road, including interstate highways.
• It is illegal to change lanes across a double yellow or double white solid line.
• If a school bus stops on a two-way road to drop off or pick up children, traffic travelling in both directions must stop. On a divided highway, only traffic travelling in the same direction need stop.
• Don't drink even one beer. Driving under the influence (DUI) is treated very seriously; violators can be fined hundreds of dollars or even imprisoned for a short period.

One of many car rental agencies

Old style petrol station at Burt Reynolds' Ranch on the Treasure Coast

PETROL

Unleaded petrol (or "gas") is used by most modern cars in the US. Petrol comes in three grades – regular, super and premium – and diesel fuel is usually also available.

Fuel is very cheap by most standards, but the price varies a great deal according to the location and service. Stick to self-service unless you want to pay an extra fee (charged per gallon) for an attendant to fill your tank, check the oil and clean the windscreen.

Petrol prices are marked inclusive of tax per gallon – the US gallon, that is, which is 3.8 litres, about a litre less than an Imperial gallon. At most petrol stations you can pay with cash, a credit card or travellers' cheques, though some places (mainly in rural areas) take cash only. Occasionally you are expected to pay in advance.

If you intend to drive along back roads, make sure the car is topped up with oil, petrol and water, as you won't come across many filling stations.

BREAKDOWNS

If your vehicle breaks down, pull off the road, turn on the emergency indicators and wait for the police. On expressways you can make use of the emergency phones *(see p349)*. If you are travelling alone, you may choose to rent a mobile phone – offered at a small cost by most car rental firms.

If you have hired a car, you will find an emergency number on the rental agreement, so try that first; in the event of a serious breakdown, the rental agency will provide a new vehicle. The **American Automobile Association** (AAA) provides its own breakdown vehicles and will assist its members. Alternatively, call the State Police or your credit card's emergency number.

Time elapsed shown here

Insert coins here

Turn handle to register coins

Parking meter

PARKING

Finding a parking space is rarely a problem at theme parks and other major tourist attractions, shopping malls, or in most downtown districts. The main places where you may have difficulty are in the vicinity of city beaches – for example in Fort Lauderdale or South Beach *(see p362)*.

You'll find small and multi-storey car parks in cities, but usually you'll have to use parking meters. When you find a space (ideally in the shade), feed the meter generously: the fee varies from 25c to $1 per hour. Overstay and you risk a substantial fine or the possibility of your car being wheelclamped or towed away. Be sure to read parking signs carefully. Restrictions are normally posted on telephone poles, street lights or roadside

---

SAFETY FOR DRIVERS

Miami has the worst reputation for crime against motorists, but take care wherever you are. Various measures have been introduced to safeguard foreign drivers. For example, the registration plate code identifying rental cars was dropped, and in Miami road signs were improved: an orange sunburst sign guides drivers along the main routes to and from the airport. Here are a few tips to help you stay safe:

• If arriving in Florida by air at night, you could arrange to pick up your rental car the next morning in order to avoid driving in unfamiliar territory after dark.
• Avoid having handbags or other valuable items visible inside the car; pack them out of sight in the boot.
• Keep car doors locked, especially in urban areas.
• Ignore any attempt by a pedestrian or motorist to stop you, e.g. by pointing out some alleged fault on your car or, less subtly, by ramming you from behind. Another ruse is to stand by a "broken-down" vehicle, signalling for help.
• If you need to refer to a map in a city, don't stop until you are in a well-lit and preferably busy area.
• Avoid sleeping in the car off the highway, though some rest areas on expressways have security patrols.
• Avoid taking short cuts in urban areas. Stick to the main highways if possible.

Sunburst signs for visitors to Miami

Tandems and bikes for hire in cycle-friendly Palm Beach

walls or kerbs. Cars should not be parked within 10 ft (3 m) of a fire hydrant: this is the surest way to get towed away.

For those prepared to pay, valet parking is available at many hotels and restaurants.

CYCLING

CYCLING IS BECOMING more and more popular as a recreational activity *(see p343)* or as a means of keeping fit, but on the whole bicycles are not used as a practical form of transport. Cycling in most urban areas is not particularly agreeable, not least because drivers are not accustomed to sharing the road with bikes, and indeed can be hazardous.

The places best suited to cyclists are smaller cities or seaside resorts such as South Beach, Key West, Palm Beach or St Augustine – where the roads aren't too busy and where car parking can be a problem. Bikes can be hired for around $10–15 per day. Rollerblading is also very popular in these holiday areas, and skates are easy to hire.

MOTORCYCLE HIRE

IF CRUISING FLORIDA'S streets and highways on a Harley-Davidson is your dream, you may want to visit **Iron Horse Rentals**, which has branches in Fort Lauderdale, Orlando, Miami and Tampa. Charges are around $135 for 24 hours, plus a deposit of $500; the minimum age is 21. **Rolling Thunder** in Coral Gables, Miami, offers a similar range of motorbikes for hire.

RV RENTAL

RECREATIONAL vehicles (RVs), or mobile homes are great for groups or families. It costs $300 upwards to hire one for a week. RV rental outlets are surprisingly scarce. The largest in the United States is **Cruise America**, which also has agents abroad. **Sundance Motorhomes** is the other alternative for renting RVs.

Hire conditions are usually similar to those for car rental *(see p357)*. Size and facilities vary greatly, but most RVs have every imaginable mod con.

The car ferry at Mayport *(see p195)*, a short cut across the St Johns River

Travelling Around Florida

VISITORS TO FLORIDA who rely on public transport will find their horizons rather restricted. The rail network is particularly limited, leaving Greyhound buses – which link most sizeable towns – as the main form of long-distance land transport. Places outside the main urban areas will often elude those without cars. Some local bus services are good, but you'll need time and flexibility to make use of these. Public transport within cities is more useful. Here, the emphasis is on serving commuters rather than visitors, but the main tourist centres have some services that cater to the needs of sightseers.

Spanish Revival-style Tri-Rail station in West Palm Beach

Anyone planning to do more than a couple of journeys by train might consider buying a rail pass, which gives unlimited travel during a set period of time; this must be bought from an Amtrak agent abroad before you arrive; overseas agents can also send out time-tables for both national and regional services.

Florida's only other train service is **Tri-Rail**, which links 15 stations between Miami airport and West Palm Beach, including Fort Lauderdale and Boca Raton. Intended primarily for commuters, the trains are also useful for tourists. Services run more or less hourly, with reduced sevices at weekends. One-way fares range from about $2 to $6, depending on the number of zones you pass through, and transfers to Miami's Metrorail and Metromover services (see p362) are free.

Tri-Rail also runs guided tours, to South Beach and Worth Avenue, for example, as well as special trips to big games at the Orange Bowl Stadium in Miami.

ARRIVING BY TRAIN

THE USE OF RAILWAYS in the US is dwindling, but there are still connections between major cities. The national passenger rail company, **Amtrak**, serves Florida from both the east and west coasts. There are three daily services from New York City. The Silver Meteor and Silver Palm run south via Washington DC down to Jacksonville and Miami, taking over 25 hours. The Silver Star travels the same route as far as Orlando, from where it veers west to Tampa.

The Sunset Limited, complete with deluxe cabins and movie entertainment, covers the 3,066 miles (4,933 km) from Los Angeles to Sanford near Orlando, stopping at Phoenix and New Orleans.

If you want to travel by train but take your own car, there is Amtrak's Auto Train, which runs daily from Lorton in Virginia to Sanford, taking about 18 hours.

A cheap flight can work out cheaper than the equivalent rail fare. You'll often do best to buy a rail pass.

EXPLORING BY TRAIN

AMTRAK TRAINS serve only a limited number of towns and cities in Florida (see the map on pages 12–13). Other than Tampa, the Gulf Coast is linked only by Amtrak buses, known as "Thruway" buses. These run from Winter Haven, near Orlando, to Fort Myers via St Petersburg and Sarasota, with guaranteed connections with Amtrak rail services.

Rail fares do not compete well with those of Greyhound, but journeys are obviously more relaxing than on a bus. When travelling overnight, you can choose between the ordinary (but reclining) seats of "coach class" and a cabin.

LONG-DISTANCE BUSES

WHETHER YOU are travelling from other parts of the country or within Florida, **Greyhound** buses offer the cheapest way to get around. Some services are "express", with few stops en route, while others serve a greater number of destinations.

A few routes have "flag stops", where a bus may stop to deposit or collect passengers in places without a bus station; pay the driver direct or, if you want to book in advance, go to the nearest Greyhound agent – usually in a local store or post office.

An air-conditioned Greyhound bus, serving the Florida Keys

Passes provide unlimited travel for set periods of time (from between four and sixty days), but are useful only if you have a very full itinerary. Overseas visitors should also note that passes are cheaper if bought from a Greyhound agent outside the United States.

A complete bus timetable is not available, but agents can send out photocopies of requested services.

LOCAL AND CITY BUSES

BUS SERVICES operated by local authorities can be useful for short hops within county boundaries, although services are rarely frequent enough for sightseeing trips. You can travel between many of the cities of southeastern Florida by stringing together local buses, but you'll need to allow plenty of time.

There is more scope to take advantage of buses within cities, and shuttle buses are useful for travelling to and from the airports in Orlando and Miami *(see p355)*. Buses in the US do not have conductors, so always have the right money, ticket or token to give the driver (or put in the box) as you board.

TAXIS

TAXIS (more often called "cabs") are easily found at airports, transport terminals and major hotels. Taxi ranks are rare elsewhere, and since cabs do not tend to cruise around city streets, it is best to order one by phone: numbers are listed in the *Yellow Pages*. Alternatively, ask someone at your hotel to call a taxi for you – although you may be expected to pay them a tip for doing this.

If you are travelling off the beaten track in a city, it will help to have your destination marked on a map. Not all drivers know their way

A Key West taxi – painted pink rather than the usual yellow

Horse and carriage, a pleasant way to go sightseeing in St Augustine

around. All taxi fares should be metered according to the distance travelled. Some cabs accept credit cards, but you should check in advance.

WATER TAXIS

IN SEVERAL CITIES water taxis add a new dimension to urban travel. You'll find them in Miami, Jacksonville, Tampa and Fort Lauderdale. Routes are generally geared to tourists and as a result they are fairly limited in scope – linking hotels, restaurants, and shops, for example. However, they are fine for sightseeing.

Some operate as regular shuttle services, as is the case across the St Johns River in Jacksonville, while others, such as those in Tampa and Miami, can only be summoned by phone. Fares are usually $5–10, which you pay on board.

TRANSPORT FOR TOURISTS

MOST POPULAR tourist centres provide special transport for visitors. This often comes in the form of old-fashioned trolley buses: Tallahassee has a replica streetcar with wooden seats and brass handrails. In Daytona Beach and Fort Lauderdale tourist trolleys are a useful link between downtown and the beach.

A familiar sight in Key West is the Conch Train, which consists of open-sided coaches towed by a butane-powered jeep disguised as an old locomotive. St Augustine has a similar train, as well as horse-drawn carriages, which can be hired in downtown Orlando too.

UNDERSTANDING CITIES

YOU SHOULD NOT think of "downtown" as the heart of a city; though it may be the hub of business, most people spend their leisuretime elsewhere. Most large cities are arranged on a grid pattern, with numbered streets taking their orientation from the junction of two main axes downtown – as in Miami *(see p363)*.

Americans tend not to walk anywhere, but as a sightseer you'll find it hard to avoid. At pedestrian crossings, be sure to obey the "Walk", "Don't Walk" or "Wait" signals.

Signals at a pedestrian crossing, ordering you to proceed or stop

Travelling Around Miami

PUBLIC TRANSPORT in Miami is run by the Metro-Dade Transit Agency, which operates the buses, the Metrorail commuter train network and Downtown's elevated Metromover. There is also a limited water taxi service, which can be a pleasant way to get around, but it is hard to make the most of Miami without a car unless you're happy to stay put in South Beach. However you travel, pay heed to the safety tips on pages 348 and 358.

The Metromover, which loops around downtown Miami

ARRIVING IN MIAMI

FOR INFORMATION on getting away from Miami airport, see page 355. If you arrive at the **Amtrak** station, just north of the airport, or at one of the **Greyhound** terminals, there are no car rental outlets but plenty of taxis and a choice, if limited, of buses going to Downtown and Miami Beach.

Arriving by car is relatively hassle-free. I-95, the main road from the north, heads straight through Downtown before joining US 1, which continues south skirting Coral Gables. Route A1A is a slower way in from the north, but takes you direct into South Beach. From the west, US 41 runs through Little Havana to the coast, where it links up with the main north-south routes.

Amtrak Station
8303 NW 37th Ave.
℃ (305) 835-1222.

Greyhound Stations
Airport, 4111 NW 27th St.
℃ (305) 871-1810.
Bayside, 700 Biscayne Blvd.
℃ (305) 379-7403.
North Miami, 16560 NE 6th Ave.
℃ (305) 945-0801.

METRORAIL AND METROMOVER

METRORAIL, a 21-mile (34-km) train line between the northern and southern suburbs of Miami, is of limited use to visitors. However, it provides a useful link between Coral Gables or Coconut Grove and the downtown area. Services run daily every ten minutes or so from 6am until midnight.

You can transfer free from Metrorail to the Tri-Rail line *(see p360)* in Hialeah, and also to the Metromover system at Government Center station (where you can pick up transport maps and information on rail routes).

The Metromover connects the heart of Downtown with the Brickell and Omni business districts on two elevated loop lines. Although the service is underused by local people, the Inner Loop provides a good way to see the downtown area *(see pp70–71)*. Cars operate continually from 6am to midnight. Make sure that you have coins ready for the turnstile as you enter the station.

Metro-Dade Transit Information
℃ (305) 638-6700.

METROBUS

MIAMI'S METROBUS network serves most places of interest, but the frequency of services varies greatly, being much reduced at weekends. Many of the services converge on Flagler Street and Government Center, Downtown, which is a good place to pick up buses.

There are express routes, which cost about double the usual fare. If you need to change buses, ask for a free transfer when you get on the first bus; you pay as you board, so have the right change ready. Transfers to the Metrorail or Metromover cost extra.

Metrobus stop

TAXIS

TAXIS ARE OFTEN the best way to get around at night, even if you have a car; you may feel nervous about navigating after dark, and parking can be a problem in some areas.

Taxis charge approximately $2 per mile; the trip from South Beach to Coconut Grove, for example, will cost around $15. Don't try to hail a passing cab from the kerb *(see p361)*; it is best to order one by phone. **Metro Taxi** and **Central Cab** are both reliable.

Metro Taxi
℃ (305) 888-8888.

Central Cab
℃ (305) 532-5555.

A typical Metromover station, with a plan of the network by the entrance

WATER TAXIS

MIAMI'S WATER TAXI operates two routes from Bayside Marketplace: a request service (11am–1am) runs east to South Beach, with stops at Lincoln Road and the 5th Street marina, and a cheaper shuttle service goes up the Miami River as far as the Orange Bowl Stadium, stopping at various restaurants and hotels en route. The latter runs every 30 minutes between 10am and 1am. Day passes are available.

Water Taxi
🔲 (954) 467-6677.

TRAVELLING BY CAR

DRIVING IN MIAMI is not as intimidating as you might think. Biscayne Bay is a useful reference point, and you can't go far wrong if you stick to the main through routes.
Parking is straightforward, but it can be a nightmare in South Beach. At weekends forget it; at other times bring change for the meters, which operate from 9am to 9pm, and pay heed to the signs threatening to tow away your vehicle. You can contact the **Miami Parking System** and the **Miami Beach Parking Department** for directions to specific parking lots.

Miami Beach Parking Department
🔲 (305) 673-7505.

Miami Parking System
🔲 (305) 373-6789.

STREET ADDRESSES

MIAMI IS SPLIT into four by the junction of Miami Avenue and Flagler Street in Downtown. Avenues, which run north-south, and streets, running east-west, start their numbering here. The coordinates NE, SE, NW and SW, which prefix street names in Miami, change depending on which side of the main two axes the road is.
In Miami Beach, the southernmost street is 1st Street; the numbers then simply increase as you move northwards.

Travelling in Florida's Other Cities

IN THE MOST POPULAR TOURIST CENTRES, quaint trolley buses and carriages designed to cater for tourists provide a relaxing way to sightsee *(see p361)*. In the bigger cities of Jacksonville and Tampa and in the Orlando area, however, it is worth familiarizing yourself with some of the alternative forms of transport.

ORLANDO

YOU CAN SURVIVE in Orlando better than in other areas without a car thanks to the excellent **Lynx Buses**, which serve the airport, downtown Orlando, International Drive and Walt Disney World. If you need a transfer, ask for one when you board the first bus.
I-Ride minibuses, which are also operated by Lynx, ply International Drive between Wet 'n Wild and Sea World. Buses run every ten minutes from 7am to midnight. Passes are good value and mean that you don't always have to have change handy. Passes and timetables are available from the Lynx bus station in downtown Orlando (near Church Street Station) and from Walgreens stores on International Drive. Taxis are plentiful but costly. Private shuttle buses are much cheaper, especially for the trip from I Drive to Walt Disney World, but you need to book ahead for these.

Orlando's Lynx buses logo

Lynx Buses
🔲 (407) 841-8240.

JACKSONVILLE

JACKSONVILLE is best suited to the motorist. The fairly new **Automated Skyway Express**, or ASE, is a monorail line that currently serves only Downtown; however, there are plans to extend the line.
Jacksonville also has a **Water Taxi** service between the north and south banks of the St Johns River. Shuttle services operate between 10–11am and 4–6pm,

Jacksonville's water taxi, ready to cross the St Johns River

though times depend on the weather. For other destinations, you should rely on the buses operated by the **Jacksonville Transit Authority**, whose terminus downtown is on Kings Road, about eight blocks north of Jacksonville Landing.

Automated Skyway Express
🔲 (904) 632-5531.

Water Taxi
🔲 (904) 733-7782.

Jacksonville Transit Authority
🔲 (904) 630-3100.

TAMPA

DOWNTOWN TAMPA is quite compact, but without a car you'll need to use the local HARTline buses *(see p245)* to travel to outlying sights such as Busch Gardens. These depart from the terminal on Marion Street and run roughly every half hour along most routes, from about 5am to 8pm. There is also a trolley bus connection to Ybor City.
Water taxis in Tampa run a request service, stopping at a number of downtown attractions *(see pp244–5)*.

A tourist
trolley bus
in Tampa

General Index

Acknowledgments

DORLING KINDERSLEY would like to thank the following people whose contributions and assistance have made the preparation of this book possible.

MAIN CONTRIBUTORS

RICHARD CAWTHORNE is a freelance travel writer who specializes in the United States.

DAVID DICK is a postgraduate at University College London, specializing in US history.

GUY MANSELL writes travel articles for British magazines and newspapers, including *The Sunday Telegraph*, as well as guidebooks.

FRED MAWER is a travel journalist who contributes regularly to the *Daily Telegraph* and the *Mail on Sunday*. He is also the author of half a dozen guidebooks and has contributed to various Eyewitness guides.

EMMA STANFORD has travelled extensively in Florida and has written several books and articles about the state. She has written guidebooks for Berlitz, the AA and Fodor's.

PHYLLIS STEINBERG lives in Florida. She writes about food, travel and lifestyle for various Florida and US magazines and newspapers.

OTHER CONTRIBUTORS AND CONSULTANTS

Frances and Fred Brown, Monique Damiano, Todd Jay Jonas, Marlena Spieler, David Stone.

ADDITIONAL PHOTOGRAPHY

Dave King, Clive Streeter, James Stevenson.

ADDITIONAL ILLUSTRATIONS

Julian Baker, Joanna Cameron, Stephen Conlin, Gary Cross, Chris Forsey, Paul Guest, Stephen Gyapay, Ruth Lindsay, Maltings Partnership, Paul Weston.

CARTOGRAPHY

Malcolm Porter, David Swain, Holly Syer and Neil Wilson at EMS Ltd (Digital Cartography Dept), East Grinstead, UK.

PROOF READER

Stewart Wild

INDEXER

Hilary Bird

EDITORIAL ASSISTANCE

Cathy Day, Kim Kemp, Desiree Kirke.

DESIGN ASSISTANCE

Louise Boulton, Leanne Hogbin, Harvey de Roemer, Ingrid Vienings.

SPECIAL ASSISTANCE

Dorling Kindersley would like to thank all the regional and local tourist offices in Florida for their valuable help. Particular thanks also to: Rachel Bell, Busch Gardens; Alison Sanders, Cedar Key Area Chamber of Commerce; Marie Mayer, Collier County Historical Museum, Naples; Mr and Mrs Charlie Shubert, Coombs House Inn, Apalachicola; Nick Robbins, Crystal River State Archaeological Site; Emily Hickey, Dali Museum, St Petersburg; Gary B van Voorhuis, Daytona International Speedway; James Laray, Everglades National Park; Sandra Barghini, Flagler Museum, Palm Beach; Ed Lane, Florida Geological Survey, Florida Department of Environmental Protection, Tallahassee; Dr James Miller, Archaeological Research, Florida Department of State, Tallahassee; Florida Keys National Marine Sanctuary; Jody Norman, Florida State Archives; Damian O'Grady and Tanya Nigro, Florida Tourism Corporation, London; Larry Paarlberg, Goodwood Plantation, Tallahassee; Dawn Hugh, Historical Museum of Southern Florida; Ellen Donovan, Historical Society of Palm Beach County; Melissa Tomasso, Kennedy Space Center; Valerie Rivers, Marjorie Kinnan Rawlings State Historic Site, Cross Creek; Carmen Smythe, Micanopy County Historian; Bob McNeil and Philip Pollack, Museum of Florida History, Tallahassee; Frank Lepore and Ed Rappaport, National Hurricane Center, Miami; Colonel Denis J Kiely, National Museum of Naval Aviation, Pensacola; Richard Brosnaham and Tom Muir, Historic Pensacola Preservation Board; Ringling Museum of Art, Sarasota; Ardythe Bromley-Rousseau, Salvors Inc, Sebastian; Arvin Steinberg; Wit Tuttell, Universal Studios; Holly Blount, Vizcaya, Miami; Melinda Crowther, Margaret Melia and Joyce Taylor, Walt Disney Attractions, London.

PHOTOGRAPHY PERMISSIONS

Dorling Kindersley would like to thank the following for their assistance and kind permission to photograph at their establishments: The Barnacle Historic Site; © 1996 FL Cypress Gardens, Inc; all rights reserved, reproduced by permission; © Disney Enterprises, Inc; Dreher Park Zoo: The Zoo of the Palm Beaches; Fish and Wildlife Service, Department of the Interior; Florida Park Service; Harry P Leu Gardens, Orlando, FL; Key West Art and Historical Society: Lighthouse Museum and East Martello Museum; Metro-Dade Culture Center, Historical Museum of Southern Florida; Monkey Jungle Inc, Miami, FL; National Park Service, Department of Interior; Pinellas County Park Department; National Society of the Colonial Dames of America in the State of Florida; Suncoast Seabird Sanctuary Inc, Indian Shores, FL; and all other museums, churches, hotels, restaurants, shops, galleries and sights too numerous to thank individually.

PICTURE CREDITS

t = top; tl = top left; tlc = top left centre; tc = top centre; trc = top right centre; tr = top right; cla = centre left above; ca = centre above; cra = centre right above; cl = centre left; c = centre; cr = centre right; clb = centre left below; cb = centre below; crb = centre right below; bl = bottom left; b = bottom; bc = bottom centre; bcl = bottom centre left; br = bottom right; d = detail.

DORLING KINDERSLEY would like to thank the following individuals, companies and picture libraries for their kind permission to reproduce their photographs:

AISA, Barcelona: 193b; Museo de America 42cl; © Disney Enterprises, Inc 146–7, 154–5; Vidler 109t, 122t; MUSEUM OF AFRICAN AMERICAN ART, Tampa: *Vendor with Flowers*, Ellis Wilson (1945) 245t; ALLSPORT, UK: Steve Swope 31b; Allsport, USA/Scott Halleran 94t; Shaquille O'Neal/Christian Laettner 31cr; APPLETON MUSEUM OF ART, Ocala: *Jeune Bergere (Young Sheperdess)*, William Adolphe Bouguereau (1825–1905), French. Oil on canvas 208t; ARCHIVE PHOTOS, New York: 47cla, 50clb; Bert & Richard Morgan 114b; MUSEUM OF ART, Fort Lauderdale: *Big Bird with Child*, Karel Appel (1972) © DACS 1997 128t; MUSEUM OF FINE ARTS, St Petersburg: *Poppy*, Georgia O'Keeffe (1927) © ARS, NY and DACS, London 1998 241t; TONY ARRUZA: 21cb, 24cbl, 36, 124t, 136b, 276c, 283b, 337t; AVALON HOTEL, Miami: 59tl.

LARRY BENVENUTI: 279cr; BIBLIOTECA NACIONAL, Madrid: *Codice Osuna* 41cb; BRITISH MUSEUM: 39t, 43cr; THE BRIDGEMAN ART LIBRARY, London: *The Agony in the Garden (Christ in the Garden of Olives)*, 1889 by Gauguin, Paul (1848–1903), Norton Gallery, Palm Beach 123t; BUSCH ENTERTAINMENT CORP: 2–3, 104b, 167c, 250b, 251t, 251bra, 251b.

JOHN CARTER: 19b, 354c; © Disney Enterprises, Inc 140–41, 142t, 148t; Courtesy of THE CHARLESTON MUSEUM, Charleston, South Carolina: Osceola portrait 44ca; ROBERT CLAYTON: 52–53, 285t, 358b, 360b, 362tr, 362b; PAT CLYNE: 110t; BRUCE COLEMAN, London: Atlantide SDF 280t; Erwin & Peggy Bauer 275br; Raimund Cramm GDT 180cla; Jeff Foott Productions 23bl; © John Shaw 23cl; George McCarthy 23t; LIBRARY OF CONGRESS, LC-USF33-30491-M3 49cr; CORBIS: 41t, 42–3c; CULVER PICTURES, INC, New York: 46cl, 49t, 53 (inset).

SALVADOR DALI MUSEUM, St Petersburg: 242t; All works of art by Salvador Dali © DEMART PRO ARTE BV/DACS 1997, *Nature Morte Vivante* 242ca, *The Sick Child* 242cb, *Cadaques* 242b, *Don Quixote y Sancho Panza* 243t, *Discovery* 243ca, *Daddy Longlegs of the Evening–Hope* (1940) 243cb; Salvador Dali by Marc Lacroix 243b; © INTERNATIONAL SPEEDWAY CORPORATION, Daytona: 204t, 205c, 205b; Nascar 205cb; DAVID DYE, University of Memphis: South Florida Museum 38cr, 41cla.

MARY EVANS PICTURE LIBRARY: 103 (inset); C Sheppard 9 (inset); ET ARCHIVE: Natural History Museum 43cla.

MEL FISHER MARITIME HERITAGE SOCIETY, Key West, Photograph by Dylan Kibler © 1993 40t; © HENRY MORRISON FLAGLER MUSEUM, Palm Beach: 47t, 120tl, 120c, 120b, 121t, 121ca, 121cb; Archives 120tr, 121b.

PET GALLAGHER: 18b; GENESIS SPACE PHOTO LIBRARY: NASA 184bl, 184br, 185br, 186cb, 186c, 186tl; GIRAUDON, Paris: Bridgeman Sir Francis Drake portrait, Olivier Isaac (1540–1596) 41cr; Laurus 37b; THE GRANGER COLLECTION, New York: 44clb, 44crb, 44t, 47crb, 48cl, 48t; THE RONALD GRANT ARCHIVE: © King Feature Syndicated 168bl. ROBERT HARDING PICTURE LIBRARY: Liason 50–51c; © THE MIAMI HERALD: © Al Diaz 31cl, 122b; Chuck Fadely & Art Gallery 90t; © Guzy 51cla; © Charlie Trainor 75cr; HENRY HIRD: 200b; DIVISION HISTORICAL RESOURCES, STATE DEPARTMENT, Tallahassee:

39crb, 110c; Courtesy of HIBEL MUSEUM OF ART, Palm Beach, FL: *Brittany and Child*, oil, gesso, and gold leaf on silk, Edna Hibel 24½" x 20½" (1994) 117c; HISTORICAL MUSEUM OF SOUTHERN FLORIDA, Miami: 48cb, 49clb, 50c, 61tr, 72t, 271t.

THE IMAGE BANK, London: 10b, 19c, V Chapman 48–9c; IMAGES COLOUR LIBRARY: 15t, 49cra, 55ba, 272br, 285b; INDEX STOCK PHOTOGRAPHY, INC, New York: 21b, 32c, 32t, 34t, 34b, 35c, 46t, 117b, 169b, 172c, 332c, 336c; © Bill Bachmann 22cl; © James Blank 15b, 268c; J. Christopher 25cr; © Henry Fichner 23cr; © Warren Flagler 51cra; Scott Kerrigan 281cr; Larry Lipsky 165bl, 277br; Wendell Metzen 30t, 30b, 180ca, 274t; © M Timothy O'Keefe 290–91; Jim Schwabel 16, 167t, 257t, 269t, 270t; Scott Smith, 94c; Steve Starr 24bra, 246bl; M. Still 277t; Randy Taylor 32b; ARCHIVO DE INDIAS, Seville: 40cb; INDIAN TEMPLE MOUND: 38cl.

MIAMI WORLD JAI-ALAI: 31t; Michael Fineman 133b.

KENNEDY SPACE CENTER – VISITORS CENTER, Cape Canaveral: 182t, 183ca, 183cb, 187c; KEN LAFFAL: 21t, 54b, 105t, 113b, 336t; FRANK LANE PICTURE LIBRARY: © Dembinsky 22bla, 279b; © David Hosking 17b, 22br, 23br, 180t, 274cr; Maslowski 112c; © Leonard Lee Rue 23crb; LIGHTNER MUSEUM, St Augustine, FL: 47bla; LOWE ART MUSEUM: 81c.

BARRY MANSELL: 271c; MACMILLAN PUBLISHERS: Pan Books *Native Tongue* and *Tourist Season* Carl Hiassen 82b; MARVEL ENTERTAINMENT GROUP, NY: Spider-Man TM and © 1996, Marvel Characters, Inc. All rights reserved 126t; FRED MAWER, London: 73t, 77t, 132b, 137t, 178t, 182cb.

© NASA: 186tr, 187t; MUSEO NAVAL, Spain: 26cl; PETER NEWARK'S PICTURES: American Pictures 43clb; Historical Pictures 27cb; Military Pictures 45cb; THE NEW YORK PUBLIC LIBRARY: Print Collection, Miriam and Ira D Wallach Division of Art, Prints and Photographs, Astor, Lenox and Tilden Foundations 40–41c; JESSE NEWMAN ASSOCIATES: 115br; GLENN VAN NIMWEGEN, Wyoming: 276ca, 277bl; Northampton Museums and Art Gallery: 42t. N.O.O.A.: National Hurricane Center, Miami 24-5, 25t.

ORONOZ, Madrid: 40ca.

THE PALM BEACH POST, FL: © Allen Eyestone 51clb; © Thomas Hart Shelby 114cl; © Greg Lovett 33c; © Loren Hosack 115bl, 118b; © EA Kennedy III 20b; © Mark Mirko 35b; © Bob Shanley 184t; © Sherman Zent 33b; PICTURES COLOUR LIBRARY: 289b; PLANET EARTH PICTURES: 279t; Kurt Amsler 236t; Peter Gasson 23bla; © Brian Kenney 22cr, 22bl, 23cla, 180cra, 274cl, 272bl, 273ca, 275t, 275c, 275bl, David Maitland 22cra; Doug Perrine 278cr, 279t; Mike Potts 274b; Nancy Sefton 278bl.

QUADRANT PICTURE LIBRARY: © Anthony R Dalton 51crb.

MIKE RASTELLI, Ocala: 261b; REX FEATURES: © Sipa-Press 51t; Kevin Wisniewski 75t; THE JOHN AND MABLE RINGLING MUSEUM OF ART, Sarasota: 258b, 259t; Bequest of John Ringling, *The Building of a Palace*, Piero di Cosimo (1515–1520) 257c, *Abraham and Melchizedek*, Peter Paul Rubens (c.1625) 257b.

SEA WORLD: 5t, 114c, 164t, 164c, 165cra, 165br; SMITHSONIAN INSTITUTION: Department of Anthropology catalogue no. 240915 38clb; FLORIDA STATE ARCHIVE, Tallahassee: 43t, 45t, 45ca, 46b, 49ca, 116br, 119t, 205ca, 217b, 247b, 249t: Museum of Florida History 49crb, 111b; TONY STONE IMAGES: Daniel McCulloch 50t; Stephen Krasemann 266; Randy Wells 272c; SUPERSTOCK: 174t.

TAMPA THEATRE: 337b; FLORIDA DEPARTMENT OF COMMERCE, DIVISION OF TOURISM: R Overton 39cra.

© UNIVERSAL STUDIOS: 168c, 168br, 169t, 171b, 172b.

PROF L GLENN WESTFALL, FL: 46–7; BILL WISSER, Miami: 65t; WOLFSONIAN FOUNDATION, Miami: Mitchell Wolfson, JR Collection 65b.

Front endpaper: All special photography except TONY STONE: Stephen Krasemann br.

Jacket: All special photography except INDEX STOCK PHOTOGRAPHY, NY: back br; PLANET EARTH PICTURES: Flip Schulke back bl; SEA WORLD: front cr.

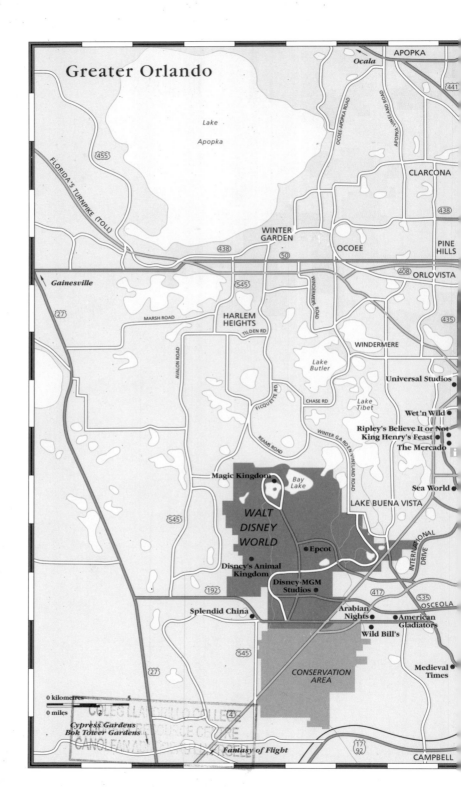

Greater Orlando

Ocala

APOPKA

441

Lake

Apopka

455

CLARCONA

438

FLORIDA'S TURNPIKE (TOLL)

WINTER
GARDEN

OCOEE

50

PINE
HILLS

Gainesville

545

408 ORLOVISTA

27

MARSH ROAD

HARLEM
HEIGHTS

TILDEN RD

WINDERMERE ROAD

435

AVALON ROAD

FICQUETTE RD

CHASE RD

*Lake
Butler*

WINDERMERE

*Lake
Tibet*

Universal Studios ●

Wet 'n Wild ●

REAMS ROAD

WINTER GA RD EN-VINELAND ROAD

Ripley's Believe It or Not ●
King Henry's Feast ●
The Mercado ●

i

Magic Kingdom ●

*Bay
Lake*

Sea World ●

545

*WALT
DISNEY
WORLD*

LAKE BUENA VISTA

● **Epcot**

INTERNATIONAL DRIVE

**Disney's Animal
Kingdom** ●

192

**Disney-MGM
Studios** ●

417

535

OSCEOLA

Splendid China ●

**Arabian
Nights** ●

● **American
Gladiators**

● **Wild Bill's**

545

27

*CONSERVATION
AREA*

**Medieval
Times** ●

0 kilometres   5

0 miles   2

*Cypress Gardens
Bok Tower Gardens*

4

Fantasy of Flight

17
92

CAMPBELL